MOTOCOURSE

The World's Leading Road Racing Annual

HAZLETON PUBLISHING

contents

publisher
RICHARD POULTER

editor
MICHAEL SCOTT

art editor
STEVE SMALL

production manager
STEVEN PALMER

managing editor
PETER LOVERING

publishing development manager
SIMON MAURICE

business development manager
SIMON SANDERSON

sales promotion
CLARE KRISTENSEN

results and statistics
KAY EDGE

chief photographers
GOLD & GOOSE
London, England
0181-333 2244

MOTOCOURSE 1997-98

is published by
Hazleton Publishing Ltd,
3 Richmond Hill,
Richmond, Surrey
TW10 6RE, England.

Colour reproduction by
Barrett Berkeley Ltd, London, England.

Printed in England by
Butler and Tanner Ltd,
Frome.

© Hazleton Publishing Ltd 1997.
No part of this publication may be reproduced,
stored in a retrieval system or transmitted, in any
form or by any means, electronic, mechanical,
photocopying, recording or otherwise, without
prior permission in writing from
Hazleton Publishing Ltd.

ISBN: 1-874557-52-7

acknowledgements

The Editor and staff of *Motocourse* wish to thank the following for their assistance in compiling the 1997/98 edition: Anne-Marie Gerber and Marc Pétrier (FIM), Paul Butler and Neil Bird (IRTA), Denis Noyes, Fiona Bird and Renata Nosetto (Dorna/TWP), Garry Taylor, Stuart Avant and Stuart Shenton (Suzuki), Kenny Roberts and Chuck Aksland (Modenas), Wayne Rainey, Shuji Sakurada and Rupert Williamson (Yamaha), Urs Wenger (SwissAuto), Iain Mackay (HRC), Carlo Pernat and Jan Witteveen (Aprilia), Hamish Jamieson, Jeremy Burgess, Jesus Benitez, Kay Edge, Henny Ray Abrams, Gunther Wiesinger, Shigehiro Kondo, Colin Young, Jean-Paul Libert, Sheona Dorson-King, Diane Michiels, Lydia Guglielmi-Kirn and many others.

photographers

Photographs in *Motocourse 1997-98* have been contributed by:
Gold & Goose (David Goldman and Patrick Gosling), Clive Challinor, Dave Collister, Double Red Photography, Kel Edge, *Two Plus Two*/Andy Gibbs, *Flick of the Wrist*/Tom Hnatiw, Nigel Kinrade, Don Morley, *Prime Picture Agency*/Richard Richards, Tom Riles, Chris Sims, *The Motorsport Shop*/Debbie Wedes, Mark Wernham.

DISTRIBUTORS

UNITED KINGDOM	NORTH AMERICA	AUSTRALIA	NEW ZEALAND	SOUTH AFRICA
Biblios Ltd	Motorbooks International	Technical Book and Magazine	David Bateman Ltd	Motorbooks
Star Road	PO Box 1	Co. Pty	PO Box 100-242	341 Jan Smuts Avenue
Partridge Green	729 Prospect Ave, Osceola	295 Swanston Street	North Shore Mail Centre	Craighall Park
West Sussex RH13 8LD	Wisconsin 54020, USA	Melbourne, Victoria 3000	Auckland 1330	Johannesburg
Telephone: 01403 710971	Telephone: (1) 715 294 3345	Telephone: (03) 9663 3951	Telephone: (9) 415 7664	Telephone: (011) 325 4458/60
Fax: 01403 711143	Fax: (1) 715 294 4448	Fax: (03) 9663 2094	Fax: (9) 415 8892	Fax: (011) 325 4146

Moët Silver Trophy
1996 Winners :
Damon Hill
Williams Grand Prix
Renault.

MOËT & CHANDON . *Sao Paulo, Monaco, Silverstone, Hockenheim, Spa, Monza, Suzuka, Estoril ...*

MOËT
SILVER TROPHY
FORMULA ONE

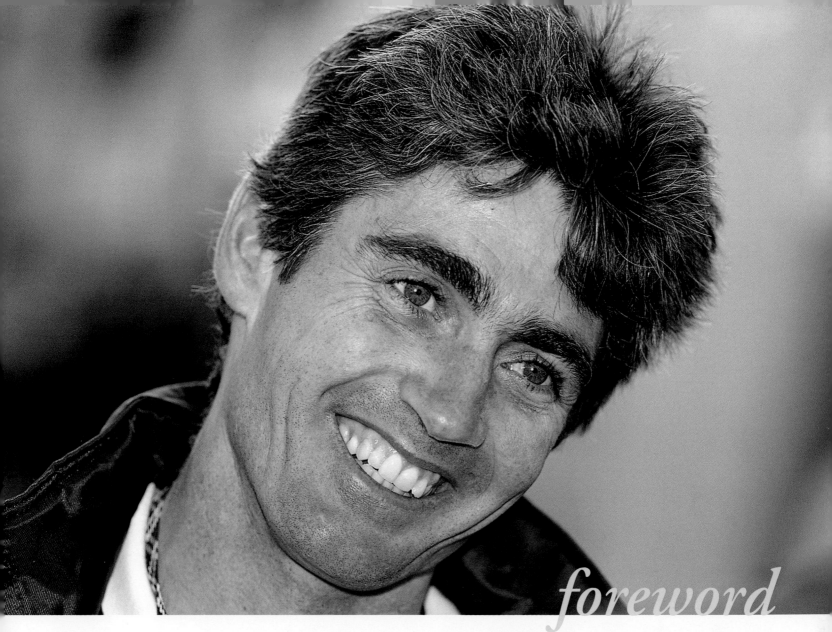

foreword

by Michael Doohan

I'VE really enjoyed this year. The bike's been fantastic at every race, so I've got to give a lot of thanks to Jerry Burgess and the crew. The guys get the bike spot on every time and that's the difference between our team and the others – they're 100 per cent into winning. I just add my own ingredient. I also have to thank them for putting up with me when I come into the pits, screaming at them! Also, it must not be overlooked that without the support of my sponsors, and the team sponsors, we could not possibly compete at this level. Then there's Dr Costa – without him, I wouldn't have won one title, let alone four.

I worked harder on my preparation for this year than I did for '96. Last season was a suck-it-and-see year – my whole approach was different because I'd already done what I wanted to do – win two championships. It was win the race in the laziest way, but I realised you can't keep doing that. Most days I would only work out for 45 minutes, but I realised I had to get my head down if I was to keep going. This year, my preparation has been more intense – like it was before '96. It's not easy to keep the domination going, but I only want to keep on racing if I can be at the front.

I hope I'm still getting better as a rider. While the motivation is there, I'll continue to try to improve. I still learn every time I ride. I feel I'm smarter than I was in '92, but I'm not as manoeuvrable on the bike after my accident. I sometimes feel restricted because I can't move around quickly enough, but I don't think that reflects in my lap times.

I never have a problem with motivation during the season. Maybe it plays on you around January when testing starts and you've been enjoying the good life, but you've got to do something in life and I love racing, so I just get my head down again. Next year will be my tenth in Grands Prix. When I first came into the paddock, I thought I'd get racing out of my system by the time I was 32, but I still feel good and I'm enjoying racing more now than ever. The racing is the easy part for me. It's the other stuff I find tough. Maybe 1998 will be my last season, but if I do keep going, '99 will 100 per cent definitely be my last.

I'm sure that the readers of this quality book will gain a clear insight into what, for me, was an exceptional race season.

editor's
INTRODUCTION

Tadayuki Okada heads a Honda express in France. While Honda's domination of the 500 class currently appears unchallenged, the rise of a group of Japanese riders to a similar position could be a feature of Grand Prix racing in the years ahead.

SUPERLATIVES all spent a year or more past, one watched Doohan's progress through 1997 without surprise, in a state of comfortable awe. This was the only possible response to history in the making, as the records tumbled and his stature grew.

The background to this pre-eminence was coloured orange and blue. The phalanx of Hondas that took almost total control of the 500 class wasn't always all-Repsol, but it happened often enough to become a habit. Hondas ruled everywhere, winning every race. And their rivals from Japan and Europe were left floundering, looking for the main part rather silly.

It is not, as some suggest, the weaknesses of the other factories and teams that made it easy for Mick Doohan and Honda. It is that Doohan and HRC together have made it very, very hard for them.

None of this, of course, will last forever. The Hondas, appropriately, also spearheaded the Samurai Sanction, set to be the next big thing. After the USA, after Australia, we seem to have started into a new era, of success for riders from the country where the motor cycles are made. How else to explain that Japanese riders were second, third, fifth and seventh in the 500 championship? It is, in retrospect, the inevitable consequence of a steady invasion, starting with the 125 class, staging via the 250s to arrive in seasoned strength in the 500 class. In the nature of these things, the Japanese invasion has only just begun.

There was more of the same in the Superbikes too. While enigmatic John Kocinski forged his way to his first world title since 1990, there was a generation of four-stroke talent lying in wait in Japan, to pounce when they got to Sugo.

Japan, Australia and Britain are three countries where four-stroke racing thrives. Indeed, in Britain a booming domestic Superbike championship led to a massive racing revival. This was not only reflected in increased TV coverage, but by a (faintly oxymoronic) vast increase in trackside crowds.

At the same time, though there were just two British riders in the GPs, and none in the 500 class, their presence in Superbikes remained not merely strong, but almost pre-eminent. Consequently, and even though Fogarty didn't win the title, the production-based series gained yet more in public popularity.

Motocourse thoroughly approves of Superbikes – competitive racing on sweet-sounding racers closely related to sports road bikes; and reflects the strong British interest with extra coverage in this edition.

Yet it is important to be aware that the British skewing of emphasis away from GPs to Superbikes remains something of a national peculiarity: elsewhere the older GP series for specialised racing machines retained unquestioned seniority. A generation of British riders has become increasingly isolated, and though only the most eccentric among them does not wish ultimately to be 500 cc World Champion, the world has gone on without them.

Last year, we celebrated a return of confidence not only to racing, but to motor cycling in general; 1997 did not always confirm that confidence. The overall prospects remain encouraging, but racing will have to change to make the most of them, and that will be difficult. It is, however, even harder to see how the factories, the fans and the TV audience can sustain two separate World Championship series.

In the meanwhile, Grand Prix racing remained the ultimate edifice, and Mick Doohan one of its all-time top practitioners. He was ably backed by a performance of similar stature by Max Biaggi in the 250s, while the 125s threw up a new hero in their champion, Valentino Rossi.

History is just what happened. And there was plenty of it in 1997.

Michael Scott
Wimbledon
London

GSX-R750

Still crazy after all these years

www.suzuki.co.uk

At the risk of stating the obvious the GSX-R750 doesn't stay still for long. Since we launched the first model 13 years ago we've continually developed, modified, enhanced and improved our race replica breed. So much so that we cleaned up in the 1997 World Endurance Championship, winning both the rider's and manufacturer's titles. Now we've added fuel injection, the GSX-R750 is more powerful, lighter and more advanced than ever before, widening the gap ahead of the competition. People thought we were mad when we launched such an advanced and outrageous motorcycle. Who's crazy now?

24 hour hotline: 01892 707001
Suzuki Information Department, P.O. Box 56, Tunbridge Wells, Kent TN1 2XY.

SUZUKI

Ride the winds of change

Designed for the experienced rider only

THE EYES

A large, eerie, deserted warehouse in the middle of a run-down industrial zone in Milan was the unusual church which sprang to life with the ground-shaking, deafening roar of a new bike as the 360-strong congregation of international press and Yamaha top brass burst into applause.

So it was that code-name 'O8R' became the YZF-R1 and was presented to the world – small but perfectly formed!

Lighter and more powerful than any other large capacity supersport machine ever built, the Yamaha YZF-R1 is destined to change the high performance motorcycle scene for ever. Totally new from the ground up, the awesome R1 is driven by an ultra-compact 998cc slant-block 20-valve engine that kicks out a class-leading 150bhp! Razor sharp handling is assured thanks to the newly developed short wheelbase Deltabox II aluminium chassis – and weighing in at only 177kg this no-compromise machine is engineered to deliver the ultimate supersport riding experience!

Fittingly enough on that memorable night of high-tech laser wizardry and high emotion, the 'godfather' that held Yamaha's precious new-born for all to see was a silver-suited Scott Russell. The very same evening the bleach-blond Georgian had signed his life to Yamaha for another two years to try and regain the Superbike World Championship he won in 1993. He is the new embodiment of Yamaha racing – dedicated, skilful, professional and always giving 100% on one side; fun, friendly and a little bit naughty on the other! So who better to launch a bike which draws on Yamaha's racing spirit and heritage and is truly 'a race apart'?

After the launch it was off to the Varano circuit on the outskirts of Milan, the R-1 loaded on the back of a van with Russell in the front – reminiscent of the uncomplicated times when Russell first started racing and in stark contrast to the way he does it today. The van then pulls into its allotted garage but he has to wait for the sound of the fleet of skidding Alfa Romeos, in the hands of their advanced driving school pupils, to subside before he can take to the track.

'I'll just do a couple of laps to check out the circuit,' he says, starting her up, dropping his visor and off he goes. Steady away on the cold tyres. First gear around the first hairpin. By the time he's back on the start-finish straight on the tight 1.8km track he's starting to wind it up and pulls a big wheelie right the way down it. Then that's it. He's off now. As the in-line four cylinder, 20-valve engine screams into the 150bhp zone the Alfa pupils interrupt their lunch to gather on a balcony, crossing from one side to the other to watch as the beautiful and compact R1 flies past in the hands of one of the world's best riders.

'Mr Daytona', as we know, is a showman and he seems to be enjoying himself and is aware that he's got a crowd – wheelies, burn-outs and an awesome display of the bike's speed and handling. He's been warned not to overdo it though. This R1's lightweight aluminium Deltabox II chassis number ends 001 – the first of a batch of pre-production models. It's currently on a busy European tour of duty to promote the new model and the next stop is the South of France to be ridden around the Paul Ricard circuit by Christian Sarron at the Bol d'Or. It keeps pretty good company, this R1.

HAVE IT

Russell comes flying along the straight for the fourth time, brakes hard and downshifts with the engine growling and the exhaust letting out beautifully rounded, deep pops. 'This thing's as fast as hell for a street bike' is the family edit of what he said. His eyes fired up and a big smile on his face, he is speaking faster than he has all day. 'This is fun! These short dashes in first are incredible. It's just got so much power'. Now, of course, you can read 'advertisement feature' on the top of this page and say to yourself that Yamaha isn't going to say that he didn't like it. But these are his comments, word for word... honest.

The show for the Alfa pupils continued for the hour with the photographer snapping away. 'Who is riding it?' one of them shouted over. They all nodded sagely as if the fact that the answer was Scott Russell explained everything. They did seem to know who he is and given the Italians' love of bike racing and Russell's high profile this isn't hard to believe.

'I want one of these', he exclaimed as he took his helmet off. 'I don't ride a street bike very often and when I do I usually find they're heavy and don't have much power compared to what I race but this is the best street bike I've ever ridden.' What Scott races is the Yamaha YZF750, the longest serving machine in the World Superbike arena but one which acquits itself admirably. It is a 750cc racing machine which weighs in at 162kg (to comply with the FIM's minimum weight limit for the class) and produces over 160bhp and approximately 300km/h.

Constructed with the vast knowledge gained from Yamaha's experience in racing factory Superbikes and 34 years of winning Grand Prix races, the new R1's engine and chassis performance is virtually in the same league as Scott's race bike – without modifications and tweaks!

But these figures alone don't tell you the whole story: a more detailed examination of this full-on supersport motorcycle reveals just how much effort and imagination have gone into creating the most exciting machine to be launched for many years. From its extremely light and compact 998cc powerplant and compact, high-rigidity 1395mm wheelbase Deltabox II chassis through to longer stroke upside down front forks, an 'intelligent' EXUP system and lightweight one-piece brake calipers, the Yamaha R1 combines cutting-edge innovation with some of the highest levels of build quality witnessed in the class.

'The first time I rode the R1,' continued Scott, 'was on a big, fast race track.' Monza to be precise – where Scott and teammate Colin Edwards II were caught testing the bike leading to the first pictures of the new Yamaha being displayed in magazines around the world. 'It felt good then but around here you really get a feel for the thing because it's short and tight. There's so much power there so you can use it coming out of these turns. It's good, smooth power and it comes in early down at low rpm. In fact it's got good delivery at bottom, mid and top. I guess you expect that from a big bike like this but it really does feel impressive.

'The handling's really good too. It feels real stable through the corners. The back end sits down a little bit when you get in the corners and it was turning

I started racing supersport production.

'I sort of stopped on the road then because I had turned my road-bike into a racer – taken the headlamps off and stuff. Every now and again I would change it back and take it on the road again. Then when you're racing factory

bikes, street bikes don't feel that exciting any more. But doing what we do we get to ride quite a few different new models and stuff.'

And the verdict: 'Yamaha has done a really good job. Everyone should have one of these in their garage! I was going to see if I could get a Royal Star for back home but I definitely want an R1 now. I'll keep the 750 to race but I'll have one of these at home. The thing works good enough to take it off to a track at home and just do some laps. And it makes me want to go street riding again. A couple of my buddies at home have supersport bikes and on a track I'm just gonna smoke 'em!'

So any messages for his employers? 'Yeah, I really want one of these with a 750 engine! I think this package would be real hard to beat in Superbikes.'

round itself a bit but we haven't adjusted anything on this bike. It's so light that it works really well. For a 1000 it's amazing that it's so small and light. Powerful bikes need good brakes and these are excellent. I'm used to the pretty trick stuff we get in World Superbikes so I was surprised to find such good brakes on a road bike.'

He's obviously impressed, but what's he comparing it to? 'I started riding a bike in 1984. I rode to work every day and then at the weekends we would go and practise in the mountains. The main goal was to try and look like a racer. We used to rent all the GPs on video and watch Roberts, Lawson, Spencer and all that. Then we would go out, find a couple of corners and practise. Two years later

THE EYES HAVE IT

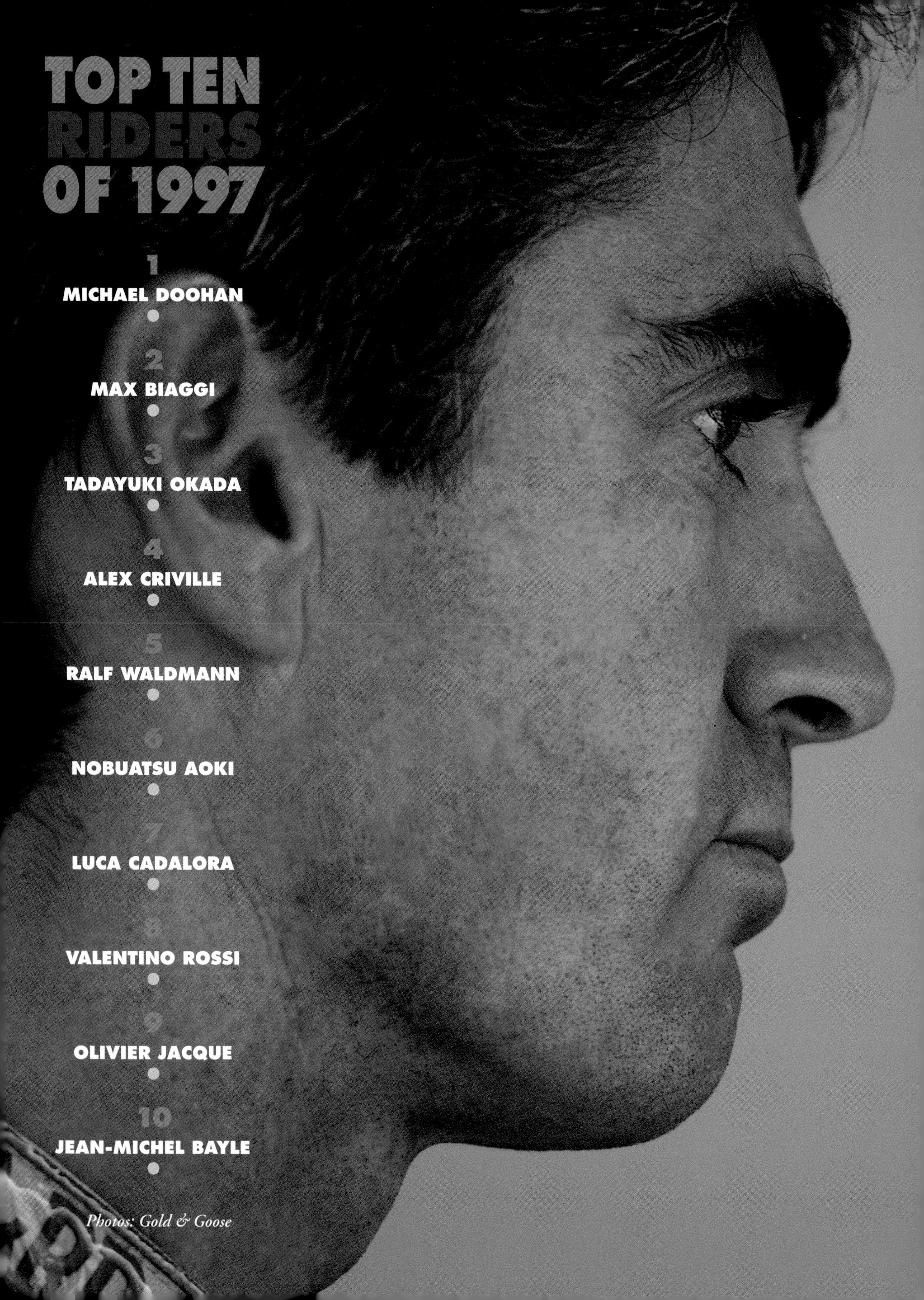

TOP TEN RIDERS OF 1997

1

MICHAEL DOOHAN

2

MAX BIAGGI

3

TADAYUKI OKADA

4

ALEX CRIVILLE

5

RALF WALDMANN

6

NOBUATSU AOKI

7

LUCA CADALORA

8

VALENTINO ROSSI

9

OLIVIER JACQUE

10

JEAN-MICHEL BAYLE

Photos: Gold & Goose

1 MICK DOOHAN

TEAM REPSOL HONDA
1997 World Championship – 1st (500 cc)
Race wins – 12 (Malaysia, Japan, Italy, Austria, France, Netherlands, Imola, Germany, Brazil, Great Britain, Czech Republic, Catalunya)
Pole positions – 12
Career GP wins – 46 (500 cc)
Born 4 June 1965, Brisbane, Australia

If the mark of a World Champion is that he never gives up, Doohan is your man. Even when there was nobody there to hold a candle, he never slackened. Mick wanted to dominate not only every race, but also every practice and every warm-up. And he was prepared to work flat out all year long.

The list of his accomplishments included a growing number of new records...the most consecutive pole positions, the most 500 class wins per season...while his 46th GP win took him well past Hailwood towards Agostini in the 500s.

Not listed are the injuries he has overcome to get there, or the phenomenal dedication that has kept him competitive even without any serious challengers.

Challenger-wise, 1997 was better than 1996, at least once or twice during the year. Since Mick throughout rode a unique 'Screamer' Honda against the Big Bangs of his rivals, one could never be sure how equal the contest was. Especially after Doohan said, late in the year, that the Big Bang was superior in almost every way, and a big part of his switch had been 'to mess with the other Honda riders'.

Mick pretends to be matter of fact, but revelled in surrounding himself in mystery in this way. All part of the complex nature of a man who describes himself as 'laid back, but intense', and who happens also to be one of the all-time giants of motor cycle racing.

MAX BIAGGI

TEAM MARLBORO KANEMOTO HONDA
1997 World Championship – 1st (250 cc)
Race wins – 5 (Malaysia, Italy, Imola, Czech Republic, Indonesia)
Pole positions – 3
Career GP wins – 29 (250 cc)
Born 26 June 1971, Rome, Italy

Melodramatic to the last, Max produced a wonderfully sustained intensity from the start of this year to the finish. When things weren't going right with his bike or his team, he would be quick to lay the blame. When things did go well, you were left in no doubt that it was due to his marvellous riding. The strange thing was how difficult it was not to agree!

His year began with a vow to defeat Aprilia, to prove it was the rider not the bike that had won three years in a row. A minor muddle in Aprilia's own technical development intervened to help him from the beginning, but by the end of the year it really was more like a personal struggle by one man against one machine – that of Tetsuya Harada.

Max had another difficulty. It just so happened that the competition was really fierce. He was obliged to go for the title in a season with some of the closest finishes ever recorded – not just between two riders, but three or four.

This makes his narrow victory all the more impressive. The other 250 riders will have reason to feel relieved if he goes to 500s as planned next year.

TADAYUKI OKADA

TEAM REPSOL HONDA

1997 World Championship – 2nd (500 cc)	
Race wins – 1 (Indonesia)	
Pole positions – 3	
Career GP wins – 3 (1 500 cc, 2 250 cc)	
Born 13 February 1967, Ibaragi Prefecture, Japan	

Tady's first year on the V4 – only his second in the 500 class – opened with three pole positions, and continued in similar vein, making clear just how good was the bike that Doohan had developed for Honda.

As the year wore on, Okada's own contribution became clearer. Driven by self-confidence and ambition that has, in lesser riders, disintegrated up against the implacable fortress of the reigning champion, Tady kept on getting better.

He even survived a mid-season spell of painful crashes, never faltering in his determination. He was also the only other Honda rider prepared to try racing the 'Screamer' engine, though the results were poor, lending credence to Doohan's suggestion that it only proved his gullibility.

In the end, though, he was the only rider all year who beat Mick in a straight fight. That counts for a great deal.

ALEX CRIVILLE

TEAM REPSOL HONDA

1997 World Championship – 4th (500 cc)	
Race wins – 2 (Spain, Australia)	
Pole positions – 0	
Career GP wins – 11 (6 500 cc, 5 125 cc)	
Born 4 March 1970, Seva, Spain	

For a man who can wheel an NSR round a track as fast as anybody, Criville is a curiously uninspiring rider – the more so as his attack during the season became blunted, his determination dismantled by Doohan's obduracy. He was even starting to complain of mysterious horsepower shortages when his horrible Assen crash cut it all short.

His left hand was badly injured, and he could have been excused for taking the rest of the season off, to achieve full recovery without further risks. To his credit (at least in racing circles), he eschewed that soft option, and forced the pace to get back on a bike as soon as possible.

But the greatest credit must go to his performances after that, culminating in an admittedly lucky win in Australia. All the same, a win is a win.

Criville's skill is not in question. Nor is his determined approach to fitness and training. Now we have also been shown he lacks nothing in terms of courage. If he could just find a little more on-track aggression, he could be a genuinely major player.

RALF WALDMANN

TEAM MARLBORO HONDA

1997 World Championship – 2nd (250 cc)	
Race wins – 4 (Spain, Great Britain, Catalunya, Australia)	
Pole positions – 4	
Career GP wins – 18 (12 250 cc, 6 125 cc)	
Born 14 July 1966, Hagen, Germany	

An ebullient and popular character, Waldie did reinforce one racing record in yet another unfortunate year. He is now even more firmly the rider who has won the most GPs without ever winning the championship.

His second to Biaggi this year was once again decided at the last race, but Ralf put together a strong season running up to it and, but for a couple of hiccups, the two-point deficit might easily have gone the other way.

By the end of the season elements within his team voiced their disappointment in the result. The canon ran that his approach, to put it kindly, was not that of 'a thinking rider'.

But what a heart. The man who once crashed, remounted and won the race (Japan, 1995) did some of the same in 1997, and his charge through from the gravel pit at Catalunya to ultimate victory was surely the best race of a long career.

NOBUATSU AOKI

TEAM RHEOS ELF FCC TECHNICAL SPORTS HONDA

1997 World Championship – 3rd (500 cc)	
Race wins – 0	
Pole positions – 0	
Career GP wins – 1 (250 cc)	
Born 31 August 1971, Sumaga Prefecture, Japan	

Rookie of the year, and surprise of the year too. Nobu won a single 250 GP in six years in the class, and no fireworks were expected when he moved to 500s on a year-old NSR V4. Instead, he started the year with a front-row grid position, and followed that with an ever-lengthening string of solid results.

At Imola he led a 500 cc GP for the first time, and by the latter part of the season he was a strong contender to finish second overall.

Eldest of the three 'Fireball Brothers', Aoki is quiet but speaks good English, and he has a gentle but well-developed sense of humour. He's a respected leading-edge member of the Samurai Sanction – the Japanese invasion of the 500 class. He's also respected as an analytical rider, as well as being fast and very reliable.

Is there more to come in his second year on a 500? Suzuki clearly think so, having snapped him up to lead their drive out of this year's doldrums.

15

7

LUCA CADALORA

TEAM RED BULL YAMAHA

1997 World Championship – 6th (500 cc)

Race wins – 0

Pole positions – 0

Career GP wins – 34 (8 500 cc, 22 250 cc, 4 125 cc)

Born 17 May 1963, Modena, Italy

He's a strange one, is Luca – a complex character whose motivation is often puzzlingly effete, in a peer group where motivation is the single most important and binding characteristic.

This year he did more for his reputation than the lack of wins suggests. Apart from a moody spell mid-season, triggered perhaps by all the uncertainty after the team's original sponsor ran out of money, he also suffered a couple of mechanical glitches. By and large, though, he seemed more willing to race for glory than previously. And once Yamaha came up with some better engine parts, he was a much more serious candidate for victory.

Measure his performance against the Hondas and it is not impressive. Against the other Yamahas, however, Luca positively towered. Only he could make the V4 YZR look like a genuinely competitive motor cycle rather than a bundle of puzzling flaws. In the process, he had the same effect on the impression he gives of himself.

VALENTINO ROSSI

TEAM NASTRO AZZURRO APRILIA

1997 World Championship – 1st (125 cc)

Race wins – 11 (Malaysia, Spain, Italy, France, Netherlands, Imola, Germany, Brazil, Great Britain, Catalunya, Indonesia)

Pole positions – 4

Career GP wins – 12 (125 cc)

Born 16 February 1979, Urbino, Italy

He may only have ridden a 125 yet, in his second full season, adorable teenager Rossi showed not only heaps of riding talent but also a deep well of aggressive confidence and an ocean of fun. He deployed a range of tactics that the other 125 riders found devastating – and there are some tough racers down there in the front pack.

Guided by some of Italian racing's most powerful men, the youngster is set to do more than emulate the success of his equally colourful father Graziano, who burst into racing with three wins on a Morbidelli, only to run into injuries that effectively ended his GP career.

Having romped to 11 wins en route to a thundering overall championship victory, Valentino is now off to the 250 class. He will have plenty to prove. Let's hope he continues to find it all so infectiously enjoyable.

OLIVIER JACQUE

9

TEAM CHESTERFIELD ELF TECH 3 HONDA
1997 World Championship – 4th (250 cc)
Race wins – 2 (Austria, Brazil)
Pole positions – 5
Career GP wins – 3 (250 cc)
Born 29 August 1973, Villerupt, France

If he hadn't broken his collarbone in practice in Japan, Olivier Jacque would surely have played the role of fourth man in the title struggle.

A string of five pole positions showed his mastery of the Honda; some mistakes in tyre choice (not always his or his team's fault) and a silly unforced crash also showed his immaturity.

More obvious, however, was his combination of talent and aggression. Fearless to the last, his tactics earned the tag 'Jacque Attack' from Waldmann, and the fast Frenchman smilingly lived up to it for the rest of the season.

Jacque had a companion on his path to world glory – Regis Laconi, who actually beat him back home in France. 'OJ' got the better breaks in GP racing, but not even Laconi could say he hasn't made the most of them.

JEAN-MICHEL BAYLE

TEAM MARLBORO ROBERTS MODENAS
1997 World Championship – 18th (500 cc)
Race wins – 0
Pole positions – 0
Career GP wins – 0
Born 1 April 1969, Manosque, France

10

Nobody could have ridden the Modenas harder than Bayle. Some might add that nobody on this list had a harder bike to ride. Not because he couldn't make it fly – his front row at Brno showed that he could, and he was on target for something similar at Donington when he met the accident he was courting with such daring.

It was breakages and failures that meant Bayle didn't come up with much in the way of race results, and never for want of trying. The man they once called 'Snayle' had a broad canvas upon which to illustrate the depth of the intelligence and determination which once made him utterly dominant in Supercross; in spite of being almost constantly thwarted, he kept coming back for more.

Bayle has escaped from the alternative route back to factory V4s to head the Rainey Yamaha team for 1998. Just watch him go.

AN

LUCKY STRIKE

EVEN DOZEN

Introduction & farewell

LUCKY STRIKE has been racing motorcycles at the highest level for 12 years. A round dozen seasons that have taken the famous bull's-eye logo to the heights of victory and the depths of despair.

Racing's like that. Always intense. Sometimes heartbreaking. Often uplifting. But always, always, exciting.

Lucky Strike knew it would be a special experience when they embarked on the adventure. They joined forces with a newcomer to the class, former triple World Champion Kenny Roberts, now operating his own 500-class team for the first time.

The new partners were instant high achievers. The riders were regulars on the top-three rostrum; their high-profile presence in the paddock made an instant impact.

Lucky Strike and Kenny Roberts together achieved greatness in four years of professionalism, and were twice runners-up in the 500cc championship – the prize every motorcycle racer values above all others.

Both would go on to win that crown – but not together. For Lucky Strike had found a new partner: the factory Suzuki team, with star rider Kevin Schwantz. The combination was to create a defining moment for the team, and for the sport. Schwantz and the Lucky Suzuki together forged a path to victory which was marked by swashbuckling style and lashings of true grit.

That coveted crown was finally theirs in 1993. Lucky Strike had won at last.

Victory was sweet – celebrated in fitting style with a gala banquet for Schwantz in Paris. But victory was not everything for the sponsors.

What mattered more was that the Suzuki team and its enormously popular hero Kevin Schwantz were forging an awareness of a special sort of brand image.

Racing the way they went racing meant the Lucky Strike message was spread far and wide across the world. And the image associated was of rugged individualism and self-reliance in a high-risk, high-speed, freedom-loving sport.

Lucky Strike has drawn much from that image over the years. It is something greater than the year-by-year ups and downs of racing.

The world changes, and concepts of marketing change with it. The owners of the Lucky Strike brand now see their own image changing, and they are altering their sponsorship programme accordingly. The 1997 season brings an end to this particular adventure for Lucky Strike. The famous logo is moving on.

They leave racing with goodwill on both sides, and a hatful of memories. Not just the triumph of Kevin Schwantz's crown, but of a thousand moments and incidents, setbacks and fightbacks, pain and victory . . .

These pages celebrate a dozen unforgettable years.

THE GREATEST YEAR – KEVIN SCHWANTZ

'93

Top: Kevin Schwantz on his way to the coveted 500cc crown in 1993. **Above:** Kevin and the number 34 plate which he made his own. **Opposite:** Schwantz rides the Lucky Strike Suzuki in 1994. As champion, he became number 1, but you can still see 34 tucked away at the bottom of the figure.

Several great riders have been Lucky Men – as the racers in the new bull's-eye leathers were soon nicknamed. None is so immediately associated with the tag as Kevin Schwantz.

The gangling six-footer from Texas was a giant of the sport in every way.

He abounded in natural talent, and rode a 500 with gleeful abandon. He'd make it do the apparently impossible; and in a time of golden talent he piled up pole positions, lap records and race wins as if there were no tomorrow.

When he didn't win, however, he'd often crash in the attempt. It was a bad habit for a man who would be champion. And while Kevin took alternating views from the top of the rostrum or the back of an ambulance, Wayne Rainey – himself a former Lucky Man – racked up three titles in a row.

This devil-may-care style did win the Texan a huge army of adoring fans. The archetypal Lucky Man was a star wherever he went. Even non-motorcycle people had heard of Revvin' Kevin Schwantz.

Kevin himself was a complex character.

One side was what everybody saw: a gun-totin', fun-lovin' cowboy who'd grown up around motorcycles, and chose the number 34 because it had been used in US dirt-track racing by his uncle, Daryl Hurst. This was the Schwantz who would tumble out of the lead of one race, and be back a fortnight later wearing a plaster cast on his wrist and a grin as wide as Texas.

The other was a brooding, introspective character who stayed mainly behind the closed door of his palatial motorhome (he was always a pace-setter in this area, too). This Schwantz blamed himself bitterly for his errors. And it was this side of his character which eventually won him the title: deliberately pushing his natural win-it-or-bin-it approach into the background in favour of uncharacteristic consistency, and the steadily accumulating tally of points that went with it.

He never lost his masterly riding style. Kevin could excel in almost any conditions. His trademark was wilful domination of the motorcycle. At times the Lucky Strike Suzuki would look like a bucking bronco as he forced it through a corner faster than the tyres and chassis could manage. Another hallmark was ultra-late braking, stealing positions from rivals by scorching past at impossible speeds, the back wheel up in the air and the front forks squirming. Yet in wet weather, he was also often unbeatable, deploying an unexpected smoothness and finesse. And his greatest successes came at technical circuits where riding skill was the most important factor – tracks like Suzuka, where he won four times, Donington Park (four wins) and Assen (three).

His personal selection of his best-ever race reflects this. It was not his stunning German GP win of 1991, when he sensationally outbraked his career-long rival Wayne Rainey on the final run into the stadium section – a frequently replayed TV moment. He rather recalls the Japanese GP of the same vintage year, where he dropped back to fourth from a fierce battle for the lead with handling problems. Then he found a way to adapt his cornering lines to turn weakness into strength, and came back to win.

Kevin's title victory coincided with another injury. Through no fault of his own, he and Lucky Strike Suzuki team-mate Alex Barros were both knocked off on the first lap of the 1993 British GP . . . by none other than Mick Doohan, the currently dominant figure in Grand Prix racing. Schwantz finished the year riding with a broken wrist, while Barros went on to claim his first 500-class victory in the final round.

The next year, further wrist injuries spoiled his title defence. The cumulative effect was to bring his career to a premature close halfway through 1995.

Kevin first came GP racing full time in 1988. He won his very first race as a full-time World Championship contender, and went on to rack up 24 more victories, against some of the toughest opposition of all time. It was a Golden Age of Grand Prix racing, and Schwantz's will not be the only name to remain as a reminder of it.

The number 34 – familiar to all emblazoned on a Lucky Strike logo – will also be his in perpetuity. It was officially retired from the 500 class as he announced his own retirement.

IN AT THE TOP - HOW THE ADVENTURE BEGAN

Lucky Strike's arrival in racing in 1986 meant a brand-new works team in an expanding sport. It also meant the return of Kenny Roberts as a team owner in the top 500 class, two years after retiring from his own glorious racing career.

Kenny had in fact run a 250 team in 1984 – a relatively low-key, low-budget effort with rookie rider Wayne Rainey on a production Yamaha. He had learned one important lesson: if you want to go racing for the World Championship, you have to do it properly.

Partnership with Lucky Strike was doing it properly.

The new sponsors brought with them a huge amount of prestige, and gave Roberts the budget he required to do the job in the way he knew it needed to be done.

Roberts brought much to the partnership. As well as his vast racing acumen and determination to succeed, he was a larger-than-life character who understood perfectly the changing needs of an increasingly professional sport. He lent his image wholeheartedly to Lucky Strike, and together they were established from the very beginning as leading players in the smart and prosperous new paddocks of the Grand Prix series.

Out on the racetracks, the new Yamaha team threw themselves into the task with gusto. In their first year, Randy Mamola recorded one win and he and team-mate Mike Baldwin were third and fourth overall. In 1987, Mamola ran a strong second in the championship, with three more victories.

Then came the big shake-up, with one-time GP winner Kevin Magee and Wayne Rainey (a double US champion) joining the squad for 1988.

Both "rookies" won a race in their first full seasons, but it was Rainey who emerged as the driving force in 1989. Riding with his unique combination of consistency and determination, he forged into the lead in the title points. This was a lead he was to hold until the third round from the end, when an entirely uncharacteristic race crash handed not only the Swedish GP, but also eventually the title to four-times champion Eddie Lawson.

For Lucky Strike, the Yamaha years were more than merely formative. They established the crimson roundel instantly as a major force on the track and in the paddock.

AFTER SCHWANTZ – DARYL BEATTIE COMES CLOSE, RUSSELL LEARNS FAST

Times have been tough for Team Lucky Strike Suzuki since Kevin Schwantz retired – not just because of his departure, but also due to a series of unlucky coincidences. It has been tough for other teams too, an upsurge in performance from Honda leaving its rivals struggling to get back on terms.

The Suzuki squad survived the loss of their great star well at first. Australian rider Daryl Beattie had been recruited to keep him company in 1995, and even

before Schwantz announced his surprise departure, had defeated Doohan and his Honda in the Japanese GP. He followed this with another win in Germany. Doohan had twice crashed, and Daryl now led the World Championship.

In retrospect, his first year as a Lucky Man was also his best, even though he did not stay ahead to the bitter end. Daryl's progress was interrupted by a rare crash in practice at Assen, but it took Doohan until the end of the year before he caught up on points and then finally outdistanced Beattie.

Since that time, Beattie has had misfortune pile on misfortune. Testing barely days before the start of the next season – when he had realistic ambitions to follow up his second position overall in the 1995

championship with a win – he crashed heavily and suffered debilitating concussion. He had not fully recovered when another crash led to further head injuries.

He returned with a clean bill of health for 1997, but struggled all season to recapture the essential confidence that would bring him and Lucky Strike Suzuki back to the front, where they belonged.

Beattie's major companion in 1995 and 1996 was another American, drafted in mid-season to replace Schwantz. Scott Russell was a former Superbike World Champion whose best result in his 18 months with the team was third place. He also brought a spirited approach to racing that enlivened his time with the team.

Top results proved elusive in Lucky Strike's final year with the team, for a variety of reasons. A dozen years of ex-

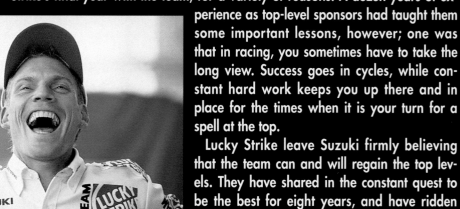

perience as top-level sponsors had taught them some important lessons, however; one was that in racing, you sometimes have to take the long view. Success goes in cycles, while constant hard work keeps you up there and in place for the times when it is your turn for a spell at the top.

Lucky Strike leave Suzuki firmly believing that the team can and will regain the top levels. They have shared in the constant quest to be the best for eight years, and have ridden the highs and lows with the factory team. It's been a hell of a ride.

LUCKY MEN – A PARADE OF LUCKY STRIKE RIDERS

Randy Mamola – 1986-7
Founder member, first GP winner, best of second overall.

Mike Baldwin – 1986-7
Other half of the new all-American team.

Kevin Magee – 1988-90
Joined on a Yamaha, stayed on with Suzuki – but was eliminated by a heavy crash.

Wayne Rainey – 1988-9
Almost took Lucky's first title in his second year – went on to win three times in different colours.

Kevin Schwantz – 1990-5
Longest serving and most illustrious. World Championship in 1993 was long overdue.

Niall Mackenzie – 1990
Scotsman took over from injured Magee, finished fourth overall.

Didier de Radigues – 1991
Belgian all-rounder spent one year in the shadow of Schwantz.

Doug Chandler – 1992
American champion frequently challenged his team-mate, just missed winning a GP.

Alex Barros – 1993-4
First year was his best, including one race win.

Daryl Beattie – 1995-7
Title runner-up in 1995, Beattie's consistency won him two GPs with the team.

Scott Russell – 1995-6
Ex-Superbike champion quickly learned how to ride a 500.

Anthony Gobert – 1997
Wild child from Superbikes promised much, but it ended prematurely in scandal.

LUCKY MEN
IN THE 250 CLASS

Martin Wimmer - 1991
Experienced German development racer gave new 250 Suzuki a promising debut.

Wilco Zeelenberg - 1992
Cheerful Dutchman ran strongly, but suffered injury problems.

Herri Torrontegui - 1992
Youthful Spaniard learned a lot in his first works team year.

John Kocinski - 1993
Big hopes ended in broken promises and a mid-season termination.

Simon Crafar - 1993
New Zealander, now racing Superbikes, took over for the rest of the year.

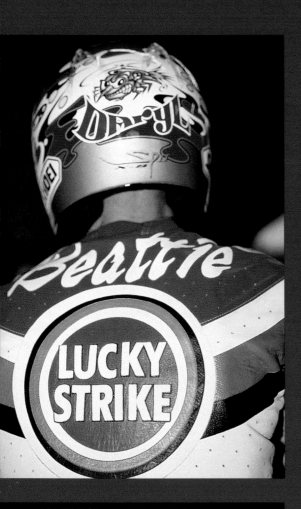

QUARTER-LITRE
INTERLUDE

Team Lucky Strike Suzuki also played its part in the second category of racing – the 250cc class. For three years, a smaller offshoot team ran one or two machines backed, like the 500 team, directly by the factory.

The 1991 season was a year of development, with the experienced Martin Wimmer (above) taking the new bike to ninth in the championship with a best finish of fifth. The following year, Dutch GP winner and Spanish 80/125cc star Herri Torrontegui campaigned the machines with mixed fortunes. Wilco Zeelenberg just missed the rostrum with a fourth and two fifth places, and finished 11th overall.

Then came 1993 – the crucial season. Former 250 World Champion and 500 GP winner John Kocinski (right) was recruited as the sole rider. The title was the goal. The effort foundered mid-season, however, following an angry outburst by the rider at the Dutch TT. He had finished a close third and broken the lap record, but that fit of temperament was the beginning of a premature end to the year.

Denied the GP success it craved, the Suzuki factory quit the 250 class at the end of that season. The V-twin 250 continued to race – and win championships – in the highly competitive domestic All-Japan series, and returned to GP racing in 1997.

COMMERCIAL GOOD SPORTS

Lucky Strike has been an important part of a remarkable period of growth for the World Championships – both commercially and geographically.

In the team's first year, 1986, the championship comprised 11 rounds, all in Europe. The annual Swedish GP was considered something of a long haul.

A dozen years later, the series has grown to 15 rounds, spanning South America and the Far East plus South-East Asia and Australia – and of course the European racing heartland.

Along with the broader horizons have come vastly increased worldwide audiences. As well as the first-hand spectators, there has been an explosion of TV viewers, with the global audience now counted in hundreds of millions.

The sport has become more professional, too – one outward sign being readily seen in a modern Grand Prix paddock. Twelve years ago the crisp and extensive Lucky Strike awnings stood out from a businesslike but relatively informal gathering behind the pits. Since then, a modern and hugely impressive mobile village on wheels has sprung up around the sponsors' tents and team vehicles.

Lucky Strike are satisfied with their 12-year motorcycle racing adventure. It has brought many dividends, created a broad platform for future endeavours, and set a standard both for motorcycle racing and for the sponsors themselves.

Above all, though, it's been 12 years of heart-in-mouth excitement which has left an indelible mark on the sport of Grand Prix racing.

A GALAXY OF WINS
LUCKY STRIKE GRAND PRIX RECORDS

YEAR – MACHINE	RIDER	RACE WINS	TITLE POSITION
1986 – ROBERTS YAMAHA YZR	Randy Mamola	1 Belgium	Third
	Mike Baldwin	-	Fourth
1987 – ROBERTS YAMAHA YZR	Randy Mamola	3 Japan/France/San Marino	Second
	Mike Baldwin	-	18th
1988 – ROBERTS YAMAHA YZR	Wayne Rainey	1 Great Britain	Third
	Kevin Magee	1 Spain	Fifth
1989 – ROBERTS YAMAHA YZR	Wayne Rainey	3 USA/Germany/Holland	Second
	Kevin Magee	-	Fifth
1990 – SUZUKI RGV GAMMA	Kevin Schwantz	5 Germany/Austria/Holland/France/GB	Second
	Niall Mackenzie	-	Fourth
	Kevin Magee	-	21st
1991 – SUZUKI RGV GAMMA	Kevin Schwantz	5 Japan/Germany/Holland/GB/Le Mans	Third
	Didier de Radigues	-	Eighth
1992 – SUZUKI RGV GAMMA	Kevin Schwantz	1 Italy	Fourth
	Doug Chandler		Fifth
1993 – SUZUKI RGV GAMMA	Kevin Schwantz	4 Australia/Spain/Austria/Holland	First
	Alex Barros	1 FIM (Jarama)	Sixth
1994 – SUZUKI RGV GAMMA	Kevin Schwantz	2 Japan/GB	Fourth
	Alex Barros	-	Eighth
1995 – SUZUKI RGV GAMMA	Daryl Beattie	2 Japan/Germany	Second
	Kevin Schwantz	-	15th
	Scott Russell	-	13th
1996 – SUZUKI RGV GAMMA	Daryl Beattie		18th
	Scott Russell		Sixth
1997 – SUZUKI RGV GAMMA	Daryl Beattie	-	11th
	Anthony Gobert	-	15th

TOTAL WINS 29

KEEPING UP APPEARANCES

THE STATE OF RACING

by Michael Scott

Photos: Gold & Goose

Huge crowds at Jerez *(left)* proved the strength of GP racing in Dorna's home country – and Valentino Rossi helped keep them entertained – but empty grandstands in Austria *(below left)* were a forlorn sight.

Wayne Rainey *(right)*, an outspoken critic, recommends a move to ban slick tyres.

Far right: Dorna managing director Carmelo Espeleta – beleaguered boss of the GPs.

THE Brave New World Championship of 1992 made a conscious effort for motor cycle Grand Prix racing to follow F1 car racing into the realms of professionalism, big business and high finance. Five years later, in spite of sterling efforts and high-level support, reality has fallen short of the dream.

Lacking a dictator – benevolent or otherwise – and pulled this way and that by conflicting short-term interests, the new GP package has meandered along, keeping up appearances while remaining endemically financially precarious. It has at least kept moving...but this past season has wandered further than ever onto stonier ground. Dorna can cite notable growth in Spain, among some positive points, but the loss of a major sponsor and of definitely one (Austria) and maybe more European races cannot be blithely ignored.

There was another factor in the comparison with the car GPs – the racing itself, in the premier 500 class at least. And for once the cars came closer than the bikes. This might ordinarily be considered circumstantial – but here again the management factor was crucial.

In general 1997 was a good year, in all three classes, in spite of Doohan's dominance. One knew who would win most of the 500 races, and that the equally dominant Hondas would in all likelihood fill the top five places; but there was more than a little uncertainty as to their order, and they were several times very close. The course of natural evolution was bringing up a new generation.

Car racing changes went beyond evolution. After a series of rules limiting technology, what had reliably been a distant and processional contest has become much closer and much more absorbing. Not only did the championship itself run until the last race, but the results at that final round at Jerez put the first four finishers within two seconds, and the first six within 4.5 seconds.

Though small beer by the standards of the 250 and 125 classes, there was not a single 500 race that came that close during 1997. And even before this, critics were already wondering why the bike racing authorities were not exercising the same sort of control over technical rules – and also behind the scenes over rider switches and other matters – to restore closer racing to the 500 class.

It was yet more proof that the business of Grand Prix racing did not become much more businesslike during 1997. With leaseholders Dorna still under severe financial pressure, and the FIM landlords locked in a continuation of their own endemic power struggles, nobody had the time, the vision or the strength of will to exert a firm hand on the tiller.

The result, as the season ended, was an uneasy prospect, where serious worries weighed against genuine progress in other areas. Perhaps the most visible worry was the departure of Lucky Strike who, rather understandably, found nothing much to excite them after 12 years of high-level support had tailed off with two disastrous seasons for Suzuki. With a new man in charge, they were off to Formula One. On the other hand, prospects were brightened after the season when a second Malaysian company stepped in to support an alternative to the Japanese works bikes. Under the formerly East German brand name MZ (now MuZ), the Elf V4 will return next year with a higher profile and bigger funding from the Hong Leon group, alongside fellow-Malaysians Modenas.

Always assuming Modenas are still there, of course. After a difficult first year Kenny Roberts ended his season with the threat, during tricky sponsorship negotiations, that they might not return.

It is clearly Dorna's job to apply this overall control. Luminary Roberts was particularly vocal during the year, criticising Dorna's lack of vision as well as their Spanish-oriented TV coverage. Some felt he had an axe to grind, having sought and been refused a contribution from Dorna to help his Modenas venture, on the grounds that a new team ought to be encouraged in the commercial interests of all. Others thought he had a good point, for the massive success of GP racing in Spain, when set against the dismal crowds in such disparate spots as Germany, Brazil, France and Austria (and the generally buoyant numbers of spectators for Superbike races), was as much an indictment of Dorna's provincialism as a beacon of success.

Here the example of Formula One becomes important, and the Svengali role played by its control-freak controller Bernie Ecclestone (tsar to the cars, expensive erstwhile friend to the

bikes). By various means, technical and also by a different sort of machination, situations like this are massaged towards resolution. Many thought that Dorna sorely felt the lack of such a figure – though one could also feel sympathy for managing director Carmelo Espeleta, financially beleaguered, under pressure both from IRTA and (sometimes conflictingly) from individual sponsors and team owners, and reporting not to an enthusiastic chairman of the board, but to a bunch of deeply conservative bottom-line bankers with a very firm grip on the purse-strings.

Many and various were the solutions offered – though suggestions as to who was going to pay for them were not so common. Some attacked the TV coverage which, in English-speaking Europe and several other important places, came free on Eurosport, but suffered from overkill, showing all timed practice sessions in full for all classes (the sort of blanket coverage more likely to irritate potential new viewers than to attract them); and was clearly on a very tight budget. Once again it compared badly with the Superbikes, for which viewers had to pay on Sky Sports. The coverage often also showed a strong bias, predominantly Spanish, where certain sponsors' bikes were shown assiduously, regardless of interest or achievement, while others passed virtually ignored.

Other suggestions included a general refocusing, most particularly at the cost of the 125 class. The impetus for this came from a faction inside IRTA, and bore fruit at the FIM Congress, with the introduction of age limit and other rules that clearly limit the smallest (and often irritatingly the most exciting) class to just one of its current roles...as a nursery feeder class for 250s and ultimately 500s. The new rules give the current lions of the class only two more years (three if 1997 was their first year); eliminate anybody over 25 in the future; and compel the championship winner to move out of the class directly so that there will be no more multiple – or even double – champions.

Another idea – improve the show, and let the technology go hang – echoed Formula One and was supported by, among others, Wayne Rainey: the banning of slick tyres, with treaded tyres compulsory not only at GPs, but throughout racing. This would level

the playing field in the same way as rainy conditions, and should guarantee closer and more spectacular action. The crowds would hardly have time to notice the fact that lap times were slower as the best riders in the world rediscovered how to slide a two-stroke GP bike...

Then there were those who wanted more sinister interference. People looked again at car racing, and the web of conspiracies (real or otherwise) by which Ecclestone is said to guide the placement of drivers. There was a growing body of opinion that bike racing needed the same thing, and a nucleus of complaint that Doohan had not been firmly moved to Yamaha or Suzuki from Honda, and that Kocinski had not been brought back from the Superbike wilderness. At year's end, it looked as though Kocinski would be back, and on a works Honda – and 'sources close to Dorna' claimed credit for the expected move. However, this may be a poisoned chalice – one can imagine the same voices raised in complaint against unsporting manipulation, should this trend go much further.

All the same, GP racing was not without comfort. Particularly when they compared themselves not with cars, but with the rival Superbike series. The acquisition of ex-Superbike stars Corser and Gobert may have proved little beyond the fact that V4 two-strokes are indeed rather hard to ride, and both departed (for various reasons) back to four-stroke racing for 1998. The consolation came only through *schadenfreude*: while the GPs had solved their problem of shrinking grids – first with the generation of works-replica ROC and Harris V4s, and then with the handy and slightly more competitive new V-twin Hondas – now the Superbikes were running into the same country, with privateers melting away and only 12 full-time works entries.

A dearth of a support level of Superbike privateers is nothing to be happy about, however. Nor is the fact that the upstart four-stroke series and the traditionally senior two-strokes should be competing for an apparently diminishing cake.

It seemed that international motor cycle racing took two steps backward and only one forward during 1997. But at least it's still on its feet, and by identifying the malaise and the reasons for it, there is room to reverse the trend.

In 1997, Dave Morris rode his Chrysalis BMW F650 to a convincing
victory in the single-cylinder class at the Isle of Man TT. To experience

1sTT.

BMW's superior engine technology for yourself, race round to your nearest BMW dealer.

The Ultimate Riding Machine

BIG BANG – OR BIG RED HERRING?

WHAT is the verdict? Big Bang, the narrow firing order engine, has brought no decisive drop in lap times, despite being hailed as grip- and confidence-boosting technology. Mick Doohan has run the 1997 season without its supposed benefits, hounded by Big Bang-equipped rivals, and yet he is 500 cc World Champion yet again. This leaves the onlooker decidedly undecided.

Before 1992, all 500 cc fours in GP racing fired two cylinders together, then fired the other pair 180 degrees later. This twice-per-revolution firing gave them their high, musical exhaust note. The 180 degree firing order offered a smooth power flow and good crankshaft balance with a single crank or two. Smooth power makes sense mechanically, for it reduces peak loads on clutches, gears and drivechain. In the late 1980s tyre grip became peaky, and the steep torque onset of 500 cc engines was about to be tamed by

electronic engine controls. Lower-gear corner exits in 1988-90 were hectic as riders sought the fine line between peak grip and violent high-side. Many were injured, and the sporting press raised its ancient cry of 'too fast for human reflexes'. In panic, everyone strove to 'save' 500 cc racing. The FIM raised the minimum weight limit. Tyre companies built more warning into their tyres. Engine controls proliferated. Honda campaigned for a displacement cut to 375 cc.

Then came a surprise. In 1992, Honda fielded its narrow firing angle or 'Big Bang' engine, which seemed to promise extra rear tyre grip during off-corner acceleration and gave riders the confidence to apply throttle even at high angles of lean. Everyone copied it instantly. In a narrow firing angle engine, only 70 degrees or less elapse between the firings of the two cylinder pairs, with 290 or more degrees of 'silence' thereafter, before the firing

cycle repeats. This gave the engine its distinctive low tone, more like that of a big motocross single.

In pre-season testing Mick Doohan resisted the innovation, finding it harder to steer the bike by breaking the back tyre loose with throttle. Wayne Gardner likened the new technology to racing a front-drive automobile; in a rear-drive car, the harder you gas it, the more sideways it becomes. But in a front-drive car the throttle straightens the car out. You feel, Gardner said of the Big Bang, as if you're being pulled through the corner.

Kevin Schwantz has said the back end hooks up so hard it feels like it's hit a berm. Eddie Lawson and Freddie Spencer described it as putting an end to no-warning rear-end breakaways.

There were a few Banger drawbacks. Drivetrains needed redesign to handle the larger torque transients. Because lumpy power created new tyre-related power losses, there was some drop in

top speeds. Despite this, Big Bang quickly became the new orthodoxy.

Since then, Big Bang 500s have voided the truism that 125 and 250 men cannot handle 500s. Talent spilled into 500 from the lower classes. None of these men is yet a master, but they have harried Doohan and they have won races. Asked why ex-250 riders can now cut the mustard, Schwantz replied, 'Because they (Big Bangers) break loose just like a 250.' Moving his hand slightly sideways with a 'BRRT' sound, he indicated that the breakaway is small and controllable.

Exiting a corner in the vicinity of 70-80 mph, with its engine turning perhaps 180 revs per second, a bike with a 180 degree crank delivers a power pulse for about every 3 in. that the tyre rolls forward. Because the tyre footprint is approximately twice this 3-in. length, the engine is firing twice during the time that a given element of rubber lies in the footprint. Power flow is basically smooth.

Doohan switched back to the older type of engine this year, but his fellow pilots stayed with the Big Bang. Here Criville and Abe enjoy its amenable power, while Aoki chases on a V-twin. The black tyre marks show riders still use wheelspin to steer a 500, but Doohan's 'Screamer' has already left them behind.

With the narrow firing order torque is not smooth but varies significantly in waves. With a 70 degree firing angle, and with a power stroke of just over 80 degrees, this makes one engine revolution into about one-third power, two-thirds coasting. At the corner-exit speed of our example, the rear tyre receives a pulse about every 7 in. that it rolls - one pulse per tyre footprint length. In effect, the tyre lays down a fresh footprint, then the engine loads it with a torque pulse.

How could this improve either control or grip? Honda's official explanation is that narrow firing angle works like anti-lock brakes in reverse. Anti-lock preserves directional control by cyclically unlocking the braked wheel just enough to keep it turning - and steerable. Big Bang, by pausing between torque pulses, probably does stop sideways sliding in much the same way - by allowing the tyre to roll forward several inches without

applied torque, so it regains any side grip it had lost during the previous engine torque pulse.

This doesn't answer the question of how the bike can accelerate without spinning, when engine torque is varying. If the tyre spins unpredictably when torque is smooth, won't it break away instantly when the torque is served up in lumps? Rubber is weird stuff. The materials people call its behaviour 'visco-elastic'. When you stress a piece of steel, it acts like a simple spring. But when you stress rubber, it acts more like a spring connected to a shock absorber. When you push or pull it, the spring changes length promptly, but it takes time for the viscous component - the shock absorber - to move. When rubber is stressed, it takes time for it to take new shape under the new load.

In an ideal tyre, every element of tread in the footprint would share equally in generating traction, but this is hard to achieve, even with radial construction. As a tyre rolls through a corner, tread laid down at the leading edge of the footprint has little stress in it, but stress increases as it moves from leading to trailing edge, through the footprint distorted by side force. Pure cornering - neither accelerating nor braking - produces a characteristic stress distribution in the footprint. Every racer has experienced the effects of an extreme version of this stress distribution in tyres without being aware of it; cornering onto slippery track, the steering 'goes light'. This is because the more stressed rear part of the footprint is the first to lose grip on the slippery track, and the steering lightness that is felt results from the lost leverage of that rear part of the tyre footprint.

Accelerating out of a turn, a rider can apply throttle only as he raises the machine; at full lean, all of the tyre's grip is used to make the machine turn, and none is left over with which to begin acceleration. But, as the rider lifts the bike, less side grip is demanded of the tyre and the difference can be used for acceleration. If the power flow is smooth, as from a 180 'Screamer' engine, the stress pattern in the footprint changes to include the stress imposed by steady engine torque. Instead of pointing sideways, the resulting combined stress now points at some intermediate angle - part forward, part sideways.

The effects of this combined stress can be seen on a race tyre that has done some mileage: the texture of wear is always at right angles to the imposed tractive stress. At tread centre the tex-

ture lines are parallel with the axle, but as they extend up the sides of the tread they turn more and more, indicating the combination of side force and engine thrust. If the rider is at the limit, the combined turning/accelerating load produces active sliding at the rear of the footprint. The rider modulates the throttle to keep the combined load at maximum as he lifts the machine, accelerating harder all the time. If he makes a mistake, the rear tyre spins up and may lose both forward traction and side grip altogether.

Now imagine pulsed power from a Big Bang engine in the same situation. Between torque peaks the tyre lays down a footprint carrying mainly stress imposed by cornering side load on it. Because the rider is lifting up to accelerate, this stress is less than maximum. Now the wheel rim accelerates, as the next engine torque pulse sweeps up toward its maximum. The radial cord fibres in the tyre sidewalls pull suddenly on the footprint, but the visco-elastic nature of rubber prevents the footprint from being instantly deformed by this pull. Because the footprint was laid down in the absence of maximum torque, the stress pattern in it is more uniform. As a result, the torque pulse is applied more equally to all parts of the footprint.

Where a steady stress distribution would have time to deform the footprint and possibly break it loose, the Big Bang torque pulse is applied too quickly for that to happen. The tyre grips. And even if the footprint finally gives way, beginning to slide as a whole, the torque pulse then dwindles enough that, as the tyre rolls forward, it regains grip. The rear of the bike does not slide sideways. Another torque pulse arrives. This process is like the ascent of a mountain climber; carefully he sets his pitons into the rock, and once they are secure, he uses them to pull himself up. The tyre lays down a low-stress footprint, and then it loads it - in rapidly repeating cycles.

The security of Big Bang grip has caused a convergence in riding style between 250 and 500 - a convergence that old-timers deplore. Doohan himself says that the on-board computer shows he applies power very gradually and early - a far cry from the decisive, generous application of engine torque described by rear-steer classicists. It is much more like the gradual power application practised by the high corner speed, front-steer 250 contingent.

Technology and riding style are linked in a circle of causation. The coming of high power and tyre grip

after 1972 made bikes hard to steer, forcing centres of gravity to be shifted forward; compare rider and engine position between 1967 and 1977. This forward weight shift, by imposing more load on front tyres, made motor cycles less stable when braking or off-throttle. Riders responded with an on-throttle style that relieved the small front tyre of some of this load; acceleration moved it onto the larger rear tyre. When radial tyre development brought huge but touchy rear tyre grip, there was a rash of corner-exit high-side accidents. Big Bang technology has been the most successful response to this.

Sceptics remind us that, despite the supposedly increased traction, lap times have not fallen much if at all with Big Bang - the exception being Phillip Island, which until 1997 had not hosted a 500 GP in years. Have tyres gone backwards in the interests of a wider, more controllable traction peak? Is it, as Kenny Roberts has suggested, the higher minimum weight and a younger field of riders who flunked rear-steer training? Or is it an actual loss of rear-steerability, once the centrepiece of a 500 cc master's style?

Big Bang grip discourages old-style rear-steer, but the resulting sustained acceleration unloads front tyres as it did after 1972, making front-steer equally difficult - as it always has been for two-stroke 500s. Doohan's mastery makes it possible for him to use either style of engine, but others are not so blessed. Now he has said that he chose the older engine type this year simply to play with his rivals' minds. He would have something they didn't, something outside their experience or skills, giving him a psychological advantage. Fair enough - we expect competition on all levels from a master.

This leaves 500 cc performance stuck between chancy rear-steer as it existed in 1991, and the current super-powerful Big Bang motor cycle that is predictable but not easily steered from either end. This is like comparing the F-104 with the F-16. Both are fast aircraft, but the F-16's flight technology makes routine of manoeuvres that require a master pilot in the 104.

A straightforward technology of raw grip and raw power achieved the record 500 cc lap times of 1991, but at high cost in rider risk. Now a subtler, more mature technology, Big Bang, has made it possible to do those lap times - and in some cases better them - in relative security and to put them within the capability of a wider field of competitors. This is progress; but serving social rather than strictly technical goals.

by Kevin Cameron

Remember your 1ˢᵗ sexual experience?

Chances are that you do. It's something you never forget, even if you want to.

It's there, along with the first time you cycled down the road without stabilisers

and the first time you stayed out all night.

Ask anyone who's ridden the Road King® Classic and they would add this to their

'list of things to tell their grandchildren'. All the reassurances of a modern bike,

but the look and feel that you're sitting on a piece of American heritage. The rumble

of the V-twin, the heads turning as you go through town after town-

these aren't things you forget in a hurry.

And we have a suspicion, once you've tried it,

it's something you'll want to do again and again.

Call **0345 883 1340** today

for more information on the 1998 Harley-Davidson® motorcycle range

now available from £4,995 on the road, at your authorised dealer.

http://www.harley-davidson.com

Road King® Classic shown from £12,995.

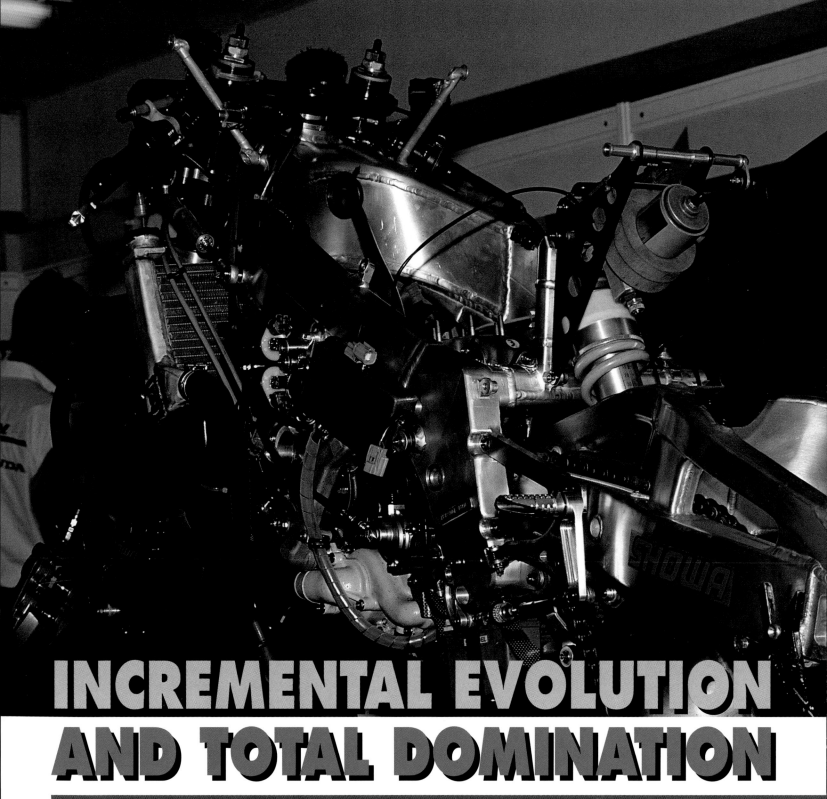

INCREMENTAL EVOLUTION
AND TOTAL DOMINATION

THE strangest thing about the domination of the V4 Honda in the 500 class was not the blanket coverage, but that it was achieved by positively eschewing technical changes. If the men in the pits are to be believed, the NSR of 1997 had only the smallest evolutionary changes compared with last year's winning machines, and not that many since 1992.

By logical progression, then, the mistake made by their rivals was to attempt progress. Beaten last year, both Suzuki and Yamaha went back to their drawing boards. What they came back with was – in one way or another – beaten even more badly than what they had before.

To the drawing board also for Team Roberts, in the biggest possible way – with their all-new three-cylinder machine. Not surprisingly, the Mode-

nas suffered from several flaws – this might be considered endemic to a first prototype of a design that broke with convention in a number of respects. Its biggest flaw, perhaps, was over-inflated expectations, and while it performed creditably on several occasions (though seldom for very long), it fell so far short of the hype that it looked to be a lot more disappointing than it actually was. The season ended back at the drawing boards yet again.

The all-European rivals were to have a difficult year. Development of the Elf 500 V4 ran into a number of intractable problems; Aprilia's V-twin, on the other hand, improved in leaps and bounds, without solving its biggest problem – how to leave the line fast enough to race up front. If GPs had rolling starts the Italian bike's results would be very different!

HONDA

This was the V4 NSR's fifth year in its present form, with only detail changes. Yet it seemed that something had crystallised in the design, for the NSR was exceptionally user-friendly, rewarding (with only one exception) the old hands and welcoming newcomers. Attainment of that ideal has been a slow but inexorable process over more than a decade, and the current state of bliss entails a marriage between the vast resources and fertile imaginations of HRC's engineering department and the matter-of-fact development criteria and strength of character of their leading rider.

It is a truism that every race-developed motor cycle is tailored around that factory's top rider. It is Honda's great good fortune that Mick Doohan's preferences for drivability – in contrast to their long-standing penchant for

out-and-out top speed – have resulted in a motor cycle that is not only the most powerful 500, but also the bike with the most amenable manners and well-rounded character.

The biggest change for 1997 applied only to Doohan's machine, and entailed reverting to an evenly spaced firing order, with cylinder pairs firing 180 degrees apart, rather than the '70 to 90 degrees' of the Big Bang. According to Doohan's chief engineer, Jeremy Burgess, the engines were otherwise identical, and completely interchangeable within the chassis, which has itself undergone only minor changes since 1992.

Doohan's switch – analysed below and in greater detail elsewhere in *Motocourse* – must be measured against the full picture of NSR motor development. The current generation dates back to 1992, and the arrival of

Chris Sims

Honda's V4 NSR, revealed in all its glory. Steady evolution has polished and refined the design to a high degree. One change for this year was a larger capacity rear damper unit, clearly seen in this picture.

Below: Stripped for action, Okada's V-twin NSR500-V Honda was the factory development prototype, and received updates and revisions all year long.

itself, explains Burgess. 'They were modified for more top-end power. (Shinichi) Itoh and Daryl Beattie were not able to see that this was not a good idea. Mick insisted that the 1992 bike was better.' After some experiments using the 1992 cylinders he was happier, and 'since that time it's been a logical development by Mick each year to try to get more bottom power and more drivability.'

In pre-season tests this year, this quest was continued. 'We don't play a lot with exhaust pipes like some teams do. We worked mainly on reed valves and cylinders. This year we started by testing back to back with 1996 and '97 cylinders, and there were only small differences. They were on and off and on and off – the '97 cylinder with the '96 reed, and so on – and though it wasn't brilliant we were learning things.'

Knowledge is power, and HRC have extensive knowledge of the NSR. Doohan's team within HRC also have a tremendous familiarity, invaluable in finding quick ways to deal with problems at various tracks. 'We can make a small change to the bellmouths of the carburettors, and get an instant response from the rider. But if you look at, say, Kenny's (Modenas) team, they haven't even finalised carburettors yet.'

The heat had gone off electronic development, said Burgess, compared with a couple of years ago, when there was more experimentation. Again this is Mick's preference. 'We don't even fit the three-way switch' (which provides a selection of pre-mapped ignition curves and other engine management functions) 'to Mick's bike. You tend to run the same programme all the time, so you're just carrying extra weight.'

Chassis-wise, Doohan also has a few differences. 'The suspension was updated last year and this year – we moved to bigger volumes of oil and gas in the rear shock, just for a smoother ride. Mick runs the steel front forks rather than the carbon forks, which have a thicker-walled tube and therefore less air/oil volume. So, for example, when he's braking and turning at the same time he gets that little bit of extra stroke where there seems to be a bit of a lock situation with the carbon.'

The puzzle of the year, at the start, was Mick's reversion to the old firing order – by reputation this should have resulted in tyre-destroying wheelspin. That view did not take into account the other big differences wrought to the power curve since that time. 'It is quite wrong to think of this as a revival of the old engine,' says Burgess. 'The power characteristics are completely different.' Even so, Burgess was apprehensive. 'Mick decided to ride with that engine, and I was somewhat cautious about Malaysia. But when we got through there with no tyre problem I thought we were on our way.'

Doohan cited a 'more direct connection between the throttle and the back tyre' as his reason for the change. Late in the season he introduced another component – that he'd changed also 'to mess with the other riders'. Burgess gives credence to the first reason. 'The 180 has less engine braking and it freewheels a lot better. That makes it smoother running into the corners. Conversely, when you open the throttle it comes on with less of a surge. So it actually highlights what Mick is very good at – which is corner speed. That's why he liked it. In other areas, when it first starts to spin, it'll spin up quicker

than the Big Bang. Throttle control is the essence of the whole thing, and our data-logging shows how much better Mick's throttle control is than our other riders.

'We've had some harmonic frequency problems with it, and you can see it lurching at the starts a bit, when it's in the high rpm. That's caused by the clutch, and I think that can be cured, by going to a carbon-fibre clutch perhaps. For Mick, purely to make the lever lighter for when he's also using the thumb brake, we've gone from a six-plate to an eight because it has less pressure on the springs. The harmonic frequency of the 180 motor would vibrate the clutch plates when they were lifted, and that caused the drag and starting problems. It also gave us some problems back-shifting. We changed the backlash in some of the gears in the last month of the season, and we seem to be on top of that.'

A clutch plate breakage at Imola was blamed on the vibration, and it caused some knock-on problems in pre-race warm-up, solved for the race (q.v.). The only other failure was a broken exhaust valve linkage at Jerez, which at the time was also blamed on harmonic vibrations. Not so, revealed Burgess. 'The valve plate that broke was the wrong material. Somebody had made it out of the wrong stainless steel. Everybody's was checked after that, and that part could have failed on the other engine too.'

HRC also continued intensive development on the V-twin, so that Takuma Aoki's factory-backed bike received continual updates and revisions to make it a very different machine from the production bikes sold to the privateers.

Gold & Goose

by Michael Scott

the Big Bang. At the same time as the revolutionary new firing order – immediately copied by all other V4 manufacturers – came a raft of improvements. As Burgess says: 'The big step was the crankshaft timing but, at the same time, the cylinder was massively modified and changed.' Honda's new user-friendly tuning was a long way away from what had gone before, with its 'very peaky engine and very straightline oriented machine'.

Since then, the engine had only developed in detail, the major change being the adoption of ram-air induction in 1993. Typically, Doohan rejected this at first, only later adopting a simplified form which dispensed with the fuel pump, equalising pressure in the fuel tank to match the airbox by the simple means of a balance tube. This was more because of his dislike of the 1993 cylinders than the airbox

DIFFERENT BIKES,

MICK DOOHAN 500cc WORLD CHAMPION, NSR500V.

JOHN KOCINSKI WORLD SUPERBIKE CHAMPION, RC45.

PAUL BROWN SHELL ADVANCE SUPERSPORT 600 CHAMPION, CBR600.

STEFAN EVERTS 250cc MOTOCROSS WORLD CHAMPION, CR250.

MICHAEL RUTTER NORTHWEST 200 WINNER, CBR600.

IAN SIMPSON JUNIOR T.T. WINNER, CBR600. (NEW LAP AND RACE RECORD 119.86 mph)

OUR OTHER 1997 SUCCESSES INCLUDE: DARREN BARTON, SHELL ADVANCE 125cc BRITISH CHAMPION. IAN LOUGHER, ULTRA
PHIL McCALLEN, PRODUCTION T.T. WINNER, CBR900RR FIREBLADE AND SENIOR T.T. WINNER, RC45 - ALL TOGETHER NOT

DIFFERENT CLASS.

PHIL McCALLEN T.T. FORMULA 1 WINNER, RC45.

JOEY DUNLOP LIGHTWEIGHT T.T. WINNER, RS250R.

JOAKIM KARLSSON BRITISH OPEN MOTOCROSS CHAMPION, CR250.

JAMES TOSELAND CB500 CUP CHAMPION, CB500.

MAX BIAGGI 250cc WORLD CHAMPION, NSR250.

SHINICHI ITO AND TOHRU UKAWA (PICTURED) SUZUKA 8 HOURS WINNERS, RC45.

IGHTWEIGHT T.T. WINNER. SCOTT SMART, SHELL ADVANCE 250cc BRITISH CHAMPION.
AD YEAR.

FOR MORE INFORMATION ON THE 1998 RANGE OF HONDA MOTORCYCLES CALL 0345 585570 FOR A FREE BROCHURE.

HONDA
REAL RIDERS RIDE HONDA.

YAMAHA

Honda had some reason to be happy with what they already had. Yamaha had reason to be dissatisfied, and they instituted a thorough redesign of both chassis and engine. Their downfall was that when they had given their best shot to an alternative and improved machine, it failed to live up to expectations – and they were obliged to take several steps backwards after new cylinder designs could not be made race-ready in time. The end result was that, for the first time in 34 years, the great sporting Japanese factory did not win a single race in any GP class.

The target, according to Grand Prix manager Shuji Sakurada, had been improved engine performance across the board, with an increase in total horsepower as well as stronger bottom end and a good connection between the two.

The major thrust came in cylinder port design, with two different types under experiment – a 'T-port' (comprising a pair of tall and narrow ports side by side) and 'sub-exhaust ports', a pair of smaller ports on either side of the main oval, opening later to boost port area at the bottom of the stroke. The aim of the latter was to introduce an element of asymmetry to the ports, giving a handle on overall gas flow control. 'It's not a completely different direction, but it represents a big step,' said Sakurada-san, adding that they'd experimented also with different types of powervalve. Working with simulations, on the test bench, and with riders Cadalora and Gibernau, 'The new designs have not been successful – yet – but we are still continuing.'

Yamaha's bike was always considered to be a well-rounded machine, but the factory felt there was a weakness in corner entry. 'The Yamaha has good grip in the open-gas area – the middle to the exit of the corner. This has always been some advantage – now we are working on rider confidence going into the corners.' Yamaha were in any case revising chassis settings after the switch in 1996 from Dunlops to Michelins. 'The requirements of the chassis are different. We believe we have been quite successful. It's been a difficult evolution, but sometimes Luca's performance has been very close to that of the Hondas.'

Although changed geometrically and in engine position, this year's chassis matched last year's for stiffness. The changes accommodated a revision to engine architecture. The V-angle was slightly increased, creating more space for induction equipment – especially the ram-fed airbox. This was still under development, with attention to levelling the pressure. 'We need some improvement in this area.'

The other significant change was the reintroduction of magnesium crankcases in time for the German GP – a race that Luca led convincingly in

the early laps, before falling off. Yamaha had used both magnesium and aluminium between 1993 and 1996 but had had problems with magnesium, including a short life. New metallurgy had solved that problem, said Sakurada-san, and magnesium was better in respect of matching heat expansion and maintaining bearing clearances to make the engine rev more freely. Most important was the weight saving, improving overall distribution to make the bike steer better.

For Yamaha, working to find more and more performance out of such a long-established design had already led them deep into the territory of diminishing returns. 'The design of the racing two-stroke engine is now very mature, and there is not so much room for sudden improvements,' said Sakurada, adding a possible pointer to future developments. 'Mainly we are thinking about the conditions inside the expansion chambers. New electronic developments may help in this area. We also tested electronic traction control this year – but if the engine power delivery is correct, we don't think it is necessary.'

SUZUKI

Suzuki's year was, according to team manager Garry Taylor, 'disastrous'. Problems with the new bike and the two riders chased each other in circles, and trackside progress was as frustratingly absent as were rostrum finishes.

The rider component was certainly destructive. Beattie seemed detuned and was so mistrustful of the overall feel of the machine that his contribution was negligible. He saw it differently – feeling that the bike had built-in problems that the factory didn't seem prepared to fix. Gobert, as a 500 class (and indeed almost a two-stroke) novice simply didn't have the experience. Between the two of them, the year was more or less wasted in terms of development. Back at the factory, however, the new engine showed up well on the test bench while test rider Yukio Kagayama in particular set increasingly promising test times.

The new bike was conceived after Suzuki had considered the merits of the V-twins and forthcoming three-cylinder designs. They had decided that the balance of power would still favour a V4, but only if its potential was maximised. Or in this case minimised, taking the bike to the absolute minimum size and weight to improve manoeuvrability. The all-new XR-87 was in every way an evolution of previous year's bike, but there were no interchangeable parts. It was smaller and more compact in every regard: engine size and weight, chassis size and bodywork. It was completed in time for pre-season tests, and many changes meant it could be fairly considered as an all-new bike.

In one important regard it was the direct opposite of the Honda. Where the NSR had been subject to the continuous development of one exceptional rider (not to mention further input from as many as five or six other riders every year), Suzuki's continuity had been broken with the departure of Kevin Schwantz midway through 1995. Beattie was in place to pick up the threads, but then he missed most of 1996 with a series of troublesome head injuries, returning only in 1997 with a clean bill of health.

Thus the XR-87 was an engineers' rather than a rider's bike, conceived on the drawing board to offer theoretical advantages, without the benefit of a consistent development rider to assess the changes while they were in progress.

Beattie mistrusted the new chassis from the start, and by the second race switched to a hybrid bike that had been a halfway house during testing – with the slightly more powerful new motor in a modified '97 chassis. Halfway through the season, having achieved little or no progress with that bike, he switched to the full XR-87, with similar results.

He complained that the bike was both hyper-sensitive to chassis settings, and inconsistent in its responses to adjustments, and that it was lacking in every area of cornering ability, from turn-in to exit. It was capable of fairly good lap times, but only when it had the track to itself. He needed lots of room – in close company he wasn't able to open the throttle early enough to race it out. Oddly, he often set his best lap times at the end of the races, commenting: 'I feel more confident when the tyres have started sliding around.'

The team in turn wondered about his own apparent lack of commitment, while all the time awaiting a breakthrough as they pursued a normal programme of engine improvements and suspension adjustments, including different rear linkages. They switched early on from their long-standing use of AP Racing brakes to Brembos, widely used in the paddock – also without improvement.

Among this atmosphere of puzzlement and search for scapegoats, Gobert was himself at odds with the front forks, which did not work well under his hard-braking style. They would feel as though they bottomed out, though this was only sometimes the case.

The only ray of light came at the end of the year, when Peter Goddard came in as a substitute and seemed to achieve a promising development direction – a clutching at straws, given that he achieved little better in terms of qualifying or finishing positions; and when in the final round tester Kagayama produced a relatively storming performance. This was followed by productive test sessions

when 1998 signing Nobuatsu Aoki tested the bike for the first time.

Plans for next year included promises from the factory of a thorough programme of improvements, as well as a complete change in rider line-up.

APRILIA

After their best season so far, Aprilia's seminal 'super-250' V-twin grew to almost full size, and its performance improved with it. Doriano Romboni was on the front row of the grid four times and even challenged for pole – and at Assen he achieved the bike's first-ever rostrum.

The increase in size came in stages said designer Jan Witteveen, as their experience and improved metallurgy allowed them to increase the size of the cylinders without losing the revvability that was, for him, the key to success. 'We started the year at 410 cc, then went to 460 cc, then to 480 cc. After the season we have been testing with a full 500, with good results,' he said.

Both bore and stroke had been increased, the former more than the latter, to make the motor even more over-square, Witteveen continued. This limited the increase in piston acceleration, while new materials and techniques limited the increase in piston weight. This is still the limiting factor in rpm, the Dutch designer admitted, 'but we have lost only 100 to 150 rpm compared with the 410.'

On the other hand, gains in power and torque had been significant...up by season's end by some ten horsepower to give a total of 'more than 140', according to Witteveen.

The reason for the bike's existence – 1997 was its fourth year – is to brake and corner faster than the V4s, while the latest revisions brought it much closer on top speed on all but the longest straights. Intermediate-size Dunlop tyres worked well with the machine to give some notably strong performances, especially in the later stages of the race, when the V4s' tyres had started to feel the pace. But one bugbear remained – poor starts would time and again render all Romboni's practice efforts worthless, as he'd be passed on all sides by V4s and Honda V-twins.

Witteveen agrees it is a last remaining weakness in the package, but thinks it may have been exaggerated by the notorious Romboni nerves. 'It is hard to pontificate when you have only one rider. We practised the starts over and over at our test sessions, and we could compare times and acceleration with what happened in the races. When Romboni was alone, the results were always quite good. It was only when he was surrounded by other bikes that he had these problems.'

The factory are expected to support the project for one more year in 1998, although the actual racing team may be independently run.

Gold & Goose

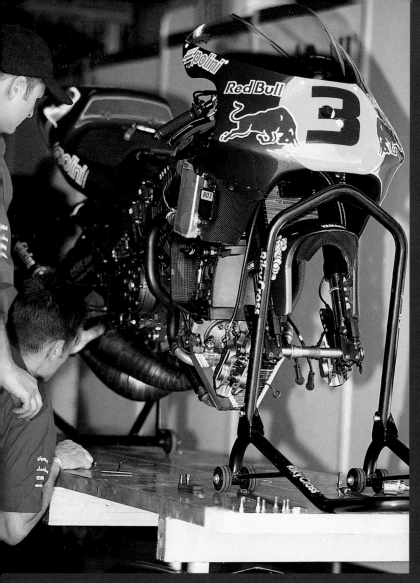

Chris Sims

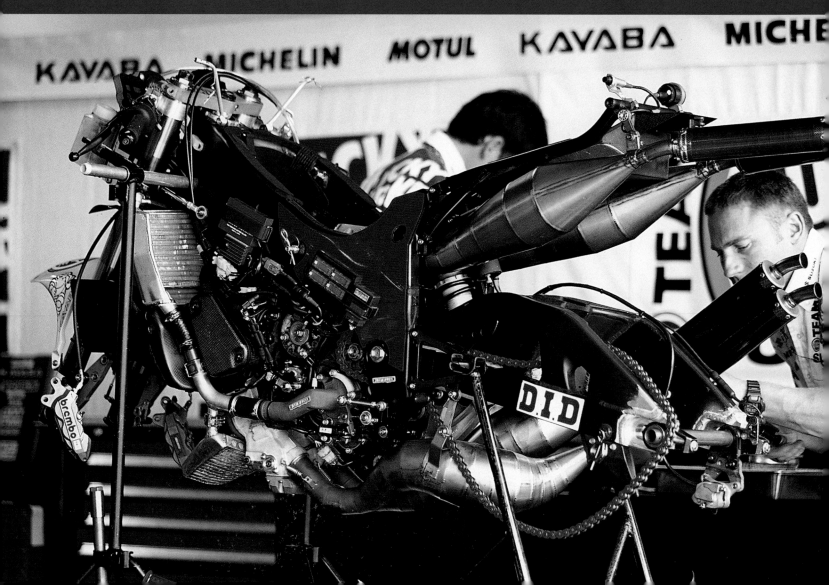

Left: The Elf 500 followed convention in all areas except internal engine design.

Below left: The Modenas was different in many areas – rare strip-down shot shows special carburettors and recirculating fuel system with belly tank. Radiator is under the seat, fed by internal ducts.

Right: The Elf's gold Ohlins forks were state-of-the-art.

Chris Sims

ELF

The alternative V4 did most things differently from the Japanese. Sharing a single-crankshaft layout with the NSR Honda and fitted during 1996 with a similar balance shaft and 'clap-valve' exhaust power system, the Elf departed thereafter from convention. The cylinder pairs shared common crankcases, eliminating two main bearings to reduce friction and overall size, and used 180 degree rather than Big Bang firing order. The née Swissauto/née BRM motor screamed like Doohan's Honda.

Already rich in top-end power, the team had experimented with close firing order the previous year and in the winter, but had stuck with the Screamer, following the one-time HRC wisdom that if you start off with plenty of speed, you can sort the rest out later. Doohan's similar choice was a further encouragement. Said designer Urs Wenger later: 'I guess when Okada tried the Screamer and it didn't work we realised we should have persevered with our own Big Bang. We should have tested it more thoroughly last year. We noticed that our bikes would lose ground in the second half of the race, because of tyre wear and poor traction.'

Both riders fell off rather more often than was comfortable – Borja nine times. This pointed to drivability problems, but Wenger defends the wheelspin-prone engine. 'We all agreed the drivability problems were only 20 per cent engine and 80 per cent chassis – a matter of settings. We had no budget for overseas tests before the season, and our two tests at Jerez were rained off. That left us with problems all season.'

In any case, a switch to an electric fuel pump midway through the year improved drivability, especially at the crucial moment of opening the throttle. 'We use the same Mikuni carburettors as Yamaha, and they told us that with the airbox fitting a fuel pump improved response.' This proved to be the case. 'It was one of the biggest steps we made.' But it brought other problems.

'The pump drained the battery, so we had to fit a generator, with a smaller battery.' Generator failure caused one of Borja's three breakdowns; another was caused when a low-budget exhaust pipe split. Other reliability problems cost the machine several top ten finishes as it faded towards the end.

'Improving reliability is the major aim for the winter tests, and we hope to perform extensive overseas tests. We will also have a separate testing team, running away from the GP tracks,' said Wenger, whose budget problems appeared to have been solved by new backers.

For its first two years the project was backed by Elf, with technical preparation by Serge Rosset's ROC establishment.

From next year, it has been taken under the wing of the Malaysian-owned former East German MuZ (formerly MZ) firm, and will race as an MuZ.

Rosset will remain involved for one more year. He retains some optimism. 'We had a budget of $3 million and a staff of ten, compared with Team Roberts's budget of $14 million and a staff of 80. I don't think we did too badly.'

MODENAS

The Modenas was the freshest and most original machine in the field. Technically unusual, the first three-cylinder machine since Honda's NS of more than ten years before, its provenance was unique. In the manner of Formula One car racing, and using the same England-based infrastructure in the 'F1 belt' around Banbury, it bore the name of a Malaysian manufacturer (of commuter bikes) but was produced entirely by racing specialists. The all-important engine was built by TWR (Tom Walkinshaw Racing) – and it was the high-profile touring cars-to-Formula One outfit's first-ever two-stroke.

It was also the most rushed – built in a matter of months and consuming midnight oil at a prodigious rate. Even then it was barely ready for the first race, and once the season was under way elements of the plan – including aerodynamics – already running behind schedule had to be shelved completely as the team fought to cope with the daunting task of achieving reliability and raceworthiness for a set of still-experimental ideas.

The clean sheet of paper gave Team

Roberts the chance not only to incorporate their own long-standing ideas but also to produce a highly integrated design. Built down to a size as well as the 115 kg weight limit (saving 15 kg against the fours), the Modenas's first departure from convention was in the rear-mounted ducted radiator, giving the cowling a uniquely clean and compact frontal aspect. Wind-tunnel tests during the season showed many errors in the seat-of-the-pants design, but there was no chance by then to change it much, and the principle remained right.

Suspension and running gear followed convention. The other departure was in the engine. It was not merely a V-three. It was actually a lopsided triple, marrying a V-twin in which the cylinders shared a common crankcase and fired simultaneously with a third cylinder tacked on the side. Its compact dimensions left no room for conventional carburettors, and 'KR' instruments were specially designed. These were to a still-secret design, substituting float bowls with a recirculating pumped system – 'not fuel injection', according to Roberts. 'Just a different way of getting fuel into a hole.'

Power was not revealed, but it was 'sufficient' for the machine to exploit a higher cornering speed, at least in theory. To this very end it had been designed to use 250-size rear tyres, or at least an intermediate size like that used by Aprilia's V-twin. As it turned out, they ran on full-size (6-in. rim width) 500 cc rears right until the last race of the season, although with their lighter weight and lower power output

the three-cylinder bikes were able to use softer constructions than the V4s.

The Modenas's main weakness was endemic to its design. The lopsided layout caused vibration so severe that it snapped footrest hangers, frothed the fuel and the coolant, chafed through wiring, caused component failures – and in general subjected the bike (and its riders) to a constant destruction test.

The fuel problems were constant but erratic. 'One time it will carburate fine. Next time it goes out it misfires and comes back in spitting fuel everywhere,' said Roberts, who arranged during the year for an alternative set-up using conventional float bowls, but did not use it. Why should it be different, when the vibration was the cause of the problems?

Cooling was also a bugbear, with flow to the rear radiator falling short of requirements. Roberts blamed cavitation and matters improved with careful attention to the pumping arrangements – but the extra degrees never really went away, adding to reliability problems and costing horsepower throughout.

The vibration was clearly a design fault. Roberts has stated that the engine needs a redesign if he is to bring it back next year, and insists that even if the shared crankcase design is retained (by no means a certainty), there will be another main bearing between the crankshaft throws. And a balance-shaft. 'Even if we don't use it, there'll be space for one.'

This belt-and-braces fix would cost weight, size and internal friction; Kenny's vehemence reveals the extent of the problem. He blames misleading information from the crankshaft suppliers, who had promised the shafts would be stiff enough that they would not vibrate.

Given these development problems and the tight schedule, though, the Modenas made a highly promising showing, including a front-row qualifying position for Bayle at Brno. It was, after all, a first prototype undergoing development in public in the white heat of the World Championship. Yet the project was regarded as something of a failure. This was for a non-technical reason.

The Modenas project was saddled with overly high expectations, the result of high-profile big-money backing from Marlboro as well as Kenny's own ambitions. The team had bitten off more than they could chew in making it competitive in its first year. This cost results and, at year's end, it looked like it might also cost the Marlboro backing. Kenny Roberts ended his hardest-ever season seeking an even bigger-spending sponsor to assure the continuance of the Modenas. 'This year, I did it because I wanted to,' he said. 'Next year, it has to be done as a business.'

LEAN

LET THE FEAST BEGIN - CAN'T GIVE IT UP CAN YOU? YOU'VE TRIED THE ALTERNATIVES, THE LOW CALORIE, LOW ENERGY COMPROMISES. YOU KNEW - IN YOUR BONES - REAL BEEF COMES FROM A RARE BREED - AND LEAN BEEF RARER STILL.

LOW FAT, HIGH ENERGY - INTRODUCING THE 1998 KAWASAKI ZX-9R AND ZX-6R, REAL BEEF - STRAIGHT FROM THE CRATE. WE'VE TAKEN A LONG HARD LOOK AT TWO OF THE WINNINGEST BIKES ON THE STREET, CARVED POUNDS OFF AND RELEASED EVEN MORE RAW POWER TO CREATE THE NEXT GENERATION OF KAWASAKI SUPERSPORTS MOTORCYCLES.

RAW AND RARE - THE ZX-6R GETS RARE EARTH ALTERNATOR MAGNETS FOR A LIGHTER, SLIMMER ENGINE. WHY? YOU WOULDN'T RIDE THE ZX-6R IF YOU DIDN'T HUNGER FOR IMPOSSIBLE LEAN ANGLES WOULD YOU! DID ANYONE SAY CARBON? THINGS HAVE MOVED ON - THE SILENCER CAN ON THE ZX-9R IS ULTRA LIGHT TITANIUM. AND NOW SELECTED COVERS ON BOTH MILLS ARE SUPERBIKE SPEC MAGNESIUM FOR LOW WEIGHT AND MAXIMUM MUSCLE.

RIDE THE RANGE - SEE AND EXPERIENCE THE KAWASAKI RANGE OF MOTORCYCLES FROM 50cc > 1500cc AT YOUR OFFICIAL FRANCHISED KAWASAKI DEALER. ALL PROVIDE UNPARALLELED KAWASAKI EXPERTISE AND A RANGE OF UNIQUE BENEFITS LIKE K CARE FINANCE & INSURANCE, FREE RIDER CLUB MEMBERSHIP ON NEW MACHINES, OFFICIAL KAWASAKI CLOTHING, ACCESSORIES AND THE FULL BACK UP THAT ONLY AN APPROVED AUTHORISED DEALER CAN PROVIDE.

CALL 0800 500 245 FOR A RANGE BROCHURE.

ZX-9R

Date: 18/10/'97 Name: Marty L
Model: ZX6R / ZX9R X
Conditions: Fine & Dry - 15 h/wind-23c
Comments: Felt right straight away, awesome braking, engine cannot be faulted...I want one!

ZX9R-ZX6R PRIVATE TRACK Test (b)

flik flak   out of seat   Amazing brakes!
head down
change line
knee down!
first time
feels - good

BEEF

SUPERBIKE STYLE
MAGNESIUM ENGINE CASES

IN-FLIGHT INFORMATION
ZX-9R STYLE

ZX-9R POWERPLANT -
BIG, BRASH AND BRUTAL

LIME GREEN ZX-9R -
WE HAD TO DIDN'T WE?

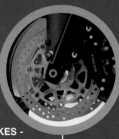

RACE BRED BRAKES -
A ZX-9R TRADEMARK

uck-in behind screen　　　ZX-6R　　　*...end - I'm in LOVE !*

cuts in - 4th...oops!　　*6th top gear*

Kawasaki

Let the good times roll.

TWO YEAR WARRANTY

Left: By the time he won the title in Brno, Rossi's fan club was a highly organised force.

Right: Fitting inside the bubble of the 125 Aprilia was rather a squeeze for the gangling teenager.

Below: Another day, another win. Rossi slaughtered the establishment in the smallest class.

VALENTINO'S DAYTIME MASSACRE

VALENTINO ROSSI PROFILE

by Michael Scott

Father and son – two generations of crazy GP winners. *Below:* Graziano was shown with his new son in the 1980-81 edition of *Motocourse.*

'I like him from the beginning – because...' Aprilia's charismatic racing boss Carlo Pernat gets a faraway look in his eyes '...because he reminds me of Kevin Schwantz.'

The image is unexpected. Schwantz is a Texan cowboy – New World man incarnate. The other man we are talking about – well, more of a boy than a man – is Valentino Rossi, an ultra-modern Italian with a crazy effeminate way of dressing, and very Old World eyes.

Then it makes sense. There are a lot of similarities...beyond the way they both are all knees and elbows as they sit on a motorbike. There's the swaggering riding style, with the apparent ability to get a motor cycle to do impossible things, way beyond what anyone else is doing. There's the showmanship, the extravagant post-race antics. And there's the *joie de vivre* that so marked out Schwantz's earlier racing years, before accidents and racing's hardships took their toll.

Yet it's not enough. Schwantz was his own man in his own era. Rossi is just a kid standing on the threshold. By the time the Italian has been through the years and achievements of the now-retired American, he will have carved his own legend. He will hardly need to borrow from another.

Does he need to now? It is surely significant that, after a spell in which critics of Grand Prix racing have been complaining about a staleness, the most exciting figure in the series should be a teenage shooting star. About time one came along. Rossi has already felt the weight of the burden of hopes that he carries. During 1997 the interest of the press and the adulation of the fans exploded. 'It is a big problem for me. I don't want to be famous. I just want to have fun with my friends. I'd prefer to go for a ride to the beach.' But he shouldered it in fine style, laughing all the way.

It is Rossi and his contemporaries who must provide the power for the regeneration already begun by the heroes of the 250 class. The down side might be that Rossi may so far outshadow his contemporaries as to initiate a new era of stagnating domination, like the one prevailed over now by Doohan. This is looking too far ahead, however – the test will come in 1999, Valentino's planned second year in the 250 class, by when he will be aboard a factory Aprilia.

The world will be looking to see if he can muster the same sort of on-track superiority on bigger bikes that he did on 125s. But it is not only his riding skill which needs to survive the test. We will be watching also for the survival of his star quality. For Rossi has not only learned how to control a motor cycle, and how to pace a race – but also how to work a crowd. He was even prepared to face fines from the

FIM to continue his new-found tradition of stopping on the track and dressing up after a race victory, often as not after first climbing the fence to gesticulate like a monkey. Fancy-dress Rossi appeared as Robin Hood in England, as a medieval torturer with mace in Germany, as a great lover at Mugello (toting around an inflatable doll dressed as Claudia Schiffer), and so on...

The name of Rossi is not, of course, new to GP racing. Nor yet to long-standing *Motocourse* readers. It was back in 1979 when the colourful long-haired Graziano won three 250 GPs in succession on the Italian *garagiste*-made disc-valve Morbidelli. He only just missed the Top Ten (the then Editor ran a sort of consolation nearly-men piece to avoid hurting too many feelings, and said: 'His sudden rise leaves us slightly breathtaken.') Graziano switched to a 500 in 1980, twice making the rostrum to claim fifth in the championship, but his career fizzled out prematurely after several accidents both on the track and on the road in a car.

One of GP racing's greatest veterans, Jorge Martinez, recalls Graziano introducing him to his babe in arms in the paddock during his first GP season in 1982. It was Valentino, born on 16 February 1979, at Urbino, a medieval town near Misano. 'I should have taken my chance then and run over him,' joked the Spaniard, whose last chance of a 125 title in his final GP year was thoroughly destroyed by the same kid.

Valentino grew up with his mother in Cattolica, not far from Urbino, after his parents separated. Graziano remained in close contact, while at the same time continuing his own motor sporting

involvement rallying and more recently racing saloon cars. He firmly denies that he ever pushed his son into racing. The interest was just natural, he says. Plus it was something that a father and son could do together.

'Valentino's first memories are of the paddock, and when he was at home he played with motorbikes instead of other toys. He was three years old when I finished bike racing. He had already begun to know some riders, to look at books and photos, and to speak about motor cycles.'

He had already begun to ride them too, 'before he could ride a bicycle', continues Graziano. 'He began racing at ten in a go-kart. Then for two years it was minimoto.' When he was old enough, at 14, he started to race Sport Production – a hotly contested entry-level series on street-based 125 Aprilias and Cagivas. The next year he rode a GP class thoroughbred racing 125, and at 16 he won the Italian 125 Championship at his first attempt. At the same time, he was third in the European Championship. This was run at GP meetings but, though clearly fast enough, Valentino was too young even for a wild card GP entry.

It sounds like the path of a boy being propelled by parental ambition. Valentino sees it differently, recalling that he pestered his father endlessly before he would buy him a motor cycle good enough to race on. Of course, he was smaller then, but even so it was as tight a squeeze to fit his lanky frame onto one of the shoebox minimoto racers as it is today to fold it all up small enough to fit on a 125. Good training, no doubt.

The Italian minimoto series is con-

tested on go-kart tracks, of which there are a large number serving the coastal strip of resorts around Rimini and near the Misano race track. With a floodlit fairground feel, they are a world away from organised circuit racing – barely, one might think, connected.

Not so, insists Valentino. 'They are like 500s. They are good training. To have that much power in such a short wheelbase means that you do very long wheelies, and also that you slide them in the corners.'

Being the way he is, he is probably only half-serious – poking fun at the orthodox theory that only ex-dirt-trackers can ride 500s properly. This is entirely in keeping with his character. Turning 19 next February, he's full of teenage mischief and iconoclasm. Ask how he enjoys himself, and he replies with a grin that he likes nothing better than to get together with some friends on motor scooters to taunt the traffic police – a very Italian pastime. In fact his only serious injury so far in eight years of racing came in a road accident in 1994. He was a passenger on a motor scooter that was hit by a car. 'I had three fractures in my left leg. I still have problems with that leg now.'

Valentino delivers this information partly in English, partly through an interpreter, speaking at breakneck speed with his hands flailing constantly. He still had his long hair at the time. After the title, he had it all cropped off and briefly dyed it blue. But there's a good understanding of how to build his image amid the innocence of his youth. He is very popular with the lively Italian press, and makes sure of plenty of exposure by visiting the press room on a daily basis.

This prominence naturally butts him up against the incumbent Italian motor cycling hero Max Biaggi, and Valentino is a willing - even eager – participant in a paper war with the senior rider, whose very different personality puts him at odds with the same highly partisan journalists. The contest opened before the start of the 1997 season, with Rossi poking fun at Max on a national TV chat show (such is the popularity of bike racing in Italy), and the temperature was raised when Biaggi rebuked him in a restaurant at only the second race of the year, in Japan. Many will sympathise with the older rider's view – that the upstart is using Biaggi's own hard-earned fame to lever himself up into the public eye. Here is Valentino's side.

'I don't know Max. I only know him from the newspapers. But when I watched him before, he was never my favourite rider. There are five or six riders who are as fast as Max. I don't like the person – or my impression of the person. He is always complaining about his bike, and saying he is the best rider. In Japan, I was in a restaurant and he came up to me and said: "Stay quiet. Because I am number one." I don't care about this.'

He demonstrated this attitude whenever possible. The Claudia Schiffer ploy at Mugello was a jeering reference to reports in the winter of a relationship between Max and another supermodel, Naomi Campbell. ('We are just good friends,' said Max at the time.) Another jibe came in response to Max's continual complaints about front-fork chatter. It was quite late in the season, after yet another pole position, when Valentino smilingly

Gold & Goose

Rossi celebrated his coming of age as a champion with a cropped head and a blue-rinse tint.

Bottom: Podium popsies were never safe when Valentino was about.

attributed his success to a technical breakthrough. 'At last we have been able to develop some chatter, which seems to be important.'

Then there's the nickname he gave himself soon after he arrived in the 125 class, to find that most of the top riders he would have to beat were Japanese. In a trice, he had the name 'ROSSIFUMI' emblazoned across the back of his leathers. A good-natured joke, he insists. 'In 1994 I watched Norifumi Abe, and I liked his racing style very much. Now I also like the Japanese 125 riders. They are very funny, and I enjoyed racing with them very much.' After the Japanese GP he stayed on with the Aoki brothers for a holiday, and he admires the riding of Sakata, Ueda, Tokudome and Manako. His cordial relationship with his Japanese rivals has been a feature of 1997 – laughing and hugging each other on the race rostrums, they had also quite obviously really enjoyed racing against Rossi.

His jokes define his public personality, but it is his racing success that has put him up there. He joined GPs on an express train, and his first encounter with the big men of the class left him as breathless as he now leaves them, barely two years later. It came in 1995, when he entered a Ducados Open race which had several GP riders on the grid, including Martinez, Sakata and Öttl. 'When I saw how fast they went, I thought then it would be impossible for me ever to ride like that. The next year I went to the IRTA tests at Jerez before the season. I remember Sakata passing me going into the first corner there. In that one corner, he gained about a second on me. I tried to follow Tokudome at the same tests. He made it through the corner, but I went on straight. I realised that the World Championship riders had a different style, especially braking very deep into the corner.'

He arrived in GPs in 1996, making an immediate impact. This was not only because of his unique appearance – skinny and lanky body draped in flowing unisex clothing, Prince Valiant haircut often kept in check by an Alice

band. Valentino was clearly fast, and when his first GP victory came, at Brno, it was somewhat overdue. But he was also erratic and very accident prone, crashing frequently as he tried to master the trick of getting the bike to perform beyond its normal limits.

'Last year I had very much fun. There was no pressure, and I could amuse myself. It didn't matter where I finished, and it didn't matter if I crashed. Fifth or tenth place was okay, and to fall off was okay. This year is much different, much pressure. If I finish seventh this year, it is a terrible result, and I'm not happy.' Luckily he never did have to endure this torment, never finishing lower than sixth during the whole season.

Aprilia already had a handle on him, and from the tenth round of 1996 started to give him direct technical assistance. For 1997, his role was clear – riding the fully factory-backed bike in Nastro Azzurro colours, thus taking the place of Stefano Perugini.

The ebullient youngster rose to the challenge magnificently. If he found it

less enjoyable he never let it show. Out of 15 races, he won 11. He crashed in Japan in the closing stages, saying afterwards: 'I thought I could win the race. Now I just think I'm an idiot.' He was beaten by yards in Austria, after his major title rival Ueda found a better way through the last corners. At Brno, he needed only to finish third to clinch the title, and in the circumstances this was all he could manage. And in Australia a partial seizure dropped him to fifth. He won everywhere else, sometimes by inches and sometimes by miles. It was a fine performance.

Good enough even to please his father, whose current role at the GP tracks is as a steadying influence on his son – as steadying an influence as you can be with a plaited ponytail running down to waist level. 'As his father, every year is the best year...but though I knew he is a good fast rider, I didn't know if he was good enough to be champion. This year he raced very well – because he showed he could control the situation in a race.'

Good enough also for Pernat, who has ousted the fast but undazzling Perugini from the semi-works Nastro Azzurro 250 in favour of the kid who, at 1.7 metres, was definitely too tall for a 125. Too heavy as well, he adds. He gave away an average 10 kg to his pint-sized Japanese rivals.

Valentino speaks about the 250 with mature reserve. 'I have ridden a 250 only once, only for a few laps at a testing session. I thought it was very fast. I know the 125 well, and I have learned a lot about setting up from my team during this year. On a 250 I feel I'll be starting again from zero.'

His father agrees. 'I am not sure if he will be fast enough to race in the 250 class. As a rider, I know how many problems you can have. You have to understand them – it is something to learn.'

And does he aim to move on up after that to 500s? The youngster laughs and shakes his head, setting his pretty curls a-dancing. He doesn't even want to talk about that.

Until now, Valentino's road into racing has been a shining path, strewn with rosebuds and awash with champagne. It is important to remember, however, that it is only just starting. There are bound to be rocky patches ahead, and the way Rossi tackles them will give depth to his legend. And the way he carries the burden of the hopes of his fans, and of racing itself.

We shall see. Meanwhile, though he may only have just begun – what a beginning it was.

Nelson Piquet 1

1

Gold & Goose

Aprilia have been breeding champions for several years.

racing
line

Valentino Rossi extended Aprilia's run of World Championship titles to six by dominating the FIM 125cc World Championship in 1997.

RS
250

RSV
mille

The technology that we develop through racing has allowed us to build bikes that win World Championships on the track and world acclaim on the road.

From this heritage come our two latest models: the RS250 — a race replica of the bike that has won three 250cc World Championships — and the RSV Mille 1000cc V-Twin, making Aprilia the first European manufacturer to produce a complete model range from 50cc to 1000cc.

To ride an Aprilia is to love it.

Ask Valentino.

Or better still, ask your nearest Aprilia dealer and find out why yourself.

technologia reparto corse

aprilia

**FOR MORE INFORMATION
CALL 01581 400 660**

**APRILIA MOTO (UK) LTD
Dunragit
Stranraer
Scotland
DG9 8PN**

http://www.aprilia.co.uk

**APRILIA MOTO (UK) LTD RECOMMEND THE
USE OF PUTOLINE OILS AND DUNLOP TYRES.**

WHO'S WHO IN 1997 *by Michael Scott*

NORIFUMI ABE

500 cc: HONDA'S PARTY

In the 49th year of the World Championship series, the 500 class saw problems and solutions both, at each end of the spectrum. Potential problems included smaller grids and growing one-make domination by Honda, and the loss at the year's end of major sponsor Lucky Strike. Potential solutions included an all-new type of factory motor cycle, offering a tantalising glimpse of an alternative future modelled on F1 car racing.

Among the works teams, the triple abandonment of Yamaha by riders, sponsors and teams was a blow both heavy and unexpected. Marlboro's withdrawal of their anticipated backing came on the eve of the first official IRTA tests, leaving the factory team back in factory colours, as had happened to Honda three years before.

The Marlboro millions went instead to the Modenas alternative. Based on car GP practice, this had a name from a Malaysian commuter-bike manufacturer, and technology and working practices from the heart of the British Formula One industry. Alongside fellow-independents Elf, but with a much higher profile, this was a crucial new challenge to the Japanese tetrarchy's stronghold on the 500 class, and possibly the harbinger of a new era of specialist racing manufacturers burgeoning into a new industry. If only somebody can be found to pay for it...

The privateers had their numbers cut by new, smaller grid sizes. On the other hand, they had a new choice of machine in the NSR500-V Honda. At first, the customers came only slowly. Their numbers increased during the year, however: the machine not only filled its design brief well and at a predictable if not exactly low cost, but it was also surprisingly competitive against the ageing and dwindling squad of ROC Yamahas – the Harris variation having quietly disappeared.

The arrival of these new machines tipped the numbers equation even further towards Honda, with six V4s and five V-twins for the first race. Yamaha held ground with four works riders; likewise Suzuki with two. Two Elf 500s and two Modenas KR3s joined the class. Aprilia was again represented by just one machine. With the privateers, this brought numbers to 25, one short of a full house.

The rider pool was augmented by two top Superbike riders, Troy Corser and Anthony Gobert; Scott Russell had been lost to the four-stroke series in exchange.

HONDA
TEAM REPSOL
The official HRC squad rider numbers stayed the same as last year, but with an extra V4 and only one V-twin. Alongside three-times World Champion Mick Doohan (31 at the start of the season) and Alex Criville (27), runner-up in 1996, they had allotted two more cylinders also to Tadayuki Okada (30), a reward for his sterling efforts on the all-new twin. Rather unexpectedly, they had decided to run a factory development twin for one more season, and upon this they put their All-Japan champion Takuma Aoki (23), middle of the three 'Fireball Brothers'.

The line-up of the factory pit crews was basically unchanged, each rider having his own team but all reporting to HRC. This meant information was shared – a big advantage for development engineers, but a thorn in the side for Doohan, who felt he should be able to keep at least some of his hard-won secrets to himself.

CARLOS CHECA

TEAM MOVISTAR PONS
The biggest satellite team had a new sponsor and new dark blue-and-stars livery, but the same rider line-up. Owner Sito Pons had a strong card in Carlos Checa (24), who had won his first GP towards the end of the previous season, and was already considered one of the coming-men. Retaining Alberto Puig (30) was more complex. Still struggling after taking more than a year to return after serious leg injuries, Puig was a long way off his race-winning form of 1995. But his influence and valuable family connections linked him with the sponsorship deal and the team's very existence.

TEAM FCC TECHNICAL SPORTS
Nobuatsu (25) is the eldest of the three Aoki brothers, the most experienced but the least decorated. Now he was up to 500s after six years hovering near the top of the 250s. He was chosen by the Technical Sports crew to head their entry into the class, on year-old bikes previously used to win two GPs by Luca Cadalora.

YAMAHA
Yamaha's plans for the year only became clear retrospectively. Thrown into confusion by the unexpected withdrawal of Marlboro in mid-December 1996, they were then further deranged by the financial collapse of Promotor, sponsors of their Power Horse team. The consequences played a big part in a downbeat year.

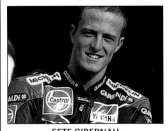
SETE GIBERNAU

TEAM RAINEY
Loris Capirossi turned his back on his contract to go 250 racing, leaving Rainey with a rider problem – whom to pair with 21-year-old Norifumi Abe? After much to-and-fro with rider suggestions (including Max Biaggi – too expensive, and Jean-Michel Bayle – committed to Team Roberts), Marlboro then backed out too. Yamaha immediately stepped in to underwrite what was intended to be their major factory team. With no stars available, Rainey directly signed up promising young Spaniard Sete Gibernau (24), fresh from a mediocre 250 year. Gibernau is the grandson of Spanish motor cycle luminary Don Francisco Bulto, founder of the Bultaco factory.

TROY CORSER

TEAM POWER HORSE/RED BULL
The other Yamaha team had something Rainey did not: a proven star rider in Luca Cadalora, at 33 the oldest man in the class. This shifted the factory's emphasis slightly once the season began, with the Italian getting the benefit of the latest parts before the other riders. By then, however, the Promotor backing team was insolvent, after an in-house cash crisis for Power Horse. Rescue came from American millionaire

sponsor Bob MacLean, and a mid-season deal with rival energy drink manufacturer Red Bull. This, however, spelled the end for the team's second rider, Australian World Superbike Champion Troy Corser (25), after protracted re-negotiations between him and MacLean fell apart. It was also (due to IRTA rules) the end of MacLean's privateer WCM team, and eventually another Australian, Kirk McCarthy (27), found himself on the second factory Yamaha for the closing races.

TEAM LUCKY STRIKE SUZUKI
Daryl Beattie (26) was finally given a clean bill of health after yet more attention to his inner ear damage following a year of vexing head injuries, and was expected back at full strength on the redesigned new bike. In a surprise move, Scott Russell's contract was not renewed – he returned to World Superbikes with Yamaha – and Anthony Gobert (21) was signed up in his place. Much was expected of the outspoken and outrageous youngster,

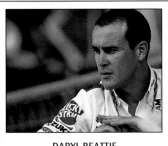
DARYL BEATTIE

and much was delivered – not all of it, though, to do with motor cycle racing. Reserve rider Peter Goddard (32) was in the end called upon to race four times during the year.

TEAM ELF
A second year with the alternative V4 saw Juan Borja (27) joined by Jurgen Fuchs (31), fresh from a strong works bike year on a 250 Honda. This was also the new bike's second full season.

JUAN BORJA

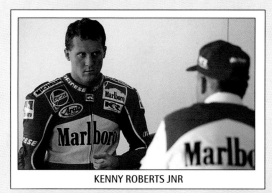

KENNY ROBERTS JNR

MAX BIAGGI

TEAM MARLBORO ROBERTS MODENAS

The whole of the impressive Team Roberts plus more manpower back at the Banbury base brought the Malaysian commuter-bike manufacturers Modenas into racing and onto the world stage with a blast of big staff, big budget and big publicity. With the motor built by Tom Walkinshaw Racing and the chassis by Team Roberts, this was a racing effort in the style of Formula One.

Roberts took the Marlboro sponsorship with him as well as two of the three riders he'd had on Yamahas the year before – Jean-Michel Bayle (28) and his elder son, Kenny Roberts Junior (23). Let the adventure begin.

DORIANO ROMBONI

IP APRILIA

Stay of execution gave the original V-twin one more year, with Doriano Romboni (28) again the rider. Technical development continued along with a full factory effort.

PRIVATEERS

TEAM GRESINI HONDA

The team owned by former 125 champion Fausto Gresini took the plunge as one of the first customers for a V-twin. Rider Alex Barros, still only 26 but vastly experienced, numbered factory Hondas, Suzukis and Cagivas in his CV, as well as several years on smaller bikes. Erratically strong, he was an interesting prospect.

TEAM MILLAR MQP HONDA

The private team backed by Irishman Joe Millar dropped last year's rider Eugene McManus and took up with Dutch 250 privateer Jurgen van den Goorbergh (27) instead. They had a Yamaha already, and ordered a V-twin Honda, with the notion that they might use one or the other for different circuits. The idea was shelved after the first back-to-back tests, as was the old YZR.

REGIS LACONI

TEAM ELF TECMAS HONDA

Regis Laconi's blue Tecmas Honda had been a major feature of the privateer battles in the 250 class last year. Now the youngster (21) moved up a class with the same team.

SOVEREX FP RACING HONDA

French privateer Fred Protat (30) started the season on an ageing ROC Yamaha, but switched to a Honda before the middle of the year. Injuries sustained in a pre-season crash left him below form from the start, however.

WCM ROC YAMAHA

Australian ex-Superbike rider Kirk McCarthy was another V4 private foot-soldier who did not finish the year on the bike with which he started – which was the ageing ex-Mackenzie ex-Hodgson ROC run by US entrant Bob MacLean.

TEAM MILLET RACING/TEAM PEDERCINI/ROC

Belgian Laurent Naveau (30) and Italian Lucio Pedercini (24) were the last surviving independent privateers to run a full season on ROC Yamahas.

LAURENT NAVEAU

250 cc: V-TWINS AND VENDETTAS

The 250 class represented a maelstrom of malice, a refectory of revenge – a dish that was eaten anything but cold in a year that promised (and delivered) much.

This wasn't just Honda versus Aprilia. It was Biaggi changing sides, in a one-man crusade against the Italians with whom he had won for the previous three years. And it was also Harada joining the opposition, after his own disappointments with Japan Inc. over the past two years. His own mechanical adversary, Yamaha, withdrew from the whole contest – rather prudently, as it transpired.

HONDA

As with the 500s, Hondas swamped the grids – at least up at the front. Like last year, HRC policy was to operate only 'satellite' lease teams equipped with the factory NSR, although favourite rider Tohru Ukawa did have a direct link with HRC.

TEAM MARLBORO KANEMOTO

Newest kids on the block, but actually a replay of 1993, when Erv and Max played together on a Honda in Rothmans paint. The big difference this time was the tyres as well as the dayglo paint job – the earlier rebellion against Aprilia had foundered on Biaggi's dislike of the Michelin tyres which came with the deal. Now he was on Dunlops, class favourites in any case, and familiar to him from his Aprilia years. Biaggi (25) brought the number one plate with him to Honda, along with a heap of talent and attitude.

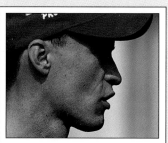

RALF WALDMANN

TEAM MARLBORO HONDA GERMANY

Paintwork changed also for the reduced-size ex-HB team, but otherwise it was business as usual for 1996 runner-up Ralf Waldmann (30), now in his 11th GP year. The reduced budget also cut his own resources – while

other NSR riders had two bikes to choose from, Ralf remained One-Bike Waldie throughout the year.

TEAM BENETTON HONDA

Tohru Ukawa (23) made a good impression in 1996 – albeit sometimes against the crash barrier. Back with the same squad, he now brought track knowledge and GP experience to an already strong package. As ever, in line with HRC's normal practice, his machine was fitted with Michelin tyres – only two other Honda riders and one privateer followed suit.

TOHRU UKAWA

TEAM ELF CHESTERFIELD

The French-based Tech 3 outfit were the only two-rider squad among the factory runners – but only Olivier Jacque (23) rode a factory bike. Silver-coloured team-mate William Costes (24) had a kitted RS250 for his debut season, in between endurance races.

FORTUNA HONDA

Spain is fortunate in having a distinct ladder for good riders, backed by sponsors. At least for some riders – the lucky one here being Emilio Alzamora (23), fresh from some strong rides on a 125. He was the second NSR rider to use Michelins.

EMILIO ALZAMORA

LORIS CAPIROSSI

HARUCHIKA AOKI

MATTEONI RACING HONDA

Financial scandal dismantled the Pileri team's 250 plans, leaving signed-up former double 125 World Champion Haruchika Aoki – youngest Fireball at 21 – with his plans in ruin, until Matteoni stepped into the breach. Haruchika got the final works NSR, and also used Michelin tyres.

APRILIA

Biaggi's reign at Aprilia had imposed an austerity they were glad to be rid of. He had always demanded a one-man factory team; now they could have the two-rider outfit they preferred. They also officially supported ex-125 protégé Stefano Perugini, with diluted largesse trickling to selected privateers.

TETSUYA HARADA

APRILIA RACING TEAM

Aprilia lost the expected Marlboro backing when they lost Biaggi: their two factory bikes appeared in sinister black livery, two riders with three World Championships between them. It soon became obvious that Tetsuya Harada was the senior of them, the 1993 champion now 26 and intent on reversing his sliding fortunes. Loris Capirossi (24) had two 125 titles to boast of, and had been Harada's closest rival in 1993, as well as a 500 class winner last year.

NASTRO AZZURRO APRILIA

Factory supported, but not on a full works bike, Stefano Perugini (22) was in a similar position last year in the 125 class. Firmly on the Aprilia ladder, this would be a year in which he must prove himself worthy of further patronage.

NORIYASU NUMATA

SUZUKI

The return of the other Japanese works bike to the class came also in black livery, after Dutchman Arie Molenaar's sponsorship plans became unhinged. The Suzuki was a GP enigma. In three years, until its withdrawal at the end of 1993, it never quite scaled the heights and never won a GP, even in the hands of former champion John Kocinski. Yet it had continued to achieve success in the very competitive domestic series. Team Molenaar operated closely with the factory, fielding the former All-Japan 250 champion Noriyasu Numata (30) in his first GP year, alongside British hopeful Jamie Robinson (21).

JAMIE ROBINSON

PRIVATEERS

Yamaha backed out at factory level, although they did support privateer entries from ex-Honda man Luis D'Antin (33) and team-mate José Luis Cardoso (22) in a Spanish team, as well as the Japanese Edo Racing's Osamu Miyazaki (31), who had ridden an Aprilia last year, and his team-mate Franco Battaini (24), from Italy.

Most privateers chose Honda RS machines, with the focus on the FCC Technical Sports bike of 22-year-old Takeshi Tsujimura, with indistinct but apparently valuable links with HRC. Of the rest, it transpired that ex-500 privateer Jeremy McWilliams (33) would play a leading role on the Queens University Belfast (QUB) Honda.

TAKESHI TSUJIMURA

JEREMY McWILLIAMS

Others to pedal RS Hondas were Cristiano Migliorati (28) for Team Axo – another ex-500 privateer – and 25-year-old Luca Boscoscuro (Dee Cee Racing Team), both from Italy.

Private Aprilias were the choice of the remaining six privateers. Chief among them was Sebastian Porto from Argentina. The fast 18-year-old had changed his name from Porco (meaning

KURTIS ROBERTS

Pig), but was otherwise as full of crackling as last year. Switzerland's Oliver Petrucciani (27) lined up for another year on a Mohag Aprilia; former Thunderbike heroes the Gavira brothers – Idalio (26) and Eustaquio (24) – joined in on Mobil 1 Aprilias. Giuseppe Fiorillo (27), injured at the start of the year, rode a Radiant Aprilia.

The last Aprilia privateer had a high profile, for a rank novice. Kenny Roberts's younger son Kurtis (18) started the year with a pair of Aprilias, then switched to Hondas after unsatisfactory results. Much attention would be paid to his finishing positions, while impecunious rivals who could barely afford one bike wondered at a novice whose wealthy dad would buy him four during the course of the season.

125 cc: COME YOUNG, COME OLD...

There was only one true works bike in the smallest class – Valentino Rossi's Nastro Azzurro Aprilia. Even then, it was more breathed upon than really different, though small things mean a lot down here. Rossi, at 18 when the season started, was the youngest rider in any class to complete it. The oldest man was also on a 125 – Jorge Martinez (Airtel Aprilia), who turned 35 in August.

JORGE MARTINEZ

GARRY McCOY

Jurgen van den Goorbergh on the V-twin Team Millar Honda – one privateer squad that did survive.

NOBORU UEDA

MASAKI TOKUDOME

CHANGING RULES, CHANGING NUMBERS

There were some significant rule changes for 1997.

One concerned the number of permanent entries, which was cut in each class to just 26. This would open the way for up to six wild card riders in each class.

Controversial from the start, the impact on the 500 class was particularly damaging to the privateers.

While six wild cards did appear from time to time in the smaller classes, there were never more than one or two on 500s, and frequently none at all. This was not surprising, since there are no parallel national championships offering a pool of machines and riders.

The result was depleted grids, which was especially ironic for a number of 500 class privateers who had been refused entries. It would be nice to say that this trimmed the dead wood. Instead, many of the better privateers were lost to 250s and World Superbikes – and the same people came last as would have come last anyway.

The other significant rule change was to cancel the controversial one-bike rule in the 250 class – though it remained for the 125s.

The change, after two years, was the result of pressure from the works teams, and on safety grounds.

Hondas dominated on numbers – 12 in all, led by the HRC-kitted fancy men from Japan: Tomomi Manako (24) and Noboru Ueda (30). Italians Lucio Cecchinello (27), Roberto Locatelli (22) – down from 250s – and fast newcomer Mirko Giansanti (20) also had HRC-boosted bikes, as did another Japanese newcomer, Masao Azuma (26).

TOMOMI MANAKO

Other small Honda teams did not have full kits, including German former champion Dirk Raudies (32), Frenchman Fred Petit (21), Josep Sarda (24) from Spain and Jaroslav Hules, the Czech youngster of 22 who made a wild card debut last year.

As ever, various Aprilia teams boasted of degrees of factory support, all the while eyeing each other suspiciously. Muddied waters made it uncertain just how special were the specials, and vice versa.

Masaki Tokudome (26) moved to Docshop racing with one of the better specials; Martinez also had a fast Aprilia, unlike his famous-name team-mate Angel Nieto Junior, who at 20 was

KAZUTO SAKATA

clearly not going to be the man his 13-times World Champion father was.

Australian Garry McCoy (24) had Marlboro backing for his kitted bike. Another speedy machine belonged to Kazuto Sakata (30), the tough former champion; one more went to Peter Öttl. The 33-year-old German was to have a misfortunate season, however, and his place was taken by Manfred Geissler (26), whose Honda eventually ended up being ridden by Malaysian wild card Shahrol Yuzy (21), after a brief occupancy by former East German and new bright hope Steve Jenkner (20) – who also ended up on an Aprilia by the finish! Xavier Soler (23) replaced out-of-sorts teenage former GP winner Ivan Goi as McCoy's team-mate.

Yamaha's ranks were relatively swollen, with the German Kurz Yamaha team fielding two riders – the impressive orange-haired Youichi Ui (24) and Spaniard Juan Enrique Maturana (23). Yoshiaki Katoh (31) remained as an old Yamaha soldier, with Gino Borsoi (23) as his Team Semprucci team-mate.

TYRED AND EMOTIONAL

Tyre wars were not evenly divided – with Michelins set to win every GP in the 500 class, Dunlops every race in the 250 and 125 classes.

The Anglo-Japanese company still did not have any V4 motor cycles on its books, but the presence of Dunlops in the 500 class was stronger than last year, when they had only the lone V4 Aprilia. This year the Italian bike was joined by a pair of V-twin Hondas, ridden by Regis Laconi and Jurgen van den Goorbergh.

All the remaining 500 cc machines used Michelin tyres.

Dunlop did not quite have a stranglehold on the 250 class, but were clearly dominant. Non-believers on Michelins were led by HRC rider Tohru Ukawa and compatriot Haruchika Aoki, while Alzamora likewise used the French tyres. So too did privateer Porto.

In the evenly matched 125 class, tyre loyalties shifted through the season. Dunlop already held the high ground, but Michelin had recruited several riders for the start of the year, while two others used Bridgestone – Manako and Geissler. This pair switched to Dunlops at the third GP, leaving Bridgestone with no more GP customers. Then came the Michelin men, one by one: Tokudome in Germany, Cecchinello at Imola, Sakata at Assen, and finally Dirk Raudies at Donington Park. This left Martinez and McCoy among the only fast men still on the French rubber.

Probably the best Superbike in the world

Judge for yourself

You have to see the new TL1000R to believe it. Aggressive aerodynamic styling, race derived aluminium chassis, six piston calipers and an awesome 996cc, liquid cooled V-Twin that delivers 135ps @ 9,500rpm. Every last drop of Suzuki Superbike experience is shoehorned into the TL1000R. The best Superbike in the world? Probably. Will you be impressed? Definitely.

24 hour hotline: 01892 707001
Suzuki Information Department, P.O. Box 56, Tunbridge Wells, Kent TN1 2XY

www.suzuki.co.uk

Ride the winds of change

1997 GRANDS PRIX

MALAYSIAN
grand prix

500 cc	DOOHAN
250 cc	BIAGGI
125 cc	ROSSI

THERE was, of course, a frisson of doubt: Shah Alam is a tyre-sensitive circuit, and the Screamer engine was supposed to be hard on tyres. Even so, certainly in retrospect, everyone expected Doohan to win. Everyone except the diehard clutch of Spanish Criville supporters, anyway. Mick would do the same thing, his supporters felt, whether he had a 180-degree engine or a Big Bang – or indeed a Yamaha or something else instead of a Honda. The magic lay in the name on the leathers.

It had been a masterly performance. Instead of being rough on tyres, the smoother power of the evenly spaced engine worked the other way. It wasn't the firing interval that really mattered, insisted crew chief Jerry Burgess. The important thing – masked by the simultaneous introduction of the Big Bang in 1992 – was that other engine changes (cylinders, electronics, etc.) made the power torquier and more malleable no matter what the crankshaft timing. Mick's Screamer was a new, different engine rather than a simple revival of the old tyre-shredder motors of 1991 and before. Doohan used it to smash Kocinski's pre-Big Bang lap record, then said: 'I wanted to get back that direct relationship between the throttle and the back wheel. That's been successful. The new engine played a big part in winning. It meant I didn't need to spin the rear wheel to get away. That preserved the tyre.'

The bigger surprise at the first GP of the year was how the Hondas had, over the winter, achieved a blanket domination. This embraced new riders and old, V-twins and V-fours alike. This time round, the magic lay in the name on the fuel tank.

Whatever the reason for this (exotic materials? electronic traction control? computerised force fields? a pact with the Devil?), it left the rest looking like dolts. The reworked Yamahas, redesigned Suzukis and drawing-board-fresh Modenas KR3s just didn't count. For those to whom one swallow makes a summer, or who had no faith in the immutability of endless change, the season was already a foregone conclusion.

The preceding and increasingly prolonged independent test sessions had warned of this, though it had been possible to ignore the portents, blaming variable weather etc. for the fact that Honda had been setting the times everywhere, with Mick and his one-man Screamer invariably fastest. Thus there were still many open questions, before the level playing field rammed the message home.

Suzuki had a new bike, and a new rider. Anthony Gobert's debut was eagerly awaited. The script dictated a damp squib. The flame-haired shooting star of Superbikes had been knocked about by a series of testing spills (he'd been faster than Beattie pretty much throughout), at least one of which was because of a seized engine, and all of which had imposed further damage on his already troublesome right collarbone. A fortnight before, this had been fitted with a second, larger, metal plate. He couldn't shake hands and, not surprisingly, it took only a few laps of practice to show that he couldn't ride a 500 either. He stayed, adding to the other side of his colourful reputation, but that was the last we saw of him on a bike for a while.

Beattie represented a series of questions, each hinging upon the other. Had he recovered? If not, how long would he continue? If so, was the new bike any good? If not, could he fix it? And so on. None of these were answered in the baking humidity of the increasingly seedy track, due for replacement within two years.

Yamaha had two teams, each with their own private turmoils. Rainey's sponsorship crisis had been ameliorated by a last-ditch top-up from the south-east Asian wing of the Marlboro empire, and his bikes would carry the chevron here and also in Indonesia. But he was short of real rider strength, with one class novice – Gibernau – and the always erratic Abe. Power Horse were already running out of money, the team riddled with growing doubts. At the same time, while Cadalora could always spring a surprise, Corser had apparently not taken instinctively to the 500. After trundling to US and World Superbike victory on a loping Ducati V-twin, he was finding the YZR a bit of a handful.

But there didn't seem much doubt about the Modenas. Circumstances had brought Roberts and his men to the grid too early: simple as that. Accumulated delays meant that the new 'bent-Boxer' triple had so far not been tested in anger, let alone brought to race-readiness. But the bike was running on Malaysian money, and for this among many reasons needed to at least make a showing. An embarrassing failure was a very real possibility. That it did not take place was a credit to Kenny Roberts and his team, as well as a blessing from a kindly fate.

This left the squad of Hondas. There were plenty, but apart from Mick and Alex they were a crop of new boys, one way and another. When all of them did astonishingly well in practice, with the two new V4 riders Okada and N. Aoki on pole and third respectively, their rivals were left to hollow reassurances that the first GP, and especially this tyre-punishingly overheated Malaysian round, were never typical.

The 250 class added personal intrigue and rivalry in a thoroughly Italian way, to make it much more besides. This first confrontation between Biaggi and his ex-colleagues at Aprilia was another decisive battle. As Max said later: 'I change my team. I change my bike. I change everything. The result is the same.' But his usual runaway win here had more to do, this year, with canny tyre choice on a damp but drying track. Max had changed to his cut-slick combination on the line, delaying the start. In the spirit of things, Aprilia's response was to slap in a protest against this delay. Rather than the disqualification that some wilder elements may have desired, however, he was merely fined 5000 Swiss francs; a trifle after this first important victory.

Opposite: The Screamer's delight: Nobuatsu checks the quality of the bubbly while Mick enjoys realising the wisdom of his decision.

Debutants in trouble.
Above: Kenny Roberts and the Modenas man wished the season was still months away.
Left: Anthony Gobert's underwear was fitter than his collarbone, as he shows Troy Corser.
Below: And Corser fell in practice – his first public outing on the Yamaha.

Photos: Gold & Goose

Happy, darling? Two men were needed to replace Max at Aprilia, and Capirossi and Harada were both of them.

Opposite page, main picture: One finger on the clutch, Puig shows Abe how to power-slide a 500.

Opposite page, top left: Good friends off the track, deadly rivals on it. 125 stars Sakata, Rossi and Ueda live the cliché.

Opposite page, top right: Last year's winner Cadalora had changed horses, lost power.

500 cc RACE – 33 LAPS

Criville led the first lap, then pole-qualifier Okada forged past in the last corner to lead the second. Almost simultaneously he was shaking his head violently as he passed his pit crew, and rapidly started to drop back. The driveshaft to his exhaust powervalve had broken, costing him revs and the chance of a dream V4 debut.

One rookie down. Another will be along in a moment: T. Aoki was now mounted on Okada's old V-twin, and like his predecessor last year he also led, forcing through from sixth on lap one, Doohan tucked up behind, N. Aoki pushing past Criville into third in the all-Honda parade.

All this forced Doohan to abandon his plan to cat-and-mouse Criville. Safer instead to leave this unseemly high-risk 125-style brawling behind. He made the pass round the outside at the end of the straight – one of the fastest corners in GP racing – and led from lap four to the end. Takuma succumbed to brother Nobuatsu on the same lap; and by the time Criville managed to find a way past both of the Aokis, to take second on lap 11, Mick was already a clear second ahead, and pulling away. His best lap – a new record – came early in the process, but even at the end he was clearly not having any of the feared tyre problems.

Criville drew away steadily from N. Aoki as well, in brotherly combat with Takuma's twin. But his tyres were shot, and by the finish he was slowing dramatically. Given a lap or two more, Nob may even have been in front – Takuma having dropped away with his own tyre problems.

Cadalora was riding cleverly behind. He was all over Checa's Honda in the corners, but lacked the acceleration to overtake. He waited for the inevitable mistake, which came with eight laps left, then charged past to claim fourth from Takuma.

Checa narrowly hung on to sixth, fading to be all but overwhelmed by his team-mate Puig and practice crasher Abe, who were back and forth for most of the race.

Gibernau's ninth was a creditable debut, holding off the stricken Okada and Barros in his V-twin debut; Laconi was 12th in another impressive debut – of course this track is good for V-twins. Corser was a 'so-so' 13th after an early collision and near off-track excursion.

Borja was 14th on the Elf, battling all weekend with jerky throttle response, while Jurgen van den Goor-

bergh took the last point in his class debut, last man not to be lapped out of 17 finishers.

Retirements aplenty: Bayle's Modenas first out with crankshaft failure; Fuchs pitting two laps later, too battered from a practice crash to continue; Beattie had started on the third row, and retired after dropping back even more. Then Junior pitted with 22 laps remaining: a washer had come adrift in the rear suspension and the tyre was ruined.

Gramigni pulled in too, so far off the pace by the 11th lap that it wasn't worth continuing; McCarthy's first GP ended early with a broken battery lead.

250 cc – 31 LAPS

Tropical storms of varying intensity come and go very quickly in Malaysia – quickly enough for almost anything to happen in the ten or more minutes between leaving the pits and starting the race. This time, almost everybody bargained on the heavy-spotted rain to continue, but for an intermediate front and a hand-cut or intermediate rear to be sufficient on the well-drained surface. Only Biaggi and Waldmann discerned the imminent passing of the cloud, the former so late that his mechanics were still working when supposed to clear the

grid at the three-minute board, delaying the procedure somewhat.

The choice was perfect, and Biaggi was simply untouchable. The expected close race was stretched to breaking point in hopeless pursuit, with Harada reduced to best of the rest as he displaced Jacque's Honda from second after four laps. The Japanese star had transferred all his smoothness and style from Yamaha to Aprilia and was a joy to watch. But as the growing gap confirmed, he wasn't in the same league as Max, and conditions turned increasingly against his tyre choice. Jacque was hanging grimly onto third, seething at the knowledge that his own request for a hand-cut slick front like Biaggi's had been over-ruled by his team boss Hervé Poncharal.

Ukawa was slipping away behind, to come into the grips of rookie Haruchika Aoki; Waldmann, meanwhile, racing in pain after breaking bones in his right hand in two practice crashes, was having a real adventure. Near the front after the start, the track still streaked with damp, he lost the front and ran into the gravel, rejoining in 17th. In spite of braking difficulties with his injured hand he charged back through the field to join battle for fourth before half-distance. As Ukawa unhappily dropped off behind the experienced German hung on Aoki's back wheel,

knowing with his tyre advantage he could nip past on the final lap.

The other ex-125 star, Alzamora, was seventh, prevailing over top privateers Migliorati and McWilliams, a strong pair of ex-500 men.

Only 15 finished, so there were points for all. Capirossi was not among them: he'd started badly but picked his way through to set about Aoki, then pitted with his power curve going flat. Perugini had already done the same with his heat-troubled Aprilia.

Crashes started with wide-eyed rookie Kurtis Roberts, knocked off on his first-ever GP lap. Idalio Gavira, William Costes and Porto all crashed without any help.

Fall of the day, and best hard-luck story, came from Jamie Robinson, storming in his works-bike debut. He'd just passed Suzuki team-mate Numata (who'd had his mechanics up all night after a fiery practice crash), but could not know that the Japanese rider was having brake trouble. He found out at the next bend, when he was hit so hard from behind that he went somersaulting through the air, lucky to hobble away with minor foot fractures. Numata continued to finish 14th.

125 cc – 29 LAPS

First and best race of the day started with a four-strong battle for the lead, terminated when Manako and Ui, losing touch somewhat, collided. Ui crashed, Manako survived back in the midfield, which left the Aprilias of Rossi and Sakata battling up front.

Rossi had Dunlops, Sakata Michelins, the latter clearly not working quite so well and putting the tough little former champion under severe pressure. Each tried to break away, Sakata first before half-distance, Rossi later. Each time the other clawed back the advantage. Rossi used the backmarkers well to get a breathing space for the last lap; Sakata hurled himself in pursuit and tried to overtake at the end of the back straight. He was riding way over the edge, though, and Rossi was able to slip in front when it really mattered, on the inside at the last corner.

Ueda conquered a big brawl to take third, with new Honda rider Mirko Giansanti hanging impressively on his tail. The luckless Tokudome had seemed sure of the last rostrum spot, but his tyres were shot and he was relegated to fifth on the second-last lap.

Martinez held off Manako, Katoh and Petit; fancied former winner McCoy retired with a water leak after a strong start.

MALAYSIA AIRPORTS

MARLBORO MALAYSIAN GRAND PRIX
KUALA LUMPUR
Shah Alam Circuit
11 - 13 April 1997

GP250
CHAMPION

Marlboro Malaysian
Grand Prix

MARLBORO
MALAYSIAN
GRAND PRIX
13 APRIL 1997

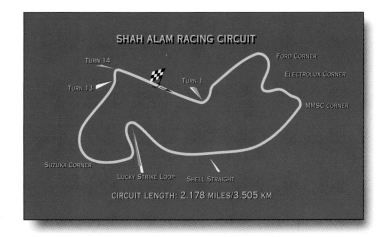

SHAH ALAM RACING CIRCUIT

TURN 14 FORD CORNER
TURN 13 ELECTROLUX CORNER
TURN 1
MMSC CORNER
SUZUKA CORNER
LUCKY STRIKE LOOP SHELL STRAIGHT

CIRCUIT LENGTH: 2.178 MILES/3.505 KM

500 cc
33 laps, 71.874 miles/115.665 km

Pos.	Rider (Nat.)	No.	Machine	Laps	Time & speed
1	Michael Doohan (AUS)	1	Honda	33	47m 11.545s 91.376 mph/ 147.055 km/h
2	Alex Criville (E)	2	Honda	33	47m 23.341s
3	Nobuatsu Aoki (J)	18	Honda	33	47m 24.948s
4	Luca Cadalora (I)	3	Yamaha	33	47m 33.776s
5	Takuma Aoki (J)	24	Honda	33	47m 34.154s
6	Carlos Checa (E)	8	Honda	33	47m 46.060s
7	Alberto Puig (E)	9	Honda	33	47m 46.413s
8	Norifumi Abe (J)	5	Yamaha	33	47m 46.453s
9	Sete Gibernau (E)	20	Yamaha	33	47m 54.678s
10	Tadayuki Okada (J)	7	Honda	33	47m 55.398s
11	Alex Barros (BR)	4	Honda	33	47m 55.723s
12	Regis Laconi (F)	55	Honda	33	48m 06.364s
13	Troy Corser (AUS)	11	Yamaha	33	48m 06.978s
14	Juan Borja (E)	14	Elf 500	33	48m 07.708s
15	Jurgen v.d. Goorbergh (NL)	21	Honda	33	48m 23.536s
16	Lucio Pedercini (I)	17	Yamaha	32	47m 51.614s
17	Laurent Naveau (B)	25	Yamaha	32	47m 58.031s
	Kirk McCarthy (AUS)	22	Yamaha	18	DNF
	Alessandro Gramigni (I)	39	Aprilia	11	DNF
	Kenny Roberts Jnr (USA)	10	Modenas	11	DNF
	Daryl Beattie (AUS)	6	Suzuki	7	DNF
	Frédéric Protat (F)	15	Yamaha	5	DNF
	Jurgen Fuchs (D)	16	Elf 500	4	DNF
	Jean-Michel Bayle (F)	12	Modenas	2	DNF

Fastest lap: Doohan, 1m 24.840s, 92.415 mph/148.727 km/h (record).
Previous record: John Kocinski, USA (Yamaha), 1m 25.100s, 92.133 mph/148.273 km/h (1991).

Qualifying: 1 Okada, 1m 23.485s; **2** Doohan, 1m 23.904s; **3** N. Aoki, 1m 24.182s; **4** Criville, 1m 24.195s; **5** Cadalora, 1m 24.282s; **6** T. Aoki, 1m 24.302s; **7** Barros, 1m 24.417s; **8** Checa, 1m 24.556s; **9** Puig, 1m 24.900s; **10** Abe, 1m 25.195s; **11** Corser, 1m 25.277s; **12** Beattie, 1m 25.331s; **13** Laconi, 1m 25.636s; **14** Gibernau, 1m 25.917s; **15** van den Goorbergh, 1m 26.232s; **16** Borja, 1m 26.296s; **17** Bayle, 1m 26.654s; **18** Gramigni, 1m 26.706s; **19** Roberts Jnr, 1m 26.838s; **20** Pedercini, 1m 26.906s; **21** Protat, 1m 26.923s; **22** McCarthy, 1m 27.165s; **23** Fuchs, 1m 27.864s; **24** Naveau, 1m 28.864s.

Fastest race laps: 1 Doohan, 1m 24.840s; **2** Criville, 1m 25.232s; **3** N. Aoki, 1m 25.308s; **4** T. Aoki, 1m 25.320s; **5** Checa, 1m 25.560s; **6** Cadalora, 1m 25.564s; **7** Puig, 1m 25.818s; **8** Barros, 1m 25.870s; **9** Abe, 1m 25.883s; **10** Okada, 1m 26.161s; **11** Gibernau, 1m 26.340s; **12** Corser, 1m 26.368s; **13** Laconi, 1m 26.667s; **14** Borja, 1m 26.843s; **15** Beattie, 1m 26.864s; **16** van den Goorbergh, 1m 26.995s; **17** Pedercini, 1m 27.531s; **18** Bayle, 1m 27.635s; **19** McCarthy, 1m 27.685s; **20** Roberts Jnr, 1m 27.694s; **21** Gramigni, 1m 28.084s; **22** Naveau, 1m 28.575s; **23** Fuchs, 1m 29.070s; **24** Protat, 1m 29.770s.

World Championship: 1 Doohan, 25; **2** Criville, 20; **3** N. Aoki, 16; **4** Cadalora, 13; **5** T. Aoki, 11; **6** Checa, 10; **7** Puig, 9; **8** Abe, 8; **9** Gibernau, 7; **10** Okada, 6; **11** Barros, 5; **12** Laconi, 4; **13** Corser, 3; **14** Borja, 2; **15** van den Goorbergh, 1.

Main picture: Biaggi shows off his winning choice of (well-worn) cut-slick tyres.

Inset, top: Kurtis Roberts's first GP lasted less than one lap.

Inset, middle: Suzuki's 250 return: Numata heads Robinson in practice; in the race they collided.

Inset, bottom: Gold for Max – new team, same result.

250 cc
31 laps, 67.518 miles/108.655 km

Pos.	Rider (Nat.)	No.	Machine	Laps	Time & speed
1	Max Biaggi (I)	1	Honda	31	45m 29.692s 89.041 mph/ 143.297 km/h
2	Tetsuya Harada (J)	31	Aprilia	31	45m 43.562s
3	Olivier Jacque (F)	19	Honda	31	46m 01.026s
4	Ralf Waldmann (D)	2	Honda	31	46m 04.291s
5	Haruchika Aoki (J)	7	Honda	31	46m 04.449s
6	Tohru Ukawa (J)	5	Honda	31	46m 33.290s
7	Emilio Alzamora (E)	26	Honda	30	45m 32.751s
8	Cristiano Migliorati (I)	8	Aprilia	30	45m 43.195s
9	Jeremy McWilliams (GB)	11	Honda	30	45m 48.762s
10	Oliver Petrucciani (CH)	25	Aprilia	30	45m 52.063s
11	Osamu Miyazaki (J)	18	Yamaha	30	45m 55.409s
12	Eustaquio Gavira (E)	28	Aprilia	30	46m 04.102s
13	Franco Battaini (I)	21	Yamaha	30	46m 06.394s
14	Noriyasu Numata (J)	20	Suzuki	30	46m 11.986s
15	Luca Boscoscuro (I)	10	Honda	30	46m 36.241s
	Sebastian Porto (ARG)	27	Aprilia	25	DNF
	Loris Capirossi (I)	65	Aprilia	16	DNF
	Jamie Robinson (GB)	14	Suzuki	14	DNF
	William Costes (F)	16	Honda	10	DNF
	Idalio Gavira (E)	29	Aprilia	8	DNF
	Luis D'Antin (E)	6	Yamaha	8	DNF
	Takeshi Tsujimura (J)	12	Honda	8	DNF
	Stefano Perugini (I)	15	Aprilia	3	DNF
	José Luis Cardoso (E)	17	Yamaha	3	DNF
	Kurtis Roberts (USA)	22	Aprilia	0	DNF

Fastest lap: Biaggi, 1m 26.835s, 90.291 mph/145.310 km/h.
Lap record: Max Biaggi, I (Aprilia), 1m 25.994s, 91.174 mph/146.731 km/h (1996).

Qualifying: 1 Biaggi, 1m 25.380s; **2** Harada, 1m 25.740s; **3** Ukawa, 1m 26.319s; **4** Jacque, 1m 26.400s; **5** Capirossi, 1m 26.620s; **6** Tsujimura, 1m 26.793s; **7** Waldmann, 1m 26.875s; **8** Numata, 1m 27.110s; **9** Perugini, 1m 27.224s; **10** Aoki, 1m 27.242s; **11** Alzamora, 1m 27.436s; **12** Migliorati, 1m 27.528s; **13** Porto, 1m 27.547s; **14** D'Antin, 1m 27.658s; **15** Robinson, 1m 27.816s; **16** Cardoso, 1m 28.303s; **17** McWilliams, 1m 28.620s; **18** Miyazaki, 1m 28.666s; **19** Boscoscuro, 1m 29.062s; **20** Petrucciani, 1m 29.215s; **21** Battaini, 1m 29.509s; **22** Costes, 1m 29.663s; **23** E. Gavira, 1m 30.403s; **24** I. Gavira, 1m 30.620s; **25** Roberts, 1m 31.577s.

Fastest race laps: 1 Biaggi, 1m 26.835s; **2** Harada, 1m 27.715s; **3** Jacque, 1m 27.778s; **4** Waldmann, 1m 28.128s; **5** Aoki, 1m 28.143s; **6** Ukawa, 1m 28.390s; **7** Capirossi, 1m 28.993s; **8** Migliorati, 1m 29.281s; **9** Alzamora, 1m 29.454s; **10** Petrucciani, 1m 30.387s; **11** Porto, 1m 30.444s; **12** McWilliams, 1m 30.450s; **13** Numata, 1m 30.456s; **14** Miyazaki, 1m 30.490s; **15** Robinson, 1m 30.578s; **16** E. Gavira, 1m 30.644s; **17** Costes, 1m 30.938s; **18** Battaini, 1m 30.978s; **19** I. Gavira, 1m 31.122s; **20** Boscoscuro, 1m 32.041s; **21** Perugini, 1m 32.611s; **22** Tsujimura, 1m 35.867s; **23** D'Antin, 1m 36.198s; **24** Cardoso, 1m 41.033s.

World Championship: 1 Biaggi, 25; **2** Harada, 20; **3** Jacque, 16; **4** Waldmann, 13; **5** Aoki, 11; **6** Ukawa, 10; **7** Alzamora, 9; **8** Migliorati, 8; **9** McWilliams, 7; **10** Petrucciani, 6; **11** Miyazaki, 5; **12** E. Gavira, 4; **13** Battaini, 3; **14** Numata, 2; **15** Boscoscuro, 1.

125 cc
29 laps, 63.162 miles/101.645 km

Pos.	Rider (Nat.)	No.	Machine	Laps	Time & speed
1	Valentino Rossi (I)	46	Aprilia	29	48m 09.930s 78.677 mph/ 126.619 km/h
2	Kazuto Sakata (J)	8	Aprilia	29	48m 10.924s
3	Noboru Ueda (J)	7	Honda	29	48m 42.128s
4	Mirko Giansanti (I)	32	Honda	29	48m 46.763s
5	Masaki Tokudome (J)	2	Aprilia	29	48m 47.432s
6	Jorge Martinez (E)	5	Aprilia	29	48m 55.852s
7	Tomomi Manako (J)	3	Honda	29	48m 56.288s
8	Yoshiaki Katoh (J)	62	Yamaha	29	48m 56.836s
9	Frédéric Petit (F)	19	Honda	29	49m 08.660s
10	Lucio Cecchinello (I)	10	Honda	29	49m 09.547s
11	Jaroslav Hules (CS)	39	Honda	29	49m 14.796s
12	Masao Azuma (J)	20	Honda	29	49m 27.468s
13	Ivan Goi (I)	26	Aprilia	29	49m 31.896s
14	Dirk Raudies (D)	12	Honda	29	49m 34.711s
15	Josep Sarda (E)	25	Honda	29	49m 41.365s
16	Gianluigi Scalvini (I)	21	Honda	29	49m 49.947s
17	Roberto Locatelli (I)	15	Honda	29	49m 49.998s
18	Manfred Geissler (D)	33	Honda	28	48m 10.955s
19	Angel Nieto Jnr (E)	29	Aprilia	28	49m 29.465s
20	Chao Chee Hou (MAL)	43	Yamaha	28	48m 56.190s
21	Steve Jenkner (D)	22	Aprilia	27	48m 22.724s
22	Gino Borsoi (I)	24	Yamaha	27	49m 06.344s
	Shahrol Yuzy (MAL)	42	Honda	18	DNF
	Juan Enrique Maturana (E)	17	Yamaha	13	DNF
	Youichi Ui (J)	41	Yamaha	12	DNF
	Peter Öttl (D)	88	Aprilia	5	DNF
	Garry McCoy (AUS)	72	Aprilia	2	DNF
	Paholayuth Kalachan (THA)	45	Yamaha	0	DNF

Fastest lap: Rossi, 1m 37.824s, 80.148 mph/128.986 km/h.
Lap record: Emilio Alzamora, E (Honda), 1m 31.594s, 85.600 mph/137.760 km/h (1996).

Qualifying: 1 Rossi, 1m 30.720s; **2** Tokudome, 1m 31.007s; **3** Ui, 1m 31.389s; **4** Martinez, 1m 31.698s; **5** Katoh, 1m 31.766s; **6** Ueda, 1m 31.830s; **7** Manako, 1m 31.964s; **8** McCoy, 1m 32.011s; **9** Petit, 1m 32.016s; **10** Sakata, 1m 32.057s; **11** Locatelli, 1m 32.058s; **12** Cecchinello, 1m 32.079s; **13** Yuzy, 1m 32.271s; **14** Giansanti, 1m 32.313s; **15** Goi, 1m 32.493s; **16** Raudies, 1m 32.512s; **17** Azuma, 1m 32.564s; **18** Öttl, 1m 32.588s; **19** Hules, 1m 32.686s; **20** Scalvini, 1m 33.108s; **21** Sarda, 1m 33.409s; **22** Geissler, 1m 33.490s; **23** Maturana, 1m 33.525s; **24** Nieto Jnr, 1m 33.530s; **25** Borsoi, 1m 33.542s; **26** Jenkner, 1m 33.640s; **27** Kalachan, 1m 35.194s; **28** Chee Hou, 1m 37.501s.

Fastest race laps: 1 Rossi, 1m 37.824s; **2** Sakata, 1m 37.834s; **3** Giansanti, 1m 38.583s; **4** Ueda, 1m 38.644s; **5** Tokudome, 1m 39.471s; **6** Cecchinello, 1m 39.604s; **7** Martinez, 1m 39.607s; **8** Manako, 1m 39.616s; **9** Katoh, 1m 39.905s; **10** Goi, 1m 40.084s; **11** Hules, 1m 40.086s; **12** Petit, 1m 40.128s; **13** Azuma, 1m 40.146s; **14** Sarda, 1m 40.203s; **15** Ui, 1m 40.316s; **16** Raudies, 1m 40.407s; **17** Scalvini, 1m 40.614s; **18** Locatelli, 1m 40.692s; **19** Geissler, 1m 41.161s; **20** Nieto Jnr, 1m 42.110s; **21** Yuzy, 1m 42.172s; **22** Maturana, 1m 42.967s; **23** Chee Hou, 1m 43.042s; **24** Borsoi, 1m 43.356s; **25** Öttl, 1m 44.500s; **26** Jenkner, 1m 45.736s; **27** McCoy, 1m 59.790s.

World Championship: 1 Rossi, 25; **2** Sakata, 20; **3** Ueda, 16; **4** Giansanti, 13; **5** Tokudome, 11; **6** Martinez, 10; **7** Manako, 9; **8** Katoh, 8; **9** Petit, 7; **10** Cecchinello, 6; **11** Hules, 5; **12** Azuma, 4; **13** Goi, 3; **14** Raudies, 2; **15** Sarda, 1.

500 cc	DOOHAN
250 cc	KATO
125 cc	UEDA

FIM WORLD CHAMPIONSHIP • ROUND 2

JAPANESE
grand prix

Far left: Look back in humour – promo girls show retro charm.

Left: Beattie and race engineer Hamish Jamieson pool fingers to count the chassis changes.

Bottom left: Doohan hunted down Okada, then fended off Criville – catching up in the background.

ALMOST everybody has some reason to relish Suzuka. Many riders have Eight Hour experience and deep track knowledge. For those with powerful motor cycles, it is one of the few places where they can really let them run. For those without, it's also a circuit where riding skill can make up for all sorts of deficits. There's the pressure of the gaze of the factory bosses, under which the stronger riders thrive. Finally there are the fast and numerous wild cards, who fulfil all the criteria above except perhaps the last.

This race also offers comfort for the underprivileged. Or at least it has in the past. It's early enough in the season for those who are struggling to believe there is still hope. Early trends may turn out to be false trails.

This season, however, was already turning out to be different. It required blind optimism not to be struck by the best-ever team result in racing history. Repsol Hondas filled the rostrum and fourth place as well. And there were other Hondas too – taking the top six places in practice, the race and the points. Blind optimism was something very few were prepared to espouse, as their hopes and dreams fell apart all too visibly.

Nobody suffered more than Beattie. A cautious man for a GP winner, he'd come to his own conclusion even before the first race. It wasn't him. It was the bike. Bereft of his development input last year, the new model was a drawing-board special which, he was convinced, not only preserved the old handling balance problem, it had also introduced a wobble and weave that was all its own. He wasn't prepared to hang it out until the bike was up to it, and had told the team so in no uncertain terms in Malaysia.

This left Suzuki with a major dilemma. Maybe Beattie was right. Maybe not. There was no way to tell. Gobert was being kept off games again, amid many wild rumours of imminent sacking, officially for his collarbone to recover. His place was taken by veteran Australian all-rounder and reigning Superbike champ Peter Goddard, who flew in directly from victory at the Le Mans 24 Hours. Goddard is a respectable rider, but hardly in the forefront of GP development.

Suzuki were left to cast around in all directions. So while Goddard stuck to the new XR87, Daryl's crew went backwards and forwards with endless variations so that (as one mechanic joked), 'We took so many chassis to scrutineering that they almost gave us a pack of stickers to put on for ourselves.' These included the disinterred hybrid halfway-house development bike used in early tests, marrying this year's engine with last year's chassis – which was in turn the same as that of Beattie's race-winning 1995 bike. This he raced, but all to little avail, retiring with brake failure after just eight laps. In any case, after testing seizures, the engines were being run well on the rich side of crisp for safety, and he was more than 10 km/h down on top speed.

Over at Yamaha there were other things that their people hoped would not also become trends for the season. Last year's winner, Abe, was still floundering in the attempt to regain form, racing gamely but well out of the hunt. The Power Horse lot, meanwhile, were getting worried about money. In a sea of rumours of impending bankruptcy Cadalora awaited his first cheque (raising a smile at Team Kanemoto, with Erv still awaiting fulfilment of Luca's promise to underwrite last year's team), while Corser was still waiting for last year's World Superbike Championship bonus. He had other problems beyond mere money, though, falling again in his struggle to tame the two-stroke.

Wild cards played only a small part in the 500 class – Norihiko Fujiwara rode the Yamaha, surviving a heavy practice crash; but last-year's erstwhile race leader Katsuaki Fujiwara was kept back by Suzuki for All-Japan Superbike duties. The 250 class was full of them, as usual, all of them very fast, and one of them ultimately unbeatable. It was a remarkable race for Daijiro Kato, just 20 and still recovering from a serious car crash that had left him with head as well as hip injuries. He'd already missed the first national round as a result – his one GP of the year was also his first outing since last season. A tiny waif dwarfed by his own shock of hair, Kato was asked by the post-race TV interviewer which high school he had attended. With the classic symptoms of recent and heavy concussion, he could not remember.

The GP regulars had their own hero too. Biaggi's warfare against Aprilia had him under pressure, the more acute because he was facing Harada on his old bike, at a track where the Japanese rider is reliably magnificent. Max also had pressure from his fellow-Honda riders, but was in turn putting pressure on Kanemoto and HRC, and himself. He was trying new factory engine parts early in practice when the bike seized in the esses, hurling him under the adjacent air-fence and into the barrier at barely diminished speed. He suffered a severe shoulder dislocation, among other things. But there is a depth to Biaggi that his many critics cannot ignore. He raced anyway, and not merely to cruise around, producing a strong finish in a fierce battle. The points were especially welcome, since Olivier Jacque left Japan with none. He fell at low speed in race-morning warm-up, breaking his collarbone and eliminating himself forthwith.

Above: Wild card Kato: 'I just wanted to finish. It happened that I won.'

Right: Tady Okada claimed a second pole position in his second race on a V4.

Below: Tsujimura puts his production Honda between the works machines of Ukawa (5) and Waldmann, Kagayama's Suzuki hanging on behind.

500 cc RACE – 21 LAPS

The front row comprised the same four as in Malaysia: Okada on pole again, Doohan negligibly slower, Criville, then Nobuatsu Aoki. Two veterans, two V4 novices. All on Hondas.

Okada got the jump, and charged off as if for a five-lap sprint, gaining a deceptively comfortable four-second cushion after four laps, with Nobuatsu bound for glory on his tail, soon displaced by Criville, then Takuma Aoki on the V-twin. Doohan was at the back of this brawl, with Abe following rather desperately, soon to be outpaced.

Doohan looked to be in a vulnerable position after a rather average start, with Okada vanishing and the youngsters likely as not to bump into each other. Mick rectified this promptly, passing both Aokis in one swooping move into the Spoon Curve, outbraking Criville into Degner next time round. Now he firmly reeled in Okada, setting a new record on the way, then passed him, also into the Spoon, to take the lead on lap ten. He promptly slowed the pace, and the second half of the race began with Okada and Criville following him round in close formation, the Aoki brothers losing ground behind. Checa was battling with Abe, then came Fujiwara and Puig. This last pair were joined by Cadalora, Gibernau and Goddard, the Australian climbing up to tenth briefly before losing ground again.

This was by far the best yet by a Suzuki; Beattie never got higher than 20th and developed brake problems early in the race. He decided to press on anyway to get some miles up, then almost crashed when they failed completely.

Corser and Borja had also been at the back of the group. The Spaniard crashed on lap 12, missing his braking point for the first corner; the Australian followed him into the gravel trap, as if mesmerised.

As Okada started to lose touch, Criville took second on lap 16 for a replay of many of last year's races. Not so much stalk and pounce, more just stalk and stalk. It was also a direct confrontation between the old Big Bang engine and the sizzling Screamer. But this is not a tyre-sensitive track, and the machine differences were inconclusive. Not so the differences between the riders. Doohan was faster on the first part of the lap; Criville could use his draught to be quicker on the latter part, and he was clearly poised for a last-lap attack.

What settled the issue was sheer force of character. Criville made a convincing attempt to pull past into the final chicane, but Mick would have none of it. He held the inside line, and passed the flag four-tenths ahead, with Okada now well out of touch but a safe third.

On the last lap, Checa and Abe had caught the brotherly Aoki battle, just too late to do anything about it. They finished within one second. Some way back, Puig waited until the last lap to nip past Fujiwara. Then came Barros, delighted to put his twin ahead of Cadalora. Impressive Laconi's twin was right behind, with Goddard next in 13th.

Bayle's Modenas only lost touch with this midfield scrap in the later laps. Team-mate Kenny Junior's race had ended after six laps for an odd reason: the fairing belly-pan had been dragging on the ground so badly it was lifting the front wheel off the road. He pitted rather than repeat his practice crash, which had been caused by a water leak. The first finish and first points for the team left Roberts trying hard to stay looking grim as he insisted 'It's not as good as I expected,' adding: 'We put Bayle on soft tyres because we didn't expect him to finish.'

McCarthy finished his ROC as top V4 privateer, conceding the last point to Jurgen van den Goorbergh's V-twin. There was only one other finisher, Pro-tat's ROC, Naveau and Perdercini having crashed out.

250 cc RACE – 19 LAPS

Harada claimed his usual Suzuka pole with team-mate Capirossi on the far end. In between, rather surprisingly, were the private Honda of Tsujimura – benefiting hugely from his switch to Dunlops from Bridgestone – and wild card Kato. Jacque was on row two, but a non-starter; Biaggi on row four, further depleting the potential leading group. Even so, the rough-and-tumble gang still comprised six bikes at the race's halfway point, with Harada and Ukawa most prominent, swapping back and forth

repeatedly. Ukawa frequently passed at the chicane, seeming to reveal his last-lap tactics, for it was surely here the race would be won or lost.

The first to leave the group, dropping off the back, was Suzuki-mounted wild card Kagayama; practice crasher Numata's full-time Suzuki was battling through the field after running off the track on lap one. Now Kagayama did the same, also at the Spoon, regaining solid ground a safe sixth but out of touch.

Then Waldmann gradually fell away, in pain and short of grip. He had seemed perfectly poised to attack at the finish but couldn't match the pace. Fifth place for him.

Ahead, and once or twice actually leading, was Tsujimura, seemingly quite on terms with the works bikes until the closing laps, when he too was dropped.

This left three to continue this fine race-long battle, for Kato was clearly not overwhelmed by his companions, and took the occasional turn to put his front wheel ahead of both Ukawa and Harada.

To cut a long story short, Harada seemed to have it all well summed up. With four laps remaining he pushed up the pace and eased gradually ahead. As he started the penultimate lap he had 1.7 seconds in hand, the race apparently in his pocket. Even when he lost half a second, he seemed safe.

Not so. Apparently he was caught napping as the storming Honda pair pulled each other along, and they both appeared alongside him at the chicane. Ukawa led through that, but Kato pulled a master-stroke on the final right-hander to be just ahead over the line. The first three were covered by three-tenths of a second. What a finish.

Later, Harada was somewhat exonerated when his claim of a sudden loss of power on the final lap turned out to be something of an Aprilia syndrome. At the time, this was blamed on low fuel levels in the pumped system, but something similar had spoiled

Capirossi's efforts in the second lap as well, and inexplicable sudden temporary power lapses would recur as the season wore on.

It was still a brilliant win for Kato, who said – rather endearingly – 'I just wanted to finish. It happened that I won.'

A long way behind Kagayama Biaggi won a strong fight for seventh, holding off Aoki, Numata, wild card Matsudo and a fading Capirossi. For a rider whose injuries were described as 'serious' the day before the race by Dr Costa, this was truly heroic.

Porto was 12th, top privateer; the next pack saw wild card Ogura narrowly beat the Suzukis of Jamie Robinson and Choujun Kameya.

Yamaha wild card Kensuke Haga crashed out spectacularly from the Biaggi battle, lucky not to be hurt; Perugini was another to fall. Emilio Alzamora had fallen early in practice, breaking his wrist to miss the next two races.

Thus were Harada's hopes of a home win spiked, while Max scored more than merely nine valuable title points.

125 cc – 18 LAPS

Noboru Ueda combined clever tactics, luck and a marvellously aggressive charge through the field to win his first GP in three years. The Honda rider noticed a slight wind change in the sighting lap and pitted to change his rear sprocket. It took longer than he expected, and he only just made it to the grid after the warm-up lap, to start right at the back. Then he flew through the whole field to join the close eight-bike battle for the lead at half-distance.

Rossi was prominent in this pack and planning his last-lap move when he crashed at the chicane on the penultimate lap. 'I thought I could win,' he said later. 'Now I just think I'm an idiot.'

This left three Japanese riders to break away for a breathtaking battle to the line, with Ueda narrowly defeating Sakata's Aprilia and Nakajo's Honda. Most of the earlier group were still close behind – Azuma inches ahead of Martinez and Katoh.

McCoy was seventh; Tokudome had been with the leaders, but for a second weekend fell back in the closing stages with mechanical trouble, finishing 13th.

Ueda first came to attention when he won the 1991 race here as a local rider, and was invited to join the rest of the series. Now he again led the championship – a popular result with the crowd.

MARLBORO GRAND PRIX OF JAPAN

20 APRIL 1997

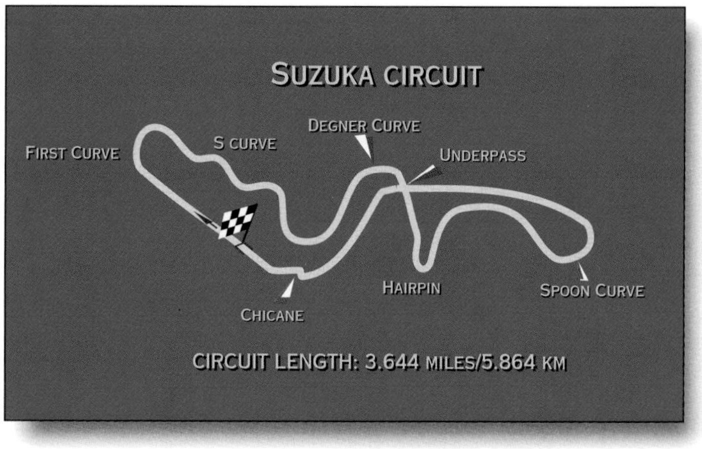
SUZUKA CIRCUIT
FIRST CURVE
S CURVE
DEGNER CURVE
UNDERPASS
HAIRPIN
SPOON CURVE
CHICANE
CIRCUIT LENGTH: 3.644 MILES/5.864 KM

500 cc

21 laps, 76.524 miles/123.144 km

Pos.	Rider (Nat.)	No.	Machine	Laps	Time & speed
1	**Michael Doohan (AUS)**	1	Honda	21	45m 11.995s 101.572 mph/ 163.465 km/h
2	**Alex Criville (E)**	2	Honda	21	45m 12.426s
3	**Tadayuki Okada (J)**	7	Honda	21	45m 18.042s
4	**Takuma Aoki (J)**	24	Honda	21	45m 35.614s
5	**Nobuatsu Aoki (J)**	18	Honda	21	45m 35.890s
6	**Carlos Checa (E)**	8	Honda	21	45m 36.397s
7	**Norifumi Abe (J)**	5	Yamaha	21	45m 36.710s
8	**Alberto Puig (E)**	9	Honda	21	45m 55.908s
9	**Norihiko Fujiwara (J)**	51	Yamaha	21	45m 55.998s
10	**Alex Barros (BR)**	4	Honda	21	46m 10.866s
11	**Luca Cadalora (I)**	3	Yamaha	21	46m 11.600s
12	**Regis Laconi (F)**	55	Honda	21	46m 11.874s
13	**Peter Goddard (AUS)**	27	Suzuki	21	46m 12.629s
14	**Jean-Michel Bayle (F)**	12	Modenas	21	46m 29.969s
15	**Jurgen v.d. Goorbergh (NL)**	21	Honda	21	46m 47.149s
16	Kirk McCarthy (AUS)	22	Yamaha	21	46m 50.303s
17	Frédéric Protat (F)	15	Yamaha	20	45m 24.967s
	Jurgen Fuchs (D)	16	Elf 500	14	DNF
	Sete Gibernau (E)	20	Yamaha	12	DNF
	Juan Borja (E)	14	Elf 500	11	DNF
	Troy Corser (AUS)	11	Yamaha	11	DNF
	Daryl Beattie (AUS)	6	Suzuki	8	DNF
	Kenny Roberts Jnr (USA)	10	Modenas	6	DNF
	Lucio Pedercini (I)	17	Yamaha	6	DNF
	Laurent Naveau (B)	25	Yamaha	6	DNF
	Alessandro Gramigni (I)	39	Aprilia		DNS

Fastest lap: Doohan, 2m 07.782s, 102.654 mph/165.206 km/h (record).

Previous record: Norifumi Abe, J (Yamaha), 2m 09.089s, 101.651 mph/163.534 km/h (1996).

Qualifying: **1** Okada, 2m 07.952s; **2** Doohan, 2m 08.017s; **3** Criville, 2m 08.403s; **4** N. Aoki, 2m 08.469s; **5** T. Aoki, 2m 08.540s; **6** Checa, 2m 08.617s; **7** Fujiwara, 2m 09.409s; **8** Puig, 2m 09.524s; **9** Abe, 2m 09.548s; **10** Gibernau, 2m 09.717s; **11** Corser, 2m 09.790s; **12** Barros, 2m 09.795s; **13** Bayle, 2m 09.896s; **14** Cadalora, 2m 10.029s; **15** Roberts Jnr, 2m 10.038s; **16** Laconi, 2m 10.040s; **17** Borja, 2m 10.450s; **18** Goddard, 2m 10.896s; **19** McCarthy, 2m 11.222s; **20** Beattie, 2m 11.336s; **21** van den Goorbergh, 2m 12.244s; **22** Fuchs, 2m 12.258s; **23** Gramigni, 2m 13.414s; **24** Pedercini, 2m 13.416s; **25** Protat, 2m 14.182s; **26** Naveau, 2m 14.520s.

Fastest race laps: **1** Doohan, 2m 07.782s; **2** Criville, 2m 08.238s; **3** Okada, 2m 08.440s; **4** T. Aoki, 2m 08.830s; **5** N. Aoki, 2m 09.164s; **6** Checa, 2m 09.318s; **7** Abe, 2m 09.366s; **8** Cadalora, 2m 10.015s; **9** Puig, 2m 10.232s; **10** Goddard, 2m 10.292s; **11** Borja, 2m 10.321s; **12** Fujiwara, 2m 10.405s; **13** Gibernau, 2m 10.435s; **14** Corser, 2m 10.506s; **15** Bayle, 2m 10.765s; **16** Laconi, 2m 10.824s; **17** Barros, 2m 10.906s; **18** Roberts Jnr, 2m 11.609s; **19** McCarthy, 2m 12.306s; **20** van den Goorbergh, 2m 12.324s; **21** Beattie, 2m 12.565s; **22** Fuchs, 2m 13.975s; **23** Protat, 2m 14.082s; **24** Pedercini, 2m 15.275s; **25** Naveau, 2m 17.597s.

World Championship: **1** Doohan, 50; **2** Criville, 40; **3** N. Aoki, 27; **4** T. Aoki, 24; **5** Okada, 22; **6** Checa, 20; **7** Cadalora, 18; **8** Abe and Puig, 17; **10** Barros, 11; **11** Laconi, 8; **12** Fujiwara and Gibernau, 7; **14** Corser and Goddard, 3; **16** Bayle, Borja and van den Goorbergh, 2.

Main picture: Noboru Ueda read the wind right to come from last to first at his home GP.

Inset: Rossi surprised himself and his motor bike by throwing the race away.

Photos: Gold & Goose

250 cc

19 laps, 69.236 miles/111.416 km

Pos.	Rider (Nat.)	No.	Machine	Laps	Time & speed
1	**Daijiro Kato (J)**	35	Honda	19	41m 42.226s 99.603 mph/ 160.296 km/h
2	**Tohru Ukawa (J)**	5	Honda	19	41m 42.434s
3	**Tetsuya Harada (J)**	31	Aprilia	19	41m 42.544s
4	**Takeshi Tsujimura (J)**	12	Honda	19	41m 43.234s
5	**Ralf Waldmann (D)**	2	Honda	19	41m 47.790s
6	**Yukio Kagayama (J)**	38	Suzuki	19	42m 03.264s
7	**Max Biaggi (I)**	1	Honda	19	42m 10.107s
8	**Haruchika Aoki (J)**	7	Honda	19	42m 10.147s
9	**Noriyasu Numata (J)**	20	Suzuki	19	42m 10.544s
10	**Naoki Matsudo (J)**	36	Yamaha	19	42m 12.400s
11	**Loris Capirossi (I)**	65	Aprilia	19	42m 19.940s
12	**Sebastian Porto (ARG)**	27	Aprilia	19	42m 24.058s
13	**Naoto Ogura (J)**	39	Yamaha	19	42m 32.124s
14	**Jamie Robinson (GB)**	14	Suzuki	19	42m 32.810s
15	**Choujun Kameya (J)**	37	Suzuki	19	42m 32.940s
16	Jeremy McWilliams (GB)	11	Honda	19	42m 49.287s
17	Luis D'Antin (E)	6	Yamaha	19	42m 54.570s
18	Oliver Petrucciani (CH)	25	Aprilia	19	42m 55.194s
19	Luca Boscoscuro (I)	10	Honda	19	42m 55.895s
20	José Luis Cardoso (E)	17	Yamaha	19	42m 56.239s
21	Franco Battaini (I)	21	Yamaha	19	43m 14.596s
22	Cristiano Migliorati (I)	8	Honda	18	42m 01.620s
	Osamu Miyazaki (J)	18	Yamaha	14	DNF
	William Costes (F)	16	Honda	12	DNF
	Kensuke Haga (J)	33	Yamaha	10	DNF
	Kurtis Roberts (USA)	22	Aprilia	6	DNF
	Stefano Perugini (I)	15	Aprilia	4	DNF
	Eustaquio Gavira (E)	28	Aprilia	3	DNF
	Idalio Gavira (E)	29	Aprilia		DNS
	Olivier Jacque (F)	19	Honda		DNS

Fastest lap: Harada, 2m 10.253s, 100.707 mph/162.072 km/h (record).

Previous record: Max Biaggi, I (Aprilia), 2m 10.492s, 100.522 mph/161.775 km/h (1996).

Qualifying: **1** Harada, 2m 09.541s; **2** Tsujimura, 2m 09.647s; **3** Kato, 2m 09.822s; **4** Capirossi, 2m 09.885s; **5** Jacque, 2m 10.132s; **6** Kagayama, 2m 10.244s; **7** Ukawa, 2m 10.540s; **8** Perugini, 2m 10.584s; **9** Matsudo, 2m 10.586s; **10** Kameya, 2m 10.967s; **11** Miyazaki, 2m 11.033s; **12** Numata, 2m 11.148s; **13** Waldmann, 2m 11.154s; **14** Haga, 2m 11.678s; **15** Biaggi, 2m 11.830s; **16** Porto, 2m 11.877s; **17** Ogura, 2m 11.881s; **18** Aoki, 2m 12.007s; **19** Robinson, 2m 12.008s; **20** McWilliams, 2m 12.977s; **21** D'Antin, 2m 13.099s; **22** Cardoso, 2m 13.561s; **23** Petrucciani, 2m 13.738s; **24** Boscoscuro, 2m 13.808s; **25** Battaini, 2m 14.372s; **26** Costes, 2m 14.411s; **27** Migliorati, 2m 14.773s; **28** I. Gavira, 2m 15.563s; **29** E. Gavira, 2m 16.190s; **30** Roberts, 2m 16.632s.

Fastest race laps: **1** Harada, 2m 10.253s; **2** Kato, 2m 10.276s; **3** Ukawa, 2m 10.516s; **4** Tsujimura, 2m 10.756s; **5** Kagayama, 2m 10.918s; **6** Waldmann, 2m 11.060s; **7** Numata, 2m 11.499s; **8** Haga, 2m 11.565s; **9** Biaggi, 2m 11.570s; **10** Aoki, 2m 11.574s; **11** Capirossi, 2m 11.694s; **12** Perugini, 2m 11.816s; **13** Matsudo, 2m 11.982s; **14** Porto, 2m 12.673s; **15** Ogura, 2m 12.766s; **16** Kameya, 2m 12.924s; **17** Miyazaki, 2m 13.024s; **18** Robinson, 2m 13.111s; **19** McWilliams, 2m 13.522s; **20** Migliorati, 2m 14.101s; **21** Petrucciani, 2m 14.102s; **22** D'Antin, 2m 14.222s; **23** Cardoso, 2m 14.386s; **24** Boscoscuro, 2m 14.452s; **25** Costes, 2m 14.656s; **26** Battaini, 2m 14.922s; **27** Roberts, 2m 16.995s; **28** E. Gavira, 2m 18.906s.

World Championship: **1** Harada, 36; **2** Biaggi, 34; **3** Ukawa, 30; **4** Kato, 25; **5** Waldmann, 24; **6** Aoki, 19; **7** Jacque, 16; **8** Tsujimura, 13; **9** Kagayama, 10; **10** Alzamora and Numata, 9; **12** Migliorati, 8; **13** McWilliams, 7; **14** Matsudo and Petrucciani, 6; **16** Capirossi and Miyazaki, 5; **18** E. Gavira and Porto, 4; **20** Battaini and Ogura, 3; **22** Robinson, 2; **23** Boscoscuro and Kameya, 1.

125 cc

18 laps, 65.592 miles/105.552 km

Pos.	Rider (Nat.)	No.	Machine	Laps	Time & speed
1	**Noboru Ueda (J)**	7	Honda	18	41m 48.072s 94.141 mph/ 151.505 km/h
2	**Kazuto Sakata (J)**	8	Aprilia	18	41m 48.437s
3	**Hideyuki Nakajo (J)**	31	Honda	18	41m 48.578s
4	**Masao Azuma (J)**	20	Honda	18	41m 50.226s
5	**Jorge Martinez (E)**	5	Aprilia	18	41m 50.236s
6	**Yoshiaki Katoh (J)**	62	Yamaha	18	41m 50.326s
7	**Garry McCoy (AUS)**	72	Aprilia	18	41m 53.952s
8	**Kazuhiro Takao (J)**	34	Honda	18	41m 57.303s
9	**Gianluigi Scalvini (I)**	21	Honda	18	42m 10.290s
10	**Frédéric Petit (F)**	19	Honda	18	42m 10.356s
11	**Roberto Locatelli (I)**	15	Honda	18	42m 12.046s
12	**Tomomi Manako (J)**	3	Honda	18	42m 12.607s
13	**Masaki Tokudome (J)**	2	Aprilia	18	42m 23.522s
14	**Ivan Goi (I)**	26	Aprilia	18	42m 23.775s
15	**Gino Borsoi (I)**	24	Yamaha	18	42m 23.819s
16	Jun Inageda (J)	37	Honda	18	42m 24.316s
17	Katsuji Uezu (J)	36	Yamaha	18	42m 24.367s
18	Mirko Giansanti (I)	32	Honda	18	42m 25.216s
19	Josep Sarda (E)	25	Honda	18	42m 35.534s
20	Yuzo Fujioka (J)	38	Honda	18	42m 35.620s
21	Steve Jenkner (D)	22	Aprilia	18	42m 52.593s
22	Angel Nieto Jnr (E)	29	Aprilia	18	43m 08.132s
23	Manfred Geissler (D)	33	Honda	18	43m 08.242s
24	Juan Enrique Maturana (E)	17	Yamaha	18	43m 08.413s
	Valentino Rossi (I)	46	Aprilia	16	DNF
	Jaroslav Hules (CS)	39	Honda	7	DNF
	Lucio Cecchinello (I)	10	Honda	6	DNF
	Peter Öttl (D)	88	Aprilia	4	DNF
	Dirk Raudies (D)	12	Honda	0	DNF
	Toshiaki Ozawa (J)	35	Honda	0	DNF
	Youichi Ui (J)	41	Yamaha	0	DNF

Fastest lap: Tokudome, 2m 17.462s, 95.425 mph/153.572 km/h.

Lap record: Kazuto Sakata, J (Aprilia), 2m 17.055s, 95.709 mph/154.029 km/h (1996).

Qualifying: **1** Ueda, 2m 16.879s; **2** Martinez, 2m 17.042s; **3** Tokudome, 2m 17.178s; **4** Ui, 2m 17.233s; **5** Sakata, 2m 17.719s; **6** Manako, 2m 17.912s; **7** Rossi, 2m 18.011s; **8** Fujioka, 2m 18.093s; **9** Katoh, 2m 18.123s; **10** Takao, 2m 18.255s; **11** McCoy, 2m 18.527s; **12** Locatelli, 2m 18.694s; **13** Azuma, 2m 18.705s; **14** Cecchinello, 2m 18.763s; **15** Nakajo, 2m 18.797s; **16** Jules, 2m 19.020s; **17** Uezu, 2m 19.197s; **18** Scalvini, 2m 19.335s; **19** Ozawa, 2m 19.380s; **20** Raudies, 2m 19.407s; **21** Öttl, 2m 19.448s; **22** Petit, 2m 19.555s; **23** Borsoi, 2m 19.668s; **24** Inageda, 2m 20.472s; **25** Sarda, 2m 20.949s; **26** Maturana, 2m 22.186s; **27** Giansanti, 2m 22.307s; **28** Geissler, 2m 22.316s; **29** Goi, 2m 22.641s; **30** Jenkner, 2m 22.808s; **31** Nieto Jnr, 2m 23.290s.

Fastest race laps: **1** Tokudome, 2m 17.462s; **2** Takao, 2m 17.525s; **3** Ueda, 2m 17.554s; **4** McCoy, 2m 17.784s; **5** Sakata, 2m 17.797s; **6** Azuma, 2m 17.806s; **7** Katoh, 2m 17.949s; **8** Martinez, 2m 18.146s; **9** Rossi, 2m 18.152s; **10** Nakajo, 2m 18.282s; **11** Manako, 2m 18.467s; **12** Petit, 2m 19.008s; **13** Cecchinello, 2m 19.080s; **14** Locatelli, 2m 19.181s; **15** Scalvini, 2m 19.184s; **16** Borsoi, 2m 19.491s; **17** Uezu, 2m 19.495s; **18** Fujioka, 2m 19.507s; **19** Inageda, 2m 19.553s; **20** Goi, 2m 19.716s; **21** Giansanti, 2m 19.822s; **22** Öttl, 2m 19.874s; **23** Hules, 2m 20.159s; **24** Sarda, 2m 20.400s; **25** Jenkner, 2m 21.536s; **26** Maturana, 2m 21.846s; **27** Geissler, 2m 21.868s; **28** Nieto Jnr, 2m 22.249s.

World Championship: **1** Ueda, 41; **2** Sakata, 40; **3** Rossi, 25; **4** Martinez, 21; **5** Katoh, 18; **6** Azuma, 17; **7** Nakajo, 16; **8** Tokudome, 14; **9** Giansanti, Manako and Petit, 13; **12** McCoy, 9; **13** Takao, 8; **14** Scalvini, 7; **15** Cecchinello, 6; **16** Goi, Hules and Locatelli, 5; **19** Raudies, 2; **20** Borsoi and Sarda, 1.

Photos: Gold & Goose

SPANISH
grand prix

'WE'VE started to achieve our targets. But Honda has taken a big leap. Maybe our triple's not good enough to beat the V4s. If so, then we'll build a V4, if that's what it takes.' Kenny Roberts gave his first Modenas press conference at Jerez, and it was a practised performance, a steady sell for the massive project of race-developing a prototype machine in the heat of the world championship under the full public gaze. It almost made one want to invest right there.

Away from the rigmarole, the Modenas's problems were both prosaic and exotic. Overheating was robbing them of power and speed – they were 20 km/h off the Hondas down the straight. A new magnesium water-pump to the underseat ducted radiator didn't help – for some reason, possibly cavitation, the system just wasn't flowing fast enough. The team were staying on at Jerez for much-needed track time to address this and other problems.

But was it really true about Honda's great leap? Kenny said their on-board telemetry showed that the Modenas had achieved their prime objective, adding 10 km/h to mid-corner speed compared with last year's Yamahas. But, he added, the Hondas had somehow found a similar corner speed improvement as well. And then they just blasted away on the way out.

Certainly Honda's rampancy in the results bore this out. The stopwatches were not so conclusive. There were more riders in the front group, sure enough, pushing each other, and Okada's pole time (his third in succession!) was the fastest-ever lap, by a few tenths. But Schwantz's 1994 record remained intact, and the race average was in fact slower than last year's, even though the race ran full speed all the way, with no pitch invasion this time.

None of this mattered too much to the vast crowds who thronged the dusty hillsides. They'd only come to see one thing – Alex Criville exacting revenge over Michael Doohan for his defeat last year. Motor cycling ranks with cycling and football in the Spanish sporting spectrum, and King Juan Carlos was present at Jerez, as at a number of previous GPs. When the Spanish elevate someone to the role of national hero, blind support is part of the package. Thus there were few who, in their hearts, did not somehow find a way to blame the obviously innocent Australian for the track invasion in 1996, and for Criville's futile last-corner crash.

The fans got what they came for, and left well satisfied. A win is a win, even if it began to look a bit hollow when put under scrutiny. For the truth of the matter was that Mick had been riding with one cylinder tied behind his back. The different patterns of vibration of the Screamer fed a new harmonic that found a weakness in the exhaust powervalve linkage. The drive to one cylinder had snapped. Doohan later put the finger on a handling problem as well. 'I could have lived with the shortage of power, but when I tried to use more corner speed to compensate, the bike became unstable.'

This quirk notwithstanding, the story of the season continued without much change at the first of the European rounds. Honda's rivals were still a bit bemused by it all. The Power Horse problem inched further towards solution, with American millionaire and long-standing racing backer Bob MacLean taking over (putting *Motocourse* Technical Editor Peter Clifford in charge). The details were far from finalised, and the team ran in Power Horse livery for one last time.

Corser was still struggling. The YZR500 was proving a good deal harder than he'd expected, after his lolloping Ducati, and he was increasingly desperately chasing that crucial fine line of front-wheel adhesion. He stepped over the mark in practice and again in the race. The pressure was tough on the latest would-be Wollongong Wild One.

Over at Suzuki, Gobert was being 'rested' again, giving Goddard another outing; Beattie, meanwhile, switched to Brembo brakes from the team's long-standing AP Racing equipment. He had a different bike, using the same new motor/old chassis formula as the test mule he'd raced in Japan. This had been a show bike at the GP, but was spirited away for reworking. Now a cross-reference of numbers showed it was in fact the chassis on which Daryl had won the German GP in 1995, his and the team's last win.

Elf were attracting rather less attention with the high-profile Modenas as the new alternative to Japan. Considering that they were struggling as much as anybody else – and maybe more – this might have been welcome. They had a batch of new parts here too, including lightweight magnesium crankcases, but they did not use them since they had other problems to solve. New rider Fuchs was just struggling, period; Borja was plagued by the continuing difficulty of snatchy throttle response. Modified carburettors and throttle linkages varied flow speeds and opening rates. But it all came to nothing for the Spanish rider, with a breakdown on the warm-up lap.

There is one other alternative, however, and Doriano Romboni was back to wheel the Aprilia around. Simultaneously came confirmation that the bike had grown again. Originally 410 cc, then 430, it was now 460 cc, for a valuable gain of eight horsepower. Still regaining strength, Romboni was low key in practice but rode a storming race to finish top non-Honda, if not actually first V-twin.

There were active peace moves from Aprilia, on the instructions of chairman Ivan Beggio, to defuse the war against Biaggi. Symptoms had been the protest in Malaysia, and lots of bad blood – with a particular row about Max's use of Ferrari-developed carbon-fibre wheels. Aprilia thought they had an exclusive contract, but Max had secured a private deal. Now team boss Carlo Pernat had been told to back off. As if Biaggi wasn't facing enough hostility from his Honda colleagues. Waldmann and Jacque had both been complaining bitterly that Max had been given a Mk2 frame before the season, while they were stuck with the first version. Now each had a new one, with Waldmann leaving his in the crate until he could test it, but Jacque getting straight on board. Biaggi's response: 'I've been riding the first version all year anyway.'

500 cc	CRIVILLE
250 cc	WALDMANN
125 cc	ROSSI

Winners and losers. Criville *(opposite page)* and his adoring fans didn't know yet why he'd won, only that he had. Goddard *(above)* was an early faller in his second outing as Gobert's substitute.

500 cc RACE – 27 LAPS

Okada took pole again, his third in a row, and once again it was the same four on the front row. Home heroes Puig and Checa were next, Cadalora best of the non-Hondas in seventh.

Criville had crashed at a good speed on Friday, blaming the wind; but he made no mistakes in the race. He got away first, and was never headed. What's more, while he and the crowd waited for Doohan's challenge, the Australian seemed instead to be biding his time behind Okada and Checa.

Third wasn't good enough for Checa, out for glory; and he was out of the saddle twice on the fourth lap as he tried to find a way ahead. Then he made it. And Criville was just beyond. It was all too much. Half a lap later, before the back straight, he slid again – and this time it was terminal. It was not to be his turn to meet the king again today.

Criville made the most of this break over Okada, riding quickly and

smoothly to pull away inexorably. He set best lap of the race eighth time round, half a second off the record; by when he had a second in hand. And, as all his dreams came true, he kept on stretching away, up to eight seconds with five laps left. He only needed to stay on.

And Doohan? Biding his time was one thing, but he was gradually losing ground to Okada in second, and that surely wasn't right. At half-distance he was more than two seconds adrift, and though he did start to reel his Japanese rival in towards the finish, he only caught him with less than three laps to go. Then, when he dived past under brakes at the end of the back straight, Tady promptly passed him back into turn one at the start of the next lap.

Down on power and road-holding, Doohan did everything he knew to get back in front and stay there across the line. He only managed it by hundredths, and a few feet further on the positions would have been re-

versed, with Okada surging past. Having ridden much harder than he usually has to when he wins, Doohan said later: 'I feel lucky to have finished where I did.'

A long way back came the fourth member of the Repsol team, Takuma Aoki, who had pushed his V-twin past his brother Nobuatsu's V4 on lap 21, finishing some two seconds clear.

The rest were fighting over sixth place, and the group had grown to four as the race wore on. Gibernau was feeling the Spanish effect for the race of his life, passing experienced team-mate Abe, who was busy enough chasing his own front wheel around, the pair of them catching Barros for a lively battle.

Romboni, meanwhile, was charging through. He'd finished the first lap in 19th, planning to pace himself in his first ride for many months,'but the bike was going so well I thought I'd make a race of it.' And how. He joined the battle for sixth with five laps left, and made short work of getting to the

front of it, finishing up with Abe, Barros and Gibernau right behind.

Laconi impressed again, starting well then losing ground only gradually, to fend off Cadalora's Yamaha for tenth, ahead by three seconds. Later, Luca said that he'd ridden the whole race without a rear brake.

Beattie dropped off the back of this group to finish an unhappy 12th. Bayle had been ahead of him on the Modenas, but fell away to within one second of van den Goorbergh; McCarthy took the last point. There were four more finishers: Fuchs, Pedercini, Roberts Junior and Naveau, the second-last named giving Modenas their first two-bike finish.

Goddard was the first of several crashers. Starting from 23rd and trying to make up time, he fell heavily on the second lap, just a few corners earlier than compatriot Corser. Then Puig completed a disastrous day for Sito Pons's MoviStar team, falling after eight laps while trying to escape the gang and set off after the leaders.

Lap one of the first European round, with Criville already leading Okada, Nobuatsu Aoki, the doomed Checa, Doohan, Barros and Takuma Aoki. Privateer Laconi (55) is prominent as usual.

Below: Bayle moves inside the unhappy Beattie, but the positions were reversed again at the finish.

250 cc RACE – 26 LAPS

Qualifying was hectic, with Capirossi fastest, only to be ousted by both Waldmann and Harada, the first three within two-tenths. Redoubtable Biaggi was a relatively distant fourth, after surviving another high-speed crash on Friday. 'I landed on my other shoulder,' he smiled. Jacque was in pain and off the pace; Alzamora worse still, withdrawing after a couple of laps of practice. It could still have been a good race without them, however, but for a couple of early incidents.

In the first corner, as Jacque led Waldmann through, privateer Boscoscuro was blamed for a chain reaction that sent Capirossi piling straight into Ukawa up near the front. The Japanese rider remounted; the luckless Italian was out.

Then, on the second lap, after Biaggi had moved into third past Harada, he was knocked flying by his Japanese rival in a piece of rather hard riding that was analysed over and over again that evening, without anyone being able to put a harsher interpretation on it. Max went pounding across the gravel at speed, fighting to retain control and rejoining way down in 22nd place.

Jacque, full of painkillers and adrenaline, might have made a race of it but for an extraordinary and (for Dunlop) rather embarrassing problem. His tyre choice was fine, but due to a contaminated mould the actual compound didn't match the number on the side. Sliding around, he was soon moving inexorably backwards. Waldmann passed without difficulty on the third lap, and ran away for his first win of the year.

Harada had not come out of the collision unscathed. An exhaust was damaged, and he dropped right back to seventh. It didn't get any worse, however, and he managed to move steadily forwards again, catching the sliding Jacque just before half-distance to secure a lucky second.

Meanwhile Biaggi was charging through. On lap 13 he caught a gang of three disputing fourth place and moved straight through. Tsujimura and Aoki came with him, all three then despatching Jacque. Perugini was slightly behind, but he too passed the Honda rider to take sixth.

On the last lap Jacque lost even more ground, and only just held on to seventh from Numata's Suzuki. The Jerez first-timer had outpaced McWilliams towards the finish; he in turn had fended off the Yamahas of Cardoso and D'Antin by inches, with a third Yamaha, that of Miyazaki, less than two seconds behind.

Ukawa had fought his way back up to seventh before retiring with two laps left, suffering from engine problems. Migliorati and Porto were among several crashers; Kurtis Roberts did not finish the first lap after a fuel breather blocked.

125 cc RACE – 23 LAPS

Martinez had the vast crowd in ecstasy as he led away from pole position, fending off an early challenge from Tokudome. Then Ueda's notably fast Honda came past, with Tokudome and Manako close behind.

Rossi meanwhile was surging through. Fifteenth after the first lap, he was passing people as though he had a special dispensation from the laws of physics, an extra 50 cc, or an indecent amount of talent. He joined the leaders on lap nine, and was in front two laps later.

They all stayed together. Martinez, Ueda and (briefly) Manako all led at various points, preparing for a last-lap showdown.

By the finish, Tokudome and Manako had slipped back slightly, but the other three were locked together. It was Rossi who fought the hardest, far enough ahead into the final hairpin to defend his lead, with Ueda and Martinez packed up behind.

German veteran Peter Öttl prevailed over his group for sixth, outstripping Sakata at the finish. McCoy had got away with the leaders, but dropped back to retire with engine problems.

Photos: Gold & Goose

FIM WORLD CHAMPIONSHIP • ROUND 3

LUCKY STRIKE SPANISH GRAND PRIX

4 MAY 1997

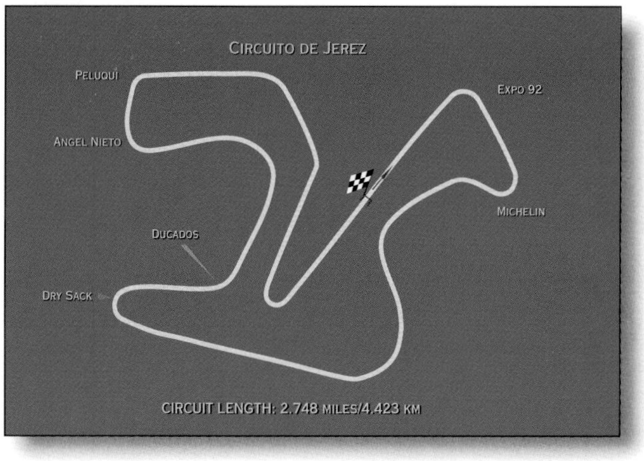
CIRCUITO DE JEREZ
PELUQUÍ
EXPO 92
ANGEL NIETO
MICHELIN
DUCADOS
DRY SACK
CIRCUIT LENGTH: 2.748 MILES/4.423 KM

500 cc

27 laps, 74.196 miles/119.421 km

Pos.	Rider (Nat.)	No.	Machine	Laps	Time & speed
1	**Alex Criville (E)**	2	Honda	27	47m 30.624s 93.711 mph/ 150.814 km/h
2	**Michael Doohan (AUS)**	1	Honda	27	47m 36.260s
3	**Tadayuki Okada (J)**	7	Honda	27	47m 36.294s
4	**Takuma Aoki (J)**	24	Honda	27	47m 53.327s
5	**Nobuatsu Aoki (J)**	18	Honda	27	47m 59.038s
6	**Doriano Romboni (I)**	19	Aprilia	27	48m 02.386s
7	**Norifumi Abe (J)**	5	Yamaha	27	48m 03.110s
8	**Alex Barros (BR)**	4	Honda	27	48m 03.930s
9	**Sete Gibernau (E)**	20	Yamaha	27	48m 04.181s
10	**Regis Laconi (F)**	55	Honda	27	48m 12.606s
11	**Luca Cadalora (I)**	3	Yamaha	27	48m 15.626s
12	**Daryl Beattie (AUS)**	6	Suzuki	27	48m 20.393s
13	**Jean-Michel Bayle (F)**	12	Modenas	27	48m 23.081s
14	**Jurgen v.d. Goorbergh (NL)**	21	Honda	27	48m 24.084s
15	**Kirk McCarthy (AUS)**	22	Yamaha	27	49m 01.881s
16	Jurgen Fuchs (D)	16	Elf 500	27	49m 07.092s
17	Lucio Pedercini (I)	17	Yamaha	27	49m 09.620s
18	Kenny Roberts Jnr (USA)	10	Modenas	27	49m 11.870s
19	Laurent Naveau (B)	25	Yamaha	26	47m 42.880s
	Alberto Puig (E)	9	Honda	8	DNF
	Frédéric Protat (F)	15	Yamaha	6	DNF
	Carlos Checa (E)	8	Honda	5	DNF
	Troy Corser (AUS)	11	Yamaha	2	DNF
	Peter Goddard (AUS)	27	Suzuki	2	DNF
	Juan Borja (E)	14	Elf 500		DNS

Fastest lap: Criville, 1m 44.564s, 94.621 mph/152.278 km/h.
Lap record: Kevin Schwantz, USA (Suzuki), 1m 44.168s, 94.981 mph/152.857 km/h (1994).

Qualifying: **1** Okada, 1m 43.403s; **2** Doohan, 1m 43.560s; **3** Criville, 1m 43.712s; **4** N. Aoki, 1m 43.874s; **5** Puig, 1m 43.890s; **6** Checa, 1m 44.054s; **7** Cadalora, 1m 44.068s; **8** T. Aoki, 1m 44.127s; **9** Laconi, 1m 44.250s; **10** Romboni, 1m 44.578s; **11** van den Goorbergh, 1m 44.582s; **12** Barros, 1m 44.901s; **13** Borja, 1m 44.905s; **14** Bayle, 1m 45.132s; **15** Gibernau, 1m 45.592s; **16** Abe, 1m 45.600s; **17** Beattie, 1m 45.620s; **18** Corser, 1m 45.897s; **19** McCarthy, 1m 46.475s; **20** Fuchs, 1m 46.570s; **21** Pedercini, 1m 46.752s; **22** Roberts Jnr, 1m 46.790s; **23** Goddard, 1m 47.295s; **24** Naveau, 1m 47.652s; **25** Protat, 1m 50.323s.

Fastest race laps: **1** Criville, 1m 44.564s; **2** Okada, 1m 44.643s; **3** Checa, 1m 44.697s; **4** N. Aoki, 1m 44.783s; **5** Doohan, 1m 44.902s; **6** T. Aoki, 1m 45.414s; **7** Puig, 1m 45.597s; **8** Abe, 1m 45.820s; **9** Gibernau, 1m 45.878s; **10** Romboni, 1m 45.939s; **11** Barros, 1m 45.942s; **12** Laconi, 1m 46.085s; **13** Cadalora, 1m 46.337s; **14** van den Goorbergh, 1m 46.537s; **15** Beattie, 1m 46.609s; **16** Bayle, 1m 46.653s; **17** Corser, 1m 46.950s; **18** McCarthy, 1m 47.376s; **19** Goddard, 1m 47.830s; **20** Pedercini, 1m 47.958s; **21** Roberts Jnr, 1m 48.276s; **22** Fuchs, 1m 48.383s; **23** Naveau, 1m 48.903s; **24** Protat, 1m 49.361s.

World Championship: **1** Doohan, 70; **2** Criville, 65; **3** N. Aoki and Okada, 38; **5** T. Aoki, 37; **6** Abe, 26; **7** Cadalora, 23; **8** Checa, 20; **9** Barros, 19; **10** Puig, 17; **11** Gibernau and Laconi, 14; **13** Romboni, 10; **14** Fujiwara, 7; **15** Bayle, 5; **16** Beattie and van den Goorbergh, 4; **18** Corser and Goddard, 3; **20** Borja, 2; 21 McCarthy, 1.

250 cc

26 laps, 71.448 miles/114.998 km

Pos.	Rider (Nat.)	No.	Machine	Laps	Time & speed
1	**Ralf Waldmann (D)**	2	Honda	26	46m 03.640s 93.081 mph/ 149.799 km/h
2	**Tetsuya Harada (J)**	31	Aprilia	26	46m 16.364s
3	**Max Biaggi (I)**	1	Honda	26	46m 23.068s
4	**Takeshi Tsujimura (J)**	12	Honda	26	46m 33.897s
5	**Haruchika Aoki (J)**	7	Honda	26	46m 34.384s
6	**Stefano Perugini (I)**	15	Aprilia	26	46m 40.120s
7	**Olivier Jacque (F)**	19	Honda	26	46m 45.600s
8	**Noriyasu Numata (J)**	20	Suzuki	26	46m 50.040s
9	**Jeremy McWilliams (GB)**	11	Honda	26	47m 01.299s
10	**José Luis Cardoso (E)**	17	Yamaha	26	47m 01.467s
11	**Luis D'Antin (E)**	6	Yamaha	26	47m 01.928s
12	**Osamu Miyazaki (J)**	18	Yamaha	26	47m 03.964s
13	**Oliver Petrucciani (CH)**	25	Aprilia	26	47m 06.871s
14	**Franco Battaini (I)**	21	Yamaha	26	47m 07.224s
15	**Luca Boscoscuro (I)**	10	Honda	26	47m 11.470s
16	Jamie Robinson (GB)	14	Suzuki	26	47m 19.350s
17	Eustaquio Gavira (E)	28	Aprilia	26	47m 30.638s
18	Oscar Sainz (E)	49	Aprilia	26	47m 31.010s
19	William Costes (F)	16	Honda	26	47m 34.994s
	Tohru Ukawa (J)	5	Honda	24	DNF
	Ismael Bonilla (E)	50	Honda	22	DNF
	Jesus Perez (E)	51	Honda	12	DNF
	Idalio Gavira (E)	29	Aprilia	11	DNF
	Giuseppe Fiorillo (I)	99	Aprilia	10	DNF
	Salvador Martin (E)	52	Aprilia	8	DNF
	Sebastian Porto (ARG)	27	Aprilia	5	DNF
	Cristiano Migliorati (I)	8	Honda	1	DNF
	Kurtis Roberts (USA)	22	Aprilia	0	DNF
	Loris Capirossi (I)	65	Aprilia	0	DNF

Fastest lap: Waldmann, 1m 45.483s, 93.797 mph/150.951 km/h.
Lap record: Max Biaggi, I (Aprilia), 1m 45.270s, 93.987 mph/151.257 km/h (1996).

Qualifying: **1** Waldmann, 1m 44.770s; **2** Harada, 1m 44.895s; **3** Capirossi, 1m 44.944s; **4** Biaggi, 1m 45.408s; **5** Ukawa, 1m 45.734s; **6** Jacque, 1m 45.809s; **7** Perugini, 1m 46.100s; **8** Tsujimura, 1m 46.118s; **9** Numata, 1m 46.526s; **10** Aoki, 1m 46.771s; **11** D'Antin, 1m 46.855s; **12** McWilliams, 1m 46.920s; **13** Porto, 1m 46.956s; **14** Migliorati, 1m 46.992s; **15** Petrucciani, 1m 47.122s; **16** Cardoso, 1m 47.147s; **17** Robinson, 1m 47.343s; **18** Boscoscuro, 1m 47.442s; **19** Battaini, 1m 47.599s; **20** Roberts, 1m 47.675s; **21** Miyazaki, 1m 47.745s; **22** Sainz, 1m 47.809s; **23** Costes, 1m 48.023s; **24** I. Gavira, 1m 49.645s; **25** E. Gavira, 1m 50.116s; **26** Fiorillo, 1m 50.569s; **27** Bonilla, 1m 50.884s; **28** Perez, 1m 51.603s; **29** Martin, 1m 51.668s.

Fastest race laps: **1** Waldmann, 1m 45.483s; **2** Biaggi, 1m 45.581s; **3** Harada, 1m 45.914s; **4** Jacque, 1m 45.920s; **5** Ukawa, 1m 46.168s; **6** Aoki, 1m 46.582s; **7** Perugini, 1m 46.689s; **8** Tsujimura, 1m 46.714s; **9** Numata, 1m 47.024s; **10** Cardoso, 1m 47.502s; **11** McWilliams, 1m 47.566s; **12** D'Antin, 1m 47.614s; **13** Boscoscuro, 1m 47.643s; **14** Porto, 1m 47.724s; **15** Miyazaki, 1m 47.775s; **16** Robinson, 1m 47.889s; **17** Battaini, 1m 47.906s; **18** Petrucciani, 1m 47.970s; **19** Costes, 1m 48.572s; **20** E. Gavira, 1m 48.723s; **21** Sainz, 1m 48.822s; **22** Fiorillo, 1m 49.492s; **23** I. Gavira, 1m 49.667s; **24** Bonilla, 1m 50.128s; **25** Perez, 1m 51.068s; **26** Martin, 1m 52.652s; **27** Migliorati, 1m 55.480s.

World Championship: **1** Harada, 56; **2** Biaggi, 50; **3** Waldmann, 49; **4** Aoki and Ukawa, 30; **6** Tsujimura, 26; **7** Jacque and Kato, 25; **9** Numata, 17; **10** McWilliams, 14; **11** Kagayama and Perugini, 10; **13** Alzamora, Miyazaki and Petrucciani, 9; **16** Migliorati, 8; **17** Cardoso and Matsudo, 6; **19** Battaini, Capirossi and D'Antin, 5; **22** E. Gavira and Porto, 4; **24** Ogura, 3; **25** Boscoscuro and Robinson, 2; **27** Kameya, 1.

125 cc

23 laps, 63.204 miles/101.729 km

Pos.	Rider (Nat.)	No.	Machine	Laps	Time & speed
1	**Valentino Rossi (I)**	46	Aprilia	23	42m 30.676s 89.216 mph/ 143.579 km/h
2	**Noboru Ueda (J)**	7	Honda	23	42m 31.034s
3	**Jorge Martinez (E)**	5	Aprilia	23	42m 31.176s
4	**Masaki Tokudome (J)**	2	Aprilia	23	42m 32.019s
5	**Tomomi Manako (J)**	3	Honda	23	42m 32.184s
6	**Peter Öttl (D)**	88	Aprilia	23	42m 38.750s
7	**Kazuto Sakata (J)**	8	Aprilia	23	42m 41.307s
8	**Roberto Locatelli (I)**	15	Honda	23	42m 45.236s
9	**Masao Azuma (J)**	20	Honda	23	42m 49.245s
10	**Yoshiaki Katoh (J)**	62	Yamaha	23	42m 50.767s
11	**Ivan Goi (I)**	26	Aprilia	23	42m 52.262s
12	**Mirko Giansanti (I)**	32	Honda	23	42m 55.143s
13	**Frédéric Petit (F)**	19	Honda	23	42m 55.520s
14	**Jaroslav Hules (CS)**	39	Honda	23	42m 55.586s
15	**Lucio Cecchinello (I)**	10	Honda	23	42m 57.790s
16	Alfonso Gonzalez (E)	48	Aprilia	23	43m 16.947s
17	Manfred Geissler (D)	33	Honda	23	43m 17.522s
18	Steve Jenkner (D)	22	Aprilia	23	43m 17.573s
19	Juan Enrique Maturana (E)	17	Yamaha	23	43m 17.598s
20	Dirk Raudies (D)	12	Honda	23	43m 18.267s
21	Gianluigi Scalvini (I)	21	Honda	23	43m 25.842s
22	Youichi Ui (J)	41	Yamaha	23	43m 35.052s
23	Gino Borsoi (I)	24	Yamaha	23	43m 56.544s
24	Angel Nieto Jnr (E)	29	Aprilia	23	44m 01.387s
25	Vicente Esparragoso (E)	51	Yamaha	23	44m 13.995s
26	Josep Sarda (E)	25	Honda	23	44m 14.125s
	Alvaro Molina (E)	52	Honda	12	DNF
	José Ramon Ramirez (E)	49	Yamaha	6	DNF
	Garry McCoy (AUS)	72	Aprilia	4	DNF
	Jeronimo Vidal (E)	50	Aprilia	2	DNF
	David Garcia (E)	47	Honda		DNS

Fastest lap: Rossi, 1m 49.604s, 90.270 mph/145.275 km/h.
Lap record: Kazuto Sakata, J (Aprilia), 1m 49.400s, 90.439 mph/145.547 km/h (1996).

Qualifying: **1** Martinez, 1m 49.582s; **2** McCoy, 1m 49.842s; **3** Tokudome, 1m 49.870s; **4** Ueda, 1m 49.946s; **5** Ui, 1m 50.079s; **6** Rossi, 1m 50.424s; **7** Cecchinello, 1m 50.445s; **8** Öttl, 1m 50.476s; **9** Katoh, 1m 50.589s; **10** Sakata, 1m 50.597s; **11** Manako, 1m 50.673s; **12** Petit, 1m 50.728s; **13** Scalvini, 1m 50.792s; **14** Hules, 1m 50.957s; **15** Azuma, 1m 51.120s; **16** Giansanti, 1m 51.298s; **17** Goi, 1m 51.325s; **18** Locatelli, 1m 51.368s; **19** Raudies, 1m 51.387s; **20** Sarda, 1m 51.521s; **21** Maturana, 1m 51.642s; **22** Geissler, 1m 51.828s; **23** Jenkner, 1m 51.954s; **24** Gonzalez, 1m 52.320s; **25** Borsoi, 1m 52.754s; **26** Nieto Jnr, 1m 52.758s; **27** Molina, 1m 53.085s; **28** Esparragoso, 1m 53.089s; **29** Ramirez, 1m 53.171s; **30** Garcia, 1m 53.219s; **31** Vidal, 1m 53.564s.

Fastest race laps: **1** Rossi, 1m 49.604s; **2** Manako, 1m 49.862s; **3** Tokudome, 1m 50.046s; **4** Martinez, 1m 50.060s; **5** Ueda, 1m 50.064s; **6** Locatelli, 1m 50.071s; **7** Ui, 1m 50.265s; **8** Sakata, 1m 50.369s; **9** Öttl, 1m 50.434s; **10** Cecchinello, 1m 50.454s; **11** Azuma, 1m 50.575s; **12** Petit, 1m 50.578s; **13** Giansanti, 1m 50.685s; **14** Hules, 1m 50.686s; **15** Goi, 1m 50.714s; **16** Katoh, 1m 50.868s; **17** Jenkner, 1m 50.988s; **18** Scalvini, 1m 51.020s; **19** Sarda, 1m 51.058s; **20** Gonzalez, 1m 51.067s; **21** Geissler, 1m 51.822s; **22** Maturana, 1m 51.892s; **23** Raudies, 1m 51.926s; **24** McCoy, 1m 52.202s; **25** Borsoi, 1m 52.835s; **26** Esparragoso, 1m 53.240s; **27** Nieto Jnr, 1m 53.329s; **28** Molina, 1m 53.352s; **29** Ramirez, 1m 53.550s; **30** Vidal, 1m 57.129s.

World Championship: **1** Ueda, 61; **2** Rossi, 50; **3** Sakata, 49; **4** Martinez, 37; **5** Tokudome, 27; **6** Azuma, Katoh and Manako, 24; **9** Giansanti, 17; **10** Nakajo and Petit, 16; **12** Locatelli, 13; **13** Goi and Öttl, 10; **15** McCoy, 9; **16** Takao, 8; **17** Cecchinello, Hules and Scalvini, 7; **20** Raudies, 2; **21** Borsoi and Sarda, 1.

Man on the way up: Waldmann's first win of the year ensured he was to be a serious title contender from now on.

Gold & Goose

ITALIAN
grand prix

HOW blessed is Italy. How apt that it should follow Spain in starting the European season. Two consecutive races like these constitute a Grand Prix feel-good factory.

Italy exceeds even Spain in having plenty of everything. Each have two GP rounds, a galaxy of star riders and partisan crowds who actually enjoy going to the races. Not to mention good racing weather. Spain has a keen king; Italy has better race tracks; Spain has more fans; Italy better restaurants. And, rather more germane, Italy has Aprilia, a real-life successful manufacturer battling the Japanese head-on and, as often as not, winning out.

A fine crowd of 60,000 or more Italians made the journey to the track in the Tuscan foothills. And what a day they had. The vastly entertaining and rightly popular Rossi claimed a superlative victory in the 125 class. He celebrated by stopping at the side of the track to pick up an inflatable doll, dressed (and named) as supermodel Claudia Schiffer. This was a taunt aimed at that other Italian hero, Biaggi, who did nothing to discourage winter reports of his own liaison with Naomi Campbell. The gangling teenager had recently been making something of a media thing of poking fun at Max, and everybody at the trackside understood the joke.

Max rose above all this, having other things to think about. In the closest 250 finish in GP history three bikes ran almost abreast across the line; all were ridden by Italians, and two out of three were Aprilias.

Italy has 500 riders too. And while Romboni fell short of the promise he'd shown at Jerez and followed up in practice, Cadalora produced one of those superlative rides he manages from time to time, to claim second place. As the first non-Honda on the rostrum all year, this was almost as good as winning.

Mugello is, of course, one of the best tracks of the year. Fast, long, scenic, technically challenging, with a big wide last corner followed by a blinding sprint to the flag that is tailor-made for epic finishes. Its only real fault is that the almost continual ess-bends, taken in one gear (third or fourth), are not conducive to overtaking. There's generally just the one fast line.

It's still a rider's track, with a sensitive surface made more difficult by the recurring climbs and drops, ever ready to punish the unwary. Thus although the 500 race started, as most of them have this year, with a four-strong Repsol Honda armada pushing away ahead, all but one of them – Doohan, who equalled Hailwood's tally of 37 class wins – made off-course excursions. Criville went farming, rejoining well out of touch, while Takuma Aoki fell off in the closing stages.

The incident of the race, however, involved Okada and Doohan. The pair were disputing the lead, and Okada was in front when he pushed harder than the track would allow – the grip was delicate, and his touch too brutal. The penalty was swift: a high-speed highsider that threw him out of the saddle to come crunching down face first onto the screen, feet high above him. Amazingly he kept hold of the bars, landing partially alongside the machine to execute an amazing gravel-trap remount without falling off. It was only to tour back to the pits to retire, however, for he'd fractured a bone in his wrist.

Doohan's involvement was peripheral but potentially catastrophic. Poised confidently behind and outside when the aerobatics began, he was convinced Okada was gone and that he was about to be knocked flying as well. He was so surprised to be still on his wheels that 'it took me half a lap to get my rhythm back'.

Other riders shone including, at last, Beattie. Tests after Jerez had brought him to a better relationship with the bike, and while he was never particularly fast, he was both consistent and obstinate, which earned a respectable fifth place. Meanwhile a chastened Gobert was back for his GP debut, talking very sensibly about keeping safety in the forefront of his mind to protect his long-troublesome collarbone. He rode very sensibly too, to finish in the points, even resisting the considerable temptation to try and stay with ex-four-stroke rival Troy Corser when he came by.

This was a minor triumph for the troubled Troy, whose Yamaha was now in Red Bull colours as the MacLean takeover progressed. With his record, even a finish was a minor triumph at this stage, sad to say.

Bayle brought his Modenas home eighth, the first top ten for the bike, on a day when the hitherto disfavoured scored some decent points. If this was largely because of the high rate of attrition – well, you have to finish races as well as go fast.

Something significant happened at the back too, when French privateer Fred Protat swapped his V4 ROC for a V-twin Honda. Another nail in the coffin of the privateer V4s, perhaps, which have now served their usefulness.

500 cc	**DOOHAN**
250 cc	**BIAGGI**
125 cc	**ROSSI**

Opposite, main picture: Biaggi narrowly in control of the 250s – a daunting task. He leads Harada and Capirossi, with Ukawa (purple helmet) and Jacque (19) close behind.

Insets, from left: Doriano Romboni broke Honda's front-row stranglehold, then stumbled. Cadalora earned the adoration; Lucchi enjoyed his moments of glory.

Below: Now in Red Bull livery, Corser earned his second points of the year.

Bottom: Dunlop's top man Jeremy Ferguson – more tyred than emotional.

Photos: Gold & Goose

500 cc RACE – 23 LAPS

Practice was a little slower than last year, with grip in short supply; and there was a minor reshuffle up front. Doohan claimed his first pole of the season, but Criville and Okada were still up with him. Nobuatsu was missing, though, as Romboni made the best of his power-boosted Aprilia to slot into fourth overall.

The early laps were familiar enough, the three Repsol V4s up front, Aoki's V-twin getting left down the straight, then catching up again within two or three corners.

Okada was the first leader, Mick nosing past here and there only to be outbraked into turn one on two consecutive laps. 'I could pass him easily, but I didn't feel like braking that deep that early in the race,' said Mick. Then, on the seventh time round, Criville left the party, doing a fraught bucking bronco act across the gravel before recovering to rejoin in 12th.

This promoted Nobuatsu's blue V4 to fourth even as he lost ground on the front men; meanwhile, a little way back, Checa and Abe had been joined by Cadalora, who'd got away badly to finish lap one 15th. Then Checa crashed once again, while the smooth-riding Italian started to close on fourth place.

Okada's narrow escape followed shortly, leaving Doohan almost two seconds ahead of Takuma's twin. He quickly made use of the advantage, stretching it to a winning margin of ten seconds.

Cadalora caught Nobuatsu quickly, but took three laps before running inside him to pull away steadily, promoted to second when Takuma fell on the 16th lap. There was no chance of catching Mick, but Nobuatsu careered across the dirt on the 20th lap, rejoining too far back to be a threat for second.

The next group saw Beattie, 11th on lap one, bring Laconi's V-twin with him as he closed steadily on Barros and Abe. Riding with typical self-containment he picked his way to the head of the group on lap 16. Criville's much faster Honda blasted past on the straight to put Daryl an eventual fifth: good on paper, if not enough to satisfy the Australian.

Laconi yielded his place in this group when an exhaust spring broke, and he lost power. He succumbed to Bayle, whose Modenas triple ran well all race for the first time all season – and the last time for several more races. Gibernau was a long way back, but also passed the flagging Laconi.

Romboni ended up 11th. He'd got an awful launch, finishing the first lap down in 18th. Trying too hard to recover, he did the gravel gallop on lap four, dropping .to last before slicing through once again.

Corser got a steady finish, another 35 seconds behind. He'd passed Gobert before half-distance, and gradually drew away from the high-profile GP new boy, in his first race since last October.

McCarthy was 14th and top privateer, with Pedercini the last rider on the same lap as the leader. Then came Naveau, and Protat's new Honda in last place.

Puig pulled into the pits with 20 laps left, his spirit apparently broken by his inability to perform. 'It made no sense to continue. I don't know what is wrong. Only that it is something serious,' he said later.

Both Elfs failed, Borja's while in the top ten in the early laps; Kenny Junior pitted his Modenas with a complicated malady – ruinous rear tyre wear caused by too much engine braking and snatchy throttle response. Van den Goorbergh also pitted his V-twin with engine problems that had troubled him for most of the weekend.

250 cc RACE – 21 LAPS

Marcellino Lucchi had to wait until he was a 40-year-old wild card before getting his first pole position. The Aprilia factory tester was in an awkward spot. One role was to try and beat Biaggi, but at the same time he ought not to do so at the expense of Harada or Capirossi, all of whom were on the front row with him. And, at the same time, here was a rare chance to win on his own account.

Biaggi won the drag to turn one, clashing fairings with Capirossi as he heeled in to seize the line. That was the first blow of many as Capirossi pushed past on lap two to begin a back-and-forth battle. Harada's second black Aprilia was in close attendance, with Lucchi's silver factory test Aprilia right up behind.

Biaggi was relieved that he could run with the Aprilias: Kanemoto had made a carburation change before the race, 'but he is a clever guy. It was in the right direction,' he said.

At the start of the fourth lap Harada abruptly stuck his leg out past the pits and rattled to a stop. A piston had disintegrated – an unprecedented failure, said Aprilia.

But there was still Lucchi, and then also Waldmann, who caught up convincingly and swept through the group to take the lead briefly at the start of lap eight. Max watched his rear wheel for the rest of that lap, then moved back ahead before they crossed the line again.

Waldmann was not to be a factor, however. His preferred Mk1 chassis had developed a crack, and he'd been forced to switch to the Mk2 version. 'It handled okay, but my real problem was a lack of straightline speed. I burned up my tyres in the corners keeping up.'

Max still had his hands full. 'The Aprilias were faster on the straight, and I also found that my bike was unstable on the quicker corners. I gave 110 per cent to stay where I was.'

Which was soon to be behind Lucchi, who first nosed ahead on the 14th lap, at the first ess at the top of the hill, only to run wide on the second part, giving Max an opening.

It was sheer speed and power that carried Lucchi by again, past the pits on lap 15, and he took his hand off the bars to wave at Max as he did so. 'I did it to apologise for passing on the straight,' he smiled afterwards. He led for two laps, then Max was in front again after a slide and a near high-side dropped Lucchi briefly behind Waldmann.

Now the pace got hotter, with Capirossi nosing ahead and the three Italians pulling away from the German as they gunned for the finish. Max stayed in front, under torrid pressure. He was still there as they started the last lap. 'This was the time for us, and nobody wanted to give up,' he said.

And it was fierce, with Capirossi attacking determinedly all the way, on the edge of crashing. He came alongside on the penultimate corner, but Max held his line and was ahead at the exit. Just one corner left.

Again Capirossi tried a run round the outside, and he did get ahead. But he was too fast, and Max could put the power on earlier. Both Max and Lucchi were ahead of him as they crossed the line almost three abreast. Less than a tenth of a second covered the trio.

Waldmann was a safe fourth; Jacque battled chatter problems all weekend to take a lonely fifth. Earlier he'd been scrapping with Tsujimura and Ukawa, until the former seized and retired and the latter crashed. Numata was equally alone in sixth, his best so far in Suzuki's return year. Some way back Perugini narrowly fended off second Suzuki rider Robinson – a career best for him as well. Fellow-Briton McWilliams led the privateers home for ninth. Then came Porto, narrowly ahead of D'Antin, Boscoscuro, Battaini and Aoki. Miyazaki took the final point.

Kurtis Roberts crashed spectacularly, after running with McWilliams in his best-yet GP.

125 cc RACE – 20 LAPS

Rossi's victory was consummate: a brilliant tactical race. First he stretched the pace to test the opposition. Martinez and Tokudome went with him, the Japanese rider leading a couple of times in the close-packed trio. Then Rossi slowed the pace for a lap before reeling off a couple of fast ones for a successful breakaway. It was some going for a teenager.

As the race progressed, Martinez and Tokudome were caught up by a pack of four, so that the last lap was a giant battle, six bikes jousting back and forth, all looking for an advantage.

All six crossed the line within half a second, and it took timekeepers a while to come up with the final order. Martinez held on to second by the narrowest of margins, with McCoy third. Then came Ueda – through from another poor start – Manako, Sakata and the luckless Tokudome.

McCoy had a good story to tell. He thought he'd timed it right to lead the group for second, but as he swerved out of Manako's draft the Japanese rider cut across him and they touched briefly. 'His backside operated my clutch, and I was just revving away going nowhere. Next time, I'll have to stand on his rear brake to pay him back,' the cheerful Australian said.

POLINI

ITALIAN
GRAND PRIX

18 MAY 1997

AUTODROMO INTERNAZIONALE DEL MUGELLO

CIRCUIT LENGTH: 3.259 MILES/5.245 KM

---

500 cc

23 laps, 74.957 miles/120.635 km

Pos.	Rider (Nat.)	No.	Machine	Laps	Time & speed
1	Michael Doohan (AUS)	1	Honda	23	44m 06.442s 101.968 mph/ 164.101 km/h
2	Luca Cadalora (I)	3	Yamaha	23	44m 16.498s
3	Nobuatsu Aoki (J)	18	Honda	23	44m 23.791s
4	Alex Criville (E)	2	Honda	23	44m 25.587s
5	Daryl Beattie (AUS)	6	Suzuki	23	44m 27.531s
6	Alex Barros (BR)	4	Honda	23	44m 27.835s
7	Norifumi Abe (J)	5	Yamaha	23	44m 35.632s
8	Jean-Michel Bayle (F)	12	Modenas	23	44m 35.856s
9	Sete Gibernau (E)	20	Yamaha	23	44m 37.146s
10	Regis Laconi (F)	55	Honda	23	44m 43.454s
11	Doriano Romboni (I)	19	Aprilia	23	44m 57.664s
12	Troy Corser (AUS)	11	Yamaha	23	45m 31.998s
13	Anthony Gobert (AUS)	23	Suzuki	23	45m 40.052s
14	Kirk McCarthy (AUS)	22	Yamaha	23	45m 50.159s
15	Lucio Pedercini (I)	17	Yamaha	23	46m 03.075s
16	Laurent Naveau (B)	25	Yamaha	22	44m 08.606s
17	Frédéric Protat (F)	15	Honda	22	45m 05.624s
	Takuma Aoki (J)	24	Honda	15	DNF
	Jurgen v.d. Goorbergh (NL)	21	Honda	14	DNF
	Kenny Roberts Jnr (USA)	10	Modenas	12	DNF
	Tadayuki Okada (J)	7	Honda	10	DNF
	Juan Borja (E)	14	Elf 500	7	DNF
	Carlos Checa (E)	8	Honda	6	DNF
	Jurgen Fuchs (D)	16	Elf 500	4	DNF
	Alberto Puig (E)	9	Honda	3	DNF
	Francesco Monaco (I)	53	Paton	3	DNF

Fastest lap: Doohan, 1m 54.144s, 102.788 mph/165.422 km/h.
Lap record: Michael Doohan, AUS (Honda), 1m 54.829s, 103.073 mph/165.880 km/h (1993).

Qualifying: 1 Doohan, 1m 53.387s; 2 Criville, 1m 53.789s; 3 Okada, 1m 53.968s; 4 Romboni, 1m 54.008s; 5 N. Aoki, 1m 54.249s; 6 T. Aoki, 1m 54.270s; 7 Cadalora, 1m 54.372s; 8 Checa, 1m 54.610s; 9 Barros, 1m 54.830s; 10 Bayle, 1m 55.046s; 11 Beattie, 1m 55.426s; 12 van den Goorbergh, 1m 55.546s; 13 Abe, 1m 55.603s; 14 Gibernau, 1m 55.662s; 15 Borja, 1m 55.841s; 16 Puig, 1m 55.964s; 17 Laconi, 1m 56.094s; 18 Roberts Jnr, 1m 56.203s; 19 McCarthy, 1m 56.474s; 20 Gobert, 1m 56.489s; 21 Fuchs, 1m 56.895s; 22 Corser, 1m 57.028s; 23 Pedercini, 1m 57.359s; 24 Naveau, 1m 58.089s; 25 Protat, 1m 58.401s; 26 Monaco, 1m 59.197s.

Fastest race laps: 1 Doohan, 1m 54.144s; 2 Okada, 1m 54.205s; 3 Cadalora, 1m 54.358s; 4 Criville, 1m 54.421s; 5 N. Aoki, 1m 54.476s; 6 T. Aoki, 1m 54.580s; 7 Checa, 1m 55.078s; 8 Abe, 1m 55.093s; 9 Beattie, 1m 55.114s; 10 Barros, 1m 55.138s; 11 Gibernau, 1m 55.206s; 12 Laconi, 1m 55.268s; 13 Romboni, 1m 55.518s; 14 Bayle, 1m 55.663s; 15 Roberts Jnr, 1m 56.284s; 16 Gobert, 1m 56.922s; 17 Corser, 1m 57.557s; 18 van den Goorbergh, 1m 57.576s; 19 Borja, 1m 57.737s; 20 Fuchs, 1m 58.052s; 21 McCarthy, 1m 58.094s; 22 Pedercini, 1m 58.143s; 23 Puig, 1m 58.696s; 24 Naveau, 1m 58.943s; 25 Protat, 2m 00.541s; 26 Monaco, 2m 00.764s.

World Championship: 1 Doohan, 95; 2 Criville, 78; 3 N. Aoki, 54; 4 Cadalora, 43; 5 Okada, 38; 6 T. Aoki, 37; 7 Abe, 35; 8 Barros, 29; 9 Gibernau, 21; 10 Checa and Laconi, 20; 12 Puig, 17; 13 Beattie and Romboni, 15; 15 Bayle, 13; 16 Corser and Fujiwara, 7; 18 van den Goorbergh, 4; 19 Gobert, Goddard and McCarthy, 3; 22 Borja, 2; 23 Pedercini, 1.

Above left: Second-placed Cadalora shakes on it with Criville behind Doohan; Barros is just passing.

Left: The crowd's colourful fireworks echoed newly re-arrived Gobert's tonsorial tints.

---

250 cc

21 laps, 68.439 miles/110.145 km

Pos.	Rider (Nat.)	No.	Machine	Laps	Time & speed
1	Max Biaggi (I)	1	Honda	21	40m 47.548s 100.666 mph/ 162.007 km/h
2	Marcellino Lucchi (I)	34	Aprilia	21	40m 47.598s
3	Loris Capirossi (I)	65	Aprilia	21	40m 47.616s
4	Ralf Waldmann (D)	2	Honda	21	40m 51.722s
5	Olivier Jacque (F)	19	Honda	21	41m 06.733s
6	Noriyasu Numata (J)	20	Suzuki	21	41m 31.167s
7	Stefano Perugini (I)	15	Aprilia	21	41m 38.995s
8	Jamie Robinson (GB)	14	Suzuki	21	41m 39.100s
9	Jeremy McWilliams (GB)	11	Honda	21	41m 41.819s
10	Sebastian Porto (ARG)	27	Aprilia	21	41m 42.554s
11	Luis D'Antin (E)	6	Aprilia	21	41m 42.554s
12	Luca Boscoscuro (I)	10	Honda	21	41m 43.531s
13	Franco Battaini (I)	21	Yamaha	21	41m 44.282s
14	Haruchika Aoki (J)	7	Honda	21	41m 45.051s
15	Osamu Miyazaki (J)	18	Yamaha	21	41m 59.628s
16	Oliver Petrucciani (CH)	25	Aprilia	21	42m 16.249s
17	William Costes (F)	16	Honda	21	42m 16.585s
18	Idalio Gavira (E)	29	Aprilia	21	42m 41.388s
19	Walter Tortoroglio (I)	55	Aprilia	21	44m 00.258s
	Fabio Carpani (I)	54	Aprilia	20	DNF
	Tohru Ukawa (J)	5	Honda	16	DNF
	Cristiano Migliorati (I)	8	Honda	15	DNF
	Takeshi Tsujimura (J)	12	Honda	9	DNF
	José Luis Cardoso (E)	17	Yamaha	7	DNF
	Kurtis Roberts (USA)	22	Aprilia	5	DNF
	Emilio Alzamora (E)	26	Honda	5	DNF
	Eustaquio Gavira (E)	28	Aprilia	4	DNF
	Oscar Sainz (E)	49	Aprilia	4	DNF
	Tetsuya Harada (J)	31	Aprilia	3	DNF
	Davide Bulega (I)	53	Aprilia		DNS

Fastest lap: Waldmann, 1m 55.416s, 101.656 mph/163.599 km/h.
Lap record: Max Biaggi, I (Aprilia), 1m 54.925s, 101.090 mph/164.298 km/h (1996).

Qualifying: 1 Lucchi, 1m 54.474s; 2 Capirossi, 1m 54.854s; 3 Biaggi, 1m 55.212s; 4 Harada, 1m 55.235s; 5 Ukawa, 1m 56.214s; 6 Jacque, 1m 56.420s; 7 Waldmann, 1m 56.448s; 8 Numata, 1m 56.848s; 9 Tsujimura, 1m 57.020s; 10 Perugini, 1m 57.073s; 11 Robinson, 1m 57.126s; 12 Aoki, 1m 57.491s; 13 Battaini, 1m 57.676s; 14 Migliorati, 1m 57.687s; 15 Porto, 1m 57.902s; 16 Cardoso, 1m 57.956s; 17 D'Antin, 1m 58.056s; 18 Miyazaki, 1m 58.074s; 19 Bulega, 1m 58.163s; 20 McWilliams, 1m 58.406s; 21 Petrucciani, 1m 58.604s; 22 Costes, 1m 58.747s; 23 Carpani, 1m 59.048s; 24 Roberts, 1m 59.290s; 25 Boscoscuro, 1m 59.962s; 26 I. Gavira, 1m 59.970s; 27 Alzamora, 2m 00.528s; 28 E. Gavira, 2m 00.734s; 29 Tortoroglio, 2m 00.764s; 30 Sainz, 2m 01.282s.

Fastest race laps: 1 Waldmann, 1m 55.416s; 2 Lucchi, 1m 55.683s; 3 Biaggi, 1m 55.712s; 4 Capirossi, 1m 55.730s; 5 Tsujimura, 1m 55.907s; 6 Ukawa, 1m 56.343s; 7 Jacque, 1m 56.386s; 8 Harada, 1m 56.462s; 9 Robinson, 1m 57.279s; 10 Numata, 1m 57.330s; 11 Aoki, 1m 57.423s; 12 Perugini, 1m 57.490s; 13 Battaini, 1m 57.693s; 14 D'Antin, 1m 57.740s; 15 Cardoso, 1m 57.760s; 16 McWilliams, 1m 57.826s; 17 Boscoscuro, 1m 57.872s; 18 Porto, 1m 57.998s; 19 Migliorati, 1m 58.054s; 20 Miyazaki, 1m 58.642s; 21 Roberts, 1m 58.742s; 22 Petrucciani, 1m 59.038s; 23 Costes, 1m 59.174s; 24 I. Gavira, 1m 59.704s; 25 Tortoroglio, 2m 01.092s; 26 Alzamora, 2m 01.181s; 27 Carpani, 2m 01.441s; 28 Sainz, 2m 01.494s; 29 E. Gavira, 2m 01.892s.

World Championship: 1 Biaggi, 75; 2 Waldmann, 62; 3 Harada, 56; 4 Jacque, 36; 5 Aoki, 32; 6 Ukawa, 30; 7 Numata, 26; 8 Tsujimura, 26; 9 Kato, 25; 10 Capirossi and McWilliams, 21; 12 Lucchi, 20; 13 Perugini, 19; 14 D'Antin, Kagayama, Miyazaki, Porto and Robinson, 10; 19 Alzamora and Petrucciani, 9; 21 Battaini and Migliorati, 8; 23 Boscoscuro, Cardoso and Matsudo, 6; 26 E. Gavira, 4; 27 Ogura, 3; 28 Kameya, 1.

---

125 cc

20 laps, 65.180 miles/104.900 km

Pos.	Rider (Nat.)	No.	Machine	Laps	Time & speed
1	Valentino Rossi (I)	46	Aprilia	20	40m 40.093s 96.166 mph/ 154.764 km/h
2	Jorge Martinez (E)	5	Aprilia	20	40m 43.404s
3	Garry McCoy (AUS)	72	Aprilia	20	40m 43.406s
4	Noboru Ueda (J)	7	Honda	20	40m 43.473s
5	Tomomi Manako (J)	3	Honda	20	40m 43.487s
6	Kazuto Sakata (J)	8	Aprilia	20	40m 43.490s
7	Masaki Tokudome (J)	2	Aprilia	20	40m 43.980s
8	Lucio Cecchinello (I)	10	Honda	20	40m 47.688s
9	Frédéric Petit (F)	19	Honda	20	40m 57.670s
10	Youichi Ui (J)	41	Yamaha	20	40m 57.712s
11	Masao Azuma (J)	20	Honda	20	41m 17.396s
12	Gianluigi Scalvini (I)	21	Honda	20	41m 17.496s
13	Ivan Goi (I)	26	Aprilia	20	41m 17.524s
14	Roberto Locatelli (I)	15	Honda	20	41m 17.572s
15	Yoshiaki Katoh (J)	62	Yamaha	20	41m 17.602s
16	Mirko Giansanti (I)	32	Honda	20	41m 17.896s
17	Manfred Geissler (D)	33	Honda	20	41m 18.219s
18	Juan Enrique Maturana (E)	17	Yamaha	20	41m 18.228s
19	Josep Sarda (E)	25	Honda	20	41m 58.776s
20	Dirk Raudies (D)	12	Honda	20	41m 58.818s
21	Roberto Bellei (I)	58	Honda	20	41m 58.946s
22	Steve Jenkner (D)	22	Aprilia	20	42m 01.248s
23	Angel Nieto Jnr (E)	29	Aprilia	20	42m 28.711s
24	Simone Sanna (I)	57	Aprilia	19	40m 40.692s
	Igor Antonelli (I)	53	Honda	18	DNF
	Marco Borciani (I)	54	Honda	13	DNF
	Peter Öttl (D)	88	Aprilia	8	DNF
	Federico Cerroni (I)	55	Aprilia	5	DNF
	Gino Borsoi (I)	24	Yamaha	1	DNF
	Marco Masetti (I)	56	Honda	1	DNF

Fastest lap: Ueda, 2m 00.555s, 97.322 mph/156.625 km/h (record).
Previous record: Akira Saito, J (Honda), 2m 01.139s, 96.854 mph/155.871 km/h (1996).

Qualifying: 1 Martinez, 2m 00.863s; 2 Ui, 2m 01.212s; 3 Rossi, 2m 01.217s; 4 Tokudome, 2m 01.324s; 5 Ueda, 2m 01.557s; 6 McCoy, 2m 01.613s; 7 Sakata, 2m 01.718s; 8 Cecchinello, 2m 01.769s; 9 Manako, 2m 01.960s; 10 Locatelli, 2m 02.625s; 11 Scalvini, 2m 02.716s; 12 Maturana, 2m 02.789s; 13 Öttl, 2m 02.898s; 14 Azuma, 2m 02.901s; 15 Katoh, 2m 02.906s; 16 Petit, 2m 02.908s; 17 Raudies, 2m 03.006s; 18 Geissler, 2m 03.018s; 19 Giansanti, 2m 03.364s; 20 Borciani, 2m 03.383s; 21 Goi, 2m 03.635s; 22 Antonelli, 2m 03.914s; 23 Borsoi, 2m 04.796s; 24 Cerroni, 2m 05.052s; 25 Sarda, 2m 05.502s; 26 Bellei, 2m 05.677s; 27 Sanna, 2m 05.759s; 28 Jenkner, 2m 05.810s; 29 Nieto Jnr, 2m 06.242s; 30 Masetti, 2m 06.370s.

Fastest race laps: 1 Ueda, 2m 00.555s; 2 Tokudome, 2m 00.900s; 3 Martinez, 2m 00.933s; 4 Rossi, 2m 00.951s; 5 Manako, 2m 01.064s; 6 Sakata, 2m 01.144s; 7 McCoy, 2m 01.275s; 8 Petit, 2m 01.313s; 9 Cecchinello, 2m 01.399s; 10 Ui, 2m 01.493s; 11 Öttl, 2m 02.177s; 12 Maturana, 2m 02.207s; 13 Locatelli, 2m 02.278s; 14 Goi, 2m 02.337s; 15 Azuma, 2m 02.554s; 16 Giansanti, 2m 02.589s; 17 Katoh, 2m 02.623s; 18 Scalvini, 2m 02.685s; 19 Geissler, 2m 02.714s; 20 Borciani, 2m 02.810s; 21 Raudies, 2m 04.197s; 22 Sarda, 2m 04.367s; 23 Bellei, 2m 04.612s; 24 Antonelli, 2m 04.667s; 25 Jenkner, 2m 04.695s; 26 Cerroni, 2m 05.082s; 27 Nieto Jnr, 2m 05.398s; 28 Sanna, 2m 07.146s; 29 Borsoi, 2m 17.232s; 30 Masetti, 2m 17.395s.

World Championship: 1 Rossi, 75; 2 Ueda, 74; 3 Sakata, 59; 4 Martinez, 57; 5 Tokudome, 36; 6 Manako, 35; 7 Azuma, 28; 8 Katoh and McCoy, 25; 10 Petit, 23; 11 Giansanti, 17; 12 Nakajo, 16; 13 Cecchinello and Locatelli, 15; 15 Goi, 13; 16 Scalvini, 11; 17 Öttl, 10; 18 Takao, 8; 19 Hules, 7; 20 Ui, 6; 21 Raudies, 2; 22 Borsoi and Sarda, 1.

AUSTRIAN
grand prix

500 cc	DOOHAN
250 cc	JACQUE
125 cc	UEDA

AUSTRIA was a turning point last year. Short of practice after heavy rain, Criville took a better guess at tyres than Doohan – and beat him for the first time ever. From that single event came the confidence for the next win at Brno, and the belief in Criville's camp that he was a serious title contender for 1997.

This year's race at the A1-Ring marked another turning point, back in the other direction. As Doohan continued on his streak of wins (his 38th took him one past Mike Hailwood's 500 class total, to second behind Agostini's 68), Criville fluffed and faltered, losing second place after missing his braking point and taking to the escape road. He also voiced for the first time the complaint that somehow Doohan's bike was superior to his. It accelerated harder, and his slip had come because he was having to brake so late to stay in touch. One implication was that HRC were covertly favouring the defending cham-

pion, at Criville's expense. This was plausible only to the most partisan of Criville's supporters. Austria revealed the first outward sign that things were falling apart for the Spanish young pretender.

In fact, it went back further. After the Italian GP, Criville had tested the 180-degree engine at Mugello, ostensibly at the request of HRC, who wanted his opinion on Doohan's gearshifting problems. Once again, he didn't like it, saying in Austria: 'I've decided definitely now that I will stick to the Big Bang, that I know.' This represented an important psychological staging post. From now on, both riders would know: Alex can only win on the Big Bang; Mick can win on either.

Not that the Spaniard didn't push hard. The lap record was broken repeatedly, the last time by Doohan on his final lap, running away from a phantom. He didn't realise Alex wasn't there.

Spectators were another race-day phantom. The organisers claimed 40,000, but informed estimates put the figure below 20,000. It was hard to know exactly why, because a reasonable number of people had made the journey to the foothills last year, in spite of the awful weather that had threatened cancellation. This time it was dry if rather cold, but the fans stayed home. Perhaps having seen the track once they were not inspired.

Nor is it inspiring for the riders. The new A1-Ring comprises a handful of slow corners, only two turning left, linked by drag

strips. Horsepower comes in handy here, and an elbow or two under hard braking, especially at the top of the hill. And fists as well – though these are usually deployed after the accident.

Fisticuffs were involved at both ends of the 250 race. The first fight came after Boscoscuro was accused of triggering a multiple pile-up by charging too precipitately into the first corner, just as he had in Spain. This time he knocked down Lucchi, back for another outing, as well as McWilliams and Cardoso. Lucchi extracted revenge for all by taking a swing at the young hothead.

At the finish Waldmann had to be held back by his team manager, Dieter Stappert, for fear that he would attack Olivier Jacque. He was enraged by the Frenchman's last-lap tactics, saying threateningly: 'At Jerez and here, it seems Jacque wants to create a new style of riding, using his body and legs as well as the bike. It is not fair and it is not safe. But I can do that too. In the future, I will be prepared to use more body power.' It took him a week to settle down and admit to himself that he shouldn't have left Jacque the space for what others saw as a hard but fair manoeuvre.

And it certainly looked as though Capirossi tried to punch Biaggi, after his hated fellow-Italian stole third on the line with a very aggressive near-collision on the run

to the flag. One could hardly have blamed him, given the extravagantly explicit rudeness of the gesture he received from Max as he made the successful pass.

The knockabout stuff was put into proportion, however, when the exciting French privateer Regis Laconi was seriously injured in a carbon-copy first-corner melee in the 500 class. Much too late on the brakes, he'd fallen under the wheels of several rivals, two of whom ran over him. He was rushed to hospital with internal injuries for immediate surgery, and was unconscious for five days before beginning a slow recovery.

Faces were looking increasingly strained at Modenas, where this week's problem was vibration. Plus the usual misfires and stoppages. There was a new, more bulbous fairing, as well as a higher-inertia crankshaft for Junior, to address his problem of rear-wheel lock-ups. The response time to re-engineering requests was impressively fast; but the response of the motor cycle to the improvements still obstinately slow. 'The engine doesn't run in the chassis like it does on the dyno,' said team boss Roberts.

Talking of obstinately slow, the Austrian wild cards set new standards. One 125 rider, Wolfgang Brandstette, was disqualified from the class after running 14 seconds slower than pole in the first practice; another in the 250 class, one Robert Zwidl, withdrew even before the first timed session. Nor were the rest much better, leading to the memorable quip from German Elf rider Jurgen Fuchs, 'Can you tell me who is delivering the mail in Austria today?'

Opposite page, top: Avenging his defeat last year, Doohan made himself uncatchable by Criville, and brought him undone.

Far left: Jacque hunts down Waldmann, for a 'body-power' attack.

Left: The race went on, Doohan heading Okada and the rest, although Laconi was still being treated by the trackside.

Above: 'And when I just raise this finger, it means...' Doohan amuses Bayle and Gibernau with a lesson in Strine hand-gestures.

Top: Okada conquered his own pain to lead Nobuatsu Aoki and Cadalora.

Photos: Gold & Goose

Waldmann glowers as OJ and team boss Hervé Poncharal celebrate the success of the Jacque Attack. Biaggi has his own reasons to smile.

Opposite: Gobert found himself in the top ten for the first time after outriding Puig.

500 cc RACE – 28 LAPS

Practice came alive in the last 15 minutes, with Checa, Okada and Doohan swapping pole back and forth. Mick started and finished on top. Okada was second but crashed heavily trying to reverse the situation, when the wind got under the bike while it was leaned right over. Cadalora was fifth on the first non-Honda; Gobert outqualified Beattie by one place, in his second GP, to lead row three.

Okada led off the line, but Doohan took over almost at once to head the V4 Honda Armada at the end of lap one – himself, Okada, Criville, N. Aoki, Checa. It wasn't until lap seven that Criville slipped into second, and now the two rivals began to pull away, almost taking turns to break the lap record repeatedly.

The Spaniard challenged several times, but to little effect. Then, in the closing stages, Mick showed his sheer authority, gaining just over a second as they started the penultimate lap. And for the first time all year it unnerved Criville.

He complained later that Mick's bike accelerated harder than his, so he was being forced to make it all up under brakes. The risks involved became clear as he braked too late, picking the bike up and weaving between the bollards onto the escape road at the first of the track's two left-handers. It took him ages to get turned around, and the rest of the pursuit pack flashed past.

Checa had led this gang from laps nine to 19 before falling away, his tyres over-used. Now the group comprised Okada, Aoki and Cadalora, who had caught up by half-distance. All were inspired by the new prospect of second place, and the last lap and a half were hectic. Okada also broke the old record as he ignored the pain to stay narrowly ahead – he had to be lifted off the bike after the race, barely able to walk; Cadalora, at a disadvantage on this horsepower track, managed to get ahead of Aoki, only to be repassed on the next and final lap. Luca was having one of his inspired days, however, and outbraked the 500 class first-timer into the final bends to claim a second successive top three finish, his last for some time to come.

The disheartened Criville was three seconds shy, in fifth, with Checa another three seconds down.

Gobert was a long way back. The rookie started strongly, but was then caught and passed by Puig. The Australian followed him for the rest of the race, making up his acceleration deficit under brakes and on corner speed. 'I knew I could pass him again,' he said later, and he did so under brakes.

Team-mate Beattie was struggling, still fiddling back and forth with chassis settings throughout the weekend. He could do nothing about Abe's Yamaha or even Romboni's twin as the Italian came through, finishing 11th and close behind this duo.

Borja's Elf had been with the group, but he dropped back to finish a lonely 12th, ahead of a troubled Barros, who'd been losing ground throughout after a strong start. Bayle likewise had problems, culminating in running short of fuel as he struggled to the end in 14th, with Naveau picking up the final point. There were only 17 finishers, Roberts Junior retiring his Modenas after it went onto two cylinders.

Laconi's first-corner crash had eliminated four runners: van den Goorbergh and Protat had both hit the fallen rider, while Gibernau lost a footrest in the process, cruising round to the pits in high dudgeon. T. Aoki had crashed his twin heavily but alone two corners later, to be carried off concussed. Corser crashed once again as his struggle continued, after three laps.

250 cc RACE – 26 LAPS

The stop-go corners favoured the reed-valve Hondas, with Aprilia rider Capirossi complaining that the 800 m altitude made the disc-valver's low-end throttle response even more abrupt than usual. Jacque was the fastest Honda in practice, until Waldmann – riding his Mk2 chassis again, the Mk1 not ready after repairs – snatched pole in the final minutes.

Ahead of the first-corner melee, Waldmann and Jacque made the running up front, Biaggi soon starting to lose ground behind. Capirossi had been ahead of him before he was stricken with the intermittent Aprilia problem, his motor 'stalling' twice, dropping him to ninth the second time it happened, on lap three. A little way back, Ukawa and Perugini embarked on a race-long battle, the younger Aprilia rider only losing touch in the closing stages.

Jacque led several times until, on the sixth lap, he also started to lose ground, saying later that he was having trouble braking with a full fuel load. By half-distance Waldmann led by more than a second. But the Frenchman's bike was burning off fuel fast, and now started closing.

On lap 20, as Capirossi broke the record for the first time on his epic ride through the field, Jacque was starting to challenge, and on lap 22 he led for the first time. Waldmann pushed him back again, and the battle to the flag commenced.

It was resolved as they went into the turn three right-hander for the last time, both braking on the limit. Waldmann's error was to leave enough room for Jacque to run up inside him, and it was all the talented youngster needed. As Waldmann swung towards the apex, Jacque was already there, and though the German was furious at what he saw as dangerously forceful and out-of-control riding, there was nothing he could do about it. The two bikes touched, and Ralf bounced off towards the outside edge. By the time he'd recovered Jacque was gone, to win by just over half a second.

Biaggi had seemed safe in a lonely third – until Capirossi turned up, travelling at lap-record speed. At the start of the last lap he was ready to attack.

It took all of Biaggi's force of character to render the attack unsuccessful. Capirossi was inside and marginally ahead as they came out of the final corner, but Max moved right across so they almost collided, taking the last rostrum spot by three-thousandths of a second, the two bitter rivals swapping insulting gestures as they crossed the line.

Ukawa hung on to fifth. Tsujimura had been with him and Perugini, but dropped back in the closing stages to finish seventh, with Aoki in a lonely eighth.

Then came a good battle, Porto's fast private Aprilia eventually overcoming the slow-to-accelerate Suzukis. Numata stayed behind, fending off D'Antin's Yamaha. Robinson dropped off the back of the group after suffering vision problems in the closing laps.

Costes was another second behind in 13th, his first points of the season, battling privateer Franco Battaini's Edo Yamaha to the end.

Harada no-scored for a second race. As well as the Aprilia engine-stall problem, he then had an extraordinary failure of his helmet visor, which cracked. He pitted for a replacement, his hope of points remote and unfulfilled as he finished 17th, one place ahead of Kurtis Roberts.

125 cc RACE – 24 LAPS

Ueda's fight to stop the charge to glory of young hero Valentino Rossi reached apogee here after a race of inches to the line.

Tokudome was the early leader, putting in an impressive attempt at a breakaway, only to be pegged back by Ui's Yamaha and the Aprilias of McCoy and Manako. All the while, pole-qualifier Ueda was moving through from tenth at the end of lap one to join the group on lap five, promptly pushing through to take the lead from the hard-riding McCoy on lap eight.

Soon he and Rossi were moving ahead of the gang, the youngster shadowing the Honda, timing his attack for the penultimate corner where he dived inside under braking.

Ueda's tactics proved better, and his bike faster. Rossi braked a bit late for the last corner while Ueda hung back, whipping out of the Aprilia's slipstream to lead across the line by four-thousandths of a second.

An equally fierce three-way battle for third went to Manako from McCoy and Tokudome. Sakata was 12 seconds adrift in sixth, after defeating the fading Ui; Martinez had been in the leading group, but crashed out without injury with three laps left.

Photos: Gold & Goose

AUSTRIAN GRAND PRIX

1 JUNE 1997

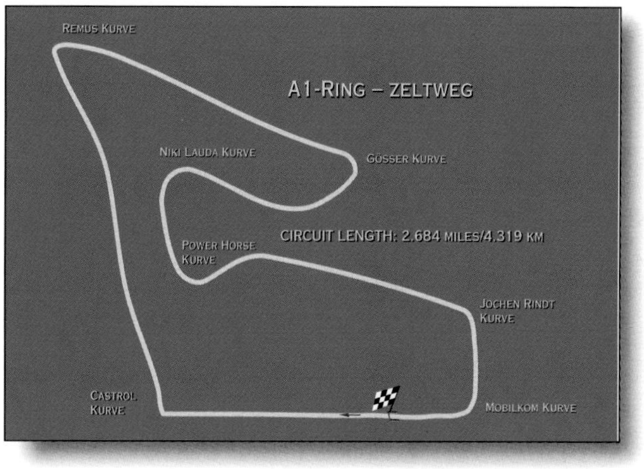
Remus Kurve
A1-Ring – Zeltweg
Niki Lauda Kurve
Gösser Kurve
Power Horse Kurve
Circuit length: 2.684 miles/4.319 km
Jochen Rindt Kurve
Castrol Kurve
Mobilkom Kurve

500 cc

28 laps, 75.152 miles/120.932 km

Pos.	Rider (Nat.)	No.	Machine	Laps	Time & speed
1	**Michael Doohan (AUS)**	**1**	**Honda**	**28**	**41m 48.665s 107.833 mph/ 173.540 km/h**
2	**Tadayuki Okada (J)**	**7**	**Honda**	**28**	**42m 10.742s**
3	**Luca Cadalora (I)**	**3**	**Yamaha**	**28**	**42m 11.136s**
4	**Nobuatsu Aoki (J)**	**18**	**Honda**	**28**	**42m 11.328s**
5	**Alex Criville (E)**	**2**	**Honda**	**28**	**42m 14.127s**
6	**Carlos Checa (E)**	**8**	**Honda**	**28**	**42m 17.314s**
7	**Anthony Gobert (AUS)**	**23**	**Suzuki**	**28**	**42m 47.675s**
8	**Alberto Puig (E)**	**9**	**Honda**	**28**	**42m 48.682s**
9	**Norifumi Abe (J)**	**5**	**Yamaha**	**28**	**42m 51.050s**
10	**Doriano Romboni (I)**	**19**	**Aprilia**	**28**	**42m 51.138s**
11	**Daryl Beattie (AUS)**	**6**	**Suzuki**	**28**	**42m 52.110s**
12	**Juan Borja (E)**	**14**	**Elf 500**	**28**	**43m 11.315s**
13	**Alex Barros (BR)**	**4**	**Honda**	**27**	**41m 59.560s**
14	**Jean-Michel Bayle (F)**	**12**	**Modenas**	**27**	**42m 10.852s**
15	**Laurent Naveau (B)**	**25**	**Yamaha**	**27**	**42m 23.297s**
16	Lucio Pedercini (I)	17	Yamaha	27	42m 45.113s
17	Kirk McCarthy (AUS)	22	Yamaha	27	42m 48.088s
	Kenny Roberts Jnr (USA)	10	Modenas	7	DNF
	Jurgen Fuchs (D)	16	Elf 500	4	DNF
	Troy Corser (AUS)	11	Yamaha	3	DNF
	Sete Gibernau (E)	20	Yamaha	1	DNF
	Frédéric Protat (F)	15	Honda	0	DNF
	Jurgen v.d. Goorbergh (NL)	21	Honda	0	DNF
	Takuma Aoki (J)	24	Honda	0	DNF
	Regis Laconi (F)	55	Honda	0	DNF

Fastest lap: Doohan, 1m 28.666s, 108.963 mph/175.359 km/h (record).

Previous record: Alex Criville, E (Honda), 1m 30.112s, 107.214 mph/172.545 km/h (1996).

Qualifying: **1** Doohan, 1m 28.803s; **2** Okada, 1m 29.113s; **3** Criville, 1m 29.310s; **4** Checa, 1m 29.399s; **5** Cadalora, 1m 29.688s; **6** N. Aoki, 1m 29.758s; **7** Puig, 1m 30.615s; **8** Barros, 1m 30.767s; **9** Gobert, 1m 30.803s; **10** Beattie, 1m 30.813s; **11** Abe, 1m 30.841s; **12** Romboni, 1m 30.906s; **13** Borja, 1m 30.941s; **14** T. Aoki, 1m 31.161s; **15** Gibernau, 1m 31.350s; **16** Laconi, 1m 31.411s; **17** Roberts Jnr, 1m 31.513s; **18** Fuchs, 1m 31.539s; **19** Bayle, 1m 31.546s; **20** McCarthy, 1m 31.827s; **21** Corser, 1m 32.334s; **22** Naveau, 1m 32.812s; **23** van den Goorbergh, 1m 32.968s; **24** Pedercini, 1m 33.140s; **25** Protat, 1m 36.601s.

Fastest race laps: **1** Doohan, 1m 28.666s; **2** Criville, 1m 28.670s; **3** Cadalora, 1m 29.527s; **4** N. Aoki, 1m 29.652s; **5** Okada, 1m 29.701s; **6** Checa, 1m 29.829s; **7** Abe, 1m 30.496s; **8** Beattie, 1m 30.692s; **9** Gobert, 1m 30.695s; **10** Romboni, 1m 30.804s; **11** Puig, 1m 30.881s; **12** Barros, 1m 31.015s; **13** Borja, 1m 31.333s; **14** Bayle, 1m 31.900s; **15** Roberts Jnr, 1m 32.026s; **16** Naveau, 1m 33.091s; **17** Fuchs, 1m 33.174s; **18** McCarthy, 1m 33.284s; **19** Pedercini, 1m 33.660s; **20** Corser, 1m 33.712s; **21** Gibernau, 2m 14.195s.

World Championship: **1** Doohan, 120; **2** Criville, 89; **3** N. Aoki, 67; **4** Cadalora, 59; **5** Okada, 58; **6** Abe, 42; **7** T. Aoki, 37; **8** Barros, 32; **9** Checa, 30; **10** Puig, 25; **11** Gibernau and Romboni, 21; **13** Beattie and Laconi, 20; **15** Bayle, 15; **16** Gobert, 12; **17** Corser and Fujiwara, 7; **19** Borja, 6; **20** van den Goorbergh, 4; **21** Goddard and McCarthy, 3; **23** Naveau and Pedercini, 1.

250 cc

26 laps, 69.784 miles/112.294 km

Pos.	Rider (Nat.)	No.	Machine	Laps	Time & speed
1	**Oliver Jacque (F)**	**19**	**Honda**	**26**	**40m 29.266s 103.403 mph/ 166.411 km/h**
2	**Ralf Waldmann (D)**	**2**	**Honda**	**26**	**40m 29.888s**
3	**Max Biaggi (I)**	**1**	**Honda**	**26**	**40m 35.678s**
4	**Loris Capirossi (I)**	**65**	**Aprilia**	**26**	**40m 35.681s**
5	**Tohru Ukawa (J)**	**5**	**Honda**	**26**	**40m 52.624s**
6	**Stefano Perugini (I)**	**15**	**Aprilia**	**26**	**40m 55.558s**
7	**Takeshi Tsujimura (J)**	**12**	**Honda**	**26**	**40m 59.257s**
8	**Haruchika Aoki (J)**	**7**	**Honda**	**26**	**41m 09.345s**
9	**Sebastian Porto (ARG)**	**27**	**Aprilia**	**26**	**41m 18.917s**
10	**Noriyasu Numata (J)**	**20**	**Suzuki**	**26**	**41m 20.712s**
11	**Luis D'Antin (E)**	**6**	**Yamaha**	**26**	**41m 20.819s**
12	**Jamie Robinson (GB)**	**14**	**Suzuki**	**26**	**41m 32.045s**
13	**William Costes (F)**	**16**	**Honda**	**26**	**41m 33.754s**
14	**Franco Battaini (I)**	**21**	**Yamaha**	**26**	**41m 34.047s**
15	**Oliver Petrucciani (CH)**	**25**	**Aprilia**	**26**	**41m 38.651s**
16	Cristiano Migliorati (I)	8	Honda	26	41m 38.876s
17	Tetsuya Harada (J)	31	Aprilia	26	41m 56.450s
18	Kurtis Roberts (USA)	22	Aprilia	25	40m 30.616s
19	Eustaquio Gavira (E)	28	Aprilia	25	41m 02.661s
20	Uwe Bolteraurer (A)	60	Honda	25	41m 23.765s
21	Thomas Stadler (A)	59	Honda	25	42m 00.614s
	Idalio Gavira (E)	29	Aprilia	22	DNF
	Osamu Miyazaki (J)	18	Yamaha	1	DNF
	Jeremy McWilliams (GB)	11	Honda	1	DNF
	Luca Boscoscuro (I)	10	Honda	0	DNF
	José Luis Cardoso (E)	17	Yamaha	0	DNF
	Marcellino Lucchi (I)	34	Aprilia	0	DNF
	Emilio Alzamora (E)	26	Honda		DNS
	Mario Zehetner (A)	64	Aprilia		DNS
	Robert Zwidl (A)	61	Aprilia		DNQ
	Jurgen Haim (A)	63	Yamaha		DNQ

Fastest lap: Capirossi, 1m 32.392s, 104.569 mph/168.287 km/h (record).

Previous record: Ralf Waldmann, D (Honda), 1m 34.866s, 101.842 mph/163.899 km/h (1996).

Qualifying: **1** Waldmann, 1m 32.607s; **2** Jacque, 1m 32.626s; **3** Biaggi, 1m 32.650s; **4** Capirossi, 1m 32.684s; **5** Perugini, 1m 32.930s; **6** Harada, 1m 32.994s; **7** Ukawa, 1m 32.998s; **8** Aoki, 1m 33.508s; **9** Tsujimura, 1m 33.635s; **10** Porto, 1m 33.908s; **11** Lucchi, 1m 34.022s; **12** Numata, 1m 34.027s; **13** Robinson, 1m 34.560s; **14** McWilliams, 1m 34.584s; **15** Boscoscuro, 1m 34.602s; **16** Costes, 1m 34.850s; **17** D'Antin, 1m 34.867s; **18** Migliorati, 1m 35.068s; **19** Battaini, 1m 35.359s; **20** I. Gavira, 1m 35.441s; **21** Petrucciani, 1m 35.486s; **22** Miyazaki, 1m 35.600s; **23** Roberts, 1m 35.633s; **24** Cardoso, 1m 35.976s; **25** E. Gavira, 1m 35.982s; **26** Alzamora, 1m 37.184s; **27** Bolteraurer, 1m 38.107s; **28** Stadler, 1m 39.462s; **29** Zehetner, 1m 40.009s.

Fastest race laps: **1** Capirossi, 1m 32.392s; **2** Waldmann, 1m 32.482s; **3** Jacque, 1m 32.597s; **4** Biaggi, 1m 32.741s; **5** Harada, 1m 32.985s; **6** Perugini, 1m 33.362s; **7** Ukawa, 1m 33.622s; **8** Tsujimura, 1m 33.684s; **9** Porto, 1m 33.928s; **10** D'Antin, 1m 33.988s; **11** Aoki, 1m 34.058s; **12** Numata, 1m 34.122s; **13** Robinson, 1m 34.795s; **14** Petrucciani, 1m 34.873s; **15** Battaini, 1m 34.987s; **16** Costes, 1m 35.104s; **17** Migliorati, 1m 35.119s; **18** Roberts, 1m 36.068s; **19** I. Gavira, 1m 36.461s; **20** E. Gavira, 1m 36.660s; **21** Bolteraurer, 1m 37.980s; **22** Stadler, 1m 39.967s; **23** Miyazaki, 2m 44.249s; **24** McWilliams, 6m 54.658s.

World Championship: **1** Biaggi, 91; **2** Waldmann, 82; **3** Jacque, 61; **4** Harada, 56; **5** Ukawa, 41; **6** Aoki, 40; **7** Tsujimura, 35; **8** Capirossi, 34; **9** Numata, 33; **10** Perugini, 29; **11** Kato, 25; **12** McWilliams, 21; **13** Lucchi, 20; **14** Porto, 17; **15** D'Antin, 15; **16** Robinson, 14; **17** Battaini, Kagayama, Miyazaki and Petrucciani, 10; **21** Alzamora, 9; **22** Migliorati, 8; **23** Boscoscuro, Cardoso and Matsudo, 6; **26** E. Gavira, 4; **27** Costes and Ogura, 3; **29** Kameya, 1.

125 cc

24 laps, 64.416 miles/103.656 km

Pos.	Rider (Nat.)	No.	Machine	Laps	Time & speed
1	**Noboru Ueda (J)**	**7**	**Honda**	**24**	**40m 19.719s 95.825 mph/ 154.216 km/h**
2	**Valentino Rossi (I)**	**46**	**Aprilia**	**24**	**40m 19.723s**
3	**Tomomi Manako (J)**	**3**	**Honda**	**24**	**40m 26.005s**
4	**Garry McCoy (AUS)**	**72**	**Aprilia**	**24**	**40m 26.140s**
5	**Masaki Tokudome (J)**	**2**	**Aprilia**	**24**	**40m 26.174s**
6	**Kazuto Sakata (J)**	**8**	**Aprilia**	**24**	**40m 38.698s**
7	**Youichi Ui (J)**	**41**	**Yamaha**	**24**	**40m 41.987s**
8	**Roberto Locatelli (I)**	**15**	**Honda**	**24**	**40m 42.703s**
9	**Gianluigi Scalvini (I)**	**21**	**Honda**	**24**	**40m 51.046s**
10	**Frédéric Petit (F)**	**19**	**Honda**	**24**	**40m 51.106s**
11	**Masao Azuma (J)**	**20**	**Honda**	**24**	**41m 13.967s**
12	**Ivan Goi (I)**	**26**	**Aprilia**	**24**	**41m 17.247s**
13	**Manfred Geissler (D)**	**33**	**Aprilia**	**24**	**41m 23.658s**
14	**Juan Enrique Maturana (E)**	**17**	**Yamaha**	**24**	**41m 25.103s**
15	**Steve Jenkner (D)**	**22**	**Aprilia**	**24**	**41m 44.264s**
16	Angel Nieto Jnr (E)	29	Aprilia	24	41m 59.717s
17	Bernd Holzleitner (A)	63	Yamaha	23	40m 45.171s
18	Harald Danninger (A)	59	Honda	23	40m 52.467s
19	Gerwin Hofer (A)	60	Honda	22	40m 55.527s
	Jorge Martinez (E)	5	Aprilia	21	DNF
	Jaroslav Hules (CS)	39	Honda	8	DNF
	Gino Borsoi (I)	24	Yamaha	5	DNF
	Georg Scharl (A)	61	Honda	4	DNF
	Lucio Cecchinello (I)	10	Honda	3	DNF
	Yoshiaki Katoh (J)	62	Yamaha	3	DNF
	Dirk Raudies (D)	12	Honda	2	DNF
	Josep Sarda (E)	25	Honda	1	DNF
	Benny Jerzenbeck (D)	77	Honda	1	DNF
	Mirko Giansanti (I)	32	Honda	0	DNF
	Wolfgang Brandstette (A)	64			DNQ
	Jochen Reichart (A)	65			DNQ

Fastest lap: Rossi, 1m 39.596s, 97.005 mph/156.114 km/h (record).

Previous record: Dirk Raudies, D (Honda), 1m 42.002s, 94.717 mph/152.432 km/h (1996).

Qualifying: **1** Ueda, 1m 40.080s; **2** Rossi, 1m 40.126s; **3** Tokudome, 1m 40.191s; **4** Sakata, 1m 40.271s; **5** Manako, 1m 40.326s; **6** McCoy, 1m 40.482s; **7** Martinez, 1m 40.796s; **8** Ui, 1m 40.899s; **9** Cecchinello, 1m 40.916s; **10** Locatelli, 1m 41.338s; **11** Petit, 1m 41.594s; **12** Goi, 1m 41.805s; **13** Raudies, 1m 41.818s; **14** Scalvini, 1m 41.832s; **15** Giansanti, 1m 41.864s; **16** Geissler, 1m 42.038s; **17** Azuma, 1m 42.200s; **18** Katoh, 1m 42.639s; **19** Maturana, 1m 42.781s; **20** Hules, 1m 42.962s; **21** Nieto Jnr, 1m 43.395s; **22** Jenkner, 1m 43.753s; **23** Borsoi, 1m 43.812s; **24** Danninger, 1m 43.940s; **25** Sarda, 1m 44.183s; **26** Holzleitner, 1m 44.962s; **27** Jerzenbeck, 1m 45.500s; **28** Hofer, 1m 48.147s; **29** Scharl, 1m 48.525s.

Fastest race laps: **1** Rossi, 1m 39.596s; **2** Ueda, 1m 39.621s; **3** McCoy, 1m 39.940s; **4** Tokudome, 1m 39.944s; **5** Manako, 1m 40.093s; **6** Sakata, 1m 40.458s; **7** Scalvini, 1m 40.820s; **8** Martinez, 1m 40.847s; **9** Locatelli, 1m 40.873s; **10** Ui, 1m 40.875s; **11** Petit, 1m 40.979s; **12** Goi, 1m 41.571s; **13** Geissler, 1m 42.110s; **14** Azuma, 1m 42.163s; **15** Cecchinello, 1m 42.309s; **16** Maturana, 1m 42.718s; **17** Jenkner, 1m 43.056s; **18** Nieto Jnr, 1m 43.810s; **19** Hules, 1m 44.031s; **20** Borsoi, 1m 44.791s; **21** Danninger, 1m 45.012s; **22** Holzleitner, 1m 45.097s; **23** Hofer, 1m 48.319s; **24** Raudies, 1m 49.563s; **25** Scharl, 1m 52.583s; **26** Katoh, 1m 53.180s; **27** Sarda, 1m 57.261s; **28** Jerzenbeck, 1m 57.543s.

World Championship: **1** Ueda, 99; **2** Rossi, 95; **3** Sakata, 69; **4** Martinez, 57; **5** Manako, 51; **6** Tokudome, 47; **7** McCoy, 38; **8** Azuma, 34; **9** Petit, 29; **10** Katoh, 25; **11** Locatelli, 23; **12** Scalvini, 18; **13** Giansanti and Goi, 17; **15** Nakajo, 16; **16** Cecchinello and Ui, 15; **18** Öttl, 10; **19** Takao, 8; **20** Hules, 7; **21** Geissler, 3; **22** Maturana and Raudies, 2; **24** Borsoi, Jenkner and Sarda, 1.

Man at work – Doohan muscles his Screamer into superlative submission.

500 cc	**DOOHAN**
250 cc	**HARADA**
125 cc	**ROSSI**

FRENCH

grand prix

GRAND
PAU

IS the Paul Ricard circuit suitable for Grand Prix motor cycle racing? The question arises for one simple reason – a grand total of 61 recorded crashes, and the subsequent ambulance toll of 13 riders, if you count in several concussions. Among these were leading 125 lights Tokudome (dislocated shoulder) and Martinez (broken wrist and finger injuries) as well as Kurtis Roberts (broken leg) and Jamie Robinson (broken wrist and broken ankle). Jeremy McWilliams crashed twice – because a water-hose split; Okada almost twice, with another miraculous high-side rescue followed by a real get-off.

The high toll was not because it rained, or because there were any multiple crashes – in fact conditions were about perfect, if a little warm. The major reason was the layout of the current version of the circuit used for GPs – a sad mockery of the sweeping majesty of the old, full Bol d'Or track, using a pair of car-park slow bends to short-circuit the magnificent Mistral Straight. The full lap takes barely 80 seconds, with first and second gears used several times. And, crucially, there are only two left-hand bends.

From the pit straight the circuit funnels into a very slow right-hander – the ideal recipe for a first-corner blancmange. The following wiggle offers the chance to short-cut the inside kerb, which peppers both pursuers and the track with pebbles. Another stop-and-go slow right then debouches onto the latter part of the Mistral, and thence to the only two real corners of the lap: the almost flat fifth-gear right Courbe des Signes, leading into a looping double apex right that turns the bikes back towards the pits, via the Pif-Paf chicane.

Only now comes the first left-hander, a good hard-leaning second-gear turn with the power on for a long time on the exit. Sweep right, then directly into the other left-hander, before the hard braking right flick back onto the pit straight.

Almost a full lap ensues before one turns left again. This allows the left-hand shoulder of the tyre to drop below full temperature, and to lose grip accordingly. High angles of lean become very risky, but in the heat of the moment it is obviously rather hard to know exactly where to draw the line. A secondary problem is more abstruse...the continual heating and cooling of that side makes the tyres 'go off' when hardly used, because of chemical decay. A case, one might think, for Daytona-style mixed compound tyres, but the tyre companies said no – and if anybody did have such a cocktail they were keeping very quiet about it.

Of course, it was also possible not to fall off – an option taken by the majority of the riders. Only narrowly so, however, in the case of one of the most frighteningly close 250 races in living memory. All the same, it is clear that the use of this track represents an erosion of safety standards; and the riders ought to be asking questions of themselves and their teams about the extent to which commercial requirements have been put ahead of their own safety.

Meanwhile, on with the show: Mick rampant, Alex sulking, the rest chasing along behind. France was the scene of a clash which may turn out to have had some significance: Doohan versus the upstart Gobert, after the former had firmly taken the inside line on the latter during practice. Gobert was obliged to lift and practise his motocross skills across the gravel trap, or (as he menacingly put it) to have held his line and taken both of them down. 'If I wasn't protecting my collarbone injury, that's what I would have done,' he said, setting a not unexpectedly over-the-top tone for his own invective, which was to continue unabated in the weeks to come. Mick laughed it off, but the pair exchanged hard words when they met by chance in Dr Costa's clinic later that evening. 'If he thinks I just turned up here yesterday, he's in for a surprise,' said Mick. 'I used to want him as my team-mate, but I don't know if there's enough room in his helmet to learn what he needs to know.'

The others were still more or less struggling. Over at Yamaha, they pulled out a '96 bike to see if that would reawaken the slumbering form of last year's Japanese GP winner Norick Abe. 'The engine is not so good, but I prefer the chassis,' said Abe, while increasingly exasperated team boss Wayne Rainey just said: 'We're trying all sorts of things right now, and that's one of them.'

His other rider was punished by a barbecued bike and the loss of large quantities of skin on his back: it took dilatory French marshals ages to reach Gibernau's bike, which was lying on its side licked by a single flame. It never really did get burning, though internal damage to carburettors and airbox was extensive.

How unlike the Modenas, with its own barbie-drama during the race. Kenny Jnr slid off, and stood up to see a distinct line of fuel leading to his bike along the crash trajectory, with a flame rushing up it in determined fashion. With the bike itself already blazing, and the high-pressure fuel system doing who-knows-what, Junior did not hesitate to salvage the family property, rushing to unclip and remove the fuel tank, at considerable risk to himself.

There were few diversions after obvious budget cutbacks, in contrast to last year's stunts and jet-cars, but a fair crowd of the faithful did make the trip down south, to be rewarded with good weather and some very fine racing indeed – the 250 class finish, with three bikes within the same quarter of a second, was a fitting end to a spell-bindingly close race.

Doohan still has his visor open as the all-Honda front row fix their eyes on the (faulty) starting lights.

Left: Harada's first win in more than a year: achieved by adding masterful blocking to his repertoire of skills.

Right: It's raining tanks and motor bikes – Kirk McCarthy runs for cover.

Photos: Gold & Goose

Tetsuya's Train: Waldmann and Biaggi were faster everywhere but the end of the straight, but Harada wasn't for being passed today. Capirossi is in the background.

Below left: Checa's second was his best so far this year.

Bottom: Screen smashed, wrist wrenched, 'important body part' impacted – Okada measures the cost of his near high-sider in practice.

500 cc RACE – 31 LAPS

One of the great sights of Paul Ricard remains – the way a slipstreaming pack of bikes disputing the lead of the 500 race split three or four abreast as they brake for the fast Signes right-hander. In the past this has been a multi-coloured spectacle. In 1997 it was a uniform orange and blue. The early stages of the race did muster the required quorum of four – and every one of them was a Repsol Honda.

Three out of those four Hondas started on the first row, with another NSR taking the other place. It was Doohan's third successive pole. Criville was less than a tenth slower, but visibly working hard at it. Then came N. Aoki and the battered Okada, with the near high-sider in practice hurting his wrist again as well as an 'important body part', followed by yet another high-speed tumble in race-morning warm-up.

Two V-twins – T. Aoki and Barros – headed Checa's V4, with Cadalora in

eighth as the best non-Honda, within two-tenths of being deposed by Romboni's V-twin Aprilia. The V4s were clocking up to 305 km/h at the end of the truncated Mistral, the best V-twin Hondas were ten or more km/h slower, but they clearly made it all up again in the turns.

Flickering starting lights caught out Doohan, who paused while the rest took off. Takuma Aoki led at first, Doohan was seventh, but it didn't take him long to join the leading quartet.

The remarkable Okada, once again full of painkillers, took over the lead on lap four as Doohan was slicing inside Criville to take third. Then Mick was in second as Takuma ran wide. He finally took the lead on the straight on lap eight, after another brief hiatus: poised to pass, 'I saw a yellow flag out of the corner of my eye, and I hit the brakes. I didn't want to incur any penalty. It took me a while to catch up again.' His fastest lap was his eighth, as he took the lead, and from then he pulled away gradually and inexorably.

Criville tried to follow him through, but Okada was hard to pass, and he had problems of his own. Then his challenge ended just before half-distance, in a replay of Austria. He left his braking too late at the end of the front straight and ran wide. Again, he said, he was mysteriously short of power. 'We need to find out why before the next race,' he said ominously.

N. Aoki and Checa had also started well, and were running close behind in company with Cadalora, T. Aoki losing places within the group as he battled with over-hard suspension settings. Cadalora was the first to go, dropping back, then pitting, then going out again for a pointless gallop after fitting a new front tyre. Checa got ahead of Criville shortly before Nobuatsu slid off gracefully at the far right-hander.

Checa quickly caught and passed Okada, and even slightly closed the gap of some three seconds to Doohan, before the Australian got the message and upped the pace again.

The first four finished within just over six seconds. Then came a long gap to Takuma Aoki, and another almost 20 seconds to a fierce three-way scrap. Abe had been ahead of Puig and Barros. A last-lap sort-out saw Puig out-brake himself. He and Abe both ran off into the dirt, letting Barros through.

The next group had seen Romboni's V-twin Aprilia narrowly leading Borja's Elf. Then Gobert, riding unwillingly 'at 70 per cent' with front suspension problems, moved past them both. On the last lap, however, he misread his pit board and eased up, giving

Borja the chance to push ahead. Romboni was another second behind.

Beattie was next, moving steadily through after clutch problems left him 22nd on the first lap. Then came Gibernau, in pain after his practice crash, but clear of the lacklustre Corser. Jurgen van den Goorbergh took the last point after he pushed his V-twin Honda clear of Jurgen Fuchs's Elf.

Another bad weekend for the Marlboro Modenas gang saw Jean-Michel Bayle soldier on after Junior's lap four crash, only to retire ten laps later. Kirk McCarthy crashed on the same lap as Roberts.

250 cc – 29 LAPS

Pole changed hands four times in the closing minutes of practice: from Jacque to Waldmann to Capirossi and then a vengeful Biaggi as the chequered flag was readied. And then came Jacque again, by two-tenths – quite a margin, under the circumstances.

Jacque took off in the lead, too, a great Gallic dash that ended after three corners. Suddenly he was off the track, on the gravel outside the fourth, heading for a parking spot by the barrier, his engine seized solid and his race over. In fact, it was his second seize of the day, and (as it transpired) for the same reason, as team owner Hervé Poncharal explained. 'In the morning he seized then went out on his spare bike. The engine was fine, but the spare is the Mk1 chassis and he prefers the Mk2. For the race, we moved the engine from the spare bike into the other chassis. We changed everything except the wiring and the ECU (Electronic Control Unit).' A fatal flaw that dealt Jacque's title chances a mortal blow: the intermittent engine management fault only showed up in intensive tests back at HRC headquarters in Tokyo.

This left Biaggi to lead Harada, Waldmann and Capirossi, Ukawa dropping off the back after a slide lost him the slipstream. Harada took the lead for the first time on lap seven, to be displaced briefly by an impetuous Capirossi, then Biaggi again.

Harada regained the lead and, remarkably, held it all the way to the end, under the severest of pressure. Clearly he was slower round the corners, the snappish disc-valve Aprilia a handful in the lower gears; as clearly, he was faster than the Hondas down the straight. The way he used the advantage showed that in his long absence from the front he had lost none of his tactical skill.

At one point Biaggi came within tenths of inches of colliding with him,

Photos: Gold & Goose

Below: Post-practice 125s gather round first-time pole-qualifier Garry McCoy (72).

Bottom: If the cap fits...Jester Rossi fills the role, Manako sees the joke. Apparently.

Photos: Gold & Goose

when the Aprilia faltered briefly between the snail-paced turns one and two; at other times both Biaggi and Waldmann nosed ahead either there or at the end of the straight, where Harada was clearly slower round the fast Signes corner. But power will tell, when it is in the hands of a master blocker, and he was even able to hold off their desperate last-lap attacks to lead across the line, Biaggi less than a tenth behind, Waldmann on his wheel. A second close finish in two races.

Capirossi fell back again, blaming a lack of front-end grip and finishing eight seconds away, comfortably clear of Ukawa. Then came a lone Haruchika Aoki, soldiering on to some more good points on sliding tyres.

Porto's fast private Aprilia forged through a big gang after a slow start to claim seventh, three seconds ahead of a battling D'Antin and the improving William Costes. Miyazaki and McWilliams were close behind.

Cardoso and Migliorati were out in a first-corner melee. Perugini, Tsujimura and Numata all had mechanical problems.

125 cc – 27 LAPS

Several fancied runners were out in practice falls, including Tokudome and Martinez, the latter requiring surgery for a broken wrist. Garry McCoy meanwhile claimed his first-ever pole position, but lost the advantage – and the crucial slipstream – when he botched his start.

Rossi found himself hounded by front-row starter Locatelli and Manako, but the former fell and the other dropped away as the young Italian upped the pace to win again. Ueda started slowly but had charged through to fourth when he fell, remounting only to tour into the pits a few laps later.

McCoy was third, after catching and passing Ui's Yamaha at two-thirds distance. This left room in the top ten for junior riders: Frenchman Fred Petit was a distant fifth behind Ui, Yoshiaki Katoh sixth and promising Italian Mirko Giansanti won the closest battle of the race for seventh, finishing ahead of fellow-countryman Scalvini, Azuma, Raudies and Maturana.

FRENCH GRAND PRIX

8 JUNE 1997

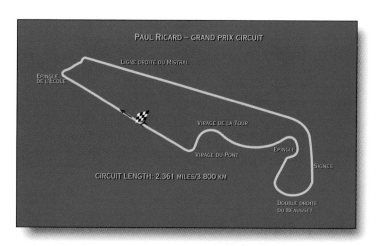

PAUL RICARD – GRAND PRIX CIRCUIT

LIGNE DROITE DU MISTRAL
EPINGLE DE L'ECOLE
VIRAGE DE LA TOUR
VIRAGE DU PONT
EPINGLE
SIGNES
CIRCUIT LENGTH: 2.361 MILES/3.800 KM
DOUBLE DROITE DU BEAUSSET

500 cc

31 laps, 73.191 miles/117.800 km

Pos.	Rider (Nat.)	No.	Machine	Laps	Time & speed
1	Michael Doohan (AUS)	1	Honda	31	42m 38.064s 103.012 mph/ 165.781 km/h
2	Carlos Checa (E)	8	Honda	31	42m 42.356s
3	Tadayuki Okada (J)	7	Honda	31	42m 43.779s
4	Alex Criville (E)	2	Honda	31	42m 44.223s
5	Takuma Aoki (J)	24	Honda	31	43m 02.291s
6	Alex Barros (BR)	4	Honda	31	43m 19.501s
7	Norifumi Abe (J)	5	Yamaha	31	43m 19.798s
8	Alberto Puig (E)	9	Honda	31	43m 22.898s
9	Juan Borja (E)	14	Elf 500	31	43m 29.985s
10	Anthony Gobert (AUS)	23	Suzuki	31	43m 30.665s
11	Doriano Romboni (I)	19	Aprilia	31	43m 31.924s
12	Daryl Beattie (AUS)	6	Suzuki	31	43m 34.255s
13	Sete Gibernau (E)	20	Yamaha	31	43m 39.108s
14	Troy Corser (AUS)	11	Yamaha	31	43m 42.637s
15	Jurgen v.d. Goorbergh (NL)	21	Honda	31	43m 55.732s
16	Jurgen Fuchs (D)	16	Elf 500	31	43m 59.036s
17	Bernard Garcia (F)	13	Honda	31	44m 01.255s
18	Frédéric Protat (F)	15	Honda	30	43m 05.829s
19	Lucio Pedercini (I)	17	Yamaha	30	43m 06.292s
	Luca Cadalora (I)	3	Yamaha	24	DNF
	Nobuatsu Aoki (J)	18	Honda	19	DNF
	Laurent Naveau (B)	25	Yamaha	17	DNF
	Jean-Michel Bayle (F)	12	Modenas	14	DNF
	Kenny Roberts Jnr (USA)	10	Modenas	4	DNF
	Kirk McCarthy (AUS)	22	Yamaha	4	DNF

Fastest lap: Doohan, 1m 21.674s, 104.077 mph/167.495 km/h (record)
Previous record: Alex Criville, E (Honda), 1m 22.022s, 103.635 mph/166.785 km/h (1996).

Qualifying: 1 Doohan, 1m 21.082s; **2** Criville, 1m 21.166s; **3** N. Aoki, 1m 21.380s; **4** Okada, 1m 21.393s; **5** T. Aoki, 1m 21.456s; **6** Barros, 1m 21.661s; **7** Checa, 1m 21.707s; **8** Cadalora, 1m 21.710s; **9** Romboni, 1m 21.916s; **10** Puig, 1m 22.282s; **11** Gobert, 1m 22.435s; **12** Abe, 1m 22.558s; **13** Roberts Jnr, 1m 22.599s; **14** Borja, 1m 22.660s; **15** Beattie, 1m 22.848s; **16** Bayle, 1m 22.892s; **17** Gibernau, 1m 23.014s; **18** van den Goorbergh, 1m 23.358s; **19** Fuchs, 1m 23.480s; **20** McCarthy, 1m 23.493s; **21** Corser, 1m 23.554s; **22** Pedercini, 1m 23.849s; **23** Garcia, 1m 23.941s; **24** Naveau, 1m 24.343s **25** Protat, 1m 24.696s.

Fastest race laps: 1 Doohan, 1m 21.674s; **2** Checa, 1m 21.866s; **3** Okada, 1m 22.046s; **4** Criville, 1m 22.071s; **5** N. Aoki, 1m 22.198s; **6** T. Aoki, 1m 22.220s; **7** Cadalora, 1m 22.327s; **8** Barros, 1m 22.747s; **9** Abe, 1m 22.756s; **10** Puig, 1m 23.097s; **11** Romboni, 1m 23.126s; **12** Borja, 1m 23.245s; **13** Beattie, 1m 23.404s; **14** Gobert, 1m 23.567s; **15** Roberts Jnr, 1m 23.605s; **16** Gibernau, 1m 23.680s; **17** Bayle, 1m 23.705s; **18** Corser, 1m 23.810s; **19** Fuchs, 1m 23.895s; **20** van den Goorbergh, 1m 24.203s; **21** Garcia, 1m 24.403s; **22** McCarthy, 1m 24.821s; **23** Protat, 1m 25.054s; **24** Pedercini, 1m 25.105s; **25** Naveau, 1m 25.584s.

World Championship: 1 Doohan, 145; **2** Criville, 102; **3** Okada, 74; **4** N. Aoki, 67; **5** Cadalora, 59; **6** Abe, 51; **7** Checa, 50; **8** T. Aoki, 48; **9** Barros, 42; **10** Puig, 33; **11** Romboni, 26; **12** Beattie and Gibernau, 24; **14** Laconi, 20; **15** Gobert, 18; **16** Bayle, 15; **17** Borja, 13; **18** Corser, 9; **19** Fujiwara, 7; **20** van den Goorbergh, 5; **21** Goddard and McCarthy, 3; **23** Naveau and Pedercini, 1.

250 cc

29 laps, 68.469 miles/110.200 km

Pos.	Rider (Nat.)	No.	Machine	Laps	Time & speed
1	Tetsuya Harada (J)	31	Aprilia	29	40m 58.961s 100.250 mph/ 161.336 km/h
2	Max Biaggi (I)	1	Honda	29	40m 59.004s
3	Ralf Waldmann (D)	2	Honda	29	40m 59.185s
4	Loris Capirossi (I)	65	Aprilia	29	41m 07.348s
5	Tohru Ukawa (J)	5	Honda	29	41m 28.663s
6	Haruchika Aoki (J)	7	Honda	29	41m 45.716s
7	Sebastian Porto (ARG)	27	Aprilia	29	41m 52.283s
8	Luis D'Antin (E)	6	Yamaha	29	41m 55.638s
9	William Costes (F)	16	Honda	29	41m 56.988s
10	Osamu Miyazaki (J)	18	Yamaha	29	41m 57.216s
11	Jeremy McWilliams (GB)	11	Honda	29	41m 57.375s
12	Franco Battaini (I)	21	Yamaha	29	41m 58.580s
13	Sebastien Gimbert (F)	66	Honda	29	42m 03.501s
14	Idalio Gavira (E)	29	Aprilia	28	41m 28.310s
15	Claudio Vanzetta (CH)	24	Aprilia	28	41m 35.463s
16	Frédéric Boutin (F)	70	Aprilia	28	42m 12.748s
	Bertrand Stey (F)	68	Honda	15	DNF
	Stefano Perugini (I)	15	Aprilia	13	DNF
	Takeshi Tsujimura (J)	12	Honda	13	DNF
	Noriyasu Numata (J)	20	Suzuki	13	DNF
	Franck Poulle (F)	67	Honda	13	DNF
	José Luis Cardoso (E)	17	Yamaha	0	DNF
	Olivier Jacque (F)	19	Honda	0	DNF
	Cristiano Migliorati (I)	8	Honda	0	DNF
	Jamie Robinson (GB)	14	Suzuki		DNS
	Eustaquio Gavira (E)	28	Aprilia		DNS
	Kurtis Roberts (USA)	22	Aprilia		DNS
	Gilles Ferstler (F)	71	Honda		DNS

Fastest lap: Capirossi, 1m 23.559s, 101.728 mph/163.716 km/h (record).
Previous record: Max Biaggi, I (Aprilia), 1m 24.189s, 100.968 mph/162.492 km/h (1996).

Qualifying: 1 Jacque, 1m 23.059s; **2** Biaggi, 1m 23.232s; **3** Capirossi, 1m 23.236s; **4** Waldmann, 1m 23.530s; **5** Ukawa, 1m 23.852s; **6** Harada, 1m 23.880s; **7** Tsujimura, 1m 24.124s; **8** Perugini, 1m 24.442s; **9** Aoki, 1m 24.477s; **10** Cardoso, 1m 25.035s; **11** Costes, 1m 25.265s; **12** Porto, 1m 25.274s; **13** D'Antin, 1m 25.361s; **14** Numata, 1m 25.493s; **15** Migliorati, 1m 25.498s; **16** McWilliams, 1m 25.590s; **17** Battaini, 1m 25.623s; **18** Gimbert, 1m 25.682s; **19** Miyazaki, 1m 25.777s; **20** Robinson, 1m 26.162s; **21** I. Gavira, 1m 26.529s; **22** Vanzetta, 1m 27.262s; **23** Stey, 1m 27.308s; **24** E. Gavira, 1m 27.961s; **25** Roberts, 1m 28.000s; **26** Ferstler, 1m 28.097s; **27** Boutin, 1m 28.403s; **28** Poulle, 1m 29.370s.

Fastest race laps: 1 Capirossi, 1m 23.559s; **2** Harada, 1m 23.842s; **3** Waldmann, 1m 23.887s; **4** Biaggi, 1m 23.918s; **5** Ukawa, 1m 24.129s; **6** Perugini, 1m 24.486s; **7** Aoki, 1m 24.728s; **8** Tsujimura, 1m 24.735s; **9** Porto, 1m 25.533s; **10** D'Antin, 1m 25.806s; **11** Costes, 1m 25.983s; **12** Miyazaki, 1m 25.989s; **13** Battaini, 1m 26.057s; **14** McWilliams, 1m 26.123s; **15** Gimbert, 1m 26.221s; **16** Numata, 1m 26.306s; **17** I. Gavira, 1m 27.352s; **18** Stey, 1m 27.650s; **19** Vanzetta, 1m 27.872s; **20** Boutin, 1m 28.822s; **21** Poulle, 1m 29.475s.

World Championship: 1 Biaggi, 111; **2** Waldmann, 98; **3** Harada, 81; **4** Jacque, 61; **5** Ukawa, 52; **6** Aoki, 50; **7** Capirossi, 47; **8** Tsujimura, 35; **9** Numata, 33; **10** Perugini, 29; **11** McWilliams and Porto, 26; **13** Kato, 25; **14** D'Antin, 23; **15** Lucchi, 20; **16** Miyazaki, 16; **17** Battaini and Robinson, 14; **19** Costes, Kagayama and Petrucciani, 10; **22** Alzamora, 9; **23** Migliorati, 8; **24** Boscoscuro, Cardoso and Matsudo, 6; **27** E. Gavira, 4; **28** Gimbert and Ogura, 3; **30** I. Gavira, 2; **31** Kameya and Vanzetta, 1.

125 cc

27 laps, 63.747 miles/102.600 km

Pos.	Rider (Nat.)	No.	Machine	Laps	Time & speed
1	Valentino Rossi (I)	46	Aprilia	27	40m 20.214s 94.830 mph/ 152.614 km/h
2	Tomomi Manako (J)	3	Honda	27	40m 23.175s
3	Garry McCoy (AUS)	72	Aprilia	27	40m 32.676s
4	Youichi Ui (J)	41	Yamaha	27	40m 37.895s
5	Frédéric Petit (F)	19	Honda	27	40m 50.616s
6	Yoshiaki Katoh (J)	62	Yamaha	27	40m 58.378s
7	Mirko Giansanti (I)	32	Honda	27	41m 04.330s
8	Gianluigi Scalvini (I)	21	Honda	27	41m 04.763s
9	Masao Azuma (J)	20	Honda	27	41m 04.959s
10	Dirk Raudies (D)	10	Honda	27	41m 09.948s
11	Juan Enrique Maturana (E)	17	Yamaha	27	41m 11.365s
12	Gino Borsoi (I)	24	Yamaha	27	41m 22.362s
13	Steve Jenkner (D)	22	Aprilia	27	41m 25.442s
14	Josep Sarda (E)	25	Honda	27	41m 25.687s
15	Angel Nieto Jnr (E)	29	Aprilia	27	41m 26.169s
16	Ivan Goi (I)	26	Aprilia	27	41m 49.325s
17	Nicolas Dussauge (F)	71	Honda	26	40m 49.364s
18	Benny Jerzenbeck (D)	77	Honda	26	41m 01.403s
19	Vincent Philipe (F)	70	Honda	26	41m 18.861s
20	Patrick Detot (F)	67	Honda	26	41m 21.076s
21	Fabien Rousseau (F)	69	Aprilia	26	41m 33.021s
	Roberto Locatelli (I)	15	Honda	22	DNF
	Noboru Ueda (J)	7	Honda	17	DNF
	Jaroslav Hules (CS)	39	Honda	9	DNF
	Eric Mizera (F)	66	Honda	8	DNF
	Mike Lougassi (F)	68	Honda	5	DNF
	Manfred Geissler (D)	33	Aprilia	4	DNF
	Lucio Cecchinello (I)	10	Honda	4	DNF
	Kazuto Sakata (J)	8	Aprilia	2	DNF

Fastest lap: Manako, 1m 28.383s, 96.232 mph/154.780 km/h (record).
Previous record: Valentino Rossi, I (Aprilia), 1m 29.263s, 95.228 mph/153.255 km/h (1996).

Qualifying: 1 McCoy, 1m 28.774s; **2** Locatelli, 1m 29.134s; **3** Rossi, 1m 29.197s; **4** Ueda, 1m 29.223s; **5** Sakata, 1m 29.231s; **6** Manako, 1m 29.366s; **7** Petit, 1m 29.524s; **8** Ui, 1m 29.542s; **9** Azuma, 1m 29.742s; **10** Geissler, 1m 29.772s; **11** Giansanti, 1m 29.995s; **12** Scalvini, 1m 30.068s; **13** Cecchinello, 1m 30.150s; **14** Raudies, 1m 30.466s; **15** Katoh, 1m 30.500s; **16** Maturana, 1m 30.737s; **17** Dussauge, 1m 30.810s; **18** Sarda, 1m 30.916s; **19** Goi, 1m 31.167s; **20** Jenkner, 1m 31.239s; **21** Borsoi, 1m 31.509s; **22** Nieto Jnr, 1m 31.689s; **23** Hules, 1m 31.757s; **24** Mizera, 1m 32.992s; **25** Jerzenbeck, 1m 33.504s; **26** Rousseau, 1m 33.517s; **27** Philipe, 1m 33.818s; **28** Detot, 1m 34.347s; **29** Lougassi, 1m 34.778s.

Fastest race laps: 1 Manako, 1m 28.383s; **2** Rossi, 1m 28.742s; **3** McCoy, 1m 28.837s; **4** Locatelli, 1m 28.940s; **5** Ueda, 1m 28.980s; **6** Sakata, 1m 29.436s; **7** Ui, 1m 29.496s; **8** Petit, 1m 29.754s; **9** Katoh, 1m 29.874s; **10** Giansanti, 1m 30.393s; **11** Scalvini, 1m 30.433s; **12** Azuma, 1m 30.483s; **13** Cecchinello, 1m 30.604s; **14** Borsoi, 1m 30.707s; **15** Jenkner, 1m 30.724s; **16** Maturana, 1m 30.734s; **17** Raudies, 1m 30.806s; **18** Hules, 1m 30.918s; **19** Sarda, 1m 31.071s; **20** Nieto Jnr, 1m 31.151s; **21** Goi, 1m 31.293s; **22** Geissler, 1m 31.350s; **23** Dussauge, 1m 32.760s; **24** Mizera, 1m 33.192s; **25** Rousseau, 1m 33.471s; **26** Jerzenbeck, 1m 33.514s; **27** Philipe, 1m 33.694s; **28** Detot, 1m 34.408s; **29** Lougassi, 1m 34.664s.

World Championship: 1 Rossi, 120; **2** Ueda, 99; **3** Manako, 71; **4** Sakata, 69; **5** Martinez, 57; **6** McCoy, 54; **7** Tokudome, 47; **8** Azuma, 41; **9** Petit, 40; **10** Katoh, 35; **11** Ui, 28; **12** Giansanti and Scalvini, 26; **14** Locatelli, 23; **15** Goi, 17; **16** Nakajo, 16; **17** Cecchinello, 15; **18** Öttl, 10; **19** Raudies and Takao, 8; **21** Hules and Maturana, 7; **23** Borsoi, 5; **24** Jenkner, 4; **25** Geissler and Sarda, 3; **27** Nieto Jnr, 1.

DUTCH
grand prix

D OOHAN had been dismantling Criville for the past several races. The final disassembly came at the Spaniard's own hands (so to speak). Trying once again extremely hard in practice, Criville fell foul of an Assen quirk of exactly the type that Doohan has railed against ever since his own such experience in 1992.

Hard on the power in fourth, travelling at upwards of 150 mph, Criville negotiated the right-hand component of a typical right-left flick, and was crossing the crown of the road to drop down again to the left-hand apex when the rear wheel went light and started to spin, and the bike began to slide sideways. By the time that grip was restored, as the bike squatted on its suspension on the other side, it was too late. Alex was thrown over the high side to land alongside the bike, still holding the left-hand clip-on, his hand trapped against the road.

It does not, at those speeds, take long for serious damage to take place. By the time he'd stopped sliding his thumb had been all but detached, and his hand was so badly damaged that all he could do was sit in the middle of the track staring at it, flabbergasted. It was a shocking sight.

It is often like this at Assen. The flowing track, the lyrical switchback curves and the elegant progress of corners lift the heart. Designed for motor cycle racing, Assen makes it beautiful. At the same time, it provides regular reminders of that other great truth – this is a dangerous sport, and should not, not ever, be taken lightly.

Assen was crucial in the 250 class as well, but this had nothing to do with the circuit itself, and everything to do with the people running the sport. The incident was the disqualification of Max Biaggi – and the arguments were still going on months later.

One must go back to the start of the season, in Malaysia, to get the full flavour. Changing weather conditions there had made tyre choice a gamble. At Assen the situation was similar – intermittent rain had interrupted practice, and returned threateningly on race day too. At Shah Alam, Max won largely because of a canny tyre change on the starting line. In the process, he delayed the start procedure, and was accordingly fined 5000 Swiss francs. Cheap at the price.

Now Max again asked for a tyre change after the sighting lap, and technicians set to work on the startline. Normally there would be enough time to swap the front wheel, but as team boss Erv Kanemoto complained afterwards, Biaggi's team is not normal, since it is divided into two factions: Kanemoto's English-speaking regulars and Max's favourite Italians. In any case, when the three-minute board was shown – the signal to clear the grid – mechanics were still at work on Biaggi's machine on the second row. This was an offence against the rules, and for the second time this year. While the rest went off for the warm-up lap, and while race director Roberto Nosetto pondered what to do about it, the Marlboro-Kanemoto mechanics were ushered off into pit lane.

By the time the race started his bike was in one piece, and Biaggi took off from the pits at the back of the field in a highly convincing manner. After only three laps he'd surged through from last place to seventh, concentrating hard on making up the deficit. However, Nosetto decided that though the pit-lane start did constitute a penalty, it was just the natural consequence of missing the warm-up lap. The second offence, of failing to clear the grid, would have to be punished separately, with a statutory stop-and-go penalty. Accordingly, he instructed Biaggi's pit to call Max in.

Max said later he'd seen the 'IN' signal, but thought it was because they were worried about something on the bike, after the hasty wheel-change. 'The bike felt fine, so I decided to stay out.' He would have expected, he added, rather more vehemence from his pit crew for such an important thing as a statutory stop. After he had ignored the signal three times, the penalty became compulsory disqualification. He was finally persuaded into the pits by a black flag carrying his number one, and stormed off in high dudgeon.

Justice had been done, and if it was harsh justice – well, this was the second offence. The converse was equally true. For a World Champion of Max's stature this was no way to lose a motor cycle race – especially since he also lost his title lead at the same time.

The question of strict application of rules came into focus for another reason. Bad weather had interrupted proceedings several times during the three days, and did so again on race day. The 500 race was stopped after 12 out of 20 laps – just short of the two-thirds distance that would have avoided the need for a restart. However, the race had been started five minutes late at the behest of the TV companies, to make way for the closing minutes of F1 car practice in France. A crucial time lapse, long enough for more than two laps...indeed for the race to have run far enough for a result to be declared. Considering the obvious risks of a restart on a wet track, not to mention the inconvenience, it was not surprising that Doohan and a number of other riders were somewhat upset.

Assen once again attracted a good crowd – back above 100,000 after slumping below last year – who were entertained on the practice days with some rumbling classic racing. This is a speciality here, for it is frowned on generally because of the habits of the Nortons, Matchlesses, Aermacchis et al. to drop things, especially oil. And with some reason, as it transpired. During the first practice outing Doohan toured back to the pits with a flat tyre, complete with big hole. Upon investigation, the Michelin men found a chunk of aluminium in there – perhaps a cylinder head fin or part of an engine cover, almost certainly shed by a classic, and potentially lethal too, being almost two inches by one inch in size.

The Modenas also shed stuff for Assen. The 'big step forward' promised all year comprised, among other things, a significant weight loss, some 8 kg courtesy of magnesium engine casings and other savings. This put the triple within a pound or two of the minimum weight of 115 kg – quite an achievement. However, a more serious problem was persistent misfiring, particularly acute (according to Bayle) at between 10,000 and 12,000 rpm, just where smooth power was needed to come out

Chief mechanic Gilles Bigot looks on anxiously as Criville, bloodied and deeply dismayed, is stretchered into the Clinica Mobile. Dr Costa is on the right.

Opposite: Under looming skies, Doohan leads Checa in the first leg.

Inset: Jolly fun for Assen crowds, back in revived numbers.

Bottom: Dad's Army bikes pleased the crowds after practice – not a dry patch in the house.

of Assen's corners. For several races after this he tended to prefer the heavy bike in any case, while in the race itself he stopped for a truly prosaic reason – one of his ignition coil wires rubbed through its insulation and short-circuited.

Assen rather unexpectedly favoured the other alternative to Japanese bikes, the Elf 500s, and for the first time it was ex-250 man Jurgen Fuchs faster than more experienced team-mate Juan Borja. 'Because', he said, 'for the first time I've had a full practice session without some sort of mechanical trouble.' He went on to score his first points of the year, equalling senior team-mate Borja's best-yet ninth place of the season at the previous round.

500 cc	DOOHAN
250 cc	HARADA
125 cc	ROSSI

Photos: Gold & Goose

Gold & Goose

Opposite (clockwise from top left): Biaggi meets the Press; Capirossi reads it. This is Superman? Cape-clad Rossi giggles becomingly. Ueda looks uncharacteristically serious as his title hopes take a blow. Harada found another way to improve his own position.

Left: Front-row first-timer Jurgen van den Goorbergh won local-hero treatment, but his race was over almost before it had begun.

Bottom: He'll never catch them in that...500s take off on Assen's wide pit straight.

500 cc RACE – 20 LAPS
(11 plus 9)

The extra 30 cc in this year's Aprilia put Romboni's top speed only 5 km/h slower at the end of Assen's relatively short back straight than the two best V4 Hondas, and faster than the rest; but the tendency to wheelie made the bike a handful as the front went light with every change of direction. Nevertheless he flew in practice, to qualify second behind Mick, and ahead of Checa, who stepped forward to take up the role of Sacrificial Spaniard so suddenly vacated by Criville.

The other sensation of practice was Jurgen van den Goorbergh, who put his private Team Millar V-twin Honda in fourth, the first front row for the production version of the bike, consigning Okada to row two, with Cadalora the first non-Honda at the far end of the same row.

The race started off much as usual, but went wrong when the rains came. It was stopped with commendable promptness, and began again with the track wet but drying. Thereafter it was very hard to follow progress, not only because of the fact that aggregate times needed to be taken into account to determine positions, rather than merely positions on the road. To complicate matters further, most riders were on wet front tyres and intermediate rears, while Romboni had gambled on cut slicks. The speed differential was considerable both at the start, when it was wet, and the other way round towards the end.

Checa took the break from the first start, was passed by Doohan into the first corner, but promptly passed him

back at the end of the back straight. He pulled away slightly, then Doohan passed him firmly under braking for the chicane at the end of lap five. He had some 3.5 seconds in hand after lap 11 – the one that counted, one lap before the red flag.

The battle was for third. Van den Goorbergh was out early, his engine seized; this left Romboni fending off Barros and the V4s of Okada and N. Aoki. Meanwhile Abe had started well and moved through to lead this group by lap six. He had Okada, Aoki and Romboni still close behind when the race was stopped; T. Aoki was losing ground behind, Puig was heading Borja and Beattie.

The track was drying fast after the statutory 30-minute break. Barros flew off on his V-twin, though barely in the top ten on aggregate; and there was all sorts of often rather pointless shuffling around behind, as the hot-heads took advantage of the conditions. Chief among these was Gobert, revelling in the slides as he swept round the outside of Doohan to take second on the road at the end of the back straight, only to be sent onto the grass and a near-crash soon afterwards by Bernard Garcia, substituting for Laconi.

As the track dried, Doohan moved forward. He was second ahead of Checa by the sixth lap, and quickly closed down on Barros to pass him and lead for a second time that day.

Behind, Checa was embroiled with Borja, until he fell, and Puig; the others were chasing along behind, T. Aoki falling early on. Romboni provided the most excitement as his tyre choice came really good at the finish. He was charging through, taking third from N. Aoki on the last lap. It was the first

rostrum for the Aprilia, and the first for a non-Japanese bike since the Cagiva in 1994.

Puig headed Barros, Beattie (only his second top ten of the season) and Roberts Jnr, who'd had his best race of the year in the second leg. Fuchs was ninth, Abe a disillusioned tenth – all his efforts in the first leg coming to nothing in the rain; then Garcia, with Okada slipping backwards in the second leg on full wet tyres.

Gobert and Corser were next; Borja remounted for the final point.

Cadalora had missed all the fun after 'steering damper problems' saw him so wide on the bend before the chicane that he had to take to the pit lane to avoid crashing. He rejoined briefly, but did not finish. Cynics pointed out that he hadn't finished a race since he'd signed a contract with the new Red Bull team...

Kirk McCarthy did not start, breaking bones in his foot in a heavy practice spill.

250 cc RACE – 18 LAPS

The first half-dozen qualified within just over one second, Jacque fastest for a second race in succession, then Capirossi, Waldmann, Harada and Perugini, with Biaggi at the back of the group, complaining again of front-end chatter.

Jacque took the immediate lead and was pulling away impressively when he crashed on the third lap. 'I lost the front wheel. I hadn't even started braking yet,' he said, blaming a last-minute switch to a harder tyre.

Now Waldmann led the Aprilias narrowly, Harada taking over second on lap seven, Capirossi just losing

touch as the Japanese rider showed the obdurate Waldmann his front wheel first one side, then the other. The game went on but Capirossi slowed substantially at the finish, his motor on one cylinder. That he remained third demonstrated how far ahead they all were.

On the last lap Harada passed Waldmann for the first time at the end of the back straight. Waldmann passed him right back again. Harada moved ahead once more into the double rights, then Waldmann pulled a stunning outbraking move into the last fast left. Too stunning. He ran wide, and left an opening for Harada to win his second successive race by a quarter of a second.

Ukawa never had a chance of catching the ailing Capirossi, since he also had mechanical problems. Then came Perugini, charging at the finish after passing top privateer Tsujimura.

Costes was an impressive seventh, heading Miyazaki and McWilliams, whose exhaust split to spoil his challenge in the closing miles. Numata's Suzuki had been with them, until he pitted with engine trouble.

A long list of retirements included Robinson and Aoki. The Japanese rider had crashed heavily in morning warm-up. He did it again in the race, taking Robinson out with him.

125 cc RACE – 17 LAPS

The first race of the day was a typical 125-fest, with 11 riders contesting the lead until the closing stages. Not among them McCoy, who led the first laps before easing back to third to let the gang get sorted out a bit. His Aprilia responded by seizing with only six laps left to the finish. 'I thought I could win that one,' he said.

Maybe so, but for the remarkable Rossi. He also led early on, one of a large number of riders to do so, but had dropped to near the back of the group after he started having brake trouble. 'Then they cooled down and started to work again, and I thought again I must attack,' he said.

He did lead the last three laps, under severe pressure, and was in fact fourth at the end of the back straight last time round, risking everything under brakes from there to the finish to claim a superb win. He celebrated by donning a superhero cape emblazoned 'Superfumi' for the slowing-down lap.

The lead group numbered eight on the last lap, covered by just over 1.5 seconds. Manako just held off Sakata for second, with Ueda another two-tenths adrift.

Gold & Goose

LUCKY STRIKE
DUTCH
GRAND PRIX
28 JUNE 1997

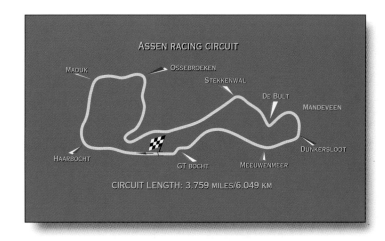

ASSEN RACING CIRCUIT

MADUK · OSSEBROEKEN · STEKKENWAL · DE BULT · MANDEVEEN · DUNKERSLOOT · MEEUWENMEER · GT BOCHT · HAARBOCHT

CIRCUIT LENGTH: 3.759 MILES/6.049 KM

500 cc
20 laps, 75.180 miles/120.980 km

Pos.	Rider (Nat.)	No.	Machine	Laps	Time & speed
1	Michael Doohan (AUS)	1	Honda	20	43m 37.954s 103.372 mph/ 166.361 km/h
2	Carlos Checa (E)	8	Honda	20	43m 48.514s
3	Doriano Romboni (I)	19	Aprilia	20	43m 56.236s
4	Nobuatsu Aoki (J)	18	Honda	20	44m 02.002s
5	Alberto Puig (E)	9	Honda	20	44m 06.059s
6	Alex Barros (BR)	4	Honda	20	44m 16.173s
7	Daryl Beattie (AUS)	6	Suzuki	20	44m 21.171s
8	Kenny Roberts Jnr (USA)	10	Modenas	20	44m 25.479s
9	Jurgen Fuchs (D)	16	Elf 500	20	44m 26.678s
10	Norifumi Abe (J)	5	Yamaha	20	44m 27.528s
11	Bernard Garcia (F)	13	Honda	20	44m 42.385s
12	Tadayuki Okada (J)	7	Honda	20	44m 43.761s
13	Anthony Gobert (AUS)	23	Suzuki	20	44m 46.807s
14	Troy Corser (AUS)	11	Yamaha	20	44m 47.519s
15	Juan Borja (E)	14	Elf 500	20	45m 31.027s
16	Laurent Naveau (B)	25	Yamaha	20	46m 54.790s
17	Frédéric Protat (F)	15	Honda	20	48m 01.305s
18	Lucio Pedercini (I)	17	Yamaha	19	44m 27.415s
19	Sete Gibernau (E)	20	Yamaha	19	44m 35.041s
	Takuma Aoki (J)	24	Honda	11	DNF
	Jean-Michel Bayle (F)	12	Modenas	9	DNF
	Luca Cadalora (I)	3	Yamaha	7	DNF
	Jurgen van den Goorbergh (NL)	21	Honda	2	DNF
	Kirk McCarthy (AUS)	22	Yamaha		DNS

Fastest lap: Checa, 2m 03.363s, 109.686 mph/176.522 km/h.
Lap record: Kevin Schwantz, USA (Suzuki), 2m 02.433s, 110.519 mph/177.849 km/h (1991).

Qualifying: 1 Doohan, 2m 02.512s; 2 Romboni, 2m 02.884s; 3 Checa, 2m 02.986s; 4 van den Goorbergh, 2m 03.537s; 5 Okada, 2m 03.827s; 6 Barros, 2m 04.308s; 7 N. Aoki, 2m 04.620s; 8 Cadalora, 2m 04.656s; 9 Fuchs, 2m 04.717s; 10 Borja, 2m 04.749s; 11 Beattie, 2m 05.357s; 12 Gobert, 2m 05.568s; 13 Corser, 2m 05.779s; 14 T. Aoki, 2m 05.792s; 15 Puig, 2m 05.834s; 16 Abe, 2m 05.836s; 17 Bayle, 2m 05.951s; 18 McCarthy, 2m 06.163s; 19 Gibernau, 2m 06.164s; 20 Garcia, 2m 06.232s; 21 Roberts Jnr, 2m 07.212s; 22 Pedercini, 2m 07.218s; 23 Naveau, 2m 08.683s; 24 Protat, 2m 10.741s.

Fastest race laps: 1 Checa, 2m 03.363s; 2 Doohan, 2m 03.517s; 3 Okada, 2m 05.074s; 4 Abe, 2m 05.260s; 5 Romboni, 2m 05.337s; 6 Borja, 2m 05.346s; 7 Barros, 2m 05.357s; 8 T. Aoki, 2m 05.394s; 9 Puig, 2m 05.487s; 10 N. Aoki, 2m 05.513s; 11 Beattie, 2m 06.187s; 12 Fuchs, 2m 06.200s; 13 Gibernau, 2m 06.230s; 14 Bayle, 2m 06.331s; 15 Roberts Jnr, 2m 06.393s; 16 Gobert, 2m 06.413s; 17 Corser, 2m 06.574s; 18 Garcia, 2m 06.618s; 19 van den Goorbergh, 2m 07.068s; 20 Cadalora, 2m 07.075s; 21 Pedercini, 2m 09.729s; 22 Naveau, 2m 10.168s; 23 Protat 2m 12.482s.

World Championship: 1 Doohan, 170; 2 Criville, 102; 3 N. Aoki, 80; 4 Okada, 78; 5 Checa, 70; 6 Cadalora, 59; 7 Abe, 57; 8 Barros, 52; 9 T. Aoki, 48; 10 Puig, 44; 11 Romboni, 42; 12 Beattie, 33; 13 Gibernau, 24; 14 Gobert, 21; 15 Laconi, 20; 16 Bayle, 15; 17 Borja, 14; 18 Corser, 11; 19 Roberts Jnr, 8; 20 Fuchs and Fujiwara, 7; 22 Garcia and van den Goorbergh, 5; 24 Goddard and McCarthy, 3; 26 Naveau and Pedercini, 1.

250 cc
18 laps, 67.662 miles/108.882 km

Pos.	Rider (Nat.)	No.	Machine	Laps	Time & speed
1	Tetsuya Harada (J)	31	Aprilia	18	38m 09.016s 106.404 mph/ 171.241 km/h
2	Ralf Waldmann (D)	2	Honda	18	38m 09.254s
3	Loris Capirossi (I)	65	Aprilia	18	38m 21.522s
4	Tohru Ukawa (J)	5	Honda	18	38m 39.679s
5	Stefano Perugini (I)	15	Aprilia	18	38m 40.594s
6	Takeshi Tsujimura (J)	12	Honda	18	38m 44.758s
7	William Costes (F)	16	Honda	18	39m 05.819s
8	Osamu Miyazaki (J)	18	Yamaha	18	39m 05.978s
9	Jeremy McWilliams (GB)	11	Honda	18	39m 06.376s
10	Luis D'Antin (E)	6	Yamaha	18	39m 16.479s
11	Franco Battaini (I)	21	Yamaha	18	39m 27.303s
12	Oliver Petrucciani (CH)	25	Aprilia	18	39m 29.452s
13	Cristiano Migliorati (I)	8	Honda	18	39m 29.760s
14	Maurice Bolwerk (NL)	73	Honda	18	40m 22.351s
15	Eustaquio Gavira (E)	28	Aprilia	18	40m 32.981s
16	Gerard Rike (NL)	74	Honda	17	38m 49.368s
17	Jaap Hoogeveen (NL)	77	Yamaha	17	39m 06.323s
18	Henk van de Lagemaat (NL)	76	Honda	17	39m 29.362s
19	Gert Pieper (NL)	78	Honda	17	39m 33.999s
	Noriyasu Numata (J)	20	Suzuki	16	DNF
	Emilio Alzamora (E)	26	Honda	8	DNF
	Max Biaggi (I)	1	Honda	6	DSQ
	Sebastian Porto (ARG)	27	Aprilia	6	DNF
	José Luis Cardoso (E)	17	Yamaha	5	DNF
	Idalio Gavira (E)	29	Aprilia	5	DNF
	Luca Boscoscuro (I)	10	Honda	3	DNF
	Giuseppe Fiorillo (I)	99	Aprilia	3	DNF
	Olivier Jacque (F)	19	Honda	2	DNF
	Jamie Robinson (GB)	14	Suzuki	2	DNF
	Haruchika Aoki (J)	7	Honda	2	DNF
	Andre Romein (NL)	75	Honda	1	DNF

Fastest lap: Jacque, 2m 06.047s, 107.351 mph/172.764 km/h (record).
Previous record: Max Biaggi, I (Aprilia), 2m 06.078s, 107.324 mph/172.722 km/h (1995).

Qualifying: 1 Jacque, 2m 05.190s; 2 Capirossi, 2m 05.577s; 3 Waldmann, 2m 05.610s; 4 Harada, 2m 05.883s; 5 Perugini, 2m 05.905s; 6 Biaggi, 2m 06.260s; 7 Ukawa, 2m 06.805s; 8 Tsujimura, 2m 07.180s; 9 Aoki, 2m 07.676s; 10 Numata, 2m 08.128s; 11 McWilliams, 2m 08.363s; 12 D'Antin, 2m 08.398s; 13 Miyazaki, 2m 08.658s; 14 Migliorati, 2m 08.807s; 15 Cardoso, 2m 09.037s; 16 Costes, 2m 09.437s; 17 Boscoscuro, 2m 09.566s; 18 Battaini, 2m 09.806s; 19 Robinson, 2m 10.197s; 20 Petrucciani, 2m 10.567s; 21 Fiorillo, 2m 10.711s; 22 Alzamora, 2m 10.805s; 23 E. Gavira, 2m 10.911s; 24 Porto, 2m 11.573s; 25 Bolwerk, 2m 12.366s; 26 I. Gavira, 2m 12.454s; 27 Rike, 2m 13.834s; 28 van de Lagemaat, 2m 15.572s; 29 Hoogeveen, 2m 15.937s; 30 Romein, 2m 17.137s; 31 Pieper, 2m 17.476s.

Fastest race laps: 1 Jacque, 2m 06.047s; 2 Waldmann, 2m 06.097s; 3 Harada, 2m 06.105s; 4 Capirossi, 2m 06.285s; 5 Perugini, 2m 07.433s; 6 Biaggi, 2m 07.448s; 7 Ukawa, 2m 07.643s; 8 Tsujimura, 2m 08.076s; 9 Miyazaki, 2m 09.035s; 10 McWilliams, 2m 09.167s; 11 Numata, 2m 09.316s; 12 Costes, 2m 09.347s; 13 D'Antin, 2m 09.688s; 14 Aoki, 2m 09.851s; 15 Robinson, 2m 09.961s; 16 Battaini, 2m 10.138s; 17 Petrucciani, 2m 10.231s; 18 Migliorati, 2m 10.447s; 19 E. Gavira, 2m 10.944s; 20 Fiorillo, 2m 11.042s; 21 Cardoso, 2m 11.359s; 22 Boscoscuro, 2m 11.582s; 23 Porto, 2m 11.681s; 24 Alzamora, 2m 11.876s; 25 I. Gavira, 2m 12.153s; 26 Bolwerk, 2m 12.489s; 27 Rike, 2m 14.639s; 28 Hoogeveen, 2m 16.425s; 29 van de Lagemaat, 2m 17.275s; 30 Pieper, 2m 18.174s; 31 Romein 2m 33.116s.

World Championship: 1 Waldmann, 118; 2 Biaggi, 111; 3 Harada, 106; 4 Ukawa, 65; 5 Capirossi, 63; 6 Jacque, 61; 7 Aoki, 50; 8 Tsujimura, 45; 9 Perugini, 40; 10 McWilliams and Numata, 33; 12 D'Antin, 29; 13 Porto, 26; 14 Kato, 25; 15 Miyazaki, 24; 16 Lucchi, 20; 17 Battaini and Costes, 19; 19 Petrucciani and Robinson, 14; 21 Migliorati, 11; 22 Kagayama, 10; 23 Alzamora, 9; 24 Boscoscuro, Cardoso and Matsudo, 6; 27 E. Gavira, 5; 28 Gimbert and Ogura, 3; 30 Bolwerk and I. Gavira, 2; 32 Kameya and Vanzetta, 1.

125 cc
17 laps, 63.903 miles/102.833 km

Pos.	Rider (Nat.)	No.	Machine	Laps	Time & speed
1	Valentino Rossi (I)	46	Aprilia	17	38m 50.264s 98.714 mph/ 158.865 km/h
2	Tomomi Manako (J)	3	Honda	17	38m 50.364s
3	Kazuto Sakata (J)	8	Aprilia	17	38m 50.548s
4	Noboru Ueda (J)	7	Honda	17	38m 50.776s
5	Youichi Ui (J)	41	Yamaha	17	38m 51.135s
6	Jorge Martinez (E)	5	Aprilia	17	38m 51.832s
7	Masaki Tokudome (J)	2	Aprilia	17	38m 51.860s
8	Roberto Locatelli (I)	15	Honda	17	38m 51.900s
9	Frédéric Petit (F)	19	Honda	17	39m 16.612s
10	Masao Azuma (J)	20	Honda	17	39m 20.979s
11	Jaroslav Hules (CS)	39	Honda	17	39m 21.083s
12	Manfred Geissler (D)	33	Honda	17	39m 29.033s
13	Gianluigi Scalvini (I)	21	Honda	17	39m 29.306s
14	Juan Enrique Maturana (E)	17	Yamaha	17	39m 29.611s
15	Ivan Goi (I)	26	Aprilia	17	39m 36.728s
16	Angel Nieto Jnr (E)	29	Aprilia	17	40m 01.931s
17	Steve Jenkner (D)	22	Aprilia	17	40m 28.063s
18	Rob Filart (NL)	73	Honda	17	40m 28.334s
19	Hans Koopman (NL)	75	Honda	17	41m 00.428s
	Peter Öttl (D)	88	Aprilia	13	DNF
	Jarno Janssen (NL)	74	Honda	13	DNF
	Garry McCoy (AUS)	72	Aprilia	11	DNF
	Gino Borsoi (I)	24	Yamaha	6	DNF
	Josep Sarda (E)	25	Honda	6	DNF
	Arno Visscher (NL)	79	Aprilia	5	DNF
	Mirko Giansanti (I)	32	Honda	5	DNF
	Dirk Raudies (D)	12	Honda	3	DNF
	Yoshiaki Katoh (J)	62	Yamaha	2	DNF
	Lucio Cecchinello (I)	10	Honda	0	DNF

Fastest lap: Manako, 2m 15.049s, 100.195 mph/161.248 km/h (record).
Previous record: Hideyuki Nakajo, J (Honda), 2m 15.629s, 99.767 mph/160.559 km/h (1995).

Qualifying: 1 Rossi, 2m 15.085s; 2 Sakata, 2m 15.805s; 3 McCoy, 2m 16.139s; 4 Ueda, 2m 16.286s; 5 Katoh, 2m 16.514s; 6 Tokudome, 2m 16.653s; 7 Locatelli, 2m 16.775s; 8 Ui, 2m 16.926s; 9 Cecchinello, 2m 17.095s; 10 Scalvini, 2m 17.155s; 11 Martinez, 2m 17.208s; 12 Manako, 2m 17.411s; 13 Hules, 2m 17.480s; 14 Giansanti, 2m 17.697s; 15 Petit, 2m 17.733s; 16 Maturana, 2m 17.888s; 17 Geissler, 2m 17.973s; 18 Azuma, 2m 18.385s; 19 Öttl, 2m 18.974s; 20 Borsoi, 2m 20.172s; 21 Raudies, 2m 20.366s; 22 Janssen, 2m 20.536s; 23 Nieto Jnr, 2m 20.701s; 24 Sarda, 2m 20.720s; 25 Goi, 2m 21.014s; 26 Koopman 2m 21.848s; 27 Filart, 2m 22.728s; 28 Jenkner, 2m 24.152s; 29 Visscher, 2m 25.645s.

Fastest race laps: 1 Manako, 2m 15.049s; 2 Rossi, 2m 15.153s; 3 Ui, 2m 15.209s; 4 Locatelli, 2m 15.431s; 5 Tokudome, 2m 15.522s; 6 Ueda, 2m 15.578s; 7 Sakata, 2m 15.678s; 8 Martinez, 2m 15.891s; 9 Öttl, 2m 16.031s; 10 McCoy, 2m 16.196s; 11 Petit, 2m 16.405s; 12 Scalvini, 2m 16.649s; 13 Giansanti, 2m 16.846s; 14 Azuma, 2m 17.095s; 15 Maturana, 2m 17.502s; 16 Hules, 2m 17.505s; 17 Geissler, 2m 17.563s; 18 Katoh, 2m 17.589s; 19 Borsoi, 2m 18.093s; 20 Sarda, 2m 18.196s; 21 Goi, 2m 18.392s; 22 Janssen, 2m 19.104s; 23 Nieto Jnr, 2m 20.064s; 24 Jenkner, 2m 20.947s; 25 Filart, 2m 20.992s; 26 Raudies, 2m 21.593s; 27 Koopman, 2m 23.221s; 28 Visscher, 2m 25.902s.

World Championship: 1 Rossi, 145; 2 Ueda, 112; 3 Manako, 91; 4 Sakata, 85; 5 Martinez, 67; 6 Tokudome, 56; 7 McCoy, 54; 8 Azuma and Petit, 47; 10 Ui, 39; 11 Katoh, 35; 12 Locatelli, 31; 13 Scalvini, 29; 14 Giansanti, 26; 15 Goi, 18; 16 Nakajo, 16; 17 Cecchinello, 15; 18 Hules, 12; 19 Öttl, 10; 20 Maturana, 9; 21 Raudies and Takao, 8; 23 Geissler, 7; 24 Borsoi, 5; 25 Jenkner, 4; 26 Sarda, 3; 27 Nieto Jnr, 1.

All-action 125s – Sakata heads Rossi, Tokudome, Martinez and Manako.

IMOLA
grand prix

500 cc	DOOHAN
250 cc	BIAGGI
125 cc	ROSSI

IMOLA had mysteriously grown since last year's visit, the overall circuit length extending to 4.930 km compared with 4.892 km previously. Some resurfacing had been done, but the track alignment remained unchanged. So where did the extra 38 metres come from?

The most elegant explanation was that the track had expanded because the weather was warmer than last year (so much warmer, in fact, that works rider Anthony Gobert did not look anything but sensible when he erected a top-of-the-range inflatable paddling pool outside his motorhome). As usual, however, the truth was more prosaic. It had simply been re-measured, and the old length found to have been wrong. As a result, the organisers discounted previous lap records – a less than logical step, since altering the nominal length does not affect the lap time, only the average speed.

Logic wasn't high on the agenda here in any case, for this return visit to the historic municipal race track with its unique suburban Italian atmosphere.

Valentino Rossi was not logical when he defied the race management's specific instructions, to enjoy yet another prolonged and hugely popular post-victory celebration.

Nor was the victorious Biaggi entirely in control of rationality when he followed Rossi's lead by climbing the main fence in front of the grandstand after failing to throw his helmet over it into the crowd. The fence has a big V-section at the top with extensive overhang on both sides – a fact Biaggi appeared not to have realised until he'd gone too far: he hung there nervously, legs dangling.

Lack of logic on a larger scale dictated that none of the cigarette-backed bikes but for Marlboro's wore any branding. This was in response to a very woolly threat relayed via IRTA from a branch of the Italian police to enforce an apparently ill-understood anti-advertising law which some said was dormant in the statute books, but which others maintained was at this stage still only a proposal. Confusion reigned, with caution prevailing for all but the best-established racing brand.

Nor, at first sight anyway, was there much logic in one of the bigger news breaks of the weekend – World Superbike Champion Troy Corser's strike. After a season of poor results and worse financial prospects the Australian rider finally went public with his complaints, revealing himself as one of the greater victims of the Inzinger/Power Horse financial debacle. He was still awaiting his bonuses for winning the title last year, he said, and was unpaid for this year as well. Three attempts to come to terms with the team's new owner, Bob MacLean, had failed, he said, with 'each new deal worse than the last'. Now, faced with what he said was 'virtually an expenses-only' offer, he wasn't going to play any more. The team's own responses were guarded, as might be expected. Yamaha, meanwhile, impounded the two works bikes with Troy's name on them, expressing support for him to the extent of insisting that he would still ride for them in the Suzuka Eight Hour, but saying also that rider contracts were entirely a matter for the teams.

How much more relentless true logic appeared, then, as applied to the rule book by Team Roberts. Although there is no restriction on the size of fuel tanks, they suffered particularly acutely from consumption problems, and were among several teams worried about making the end of the race. (In fact, with their special high-pressure electronic carbs tending to 'work good one time, then spit fuel all over the place the next', according to Kenny, they flew conventional float-bowl carbs to the track here, but ended up not using them.)

Refuelling on the grid after the sighting lap is forbidden, and a special Imola diktat closed off a potential loophole – it was declared illegal to swap fuel tanks on the line, making it impossible to fit a newly topped-up tank to buy those important extra few miles. But if they might not change their tank, there was nothing to prevent anyone from changing the complete motor cycle. Roberts Junior and Bayle accordingly pitted after the sighting lap, where the newly scrubbed tyres off their spare bikes were fitted to race bikes brimming with fuel, and they joined the warm-up lap from pit lane.

Mick Doohan, meanwhile, continued without Criville, in more relaxed mode – easing through the race, even pausing to play with Nobu Aoki, who led for a time. They headed the usual Honda armada filling the first five places. But it was not as smooth as it looked, after the different harmonic vibrations of Doohan's unique Screamer engine laid a long-winded trap that stopped the bike dead in race-morning warm-up. The trouble started when a clutch plate fractured, with the knock-on effect that one of the self-generating ignition coils (on the same shaft) also sustained some damage to one of the components in the high-rev loop, though the engine ran fine at low revs. The clutch was repaired, and the bike had been reassembled for race-morning warm-up where, on the first lap, it showed up as a high-rev/high-load misfire. Mick pitted in some agitation and jumped onto his spare (on which, by the way, he then set fastest lap of the session) while his pit crew frantically tracked the problem down. His favoured bike was ready again for the afternoon, but nobody knew if the misfire was really cured until he'd run the sighting lap just before the race.

Nobuatsu Aoki produced a good performance for a 500 class rookie, but was still almost ten seconds behind Doohan at the finish; brother Takuma finished third for his first-ever rostrum, and the first time two brothers had shared this position. But anyone hoping they'd seen the emergence of a real right-now rival for Mick by the sudden speed of Anthony Gobert, who vaulted up for his first front-row start, was disappointed when niggling problems showed that there's a lot of difference between cutting a handful of fast laps and running 25 of them all in a row.

Opposite: Some riders in this group are trying rather harder than others: Nobu Aoki leads Doohan, Checa and Takuma Aoki early in the 500 race.

Bottom far left: Corser opted for an early bath, without having really ever got dirty. The Superbike champion was one of the worse-off victims of the Power Horse team collapse.

Bottom left: Gobert's big day: on the front row of the grid, he'd then fallen off, emerging unhurt and effervescent.

Below: Kenny Roberts: his carbs were playing him up; he exacted mischievous revenge upon the rules book.

Photos: Gold & Goose

Opposite page: British Brigade: McWilliams scored a season-best seventh on the Queens University Belfast Honda, closing on Tsujimura in the privateer battle; the battered Robinson soldiered on to take the last point.

Left: Takuma Aoki celebrates his first rostrum with some post-race acrobatics.

Below: Two out of three Fireball Brothers – Nobuatsu left and Takuma right – made history on the 500 rostrum.

passed Capirossi on lap six, and after the halfway mark started to close a three-second gap on the Hondas, riding impressively. The fastest man on the track, he had chosen hard tyres and was now feeling the benefit. He set best lap as he closed on Waldmann on lap 16, then surged past him with a fine tactical move through one of the chicanes. He was now just one second adrift of the leaders – but a shock victory was not to be as the dreaded Aprilia misfire struck again. He lost six seconds in just one lap as Waldmann got back in front, and then Capirossi as well, though Loris obligingly ceded fifth to his team-mate at the finish by breaking down on the final lap. 'Max was lucky to win today,' said Harada later.

Up front, Biaggi imposed his au-

500 cc RACE – 25 LAPS

Imola is a real charger's track, but the wind can complicate matters, with day one leader Checa blaming it for his crash on Saturday. Mick ended up on top, also running off-track twice; Gobert was a sensational third, though he also crashed, the bike landing on top of him. 'It's so light compared with a Superbike I could just push it off,' he grinned later. He was the first non-Honda V4 on the front row this year. Roberts Junior also crashed, because of a seize.

Fourth-fastest Nobuatsu led away from Gobert, then Checa came charging past both almost at once, with Mick slotting into fourth.

On lap four, Gobert ran wide as his problems began – too-tight leathers were cramping his right arm, a misplaced gear pedal making his leg stiff. If only he'd run a few more consecutive laps in practice...

Next time round Mick was in second, and he took the lead into the Acque Minerale chicane on lap seven. This flustered Checa, who dropped to third and started losing ground, leaving Doohan and N. Aoki up front, to play cat and mouse for several laps; the lap times, however, showed Doohan had something in hand.

Now Mick put his ploy into action, letting Aoki through (to a cheer from the crowd) to lead for three laps. And then, having failed to force an error, he moved past again and powered on to win, setting fastest lap as he did so.

Behind these two, T. Aoki had passed Checa but could not get away, even though the V4 was suffering badly from wheelspin. Checa kept trying, finally diving past in a hopelessly

over-ambitious move with four laps left – only to run straight on into the gravel, lucky to stay on board.

Gobert was going backwards, and by lap ten he'd been caught by a hard-nosed trio: Cadalora, Okada and Abe, also losing ground gradually. The first two swept directly past the stricken Suzuki rider, Abe two laps later. Okada then passed the Italian toward the finish, the latter making a far from unique complaint of a shortage of power compared with the Honda.

Bayle looked as though he might catch Abe but faded at the end: eighth equalled his best yet. Team-mate Roberts was suffering aches after his heavy practice crash, and never did get into the points. Barros was a lone ninth, the last person to pass Gobert. Had the race been only a little longer, Gibernau and Puig, locked together almost for the full distance, might also have got by the Australian.

Then came Beattie, in another downbeat race after switching from his hybrid bike to the XR87 as raced by Gobert for the first time. Puzzlingly he'd started badly, then began going faster and faster towards the finish. His last victim was Fuchs, whom he consigned to 14th with two laps left. McCarthy took the last point.

There was only one crash – Garcia dropped Laconi's V-twin in morning warm-up and in the race.

250 cc RACE – 23 LAPS

Biaggi, fresh from his black flag, had a point to prove. So too did Jacque, without a finish since Austria despite two poles in succession. The Frenchman took pole again by fractions, but Max was more confident. Waldmann

and Ukawa made it an all-Honda front row, the Aprilias slotting in next, some way adrift at a track where slow corners make their disc-valvers difficult.

Waldmann took off like a scalded cat, pulling a second on lap one on Capirossi, Jacque and Biaggi, with Ukawa behind. But the Aprilia was just getting in the way, and Max forced into second directly, with Jacque suffering a big slide soon afterwards, running off the track and dropping briefly to fifth.

Waldmann was already running into sliding problems, and by the middle part of the race was at the back of four Hondas. Max had most of the leading, with Ukawa forcing past for one lap around half-distance, Biaggi regaining the front after a barging match lasting at least half of the next lap. It was a fine show.

Behind this quartet, Harada had

thority in the last three laps, racing his Mk2 chassis for the first time to take victory by less than seven-tenths. Jacque grimly hung on to second, blocking Ukawa's every move. The gap between them was just two-tenths at the flag. Then came Waldmann, with fourth-placed Harada more than 20 seconds down at the finish as his motor stuttered and banged.

Wild card Lucchi was another half-minute away in sixth, battling a sticky gearshift that caused him to develop cramp. Then came McWilliams, the private QUB Honda rider showing strongly to keep D'Antin's Yamaha at bay, until the Spaniard fell without injury with one lap to go. His other great privateer rival, Takeshi Tsujimura, had a huge high-side on the second lap, close behind the leaders, after a second-row start.

Manako *(right)* led for miles, but eventually had to give best to Rossi *(below)*, who milked the adoring home crowd in inimitable style.

Haruchika Aoki was a lonely eighth, then came Miyazaki's Yamaha at the head of a huge group, stretched out only slightly at the finish: Alzamora's works bike ahead of privateers Battaini, Costes, Migliorati and Cardoso. Jamie Robinson, riding hurt on the Suzuki, had been part of the group until losing revs on the final laps, dropping to 15th.

Numata was among several retirements on the other Suzuki.

125 cc RACE – 21 LAPS

Rossi started from pole but was slow off the line as Manako charged away convincingly. The young Italian was soon slicing through the pursuit pack impressively, though, second after two laps and embarking on a fine pursuit to cut a two-second lead to nothing by lap five. He passed the Honda into the first corner as they started lap six, and that was that, the pursuit becoming attenuated behind.

Sakata moved gradually away in third, while Locatelli fell back into a five-bike group behind, cut to four when the luckless Tokudome crashed out on lap 12, giving erstwhile group leader McCoy some breathing space for fourth.

At the finish, Ueda led the remnants of the pack for fifth, with Martinez and Locatelli right behind, Ui dropping back somewhat in the closing laps.

GRAND PRIX OF THE CITY OF IMOLA

6 JULY 1997

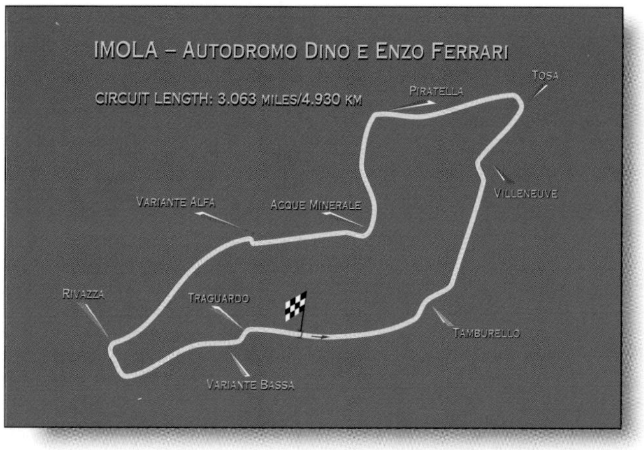
IMOLA – AUTODROMO DINO E ENZO FERRARI
CIRCUIT LENGTH: 3.063 MILES/4.930 KM
PIRATELLA
TOSA
VILLENEUVE
VARIANTE ALTA
ACQUE MINERALE
RIVAZZA
TRAGUARDO
TAMBURELLO
VARIANTE BASSA

500 cc

25 laps, 76.575 miles/123.250 km

Pos.	Rider (Nat.)	No.	Machine	Laps	Time & speed
1	Michael Doohan (AUS)	1	Honda	25	45m 58.995s 99.928 mph/ 160.819 km/h
2	Nobuatsu Aoki (J)	18	Honda	25	46m 07.643s
3	Takuma Aoki (J)	24	Honda	25	46m 19.011s
4	Carlos Checa (E)	8	Honda	25	46m 23.565s
5	Tadayuki Okada (J)	7	Honda	25	46m 24.879s
6	Luca Cadalora (I)	3	Yamaha	25	46m 25.075s
7	Norifumi Abe (J)	5	Yamaha	25	46m 28.369s
8	Jean-Michel Bayle (F)	12	Modenas	25	46m 39.876s
9	Alex Barros (BR)	4	Honda	25	46m 42.531s
10	Anthony Gobert (AUS)	23	Suzuki	25	47m 00.378s
11	Sete Gibernau (E)	20	Yamaha	25	47m 04.917s
12	Alberto Puig (E)	9	Honda	25	47m 05.770s
13	Daryl Beattie (AUS)	6	Suzuki	25	47m 12.069s
14	Jurgen Fuchs (D)	16	Elf 500	25	47m 13.714s
15	Kirk McCarthy (AUS)	22	Yamaha	25	47m 45.195s
16	Lucio Pedercini (I)	17	Yamaha	25	47m 54.875s
17	Kenny Roberts Jnr (USA)	10	Modenas	24	46m 07.389s
18	Frédéric Protat (F)	15	Honda	24	47m 00.153s
19	Francesco Monaco (I)	53	Paton	24	47m 14.787s
	Laurent Naveau (B)	25	Yamaha	18	DNF
	Juan Borja (E)	14	Elf 500	14	DNF
	Bernard Garcia (F)	13	Honda	13	DNF
	Doriano Romboni (I)	19	Aprilia	11	DNF
	Jurgen v.d. Goorbergh (NL)	21	Honda	8	DNF

Fastest lap: Doohan, 1m 49.436s, 100.771 mph/162.176 km/h (record).
Previous circuit record: Alex Criville, E (Honda), 1m 50.191s, 99.310 mph/159.824 km/h (1996).

Qualifying: 1 Doohan, 1m 48.997s; 2 Checa, 1m 49.374s; 3 Gobert, 1m 49.652s; 4 N. Aoki, 1m 49.817s; 5 Okada, 1m 49.925s; 6 T. Aoki, 1m 50.030s; 7 Abe, 1m 50.066s; 8 Cadalora, 1m 50.339s; 9 Bayle, 1m 50.348s; 10 Barros, 1m 50.491s; 11 Gibernau, 1m 50.789s; 12 Puig, 1m 50.854s; 13 Borja, 1m 51.257s; 14 Beattie, 1m 51.475s; 15 van den Goorbergh, 1m 51.530s; 16 Romboni, 1m 51.664s; 17 Fuchs, 1m 51.890s; 18 Garcia, 1m 52.514s; 19 Roberts Jnr, 1m 53.367s; 20 Pedercini, 1m 53.476s; 21 McCarthy, 1m 53.657s; 22 Naveau, 1m 55.308s; 23 Protat, 1m 55.890s; 24 Monaco, 1m 56.606s.

Fastest race laps: 1 Doohan, 1m 49.436s; 2 N. Aoki, 1m 49.754s; 3 Cadalora, 1m 50.104s; 4 Okada, 1m 50.169s; 5 T. Aoki, 1m 50.194s; 6 Checa, 1m 50.321s; 7 Gobert, 1m 50.466s; 8 Abe, 1m 50.504s; 9 Bayle, 1m 50.838s; 10 Barros, 1m 51.256s; 11 Beattie, 1m 51.384s; 12 Gibernau, 1m 51.796s; 13 Puig, 1m 51.985s; 14 van den Goorbergh, 1m 52.102s; 15 Fuchs, 1m 52.106s; 16 Borja, 1m 52.226s; 17 Garcia, 1m 52.477s; 18 Romboni, 1m 52.545s; 19 Roberts Jnr, 1m 53.313s; 20 McCarthy, 1m 53.317s; 21 Pedercini, 1m 53.339s; 22 Naveau, 1m 54.698s; 23 Monaco, 1m 56.373s; 24 Protat, 1m 56.378s.

World Championship: 1 Doohan, 195; 2 Criville, 102; 3 N. Aoki, 100; 4 Okada, 89; 5 Checa, 83; 6 Cadalora, 69; 7 Abe, 66; 8 T. Aoki, 64; 9 Barros, 59; 10 Puig, 48; 11 Romboni, 42; 12 Beattie, 36; 13 Gibernau, 29; 14 Gobert, 27; 15 Bayle, 23; 16 Laconi, 20; 17 Borja, 14; 18 Corser, 11; 19 Fuchs, 9; 20 Roberts Jnr, 8; 21 Fujiwara, 7; 22 Garcia and van den Goorbergh, 5; 24 McCarthy, 4; 25 Goddard, 3; 26 Naveau and Pedercini, 1.

250 cc

23 laps, 70.449 miles/113.390 km

Pos.	Rider (Nat.)	No.	Machine	Laps	Time & speed
1	Max Biaggi (I)	1	Honda	23	43m 17.419s 97.653 mph/ 157.157 km/h
2	Olivier Jacque (F)	19	Honda	23	43m 18.075s
3	Tohru Ukawa (J)	5	Honda	23	43m 18.235s
4	Ralf Waldmann (D)	2	Honda	23	43m 23.919s
5	Tetsuya Harada (J)	31	Aprilia	23	43m 44.562s
6	Marcellino Lucchi (I)	34	Aprilia	23	44m 11.576s
7	Jeremy McWilliams (GB)	11	Honda	23	44m 15.370s
8	Haruchika Aoki (J)	7	Honda	23	44m 17.999s
9	Osamu Miyazaki (J)	18	Yamaha	23	44m 30.232s
10	Emilio Alzamora (I)	26	Honda	23	44m 31.171s
11	Franco Battaini (I)	21	Yamaha	23	44m 31.343s
12	William Costes (F)	16	Honda	23	44m 34.345s
13	Cristiano Migliorati (I)	8	Honda	23	44m 34.450s
14	José Luis Cardoso (E)	17	Yamaha	23	44m 35.568s
15	Jamie Robinson (GB)	14	Suzuki	23	44m 44.708s
16	Oliver Petrucciani (CH)	25	Aprilia	23	44m 46.692s
17	Davide Bulega (I)	53	Aprilia	23	45m 02.953s
	Loris Capirossi (I)	65	Aprilia	22	DNF
	Luis D'Antin (E)	6	Yamaha	22	DNF
	Noriyasu Numata (J)	20	Suzuki	16	DNF
	Stefano Perugini (I)	15	Aprilia	11	DNF
	Eustaquio Gavira (E)	28	Aprilia	8	DNF
	Giuseppe Fiorillo (I)	99	Aprilia	7	DNF
	Luca Boscoscuro (I)	10	Honda	5	DNF
	Idalio Gavira (E)	29	Aprilia	5	DNF
	Sebastian Porto (ARG)	27	Aprilia	4	DNF
	Takeshi Tsujimura (J)	12	Honda	1	DNF

Fastest lap: Harada, 1m 51.872s, 98.577 mph/158.645 km/h (record).
Previous circuit record: Ralf Waldmann, D (Honda), 1m 53.594s, 96.335 mph/155.036 km/h (1996).

Qualifying: 1 Jacque, 1m 51.582s; 2 Biaggi, 1m 51.758s; 3 Waldmann, 1m 52.290s; 4 Ukawa, 1m 52.376s; 5 Capirossi, 1m 52.441s; 6 Harada, 1m 52.625s; 7 Tsujimura, 1m 52.656s; 8 Lucchi, 1m 53.075s; 9 Perugini, 1m 53.224s; 10 McWilliams, 1m 53.374s; 11 D'Antin, 1m 53.383s; 12 Fiorillo, 1m 53.933s; 13 Miyazaki, 1m 54.213s; 14 Cardoso, 1m 54.389s; 15 Battaini, 1m 54.655s; 16 Aoki, 1m 54.681s; 17 Robinson, 1m 54.949s; 18 Porto, 1m 55.063s; 19 Numata, 1m 55.063s; 20 Migliorati, 1m 55.199s; 21 Alzamora, 1m 55.352s; 22 Costes, 1m 55.438s; 23 Boscoscuro, 1m 55.742s; 24 Petrucciani, 1m 55.900s; 25 Bulega, 1m 56.203s; 26 E. Gavira, 1m 56.345s; 27 I. Gavira, 1m 57.869s.

Fastest race laps: 1 Harada, 1m 51.872s; 2 Biaggi, 1m 51.905s; 3 Jacque, 1m 52.094s; 4 Ukawa, 1m 52.102s; 5 Waldmann, 1m 52.556s; 6 Capirossi, 1m 53.005s; 7 Lucchi, 1m 53.413s; 8 D'Antin, 1m 54.061s; 9 Aoki, 1m 54.102s; 10 McWilliams, 1m 54.352s; 11 Battaini, 1m 54.420s; 12 Miyazaki, 1m 54.505s; 13 Migliorati, 1m 54.813s; 14 Alzamora, 1m 54.903s; 15 Costes, 1m 54.947s; 16 Numata, 1m 54.978s; 17 Cardoso, 1m 54.983s; 18 Petrucciani, 1m 55.303s; 19 Fiorillo, 1m 55.309s; 20 Robinson, 1m 55.435s; 21 Perugini, 1m 55.573s; 22 Bulega, 1m 56.053s; 23 Boscoscuro, 1m 56.464s; 24 E. Gavira, 1m 56.637s; 25 I. Gavira, 1m 57.850s; 26 Porto, 1m 58.480s; 27 Tsujimura, 2m 00.708s.

World Championship: 1 Biaggi, 136; 2 Waldmann, 131; 3 Harada, 117; 4 Jacque and Ukawa, 81; 6 Capirossi, 63; 7 Aoki, 58; 8 Tsujimura, 45; 9 McWilliams, 42; 10 Perugini, 40; 11 Numata, 33; 12 Miyazaki, 31; 13 Lucchi, 30; 14 D'Antin, 29; 15 Porto, 26; 16 Kato, 25; 17 Battaini, 24; 18 Costes, 23; 19 Alzamora and Robinson, 15; 21 Migliorati and Petrucciani, 14; 23 Kagayama, 10; 24 Cardoso, 8; 25 Boscoscuro and Matsudo, 6; 27 E. Gavira, 5; 28 Gimbert and Ogura, 3; 30 Bolwerk and I. Gavira, 2; 32 Kameya and Vanzetta, 1.

125 cc

21 laps, 64.323 miles/103.530 km

Pos.	Rider (Nat.)	No.	Machine	Laps	Time & speed
1	Valentino Rossi (I)	46	Aprilia	21	41m 50.114s 92.262 mph/ 148.482 km/h
2	Tomomi Manako (J)	3	Honda	21	41m 51.739s
3	Kazuto Sakata (J)	8	Aprilia	21	42m 13.665s
4	Garry McCoy (AUS)	72	Aprilia	21	42m 17.176s
5	Noboru Ueda (J)	7	Honda	21	42m 18.310s
6	Jorge Martinez (E)	5	Aprilia	21	42m 18.978s
7	Roberto Locatelli (I)	15	Honda	21	42m 19.854s
8	Youichi Ui (J)	41	Yamaha	21	42m 25.250s
9	Masao Azuma (J)	20	Honda	21	42m 44.560s
10	Mirko Giansanti (I)	32	Honda	21	42m 44.932s
11	Gianluigi Scalvini (I)	21	Honda	21	42m 46.295s
12	Yoshiaki Katoh (J)	62	Yamaha	21	42m 49.392s
13	Jaroslav Hules (CS)	39	Honda	21	42m 50.477s
14	Angel Nieto Jnr (E)	29	Aprilia	21	43m 07.445s
15	Peter Öttl (D)	88	Aprilia	21	43m 08.072s
16	Manfred Geissler (D)	33	Honda	21	43m 16.347s
17	Dirk Raudies (D)	12	Honda	21	43m 20.690s
18	Steve Jenkner (D)	22	Aprilia	21	43m 41.201s
19	Christian Pistoni (I)	84	Honda	21	43m 42.574s
20	Maurizio Cucchiarini (I)	81	Honda	20	42m 12.793s
	Ivan Goi (I)	26	Aprilia	20	DNF
	Masaki Tokudome (J)	2	Aprilia	11	DNF
	Paolo Tessari (I)	83	Honda	10	DNF
	Gabriele Debbia (I)	80	Yamaha	9	DNF
	Frédéric Petit (F)	19	Honda	7	DNF
	Josep Sarda (E)	25	Honda	7	DNF
	Gino Borsoi (I)	24	Yamaha	6	DNF
	Lucio Cecchinello (I)	10	Honda	5	DNF
	Juan Enrique Maturana (E)	17	Yamaha	5	DNF
	Igor Antonelli (I)	53	Honda	5	DNF

Fastest lap: Rossi, 1m 58.490s, 93.071 mph/149.784 km/h (record).
Previous circuit record: Valentino Rossi, I (Aprilia), 2m 00.362s, 90.918 mph/146.319 km/h (1996).

Qualifying: 1 Rossi, 1m 58.886s; 2 Manako, 1m 59.520s; 3 McCoy, 2m 00.123s; 4 Petit, 2m 00.302s; 5 Sakata, 2m 00.355s; 6 Ueda, 2m 00.371s; 7 Tokudome, 2m 00.507s; 8 Martinez, 2m 00.533s; 9 Ui, 2m 00.644s; 10 Locatelli, 2m 00.872s; 11 Katoh, 2m 01.388s; 12 Scalvini, 2m 01.603s; 13 Hules, 2m 01.751s; 14 Azuma, 2m 01.788s; 15 Cecchinello, 2m 01.936s; 16 Giansanti, 2m 02.166s; 17 Maturana, 2m 02.179s; 18 Borsoi, 2m 02.373s; 19 Debbia, 2m 02.586s; 20 Öttl, 2m 02.658s; 21 Raudies, 2m 02.715s; 22 Tessari, 2m 02.720s; 23 Nieto Jnr, 2m 02.804s; 24 Goi, 2m 02.890s; 25 Geissler, 2m 03.112s; 26 Antonelli, 2m 03.746s; 27 Sarda, 2m 04.014s; 28 Pistoni, 2m 05.245s; 29 Jenkner, 2m 05.402s; 30 Cucchiarini, 2m 05.439s.

Fastest race laps: 1 Rossi, 1m 58.490s; 2 Manako, 1m 58.532s; 3 Sakata, 1m 59.490s; 4 McCoy, 1m 59.570s; 5 Locatelli, 1m 59.680s; 6 Martinez, 1m 59.705s; 7 Ueda, 1m 59.931s; 8 Ui, 1m 59.938s; 9 Tokudome, 2m 00.148s; 10 Azuma, 2m 00.724s; 11 Petit, 2m 00.938s; 12 Giansanti, 2m 00.996s; 13 Öttl, 2m 01.000s; 14 Katoh, 2m 01.028s; 15 Hules, 2m 01.215s; 16 Scalvini, 2m 01.311s; 17 Borsoi, 2m 01.422s; 18 Tessari, 2m 01.916s; 19 Nieto Jnr, 2m 02.044s; 20 Cecchinello, 2m 02.303s; 21 Geissler, 2m 02.312s; 22 Raudies, 2m 02.518s; 23 Goi, 2m 02.546s; 24 Debbia, 2m 02.701s; 25 Jenkner, 2m 02.977s; 26 Antonelli, 2m 03.050s; 27 Pistoni, 2m 03.208s; 28 Maturana, 2m 03.353s; 29 Sarda, 2m 04.555s; 30 Cucchiarini, 2m 05.184s.

World Championship: 1 Rossi, 170; 2 Ueda, 123; 3 Manako, 111; 4 Sakata, 101; 5 Martinez, 77; 6 McCoy, 67; 7 Tokudome, 56; 8 Azuma, 54; 9 Petit and Ui, 47; 11 Locatelli, 40; 12 Katoh, 39; 13 Scalvini, 34; 14 Giansanti, 32; 15 Goi, 18; 16 Nakajo, 16; 17 Cecchinello and Hules, 15; 19 Öttl, 11; 20 Maturana, 9; 21 Raudies and Takao, 8; 23 Geissler, 7; 24 Borsoi, 5; 25 Jenkner, 4; 26 Nieto Jnr and Sarda, 3.

FIM WORLD CHAMPIONSHIP • ROUND 9

GERMAN

500 cc	**DOOHAN**
250 cc	**HARADA**
125 cc	**ROSSI**

grand prix

THE final chicane was the theme of last year's 'Ring race – whether to short-cut or not, whether it was an infringement to do so or not. This year the corner came to its senses, after another complete redesign turned it from a first-gear squabbler to something more like a second-gear sweeper. Speeds were higher and short-cuts not only more risky, but also more likely to cost time rather than gain it.

The chicane had retained another characteristic – the ability to decide a race. It happened in the 250 class, rapidly gaining in quality and interest as the 500 class remained an austere if magnificent demonstration of Mick's prowess. Now 25 laps of the highly technical Nürburgring delivered four riders into the chicane just as close as you like, for a finale that put the fourth man into the corner first across the line – and revealed much about the characters and positions of those involved, as well as the highly competitive state of the championship.

Biaggi seemed in control as he led the pack in. Jacque was barely in control as his front wheel slid in a desperate attack that pushed Max off and over the kerb. Waldmann was almost in luck as he tried to go round the pair on the outside at the exit, but it was just too far.

Harada, though, was in the perfect position. 'I thought that something might happen at the last corner, and I wanted to be ready,' he said later. As the other three tripped each other up, a black streak came through on the inside. Harada's third win of the year was in the bag, and his championship chances received a timely and worthwhile boost. He was still beaming some time later when I asked him to settle the raging argument. In his opinion, had he been clever, or lucky? 'Lucky,' he responded without hesitation. Living proof of the old assertion – in racing, you make your own luck.

The return to the 'Ring came with the usual weather – rain in practice, and for the 125 race, though the rest were dry and even sunny. Good weather for the old Nürburgring, too, where a British car magazine had assembled several supercars and a handful of racing drivers for a vain attempt on the production car lap record. Mates Mick Doohan and Daryl Beattie were among those who went to have a look, with Mick a reluctant and resolutely unimpressed passenger for a fast lap in a Ferrari... 'It's just another race track,' he said later. On the way over, he had his biggest problem of the whole weekend – he was stopped by traffic police for riding an unregistered paddock scooter without a helmet. 'Who do you think you are – Mick Doohan?'

Back in the paddock, Troy Corser's Grand Prix debut year came to a halt without a whimper, the last last chances entangled in the red tape of IRTA. In order to avoid a fine for infringing his contract with them, team owner Bob MacLean was allowed to wind up his private WCM team. Then he was able to move rider Kirk McCarthy into Red Bull to make up the required two riders. Since Yamaha had taken Troy's bikes back, McCarthy obviously had to ride the ex-WCM ROC, which was still in their mainly white colours in spite of being a Red Bull entry. Confused? No need to be, since the end result was no room for Troy. Even if he did find a way to agree terms with the team, they no longer had a saddle for him.

This race was also of negative importance for that other Australian who came GP racing out of Superbikes. Though there were clearly other reasons, Gobert would later blame his fading results on not getting on with Brembo brakes. Fitted to his bike for the first time here, they triggered a bout of rather confusing front-end problems that caused him two crashes during the weekend.

The brakes meant that, for the first time, he and team-mate Beattie were riding basically identical equipment, doubling data for the team in their continuing struggle to get the XR87 up to speed. It was still unclear just how far off the target it really was: Beattie had smashed the lap record in tests at Brno the week before, but was determinedly underwhelmed. 'That's just one lap. The bike needs to be able to do that consistently before it's competitive,' he said. More confusion after the race, in which both Suzuki riders' best laps were their last ones, leading to questions about what the experienced Beattie in particular had been doing for the rest of the race. 'I only feel confident when the tyres are sliding around,' he explained.

There was another costly fire for Team Rainey Yamaha, with Gibernau's bike flaming up for a second time this year after a practice crash. As in France, much damage had been done by the time dilatory fire marshals were in action. 'We timed them on the video – it took around 50 seconds before they got to the bike,' said Rainey later.

The 125 class saw two more riders add to the mass switch to Dunlops, Tokudome and Cecchinello following McCoy, Sakata and others away from the Michelin truck. Of the top men, only Martinez remained among the Michelin users.

The race was marked by an official one-minute silence, for a Spanish politician murdered the weekend before by ETA terrorists. This was taken as a sign of just how Spanish the whole sport was becoming. There was an opportunity later in the year to demonstrate some sort of balance, after a second tragedy was also marked by one minute's silence on the grid at Brno – this time on the day of the death of the Princess of Wales.

Finally, the early- but slow-starting GP career of 250 novice Kurtis Roberts received another boost. His supposedly ex-works Aprilias having proven disappointing, the younger Roberts had a pair of Hondas in the PJ1 pit instead. One of the leading lights to look askance at this was Ralf Waldmann, who had only one bike to play with.

Inches apart, after 70 miles of racing, the closest finish on record. Harada snatches victory from Jacque and Waldmann, with Biaggi (1) trying on his own at the left. Thirteen-hundredths of a second covered all four.

Above right: Students of body language might read much into this pit-lane conference between Anthony Gobert and race engineer Stuart Shenton.

Far left: Mist lingered in the forests, but the 500s raced under sunny skies, with Luca seizing an impressive if short-lived lead ahead of Barros, Okada, Doohan and the gang.

Grim faced after so abrupt an end to his glory, Cadalora was lucky to walk away from a massive crash. It had been his and Yamaha's best showing of the year by miles.

Right: The cream of 250 racing, squabbling over inches of tarmac: Waldmann leads Biaggi, Jacque and Harada in the ever-shuffling pack.

Bottom: Just three-tenths decided the brotherly battle in favour of Takuma (24) this time, with fraternal Fireball Nobuatsu missing the rostrum by a length or two.

500 cc RACE – 27 LAPS

Doohan was on pole for the sixth time in a row, heading Checa, Okada – sore after yet another crash, testing for the upcoming Eight Hour in Japan – and last year's winner Cadalora, who had pushed Bayle's Modenas off its first potential front-row start. He headed a second rank completed entirely by V-twins, with Takuma Aoki heading Romboni and Barros, leading a bunch of closely matched V4 times.

Cadalora made a lightning start to lead Barros, with Doohan sixth behind Abe after a short but perilous trip across the dirt at the chicane – he'd bottomed out his front forks under hard braking. Half a lap later, Cadalora's charge ended with a huge high-sider in the fast esses before the back straight. Luckily he wasn't hurt.

Okada had worked his way through behind him, and now made the most of the clear track to pull ahead as Checa pushed past Barros and T. Aoki into second. Doohan blamed another slide for the fact he was still at the back of the group. He was soon cutting through it, however, sweeping past Checa on the pit straight to take second after a much better drive out of the tricky last corner. He quickly closed the two-second gap on Okada and passed him out of the last chicane four laps on.

'It's never easy, winning races,' he said later. He just makes it look easy.

Okada was happy with second, free from any threat from behind when Checa crashed out. This left the Aoki brothers to dispute third, Takuma's twin always finding a corner just in time to hold Nobuatsu's threatening V4 at bay. Then, two laps from the end, Nobuatsu dived past into the first corner and made a run for it. All went well until the last lap, when a big slide where Cadalora had fallen gave Takuma the chance of a successful attack into the last chicane.

Barros's V-twin held off the Rainey Yamahas during the first half of the race, Abe pushing hard only to crash, Gibernau chasing behind. A little further back Bayle was battling with Borja. He had prevailed, only to drop back suddenly at half-distance, then retire two laps later. The engine had nipped up, and the crankshaft was damaged.

Behind all this Romboni was making a typical showing. He was using a very tall first gear to cut the wheelie problem, and was overwhelmed at the start, rendering his second-row qualifying position worthless. Sixteenth at the end of lap one, he was soon carving through the slower riders, taking seventh from Borja after half-distance. He quickly caught Gibernau, then whizzed past Barros, fading on too-soft tyres. By now the Aoki brothers were too far in front, and the Italian settled for fifth. Barros just held off Gibernau, for whom seventh was a career best; Borja was eighth for his best of the year so far.

Some four seconds further back a quartet became a trio with two laps left after Roberts Junior retired with electrical problems. Puig led the pack into the last lap, but Gobert knew where he would pass him. Van den Goorbergh finished hard up behind the Spaniard. Beattie was seven seconds adrift.

250 cc RACE – 25 LAPS

Waldmann was waving confidently at the end of practice, unaware that half a lap behind Jacque was carving through to his fourth pole in succession. Capirossi came through to third, Biaggi was on the far end of a close front row, complaining as ever of chatter problems.

Harada led row two from Ukawa, Perugini and Numata's Suzuki, poor acceleration for once not a disadvantage at this flowing circuit.

With clearing skies and lingering damp patches slicks were the universal choice. Jacque led away, Waldmann taking over on lap three, Biaggi, Harada and Capirossi marginally behind to close right up by lap seven before the last-named lost touch, blaming a too-hard rear tyre.

Any one of the remaining four might have won. Waldmann was making the pace, Biaggi nosing into second after half-distance, leading sporadically, Jacque also pushing ahead and Harada briefly at the front as well. Back and forth they went, and it seemed highly unlikely that anyone had anything to spare for a final sprint.

Even Biaggi's move to dominate turned out to be premature. He looked in control until Jacque appeared half-sideways alongside him at the chicane, almost bringing both of them down, baulking Waldmann and letting clever little Harada through.

All four were swerving around on the sprint to the line. Jacque was lucky to get second, Waldmann retained third, then came an angry Biaggi – less than two-tenths covered second to fourth. Biaggi's lead shrank to two points over Waldmann, and he slammed Jacque's attack as unprofessional, observing that he was able to take such risks at the cost of others only because he did not have a championship position to protect. Long-time GP watchers lost no time in reminding

him of his own similar last-lap attack on Romboni, in Germany in 1994, where he had replied to similar complaints with the memorable remark: 'This is bike racing, not classical music.'

The rest of the race barely mattered. Capirossi dropped away by almost half a minute without losing fifth; Ukawa was a lonely sixth. Then came Numata, narrowly prevailing over an inspired Jeremy McWilliams's private Honda and Haruchika Aoki's works NSR. The next close scrap was for 14th, won by Boscoscuro.

125 cc RACE – 23 LAPS

The race was a massive moral victory for Aprilia-mounted Kazuto Sakata. But sadly, he didn't win it.

Manako took an early lead on a streaming track, with Sakata on his heels, taking over at the front when the Honda rider fell on the third lap, first of eleven to tumble. By the time Rossi had moved to second, Sakata was a massive ten seconds ahead.

By this time Ueda had crashed out of fifth, and fast-starter McCoy was falling back to his eventual prang. The race became rather processional, everyone on tiptoes, the action enlivened by regular crashes.

Then, with seven laps left, Sakata's engine died and he coasted broken-hearted to a stop. Now a three-way group who'd been going for second got serious in a tentative manner, Katoh sticking close to Rossi in case he should stumble, Geissler dropping away only in the closing laps, happy to settle for a career-best third place. He was riding the injured Peter Öttl's Aprilia, and enjoying the experience.

Frenchman Fred Petit was also having fun in the wet – the great leveller and privateer's friend. He managed to fend off Cecchinello's similar Honda and Martinez's works-backed Aprilia for fourth. First-time front-row starter Mirko Giansanti was a lone seventh; a disappointed Tokudome ninth.

ADAC MOTORRAD
GERMAN
GRAND PRIX
20 JULY 1997

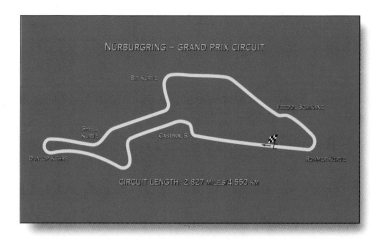

NÜRBURGRING – GRAND PRIX CIRCUIT

CIRCUIT LENGTH: 2.827 MILES/4.550 KM

500 cc
27 laps, 76.329 miles/122.850 km

Pos.	Rider (Nat.)	No.	Machine	Laps	Time & speed
1	Michael Doohan (AUS)	1	Honda	27	44m 55.117s 101.965 mph/ 164.096 km/h
2	Tadayuki Okada (J)	7	Honda	27	45m 00.807s
3	Takuma Aoki (J)	24	Honda	27	45m 19.990s
4	Nobuatsu Aoki (J)	18	Honda	27	45m 20.274s
5	Doriano Romboni (I)	19	Aprilia	27	45m 31.001s
6	Alex Barros (BR)	4	Honda	27	45m 34.024s
7	Sete Gibernau (E)	20	Yamaha	27	45m 34.658s
8	Juan Borja (E)	14	Elf 500	27	45m 47.592s
9	Anthony Gobert (AUS)	23	Suzuki	27	45m 50.400s
10	Alberto Puig (E)	9	Honda	27	45m 50.553s
11	Jurgen v.d. Goorbergh (NL)	21	Honda	27	45m 50.911s
12	Daryl Beattie (AUS)	6	Suzuki	27	45m 57.889s
13	Jurgen Fuchs (D)	16	Elf 500	27	46m 12.462s
14	Bernard Garcia (F)	13	Honda	27	46m 17.409s
15	Kirk McCarthy (AUS)	22	Yamaha	26	45m 16.108s
16	Laurent Naveau (B)	25	Yamaha	26	45m 19.022s
	Kenny Roberts Jnr (USA)	10	Modenas	25	DNF
	Jean-Michel Bayle (F)	12	Modenas	15	DNF
	Norifumi Abe (J)	5	Yamaha	12	DNF
	Carlos Checa (E)	8	Honda	11	DNF
	Lucio Pedercini (I)	17	Yamaha	10	DNF
	Luca Cadalora (I)	3	Yamaha	1	DNF
	Frédéric Protat (F)	15	Honda	1	DNF

Fastest lap: Doohan, 1m 39.051s, 102.756 mph/165.369 km/h (record).
Previous circuit record: Michael Doohan, AUS (Honda), 1m 40.219s, 101.692 mph/163.658 km/h (1996).

Qualifying: 1 Doohan, 1m 38.425s; 2 Checa, 1m 38.757s; 3 Okada, 1m 39.069s; 4 Cadalora, 1m 39.187s; 5 Bayle, 1m 39.266s; 6 T. Aoki, 1m 39.412s; 7 Romboni, 1m 39.500s; 8 Barros, 1m 39.714s; 9 N. Aoki, 1m 39.794s; 10 Beattie, 1m 40.294s; 11 van den Goorbergh, 1m 40.295s; 12 Borja, 1m 40.441s; 13 Fuchs, 1m 40.483s; 14 Gibernau, 1m 40.569s; 15 Gobert, 1m 40.575s; 16 Roberts Jnr, 1m 40.670s; 17 Abe, 1m 40.863s; 18 Puig, 1m 40.882s; 19 Pedercini, 1m 41.540s; 20 Garcia, 1m 41.591s; 21 McCarthy, 1m 42.813s; 22 Naveau, 1m 42.996s; 23 Protat, 1m 43.704s.

Fastest race laps: 1 Doohan, 1m 39.051s; 2 Okada, 1m 39.243s; 3 Checa, 1m 39.302s; 4 N. Aoki, 1m 39.664s; 5 Romboni, 1m 39.921s; 6 T. Aoki, 1m 39.963s; 7 Bayle, 1m 40.396s; 8 Abe, 1m 40.399s; 9 Barros, 1m 40.467s; 10 Gibernau, 1m 40.468s; 11 Borja, 1m 40.601s; 12 Beattie, 1m 40.686s; 13 Gobert, 1m 40.863s; 14 Roberts Jnr, 1m 40.935s; 15 van den Goorbergh, 1m 41.059s; 16 Puig, 1m 41.074s; 17 Garcia, 1m 41.630s; 18 Fuchs, 1m 41.665s; 19 Pedercini, 1m 42.995s; 20 McCarthy, 1m 43.626s; 21 Naveau, 1m 44.525s; 22 Cadalora, 1m 45.188s; 23 Protat 1m 53.867s.

World Championship: 1 Doohan, 220; 2 N. Aoki, 113; 3 Okada, 109; 4 Criville, 102; 5 Checa, 83; 6 T. Aoki, 80; 7 Barros and Cadalora, 69; 9 Abe, 66; 10 Puig, 54; 11 Romboni, 53; 12 Beattie, 40; 13 Gibernau, 38; 14 Gobert, 34; 15 Bayle, 23; 16 Borja, 22; 17 Laconi, 20; 18 Fuchs, 12; 19 Corser, 11; 20 van den Goorbergh, 10; 21 Roberts Jnr, 8; 22 Fujiwara and Garcia, 7; 24 McCarthy, 5; 25 Goddard, 3; 26 Naveau and Pedercini, 1.

250 cc
25 laps, 70.675 miles/113.750 km

Pos.	Rider (Nat.)	No.	Machine	Laps	Time & speed
1	Tetsuya Harada (J)	31	Aprilia	25	42m 36.407s 99.534 mph/ 160.185 km/h
2	Olivier Jacque (F)	19	Honda	25	42m 36.500s
3	Ralf Waldmann (D)	2	Honda	25	42m 36.513s
4	Max Biaggi (I)	1	Honda	25	42m 36.542s
5	Loris Capirossi (I)	65	Aprilia	25	43m 04.590s
6	Tohru Ukawa (J)	5	Honda	25	43m 10.732s
7	Noriyasu Numata (J)	20	Suzuki	25	43m 17.489s
8	Jeremy McWilliams (GB)	11	Honda	25	43m 18.251s
9	Haruchika Aoki (J)	7	Honda	25	43m 19.063s
10	Emilio Alzamora (E)	26	Honda	25	43m 29.577s
11	Franco Battaini (I)	21	Yamaha	25	43m 35.909s
12	Giuseppe Fiorillo (I)	99	Aprilia	25	43m 49.094s
13	Takeshi Tsujimura (J)	12	Honda	25	43m 50.888s
14	Luca Boscoscuro (I)	10	Honda	25	43m 54.185s
15	Cristiano Migliorati (I)	8	Honda	25	43m 54.420s
16	Sebastian Porto (ARG)	27	Aprilia	25	43m 54.652s
17	Luis D'Antin (E)	6	Yamaha	25	43m 54.890s
18	Osamu Miyazaki (J)	18	Yamaha	25	43m 54.926s
19	Oliver Petrucciani (CH)	25	Aprilia	25	43m 55.290s
20	William Costes (F)	16	Honda	25	43m 55.937s
21	Eustaquio Gavira (E)	28	Aprilia	25	44m 08.997s
22	Kurtis Roberts (USA)	22	Honda	24	43m 24.460s
23	Juergen Lingg (D)	86	Honda	24	43m 31.018s
24	Matthias Neukirchen (D)	87	Yamaha	24	44m 01.391s
25	Stefan Kruse (D)	85	Honda	23	43m 16.717s
	Jamie Robinson (GB)	14	Suzuki	16	DNF
	José Luis Cardoso (E)	17	Yamaha	8	DNF
	Idalio Gavira (E)	29	Aprilia	3	DNF
	Stefano Perugini (I)	15	Aprilia	1	DNF

Fastest lap: Harada, 1m 40.993s, 100.780 mph/162.189 km/h (record).
Previous circuit record: Ralf Waldmann, D (Honda), 1m 42.991s, 98.955 mph/159.253 km/h (1996)

Qualifying: 1 Jacque, 1m 40.361s; 2 Waldmann, 1m 40.785s; 3 Capirossi, 1m 40.873s; 4 Biaggi, 1m 40.986s; 5 Harada, 1m 41.378s; 6 Ukawa, 1m 41.709s; 7 Perugini, 1m 42.511s; 8 Numata, 1m 42.594s; 9 McWilliams, 1m 42.643s; 10 Aoki, 1m 42.738s; 11 Alzamora, 1m 43.081s; 12 Cardoso, 1m 43.127s; 13 Fiorillo, 1m 43.151s; 14 Petrucciani, 1m 43.157s; 15 Battaini, 1m 43.182s; 16 Robinson, 1m 43.193s; 17 Porto, 1m 43.206s; 18 Migliorati, 1m 43.423s; 19 Tsujimura, 1m 43.505s; 20 Miyazaki, 1m 43.624s; 21 Costes, 1m 43.725s; 22 I. Gavira, 1m 43.988s; 23 D'Antin, 1m 44.025s; 24 Boscoscuro, 1m 44.180s; 25 E. Gavira, 1m 45.059s; 26 Roberts, 1m 46.311s; 27 Lingg, 1m 46.621s; 28 Neukirchen, 1m 46.781s; 29 Kruse, 1m 49.639s.

Fastest race laps: 1 Harada, 1m 40.993s; 2 Biaggi, 1m 41.011s; 3 Waldmann, 1m 41.179s; 4 Jacque, 1m 41.221s; 5 Capirossi, 1m 42.170s; 6 Ukawa, 1m 42.648s; 7 Aoki, 1m 42.833s; 8 Numata, 1m 42.994s; 9 McWilliams, 1m 43.031s; 10 Alzamora, 1m 43.077s; 11 Battaini, 1m 43.488s; 12 Tsujimura, 1m 43.602s; 13 Fiorillo, 1m 43.896s; 14 Boscoscuro, 1m 43.920s; 15 Costes, 1m 43.958s; 16 Migliorati, 1m 43.977s; 17 Porto, 1m 43.982s; 18 D'Antin, 1m 44.063s; 19 Petrucciani, 1m 44.155s; 20 Miyazaki, 1m 44.180s; 21 Cardoso, 1m 44.441s; 22 Robinson, 1m 44.508s; 23 E. Gavira, 1m 44.754s; 24 I. Gavira, 1m 46.006s; 25 Roberts, 1m 47.157s; 26 Lingg, 1m 47.241s; 27 Neukirchen, 1m 47.291s; 28 Kruse, 1m 51.356s; 29 Perugini, 1m 54.621s.

World Championship: 1 Biaggi, 149; 2 Waldmann, 147; 3 Harada, 142; 4 Jacque, 101; 5 Ukawa, 91; 6 Capirossi, 74; 7 Aoki, 65; 8 McWilliams, 50; 9 Tsujimura, 48; 10 Numata, 42; 11 Perugini, 40; 12 Miyazaki, 31; 13 Lucchi, 30; 14 Battaini and D'Antin, 29; 16 Porto, 26; 17 Kato, 25; 18 Costes, 23; 19 Alzamora, 21; 20 Migliorati and Robinson, 15; 22 Petrucciani, 14; 23 Kagayama, 10; 24 Boscoscuro and Cardoso, 8; 26 Matsudo, 6; 27 E. Gavira, 5; 28 Fiorillo, 4; 29 Gimbert and Ogura, 3; 31 Bolwerk and I. Gavira, 2; 33 Kameya and Vanzetta, 1.

125 cc
23 laps, 65.021 miles/104.650 km

Pos.	Rider (Nat.)	No.	Machine	Laps	Time & speed
1	Valentino Rossi (I)	46	Aprilia	23	48m 05.749s 81.120 mph/ 130.551 km/h
2	Yoshiaki Katoh (J)	62	Yamaha	23	48m 06.318s
3	Manfred Geissler (D)	33	Aprilia	23	48m 19.272s
4	Frédéric Petit (F)	19	Honda	23	48m 45.234s
5	Lucio Cecchinello (I)	10	Honda	23	48m 45.769s
6	Jorge Martinez (E)	5	Aprilia	23	48m 45.789s
7	Mirko Giansanti (I)	32	Honda	23	49m 05.164s
8	Gino Borsoi (I)	24	Yamaha	23	49m 07.063s
9	Masaki Tokudome (J)	2	Aprilia	23	49m 09.254s
10	Juan Enrique Maturana (E)	17	Yamaha	23	49m 09.977s
11	Angel Nieto Jnr (E)	29	Aprilia	23	49m 13.417s
12	Gianluigi Scalvini (I)	21	Honda	23	49m 19.953s
13	Ivan Goi (I)	26	Aprilia	23	50m 03.592s
14	Alex Hofmann (D)	87	Yamaha	23	50m 12.088s
15	Benny Jerzenbeck (D)	77	Honda	22	48m 17.836s
16	Klaus Nohles (D)	89	Honda	21	48m 23.321s
	Roberto Locatelli (I)	15	Honda	21	DNF
	Dirk Raudies (D)	12	Honda	20	DNF
	Emanuel Buchner (D)	86	Aprilia	20	DNF
	Maik Stief (D)	91	Honda	17	DNF
	Josep Sarda (E)	25	Honda	16	DNF
	Kazuto Sakata (J)	8	Aprilia	15	DNF
	Jaroslav Hules (CS)	39	Honda	13	DNF
	Oliver Perschke (D)	90	Honda	11	DNF
	Masao Azuma (J)	20	Honda	9	DNF
	Garry McCoy (AUS)	72	Aprilia	8	DNF
	Noboru Ueda (J)	7	Honda	4	DNF
	Youichi Ui (J)	41	Yamaha	3	DNF
	Dirk Heidolf (D)	85	Honda	3	DNF
	Tomomi Manako (J)	3	Honda	3	DNF
	Steve Jenkner (D)	22	Aprilia	0	DNF

Fastest lap: Katoh, 2m 01.546s, 83.738 mph/134.763 km/h (record).
Previous circuit record: Peter Öttl, D (Aprilia), 1m 48.383s, 94.032 mph/151.330 km/h (1996).

Qualifying: 1 Rossi, 1m 47.160s; 2 Giansanti, 1m 48.331s; 3 Geissler, 1m 48.366s; 4 Martinez, 1m 48.375s; 5 Ueda, 1m 48.408s; 6 Sakata, 1m 48.746s; 7 Locatelli, 1m 49.049s; 8 Manako, 1m 49.051s; 9 Hules, 1m 49.142s; 10 Scalvini, 1m 49.187s; 11 Nieto Jnr, 1m 49.206s; 12 Petit, 1m 49.286s; 13 McCoy, 1m 49.446s; 14 Cecchinello, 1m 49.576s; 15 Raudies, 1m 49.583s; 16 Katoh, 1m 49.585s; 17 Tokudome, 1m 50.215s; 18 Goi, 1m 50.242s; 19 Borsoi, 1m 50.272s; 20 Ui, 1m 50.295s; 21 Stief, 1m 50.347s; 22 Azuma, 1m 50.787s; 23 Jenkner, 1m 50.966s; 24 Perschke, 1m 51.740s; 25 Sarda, 1m 51.875s; 26 Hofmann, 1m 52.164s; 27 Buchner, 1m 52.294s; 28 Maturana, 1m 52.441s; 29 Nohles, 1m 52.731s; 30 Heidolf, 1m 52.750s; 31 Jerzenbeck, 1m 54.081s.

Fastest race laps: 1 Katoh, 2m 01.546s; 2 Rossi, 2m 01.640s; 3 Geissler, 2m 03.105s; 4 Sakata, 2m 03.621s; 5 Petit, 2m 03.771s; 6 Martinez, 2m 03.781s; 7 Cecchinello, 2m 04.017s; 8 Scalvini, 2m 04.418s; 9 Nieto Jnr, 2m 04.484s; 10 Buchner, 2m 04.921s; 11 Giansanti, 2m 04.988s; 12 Borsoi, 2m 05.232s; 13 Maturana, 2m 05.288s; 14 Raudies, 2m 05.349s; 15 Tokudome, 2m 05.445s; 16 Stief, 2m 05.802s; 17 Locatelli, 2m 05.829s; 18 Ueda, 2m 05.909s; 19 Sarda, 2m 06.119s; 20 Azuma, 2m 06.790s; 21 Ui, 2m 06.804s; 22 McCoy, 2m 07.225s; 23 Hules, 2m 07.332s; 24 Goi, 2m 07.452s; 25 Jerzenbeck, 2m 07.596s; 26 Maturana, 2m 08.243s; 27 Manako, 2m 09.286s; 28 Perschke, 2m 10.172s; 29 Nohles, 2m 12.895s; 30 Heidolf, 2m 17.321s.

World Championship: 1 Rossi, 195; 2 Ueda, 123; 3 Manako, 111; 4 Sakata, 101; 5 Martinez, 87; 6 McCoy, 67; 7 Tokudome, 63; 8 Petit, 60; 9 Katoh, 59; 10 Azuma, 14 Ui, 47; 12 Giansanti, 41; 13 Locatelli, 40; 14 Scalvini, 38; 15 Cecchinello, 26; 16 Geissler, 23; 17 Goi, 21; 18 Nakajo, 16; 19 Hules and Maturana, 15; 21 Borsoi, 13; 22 Öttl, 11; 23 Nieto Jnr, Raudies and Takao, 8; 26 Jenkner, 4; 27 Sarda, 3; 28 Hofmann, 2; 29 Jerzenbeck, 1.

Sakata, masterly in the wet, had the 125 race sewn up – but it was Rossi who inherited the win after the former champion's Aprilia failed.

RIO
grand prix

A S is often the way with tracks reckoned dangerous, there were very few crashes at Rio. Though it was easy to see when people went off line how they would be fighting to catch front-wheel slides that would take them to the outside of the track – Gobert actually wore right through one knee-slider doing this in the race. But the track is wide and capacious, and save them they did, most of the time.

There was only one practice injury victim – Takuma Aoki, who fractured and dislocated his shoulder on Friday. His weekend, said the medical report, was over.

Practice went on, people speeding up on Saturday as a clean line developed. Then who should appear on track but Aoki: strapped up and sent out, medical opinion having veered from a definite 'No' to a definite 'Maybe'. The hapless rider, wobbling around some 30 seconds off the pace, managed only three laps before pulling in. No way. Until they told him – wait and see again tomorrow.

This tableau ended after race-morning warm-up. After another painful doddle Takuma was finally declared unfit. Long before then, however, serious questions had been raised, and were in no way answered by a voluntary and unexpected visit to the press room on Saturday evening by two doctors, one an Italian from Dr Costa's permanent mobile clinic, the other the Brazilian delegate. The two clearly disagreed. This was plain as the Italian doctor explained how they had changed their mind, to let Takuma have a go. Since it had been his job to patch him up, he had every justification in what might be discerned as a glow of pride in a job well done. Yes, Doctor. But is there not a conflict of interest – on the one hand of being charged by the patient to make him fit to race, on the other of then being the arbiter of whether he is ready to do so? No, he replied. No conflict. Well, Doctor, is it then your opinion that it is safe for a man to circulate at 30 seconds off the pace on a one-line race track? Yes, he eventually replied angrily, after many deviations. It is safe.

Glowering alongside, the Brazilian doctor – obviously having been over-ruled in this affair – was nodding and smiling at *Motocourse*'s line of questioning. Did he then think it was safe? His reply was immediate. 'No. It was not safe.'

No further questions. Except the one the riders must ask the management, and the management must ask itself. Dr Costa's Clinica Mobile – upgraded handsomely this year – is a marvellous, superlative facility of unquestioned dedication and life-saving potential, of immeasurable value to riders in physical trauma. Many of those riders then choose continued treatment from the doctor and his team – generally because he reliably offers the quickest way to get them racing again. Dr Costa does not shy away from adventurous and medically controversial techniques – his job is to patch them up and get them out. And it is an urgent job, on behalf of not only the riders but also the teams and sponsors. But can it be right that the Clinica Mobile has achieved a position so powerful that it can over-rule the second opinion of the official track doctor?

In the early days of the Brave New World Championship, IRTA appointed another doctor as an independent arbiter – an appointment that was allowed to fall away at the end of 1993. The doctor in question, a highly pragmatic neurosurgeon called Peter Richards, had a simple test of fitness. Twenty press-ups. One could not imagine the broken-shouldered Takuma Aoki passing this test.

Questions of probity and bias arose concerning another safety-related matter – the state of the track. Unsurprisingly. Perennially dogged by controversy, the Rio race had been saved from cancellation only by a complete resurfacing. The official go-ahead had come just a month before, after a late inspection by FIM officials and riders' safety officer Franco Uncini. This year's tarmac was marginally less bumpy than last year's, but was again critically 'green' and very slippery, until a grippier racing line appeared during the course of the weekend. Woe betide anyone who went off line – to overtake, for example.

Action from the riders was too little too late. They had a sparsely attended meeting after the first practice, with Doohan and Beattie taking a leading role in calling the safety of the surface into question. Doohan was eloquent in his complaint against the woolly procedure. 'If I turn up late for the start of the race, I'm fined. But they don't apply the rules to themselves. Tracks are supposed to be passed before January, not a few weeks before the race.' But it all came to nothing, beyond a few imprecations aimed at Uncini.

Another area where standards have slipped over the years, and if the riders could find a voice, they should be asking questions about this as well.

The track, as we have said, only caught out a relative handful of riders, including the other Aoki – Nobu – Checa and Borja. Both Suzuki men went down: Gobert as he continued his fruitless battle to brutalise the front suspension into submission; Beattie sliding off gracefully. It had been his first fall since the catastrophic head-banging arm-breaker in France last year which ended his season, since when he had never regained form. There was some hope that this might have broken the ice somewhat, while he observed, 'If all crashes were as painless as that one, I'd do it all the time.'

The real problem on Friday had been that a chunk of the new surface was already lifting on one corner. This set an alarming precedent. What if there were further disintegration? In the event, an overnight epoxy repair held good, as did the remainder of the large and rather sterile Nelson Piquet circuit for the rest of the weekend.

There was some motor cycle racing amid all the politics, though several leading lights were absent from the pits. Kenny Roberts was taking a break; Wayne Rainey too. Erv Kanemoto was also missing, after a family bereavement.

For the rest, business to the samba beat of the Brazilian drum. Even the time schedule was out of kilter – the 500 race ran first, to mesh with European TV schedules, where viewers cannot have been too surprised to see Doohan tiptoe over the bumps to his seventh victory in succession, running just fast enough to stay ahead of Tady Okada by the second-smallest margin of the year. This was more a measure of the precision of his overall control than a reflection of any real challenge.

For true drama they should have put the 250s on first where, in yet another twist in the championship battle, Biaggi forfeited his lead with an off-track excursion, Waldmann fell and remounted, and the wily Harada survived another collision to take second and the points lead.

The 'Defeat from the Jaws of Victory' award went, appropriately, to Brazil's own Alex Barros. After a hard race on the V-twin, he was disputing eighth with Bayle's Modenas. Determined not to be beaten at home, he made one final error and fell off on the final corner.

Photos: Gold & Goose

One man and his shadow: out on the track, Mick Doohan assumed his usual dominant position. Prior to that, he'd taken a leading role in complaints about the too-new surface. Surrounded by pressmen, he confronts riders' representative Franco Uncini *(right)*.

Far right: Dishevelled and disoriented, or just dazed and confused. Controversial crash victim Takuma Aoki has that 'where-am-I' look as press-room habitué Valentino Rossi plays with his pigtail.

500 cc	DOOHAN
250 cc	JACQUE
125 cc	ROSSI

500 cc RACE – 24 LAPS

Doohan started from pole for the seventh race in succession. Alongside, Cadalora had displaced Checa, with Okada fourth.

Doohan led away, unusually, and Okada was soon with him, the pair stretching ahead in a race of their own. In the later stages Okada was able to peer over Doohan's shoulder once or twice, but no more than that. Then, at the finish, Mick upped the pace just enough to make sure of victory.

The tactics were dictated by the gamble of tyre choice on the cooler track of the morning. Apparently morning free practice had not been enough to do this, according to Doohan. He'd been nursing a sliding front from lap six. 'I eased the pace a little to encourage Tady past, so I could put pressure on him, but when it came to it, he couldn't.' Okada's smiling response was to state the obvious: 'It's difficult to pass Mick.'

A good battle for third comprised five bikes in the early stages, until Gibernau and Bayle fell away behind. This left Abe under mounting pressure from Nobu Aoki, Fuchs and the re-

doubtable Cadalora. Before mid-distance, Aoki and Cadalora were pulling clear, and although Abe did close up again by the finish, the battle was between those two. Cadalora won it, also nursing front-end slides.

Gibernau had lost touch with the group because of engine problems, finally running out of steam with ten laps left. Bayle was meanwhile circulating steadily, the bike slower than in practice, running rich for safety after a morning blow-up.

Now Romboni was catching up: he finished the first lap 15th after a big wheelie and a couple of scary slides. 'I had to be patient until the fuel load got lighter,' he explained. He towed Barros past Bayle before stealing away for a safe seventh.

Bayle and Barros were heading for their last-lap showdown. The Brazilian explained: 'His bike was faster, so I had to work really hard to get ahead on the second last lap. He was right with me. I took a different line into the last corner to make sure he couldn't get past – but it took me onto the slippery part of the circuit.' He crashed within sight of the flag, tried to restart, but a clip-on and the gearshifter had broken off.

Laconi dropped behind this group after half-distance as they all passed the fading Gobert, soldiering on to finish another race dogged by bottoming forks and the front tucking under. In the last two laps he saw off a challenging van den Goorbergh. Sixteen seconds back was Kirk McCarthy, who had passed Beattie's works Suzuki after half-distance. The equally lacklustre Puig trailed in behind.

So what of fast qualifier Checa? Disaster on the second lap, in the leading melee, when he lost the front and fell heavily, luckily unhurt. This was his second race crash in succession. It would become a trend.

Borja crashed out after 14 laps, running well down on team-mate Fuchs. Roberts Junior retired with 18 laps left. 'The front suspension went completely solid,' he said.

250 cc RACE – 22 LAPS

Jacque won his first GP here last year, and took his fifth successive pole this time. Once again first away, he established a small but useful lead as Biaggi, Harada, Ukawa, Waldmann and Capirossi swapped back and forth, all

pulling steadily away from the lonely Perugini.

Waldmann was already in trouble. 'I had no grip from the front. There was no way I could stay with the leaders,' he said. He was sixth at the end of lap seven. Then he slid wide and went down on the long turn before the back straight. Waldie kicked the bike straight and rejoined in 18th. 'After that, it was difficult. The crash snapped off most of the gear lever, so shifting was a problem.' He gradually picked his way through to 12th and some possibly useful points.

By half-distance Harada had broken clear of the group and was working on Jacque's second-plus lead. The Aprilia's turn of speed on the straight was useful, and Olivier started to get a little ragged. At the end of lap 19 it almost ended in a freak disaster. He lost the front wheel in the last corner, managing to stay on board but with all his speed lost. Harada aimed past on the inside. His trajectory was just a shade coarse, and he drifted across Jacque's front wheel. The bikes touched momentarily, and the impact squeezed the Frenchman's brake, locking the front wheel so there was daylight under the rear.

Local hero Alex Barros thrills the home crowd as he leads fellow twin riders Romboni and Laconi. And then he had to go and spoil it all on the very last corner.

Right: Youichi Ui claimed a season's first rostrum for himself and the 125 Yamaha.

Bottom: Jacque scored his first GP win here last year. Now he repeated the experience.

He survived the melodrama to start fighting in earnest, the pair changing places twice in the last lap alone. Harada later complained of suspension trouble and bad front tyre wear. 'When we were fighting, the risk was very high. I decided second was okay, because of the way things stand in the championship.'

Six seconds behind Ukawa – fresh from Eight Hour victory – and Biaggi were battling furiously, Ukawa's bike clearly faster, but Max very determined. Then on the final lap Biaggi braked too late at the end of the long back straight and went careering across the gravel trap at high speed. He was lucky to maintain control, but Capirossi was past before he regained the track.

Aoki took seventh behind the lone Perugini, another unobtrusive top ten for the 125 champion. Tsujimura prevailed in the privateer battle, ahead of Porto and McWilliams. Migliorati had been with them but dropped away at the finish.

Waldmann passed Boscoscuro for 12th only on the last lap; the last points went to Alzamora, still far from sparkling on his works NSR, and Cardoso.

Osamu Miyazaki fell heavily on the first lap, escaping unhurt. Both Suzuki riders crashed out, Johan Stigefelt (substituting for the knocked-about Robinson) two laps earlier than Numata.

125 cc RACE – 21 LAPS

Rossi made an unusually good start and by lap three he was more than a second ahead. By lap five, however, he'd been all but overwhelmed by a pack of eight.

He and three Japanese rivals got away from this scrum, the lead changing back and forth between himself, title rival Ueda, Ui and Manako. There was no certain outcome.

With six laps to go Ueda made a run for it. Rossi went with him. The crucial move came the last time down the back straight. His bike faster, Rossi swept past, then used back-markers cleverly to break the pursuit and win by almost 1.4 seconds. Afterwards, he leaned over the front of the fairing to hug and caress his bike. It deserved it.

Ui was third, his and the Yamaha's best so far, narrowly ahead of Manako.

The battle for fifth was another epic, with any number of changes of fortune leading to a blur across the line – Sakata, Giansanti, Martinez, Cecchinello, Petit and Tokudome, covered by just seven-tenths of a second.

FIM WORLD CHAMPIONSHIP • ROUND 10

LUCKY STRIKE
RIO
GRAND PRIX
3 AUGUST 1997

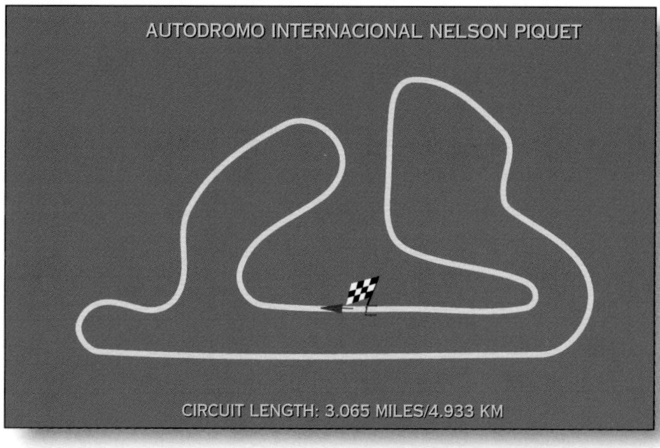

AUTODROMO INTERNACIONAL NELSON PIQUET
CIRCUIT LENGTH: 3.065 MILES/4.933 KM

500 cc

24 laps, 73.560 miles/118.393 km

Pos.	Rider (Nat.)	No.	Machine	Laps	Time & speed
1	**Michael Doohan (AUS)**	**1**	**Honda**	**24**	**45m 05.793s 97.877 mph/ 157.518 km/h**
2	**Tadayuki Okada (J)**	**7**	**Honda**	**24**	**45m 06.499s**
3	**Luca Cadalora (I)**	**3**	**Yamaha**	**24**	**45m 28.328s**
4	**Nobuatsu Aoki (J)**	**18**	**Honda**	**24**	**45m 29.286s**
5	**Norifumi Abe (J)**	**5**	**Yamaha**	**24**	**45m 29.562s**
6	**Jurgen Fuchs (D)**	**16**	**Elf 500**	**24**	**45m 35.228s**
7	**Doriano Romboni (I)**	**19**	**Aprilia**	**24**	**45m 47.467s**
8	**Jean-Michel Bayle (F)**	**12**	**Modenas**	**24**	**45m 49.906s**
9	**Regis Laconi (F)**	**55**	**Honda**	**24**	**46m 08.515s**
10	**Anthony Gobert (AUS)**	**23**	**Suzuki**	**24**	**46m 12.144s**
11	**Jurgen v.d. Goorbergh (NL)**	**21**	**Honda**	**24**	**46m 14.954s**
12	**Kirk McCarthy (AUS)**	**22**	**Yamaha**	**24**	**46m 31.186s**
13	**Daryl Beattie (AUS)**	**6**	**Suzuki**	**24**	**46m 33.008s**
14	**Alberto Puig (E)**	**9**	**Honda**	**24**	**46m 34.691s**
15	**Lucio Pedercini (I)**	**17**	**Yamaha**	**24**	**46m 56.683s**
16	Laurent Naveau (B)	25	Yamaha	23	45m 30.689s
17	Frédéric Protat (F)	15	Honda	23	45m 43.551s
	Alex Barros (BR)	4	Honda	23	DNF
	Juan Borja (E)	14	Elf 500	14	DNF
	Sete Gibernau (E)	20	Yamaha	13	DNF
	Kenny Roberts Jnr (USA)	10	Modenas	6	DNF
	Carlos Checa (E)	8	Honda	1	DNF
	Takuma Aoki (J)	24	Honda		DNS

Fastest lap: Okada, 1m 51.928s, 98.588 mph/158.662 km/h (record).
Previous record: Michael Doohan, AUS (Honda), 1m 53.602s, 97.136 mph/156.325 km/h (1996).

Qualifying: **1** Doohan, 1m 51.955s; **2** Cadalora, 1m 52.353s; **3** Checa, 1m 52.464s; **4** Okada, 1m 52.495s; **5** Romboni, 1m 52.653s; **6** Bayle, 1m 52.991s; **7** N. Aoki, 1m 53.030s; **8** Beattie, 1m 53.111s; **9** Gobert, 1m 53.196s; **10** Gibernau, 1m 53.386s; **11** Abe, 1m 53.794s; **12** Fuchs, 1m 53.927s; **13** Barros, 1m 54.091s; **14** Borja, 1m 54.185s; **15** Laconi, 1m 54.239s; **16** van den Goorbergh, 1m 54.340s; **17** Roberts Jnr, 1m 54.628s; **18** T. Aoki, 1m 54.810s; **19** McCarthy, 1m 54.918s; **20** Puig, 1m 54.949s; **21** Pedercini, 1m 55.262s; **22** Naveau, 1m 57.115s; **23** Protat, 1m 57.604s.

Fastest race laps: **1** Okada, 1m 51.928s; **2** Doohan, 1m 52.174s; **3** Cadalora, 1m 52.641s; **4** N. Aoki, 1m 52.750s; **5** Abe, 1m 53.134s; **6** Fuchs, 1m 53.144s; **7** Gibernau, 1m 53.376s; **8** Romboni, 1m 53.403s; **9** Barros, 1m 53.432s; **10** Bayle, 1m 53.475s; **11** Gobert, 1m 53.535s; **12** Laconi, 1m 54.066s; **13** van den Goorbergh, 1m 54.669s; **14** Beattie, 1m 54.951s; **15** McCarthy, 1m 55.284s; **16** Borja, 1m 55.344s; **17** Puig, 1m 55.348s; **18** Roberts Jnr, 1m 55.534s; **19** Pedercini, 1m 56.156s; **20** Checa, 1m 57.003s; **21** Naveau, 1m 57.233s; **22** Protat, 1m 57.617s.

World Championship: **1** Doohan, 245; **2** Okada, 129; **3** N. Aoki, 126; **4** Criville, 102; **5** Cadalora, 85; **6** Checa, 83; **7** T. Aoki, 80; **8** Abe, 77; **9** Barros, 69; **10** Romboni, 62; **11** Puig, 56; **12** Beattie, 43; **13** Gobert, 40; **14** Gibernau, 38; **15** Bayle, 31; **16** Laconi, 27; **17** Borja and Fuchs, 22; **19** van den Goorbergh, 15; **20** Corser, 11; **21** McCarthy, 9; **22** Roberts Jnr, 8; **23** Fujiwara and Garcia, 7; **25** Goddard, 3; **26** Pedercini, 2; **27** Naveau, 1.

In smooth flow in the late afternoon sunshine, Okada had come through his mid-season spell of crashes with his challenge stronger than ever.

Gold & Goose

250 cc

22 laps, 67.430 miles/108.562 km

Pos.	Rider (Nat.)	No.	Machine	Laps	Time & speed
1	**Olivier Jacque (F)**	**19**	**Honda**	**22**	**42m 09.114s 95.988 mph/ 154.478 km/h**
2	**Tetsuya Harada (J)**	**31**	**Aprilia**	**22**	**42m 09.347s**
3	**Tohru Ukawa (J)**	**5**	**Honda**	**22**	**42m 15.202s**
4	**Loris Capirossi (I)**	**65**	**Aprilia**	**22**	**42m 24.179s**
5	**Max Biaggi (I)**	**1**	**Honda**	**22**	**42m 31.491s**
6	**Stefano Perugini (I)**	**15**	**Aprilia**	**22**	**42m 41.002s**
7	**Haruchika Aoki (J)**	**7**	**Honda**	**22**	**42m 56.405s**
8	**Takeshi Tsujimura (J)**	**12**	**Honda**	**22**	**42m 59.846s**
9	**Sebastian Porto (ARG)**	**27**	**Aprilia**	**22**	**43m 01.922s**
10	**Jeremy McWilliams (GB)**	**11**	**Honda**	**22**	**43m 02.603s**
11	**Cristiano Migliorati (I)**	**8**	**Honda**	**22**	**43m 09.634s**
12	**Ralf Waldmann (D)**	**2**	**Honda**	**22**	**43m 13.238s**
13	**Luca Boscoscuro (I)**	**10**	**Honda**	**22**	**43m 14.456s**
14	**Emilio Alzamora (E)**	**26**	**Honda**	**22**	**43m 16.510s**
15	**José Luis Cardoso (E)**	**17**	**Yamaha**	**22**	**43m 18.466s**
16	Giuseppe Fiorillo (I)	99	Aprilia	22	43m 19.408s
17	Oliver Petrucciani (CH)	25	Aprilia	22	43m 47.011s
18	Kurtis Roberts (USA)	22	Honda	22	44m 06.277s
19	Eustaquio Gavira (E)	28	Aprilia	21	42m 10.930s
	Juan Gartner (ARG)	93	Honda	13	DNF
	Noriyasu Numata (J)	20	Suzuki	10	DNF
	Luis D'Antin (E)	6	Yamaha	9	DNF
	Johan Stigefelt (S)	23	Suzuki	8	DNF
	Idalio Gavira (E)	29	Aprilia	4	DNF
	William Costes (F)	16	Honda	1	DNF
	Osamu Miyazaki (J)	18	Yamaha	0	DNF

Fastest lap: Jacque, 1m 54.267s, 96.570 mph/155.414 km/h (record).
Previous record: Olivier Jacque, F (Honda), 1m 56.004s, 95.124 mph/153.088 km/h (1996).

Qualifying: **1** Jacque, 1m 53.870s; **2** Capirossi, 1m 54.259s; **3** Waldmann, 1m 54.469s; **4** Biaggi, 1m 54.557s; **5** Perugini, 1m 54.580s; **6** Harada, 1m 55.249s; **7** Ukawa, 1m 55.289s; **8** Migliorati, 1m 55.652s; **9** Aoki, 1m 55.759s; **10** Porto, 1m 56.021s; **11** Tsujimura, 1m 56.057s; **12** Numata, 1m 56.127s; **13** Cardoso, 1m 56.528s; **14** Fiorillo, 1m 56.699s; **15** Petrucciani, 1m 56.745s; **16** McWilliams, 1m 56.782s; **17** D'Antin, 1m 57.110s; **18** Miyazaki, 1m 57.129s; **19** Boscoscuro, 1m 57.285s; **20** Stigefeld, 1m 57.840s; **21** Costes, 1m 57.852s; **22** Alzamora, 1m 57.917s; **23** E. Gavira, 1m 58.413s; **24** Roberts, 1m 58.469s; **25** Gartner, 1m 59.631s; **26** I. Gavira, 1m 59.682s.

Fastest race laps: **1** Jacque, 1m 54.267s; **2** Harada, 1m 54.276s; **3** Biaggi, 1m 54.381s; **4** Ukawa, 1m 54.428s; **5** Capirossi, 1m 54.787s; **6** Waldmann, 1m 54.984s; **7** Perugini, 1m 55.615s; **8** Tsujimura, 1m 56.235s; **9** Aoki, 1m 56.335s; **10** Porto, 1m 56.398s; **11** Migliorati, 1m 56.433s; **12** McWilliams, 1m 56.434s; **13** Alzamora, 1m 56.799s; **14** Boscoscuro, 1m 56.813s; **15** Numata, 1m 56.970s; **16** Stigefelt, 1m 57.212s; **17** Cardoso, 1m 57.264s; **18** Fiorillo, 1m 57.404s; **19** D'Antin, 1m 57.413s; **20** Petrucciani, 1m 57.442s; **21** Roberts, 1m 58.654s; **22** E. Gavira, 1m 59.257s; **23** I. Gavira, 1m 59.751s; **24** Gartner, 2m 00.221s; **25** Costes, 2m 16.231s.

World Championship: **1** Harada, 162; **2** Biaggi, 160; **3** Waldmann, 151; **4** Jacque, 126; **5** Ukawa, 107; **6** Capirossi, 87; **7** Aoki, 74; **8** McWilliams and Tsujimura, 56; **10** Perugini, 50; **11** Numata, 42; **12** Porto, 33; **13** Miyazaki, 31; **14** Lucchi, 30; **15** Battaini and D'Antin, 29; **17** Kato, 25; **18** Alzamora and Costes, 23; **20** Migliorati, 20; **21** Robinson, 15; **22** Petrucciani, 14; **23** Boscoscuro, 11; **24** Kagayama, 10; **25** Cardoso, 9; **26** Matsudo, 6; **27** E. Gavira, 5; **28** Fiorillo, 4; **29** Gimbert and Ogura, 3; **31** Bolwerk and I. Gavira, 2; **33** Kameya and Vanzetta, 1.

125 cc

21 laps, 64.365 miles/103.593 km

Pos.	Rider (Nat.)	No.	Machine	Laps	Time & speed
1	**Valentino Rossi (I)**	**46**	**Aprilia**	**21**	**42m 32.218s 90.795 mph/ 146.121 km/h**
2	**Noboru Ueda (J)**	**7**	**Honda**	**21**	**42m 33.597s**
3	**Youichi Ui (J)**	**41**	**Yamaha**	**21**	**42m 40.699s**
4	**Tomomi Manako (J)**	**3**	**Honda**	**21**	**42m 41.233s**
5	**Kazuto Sakata (J)**	**8**	**Aprilia**	**21**	**42m 59.320s**
6	**Mirko Giansanti (I)**	**32**	**Honda**	**21**	**42m 59.458s**
7	**Jorge Martinez (E)**	**5**	**Aprilia**	**21**	**42m 59.609s**
8	**Lucio Cecchinello (I)**	**10**	**Honda**	**21**	**42m 59.672s**
9	**Frédéric Petit (F)**	**19**	**Honda**	**21**	**42m 59.800s**
10	**Masaki Tokudome (J)**	**2**	**Aprilia**	**21**	**42m 59.949s**
11	**Roberto Locatelli (I)**	**15**	**Honda**	**21**	**43m 00.199s**
12	**Steve Jenkner (D)**	**22**	**Aprilia**	**21**	**43m 09.220s**
13	**Garry McCoy (AUS)**	**72**	**Aprilia**	**21**	**43m 09.446s**
14	**Gino Borsoi (I)**	**24**	**Yamaha**	**21**	**43m 11.414s**
15	**Juan Enrique Maturana (E)**	**17**	**Yamaha**	**21**	**43m 11.732s**
16	Yoshiaki Katoh (J)	62	Yamaha	21	43m 20.839s
17	Masao Azuma (J)	20	Honda	21	43m 29.357s
18	Ivan Goi (I)	26	Aprilia	21	43m 35.266s
19	Josep Sarda (E)	25	Honda	21	43m 39.565s
20	Dirk Raudies (D)	12	Honda	21	43m 44.707s
21	Adilson Zaccari (BR)	95	Honda	20	42m 34.061s
22	Cesar Barros (BR)	92	Honda	20	42m 34.196s
23	Carlos Medeiros (BR)	97	Honda	20	43m 24.314s
24	Renato Velludo (BR)	94	Honda	20	43m 34.480s
25	Eraldo Tome (BR)	93	Honda	20	44m 21.165s
	Cristiano Vieira (BR)	96	Honda	19	DNF
	Manfred Geissler (D)	33	Aprilia	13	DNF
	Gianluigi Scalvini (I)	21	Honda	13	DNF
	Angel Nieto Jnr (E)	29	Aprilia	4	DNF
	Benny Jerzenbeck (D)	77	Honda	1	DNF
	Jaroslav Hules (CS)	39	Honda		DNS

Fastest lap: Rossi, 2m 00.074s, 91.900 mph/147.898 km/h (record).
Previous record: Haruchika Aoki, J (Honda), 2m 01.306s, 90.967 mph/146.397 km/h (1996).

Qualifying: **1** Ueda, 2m 00.287s; **2** Rossi, 2m 00.431s; **3** Martinez, 2m 00.914s; **4** Cecchinello, 2m 01.030s; **5** Petit, 2m 01.102s; **6** Tokudome, 2m 01.309s; **7** Geissler, 2m 01.324s; **8** Manako, 2m 01.466s; **9** Ui, 2m 01.554s; **10** Scalvini, 2m 01.708s; **11** McCoy, 2m 02.115s; **12** Sakata, 2m 02.128s; **13** Giansanti, 2m 02.255s; **14** Borsoi, 2m 02.804s; **15** Maturana, 2m 02.903s; **16** Goi, 2m 02.943s; **17** Hules, 2m 03.244s; **18** Raudies, 2m 03.418s; **19** Azuma, 2m 03.476s; **20** Jenkner, 2m 03.552s; **21** Katoh, 2m 03.604s; **22** Sarda, 2m 03.688s; **23** Nieto Jnr, 2m 03.940s; **24** Locatelli, 2m 04.101s; **25** Zaccari, 2m 05.450s; **26** Vieira, 2m 06.231s; **27** Jerzenbeck, 2m 09.405s; **28** Barros, 2m 09.440s; **29** Medeiros, 2m 09.496s; **30** Tome, 2m 10.465s; **31** Velludo, 2m 10.614s.

Fastest race laps: **1** Rossi, 2m 00.074s; **2** Ueda, 2m 00.318s; **3** Manako, 2m 00.815s; **4** Ui, 2m 00.954s; **5** Giansanti, 2m 01.373s; **6** Tokudome, 2m 01.403s; **7** Cecchinello, 2m 01.405s; **8** Geissler, 2m 01.442s; **9** Petit, 2m 01.533s; **10** Locatelli, 2m 01.539s; **11** Sakata, 2m 01.600s; **12** Martinez, 2m 01.605s; **13** Scalvini, 2m 01.745s; **14** Jenkner, 2m 01.874s; **15** Borsoi, 2m 01.974s; **16** Maturana, 2m 02.013s; **17** McCoy, 2m 02.358s; **18** Azuma, 2m 02.443s; **19** Katoh, 2m 02.727s; **20** Sarda, 2m 03.277s; **21** Goi, 2m 03.668s; **22** Raudies, 2m 03.814s; **23** Nieto Jnr, 2m 05.562s; **24** Vieira, 2m 06.099s; **25** Zaccari, 2m 06.172s; **26** Barros, 2m 06.311s; **27** Medeiros, 2m 08.901s; **28** Velludo, 2m 09.442s; **29** Tome, 2m 11.426s; **30** Jerzenbeck, 2m 45.528s.

World Championship: **1** Rossi, 220; **2** Ueda, 143; **3** Manako, 124; **4** Sakata, 112; **5** Martinez, 96; **6** McCoy, 70; **7** Tokudome, 69; **8** Petit, 67; **9** Ui, 63; **10** Katoh, 59; **11** Azuma, 54; **12** Giansanti, 51; **13** Locatelli, 45; **14** Scalvini, 38; **15** Cecchinello, 34; **16** Geissler, 23; **17** Goi, 21; **18** Maturana and Nakajo, 16; **20** Borsoi and Hules, 15; **22** Öttl, 11; **23** Jenkner, Nieto Jnr, Raudies and Takao, 8; **27** Sarda, 3; **28** Hofmann, 2; **29** Jerzenbeck, 1.

BRITISH
grand prix

500 cc	DOOHAN
250 cc	WALDMANN
125 cc	ROSSI

THE track official was moist and dishevelled in the sweltering heat of the large and airless press tent – no air conditioning this year, in spite of the heat wave, as austerity bit still deeper. But he was happy. 'The British Grand Prix has been saved,' he announced.

He was not referring to Mick Doohan's fourth title win in succession, though it was good that the day should be attended by such a coronation – and such good racing in all classes. He was talking about money. They had dropped ticket prices for a third year, added a good support programme and a full field of four British 250 and six 125 wild cards. The consequent improved race-day crowd of more than 30,000 meant that the promoters were at last looking at a modest return for their persistence.

If the recovery is genuine, it is a welcome sign. The British title round came to the mainland from the Isle of Man in 1977, and moved to Donington Park from Silverstone in 1987 – since when there has never been a wet race. Since the Dorna takeover, however, it had fallen on hard times. Along with the German round, it was looking increasingly like a lost cause, while the British public transferred their allegiance en masse to World Superbikes, where they had stars of their own to cheer. For the past four years there had been two British Superbike rounds, while the future of the Grand Prix was far from secure.

There were signs at Donington that the improvement may be more than a hiccup, in the shape of some promising talent among the wild cards. Darren Barton was the only 125 man to score, but Scott Smart, son of Paul, had a notably strong 250 ride to 12th, with two more Brits in the points, John McGuiness and Callum Ramsay, while Jason Vincent chased Honda V-twin regular van den Goorbergh home for 14th and two points in the 500 race.

None of the above made the impact, however, of 14-year-old Leon Haslam, son of the redoubtable ex-500 rider Ron. Racing in a production bike class under special dispensation, Leon was dwarfed by his 500 Honda twin, barely able to reach the ground as he waited on the front row for the start. In Hollywood style, he won, and on the rostrum the MC grabbed him round the waist and hoisted him up so the crowd could see more than just the top of his head. Valentino Rossi, beware.

In line with the mood of recovery, order was restored in the lap record department. Kevin Schwantz's 1991 record was – with his Assen time – the oldest on the books. Beaten often in practice, it had yet to be bettered in the race. Now Doohan slashed six-tenths off it en route to his eighth successive win. More importantly, he also destroyed Troy Corser's outright record, one-tenth faster than Schwantz had been, but set on a four-stroke Superbike Ducati last year. This was the only track in the world where a Superbike had ever beaten a GP 500.

Schwantz was on hand to witness the event. So too was Eddie Lawson, along with Bubba Shobert, the US dirt and road-race multi-champion whose Grand Prix career was ended by head injuries in only his third race: guests of old rival Wayne Rainey, whose biography was being published in a blaze of publicity at the GP. At the packed presentation party, Rainey held the crowd spellbound as he spoke about all his rivals and team-mates. Among a company numbering fourteen 500 class World Champions, he singled out Schwantz as 'the one guy I really hated', and announced to Mick Doohan: 'You'll prove you're a great rider if you sign up for Yamaha next year.'

There was deadly purpose in this. Donington Park marked a crucial stage in their negotiations for next year, which had been going on since the Japanese round. Rainey put a firm offer in front of Doohan, with a deadline of two weeks, take it or leave it. Sadly for those anxious to see Mick doing things differently, it all came to nothing.

Meanwhile, Doohan proved with breathtaking clarity why this was so important as he won the title with four races to spare. It was his tenth victory of the season, and the 44th of his career. The only thing all year which had prevented a clean sweep was that tiresome broken exhaust valve linkage in Spain. Mick was now truly a colossus. Four in a row put him in company with only Giacomo Agostini and Mike Hailwood. And all secured at one of the few tracks that he really mistrusts, for its quirky grip and fiddly part-throttle nature. As ever, he insisted the race was still the thing. 'I enjoy the instant gratification,' he said later.

Invited to dedicate his win, he nominated chief mechanic Jerry Burgess and the rest of the crew. 'They have to put up with me when I go into the pits shouting and screaming.' Beaming and talkative after the race, he continued: 'I had thought that at the age of 32 I might have got racing out of my system. But that's not the case. I'm enjoying it more now than when I was 23.'

This race marked the unravelling of vocal upstart challenger Anthony Gobert's career. He arrived a day late from an Australian holiday, blamed jet lag for his lacklustre practice, then surprised everyone by retiring after only five laps of the race, complaining that his gloves had rucked up and given him cramp. During practice he had undergone a drugs test, commissioned by his team – a condition of his contract. Nobody knew just yet that the test would prove positive...

Finally, how did the lightweight V-twins fare in the 500 class, in their redoubled numbers at the track which spawned the notion in Aprilia designer Jan Witteveen's mind? In fact, it was the Hondas that gave the best yet validation. Romboni was knocked off the front row of the grid at the last minute by Okada's V4, but Barros's Honda was already faster, to be the second such privateer bike to start in the top four. In the race it was Barros again, who scored a privateer V-twin's first-ever rostrum.

Above: **A galaxy of past rivals joined Wayne Rainey to celebrate the launch of his biography** *(from left)*: **Sito Pons, Kenny Roberts, Randy Mamola, Bubba Shobert, Eddie Lawson, Kevin Schwantz, Luca Cadalora and Mick Doohan.**

Below: **Bayle bows out while his Modenas self-destructs in the background.**

History man Doohan claimed his fourth straight title with yet another win, and joined Giacomo Agostini and Mike Hailwood in the hall of fame.

Far right: Jason Vincent made the 500 points – one of 11 British wild cards across the classes.

Alex Barros was third at V-twin-friendly Donington, and the first man to put a private V-twin Honda on the rostrum.

Bottom: Waldmann tracks Harada in the closing stages of a typically tense 250 race.

500 cc RACE – 30 LAPS

Doohan dominated, though his usual final fast practice lap was spoiled by a slide and he led Checa by less than a tenth. The crash-prone Spaniard had fallen on day one – would this be his weekend's quota? Sadly not. Scrabbling in the leading pack he was caught out by the tricky McLean's right-hander on lap three, and went flying again for a third successive non-finish.

Barros and Abe led off the line, split by the Repsol V4s before the end of the first lap. Okada was ahead, Doohan outbraked him cleanly second time round the penultimate hairpin, and was leading by lap three. Barros held station impressively, though by lap five Okada was past him and the V4s started to pull clear.

Mick deals with Japanese riders in a similar way. He likes to slow the pace to let them lead after half-distance, then reimpose his authority in the last laps. The difference this time was that when Okada led from laps 21 to 24, both were travelling at lap-record speed. Mick was obliged to break the record again to make sure of the win – even closer than the last in Rio, by less than a quarter of a second. In his first season on a V4, Okada was emerging as a serious challenger.

Abe and Barros had been joined by Nobu Aoki, with the Yamaha dropping to the back of the group. Then on lap 18 Abe passed them both, to lead as they started the run down the hill. Barros was having none of this, stealing the line for the first left-hander so firmly that the pair collided, and Abe was sent skimming across the grass in a perilous journey that lasted all the way to the exit of the Old Hairpin, where he rejoined the circuit in 11th, and extremely angry. Uncharacteristically, he went looking for Barros directly after the race, eager for confrontation – luckily Barros was engaged in the rostrum ceremonies.

By now, Cadalora's hard tyres were working, and he quickly closed on Barros, bringing Nobu Aoki with him. He then demonstrated the acceleration deficit of a V-twin, hounding Alex through the three last slow corners to surge past down the front straight. Barros did get ahead again, but with four laps left Cadalora was firmly in control, helped when Aoki also slipped past the V-twin for a short time.

With two laps remaining Cadalora's Yamaha suddenly slowed. A plug lead had come adrift and Luca rapidly dropped behind Barros and Aoki. Beattie had been holding station some ten seconds behind, enjoying an empty track to run at speeds he said later he could not have managed in a group. If the race had been one lap longer he too would have overtaken the stricken Cadalora.

The next group had been broken up by Romboni cutting through in familiar style from a slow start. Puig had followed him, but crashed out to make a full house for the MoviStar team, the only fallers in the race.

Borja was less than three seconds down, the disgruntled Abe on his heels. Then came Takuma Aoki, still painfully injured.

Hopes of a good home race for Modenas came to nothing. Bayle had been very fast in practice, but was on the ragged edge, and eventually paid the price. The fall left him too knocked about to race. Junior was 11th, still struggling with the handling.

Kirk McCarthy was 12th, riding a works Yamaha for the first time, one factory machine having been restored to the Red Bull team.

Jason Vincent learned a lot racing with van den Goorbergh, and was still right with him at the finish.

Laconi retired after a first-lap bump knocked his chain off; Gibernau gave up, after being pulled into the pits for a stop-go penalty for jumping the start, then a second time for speeding in pit lane. There wasn't much point after that.

250 cc RACE – 27 LAPS

Pole-starter Capirossi led the usual gang away, with Harada behind the four Hondas. He carved through to lead on the fourth lap, trailing Waldmann, with Capirossi losing touch, Jacque leading Ukawa and Biaggi.

Up front, a compelling battle: the Aprilia faster, the Honda better under brakes. On lap 11 Harada suddenly slowed, only to power back past Waldmann directly afterwards. Two laps later, a more obvious error. He braked too late at the chicane, running across the gravel. Waldmann now led by more than 2.5 seconds, with seven laps left.

It looked decisive, but Harada reeled off four devastating laps, setting a new record as he closed the gap to nothing for the last-lap duel. He was riding superbly on tyres that had already given their best. Using a corner line of great imagination he passed Waldmann easily at the Old Hairpin without even being near him on the track. But Waldmann stuck in his slipstream, and outbraked him into the chicane. Just two bends left.

At the right-hand hairpin, Harada regained the lead. One more corner...

Waldmann's final attack pushed Harada just a bit too hard. He ran wide, and was fighting the bike over the notorious bumps as Ralf slipped cleanly through to claim one of the best victories in his career.

Capirossi blamed his tyres for losing touch, but was clear of the battling Hondas. Jacque was stricken by a mysterious new problem – rear-wheel chatter when he opened the throttle – but fended Ukawa off nevertheless.

Biaggi was in real trouble, with his familiar front-wheel chatter. He managed to get to the front of the group by lap 15, only to crash at the McLeans right-hander next time round, the front tucking under before the bike went down. 'We've been dragging this problem round with us all year,' he said glumly, as he assessed a 22-point championship deficit.

Tsujimura rose above the midfield drama for sixth, top privateer again – the luckless Jeremy McWilliams was out with finger injuries after a practice crash. Perugini was a lone seventh. D'Antin and Aoki were scrapping behind him, until the former had a huge high-sider at the last hairpin. This put Porto ninth, after passing Numata and Battaini. Scott Smart defeated Cardoso for 12th; other wild cards John McGuiness and Callum Ramsay took the final points in fighting style. Kurtis Roberts was 18th and last.

Both Gavira brothers crashed again, likewise Boscoscuro. Robinson was called in to stop-and-go after jumping the start, and then ran off at the chicane.

125 cc RACE – 26 LAPS

Pole-qualifier Ui's Yamaha led for four laps, before rattling to a stop. This left Rossi with an apparently comfortable lead, but Manako and Tokudome were working well together and closed up before lap ten.

The trio drew away, with Tokudome leading the most. But for the last two breathtaking laps it was just Manako and Rossi, the former risking everything to keep his slender title hopes alive.

Manako led the penultimate lap. Rossi attacked but ran wide at the first corner. Manako held him off again at the Old Hairpin, the next passing point. And the next, and the next – all the way to the chicane. Finally Rossi outbraked him into the Melbourne Hairpin. Again, just one corner left...

Rossi ran in tight on the brakes, leaving 'not even enough room for a bicycle'. Manako came through anyway, but he was on the bumps and in trouble: Rossi watched him clatter to the ground in first gear as he slipped through for his ninth win of the year.

Tokudome was promoted to a season's-best second place. McCoy, who had fought through from tenth, would have been third but for another last-corner incident. Distracted by the yellow flags for Manako he ran wide, letting Ueda through.

The better survivors of a big group – Locatelli, Katoh and Giansanti – crossed the line before Manako could scramble back on board to save points for what was now a possible best of second overall in the title chase.

Photos: Gold & Goose

Right: Alberto Puig's racing muse had long since gone absent without leave. He scans the horizon hopefully.

Valentino Rossi *(far right)* made an unlikely Robin Hood in his increasingly theatrical victory celebrations. The Sheriff of nearby Nottingham did not appear.

Bottom: Works rider at last. Kirk McCarthy got the bike, the paint job and the leathers, completing his takeover of Troy Corser's vacated Yamaha berth.

THE SUN BRITISH GRAND PRIX

17 AUGUST 1997

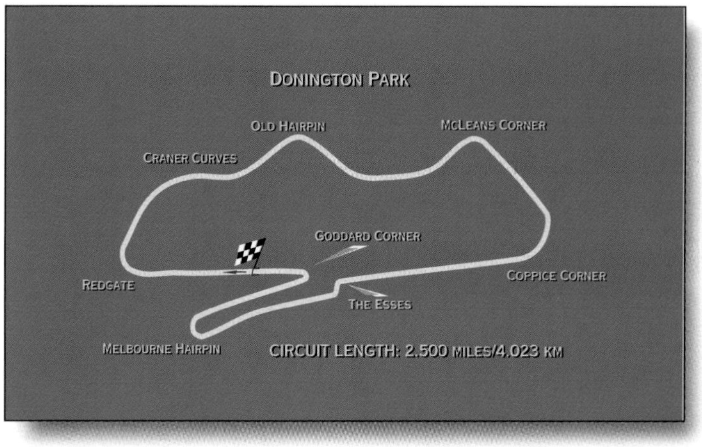

DONINGTON PARK
OLD HAIRPIN
MCLEANS CORNER
CRANER CURVES
GODDARD CORNER
REDGATE
COPPICE CORNER
THE ESSES
MELBOURNE HAIRPIN
CIRCUIT LENGTH: 2.500 MILES/4.023 KM

500 cc

30 laps, 75.000 miles/120.690 km

Pos.	Rider (Nat.)	No.	Machine	Laps	Time & speed
1	**Michael Doohan (AUS)**	**1**	**Honda**	**30**	**46m 55.378s 95.893 mph/ 154.325 km/h**
2	**Tadayuki Okada (J)**	**7**	**Honda**	**30**	**46m 55.609s**
3	**Alex Barros (BR)**	**4**	**Honda**	**30**	**47m 19.781s**
4	**Nobuatsu Aoki (J)**	**18**	**Honda**	**30**	**47m 23.669s**
5	**Luca Cadalora (I)**	**3**	**Yamaha**	**30**	**47m 26.724s**
6	**Daryl Beattie (AUS)**	**6**	**Suzuki**	**30**	**47m 27.921s**
7	**Doriano Romboni (I)**	**19**	**Aprilia**	**30**	**47m 39.850s**
8	**Juan Borja (E)**	**14**	**Elf 500**	**30**	**47m 42.423s**
9	**Norifumi Abe (J)**	**5**	**Yamaha**	**30**	**47m 43.535s**
10	**Takuma Aoki (J)**	**24**	**Honda**	**30**	**47m 58.907s**
11	**Kenny Roberts Jnr (USA)**	**10**	**Modenas**	**30**	**48m 09.568s**
12	**Kirk McCarthy (AUS)**	**22**	**Yamaha**	**30**	**48m 13.701s**
13	**Jurgen v.d. Goorbergh (NL)**	**21**	**Honda**	**30**	**48m 15.315s**
14	**Jason Vincent (GB)**	**98**	**Honda**	**30**	**48m 16.763s**
15	**Jurgen Fuchs (D)**	**16**	**Elf 500**	**29**	**47m 07.697s**
16	Lucio Pedercini (I)	17	Yamaha	29	47m 17.704s
17	Frédéric Protat (F)	15	Honda	29	48m 12.068s
18	Laurent Naveau (B)	25	Yamaha	29	48m 28.093s
	Alberto Puig (E)	9	Honda	24	DNF
	Sete Gibernau (E)	20	Yamaha	10	DNF
	Anthony Gobert (AUS)	23	Suzuki	5	DNF
	Carlos Checa (E)	8	Honda	2	DNF
	Regis Laconi (F)	55	Honda	0	DNF
	Jean-Michel Bayle (F)	12	Modenas		DNS

Fastest lap: Doohan, 1m 32.856s, 96.915 mph/155.970 km/h (record).

Previous record: Kevin Schwantz, USA (Suzuki), 1m 33.569s, 96.177 mph/154.782 km/h (1991).

Qualifying: **1** Doohan, 1m 32.872s; **2** Checa, 1m 32.935s; **3** Barros, 1m 33.132s; **4** Okada, 1m 33.239s; **5** Romboni, 1m 33.564s; **6** N. Aoki, 1m 33.681s; **7** Cadalora, 1m 33.945s; **8** Roberts Jnr, 1m 34.005s; **9** Puig, 1m 34.031s; **10** Laconi, 1m 34.108s; **11** Abe, 1m 34.157s; **12** Beattie, 1m 34.168s; **13** Borja, 1m 34.333s; **14** Bayle, 1m 34.353s; **15** T. Aoki, 1m 34.416s; **16** van den Goorbergh, 1m 34.467s; **17** Gobert, 1m 34.868s; **18** Gibernau, 1m 34.959s; **19** Fuchs, 1m 35.037s; **20** Pedercini, 1m 35.156s; **21** McCarthy, 1m 35.649s; **22** Vincent, 1m 35.905s; **23** Protat, 1m 37.619s; **24** Naveau, 1m 38.150s.

Fastest race laps: **1** Doohan, 1m 32.856s; **2** Okada, 1m 32.862s; **3** Barros, 1m 33.719s; **4** N. Aoki, 1m 33.735s; **5** Abe, 1m 33.820s; **6** Cadalora, 1m 33.913s; **7** Beattie, 1m 34.145s; **8** Romboni, 1m 34.231s; **9** Puig, 1m 34.409s; **10** Borja, 1m 34.419s; **11** T. Aoki, 1m 34.485s; **12** Checa, 1m 34.800s; **13** Gibernau, 1m 34.974s; **14** Roberts Jnr, 1m 35.140s; **15** Vincent, 1m 35.170s; **16** McCarthy, 1m 35.250s; **17** van den Goorbergh, 1m 35.490s; **18** Fuchs, 1m 35.627s; **19** Pedercini, 1m 35.932s; **20** Naveau, 1m 37.613s; **21** Protat, 1m 37.700s; **22** Gobert, 1m 37.858s.

World Championship: **1** Doohan, 270; **2** Okada, 149; **3** N. Aoki, 139; **4** Criville, 102; **5** Cadalora, 96; **6** T. Aoki, 86; **7** Barros, 85; **8** Abe, 84; **9** Checa, 83; **10** Romboni, 71; **11** Puig, 56; **12** Beattie, 53; **13** Gobert, 40; **14** Gibernau, 38; **15** Bayle, 31; **16** Borja, 30; **17** Laconi, 27; **18** Fuchs, 23; **19** van den Goorbergh, 18; **20** McCarthy and Roberts Jnr, 13; **22** Corser, 11; **23** Fujiwara and Garcia, 7; **25** Goddard, 3; **26** Pedercini and Vincent, 2; **28** Naveau, 1.

Above left: Capirossi's best race of the year saw him hold off Biaggi and Ukawa for third place.

Rossi slips through to win as Manako's last-corner attack ends in aerobatics in the background.

250 cc

27 laps, 67.500 miles/108.621 km

Pos.	Rider (Nat.)	No.	Machine	Laps	Time & speed
1	**Ralf Waldmann (D)**	**2**	**Honda**	**27**	**42m 50.897s 94.511 mph/ 152.100 km/h**
2	**Tetsuya Harada (J)**	**31**	**Aprilia**	**27**	**42m 51.030s**
3	**Loris Capirossi (I)**	**65**	**Aprilia**	**27**	**43m 02.393s**
4	**Olivier Jacque (F)**	**19**	**Honda**	**27**	**43m 06.035s**
5	**Tohru Ukawa (J)**	**5**	**Honda**	**27**	**43m 08.643s**
6	**Takeshi Tsujimura (J)**	**12**	**Honda**	**27**	**43m 26.598s**
7	**Stefano Perugini (I)**	**15**	**Aprilia**	**27**	**43m 34.778s**
8	**Haruchika Aoki (J)**	**7**	**Honda**	**27**	**43m 52.417s**
9	**Sebastian Porto (ARG)**	**27**	**Aprilia**	**27**	**43m 59.787s**
10	**Noriyasu Numata (J)**	**20**	**Suzuki**	**27**	**44m 10.053s**
11	**Franco Battaini (I)**	**21**	**Yamaha**	**27**	**44m 10.878s**
12	**Scott Smart (GB)**	**88**	**Honda**	**27**	**44m 13.480s**
13	**José Luis Cardoso (E)**	**17**	**Yamaha**	**27**	**44m 13.880s**
14	**John McGuiness (GB)**	**94**	**Aprilia**	**26**	**43m 05.320s**
15	**Callum Ramsay (GB)**	**97**	**Honda**	**26**	**43m 15.342s**
16	Steve Sawford (GB)	96	Honda	26	43m 15.762s
17	Gary May (GB)	95	Yamaha	26	43m 38.913s
18	Kurtis Roberts (USA)	22	Honda	26	43m 38.969s
	Luis D'Antin (E)	6	Yamaha	21	DNF
	Oliver Petrucciani (CH)	25	Aprilia	19	DNF
	Giuseppe Fiorillo (I)	99	Aprilia	19	DNF
	Max Biaggi (I)	1	Honda	16	DNF
	Jamie Robinson (GB)	14	Suzuki	14	DNF
	Emilio Alzamora (E)	26	Honda	13	DNF
	Osamu Miyazaki (J)	18	Yamaha	8	DNF
	Eustaquio Gavira (E)	28	Aprilia	6	DNF
	William Costes (F)	16	Honda	2	DNF
	Cristiano Migliorati (I)	8	Honda	2	DNF
	Luca Boscoscuro (I)	10	Honda	0	DNF
	Idalio Gavira (E)	29	Aprilia	0	DNF
	Jeremy McWilliams (GB)	11	Honda		DNS

Fastest lap: Harada, 1m 34.137s, 95.597 mph/153.848 km/h (record).

Previous record: Jean-Philippe Ruggia, F (Aprilia), 1m 34.888s, 94.840 mph/152.630 km/h (1993).

Qualifying: **1** Capirossi, 1m 34.346s; **2** Harada, 1m 34.552s; **3** Jacque, 1m 34.688s; **4** Waldmann, 1m 34.895s; **5** Ukawa, 1m 35.197s; **6** Biaggi, 1m 35.223s; **7** Perugini, 1m 35.248s; **8** Aoki, 1m 35.592s; **9** Tsujimura, 1m 36.026s; **10** Porto, 1m 36.295s; **11** D'Antin, 1m 36.535s; **12** Costes, 1m 36.573s; **13** Smart, 1m 36.593s; **14** Migliorati, 1m 36.650s; **15** Cardoso, 1m 36.663s; **16** Robinson, 1m 36.668s; **17** Numata, 1m 36.717s; **18** Petrucciani, 1m 36.783s; **19** Battaini, 1m 36.888s; **20** Alzamora, 1m 37.091s; **21** Boscoscuro, 1m 37.341s; **22** Miyazaki, 1m 37.348s; **23** Fiorillo, 1m 37.722s; **24** McGuiness, 1m 38.238s; **25** E. Gavira, 1m 38.486s; **26** May, 1m 38.958s; **27** Roberts, 1m 38.984s; **28** Sawford, 1m 39.073s; **29** I. Gavira, 1m 39.115s; **30** Ramsay, 1m 39.128s.

Fastest race laps: **1** Harada, 1m 34.137s; **2** Waldmann, 1m 34.580s; **3** Capirossi, 1m 34.818s; **4** Biaggi, 1m 34.965s; **5** Ukawa, 1m 34.971s; **6** Jacque, 1m 35.073s; **7** Perugini, 1m 35.665s; **8** Tsujimura, 1m 35.919s; **9** Aoki, 1m 36.131s; **10** D'Antin, 1m 36.448s; **11** Porto, 1m 36.596s; **12** Numata, 1m 36.601s; **13** Smart, 1m 37.023s; **14** Cardoso, 1m 37.045s; **15** Battaini, 1m 37.065s; **16** Robinson, 1m 37.091s; **17** Alzamora, 1m 37.339s; **18** Petrucciani, 1m 37.807s; **19** Miyazaki, 1m 38.129s; **20** Fiorillo, 1m 38.239s; **21** McGuiness, 1m 38.305s; **22** Ramsay, 1m 38.412s; **23** Sawford, 1m 38.580s; **24** E. Gavira, 1m 39.333s; **25** Roberts, 1m 39.429s; **26** May, 1m 39.610s; **27** Migliorati, 1m 41.673s; **28** Costes, 1m 43.713s.

World Championship: **1** Harada, 182; **2** Waldmann, 176; **3** Biaggi, 160; **4** Jacque, 139; **5** Ukawa, 118; **6** Capirossi, 103; **7** Aoki, 82; **8** Tsujimura, 66; **9** Perugini, 59; **10** McWilliams, 56; **11** Numata, 48; **12** Porto, 40; **13** Battaini, 34; **14** Miyazaki, 31; **15** Lucchi, 30; **16** D'Antin, 29; **17** Kato, 25; **18** Alzamora and Costes, 23; **20** Migliorati, 20; **21** Robinson, 15; **22** Petrucciani, 14; **23** Cardoso, 12; **24** Boscoscuro, 11; **25** Kagayama, 10; **26** Matsudo, 6; **27** E. Gavira, 5; **28** Fiorillo and Smart, 4; **30** Gimbert and Ogura, 3; **32** Bolwerk, I. Gavira and McGuiness, 2; **35** Kameya, Ramsay and Vanzetta, 1.

125 cc

26 laps, 65.000 miles/104.598 km

Pos.	Rider (Nat.)	No.	Machine	Laps	Time & speed
1	**Valentino Rossi (I)**	**46**	**Aprilia**	**26**	**43m 43.254s 89.194 mph/ 143.544 km/h**
2	**Masaki Tokudome (J)**	**2**	**Aprilia**	**26**	**43m 45.034s**
3	**Noboru Ueda (J)**	**7**	**Honda**	**26**	**43m 51.753s**
4	**Garry McCoy (AUS)**	**72**	**Aprilia**	**26**	**43m 52.128s**
5	**Roberto Locatelli (I)**	**15**	**Honda**	**26**	**43m 59.512s**
6	**Yoshiaki Katoh (J)**	**62**	**Yamaha**	**26**	**44m 00.251s**
7	**Mirko Giansanti (I)**	**32**	**Honda**	**26**	**44m 03.825s**
8	**Tomomi Manako (J)**	**3**	**Honda**	**26**	**44m 08.964s**
9	**Frédéric Petit (F)**	**19**	**Honda**	**26**	**44m 09.670s**
10	**Lucio Cecchinello (I)**	**10**	**Honda**	**26**	**44m 09.717s**
11	**Gianluigi Scalvini (I)**	**21**	**Honda**	**26**	**44m 11.721s**
12	**Manfred Geissler (D)**	**33**	**Aprilia**	**26**	**44m 18.167s**
13	**Masao Azuma (J)**	**20**	**Honda**	**26**	**44m 27.217s**
14	**Darren Barton (GB)**	**30**	**Honda**	**26**	**44m 35.556s**
15	**Juan Enrique Maturana (E)**	**17**	**Yamaha**	**26**	**44m 40.825s**
16	Steve Jenkner (D)	22	Aprilia	26	44m 48.002s
17	Ivan Goi (I)	26	Aprilia	26	44m 48.437s
18	Fernando Mendes (GB)	28	Honda	26	44m 57.360s
19	Angel Nieto Jnr (E)	29	Aprilia	26	44m 58.937s
20	Jason Davies (GB)	82	Honda	26	45m 15.049s
21	Alan Green (GB)	99	Honda	25	43m 48.027s
	Kazuto Sakata (J)	8	Aprilia	10	DNF
	Jorge Martinez (E)	5	Aprilia	9	DNF
	Chris Burns (GB)	98	Honda	7	DNF
	Gino Borsoi (I)	24	Yamaha	5	DNF
	Youichi Ui (J)	41	Yamaha	4	DNF
	Steve Patrickson (GB)	40	Honda	4	DNF
	Dirk Raudies (D)	12	Honda	4	DNF
	Josep Sarda (E)	25	Honda	2	DNF
	Jaroslav Hules (CS)	39	Honda	2	DNF

Fastest lap: Rossi, 1m 39.236s, 90.685 mph/145.943 km/h (record).

Previous record: Masaki Tokudome, J (Aprilia), 1m 39.704s, 90.260 mph/145.258 km/h (1996).

Qualifying: **1** Ui, 1m 39.713s; **2** Manako, 1m 39.733s; **3** Ueda, 1m 40.387s; **4** Rossi, 1m 40.419s; **5** Tokudome, 1m 40.429s; **6** Locatelli, 1m 40.566s; **7** McCoy, 1m 40.641s; **8** Katoh, 1m 40.722s; **9** Martinez, 1m 40.810s; **10** Giansanti, 1m 41.079s; **11** Petit, 1m 41.214s; **12** Sakata, 1m 41.237s; **13** Maturana, 1m 41.340s; **14** Cecchinello, 1m 41.402s; **15** Scalvini, 1m 41.517s; **16** Borsoi, 1m 41.553s; **17** Geissler, 1m 41.715s; **18** Raudies, 1m 41.814s; **19** Barton, 1m 42.012s; **20** Sarda, 1m 42.088s; **21** Jenkner, 1m 42.095s; **22** Azuma, 1m 42.414s; **23** Hules, 1m 42.493s; **24** Burns, 1m 42.639s; **25** Mendes, 1m 42.823s; **26** Nieto Jnr, 1m 42.865s; **27** Goi, 1m 43.273s; **28** Davies, 1m 43.673s; **29** Green, 1m 43.682s; **30** Patrickson, 1m 44.157s.

Fastest race laps: **1** Rossi, 1m 39.236s; **2** Manako, 1m 39.596s; **3** Tokudome, 1m 40.006s; **4** McCoy, 1m 40.334s; **5** Ueda, 1m 40.387s; **6** Giansanti, 1m 40.529s; **7** Locatelli, 1m 40.632s; **8** Sakata, 1m 40.692s; **9** Petit, 1m 40.743s; **10** Katoh, 1m 40.871s; **11** Scalvini, 1m 40.908s; **12** Cecchinello, 1m 41.035s; **13** Ui, 1m 41.077s; **14** Maturana, 1m 41.249s; **15** Azuma, 1m 41.273s; **16** Geissler, 1m 41.311s; **17** Jenkner, 1m 41.493s; **18** Barton, 1m 41.611s; **19** Martinez, 1m 41.757s; **20** Goi, 1m 42.023s; **21** Burns, 1m 42.030s; **22** Davies, 1m 42.296s; **23** Mendes, 1m 42.700s; **24** Nieto Jnr, 1m 42.844s; **25** Hules, 1m 43.253s; **26** Borsoi, 1m 43.327s; **27** Sarda, 1m 43.890s; **28** Green, 1m 44.064s; **29** Raudies, 1m 45.293s; **30** Patrickson, 1m 45.820s.

World Championship: **1** Rossi, 245; **2** Ueda, 159; **3** Manako, 132; **4** Sakata, 112; **5** Martinez, 96; **6** Tokudome, 89; **7** McCoy, 83; **8** Petit, 74; **9** Katoh, 69; **10** Ui, 63; **11** Giansanti, 60; **12** Azuma, 57; **13** Locatelli, 56; **14** Scalvini, 43; **15** Cecchinello, 40; **16** Geissler, 27; **17** Goi, 21; **18** Maturana, 17; **19** Nakajo, 16; **20** Borsoi and Hules, 15; **22** Öttl, 11; **23** Jenkner, Nieto Jnr, Raudies and Takao, 8; **27** Sarda, 3; **28** Barton and Hofmann, 2; **30** Jerzenbeck, 1.

500 cc	**DOOHAN**
250 cc	**BIAGGI**
125 cc	**UEDA**

AIN throughout practice at Brno was rather refreshing, considering more was forecast for race day. It had been so long since a really wet GP weekend – rather than just a patchy one – that there were people in the paddock who couldn't remember one, and needed to have the advantages explained.

Advantages? Oh yes. The main one being the way rain alters the balance of power. To be blunt, the 500 class is no longer just a Honda playground, with the sweet-handling Yamahas coming right back into the picture, and the nimble Suzukis also...at least in years past. And again this year, with the erratically exciting Gobert as high as third after the first day of practice, although he dropped to ninth on the second; and Beattie on the front row of the grid for the first time in well over a year.

One might expect a rider of Beattie's quality to do this. Indeed, he had been puzzlingly below expectations all year, and more people blamed the after-effects of his pair of head injuries last year than subscribed to his own view – that the bike just wasn't up to it. After all, although clearly not a Honda, it had been good enough to put Scott Russell on the rostrum here last year, while at comparable tracks Beattie wasn't matching his own old lap times whether he rode the 1996 machine or (as now) the '97 bike.

Gobert, on the other hand, was still perceived as being on the way up – and his strong ride in the wet a welcome resumption of his good form after a two- or three-race slump. He was 'feeling better in himself' he said, after being joined in Europe by his younger brother, Aaron; and he had been practising on his minibike every evening to improve throttle control, on impromptu circuits wherever he'd parked his motorhome for the night. (Given the difficulties of finding places to do this in Europe, it conjured up the spectacle of the brash young Australian belting round and round suburban back gardens, pursued by angry French, German or Austrian householders – but no matter, if it helped his riding, as seemed the case.) 'I've never minded rainy conditions – it's enjoyable spinning up the rear tyre of a 500 in the wet,' he continued. What neither he nor any team outsiders knew at this stage was that this would be his last GP.

Would it have been any different if it had rained, and he'd finished on the rostrum? A moot point, in the end, for forecasts of rain for all three days turned out to be wrong. This also changed the balance of power, introducing an element of guesswork: with only 20 minutes of morning warm-up providing the bare minimum of dry practice time prescribed by the regulations, tyre choice, gearing and suspension settings were turned into something of a gamble.

This affected some people more than others – Beattie again being one of them. Ten weeks before he'd tested at Brno and lapped under the record, though (as he was anxious to point out) it had been only a single lap, rather than a consistent improvement. Since then he'd been moving in a different direction of bike development, especially during the wet sessions. Now came the question: should he switch to that test bike, or stay with the newer version? It would seem logi-

Rain helped boost Gibernau's growing confidence after he was second fastest in the first wet practice session.

Opposite page: An unusual sight, as front-row qualifier Daryl Beattie sweeps into the first corner ahead of the pack. He was soon overwhelmed.

Bottom: Okada shadowed Doohan once again, right until the final disaster.

cal to test them back to back in the morning, but with a lap of more than two minutes, allowing time to pit and switch bikes, that would give him hardly more than four fast laps on each. This would scarcely be enough time to reach a firm conclusion, let alone think about tyre choice or the fine-tuning of suspension or gearing.

As a result, he chose to stay with the 'wet bike', and defended his decision later, even though it had surely contributed to a disastrous slump from leading into the first corner to finishing a very distant tenth out of only 14 finishers. 'In retrospect,' said team manager Garry Taylor, rather mildly given the circumstances, 'it may have been a mistake.' Then again, there's little point forcing a rider to do something against his will, and if gentle persuasion fails, there's not much room for manoeuvre.

Waldmann demonstrated a different dilemma. Unlike Biaggi and Jacque, he has only one bike. Thus, when he clashed with the Frenchman in practice in yet another 'Jacque Attack', rather than force the issue and risk both of them crashing he was obliged to lift and go whizzing across the gravel, so as to have a bike to ride for the rest of the session. The rain caused him more serious problems. 'Everything on the bike must be changed – not just the tyres and the brakes (from carbon to iron), but the gearbox and the suspension settings. It takes about 45 minutes to change the bike from wet to dry settings.' When race day dawned dry, there was just about enough time for the team to do all that; and it stayed dry all day. Had the weather been changeable, they would have been in an uncomfortable position.

Brno saw the return of Criville, rather prematurely, thought some, especially seeing how tentatively he rode the first sessions. His hand injury was livid, and he admitted it was tiring just trying to ride. But his confidence returned rapidly over the days, and he qualified on the second row. Then came a race performance nothing short of heroic. If anyone had in the past doubted the strength in depth of this soft-spoken mild-mannered second fiddler to Doohan, they could do so no more.

Other 500 news came from Aprilia – the V-twin had grown again, now to 480 cc. Still 20 cc short of the Honda, it was a big step in the right direction, but Romboni was knocked off on the first lap, so the effect was not to be felt just yet.

The 250 class remained alive by virtue of a typical bravura performance under pressure from race-winner Biaggi, while the 125 title was settled with mathematical precision by Valentino Rossi. He needed to come third if Ueda won, and that's exactly what he did. It was, however, harder to achieve than it is to say.

Photos: Gold & Goose

CZECH

grand prix

Okada got full marks for trying, after dropping his not-so-lucky seven Honda in a spirited last-lap attack.

500 cc RACE – 22 LAPS

Wet practice threw up some unusual names, with Sete Gibernau particularly impressive as he ran fastest in the second session. In the end, it was Doohan on pole, with Cadalora second and Bayle and Beattie alongside – the former giving the Modenas its first-ever front row, the latter gaining his first such position of the season.

Beattie led into turn one, but almost the full pack of works bikes came piling straight past. Except for Checa's Honda: a cracked wheel casting meant a front-wheel puncture and an early retirement.

Up front, Doohan was in control in spite of a lap one slide that had him out of the saddle. Cadalora was in pursuit, with fast-starter Gibernau soon displaced by N. Aoki. Okada was charging, however, and in second by lap five.

Mick stayed ahead by about a second for a spell, but he was sliding a lot, and decided to see what Okada could do, letting him through from lap 15 to lap 19. He then loomed ever more threateningly over Tady's shoulder before moving clearly past with three laps left.

Okada had one move left – a last-lap kamikaze attack. As Mick braked for the first fast chicane, well on the limit, the Japanese rider shot past, having decided to brake even later. With some inevitability under the circumstances, he ran straight into the gravel and crashed. 'I was already braking later than I had all lap,' said Doohan later. 'I knew he wouldn't make the corner.'

Some 15 seconds behind Cadalora was biding his time after going back and forth with Nobu Aoki. In the last lap he pulled cleanly ahead, Aoki instead coming under pressure from the remarkable Criville. He'd pulled through a four-bike pack, then gone faster and faster instead of fading away as expected. 'It's like a victory for me,' he said later. 'It was painful, and after seven laps I couldn't use the clutch. Before the start I didn't know if I could race again. Now I know I can.'

He'd overtaken Abe and Takuma Aoki on the way, pulling them along with him, and also Gibernau, who sadly ended the best ride of his life by crashing out of the group with two laps left.

Another half-minute behind came an exultant Laconi, celebrating his return to full strength by beating Barros's similar V-twin by less than two-tenths after an almost race-long battle.

Kenny Roberts Jnr had dropped away from this group in the closing stages, blaming his defeat by the twins

rather surprisingly on a lack of acceleration. Worse still, Beattie had been overwhelmed and dropped by the same group – his excuse was the Suzuki's poor mid-corner handling.

There were only 14 finishers, Jurgen van den Goorbergh heading the disgruntled Gobert, whose brakes went off on the warm-up lap and the lacklustre Puig. Naveau was last, one lap adrift.

Fuchs crashed out; likewise Romboni, after colliding with Borja on only the second lap. Borja then pulled out with his fairing flapping loose.

The race was heartbreaking for Bayle. He missed his front-row start after a rear brake caliper broke on the warm-up lap. He started on his spare from pit lane. He'd worked his way through into the points when that bike suffered a powervalve motor failure.

250 cc RACE – 20 LAPS

A slightly drier final session handed Waldmann pole over Biaggi by one-hundredth – the German's sixth pole in 11 years. Ukawa was third, happy with a new 16-in. Michelin wet front, with Capirossi alongside and Harada leading row two, both complaining that the Aprilia's notoriously snatchy throttle was a big problem in the wet on the long corners.

But it was Jacque, leaping through from row two, who pulled Waldmann and Biaggi away from Harada, Ukawa and the rest.

As the German and the Frenchman exchanged the lead, Biaggi was never higher than second. Then 'One-Bike Waldmann' obligingly started to drop away. Short of set-up time, his gearing choice was wrong ('I could hardly use sixth') and his rear ruined.

Biaggi waited until the last lap to attack. He passed Jacque in the first turn; Jacque passed him back as he ran wide on the exit. Max passed

Right: Laconi re-emphasised his strong return, holding off Barros to the flag for a worthy seventh place.

Far right: Rossi was in the thick of the early race action, with Scalvini (21) and Sakata (8) disputing the lead.

Main picture: The start of Biaggi's late season return saw him eventually outclass Olivier Jacque.

again under braking down the hill for the pair of rights into the spectator bowl. This time he emerged far enough ahead to lead for the rest of the lap.

The next battle was dramatic. Ukawa and Harada were locked in combat, and had easily passed the fading Waldmann with three laps to go. Ukawa led up the hill for the last time, but Harada went smoothly through inside when Tohru headed into the last left-right too fast. He ran wide and into the gravel, falling, then scrambling aboard again to finish fifth, behind Waldmann.

The field was strung way out behind with not a great deal happening. Tsujimura was a lone and distant sixth, then came Perugini, a skirmish between Fiorillo and Migliorati, with Porto tenth, Robinson 13th.

A number of retirements included eight not very consequential crashes, and mechanical failure not only for Numata's Suzuki, running strongly in the top ten, but also Aoki's Honda – he had been with Ukawa. Capirossi pitted, reporting handling problems. McWilliams also retired, his back wheel loose!

Biaggi's win was both impressive and timely. Although Harada's title lead extended to nine points over Waldmann, Max was definitely back in the picture now.

125 cc RACE – 19 LAPS

Rossi's practice saw him crash just after scraping onto the front row, led for a second successive race by Ui's improving Yamaha. The race itself was a huge brawl: Scalvini doing most of the leading, Rossi up front only briefly, lacking his usual domination, Locatelli in the thick of it, and a total of up to ten bikes all in the jumbled mass.

Ueda had his own agenda – he needed to win to keep his title hopes alive, though only if the Italian finished lower than third.

The last lap was one of Rossi's best of the season, considering he wasn't happy with his set-up. So too was Ueda's and he did win, fending off Manako to the line. But it was Rossi in third, and he was the champion.

The first eight finished within just over one second. Locatelli was fourth, then Cecchinello and his team-mate Scalvini. Former East German part-timer Steve Jenkner was impressively with this group, ahead of Tokudome. Then came Sakata (another early leader) and Ui, both losing touch with the gang in the closing stages.

Martinez crashed out of the group without injury with six laps left; McCoy led the next gang over the line.

Photos: Gold & Goose

CZECH GRAND PRIX

31 AUGUST 1997

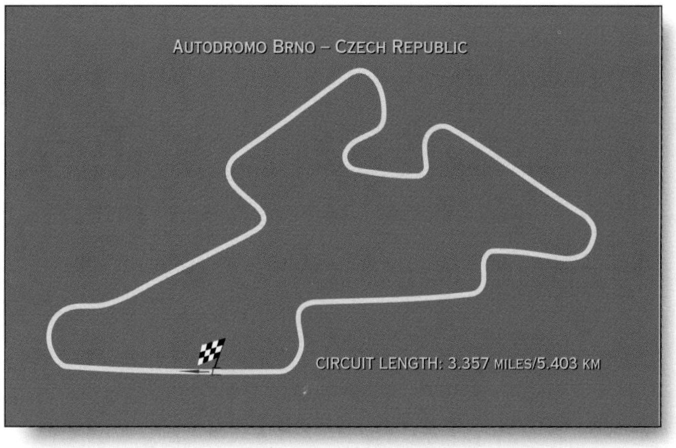
AUTODROMO BRNO – CZECH REPUBLIC
CIRCUIT LENGTH: 3.357 MILES/5.403 KM

500 cc

22 laps, 73.854 miles/118.866 km

Pos.	Rider (Nat.)	No.	Machine	Laps	Time & speed
1	**Michael Doohan (AUS)**	1	**Honda**	22	**45m 25.012s 97.576 mph/ 157.033 km/h**
2	**Luca Cadalora (I)**	3	**Yamaha**	22	**45m 39.870s**
3	**Nobuatsu Aoki (J)**	18	**Honda**	22	**45m 40.122s**
4	**Alex Criville (E)**	2	**Honda**	22	**45m 40.335s**
5	**Norifumi Abe (J)**	5	**Yamaha**	22	**45m 40.660s**
6	**Takuma Aoki (J)**	24	**Honda**	22	**45m 41.858s**
7	**Regis Laconi (F)**	55	**Honda**	22	**46m 13.790s**
8	**Alex Barros (BR)**	4	**Honda**	22	**46m 13.957s**
9	**Kenny Roberts Jnr (USA)**	10	**Modenas**	22	**46m 15.129s**
10	**Daryl Beattie (AUS)**	6	**Suzuki**	22	**46m 27.389s**
11	**Jurgen v.d. Goorbergh (NL)**	21	**Honda**	22	**46m 32.864s**
12	**Anthony Gobert (AUS)**	23	**Suzuki**	22	**47m 04.045s**
13	**Alberto Puig (E)**	9	**Honda**	22	**47m 10.609s**
14	**Laurent Naveau (B)**	25	**Yamaha**	21	**45m 41.411s**
	Tadayuki Okada (J)	7	Honda	21	DNF
	Sete Gibernau (E)	20	Yamaha	20	DNF
	Frédéric Protat (F)	15	Honda	17	DNF
	Jurgen Fuchs (D)	16	Elf 500	12	DNF
	Jean-Michel Bayle (F)	12	Modenas	10	DNF
	Lucio Pedercini (I)	17	Yamaha	8	DNF
	Carlos Checa (E)	8	Honda	4	DNF
	Kirk McCarthy (AUS)	22	Yamaha	3	DNF
	Juan Borja (E)	14	Elf 500	3	DNF
	Doriano Romboni (I)	19	Aprilia	2	DNF

Fastest lap: Doohan, 2m 02.560s, 98.614 mph/158.704 km/h (record).

Previous record: Alex Criville, E (Honda), 2m 02.791s, 98.429 mph/158.406 km/h (1996).

Qualifying: **1** Doohan, 2m 14.105s; **2** Cadalora, 2m 15.195s; **3** Bayle, 2m 15.338s; **4** Beattie, 2m 15.445s; **5** Gibernau, 2m 15.470s; **6** Checa, 2m 15.759s; **7** Criville, 2m 16.143s; **8** Laconi, 2m 16.274s; **9** Gobert, 2m 16.614s; **10** T. Aoki, 2m 16.740s; **11** Roberts Jnr, 2m 16.819s; **12** Borja, 2m 16.917s; **13** Fuchs, 2m 17.188s; **14** Romboni, 2m 17.476s; **15** Barros, 2m 17.663s; **16** Okada, 2m 17.791s; **17** Abe, 2m 18.042s; **18** N. Aoki, 2m 18.164s; **19** McCarthy, 2m 18.840s; **20** Puig, 2m 18.863s; **21** Pedercini, 2m 19.063s; **22** van den Goorbergh, 2m 19.187s; **23** Protat, 2m 24.398s; **24** Naveau, 2m 24.776s.

Fastest race laps: **1** Doohan, 2m 02.560s; **2** Okada, 2m 02.664s; **3** Abe, 2m 03.465s; **4** Gibernau, 2m 03.485s; **5** Criville, 2m 03.551s; **6** T. Aoki, 2m 03.609s; **7** Cadalora, 2m 03.733s; **8** N. Aoki, 2m 03.745s; **9** Bayle, 2m 04.792s; **10** Laconi, 2m 04.999s; **11** Barros, 2m 05.074s; **12** Roberts Jnr, 2m 05.090s; **13** Romboni, 2m 05.408s; **14** Beattie, 2m 05.503s; **15** van den Goorbergh, 2m 05.544s; **16** Checa, 2m 05.589s; **17** Fuchs, 2m 05.669s; **18** Borja, 2m 06.084s; **19** Pedercini, 2m 06.584s; **20** Gobert, 2m 06.675s; **21** McCarthy, 2m 07.517s; **22** Puig, 2m 07.622s; **23** Protat, 2m 08.836s; **24** Naveau, 2m 08.967s.

World Championship: **1** Doohan, 295; **2** N. Aoki, 155; **3** Okada, 149; **4** Cadalora, 116; **5** Criville, 115; **6** T. Aoki, 96; **7** Abe, 95; **8** Barros, 93; **9** Checa, 83; **10** Romboni, 71; **11** Beattie and Puig, 59; **13** Gobert, 44; **14** Gibernau, 38; **15** Laconi, 36; **16** Bayle, 31; **17** Borja, 30; **18** Fuchs and van den Goorbergh, 23; **20** Roberts Jnr, 20; **21** McCarthy, 13; **22** Corser, 11; **23** Fujiwara and Garcia, 7; **25** Goddard and Naveau, 3; **27** Pedercini and Vincent, 2.

Above left: Doohan watches and measures his new rival Okada after letting him through to a short-lived lead.

Biaggi: clearly a man on a mission as he rejoined the championship trail.

250 cc

20 laps, 67.140 miles/108.060 km

Pos.	Rider (Nat.)	No.	Machine	Laps	Time & speed
1	**Max Biaggi (I)**	1	**Honda**	20	**42m 06.724s 95.666 mph/ 153.960 km/h**
2	**Olivier Jacque (F)**	19	**Honda**	20	**42m 07.238s**
3	**Tetsuya Harada (J)**	31	**Aprilia**	20	**42m 16.716s**
4	**Ralf Waldmann (D)**	2	**Honda**	20	**42m 19.877s**
5	**Tohru Ukawa (J)**	5	**Honda**	20	**42m 38.500s**
6	**Takeshi Tsujimura (J)**	12	**Honda**	20	**42m 45.501s**
7	**Stefano Perugini (I)**	15	**Aprilia**	20	**42m 50.464s**
8	**Giuseppe Fiorillo (I)**	99	**Aprilia**	20	**43m 05.446s**
9	**Cristiano Migliorati (I)**	8	**Honda**	20	**43m 06.293s**
10	**Sebastian Porto (ARG)**	27	**Aprilia**	20	**43m 10.225s**
11	**José Luis Cardoso (E)**	17	**Yamaha**	20	**43m 19.127s**
12	**Emilio Alzamora (E)**	26	**Honda**	20	**43m 24.283s**
13	**Jamie Robinson (GB)**	14	**Suzuki**	20	**43m 32.345s**
14	**Osamu Miyazaki (J)**	18	**Yamaha**	20	**43m 33.195s**
15	**Franco Battaini (I)**	21	**Yamaha**	20	**43m 38.677s**
16	Eustaquio Gavira (E)	28	Aprilia	20	43m 41.017s
17	Claudio Vanzetta (CH)	24	Aprilia	20	44m 06.582s
18	Kurtis Roberts (USA)	22	Honda	19	42m 09.217s
19	Oscar Sainz (E)	49	Yamaha	19	42m 17.860s
20	Radomil Rous (CS)	42	Yamaha	19	43m 33.831s
	Luca Boscoscuro (I)	10	Honda	19	DNF
	Noriyasu Numata (J)	20	Suzuki	15	DNF
	Haruchika Aoki (J)	7	Honda	14	DNF
	Loris Capirossi (I)	65	Aprilia	7	DNF
	William Costes (F)	16	Honda	6	DNF
	Oliver Petrucciani (CH)	25	Aprilia	6	DNF
	Maurice Bolwerk (NL)	73	Honda	6	DNF
	Jeremy McWilliams (GB)	11	Honda	5	DNF
	Idalio Gavira (E)	29	Aprilia	3	DNF
	Vladimir Castka (SLK)	41	Honda	3	DNF
	Bohumil Stasa (CS)	40	Aprilia	1	DNF

Fastest lap: Waldmann, 2m 05.393s, 96.386 mph/155.118 km/h.

Lap record: Tetsuya Harada, J (Yamaha), 2m 04.684s, 96.773 mph/155.741 km/h (1995).

Qualifying: **1** Waldmann, 2m 18.982s; **2** Biaggi, 2m 18.992s; **3** Ukawa, 2m 19.525s; **4** Capirossi, 2m 19.627s; **5** Harada, 2m 19.920s; **6** Aoki, 2m 19.981s; **7** Tsujimura, 2m 20.231s; **8** Jacque, 2m 20.422s; **9** Fiorillo, 2m 20.740s; **10** Perugini, 2m 21.060s; **11** Porto, 2m 21.073s; **12** Numata, 2m 21.528s; **13** Alzamora, 2m 21.994s; **14** McWilliams, 2m 22.873s; **15** Petrucciani, 2m 23.214s; **16** Costes, 2m 23.378s; **17** Cardoso, 2m 23.540s; **18** Miyazaki, 2m 24.204s; **19** Boscoscuro, 2m 24.235s; **20** Battaini, 2m 24.813s; **21** Migliorati, 2m 25.345s; **22** Bolwerk, 2m 25.350s; **23** E. Gavira, 2m 25.765s; **24** Roberts, 2m 25.916s; **25** Stasa, 2m 25.961s; **26** Robinson, 2m 26.020s; **27** Castka, 2m 26.634s; **28** Rous, 2m 28.011s; **29** Sainz, 2m 28.160s; **30** Vanzetta, 2m 28.551s; **31** I. Gavira, 2m 28.858s.

Fastest race laps: **1** Waldmann, 2m 05.393s; **2** Biaggi, 2m 05.501s; **3** Jacque, 2m 05.543s; **4** Harada, 2m 05.664s; **5** Ukawa, 2m 05.950s; **6** Aoki, 2m 06.226s; **7** Numata, 2m 07.148s; **8** Perugini, 2m 07.169s; **9** Tsujimura, 2m 07.325s; **10** Capirossi, 2m 07.656s; **11** Fiorillo, 2m 08.469s; **12** Porto, 2m 08.497s; **13** Migliorati, 2m 08.504s; **14** Alzamora, 2m 08.803s; **15** McWilliams, 2m 09.019s; **16** Cardoso, 2m 09.086s; **17** Battaini, 2m 09.104s; **18** Miyazaki, 2m 09.431s; **19** E. Gavira, 2m 09.584s; **20** Robinson, 2m 09.603s; **21** Boscoscuro, 2m 09.692s; **22** Petrucciani, 2m 09.859s; **23** Costes, 2m 10.138s; **24** Castka, 2m 10.716s; **25** I. Gavira, 2m 11.118s; **26** Vanzetta, 2m 11.240s; **27** Roberts, 2m 11.557s; **28** Bolwerk, 2m 11.681s; **29** Sainz, 2m 11.853s; **30** Rous, 2m 15.761s; **31** Stasa, 2m 21.538s.

World Championship: **1** Harada, 198; **2** Waldmann, 189; **3** Biaggi, 185; **4** Jacque, 159; **5** Ukawa, 129; **6** Capirossi, 103; **7** Aoki, 82; **8** Tsujimura, 76; **9** Perugini, 68; **10** McWilliams, 56; **11** Numata, 48; **12** Porto, 46; **13** Battaini, 35; **14** Miyazaki, 33; **15** Lucchi, 30; **16** D'Antin, 29; **17** Alzamora and Migliorati, 27; **19** Kato, 25; **20** Costes, 23; **21** Robinson, 18; **22** Cardoso, 17; **23** Petrucciani, 14; **24** Fiorillo, 12; **25** Boscoscuro, 11; **26** Kagayama, 10; **27** Matsudo, 6; **28** E. Gavira, 5; **29** Smart, 4; **30** Gimbert and Ogura, 3; **32** Bolwerk, I. Gavira and McGuiness, 2; **35** Kameya, Ramsay and Vanzetta, 1.

125 cc

19 laps, 63.783 miles/102.657 km

Pos.	Rider (Nat.)	No.	Machine	Laps	Time & speed
1	**Noboru Ueda (J)**	7	**Honda**	19	**42m 13.666s 90.634 mph/ 145.861 km/h**
2	**Tomomi Manako (J)**	3	**Honda**	19	**42m 13.836s**
3	**Valentino Rossi (I)**	46	**Aprilia**	19	**42m 13.994s**
4	**Roberto Locatelli (I)**	15	**Honda**	19	**42m 14.442s**
5	**Lucio Cecchinello (I)**	10	**Honda**	19	**42m 14.529s**
6	**Gianluigi Scalvini (I)**	21	**Honda**	19	**42m 14.626s**
7	**Steve Jenkner (D)**	22	**Aprilia**	19	**42m 14.720s**
8	**Masaki Tokudome (J)**	2	**Aprilia**	19	**42m 14.828s**
9	**Kazuto Sakata (J)**	8	**Aprilia**	19	**42m 17.108s**
10	**Youichi Ui (J)**	41	**Yamaha**	19	**42m 19.728s**
11	**Garry McCoy (AUS)**	72	**Aprilia**	19	**42m 25.245s**
12	**Mirko Giansanti (I)**	32	**Honda**	19	**42m 25.422s**
13	**Manfred Geissler (D)**	33	**Aprilia**	19	**42m 25.551s**
14	**Jaroslav Hules (CS)**	39	**Honda**	19	**42m 26.467s**
15	**Frédéric Petit (F)**	19	**Honda**	19	**42m 26.955s**
16	Juan Enrique Maturana (E)	17	Yamaha	19	42m 43.190s
17	Marco Melandri (I)	13	Honda	19	42m 43.288s
18	Josep Sarda (E)	25	Honda	19	42m 48.987s
19	Dirk Raudies (D)	12	Honda	19	43m 17.983s
20	Emanuel Buchner (D)	86	Aprilia	19	43m 18.183s
21	Igor Kalab (CS)	35	Honda	19	43m 57.995s
	Jorge Martinez (E)	5	Aprilia	13	DNF
	Gino Borsoi (I)	24	Yamaha	10	DNF
	Masao Azuma (J)	20	Honda	9	DNF
	Angel Nieto Jnr (E)	29	Aprilia	8	DNF
	Yoshiaki Katoh (J)	62	Yamaha	4	DNF
	Michal Brezina (CS)	34	Honda	4	DNF
	Chris Burns (GB)	98	Honda	3	DNF
	Ivan Goi (I)	26	Aprilia	2	DNF

Fastest lap: Ueda, 2m 11.669s, 91.791 mph/147.724 km/h.

Lap record: Kazuto Sakata, J (Aprilia), 2m 11.305s, 91.893 mph/147.888 km/h (1995).

Qualifying: **1** Ui, 2m 25.891s; **2** Tokudome, 2m 27.619s; **3** Rossi, 2m 27.842s; **4** Sarda, 2m 28.020s; **5** Sakata, 2m 28.309s; **6** Katoh, 2m 28.496s; **7** Scalvini, 2m 28.637s; **8** Maturana, 2m 29.651s; **9** Borsoi, 2m 29.867s; **10** Hules, 2m 30.115s; **11** Petit, 2m 30.230s; **12** Cecchinello, 2m 30.300s; **13** Ueda, 2m 30.356s; **14** Manako, 2m 30.466s; **15** Geissler, 2m 30.497s; **16** Nieto Jnr, 2m 30.530s; **17** Martinez, 2m 30.631s; **18** Locatelli, 2m 30.717s; **19** Jenkner, 2m 31.109s; **20** Buchner, 2m 31.305s; **21** Melandri, 2m 32.267s; **22** Giansanti, 2m 32.931s; **23** McCoy, 2m 33.380s; **24** Raudies, 2m 33.457s; **25** Burns, 2m 33.652s; **26** Goi, 2m 36.075s; **27** Azuma, 2m 36.243s; **28** Brezina, 2m 36.812s; **29** Kalab, 2m 40.112s.

Fastest race laps: **1** Ueda, 2m 11.669s; **2** Tokudome, 2m 11.809s; **3** Manako, 2m 11.991s; **4** Locatelli, 2m 12.075s; **5** Rossi, 2m 12.079s; **6** Sakata, 2m 12.101s; **7** Jenkner, 2m 12.131s; **8** Ui, 2m 12.269s; **9** Cecchinello, 2m 12.400s; **10** McCoy, 2m 12.454s; **11** Giansanti, 2m 12.500s; **12** Martinez, 2m 12.525s; **13** Scalvini, 2m 12.587s; **14** Hules, 2m 12.669s; **15** Geissler, 2m 12.885s; **16** Petit, 2m 13.101s; **17** Melandri, 2m 13.409s; **18** Nieto Jnr, 2m 13.793s; **19** Maturana, 2m 13.857s; **20** Azuma, 2m 13.998s; **21** Sarda, 2m 14.102s; **22** Katoh, 2m 14.343s; **23** Borsoi, 2m 15.454s; **24** Buchner, 2m 15.702s; **25** Raudies, 2m 15.741s; **26** Burns, 2m 16.290s; **27** Kalab, 2m 17.767s; **28** Brezina, 2m 22.143s; **29** Goi, 2m 24.605s.

World Championship: **1** Rossi, 261; **2** Ueda, 184; **3** Manako, 152; **4** Sakata, 119; **5** Tokudome, 97; **6** Martinez, 96; **7** McCoy, 88; **8** Petit, 75; **9** Katoh, Locatelli and Ui, 69; **12** Giansanti, 64; **13** Azuma, 57; **14** Scalvini, 53; **15** Cecchinello, 51; **16** Geissler, 30; **17** Goi, 21; **18** Hules, Jenkner and Maturana, 17; **21** Nakajo, 16; **22** Borsoi, 15; **23** Öttl, 11; **24** Nieto Jnr, Raudies and Takao, 8; **27** Sarda, 3; **28** Barton and Hofmann, 2; **30** Jerzenbeck, 1.

CATALUNYAN

grand prix

Catalunya's sinuous corners showed the 250s off to advantage. Early in the race, Waldmann heads Jacque, Ukawa, Biaggi, Harada, Capirossi and Tsujimura.

Right: The full range of Spanish pit-lane popsies sometimes asked a lot of the eyes of the beholders.

Photos: Gold & Goose

500 cc	**DOOHAN**
250 cc	**WALDMANN**
125 cc	**ROSSI**

T HE finish of the European season had no air of finality in the one class left with a championship still to decide. The trio in the running for the title reshuffled their running order once again, and closed up to a spread of only nine points from new leader Waldmann to menacing third-placed man Biaggi. This result came after what was without question the ride of the German contender's life.

Ralf, with 11 years of 125 and 250 racing, has the most experience of the three, but the least success. For this and other reasons some don't take him too seriously, even now, after a year in which he had shown a fine and still-improving skill. He seems to foster this attitude with his own conspicuous lack of gravitas. Ralf likes to laugh and joke, and along with a pretty good record of 16 GP wins so far has been known to do silly things. A personal piece of history shows an adventurous spirit – in 1995 he became the first rider in 30 years to fall off, remount and then win a race – the last being Mike Hailwood at the Isle of Man. His cavalier approach makes errors under pressure a bit easier to forgive.

Not so much this time, however. He had qualified on pole and taken off in a strong lead of better than a second after three laps. Then he ran off the track once again. In his usual style he fought to stay on board, and bumped back on to regain the ribbon down in ninth place. Given the close and competitive running so far this year, it should have been all over: Waldie looked far out of the reckoning. Even in the unlikely event that he could catch up again, his tyres would surely be ruined in the effort.

But this was Ralf's day for breaking all the rules, and the progress of his dayglo Honda was marvellous to watch. He took it all the way to the front again, and then on the final lap escaped a final threat from Biaggi when the Italian made a little slip. It was a performance of the greatest bravura, fittingly rewarded with a small but distinct World Championship lead.

All coinciding, it seemed to close observers, with the development of a new depth of relationship between the two Honda riders. For most of this season the 250 class has been boiling with mutual antipathy: deadly rivals on the track, deadly enemies off it. There was genuine hatred involved. Now a sort of joshing comradeship was to be observed between Ralf and Max, at least during their joint public appearances, showing a growing underlying affection instead.

The title settled, the 500 class had moved on to notions of the near future, leaving change and decay for the rest of the year. This took many forms.

There was the disintegration of the now annual 'Mick Doohan to Yamaha' scenario, reckoned to be highly desirable by all concerned. This year's offer had come from Wayne Rainey, as two years before, and Wayne and the Yamaha factory between them had met every one of Mick's requests. They awaited only his agreement, but there was a deadline. This had passed on the night of the Czech GP. The offer was, insisted Rainey, now closed; and indeed he seemed to mean it, as he pushed straight ahead with 'Plan B' – reaching agreement at Catalunya with disaffected Team Roberts rider Jean-Michel Bayle to head the 1998 factory Yamaha team.

In public, at least, Doohan refused to take this seriously, insisting the offer was still open and, if it was not, then Yamaha were at fault: 'I wanted to give Honda a chance to respond, as a matter of courtesy, and I thought Yamaha might be prepared to wait a week or so. Wayne was once a rider and he never left Yamaha. He talked many times with other people but had the courtesy to always see what Yamaha had available. And, correct me if I'm wrong, but he's still with Yamaha. Now I wonder just how determined they were about wanting me, and wanting to win the World Championship.'

There was distinct decay at the level of sponsorship. Nobody admitted it openly here, but Lucky Strike were waiting until the day after the race to announce their withdrawal from GPs after 12 years of top-level backing. Disturbing leaks issued also from Marlboro's little paddock mini-suburb of double-decker buses, teeming for the occasion with top brass...that they planned to furl their international sponsorship umbrella, and that future sponsoring would be done by individual regions.

Deconstruction of another kind prevailed in one segment of home sponsor Repsol's vast Honda pit. Tests at Brno after the last race had left Okada impressed with Doohan's so far exclusive 180-degree 'Screamer' engine, upon which he had improved his lap times. Now he was having a go at it for this race. This prompted a cackle of laughter from Doohan, who broke cover with a fresh disclosure, that his switch to this motor had to a large extent been a great red herring, his purpose as much to bamboozle his own team-mates as to find any advantage. Criville had tested it once and 'been smart enough to stick with the Big Bang...though he came back and tested it again'. There's more to it all, of course, but it threw an unkind light on Okada's subsequent struggles in the race.

Finally, this was where the Gobert scandal became public. He'd been informed of his sacking the previous Friday, and had promptly broken his leg that evening, according to unconfirmed reports. The row was on at home in Australia, where his manager/mother had issued an angry statement denying any involvement in drugs and falsely accusing the Suzuki team of telling the world's press before telling the victim himself. Meanwhile IRTA chief executive Paul Butler was talking about formalising a list of banned substances, to be put in the rule book; and Troy Corser was (rather unaccountably) declining an offer to take over Gobert's bike for the last three races. Instead, Peter Goddard flew in, but would not actually ride until the next round in Indonesia. He had a World Endurance title to win first.

Criville and Okada share a joke. The laugh was on Tady, and it really was a Screamer.

Cadalora *(left)* missed the rostrum by just over a second: he was making the Yamaha look better more and more often now.

Right: To repeat his win last year, Checa had to beat not only Doohan but also his own tendency to push too hard. He stayed on board and accepted second – enough to leave him and his home crowd delighted all the same.

Bottom: Criville was back on the podium after a spirited battle with Cadalora on the last lap.

500 cc RACE – 25 LAPS

Doohan's tenth pole in a row broke Spencer's record, but he was only just over one-tenth ahead of last year's winner Checa, with Nobu Aoki and Romboni right alongside. Okada led row two on the Screamer from Cadalora's Yamaha, Criville and Roberts's Modenas – his best yet so far this year, after major chassis setting modifications at Brno tests.

Race day was cooler than practice, however, forcing a last-minute reassessment of tyre choices. This conspired to make the race closer than ever.

Nobu Aoki's blue Honda was first out of the traps, but by the end of the lap Okada was in front, while Criville, Cadalora and Mick lined up behind him. A little way back, Checa was on his way past fast-starting Abe to close up by the time Criville moved into the lead on lap four, Doohan close behind.

Now the game began. Doohan moved past at the end of the straight to take control on lap seven. But Checa was coming, and next time round he and Criville were ahead of Mick. Aoki was still with them, Cadalora closing up from behind. A five-bike battle for the lead was something the 500 class hadn't seen for a while.

Doohan was biding his time, waiting for Criville to tire, and after 11 laps he saw his chance, through the fast climbing rights early in the lap. But Checa followed him through, and

then also took a turn up front. Criville only followed from then on; Checa and Doohan carried on fighting, changing places several times. It was not clear how much Mick had in reserve – it was obvious that he could easily pass Checa down the straight, but he couldn't get away. And the others stayed close, too, Cadalora moving into fourth on lap 18.

Mick started his big run on the penultimate lap, breaking the lap record. Even so, a little moment as his foot slipped off the footrest helped Checa stay close. He was still less than half a second adrift at the flag; Criville, Cadalora and Aoki were close behind. 'Alex and I ran almost the whole of the last lap sideways with smoke coming off the tyre. It was a lot of fun,' said Luca.

A little way back, Tak Aoki had caught and passed Okada, who was having all sorts of trouble with wheelspin. Tady showed some spirit in fighting back ahead in the closing stages.

Another good scrap a little way behind saw Roberts Junior at last enjoying the revised handling of his Modenas, to keep Borja's Elf 500 narrowly at bay. Barros had been with them until he fell with seven laps left.

Nor was this all. Only four seconds behind came Romboni, suffering from a fever but enthusiastically battling for tenth place with Laconi's V-twin Honda and Abe's Yamaha in a fight to the finish.

McCarthy's 13th was equally hard fought, under constant pressure from van den Goorbergh. Both passed the dispirited Suzuki rider Beattie, who eventually lost all hope of scoring points when Puig discovered a spurt of aggression, passing Fuchs as well to take the last point.

Bayle retired from a top-ten position with crankshaft problems; the luckless Gibernau did not finish even half a lap of his home GP, knocked off in the first-corner scramble.

250 cc RACE – 23 LAPS

Waldmann really seemed to have screwed his chances. He had a nice lead of more than a second at the end of lap three. Then he left his braking too late, and was forced to pick up the bike and run off across the gravel. Amazingly he didn't fall, but by the time he rejoined eight riders had flashed past and he was well over eight seconds adrift – a big gap in this company.

For a while interest remained on the leading pack – Harada making most of the running from Biaggi, Ukawa and Capirossi, who would fade away once again. But it was soon obvious that the real hero of this race was going to be Ralf Waldmann.

Slashing away at the record, he was right with the leaders by the tenth lap, and imposing a new discipline as he pressed them hard. Biaggi responded best, and soon the two Hondas were

heading the pack. Harada managed one more attack, using his Aprilia's tremendous speed advantage to drive ahead briefly at the start of the 19th lap. But Max and Ralf moved away again.

The last lap saw a titanic confrontation. Ralf passed into the first corner, Max got him back into the fourth turn. Waldmann repassed him at the downhill hairpin, Max lined him up for a run out of the exit. Then, suddenly, he slowed, glancing over his shoulder as he did so. Ralf was free to go for the win of his life. It turned out to be nothing more than a muffed gearchange. 'I changed from first to second, but found neutral instead,' explained Max later.

The battle for third was rather more dour. Harada belted past Ukawa under power on the front straight on the final lap, but the Honda man managed to get back in front because of his better road-holding, albeit only by inches. 'My engine was fantastically fast, but whenever I opened the throttle in the corners I would lose traction and run wide,' said Harada later.

Capirossi was a lonely fifth, Jacque sixth – he had led off the line and for the first lap because he had chosen a soft tyre – but the choice went sour on him and he dropped away. Tsujimura was a strong seventh, comfortably clear of Aoki's works Honda. A little way back, Numata prevailed over Miyazaki's Yamaha, McWilliams's production Honda and Alzamora's works bike, all in a tight group.

125 cc RACE – 22 LAPS

Locatelli was a convincing runaway starter, but by the end of the first lap Sakata had caught and passed him, and put his head down to pull steadily away. By the end of lap seven he was more than four seconds clear.

Rossi was now in second, and he started to close the gap. It was by no means certain he could catch up, but his tenth win of the year was decided on the 16th lap, when Sakata slowed with engine problems. After that, the Italian pulled away at will to win by six seconds.

Ui had crashed out of the pursuit pack early on. In the closing stages, Ueda moved ahead of the gang to claim third, strengthening his claim on second overall. Only Manako could now catch him, and he was fifth here in Spain, just pipped by Honda-mounted Giansanti. Cecchinello and Locatelli were on his back wheel. Scalvini had dropped out of this group to lead the next pack across the line, less than a tenth ahead of McCoy, Petit, Tokudome and Martinez.

FIM WORLD CHAMPIONSHIP • ROUND 13

MARLBORO CATALUNYAN GRAND PRIX

14 SEPTEMBER 1997

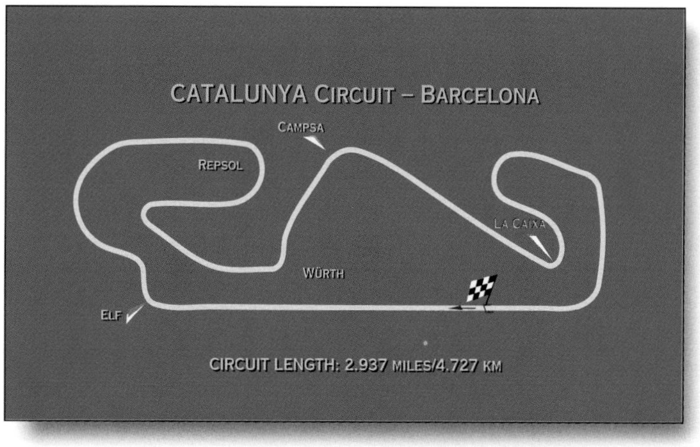
CATALUNYA CIRCUIT – BARCELONA
CAMPSA
REPSOL
LA CAIXA
WÜRTH
ELF
CIRCUIT LENGTH: 2.937 MILES/4.727 KM

500 cc

25 laps, 73.425 miles/118.175 km

Pos.	Rider (Nat.)	No.	Machine	Laps	Time & speed
1	**Michael Doohan (AUS)**	**1**	**Honda**	**25**	**44m 56.149s 98.047 mph/ 157.791 km/h**
2	**Carlos Checa (E)**	**8**	**Honda**	**25**	**44m 56.581s**
3	**Alex Criville (E)**	**2**	**Honda**	**25**	**44m 57.899s**
4	**Luca Cadalora (I)**	**3**	**Yamaha**	**25**	**44m 58.941s**
5	**Nobuatsu Aoki (J)**	**18**	**Honda**	**25**	**45m 04.308s**
6	**Tadayuki Okada (J)**	**7**	**Honda**	**25**	**45m 20.780s**
7	**Takuma Aoki (J)**	**24**	**Honda**	**25**	**45m 20.975s**
8	**Kenny Roberts Jnr (USA)**	**10**	**Modenas**	**25**	**45m 37.518s**
9	**Juan Borja (E)**	**14**	**Elf 500**	**25**	**45m 37.954s**
10	**Doriano Romboni (I)**	**19**	**Aprilia**	**25**	**45m 41.640s**
11	**Regis Laconi (F)**	**55**	**Honda**	**25**	**45m 42.587s**
12	**Norifumi Abe (J)**	**5**	**Yamaha**	**25**	**45m 43.677s**
13	**Kirk McCarthy (AUS)**	**22**	**Yamaha**	**25**	**45m 51.591s**
14	**Jurgen v.d. Goorbergh (NL)**	**21**	**Honda**	**25**	**45m 53.644s**
15	**Alberto Puig (E)**	**9**	**Honda**	**25**	**45m 57.959s**
16	Jurgen Fuchs (D)	16	Elf 500	25	45m 58.440s
17	Daryl Beattie (AUS)	6	Suzuki	25	45m 59.679s
18	Lucio Pedercini (I)	17	Yamaha	25	46m 42.515s
19	Laurent Naveau (B)	25	Yamaha	24	45m 13.761s
	Jean-Michel Bayle (F)	12	Modenas	19	DNF
	Alex Barros (BR)	4	Honda	18	DNF
	Frédéric Protat (F)	15	Honda	9	DNF
	Sete Gibernau (E)	20	Yamaha	0	DNF

Fastest lap: Doohan, 1m 46.861s, 98.951 mph/159.246 km/h (record).

Previous record: Carlos Checa, E (Honda), 1m 47.183s, 98.654 mph/158.768 km/h (1996).

Qualifying: **1** Doohan, 1m 45.990s; **2** Checa, 1m 46.126s; **3** N. Aoki, 1m 46.143s; **4** Romboni, 1m 46.297s; **5** Okada, 1m 46.507s; **6** Cadalora, 1m 46.511s; **7** Criville, 1m 46.693s; **8** Roberts Jnr, 1m 46.959s; **9** T. Aoki, 1m 47.124s; **10** Bayle, 1m 47.206s; **11** Barros, 1m 47.279s; **12** Borja, 1m 47.521s; **13** van den Goorbergh, 1m 47.651s; **14** Gibernau, 1m 47.734s; **15** Abe, 1m 48.043s; **16** Beattie, 1m 48.323s; **17** Laconi, 1m 48.401s; **18** Fuchs, 1m 48.411s; **19** Puig, 1m 48.616s; **20** Pedercini, 1m 48.966s; **21** McCarthy, 1m 49.050s; **22** Naveau, 1m 50.859s; **23** Protat, 1m 51.269s.

Fastest race laps: **1** Doohan, 1m 46.861s; **2** Checa, 1m 46.969s; **3** Criville, 1m 47.123s; **4** N. Aoki, 1m 47.243s; **5** Cadalora, 1m 47.253s; **6** Okada, 1m 47.729s; **7** T. Aoki, 1m 47.836s; **8** Borja, 1m 48.071s; **9** Roberts Jnr, 1m 48.148s; **10** Barros, 1m 48.400s; **11** Romboni, 1m 48.528s; **12** Laconi, 1m 48.921s; **13** Bayle, 1m 48.979s; **14** Abe, 1m 48.992s; **15** Fuchs, 1m 49.077s; **16** van den Goorbergh, 1m 49.160s; **17** McCarthy, 1m 49.211s; **18** Beattie, 1m 49.275s; **19** Puig, 1m 49.529s; **20** Pedercini, 1m 49.788s; **21** Naveau, 1m 51.555s; **22** Protat, 1m 51.880s.

World Championship: **1** Doohan, 320; **2** N. Aoki, 166; **3** Okada, 159; **4** Criville, 131; **5** Cadalora, 129; **6** T. Aoki, 105; **7** Checa, 103; **8** Abe, 99; **9** Barros, 93; **10** Romboni, 77; **11** Puig, 60; **12** Beattie, 59; **13** Gobert, 44; **14** Laconi, 41; **15** Gibernau, 38; **16** Borja, 37; **17** Bayle, 31; **18** Roberts Jnr, 28; **19** van den Goorbergh, 25; **20** Fuchs, 23; **21** McCarthy, 16; **22** Corser, 11; **23** Fujiwara and Garcia, 7; **25** Goddard and Naveau, 3; **27** Pedercini and Vincent, 2.

Takuma Aoki had yet another track to learn, but his close relationship with his factory V-twin made the task that much easier for another top-ten finish.

Gold & Goose

250 cc

23 laps, 67.551 miles/108.721 km

Pos.	Rider (Nat.)	No.	Machine	Laps	Time & speed
1	**Ralf Waldmann (D)**	**2**	**Honda**	**23**	**42m 05.928s 96.282 mph/ 154.951 km/h**
2	**Max Biaggi (I)**	**1**	**Honda**	**23**	**42m 06.478s**
3	**Tohru Ukawa (J)**	**5**	**Honda**	**23**	**42m 08.868s**
4	**Tetsuya Harada (J)**	**31**	**Aprilia**	**23**	**42m 08.888s**
5	**Loris Capirossi (I)**	**65**	**Aprilia**	**23**	**42m 19.688s**
6	**Olivier Jacque (F)**	**19**	**Honda**	**23**	**42m 30.093s**
7	**Takeshi Tsujimura (J)**	**12**	**Honda**	**23**	**42m 33.321s**
8	**Haruchika Aoki (J)**	**7**	**Honda**	**23**	**42m 50.326s**
9	**Noriyasu Numata (J)**	**20**	**Suzuki**	**23**	**42m 54.968s**
10	**Osamu Miyazaki (J)**	**18**	**Yamaha**	**23**	**42m 55.045s**
11	**Jeremy McWilliams (GB)**	**11**	**Honda**	**23**	**42m 55.470s**
12	**Emilio Alzamora (E)**	**26**	**Honda**	**23**	**42m 55.955s**
13	**Luis D'Antin (E)**	**6**	**Yamaha**	**23**	**43m 01.096s**
14	**José Luis Cardoso (E)**	**17**	**Yamaha**	**23**	**43m 01.194s**
15	**Franco Battaini (I)**	**21**	**Yamaha**	**23**	**43m 01.485s**
16	Cristiano Migliorati (I)	8	Honda	23	43m 02.141s
17	Luca Boscoscuro (I)	10	Honda	23	43m 21.335s
18	Sebastian Porto (ARG)	27	Aprilia	23	43m 27.320s
19	Kurtis Roberts (USA)	22	Honda	23	43m 41.300s
20	Ismael Bonilla (E)	50	Honda	22	42m 28.896s
	William Costes (F)	16	Honda	17	DNF
	Giuseppe Fiorillo (I)	99	Aprilia	13	DNF
	Stefano Perugini (I)	15	Aprilia	12	DNF
	Javier Marsella (E)	47	Honda	11	DNF
	Eustaquio Gavira (E)	28	Aprilia	9	DNF
	José de Gea (E)	48	Yamaha	7	DNF
	Jesus Perez (E)	51	Honda	7	DNF
	Manuel Luque (E)	43	Aprilia	3	DNF
	Oliver Petrucciani (CH)	25	Aprilia	2	DNF
	Jamie Robinson (GB)	14	Suzuki	1	DNF
	David Guardiola (E)	44	Honda	0	DNF

Fastest lap: Waldmann, 1m 48.681s, 97.294 mph/156.579 km/h.

Lap record: Max Biaggi, I (Aprilia), 1m 48.490s, 97.465 mph/156.855 km/h (1996).

Qualifying: **1** Waldmann, 1m 47.621s; **2** Biaggi, 1m 47.690s; **3** Ukawa, 1m 48.192s; **4** Harada, 1m 48.632s; **5** Capirossi, 1m 48.676s; **6** Perugini, 1m 49.129s; **7** Jacque, 1m 49.326s; **8** Tsujimura, 1m 49.384s; **9** McWilliams, 1m 49.437s; **10** Aoki, 1m 49.734s; **11** Numata, 1m 49.958s; **12** Miyazaki, 1m 50.269s; **13** Robinson, 1m 50.294s; **14** Costes, 1m 50.345s; **15** Migliorati, 1m 50.395s; **16** Battaini, 1m 50.430s; **17** Fiorillo, 1m 50.622s; **18** Alzamora, 1m 50.655s; **19** Petrucciani, 1m 50.694s; **20** D'Antin, 1m 50.789s; **21** Cardoso, 1m 50.862s; **22** Boscoscuro, 1m 51.184s; **23** Porto, 1m 51.924s; **24** Roberts, 1m 52.034s; **25** E. Gavira, 1m 52.424s; **26** Luque, 1m 52.973s; **27** de Gea, 1m 53.184s; **28** Marsella, 1m 53.268s; **29** Perez, 1m 53.717s; **30** Bonilla, 1m 54.701s; **31** Guardiola, 1m 55.316s.

Fastest race laps: **1** Waldmann, 1m 48.681s; **2** Biaggi, 1m 48.829s; **3** Harada, 1m 49.011s; **4** Ukawa, 1m 49.057s; **5** Capirossi, 1m 49.375s; **6** Jacque, 1m 49.440s; **7** Aoki, 1m 50.304s; **8** Tsujimura, 1m 50.535s; **9** McWilliams, 1m 50.943s; **10** Perugini, 1m 51.025s; **11** Cardoso, 1m 51.134s; **12** Numata, 1m 51.153s; **13** Migliorati, 1m 51.208s; **14** Alzamora, 1m 51.221s; **15** D'Antin, 1m 51.239s; **16** Miyazaki, 1m 51.260s; **17** Battaini, 1m 51.332s; **18** Costes, 1m 51.372s; **19** Fiorillo, 1m 51.547s; **20** Porto, 1m 51.888s; **21** Boscoscuro, 1m 51.998s; **22** E. Gavira, 1m 52.779s; **23** Petrucciani, 1m 53.496s; **24** Luque, 1m 53.526s; **25** Roberts, 1m 53.689s; **26** Marsella, 1m 53.900s; **27** de Gea, 1m 54.054s; **28** Bonilla, 1m 54.162s; **29** Perez, 1m 54.360s; **30** Robinson, 1m 57.928s.

World Championship: **1** Waldmann, 214; **2** Harada, 211; **3** Biaggi, 205; **4** Jacque, 169; **5** Ukawa, 145; **6** Capirossi, 114; **7** Aoki, 90; **8** Tsujimura, 85; **9** Perugini, 68; **10** McWilliams, 61; **11** Numata, 55; **12** Porto, 46; **13** Miyazaki, 39; **14** Battaini, 36; **15** D'Antin, 32; **16** Alzamora, 31; **17** Lucchi, 30; **18** Migliorati, 27; **19** Kato, 25; **20** Costes, 23; **21** Cardoso, 19; **22** Robinson, 18; **23** Petrucciani, 14; **24** Fiorillo, 12; **25** Boscoscuro, 11; **26** Kagayama, 10; **27** Matsudo, 6; **28** E. Gavira, 5; **29** Smart, 4; **30** Gimbert and Ogura, 3; **32** Bolwerk, I. Gavira and McGuiness, 2; **35** Kameya, Ramsay and Vanzetta, 1.

125 cc

22 laps, 64.614 miles/103.994 km

Pos.	Rider (Nat.)	No.	Machine	Laps	Time & speed
1	**Valentino Rossi (I)**	**46**	**Aprilia**	**22**	**42m 14.687s 91.778 mph/ 147.702 km/h**
2	**Kazuto Sakata (J)**	**8**	**Aprilia**	**22**	**42m 20.689s**
3	**Noboru Ueda (J)**	**7**	**Honda**	**22**	**42m 24.214s**
4	**Mirko Giansanti (I)**	**32**	**Honda**	**22**	**42m 25.872s**
5	**Tomomi Manako (J)**	**3**	**Honda**	**22**	**42m 25.883s**
6	**Lucio Cecchinello (I)**	**10**	**Honda**	**22**	**42m 25.956s**
7	**Roberto Locatelli (I)**	**15**	**Honda**	**22**	**42m 26.041s**
8	**Gianluigi Scalvini (I)**	**21**	**Honda**	**22**	**42m 33.013s**
9	**Garry McCoy (AUS)**	**72**	**Aprilia**	**22**	**42m 33.053s**
10	**Frédéric Petit (F)**	**19**	**Honda**	**22**	**42m 33.242s**
11	**Masaki Tokudome (J)**	**2**	**Aprilia**	**22**	**42m 33.290s**
12	**Jorge Martinez (E)**	**5**	**Aprilia**	**22**	**42m 33.474s**
13	**Yoshiaki Katoh (J)**	**62**	**Yamaha**	**22**	**42m 44.790s**
14	**Steve Jenkner (D)**	**22**	**Aprilia**	**22**	**43m 13.504s**
15	**Alvaro Molina (E)**	**52**	**Honda**	**22**	**43m 28.389s**
16	Gino Borsoi (I)	24	Yamaha	22	43m 28.472s
17	Dirk Raudies (D)	12	Honda	22	43m 32.888s
18	Youichi Ui (J)	41	Yamaha	22	43m 49.006s
19	Joan Montero (E)	44	Honda	22	43m 53.427s
20	Vicente Esparragoso (E)	51	Yamaha	21	42m 45.667s
21	David Ortega (E)	42	Honda	21	43m 11.380s
	Ivan Martinez (E)	45	Aprilia	5	DNF
	Angel Nieto Jnr (E)	29	Aprilia	4	DNF
	Juan Enrique Maturana (E)	17	Yamaha	3	DNF
	Jaroslav Hules (CS)	39	Honda	3	DNF
	Xavier Soler (E)	43	Aprilia	2	DNF
	Chris Burns (GB)	98	Honda	2	DNF
	Masao Azuma (J)	20	Honda	2	DNF
	Josep Sarda (E)	25	Honda		DNS
	Manfred Geissler (D)	33	Aprilia		DNS

Fastest lap: Sakata, 1m 53.773s, 92.939 mph/149.571 km/h (record).

Previous record: Tomomi Manako, J (Honda), 1m 54.307s, 92.505 mph/148.873 km/h (1996).

Qualifying: **1** Sakata, 1m 53.476s; **2** Ui, 1m 53.941s; **3** Manako, 1m 54.004s; **4** Rossi, 1m 54.091s; **5** J. Martinez, 1m 54.126s; **6** Locatelli, 1m 54.321s; **7** Tokudome, 1m 54.346s; **8** Cecchinello, 1m 54.458s; **9** Geissler, 1m 54.465s; **10** Ueda, 1m 54.510s; **11** Giansanti, 1m 54.545s; **12** Maturana, 1m 54.622s; **13** Petit, 1m 54.829s; **14** McCoy, 1m 54.920s; **15** Scalvini, 1m 55.025s; **16** Azuma, 1m 55.071s; **17** Katoh, 1m 55.210s; **18** Hules, 1m 55.397s; **19** Jenkner, 1m 55.679s; **20** Sarda, 1m 55.725s; **21** Nieto Jnr, 1m 56.113s; **22** Borsoi, 1m 56.352s; **23** Molina, 1m 56.353s; **24** Soler, 1m 57.805s; **25** I. Martinez, 1m 57.837s; **26** Esparragoso, 1m 57.873s; **27** Raudies, 1m 57.983s; **28** Montero, 1m 58.327s; **29** Burns, 1m 58.363s; **30** Ortega, 2m 00.058s.

Fastest race laps: **1** Sakata, 1m 53.773s; **2** Rossi, 1m 53.969s; **3** Scalvini, 1m 54.449s; **4** Manako, 1m 54.521s; **5** Ueda, 1m 54.560s; **6** Giansanti, 1m 54.714s; **7** Cecchinello, 1m 54.927s; **8** Locatelli, 1m 54.945s; **9** J. Martinez, 1m 54.963s; **10** Tokudome, 1m 55.020s; **11** McCoy, 1m 55.028s; **12** Katoh, 1m 55.188s; **13** Petit, 1m 55.240s; **14** Ui, 1m 56.011s; **15** Maturana, 1m 56.317s; **16** Jenkner, 1m 56.541s; **17** Molina, 1m 57.129s; **18** Borsoi, 1m 57.193s; **19** Hules, 1m 57.435s; **20** Nieto Jnr, 1m 57.603s; **21** Montero, 1m 57.650s; **22** Raudies, 1m 57.982s; **23** Esparragoso, 1m 59.020s; **24** Ortega, 2m 00.347s; **25** Azuma, 2m 02.179s; **26** Soler, 2m 05.988s; **27** I. Martinez, 2m 07.764s; **28** Burns, 2m 08.753s.

World Championship: **1** Rossi, 286; **2** Ueda, 200; **3** Manako, 163; **4** Sakata, 139; **5** Tokudome, 102; **6** Martinez, 100; **7** McCoy, 95; **8** Petit, 81; **9** Locatelli, 78; **10** Giansanti, 77; **11** Katoh, 72; **12** Ui, 69; **13** Cecchinello and Scalvini, 61; **15** Azuma, 57; **16** Geissler, 30; **17** Goi, 21; **18** Jenkner, 19; **19** Hules and Maturana, 17; **21** Nakajo, 16; **22** Borsoi, 15; **23** Öttl, 11; **24** Nieto Jnr, Raudies and Takao, 8; **27** Sarda, 3; **28** Barton and Hofmann, 2; **30** Jerzenbeck and Molina, 1.

INDONESIAN

grand prix

THE spell was broken in Sentul – but it was a prosaic and inauspicious setting for such a momentous event.

With 11 million registered motor cycles, Indonesia has the world's third-largest motor cycling population, beaten only by China and India. This is of obvious importance to the great Japanese factories, represented here by their works teams, but the motor cycling in question is a dour and utilitarian, step-thru affair, very different from what we know in the west. The recreation of racing them touches only the tiniest proportion of their users.

The second Indonesian GP was therefore rather remote from the daily life of the smoking sprawl of Jakarta, between 30 minutes and two hours from Sentul, depending on the traffic.

A great deal of that smoke comes from the 11 million motorbikes, but useful winds gave much clearer skies over Sentul than last year, also ameliorating the sweaty heat. There was good luck in that the winds were from the south, because not much more than 100 miles away were the outriggers of the scandalous fires that were not only devastating rainforest flora and fauna but also producing enough smoke to close international airports, to threaten life over a wide area, and to be blamed for at least two shipping disasters and one air crash that occurred during GP weekend alone. And we didn't get a whiff of it.

Forest fires notwithstanding, the event had a cloud of its own. Only four weeks before the race an emergency delegation comprising road-race commission boss Claude Danis and riders' representative Franco Uncini had flown out to inspect the surface, after reports that the newly laid tarmac was soggy and already starting to break up. They'd passed it fit to race, but upon arrival it still seemed too soft. In fact, though very dirty, it proved faster than last year as practice wore on, and held together mercifully well. It remained highly suspect throughout the weekend, all the same. Nothing could be done about the over-simple layout – 'drag strips with chicanes', as one rider said. With one clean line and little room for technical riding, Sentul is not much of a challenge.

The race was again attended by Premier Sukarto, and by a fair-sized crowd – though surely not as big as the 80,000 claimed. They witnessed the first straight defeat all year of the apparently unbeatable Mick Doohan. His conqueror was Okada, who led for a good chunk in the middle part of the race, then attacked with great determination, crucially passing Doohan three times in the last two laps, while Mick passed him back only twice. The victorious move was at the last corner.

Since observers were shocked and surprised at this outcome, perhaps it's understandable that Doohan was as well. His immediate response was a vulgar and derisory gesture to Okada as they slowed down after crossing the line. The flapping of his left wrist was not a blatant show for the crowds, but a private and personal message, and if the TV cameras hadn't caught him in the act it might have remained so. In the event, however, this action, and Mick's stony glares after the race, seemed somewhat unsportsmanlike, provoking debates in his absence that came to the obvious conclusion. Mick's not a good loser, and that's what makes him such a great winner.

Okada had thankfully switched back to the Big Bang for this race, and his manner of winning his first 500 GP hardly fitted Doohan's complaints that 'he copied every move I made'. In his first 500 season Tady had been quick and spirited throughout, and after a number of get-offs was becoming a fast-maturing serious threat. Not quite up to Doohan yet, but showing an aggressive streak that set him apart from Criville, his victory was widely applauded.

Above: The sponsors' gifts of free baseball caps did not extend to include spectators who'd burrowed under the wire.

Below: Okada's final lunge at last yielded a long-awaited win, and left the thwarted Doohan fuming. For Tady *(opposite page)* his team-mate's ire did not entirely take away the joy of winning.

The dramatic crescendo of the 250s orchestrated terrible things for Waldmann, wonderful things for Biaggi. Harada also hit a blip. Of all his peers, Max was now showing the greatest depth. To add to his psychological advantage, he also regained a crucial points lead.

Behind the scenes, the foment of contracts was occupying much attention. Doohan was still floating, and now rumours began of shifts by Honda (including sending Okada to the satellite Pons MoviStar team) to make room for soon-to-be World Superbike Champion John Kocinski. Cadalora was also on the loose. And at Suzuki the axe finally fell for Beattie, who had almost upon arrival heard that his contract would not be renewed. Since he'd effectively resigned in public in a mid-season interview, this was no surprise. Meanwhile Goddard had flown in to jump on the second bike. As at the Japanese GP at the other end of the year, the Australian veteran was red-rimmed and stary-eyed after a 24-hour race the previous weekend – at the Bol d'Or, where he'd secured the championship with partner Doug Polen.

Regional vagaries persisted as usual. On Friday, for example, everybody turned out almost an hour early to allow for a midday break for prayers. Everybody, that is, except some of the ambulance drivers, and in the end practice eventually got under way rather later than usual. Prayers had to be said on the move. Another problem involved Dunlop, whose fitting machines were held up by customs. Michelin lent a hand until they did arrive, shortly after practice began. 'We've done the same for them – we don't compete at that level,' said Dunlop chief Jeremy Ferguson. Meanwhile he was pleased to admit that they were eyeing renewed opportunities in the premier class with 500 cc V4 motor cycles, where they now only supply a few V-twins.

A nice young-and-old tableau was played out in the friendly 125 class. Jorge Martinez, now 37, confirmed in public after qualifying on the front row that he had decided to retire, after 16 years, four titles and 37 GP wins. He did so with an impromptu speech of great charm, describing how racing had changed over the years, and how he had had to change with it. The next day Rossi showed by how much, when he and Martinez stood together on the rostrum. The young wag wore a joke-shop head bandage – a reference to concussion in a car crash the weekend before (his father Graziano had trashed a Porsche 928 belonging to Loris Capirossi against a lamp-post on a trading estate – don't even ask how). 'I guess you can see from the race that my head is not right,' he happily announced.

500 cc	OKADA
250 cc	BIAGGI
125 cc	ROSSI

Although not a championship contender, Tohru Ukawa was frequently a front man in the 250 class, and was second here.

Below left: Go get 'em, Max. Team owner Erv Kanemoto points the way.

Below right: Norifumi Abe – so near to the rostrum, and yet so far.

500 cc RACE – 30 LAPS

Doohan added one more pole to the record – his 11th straight – a comfortable four-tenths ahead of Okada, who was off the pace until the closing minutes. Criville was third, then Romboni's Aprilia back on the front row to celebrate his 100th GP start. 'This is not a good track for a V-twin – all acceleration and speed,' he said. But the big engine meant he was 'almost as fast as the V4s'. Clutch and ignition-curve modifications were aimed at improving his slow starts – but once again the silver lightweight was left trailing, to be almost last away.

It was Okada in front, with the unusually fast-starting Doohan ahead by the second corner, Criville a close third. All highly predictable, even when Okada moved into the lead after seven laps. Doohan often lets rivals ahead for a spell to see what they're made of, and on lap 17 he regained the lead.

This time, however, Tady had a distinct horsepower advantage and, as importantly, was faster into the last corner. Mick observed this, and prepared his defence.

On the penultimate lap Okada outbraked Doohan, only to be nerfed back into second with a hard move in the next chicane. A similar attack on the final lap was repulsed even more firmly. There was just the last corner – and the unexpected outcome.

In spite of being forewarned, far from protecting his weak spot Doohan left a distinct space on the inside. Okada took it, and control of the last corner also gave him control of the run to the flag. After the crude gesture, both were grim-faced on the rostrum. 'It took some of the pleasure out of winning,' Okada later told his crew. Doohan was terse. 'I'm not making excuses. It was a hard race, but he stayed upright and he won it. I knew he was going to be hard to beat.' But he was seething with resentment at once again being obliged to 'race against my own bike'.

Criville had held third, ahead of a good battle. Cadalora and Checa were pacemakers, the Yamaha back in front on the ninth lap and starting to pull clear when a cylinder stud failed, and Luca's race was over. Checa was now under serious pressure from Nobu Aoki and Abe, with the Yamaha rider moving through step by step to head the group on lap 20. Simultaneously, Criville lost his front wheel tipping it into the first turn, recovering heroically to run across the gravel and rejoin down in sixth.

Abe had at last rediscovered his form, breaking free as Aoki also passed Checa, who blamed problems at the crucial exit from the last corner. Abe seemed set for a season-best ros-

trum finish. But Criville was far from done, and steadily picked his way through from the 24th lap – past Checa, then Aoki, then both of them closed on the tiring Abe. Criville regained third with one lap to spare, and Aoki came with him to ruin Abe's day.

Takuma Aoki was seventh, the best V-twin. Then came Gibernau, narrowly fending off Roberts Junior on the sole surviving Modenas. (Bayle had been ahead of this group, then at the back of it, before his crankshaft seized again and he narrowly escaped crashing.)

Romboni took tenth, after moving through the field steadily. Afterwards, crushed with disappointment, he declined to speak for a long time after the race.

Fuchs just held off Beattie by less than a tenth to claim 11th, the Australian having discovered some pace after spotting Goddard ahead of him, giving him a target that had to be passed. Goddard was 13th, another ten seconds down after fighting an ill-judged rear suspension change for the full race.

Puig was 14th, McCarthy right on his back wheel in 15th. There were 18 finishers.

Barros was another retirement, after slipping backwards with a handling problem. There were no crashes.

250 cc RACE – 28 LAPS

Biaggi's psychological timing was perfect, with his first pole since the Malaysian GP a full season away. 'Harada's Aprilia is like a rocket,' he said. 'But this track isn't all straights.' Jacque was alongside in a widely spaced front row, then a glum Harada and Waldmann, both with handling problems.

Biaggi repeated his Malaysian race as well – leading from the start, breaking the record on the second lap, and leading by more than six seconds at one-third distance. It was a magnificent performance after a pre-race engine swap, pushing hard all the way, and regained him the title lead as well. 'I think my strengths this year have been my refusal to give up, and my consistency. I believe you should always be constant, in life, love and motor cycle racing,' he said later, overcome by the poetry of the position.

Behind him, Ukawa took over second from Harada, then Jacque took over from him, with plenty of back-and-forth between the trio. Waldmann gradually dropped to the back of the group. By lap ten he'd lost touch, blaming a too-familiar problem of insufficient traction as he opened the throttle, costing him vital acceleration.

The three up front were battling hard. Ukawa generally had the best of it, and in the very last laps pulled a lit-

tle clear. Jacque and Harada were still close. Then on lap 23 a Jacque Attack pushed Harada wide and onto the dirty part of the track, and he lost one-and-a-half seconds. He clawed it all back for the crucial last lap.

Now came the back-markers – Petrucciani and Costes (Jacque's teammate), disputing last place. Ukawa slammed past with no trouble. Jacque also got through more or less cleanly, cool enough to give Costes a little wave – the night before they'd had a friendly argument about whether he would lap him. Harada was, unusually, out of position, and really suffered. Afterwards came a petulant outburst. Although Petrucciani had delayed him more, he delivered a blistering attack on the innocent Costes, suggesting a conspiracy to hold him up. This provoked an even angrier response from Chesterfield team manager Hervé Poncharal. 'Anyone who believes that such an arrangement could take place is an idiot,' he said. What mattered was that Jacque was 1.3 seconds ahead across the line.

Waldmann had been caught by Tsujimura and Aoki, and his lack of acceleration and the finish line's proximity to the last corner meant he finished behind both of them. It was a bitter blow to his title hopes.

Perugini was a lonely eighth, four seconds ahead of Porto's Aprilia. The pair had been battling with Numata's Suzuki before the Japanese rider fell heavily with ten laps to go, lucky to escape as walking wounded.

McWilliams was tenth, bemoaning his lack of speed; then came Migliorati. D'Antin crashed out in the early stages; Robinson retired with ten laps left in a state of near physical collapse from food poisoning.

125 cc RACE – 26 LAPS

Rossi's 11th win was in typically dominant style. His only real challenge had been the fast-starting Sakata, but there was nobody else to touch him. Winning the championship hadn't lessened his hunger for race wins in any way.

Sakata held on to second, with Martinez prevailing for once over Manako to claim third – his third rostrum of the year, and the last in a distinguished career.

Manako fell back into a five-bike fracas, and was at the rear of it with five laps left. But he timed his last-lap run almost perfectly, with only Ueda ahead of him. This secured second in the championship for Ueda, but Manako could still lose third overall to Sakata.

Tokudome was sixth, then Scalvini and Ui. McCoy was a lonely ninth, after battling with Fred Petit, before the Frenchman went off the track, rejoining lower down the field.

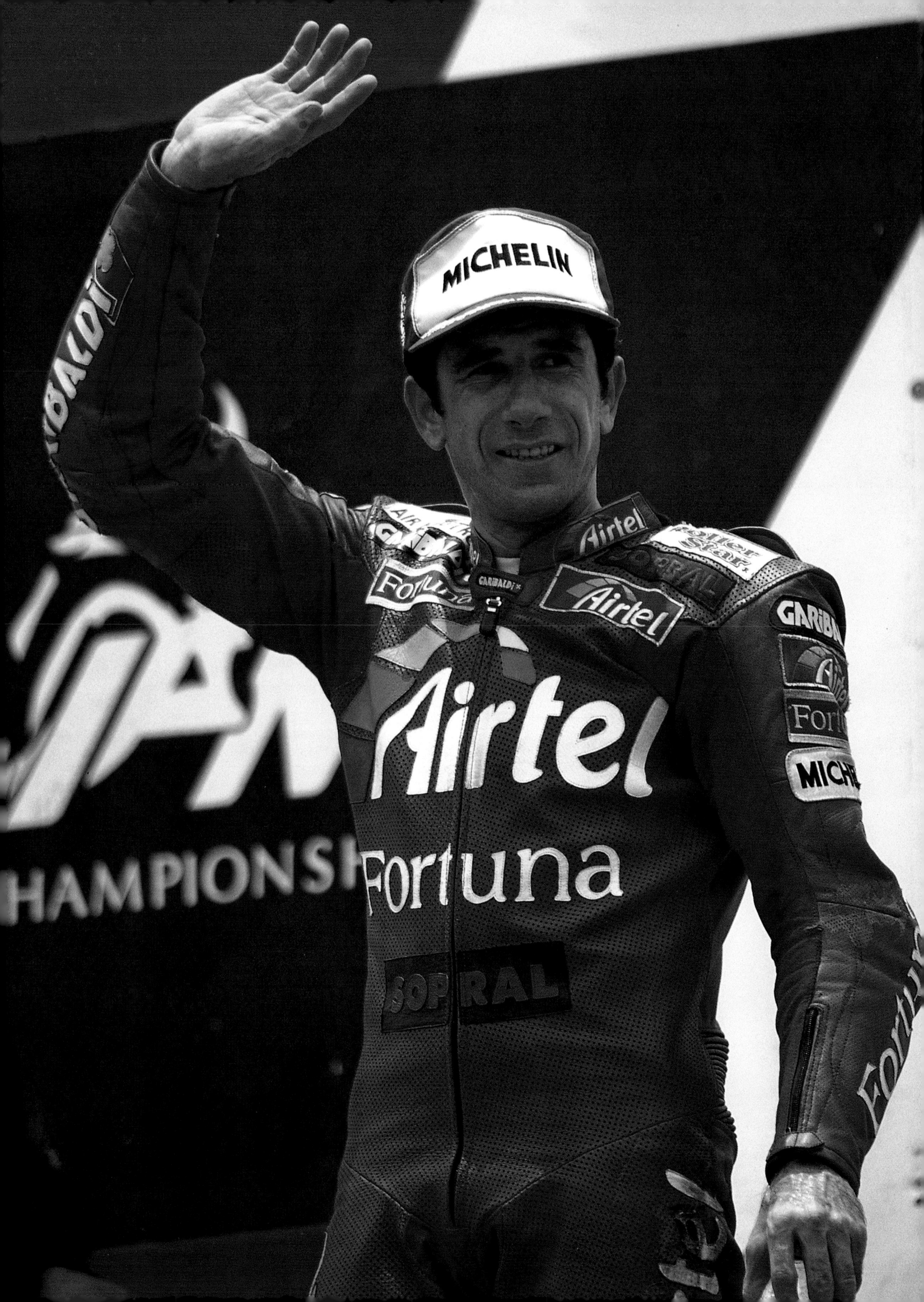

MICHELIN
Airtel
Fortuna
CHAMPIONSH

MARLBORO
INDONESIAN
GRAND PRIX
28 SEPTEMBER 1997

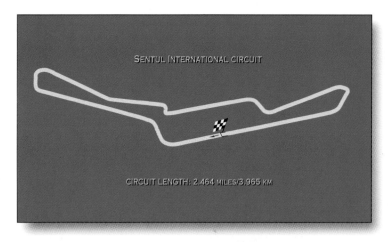

SENTUL INTERNATIONAL CIRCUIT

CIRCUIT LENGTH: 2.464 MILES/3.965 KM

500 cc

30 laps, 73.920 miles/118.950 km

Pos.	Rider (Nat.)	No.	Machine	Laps	Time & speed
1	Tadayuki Okada (J)	7	Honda	30	43m 22.010s 102.260 mph/ 164.572 km/h
2	Michael Doohan (AUS)	1	Honda	30	43m 33.001s
3	Alex Criville (E)	2	Honda	30	43m 33.793s
4	Nobuatsu Aoki (J)	18	Honda	30	43m 34.203s
5	Norifumi Abe (J)	5	Yamaha	30	43m 37.960s
6	Carlos Checa (E)	8	Honda	30	43m 52.897s
7	Takuma Aoki (J)	24	Honda	30	44m 04.067s
8	Sete Gibernau (E)	20	Yamaha	30	44m 04.822s
9	Kenny Roberts Jnr (USA)	10	Modenas	30	44m 08.536s
10	Doriano Romboni (I)	19	Aprilia	30	44m 12.826s
11	Jurgen Fuchs (D)	16	Elf 500	30	44m 12.876s
12	Daryl Beattie (AUS)	6	Suzuki	30	44m 22.060s
13	Peter Goddard (AUS)	27	Suzuki	30	44m 27.593s
14	Alberto Puig (E)	9	Honda	30	44m 27.958s
15	Kirk McCarthy (AUS)	22	Yamaha	30	44m 28.685s
16	Regis Laconi (F)	55	Honda	30	43m 56.131s
17	Lucio Pedercini (I)	17	Yamaha	29	44m 03.917s
18	Laurent Naveau (B)	25	Yamaha	29	
	Jean-Michel Bayle (F)	12	Modenas	20	DNF
	Frédéric Protat (F)	15	Honda	17	DNF
	Luca Cadalora (I)	3	Yamaha	14	DNF
	Juan Borja (E)	14	Elf 500	13	DNF
	Alex Barros (BR)	4	Honda	11	DNF
	Jurgen v.d. Goorbergh (NL)	21	Honda	11	DNF

Fastest lap: Okada, 1m 26.141s, 102.964 mph/165.705 km/h (record).
Previous record: Michael Doohan, AUS (Honda), 1m 27.139s, 101.785 mph/163.807 km/h (1996).

Qualifying: 1 Doohan, 1m 25.474s; **2** Okada, 1m 25.882s; **3** Criville, 1m 25.927s; **4** Romboni, 1m 26.005s; **5** Cadalora, 1m 26.247s; **6** Checa, 1m 26.269s; **7** N. Aoki, 1m 26.492s; **8** Abe, 1m 26.538s; **9** Fuchs, 1m 26.696s; **10** T. Aoki, 1m 26.743s; **11** Gibernau, 1m 26.755s; **12** Beattie, 1m 26.778s; **13** Roberts Jnr, 1m 26.781s; **14** Bayle, 1m 26.957s; **15** Borja, 1m 27.073s; **16** Laconi, 1m 27.092s; **17** Puig, 1m 27.319s; **18** Goddard, 1m 27.551s; **19** McCarthy, 1m 27.637s; **20** Barros, 1m 27.983s; **21** Pedercini, 1m 28.052s; **22** van den Goorbergh, 1m 28.726s; **23** Naveau, 1m 29.516s; **24** Protat, 1m 29.893s.

Fastest race laps: 1 Okada, 1m 26.141s; **2** Criville, 1m 26.157s; **3** Doohan, 1m 26.211s; **4** Cadalora, 1m 26.326s; **5** N. Aoki, 1m 26.443s; **6** Abe, 1m 26.500s; **7** Checa, 1m 26.627s; **8** T. Aoki, 1m 26.740s; **9** Roberts Jnr, 1m 26.985s; **10** Romboni, 1m 27.037s; **11** Laconi, 1m 27.193s; **12** Bayle, 1m 27.219s; **13** Gibernau, 1m 27.274s; **14** Beattie, 1m 27.359s; **15** Puig, 1m 27.443s; **16** Fuchs, 1m 27.544s; **17** Borja, 1m 27.669s; **18** McCarthy, 1m 27.851s; **19** Goddard, 1m 27.973s; **20** Barros, 1m 28.552s; **21** Pedercini, 1m 29.288s; **22** van den Goorbergh, 1m 29.759s; **23** Protat, 1m 30.156s; **24** Naveau, 1m 30.191s.

World Championship: 1 Doohan, 340; **2** Okada, 184; **3** N. Aoki, 179; **4** Criville, 147; **5** Cadalora, 129; **6** T. Aoki, 114; **7** Checa, 113; **8** Abe, 110; **9** Barros, 93; **10** Romboni, 83; **11** Beattie, 63; **12** Puig, 62; **13** Gibernau, 46; **14** Gobert, 44; **15** Laconi, 41; **16** Borja, 37; **17** Roberts Jnr, 35; **18** Bayle, 31; **19** Fuchs, 28; **20** van den Goorbergh, 25; **21** McCarthy, 17; **22** Corser, 11; **23** Fujiwara and Garcia, 7; **25** Goddard, 6; **26** Naveau, 3; **27** Pedercini and Vincent, 2.

250 cc

28 laps, 68.992 miles/111.020 km

Pos.	Rider (Nat.)	No.	Machine	Laps	Time & speed
1	Max Biaggi (I)	1	Honda	28	41m 35.549s 99.514 mph/ 160.153 km/h
2	Tohru Ukawa (J)	5	Honda	28	41m 42.141s
3	Olivier Jacque (F)	19	Honda	28	41m 43.528s
4	Tetsuya Harada (J)	31	Aprilia	28	41m 44.846s
5	Takeshi Tsujimura (J)	12	Honda	28	41m 52.741s
6	Haruchika Aoki (J)	7	Honda	28	41m 52.795s
7	Ralf Waldmann (D)	2	Honda	28	41m 53.230s
8	Stefano Perugini (I)	15	Aprilia	28	42m 21.399s
9	Sebastian Porto (ARG)	27	Aprilia	28	42m 25.120s
10	Jeremy McWilliams (GB)	11	Honda	28	42m 35.384s
11	Cristiano Migliorati (I)	8	Honda	28	42m 37.482s
12	Franco Battaini (I)	21	Yamaha	28	42m 39.266s
13	Osamu Miyazaki (J)	18	Yamaha	28	42m 41.340s
14	Loris Capirossi (I)	65	Aprilia	28	42m 43.846s
15	Luca Boscoscuro (I)	10	Honda	28	42m 57.161s
16	Oliver Petrucciani (CH)	25	Aprilia	27	41m 46.803s
17	William Costes (F)	16	Honda	27	41m 46.811s
	Giuseppe Fiorillo (I)	99	Aprilia	24	DNF
	Noriyasu Numata (J)	20	Suzuki	18	DNF
	Jamie Robinson (GB)	14	Suzuki	18	DNF
	José Luis Cardoso (E)	17	Yamaha	12	DNF
	Eustaquio Gavira (E)	28	Aprilia	10	DNF
	Luis D'Antin (E)	6	Yamaha	4	DNF
	Emilio Alzamora (E)	26	Honda	4	DNF
	Kurtis Roberts (USA)	22	Honda	0	DNF

Fastest lap: Biaggi, 1m 28.256s, 100.497 mph/161.734 km/h (record).
Previous record: Tetsuya Harada, J (Yamaha), 1m 29.696s, 98.884 mph/159.138 km/h (1996).

Qualifying: 1 Biaggi, 1m 27.438s; **2** Jacque, 1m 27.696s; **3** Harada, 1m 28.180s; **4** Waldmann, 1m 28.306s; **5** Ukawa, 1m 28.363s; **6** Tsujimura, 1m 28.464s; **7** Capirossi, 1m 28.690s; **8** Perugini, 1m 28.716s; **9** Aoki, 1m 28.935s; **10** McWilliams, 1m 29.296s; **11** Porto, 1m 29.576s; **12** D'Antin, 1m 29.733s; **13** Numata, 1m 29.804s; **14** Migliorati, 1m 29.808s; **15** Miyazaki, 1m 30.148s; **16** Battaini, 1m 30.315s; **17** Boscoscuro, 1m 30.422s; **18** Cardoso, 1m 30.528s; **19** Fiorillo, 1m 30.700s; **20** Alzamora, 1m 30.763s; **21** Petrucciani, 1m 31.017s; **22** Robinson, 1m 31.353s; **23** Costes, 1m 31.742s; **24** Roberts, 1m 31.982s; **25** Gavira, 1m 32.404s.

Fastest race laps: 1 Biaggi, 1m 28.256s; **2** Harada, 1m 28.550s; **3** Jacque, 1m 28.600s; **4** Ukawa, 1m 28.873s; **5** Tsujimura, 1m 29.060s; **6** Aoki, 1m 29.135s; **7** Waldmann, 1m 29.176s; **8** Perugini, 1m 29.938s; **9** Numata, 1m 30.072s; **10** Porto, 1m 30.107s; **11** D'Antin, 1m 30.373s; **12** McWilliams, 1m 30.393s; **13** Battaini, 1m 30.467s; **14** Capirossi, 1m 30.473s; **15** Miyazaki, 1m 30.504s; **16** Migliorati, 1m 30.517s; **17** Boscoscuro, 1m 30.979s; **18** Fiorillo, 1m 31.301s; **19** Cardoso, 1m 31.329s; **20** Robinson, 1m 31.539s; **21** Costes, 1m 31.758s; **22** Alzamora, 1m 31.768s; **23** Petrucciani, 1m 31.798s; **24** Gavira, 1m 33.083s.

World Championship: 1 Biaggi, 230; **2** Harada, 224; **3** Waldmann, 223; **4** Jacque, 185; **5** Ukawa, 165; **6** Capirossi, 116; **7** Aoki, 100; **8** Tsujimura, 96; **9** Perugini, 76; **10** McWilliams, 67; **11** Numata, 55; **12** Porto, 53; **13** Miyazaki, 42; **14** Battaini, 40; **15** D'Antin and Migliorati, 32; **17** Alzamora, 31; **18** Lucchi, 30; **19** Kato, 25; **20** Costes, 23; **21** Cardoso, 19; **22** Robinson, 18; **23** Petrucciani, 14; **24** Boscoscuro and Fiorillo, 12; **26** Kagayama, 10; **27** Matsudo, 6; **28** E. Gavira, 5; **29** Smart, 4; **30** Gimbert and Ogura, 3; **32** Bolwerk, I. Gavira and McGuiness, 2; **35** Ramsay and Vanzetta, 1.

125 cc

26 laps, 64.064 miles/103.090 km

Pos.	Rider (Nat.)	No.	Machine	Laps	Time & speed
1	Valentino Rossi (I)	46	Aprilia	26	41m 14.511s 93.192 mph/ 149.978 km/h
2	Kazuto Sakata (J)	8	Aprilia	26	41m 17.539s
3	Jorge Martinez (E)	5	Aprilia	26	41m 19.749s
4	Noboru Ueda (J)	7	Honda	26	41m 22.880s
5	Tomomi Manako (J)	3	Honda	26	41m 23.440s
6	Masaki Tokudome (J)	2	Aprilia	26	41m 23.510s
7	Gianluigi Scalvini (I)	21	Honda	26	41m 23.824s
8	Youichi Ui (J)	41	Yamaha	26	41m 23.987s
9	Garry McCoy (AUS)	72	Aprilia	26	41m 39.091s
10	Roberto Locatelli (I)	15	Honda	26	41m 45.092s
11	Masao Azuma (J)	20	Honda	26	41m 45.116s
12	Gino Borsoi (I)	24	Yamaha	26	41m 45.540s
13	Lucio Cecchinello (I)	10	Honda	26	41m 45.607s
14	Frédéric Petit (F)	19	Honda	26	41m 45.628s
15	Steve Jenkner (D)	22	Aprilia	26	41m 46.978s
16	Angel Nieto Jnr (E)	29	Aprilia	26	41m 47.364s
17	Juan Enrique Maturana (E)	17	Yamaha	26	41m 47.514s
18	Shahrol Yuzy (MAL)	42	Honda	26	41m 48.015s
19	Josep Sarda (E)	25	Honda	26	42m 10.962s
20	Jaroslav Hules (CS)	39	Honda	26	42m 11.031s
21	Yoshiaki Katoh (J)	62	Yamaha	26	42m 13.857s
	Mirko Giansanti (I)	32	Honda	18	DNF
	Manfred Geissler (D)	33	Aprilia	11	DNF
	Dirk Raudies (D)	12	Honda	10	DNF
	Xavier Soler (E)	43	Aprilia	10	DNF
	Irvan Octavianus (IND)	56	Yamaha	5	DNF
	Ahmad Jayadi (IND)	55	Yamaha	1	DNF
	Rudi Arianto (IND)	53	Yamaha		DNS

Fastest lap: Rossi, 1m 34.044s, 94.312 mph/151.780 km/h (record).
Previous record: Haruchika Aoki, J (Honda), 1m 35.068s, 93.296 mph/150.145 km/h (1996).

Qualifying: 1 Martinez, 1m 34.393s; **2** Manako, 1m 34.552s; **3** Sakata, 1m 34.649s; **4** Rossi, 1m 34.745s; **5** Giansanti, 1m 34.814s; **6** Tokudome, 1m 34.933s; **7** McCoy, 1m 34.933s; **8** Locatelli, 1m 34.943s; **9** Ui, 1m 35.008s; **10** Scalvini, 1m 35.010s; **11** Ueda, 1m 35.148s; **12** Maturana, 1m 35.275s; **13** Azuma, 1m 35.479s; **14** Petit, 1m 35.541s; **15** Borsoi, 1m 35.564s; **16** Yuzy, 1m 35.702s; **17** Cecchinello, 1m 35.758s; **18** Geissler, 1m 35.765s; **19** Jenkner, 1m 35.879s; **20** Katoh, 1m 36.046s; **21** Sarda, 1m 36.119s; **22** Hules, 1m 36.361s; **23** Raudies, 1m 37.041s; **24** Nieto Jnr, 1m 37.711s; **25** Soler, 1m 38.069s; **26** Jayadi, 1m 40.858s; **27** Arianto, 1m 41.247s; **28** Octavianus, 1m 42.759s.

Fastest race laps: 1 Rossi, 1m 34.044s; **2** Sakata, 1m 34.207s; **3** Ui, 1m 34.441s; **4** Martinez, 1m 34.507s; **5** Tokudome, 1m 34.514s; **6** Manako, 1m 34.563s; **7** Scalvini, 1m 34.693s; **8** Ueda, 1m 34.761s; **9** McCoy, 1m 35.147s; **10** Petit, 1m 35.159s; **11** Borsoi, 1m 35.308s; **12** Locatelli, 1m 35.477s; **13** Maturana, 1m 35.482s; **14** Jenkner, 1m 35.487s; **15** Nieto Jnr, 1m 35.533s; **16** Yuzy, 1m 35.551s; **17** Cecchinello, 1m 35.581s; **18** Azuma, 1m 35.595s; **19** Giansanti, 1m 35.729s; **20** Sarda, 1m 36.022s; **21** Katoh, 1m 36.196s; **22** Hules, 1m 36.200s; **23** Geissler, 1m 36.633s; **24** Raudies, 1m 37.697s; **25** Soler, 1m 37.720s; **26** Octavianus, 1m 42.871s; **27** Jayadi, 2m 08.144s.

World Championship: 1 Rossi, 311; **2** Ueda, 213; **3** Manako, 174; **4** Sakata, 159; **5** Martinez, 116; **6** Tokudome, 112; **7** McCoy, 102; **8** Locatelli, 84; **9** Petit, 83; **10** Giansanti and Ui, 77; **12** Katoh, 72; **13** Scalvini, 70; **14** Cecchinello, 64; **15** Azuma, 62; **16** Geissler, 30; **17** Goi, 21; **18** Jenkner, 20; **19** Borsoi, 19; **20** Hules and Maturana, 17; **22** Nakajo, 16; **23** Öttl, 11; **24** Nieto Jnr, Raudies and Takao, 8; **27** Sarda, 3; **28** Barton and Hofmann, 2; **30** Jerzenbeck and Molina, 1.

Jorge Martinez bids farewell – it was his last rostrum appearance in 16 distinguished years of racing.

Photos: Gold & Goose

500 cc	CRIVILLE
250 cc	WALDMANN
125 cc	UEDA

FIM WORLD CHAMPIONSHIP • ROUND 15

AUSTRALIAN
grand prix

Above: Point proven. Biaggi blasts to a historic fourth consecutive title. This time it was on a Honda. Just to prove (Max will say) it was the rider, not the bike.

Left: Waldmann won the battle, lost the war, and was generous with the champagne in defeat.

'THE GP Has Come Home' asserted the *Melbourne Age*, but it was a cold welcome from the vintage Phillip Island circuit, at the end of a vintage year of racing. Bitter winds off the Bass Strait blew only one person any good, and that was Max Biaggi – hero of the hour, the day, the weekend, the month and the year after a titanic 250 struggle. Like Doohan, it was his fourth World Championship in a row – the first time this has been achieved in the class.

Mick's own home weekend was dire. First off, after a year of keeping the wheels down, he fell in practice – a low-speed bale-out after being put off line by a slower rider. He rode the bike back and was out on it again within 20 minutes, but his first broken screen of the season was another crack in the edifice. It was followed by his first race crash since Australia last year, when Criville had knocked him down; and his first unforced error since the Nürburgring in 1995. And once again, Wayne Gardner remained the only Australian to have won his home GP at the scenic and atmospheric original circuit.

The return to the island after five years at Sydney's sterile Eastern Creek was welcomed by most. The track – laid out in the early Fifties by (among others) Vincent designer Phil Irving – is a genuine classic, an Antipodean Assen, comprising fast sweeping curves across picturesque seaside hills, and guaranteeing close 500 class racing like no other on the calendar. This was confirmed again this year – not for the lead, but in an enormous nine-bike scrap for fourth. They looked more like 125 riders than the usual 500 parade, jostling for position, then slipstreaming each other back again as they opened the throttle through sections where a 500 can really get up a good gallop.

Low track temperatures, however, led to a spate of practice accidents that called the circuit's safety into question, and highlighted the fast corners and Assen-like lack of gravel traps to slow things down once they got out of control. Crashers included not only Mick Doohan (put off line when he wrongly second-guessed a back-marker) but also Olivier Jacque (broke the front end off his better bike), Loris Capirossi (broken bones in his foot), Tohru Ukawa (dislocated shoulder), Tetsuya Harada (multiple contusions and concussion), 125 ace Garry McCoy (ran over his own leg at speed, no serious injury) and a number of lesser lights.

Jacque's team owner Hervé Poncharal was again outspoken. 'We've taken a big risk coming here at this time of year, when it is so cold. There are some very fast corners, so when you crash you're going very fast. The surface is very abrasive, so you have to run a hard compound tyre for the left-handers, but the right side hardly gets used.' A problem, surely, that the tyre engineers should be able to solve. Dunlop tyre chief Jeremy Ferguson agreed. 'No doubt we could produce a special tyre, but the conditions here are very unusual.'

The GP generated its usual eager national coverage, which took the form of a rather engineered row between Rainey and Doohan. The starting point was some remark made by Agostini to an Australian journalist when asked his views on Doohan breaking his record for wins in a season. 'Doohan is lucky because he has no opposition,' said the man who both dominated alone for years and also fought hard for many of his 17 titles in all classes.

Rainey kind of concurred, though he later complained his remarks had been truncated by TV editing to look like an attack. 'It's good for Mick, but it's bad for racing. When I was racing, you could never be sure who would win. Nowadays you wake up in the morning wondering who is going to get second.'

Mick of course defended himself vigorously, saying: 'It's easy to criticise when you've stopped racing. I've raced Rainey, Gardner, Lawson, Schwantz and I was dominating against those guys until I broke my leg in 1992.' It all got to the stage where the two felt obliged to stage a public kiss-and-make-up session for the TV cameras; but when the real issue between them was raised – the fact that their contract negotiations had come to grief for a second time during the preceding weeks – Rainey was forced to admit: 'I was kinda upset. But that's the way it is with riders.'

And talking of riders, there were a couple of new ones knocking around, and putting up a fine show. By no coincidence, perhaps, both were on Suzukis – making the bikes look a lot more competitive than for most of the year, in both the 500 and 250 classes. The 250 class hero was Australian Superbike rider Troy Bayliss, who replaced the knocked-about Numata for one race. Bayliss found enough performance in the hitherto ill-favoured V-twin to head the practice leaderboard in the final session until the closing 20 minutes, and to run with the pack of regular works men disputing third in the race. 'A bit of home track knowledge probably helps,' the 28-year-old allowed, wide-eyed with excitement at his first-ever ride on a full-race two-stroke. 'It's just a nice little bike that goes where you put it. It doesn't seem much slower than the others to me,' he added – music to the team's ears.

Next door, Japanese 250 rider Yukio Kagayama swelled the 500 team ranks with unexpected success, ending up with a fighting seventh overall. Goddard was again on the strength, and picking up the pace at his home GP. This was to have been Beattie's last race on the bike, and though narrowly the fastest Suzuki in practice, it seemed he had no stomach for the race. He called in sick on Sunday, and returned to Queensland later that same day. A rather sad end to a partnership that had been second overall two years ago.

And, another mercy, it seemed as though the Gobert affair had left few traces. Mischievous hearsay was that the man himself had threatened to show up with a busload of mates and hunt down his enemies in the British Suzuki team; in the event the only trace of the sadly disgraced rider was a practice-day banner erected by spectators opposite the Suzuki pit. It showed Goey performing a burn-out, with the caption: 'IT'S TYRE SMOKE, YOU DOPES.'

Gold & Goose

Above: Criville smiles the smile of a second-time winner, a reward for his courage in returning from horrific hand injuries two months before.

Below: How the mighty...Mick Doohan's first race crash for a year reduces his Honda to scrap as he slides harmlessly across the grass.

Debbie Wedes/The Motorsport Shop

Left: More like 125s than 500s, this was the battle for fourth. The mid-race order is Kagayama, Barros, Laconi, Romboni, Okada and Nobu Aoki.

Below left: Post-race tableau – Takuma Aoki has stopped for a flag to celebrate second; in the background Alex Barros pauses to apologise to Nobu Aoki (standing) after knocking him off.

Right: This time, it worked out for Abe – the last race was his best of the year.

Troy Bayliss *(bottom)* made a startling GP debut, equalling the hitherto ill-favoured Suzuki's best yet in his first two-stroke race.

500 cc RACE – 27 LAPS

Practice saw all sorts of conditions, culminating in a dry cool session where Doohan again dominated. The fact that he'd fallen off didn't seem to signify. His companions re-created another Honda benefit front row: Criville second, Tak Aoki third (the V-twins proved highly effective at this fast-corners track) and Okada. Then times were very close – fifth to 18th covered by a second – the Yamahas of Abe and Cadalora heading Romboni's Aprilia, Checa and the rest.

The Yamahas got away first, Abe heading Cadalora, but Doohan led by the end of lap one and was soon pulling away, riding hard as Criville moved into second after seven laps. Mick could have taken it easy, but that wasn't on this weekend's agenda. He kept on pushing; the gap kept on growing. After 16 laps, it was 7.8 seconds. And then it happened.

Turn One is a fast right-hander, with some entry bumps. It was these that stole the front wheel's adhesion, though Mick was unaware of doing anything differently from the rest of the weekend. 'Although I was pushing quite hard, I was also saving the tyres,' he said. Taken unawares, he tried desperately to regain control, riding the slide on his right knee (his weak leg). On and on he fought, but in the end it was hopeless. At the edge of the track the bike spun and he was off, sliding safely on his back to stop unhurt, shaking his head. 'I just can't believe it,' he said later.

This left Criville in the lead, but only very narrowly from Takuma Aoki, who was in turn concentrating so hard he had no time to look at his signals. He thought they were still disputing second and, when he got ahead briefly on lap 22, was unaware he was leading. 'I'd have tried harder if I'd known,' he said later, instead slackening off to tail Criville over the line by 2.2 seconds. The win was a just reward for the Spaniard, who had silenced his critics with his brave return to racing just five weeks before.

Abe at last gained the rostrum, after finishing his year rather better than he'd started it.

The battle for an eventual fourth had nine bikes charging and banging, jockeying for position, going back and forth. Amazingly, only one failed to finish. Nobu Aoki was knocked off with two laps left by an over-enthusiastic Alex Barros, who later apologised.

Goddard was an early pack leader, then Barros, then Checa. And then Romboni's V-twin, after charging through from 12th after a slow start. Next the remarkable Laconi's blue Tecmas Honda V-twin took a turn, then Kagayama for a couple of laps, suggesting that the Suzuki was not perhaps as bad as Beattie had been making it look.

At the end, Okada pushed through to head Laconi, Gibernau, Kagayama, Barros, Goddard, Checa and Romboni, the Italian heartbroken after his motor went sick on the last corner, dropping him right to the back of the pack. For the fans, however, the Phillip Island Effect had worked out once again, to give excellent close 500 cc racing.

Van den Goorbergh was 12th, with McCarthy leading Roberts Junior and Puig over the line. Bayle never got to grips with this gang.

Borja crashed out on his Elf; Cadalora pitted with 17 laps remaining after running into a typically hard-to-explain tyre problem following a good start; Fuchs retired after being called in for a stop-go penalty.

Doohan's first no-score damaged only the statistics; N. Aoki's crash lost him second overall to Okada, but he won the Rookie of the Year prize from his brother Takuma. Barros easily won IRTA's top privateer cup. And the last race of the year was a satisfyingly varied finish to a season that had been mightily impressive, but somewhat one-dimensional.

250 cc RACE – 25 LAPS

Capirossi paved the way on Friday with his own bad crash; team-mate Harada followed suit, high-siding at speed on the first corner, and rolling and tumbling to lie very still. His worst injuries were fractures to his left (gearchange) foot, and though he raced the next day, it was no longer as a potential championship winner. Waldmann also had a tumble in practice, but led the next day, until displaced at the last minute by a flying lap from Biaggi. Harada was third on the grid, with front-row first-timer Perugini fourth, enjoying the fast corners.

A very light shower as they assembled passed without wetting the track, and Harada took off in front. By the time they approached the final corners, however, it was Biaggi from the amazing Bayliss. Next time into Turn One and Waldmann swept through from fourth to first under braking. He was never headed again.

Biaggi had to work hard to stay with him, using him to get away from the pack. Having accomplished this, he eased up for the last third of the race, to reduce risks. Thus Ralf won by almost six seconds. But his feelings were more than a little mixed, after losing the title by two points. 'It was a strange feeling to be out in front but not looking forward to winning,' he said later.

Biaggi was naturally thrilled. His tactics had been perfect, almost all year. And he had avenged himself on Aprilia – all achieved with the sort of brinkmanship upon which he thrives.

The battle for third saw six riders fighting tooth and nail. Harada had most of the early leading, then Jacque worked his way up. Observers were later amused when the author of the famed Jacque Attack complained about Bayliss's out-of-control entry to the first corner. Bayliss remained in the thick of the action all race long, completely underawed by the high-class company.

Ukawa seemed to have the best of it as the race drew to a finish, in spite of his painful shoulder. Then, on the third-last lap, he was nudged by Harada under braking for the hairpin and went shooting off to rejoin out of touch, in eighth.

This left third to Jacque, Tsujimura on his back wheel, then Harada and Bayliss, with Perugini's Aprilia losing ground at the end.

Porto was a lonely ninth, with McWilliams defeating Miyazaki's Yamaha in a privateer battle for tenth.

It was the end of a classic year in the class.

125 cc RACE – 23 LAPS

Ui made a flying start, but high-sided out on Turn Two. This left Locatelli ahead, with Rossi and then Sakata taking turns as a group of six broke away. Then, just after half-distance, Rossi sat up abruptly and dropped back. It was only a momentary seizure and he was soon up to speed again, but he had no hope of catching the leaders.

Ueda broke away with three laps left, leaving Sakata and Manako battling with Locatelli: they finished in that order. Locatelli's team-mate Scalvini was fifth, then came Rossi and Cecchinello, both alone; Tokudome finally triumphed for eighth over McCoy and Giansanti.

Manako thus retained third overall from Sakata; Locatelli was Rookie of the Year after down-sizing from the 250 class in a fruitful move.

AUSTRALIAN GRAND PRIX

5 OCTOBER 1997

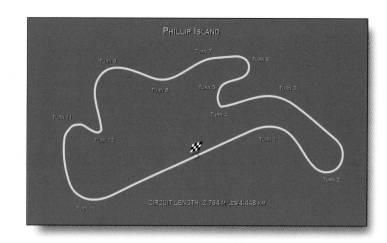

PHILLIP ISLAND

TURN 9 · TURN 7 · TURN 6 · TURN 8 · TURN 5 · TURN 3 · TURN 11 · TURN 4 · TURN 10 · TURN 1 · TURN 2 · TURN 11

CIRCUIT LENGTH: 2.764 MILES/4.448 KM

500 cc

27 laps, 74.628 miles/120.096 km

Pos.	Rider (Nat.)	No.	Machine	Laps	Time & speed
1	Alex Criville (E)	2	Honda	27	42m 53.362s 104.395 mph/ 168.008 km/h
2	Takuma Aoki (J)	24	Honda	27	42m 55.630s
3	Norifumi Abe (J)	5	Yamaha	27	43m 21.481s
4	Tadayuki Okada (J)	7	Honda	27	43m 28.592s
5	Regis Laconi (F)	55	Honda	27	43m 28.902s
6	Sete Gibernau (E)	20	Yamaha	27	43m 29.040s
7	Yukio Kagayama (J)	26	Suzuki	27	43m 29.132s
8	Alex Barros (BR)	4	Honda	27	43m 29.622s
9	Peter Goddard (AUS)	27	Suzuki	27	43m 30.157s
10	Carlos Checa (E)	8	Honda	27	43m 30.908s
11	Doriano Romboni (I)	19	Aprilia	27	43m 31.123s
12	Jurgen v.d. Goorbergh(NL)	21	Honda	27	43m 50.351s
13	Kirk McCarthy (AUS)	22	Yamaha	27	43m 54.553s
14	Kenny Roberts Jnr (USA)	10	Modenas	27	43m 55.618s
15	Alberto Puig (E)	9	Honda	27	43m 55.862s
16	Jean-Michel Bayle (F)	12	Modenas	27	44m 18.178s
17	Lucio Pedercini (I)	17	Yamaha	26	43m 22.044s
18	Frédéric Protat (F)	15	Honda	26	43m 24.478s
19	Laurent Naveau (B)	25	Yamaha	26	43m 24.622s
	Nobuatsu Aoki (J)	18	Honda	25	DNF
	Juan Borja (E)	14	Elf 500	23	DNF
	Michael Doohan (AUS)	1	Honda	16	DNF
	Luca Cadalora (I)	3	Yamaha	10	DNF
	Jurgen Fuchs (D)	16	Elf 500	6	DNF
	Daryl Beattie (AUS)	6	Suzuki		DNS

Fastest lap: Doohan, 1m 34.113s, 105.723 mph/170.144 km/h (record).
Previous record: Wayne Gardner, AUS (Honda), 1m 34.560s, 105.223 mph/169.340 km/h (1990).

Qualifying: 1 Doohan, 1m 33.135s; **2** Criville, 1m 33.961s; **3** T. Aoki, 1m 34.292s; **4** Okada, 1m 34.414s; **5** Abe, 1m 34.702s; **6** Cadalora, 1m 34.911s; **7** Romboni, 1m 34.930s; **8** Checa, 1m 34.955s; **9** Barros, 1m 35.167s; **10** Laconi, 1m 35.180s; **11** Beattie, 1m 35.273s; **12** Kagayama, 1m 35.319s; **13** van den Goorbergh, 1m 35.332s; **14** Gibernau, 1m 35.345s; **15** Goddard, 1m 35.351s; **16** N. Aoki, 1m 35.412s; **17** Roberts Jnr, 1m 35.446s; **18** Borja, 1m 35.625s; **19** Bayle, 1m 35.858s; **20** Fuchs, 1m 36.376s; **21** Puig, 1m 36.449s; **22** Pedercini, 1m 37.199s; **23** McCarthy, 1m 37.225s; **24** Protat 1m 38.297s; **25** Naveau, 1m 39.283s.

Fastest race laps: 1 Doohan, 1m 34.113s; **2** Abe, 1m 34.518s; **3** Criville, 1m 34.522s; **4** T. Aoki, 1m 34.524s; **5** Romboni, 1m 35.178s; **6** Kagayama, 1m 35.522s; **7** N. Aoki, 1m 35.607s; **8** Laconi, 1m 35.614s; **9** Gibernau, 1m 35.703s; **10** Checa, 1m 35.721s; **11** Barros, 1m 35.792s; **12** Goddard, 1m 35.806s; **13** Okada, 1m 35.836s; **14** Borja, 1m 35.911s; **15** van den Goorbergh, 1m 35.937s; **16** Roberts Jnr, 1m 36.473s; **17** McCarthy, 1m 36.491s; **18** Cadalora, 1m 36.530s; **19** Puig, 1m 36.536s; **20** Bayle, 1m 36.559s; **21** Fuchs, 1m 36.563s; **22** Pedercini, 1m 37.653s; **23** Naveau, 1m 39.025s; **24** Protat, 1m 39.159s.

Final World Championship points: see pages 144-5.

250 cc

25 laps, 69.100 miles/111.200 km

Pos.	Rider (Nat.)	No.	Machine	Laps	Time & speed
1	Ralf Waldmann (D)	2	Honda	25	40m 09.735s 103.226 mph/ 166.126 km/h
2	Max Biaggi (I)	1	Honda	25	40m 15.564s
3	Olivier Jacque (F)	19	Honda	25	40m 36.986s
4	Takeshi Tsujimura (J)	12	Honda	25	40m 37.374s
5	Tetsuya Harada (J)	31	Aprilia	25	40m 37.661s
6	Troy Bayliss (AUS)	30	Suzuki	25	40m 37.853s
7	Stefano Perugini (I)	15	Aprilia	25	40m 38.773s
8	Tohru Ukawa (J)	5	Honda	25	40m 53.329s
9	Sebastian Porto (ARG)	27	Aprilia	25	41m 08.157s
10	Jeremy McWilliams (GB)	11	Honda	25	41m 15.211s
11	Osamu Miyazaki (J)	18	Yamaha	25	41m 15.298s
12	Franco Battaini (I)	21	Yamaha	25	41m 22.114s
13	Cristiano Migliorati (I)	8	Honda	25	41m 29.285s
14	Haruchika Aoki (J)	7	Honda	25	41m 29.418s
15	Luca Boscoscuro (I)	10	Honda	25	41m 29.475s
16	Luis D'Antin (E)	6	Yamaha	25	41m 31.716s
17	Oliver Petrucciani (CH)	25	Aprilia	25	41m 50.406s
18	William Strugnell (AUS)	58	Honda	24	41m 04.164s
19	Simon Weeks (AUS)	56	Honda	24	41m 10.858s
20	Ben Reid (AUS)	84	Yamaha	24	41m 27.083s
21	Michael Clunie (NZ)	83	Yamaha	23	40m 22.158s
	William Costes (F)	16	Honda	17	DNF
	Giuseppe Fiorillo (I)	99	Aprilia	17	DNF
	Eustaquio Gavira (E)	28	Aprilia	2	DNF
	Emilio Alzamora (E)	26	Honda	2	DNF
	Jamie Robinson (GB)	14	Suzuki	1	DNF
	José Luis Cardoso (E)	17	Yamaha	1	DNF

Fastest lap: Waldmann, 1m 35.409s, 104.287 mph/167.833 km/h (record).
Previous record: John Kocinski, USA (Yamaha), 1m 36.681s, 102.915 mph/165.625 km/h (1990).

Qualifying: 1 Biaggi, 1m 34.789s; **2** Waldmann, 1m 35.116s; **3** Harada, 1m 35.953s; **4** Perugini, 1m 36.006s; **5** Jacque, 1m 36.064s; **6** Bayliss, 1m 36.259s; **7** Ukawa, 1m 36.657s; **8** Tsujimura, 1m 36.666s; **9** McWilliams, 1m 36.864s; **10** Porto, 1m 36.915s; **11** Miyazaki, 1m 36.948s; **12** Battaini, 1m 37.168s; **13** Aoki, 1m 37.208s; **14** D'Antin, 1m 37.311s; **15** Robinson, 1m 37.448s; **16** Cardoso, 1m 37.827s; **17** Boscoscuro, 1m 37.921s; **18** Migliorati, 1m 37.984s; **19** Costes, 1m 38.657s; **20** Petrucciani, 1m 38.658s; **21** Fiorillo, 1m 39.485s; **22** Gavira, 1m 40.009s; **23** Weeks, 1m 40.900s; **24** Strugnell, 1m 41.132s; **25** Alzamora, 1m 41.396s; **26** Reid, 1m 41.849s; **27** Clunie, 1m 42.928s.

Fastest race laps: 1 Waldmann, 1m 35.409s; **2** Biaggi, 1m 35.492s; **3** Perugini, 1m 36.410s; **4** Jacque, 1m 36.416s; **5** Harada, 1m 36.456s; **6** Tsujimura, 1m 36.477s; **7** Ukawa, 1m 36.520s; **8** Bayliss, 1m 36.762s; **9** Porto, 1m 37.514s; **10** McWilliams, 1m 37.976s; **11** Miyazaki, 1m 38.057s; **12** D'Antin, 1m 38.091s; **13** Battaini, 1m 38.120s; **14** Aoki, 1m 38.632s; **15** Costes, 1m 38.639s; **16** Boscoscuro, 1m 38.644s; **17** Migliorati, 1m 38.692s; **18** Petrucciani, 1m 38.852s; **19** Fiorillo, 1m 40.199s; **20** Weeks, 1m 40.864s; **21** Strugnell, 1m 41.219s; **22** Reid, 1m 42.101s; **23** Gavira, 1m 42.261s; **24** Clunie, 1m 43.560s; **25** Alzamora, 1m 45.536s; **26** Robinson, 1m 46.345s; **27** Cardoso, 1m 47.184s.

Final World Championship points: see pages 144-5.

125 cc

23 laps, 63.572 miles/102.304 km

Pos.	Rider (Nat.)	No.	Machine	Laps	Time & speed
1	Noboru Ueda (J)	7	Honda	23	38m 59.797s 97.806 mph/ 157.404 km/h
2	Kazuto Sakata (J)	8	Aprilia	23	39m 01.163s
3	Tomomi Manako (J)	3	Honda	23	39m 01.663s
4	Roberto Locatelli (I)	15	Honda	23	39m 01.700s
5	Gianluigi Scalvini (I)	21	Honda	23	39m 05.384s
6	Valentino Rossi (I)	46	Aprilia	23	39m 18.750s
7	Lucio Cecchinello (I)	10	Honda	23	39m 27.041s
8	Masaki Tokudome (J)	2	Aprilia	23	39m 35.583s
9	Garry McCoy (AUS)	72	Aprilia	23	39m 35.694s
10	Mirko Giansanti (I)	32	Honda	23	39m 36.189s
11	Juan Enrique Maturana (E)	17	Yamaha	23	39m 36.201s
12	Masao Azuma (J)	20	Honda	23	39m 36.263s
13	Jorge Martinez (E)	5	Aprilia	23	39m 44.708s
14	Yoshiaki Katoh (J)	62	Yamaha	23	39m 56.139s
15	Manfred Geissler (D)	33	Aprilia	23	39m 56.326s
16	Steve Jenkner (D)	22	Aprilia	23	39m 56.330s
17	Angel Nieto Jnr (E)	29	Aprilia	23	39m 59.829s
18	Josep Sarda (E)	25	Honda	23	39m 59.973s
19	Shahrol Yuzy (MAL)	42	Honda	23	40m 26.532s
20	Jay Taylor (AUS)	47	Honda	23	40m 31.819s
21	Hayden Bool (NZ)	52	Honda	22	40m 37.365s
22	James Armstrong (AUS)	49	Yamaha	21	40m 06.954s
	Dirk Raudies (D)	12	Honda	20	DNF
	William Strugnell (AUS)	48	Honda	13	DNF
	Xavier Soler (E)	43	Aprilia	12	DNF
	Frédéric Petit (F)	19	Honda	11	DNF
	Peter Galvin (AUS)	51	Honda	6	DNF
	Gino Borsoi (I)	24	Yamaha	1	DNF
	Jaroslav Hules (CS)	39	Honda	0	DNF
	Youichi Ui (J)	41	Yamaha	0	DNF
	Andrew Willy (AUS)	50	Yamaha	0	DNF

Fastest lap: Sakata, 1m 40.348s, 99.153 mph/159.572 km/h (record).
Previous record: Doriano Romboni, I (Honda), 1m 43.959s, 95.709 mph/154.030 km/h (1990).

Qualifying: 1 Sakata, 1m 40.680s; **2** Ui, 1m 40.762s; **3** Rossi, 1m 40.904s; **4** Ueda, 1m 41.302s; **5** McCoy, 1m 41.417s; **6** Martinez, 1m 41.422s; **7** Locatelli, 1m 41.551s; **8** Manako, 1m 41.816s; **9** Scalvini, 1m 41.946s; **10** Maturana, 1m 42.048s; **11** Petit, 1m 42.171s; **12** Giansanti, 1m 42.254s; **13** Tokudome, 1m 42.466s; **14** Borsoi, 1m 42.570s; **15** Azuma, 1m 42.684s; **16** Hules, 1m 42.694s; **17** Cecchinello, 1m 42.910s; **18** Geissler, 1m 42.985s; **19** Raudies, 1m 43.236s; **20** Katoh, 1m 43.581s; **21** Sarda, 1m 43.670s; **22** Nieto Jnr, 1m 44.090s; **23** Yuzy, 1m 44.093s; **24** Jenkner, 1m 44.422s; **25** Taylor, 1m 44.924s; **26** Soler, 1m 46.157s; **27** Willy, 1m 46.751s; **28** Strugnell, 1m 47.262s; **29** Galvin, 1m 49.329s; **30** Bool, 1m 49.813s; **31** Armstrong, 1m 50.377s.

Fastest race laps: 1 Sakata, 1m 40.348s; **2** Ueda, 1m 40.518s; **3** Rossi, 1m 40.586s; **4** Manako, 1m 40.648s; **5** Locatelli, 1m 40.789s; **6** Scalvini, 1m 41.083s; **7** Giansanti, 1m 41.471s; **8** Cecchinello, 1m 41.503s; **9** Geissler, 1m 41.870s; **10** Azuma, 1m 41.917s; **11** Tokudome, 1m 42.050s; **12** Martinez, 1m 42.169s; **13** Jenkner, 1m 42.210s; **14** Raudies, 1m 42.222s; **15** Petit, 1m 42.252s; **16** McCoy, 1m 42.276s; **17** Maturana, 1m 42.530s; **18** Sarda, 1m 42.766s; **19** Nieto Jnr, 1m 42.836s; **20** Katoh, 1m 43.012s; **21** Yuzy, 1m 43.911s; **22** Taylor, 1m 44.701s; **23** Soler, 1m 46.767s; **24** Strugnell, 1m 46.890s; **25** Bool, 1m 48.181s; **26** Galvin, 1m 50.029s; **27** Armstrong, 1m 50.451s; **28** Borsoi, 1m 52.473s.

Final World Championship points: see pages 144-5.

In a fitting finale to the season, three riders fight it out for first: Criville ahead of Takuma Aoki and Abe.

500 cc

Position	Rider	Nationality	Machine	Malaysia	Japan	Spain	Italy	Austria	France	Holland	Imola	Germany	Rio	Britain	Czech Republic	Catalunya	Indonesia	Australia	Points total
1	Michael Doohan	AUS	Honda	25	25	20	25	25	25	25	25	25	25	25	25	25	20	–	340
2	Tadayuki Okada	J	Honda	6	16	16	–	20	16	4	11	20	20	20	–	10	25	13	197
3	Nobuatsu Aoki	J	Honda	16	11	11	16	13	–	13	20	13	13	13	16	11	13	–	179
4	Alex Criville	E	Honda	20	20	25	13	11	13	–	–	–	–	–	13	16	16	25	172
5	Takuma Aoki	J	Honda	11	13	13	–	–	11	–	16	16	–	6	10	9	9	20	134
6	Luca Cadalora	I	Yamaha	13	5	5	20	16	–	–	–	10	–	16	11	20	13	–	129
7	Norifumi Abe	J	Yamaha	8	9	9	9	7	9	6	9	–	11	7	11	4	11	16	126
8	Carlos Checa	E	Honda	10	10	–	–	10	20	20	13	–	–	–	–	20	10	6	119
9	Alex Barros	BR	Honda	5	6	8	10	3	10	10	7	10	–	16	8	–	–	8	101
10	Doriano Romboni	I	Aprilia	–	–	10	5	6	5	16	–	11	9	9	–	6	6	5	88
11 =	Daryl Beattie	AUS	Suzuki	–	–	4	11	5	4	9	3	4	3	10	6	–	4	–	63
11 =	Alberto Puig	E	Honda	9	8	–	–	8	8	11	4	6	2	–	3	1	2	1	63
13	Sete Gibernau	E	Yamaha	7	–	7	7	–	3	–	5	9	–	–	–	–	8	10	56
14	Regis Laconi	F	Honda	4	4	6	6	–	–	–	–	7	–	9	5	–	11	–	52
15	Anthony Gobert	AUS	Suzuki	–	–	–	3	9	6	3	6	7	6	–	4	–	–	–	44
16 =	Juan Borja	E	Elf 500	2	–	–	–	4	7	1	–	8	–	8	–	7	–	–	37
16 =	Kenny Roberts Jnr	USA	Modenas	–	–	–	–	–	8	–	–	–	–	5	7	8	7	2	37
18	Jean-Michel Bayle	F	Modenas	–	2	3	8	2	–	–	8	–	8	–	–	–	–	–	31
19	Jurgen van den Goorbergh	NL	Honda	1	1	2	–	–	1	–	–	5	5	3	5	2	–	4	29
20	Jurgen Fuchs	D	Elf 500	–	–	–	–	–	–	7	2	3	10	1	–	–	5	–	28
21	Kirk McCarthy	AUS	Yamaha	–	–	1	2	–	–	–	1	1	4	4	–	3	1	3	20
22	Peter Goddard	AUS	Suzuki	–	3	–	–	–	–	–	–	–	–	–	–	3	7	–	13
23	Troy Corser	AUS	Yamaha	3	–	–	4	–	2	2	–	–	–	–	–	–	–	–	11
24	Yukio Kagayama	J	Suzuki	–	–	–	–	–	–	–	–	–	–	–	–	–	–	9	9
25 =	Norihiko Fujiwara	J	Yamaha	–	7	–	–	–	–	–	–	–	–	–	–	–	–	–	7
25 =	Bernard Garcia	F	Honda	–	–	–	–	–	5	–	2	–	–	–	–	–	–	–	7
27	Laurent Naveau	B	Yamaha	–	–	–	1	–	–	–	–	–	–	–	2	–	–	–	3
28 =	Lucio Pedercini	I	Yamaha	–	–	–	1	–	–	–	–	–	–	–	1	–	–	–	2
28 =	Jason Vincent	GB	Honda	–	–	–	–	–	–	–	–	–	–	–	2	–	–	–	2

GRAND PRIX DE FRANCE
CIRCUIT PAUL RICARD
8 JUIN 1997
1er 500cc

1 WORLD CHAMPIONSHIP POINTS

250 cc

Position	Rider	Nationality	Machine	Malaysia	Japan	Spain	Italy	Austria	France	Holland	Imola	Germany	Rio	Britain	Czech Republic	Catalunya	Indonesia	Australia	Points total
1	Max Biaggi	I	Honda	25	9	16	25	16	20	–	25	13	11	–	25	20	25	20	250
2	Ralf Waldmann	D	Honda	13	11	25	13	20	16	20	13	16	4	25	13	25	9	25	248
3	Tetsuya Harada	J	Aprilia	20	16	20	–	–	25	25	11	25	20	20	16	13	13	11	235
4	Olivier Jacque	F	Honda	16	–	9	11	25	–	–	20	20	25	13	20	10	16	16	201
5	Tohru Ukawa	J	Honda	10	20	–	–	11	11	13	16	10	16	11	11	16	20	8	173
6	Loris Capirossi	I	Aprilia	–	5	–	16	13	13	16	–	11	13	16	–	11	2	–	116
7	Takeshi Tsujimura	J	Honda	–	13	13	–	9	–	10	–	3	8	10	10	9	11	13	109
8	Haruchika Aoki	J	Honda	11	8	11	2	8	10	–	8	7	9	8	–	8	10	2	102
9	Stefano Perugini	I	Aprilia	–	–	10	9	10	–	11	–	–	10	9	9	–	8	9	85
10	Jeremy McWilliams	GB	Honda	7	–	7	7	–	5	7	9	8	6	–	–	5	6	6	73
11	Sebastian Porto	ARG	Aprilia	–	4	–	6	7	9	–	–	–	7	7	6	–	7	7	60
12	Noriyasu Numata	J	Suzuki	2	7	8	10	6	–	–	–	9	–	6	–	7	–	–	55
13	Osamu Miyazaki	J	Yamaha	5	–	4	1	–	6	8	7	–	–	–	2	6	3	5	47
14	Franco Battaini	I	Yamaha	3	–	2	3	2	4	5	5	5	–	5	1	1	4	4	44
15	Cristiano Migliorati	I	Honda	8	–	–	–	–	–	3	3	1	5	–	7	–	5	3	35
16	Luis D'Antin	E	Yamaha	–	–	5	5	5	8	6	–	–	–	–	–	3	–	–	32
17	Emilio Alzamora	E	Honda	9	–	–	–	–	–	–	6	6	2	–	4	4	–	–	31
18	Marcellino Lucchi	I	Aprilia	–	–	–	20	–	–	10	–	–	–	–	–	–	–	–	30
19	Daijiro Kato	J	Honda	–	25	–	–	–	–	–	–	–	–	–	–	–	–	–	25
20	William Costes	F	Honda	–	–	–	–	3	7	9	4	–	–	–	–	–	–	–	23
21	José Luis Cardoso	E	Yamaha	–	–	6	–	–	–	–	–	2	–	1	3	5	2	–	19
22	Jamie Robinson	GB	Suzuki	–	2	–	8	4	–	–	1	–	–	–	3	–	–	–	18
23	Oliver Petrucciani	CH	Aprilia	6	–	3	–	1	–	4	–	–	–	–	–	–	–	–	14
24	Luca Boscoscuro	I	Honda	1	–	1	4	–	–	–	–	2	3	–	–	–	1	1	13
25	Giuseppe Fiorillo	I	Aprilia	–	–	–	–	–	–	–	–	4	–	8	–	–	–	–	12
26 =	Troy Bayliss	AUS	Suzuki	–	–	–	–	–	–	–	–	–	–	–	–	–	–	10	10
26 =	Yukio Kagayama	J	Suzuki	–	10	–	–	–	–	–	–	–	–	–	–	–	–	–	10
28	Naoki Matsudo	J	Yamaha	–	6	–	–	–	–	–	–	–	–	–	–	–	–	–	6
29	Eustaquio Gavira	E	Aprilia	4	–	–	–	–	–	1	–	–	–	–	–	–	–	–	5
30	Scott Smart	GB	Honda	–	–	–	–	–	–	–	–	–	–	–	4	–	–	–	4
31 =	Sebastien Gimbert	F	Honda	–	–	–	–	–	3	–	–	–	–	–	–	–	–	–	3
31 =	Naoto Ogura	J	Yamaha	–	3	–	–	–	–	–	–	–	–	–	–	–	–	–	3
33 =	Maurice Bolwerk	NL	Honda	–	–	–	–	–	–	2	–	–	–	–	–	–	–	–	2
33 =	Idalio Gavira	E	Aprilia	–	–	–	–	–	2	–	–	–	–	–	–	–	–	–	2
33 =	John McGuiness	GB	Aprilia	–	–	–	–	–	–	–	–	–	–	–	–	2	–	–	2
36 =	Choujun Kameya	J	Suzuki	–	1	–	–	–	–	–	–	–	–	–	–	–	–	–	1
36 =	Callum Ramsay	GB	Honda	–	–	–	–	–	–	–	–	–	–	–	1	–	–	–	1
36 =	Claudio Vanzetta	CH	Aprilia	–	–	–	–	–	1	–	–	–	–	–	–	–	–	–	1

125 cc

Position	Rider	Nationality	Machine	Malaysia	Japan	Spain	Italy	Austria	France	Holland	Imola	Germany	Rio	Britain	Czech Republic	Catalunya	Indonesia	Australia	Points total
1	Valentino Rossi	I	Aprilia	25	–	25	25	20	25	25	25	25	25	25	16	25	25	10	321
2	Noboru Ueda	J	Honda	16	25	20	13	25	–	13	11	–	20	16	25	16	13	25	238
3	Tomomi Manako	J	Honda	9	4	11	11	16	20	20	20	–	13	8	20	11	11	16	190
4	Kazuto Sakata	J	Aprilia	20	20	9	10	10	–	16	16	–	11	–	7	20	20	20	179
5	Masaki Tokudome	J	Aprilia	11	3	13	9	11	–	9	–	7	6	20	8	5	10	8	120
6	Jorge Martinez	E	Aprilia	10	11	16	20	–	10	10	10	9	–	–	4	16	3	–	119
7	Garry McCoy	AUS	Aprilia	–	9	–	16	13	16	–	13	–	3	13	5	7	7	7	109
8	Roberto Locatelli	I	Honda	–	5	8	2	8	–	8	9	–	5	11	13	9	6	13	97
9 =	Mirko Giansanti	I	Honda	13	–	4	–	–	9	–	6	9	10	9	4	13	–	6	83
9 =	Frédéric Petit	F	Honda	7	6	3	7	6	11	7	–	13	7	7	1	6	2	–	83
11	Gianluigi Scalvini	I	Honda	–	7	–	4	7	8	3	5	4	–	5	10	8	9	11	81
12	Youichi Ui	J	Yamaha	–	–	–	6	9	13	11	8	–	16	–	6	–	8	–	77
13	Yoshiaki Katoh	J	Yamaha	8	10	6	1	–	10	–	4	20	–	10	–	3	–	2	74
14	Lucio Cecchinello	I	Honda	6	–	1	8	–	–	–	–	11	8	6	11	10	3	9	73
15	Masao Azuma	J	Honda	4	13	7	5	5	7	6	7	–	–	3	–	–	5	4	66
16	Manfred Geissler	D	Aprilia	–	–	–	–	3	–	4	–	16	–	4	3	–	–	1	31
17	Juan Enrique Maturana	E	Yamaha	–	–	–	–	2	5	2	–	6	1	1	–	–	–	5	22
18	Ivan Goi	I	Aprilia	3	2	5	3	4	–	1	–	3	–	–	–	–	–	–	21
19	Steve Jenkner	D	Aprilia	–	–	–	–	–	1	3	–	4	–	9	2	1	–	–	20
20	Gino Borsoi	I	Yamaha	–	1	–	–	–	4	–	–	8	2	–	–	4	–	–	19
21	Jaroslav Hules	CS	Honda	5	–	2	–	–	–	5	3	–	–	–	2	–	–	–	17
22	Hideyuki Nakajo	J	Honda	–	16	–	–	–	–	–	–	–	–	–	–	–	–	–	16
23	Peter Öttl	D	Aprilia	–	–	10	–	–	–	–	1	–	–	–	–	–	–	–	11
24 =	Angel Nieto Jnr	E	Aprilia	–	–	–	–	–	1	–	2	5	–	–	–	–	–	–	8
24 =	Dirk Raudies	D	Honda	2	–	–	–	–	6	–	–	–	–	–	–	–	–	–	8
24 =	Kazuhiro Takao	J	Honda	–	8	–	–	–	–	–	–	–	–	–	–	–	–	–	8
27	Josep Sarda	E	Honda	1	–	–	–	–	2	–	–	–	–	–	–	–	–	–	3
28 =	Darren Barton	GB	Honda	–	–	–	–	–	–	–	–	–	–	–	2	–	–	–	2
28 =	Alex Hofmann	D	Yamaha	–	–	–	–	–	–	–	–	2	–	–	–	–	–	–	2
30 =	Benny Jerzenbeck	D	Honda	–	–	–	–	–	–	–	–	1	–	–	–	–	–	–	1
30 =	Alvaro Molina	E	Honda	–	–	–	–	–	–	–	–	–	–	–	–	–	1	–	1

HONDA SCRATCH THEIR SEVEN-YEAR ITCH

by Stephane van Gelder

AFTER so many disheartening years chasing Ducati, it came as a surprise to see Team Castrol Honda claim their first World Superbike Championship before the season had even ended. The past few years have seen some epic title bouts, so when Honda's long sought-after prize finally came, it almost came too easily. Still, the 1997 crown stands as a clear tribute to HRC's huge determination. And to John Kocinski's huge talent.

Ever since the RC45 was first introduced, in 1994, Honda's race engineers have never stopped working to turn it into a winner. The bike's first win came in 1995 but it wasn't until last year that it really started shaking Ducati's confidence. This season Honda added the final ingredient to ensure victory: John Kocinski. The well-run Castrol Honda team did the rest by providing Kocinski with the organisational rigour he needed to stay focused all season long.

Lady Luck also played an important part in the championship: 1997 was the wettest World Superbike season on record, with the first three rounds all disrupted by heavy downpours. That gave rain master Kocinski the time he needed to adapt to the Honda's unorthodox track manners.

Over in the Ducati camp, Carl Fogarty never quite managed to get to grips with his bike. Spurned for a year in favour of a Japanese mistress, the 916 wasn't going to welcome its old partner back with open arms. Fogarty was made to work hard to try and re-establish some kind of marital harmony. Too hard. By the season's end he was crashing too often...just like he had done in 1993, when he lost the title to Kawasaki-mounted Scott Russell.

Kocinski, meanwhile, was looking more serene by the minute. He claimed his crown at Sugo – a symbolic round if ever there was one. Local hero Noriyuki Haga gave the factory Yamaha team a win that had always eluded their full-time riders. And it was here, on home ground, that Honda finally predominated over the Ducatis.

AREAS OF POTENTIAL DANGER
AND GREAT CARE SHOULD BE
EXERCISED

Photos: Gold & Goose

THE RC45 COMES OF AGE

The Bikes of 1997

BETWEEN them, John Kocinski and Aaron Slight won twelve races this year. That's one Honda win for every round of the season. Never before has the RC45 been so successful. Indeed, during the first half of the 1997 season, the RC45 won more times than it had from 1994 to 1996! Statistics like these show that HRC's V4 wonderbike really came of age in 1997.

'Honda's been setting the standard for four-stroke racers for a while,' argues Nick Goodison, John Kocinski's chief mechanic. 'The RC45 has always been the most advanced bike in the paddock. And I think it always will be because Honda are constantly looking to better everything they've got.' Goodison worked with Carl Fogarty in 1996. His interpretation of Honda's racing philosophy helps explain the RC45's supremacy and the fact that this year, for the first time, it was considered the most balanced package in World Superbikes.

An impressive achievement. When it was first introduced in 1994, the RC45 was hailed as a worthy successor to the legendary RC30. Going against the in-line four-cylinder format favoured by the other Japanese manufacturers, Honda had kept the V4 cylinder layout. But the wins failed to come and the RC45 was considered disappointing...almost a failure.

'I never really understood why the bike got such a bad rap,' remembers Aaron Slight. 'We've seen Yamaha and Suzuki come into World Superbikes and not do anything. When I first got on the Honda, in 1994, we finished third in the championship. So I think it's quite an amazing bike!'

Far from losing faith, Honda just kept refining its product. World Superbike technical regulations prevented any major changes, but the RC45 has still come a long way since its inaugural year. 'Everything's been upgraded from last year,' explains Goodison. 'The bike may look the same on the outside this year, but there's so many tiny differences it's like last year's model was the prototype and this year it's the finished product. Every little niggly thing that we had last year has been sorted now and it's a very good bike. But the only completely new system on the bike is the CBS braking system.'

Considered a marketing gimmick when it was officially presented at the first round of the season, Racing CBS actually seemed to give Aaron Slight an edge at places like Donington. 'The CBS is a mix of electrical and mechanical systems,' reveals Goodison. 'It works off a pressure sensor on the front brake which activates the whole thing and applies the rear with the front. It helps keep the bike stable on corner entry.'

Much more refined than the systems used by Honda on their production motor cycles like the CBR 1100 XX, the Racing CBS is multi-adjustable. 'We can change the power, how long it's on for and at what pressure it operates,' adds Goodison. But because it requires a separate caliper on the rear brake, John Kocinski did not use it for long. The American sometimes preferred a Doohan-style thumb-operated rear brake which also calls upon an additional rear caliper and thus prohibits the use of the Racing CBS.

Making the RC45 so competitive has taken great amounts of HRC's phenomenal R&D budget and this is reflected in the bike's complexity. It is by far the most technologically advanced Superbike, with the biggest step forward this year being the twin injector system. This has pushed power up by about ten horses and significantly improved the RC45's acceleration. Off the record, HRC engineers now boast of total power outputs in excess of 180 horsepower.

Whatever the figures, the RC45 is a technological tour de force that few people can work with. 'We're in constant touch with Japan and we really do need that back-up,' stresses Goodison. 'Without it, it would be difficult to get the best out of the bike. It's becoming so advanced now, it's getting away from the basics of bike racing as we know it. Plus you need to have worked on the bike last year to understand this year's changes. Otherwise, you simply wouldn't be able to operate the bike properly. You need to understand the computer to appreciate the tiny differences that make all the difference. These can easily go unnoticed if you don't know what you're looking for or if you can't crossover last year's information.'

The RC45's progress has shown up some of the Ducati's weaknesses which were not readily apparent before. One of the reasons Carl Fogarty switched back to Ducati this year was that he found the Honda more difficult to ride than the 916. Ironically, while the Honda got better, the 1997 Ducati changed dramatically. 'It feels a different bike to ride through the corners,' explains Fogarty. 'I remember having a very smooth flowing bike in '95 but now, in the middle of the corners, I've got a bit of a beast to ride. We've got to work really hard to get the bike set up, whereas it seemed easier in 1995.'

Nick Goodison reckons that Ducati's difficulties are a result of Honda's superior development techniques. These are highlighted by the differences in the two manufacturers' injection systems. 'The Ducati system may work, but probably it's a long way off its optimum running,' Goodison suggests. 'It works so they've just left it, whereas the Japanese are constantly looking for ways to improve their products. It's one thing to put an injection system on a bike, but to tune an injection system is a different thing altogether. I think Ducati have about three or four different chips and that's it. They have to change the whole range whereas we can change absolutely any part of the range. We can change the power curve as a whole but we can even change ignition timing for specific gears.'

This attention to detail may well be Honda's most important asset. Ducati's lack of engine and injection development was shown up at Brands Hatch, when the factory produced a new chip to alter engine character and hence improve handling. Brands pole-setter and first race winner Pier Francesco Chili was delighted with this development. 'I spoke with the engineers after Laguna and, as a result, they brought us these new parts,' Chili claimed. 'The new chip has improved handling a lot. Before, the engine speed did not come down fast enough when we slowed down for a corner. That made it hard to pitch the bike into the corner. At Laguna, I was forced to go into some corners

Opposite page: With only minor evolutionary changes, Honda's RC45 achieved its potential at last.

Below: Detail development continued on Yamaha's YZF 750, the oldest Superbike in the paddock.

a lot slower than I knew I could go and I realised that our handling problems came from the engine. The new chip has softened the power curve a bit and helped the revs come down faster.'

So what had made the Ducati's balance alter so dramatically from 1996? It seems the gradual increase in capacity and the alterations made to the 916 to adapt it to the new minimum weight have led to the bike losing its legendary smoothness. 'Our bikes are no longer the way they were meant to be,' says Virginio Ferrari, Fogarty's team manager. 'In 1994, the 916 weighed 146 kg and our engine power varied from 138 to 141 hp depending on the track. Since then, every year we've pushed power up by about 4 hp. We've had to just keep to the same level of performance since, during the same period, our minimum weight has gone up to 162 kg. Today, our engine makes about 154 hp and its character has changed drastically.'

Once again, it seems the rudimentary nature of Ducati's injection system must take the blame. Ducati has gone from last year's 54 mm throttle bodies to a huge 60 mm for 1997. 'These make power delivery a lot more aggressive low down,' says Ferrari. 'Before, power came in smoothly.' Ducati's problems have been worsened by the departure of Corser and Kocinski. Both Fogarty and Chili, Ducati's strong men for 1997, lacked experience with the '96 bike. Fogarty was riding a Honda at the time and Chili did not have constant access to full factory machinery. Fogarty had tried the 996 cc engine just before he left Ducati in 1995, at the last race of the season at Phillip Island. 'It already felt different then,' he recalls. 'I had problems with it and didn't win the last race, which annoyed me. They just put the big engine in my chassis and it altered the handling of the bike. The 996 cc is just a different bike to the 955 cc we were using at that time. Obviously it's the right way to go because the times are better, but it's just a harder bike to ride.'

There's also another aspect to the problem: the 996 cc is now heavier by design. When the FIM decided that twins should no longer enjoy a weight advantage over the fours, Ducati still had a bike that was designed to weigh 145 kg. To comply with the new regulations, the Italians simply put lead weights wherever they wanted. Altering the weight balance of the bike was child's play.

Since then, however, the factory has taken advantage of the higher minimum weight to improve the 916's reliability. A new street model, the 916 SPS, was introduced this year to homologate the 1997 race bike with a reinforced version of the 996 cc V-twin. Modifications include stronger crankcases and thicker cylinder walls. The extra weight has thus been put to good use, but the down side is that the 162 kg are now built into the race bike. Changing weight distribution is no longer a case of moving a few blocks of lead about.

True Superbike development will always be limited by the very nature of the class: the need to be based on production motor cycles. A new chassis or a new engine might be the miracle cure to a bike's lack of performance or results, but to use them a manufacturer must first homologate them on a new model. This is something which Yamaha has been reluctant to do, so that their YZF 750 remained the oldest bike in the paddock this year. Still, development has continued on the YZF. 'We've had small changes in the chassis,' disclosed Yamaha team manager Davide Brivio. 'The swing arm has changed a bit and we've improved the rear suspension and front forks thanks to our very close relationship with Ohlins. In Japan, they tried to give the engine more torque and we then concentrated on getting better top-end power. The riders now seem happy with the level of torque – our acceleration is not so bad. So our target is now to work on top-end power. Maybe we forgot about this a little bit while we were concentrating on torque in the last few years.'

Through the use of a modified

intake and lighter crankshafts, Yamaha engineers were thus able to boost acceleration between 8000 and 10,000 revs. Meanwhile, Brivio and the Yamaha factory team continued trying to wring the last few ounces of performance out of their ageing motor cycle.

'It's difficult to continue working on an engine that's been around for many years because the engineers have probably done all that it was possible to do with it,' laments Brivio. 'Every year, it gets harder and harder to increase the engine's performance. So it would be very useful for us to have a new bike. But our old engine is still very competitive.'

From the oldest Superbike to the newest: the Kawasaki and Suzuki entries both failed to make much more of an impression on the Honda-Ducati domination than Yamaha. Both the Kawasaki ZX-7R and the Suzuki GSX-R750 were introduced in 1996, but have yet to live up to expectations.

For 1997, Kawasaki introduced a whole new team into the fray and the ZX-7R was updated. 'It's the same basic homologated bike but we changed a few things on the chassis and suspension,' explains Kawasaki team manager Harald Eckl. 'The engine has different cam-timings, different cylinder heads, different pistons...small changes which, taken together, have quite a big effect.'

Indeed, the 1996 ZX-7R's chronic lack of top-end power is now a thing of the past. This was evident from the word go, when Akira Yanagawa and Simon Crafar qualified very strongly at Phillip Island. It was further highlighted by Crafar's Hockenheim performance, the Kiwi landing his first World Superbike pole at one of the fastest tracks on the calendar. With the increase in power the ZX-7R now makes around 158 hp, so Kawasaki engineers could concentrate on other parts of the rev range. 'It's important to get mid-range and make the bike as rideable as possible,' claims Eckl. 'You must get the power down on the road and if you get better traction out of corners, you get better top speeds. We've got more top-end power, more power overall, so we must now concentrate more on mid-range and bottom power.'

Suzuki's 1997 modifications were quite extensive. Lester Harris and his team dared to make drastic changes to put the GSX-R750 on a par with its competitors. 'We made some fundamental changes,' admits Harris. 'Going from Kayaba to Showa was one. It meant that all the suspension data we had from last year became useless. We had to start again. There were different suspension links, different swing arms, triple clamps...a lot of changes in an effort to make the bike turn quicker – to change the stiffness of the machine.'

In its debut season, the GSX-R proved very fickle to set up. The slightest variation in track conditions (temperature or grip, for example) from one test day to the next was enough to upset it. So Team Harris did a lot of work on suspension balance and weight distribution in an effort to get a more balanced package. They even ran a separate test programme in England, in addition to the official development work done by the factory in Japan.

Suzuki also suffered from the same plague as Kawasaki and Yamaha. Their four-cylinder has plenty of power but lacked mid-range. A host of small improvements were implemented to try and reduce internal friction this year, and the 40 mm carburettors were replaced by 42 mm units. 'There is no doubt the bike is faster this year,' claims Harris. 'But there is always a trade-off with these things and we found we had a slight deficit of mid-range power. We'd pushed it all up top and realised we had to start working on broadening the power spread.'

So 1997 did little to change the hierarchy of World Superbike racing. Yamaha, Kawasaki and Suzuki are still playing catch-up to Honda and Ducati. The big move was there at the top, with Honda finally producing a true Ducati beater.

NEW AND OLD DREAMS

Photos: Gold & Goose

Who Was Who in 1997

CONTINUITY was the word in 1997 as far as the big teams were concerned. With one major exception. German Harald Eckl replaced American Rob Muzzy at the head of Team Kawasaki Racing. Kawasaki's Japanese bosses were known to have grown increasingly dissatisfied, and rumours of a change had been flying around for a while: nobody was surprised when it was officially announced.

Eckl had been contacted during the summer of 1996. 'Last August, between two GPs, Kawasaki Germany asked me if I could see myself running the Kawasaki Superbike team in 1997,' recalls the ex-125 cc GP team manager. 'We discussed this, two months passed and they came back to tell me they wanted to work with me.'

Muzzy's partnership with Kawasaki did not end with the loss of the World Superbike team. The man behind Scott Russell's 1993 Superbike world title remained in charge of Kawasaki's Superbike efforts in America. This is an extremely successful venture for Muzzy, and Doug Chandler claimed his second consecutive national title this year.

With a three-year contract assuring him of a fair degree of professional stability, Eckl set about restructuring the Kawasaki operation. New workshops were built in Eckl's home town of Vohenstrauss, in Germany, where the team would now be based. A new hospitality unit was introduced to the paddock and efforts were made to improve public relations.

Eckl signed his contract in November, so the riders he would work with had already been lined up. Talented Kiwi Simon Crafar was kept on, his experience of the World Superbike Championship bringing a measure of stability to a changing team. Japanese newcomer Akira Yanagawa was hired as Crafar's team-mate.

There were other fundamental differences in the way the team was run this year. 'The most obvious one from last year is budget,' explained Crafar. 'We've got a lot more to play with this year, more back-up. As for team management, I think Harald is on a higher level. He doesn't care so much about what other people think. It's just what it takes to do the job and to improve the bike.'

Healthier finances and Eckl's more determined approach did not lead to an immediate title challenge from Kawasaki, although that would have been too much to ask from a team that spent the year learning to work together. In fact, Eckl's outfit acquitted themselves very well for a first season, as Yanagawa's wins clearly show. Crafar came close to winning on a number of occasions too, but he suffered an appalling run of bad luck which saw him taken out of races at critical times by other riders' crashes and by frustrating engine failures.

Still, Kawasaki continued to provide the only real alternative to the Honda-Ducati domination. The two major forces in World Superbike racing had swapped their number one riders for this year. Carl Fogarty had announced his return to Virginio Ferrari's factory Ducati team before the 1996 season even ended. Fogarty had apparently found it difficult to adapt to the strict Castrol Honda team. He also claimed that his career was now winding down and that he wanted to end it on a bike that was easier to ride than the Honda.

Bad move. In 1997 the Honda often looked a lot less of a handful than the Ducati. Fogarty and Italian Pier Francesco Chili spent half the season trying to get to grips with the latest 916's recalcitrant handling.

Following the decision by Troy Corser and the Promotor team to move to 500 GP racing rather than defend their 1996 title, Ducati chose not to run two full factory teams again this year. Most of their title hopes therefore rested on Fogarty and Chili. Although Pier Francesco Chili had stayed with the Italian Gattolone team, he now received a full factory bike and the same level of support as Fogarty. In effect, Gattolone was Ducati's second official team, albeit one the factory did not have to fund directly.

Fogarty's team-mate in the factory squad, run again by Virginio Ferrari, was fellow-Englishman Neil Hodgson. He sometimes looked good, setting pole at Donington for example, but never displayed the same potential for brilliance as Fogarty.

Fogarty had swapped places with John Kocinski and just as the Englishman craved a more relaxed atmosphere than the one he'd endured at Honda in 1996, so Kocinski hoped for a more rigorous organisation than the one he'd witnessed in Ferrari's team. Moving to Honda provided Kocinski with that well-oiled environment he had been looking for. It was also the fulfilment of a career-long ambition to work with the world's number one motor cycle manufacturer.

On paper, Honda seemed to have the strongest team for 1997. Castrol Honda team manager Neil Tuxworth had retained the services of Aaron Slight alongside Kocinski. Slight's experience is unique, as the Kiwi has ridden the RC45 since it first came out in 1994. With the bike improving every year, Slight certainly ranked among the title favourites.

Another very strong team was the Yamaha squad run by Italian importer Belgarda. Under team manager Davide Brivio's leadership, a true family atmosphere has developed at Yamaha that is unique to the World Superbike paddock. 'Since our team was set up in 1995, we've only changed one mechanic in our organisation,' boasted Brivio. 'We've not changed anyone else, apart from the riders. Not the cook in our hospitality, no one. That is very good for our team.'

Just as beneficial to morale was the arrival of 1993 World Superbike Champion Scott Russell, who had just spent a rather difficult season and a half with the Suzuki 500 Grand Prix team. Russell and long-time Yamaha ace Colin Edwards immediately built up a very good relationship. 'Since Scott's come into it, we're a real team,' rejoiced Edwards when asked to summarize the differences between this and previous years. 'It was a little bit tough with the two Japanese riders (Yasutomo Nagai in 1995 and Wataru Yoshikawa last year)

Frankie Chili and Carl Fogarty – the Briton was back on a Ducati again. *Opposite:* After 18 months in the GPs, Scott Russell was back chasing old dreams with a new fin on his helmet, but it was left to part-timer Noriyuki Haga *(right)* to take Yamaha's only race win. *Bottom left:* Virginio Ferrari had his eyes on another title for the Ducati factory team. *Below:* The new Green Gang *(from left to right):* Yanagawa, Eckl and Crafar.

because they hardly spoke any English. They spoke Japanese to the Japanese engineers and they spoke broken English to me. So I didn't really feel the communication there was spot on. Now that Scott's here we can do so much in a day's worth of testing, two or three times as much as we did before, simply because we communicate so well.'

Suzuki's GSX-R750 is by no means a winner yet, but Lester Harris and his men have shown that the bike is a potential podium finisher. Full credit for that must go to James Whitham. There were two new Suzuki riders this year, but the British rider was the true revelation. The performance of his team-mate, American Mike Hale, despite being back on a four-cylinder bike that he's always claimed suited his style more, was something of a disappointment.

It took Team Harris a lot of effort to get Whitham and the Suzuki on the podium. It also required time for the team and their Japanese bosses to learn to trust and depend upon each other. 'That's what I've been trying to do,' claimed Harris. 'To build a good enough relationship with Suzuki to allow me more leeway in what we do with the bike. The Japanese as a nation are cautious people. They take a long time to trust your judgement. But they've worked with us for a year now. They can see that we know what we are doing. They can see that our development ideas are actually going in the right direction. And as they allow us more freedom, we're seeing more results.'

Factory teams aside, there were few real competitors making up the rest of the grid. The major privateer teams were once again Bertocchi and GioCaMoto.

Bertocchi can be considered a semi-factory Kawasaki team. Piergiorgio Bontempi had a 1996 works engine in his Kawasaki until Albacete, where he was given this year's engine.

GioCaMoto also get help from the factory, and this year the Italian team hired Briton James Haydon. The season did not go well: Haydon and the team went their separate ways after Albacete and Supermono champion Makoto Suzuki took over the Gio-CaMoto Ducati for Sugo and Sentul.

Other regular privateers included Kawasaki riders Jochen Schmid and Slovene Igor Jerman, Honda-mounted Pere Riba Cabana and Ducati's Andreas Meklau. Jerman competed for the full season, the Spanish rider missed the Laguna Seca round, Schmid rode at selected meetings and Meklau was sidelined by injury for the last third of the season.

Don't forget the privateers

Privateers make racing possible. Cut out the small teams and you'll soon end up with a moribund championship. The high-profile factory teams monopolise the best riders and machinery, as well as every camera shot and TV broadcast, but they cannot exist alone. It's the privateers who fill the grids, and provide (relatively) cheap and easy access to international racing for would-be stars.

World Superbikes used to be a privateers' championship, seemingly becoming more factory oriented by natural progression. But have the Supers forgotten their roots? In a bid to please the factories, the series appears to have shunned the more modest teams and riders.

Today, World Superbikes are going down the same road that led the 500 GP class close to extinction at the turn of the decade – until Yamaha handed out competitive V4 engines to specialist manufacturers Harris and ROC, and the new order made increased start money and travel funds available to privateers.

In World Superbikes, the privateers' fund is a lot less generous – and there is a distinct lack of competitive machinery on offer. The only real option is Ducati's 916, but the Italian twin needs to be fed a constant supply of spare parts to avoid breakdowns. That gets very expensive. Too expensive for most private teams, who have thus been recycling their riders into the newly born Supersport World Series.

Long-standing Superbike outfits like GioCaMoto, Alstare or Yamaha Belgarda have taken some of their World Superbike regulars like Mauro Lucchiari, Paolo Casoli or Massimo Meregalli – and even veterans like Fabrizio Pirovano and Stéphane Mertens – down a class. All these racers prefer to be front-runners in the new championship rather than staying on in Superbikes as back-row no-hopers.

Last year, World Superbike organiser Maurizio Flammini realised that something had to be done to counteract dwindling grids. A new championship was introduced in 1997, bringing together the World and European Superbike competitors. The racing ran concurrently, with two separate point-scoring systems for the participants.

It was little more than an emergency repair job to avoid having only 12 bikes on the grid, and was a far from satisfactory solution. The huge difference in lap times between the World and European Superbikers has led to some dangerous situations arising, especially at faster tracks like Hockenheim.

Other solutions are being considered. 'I wouldn't mind giving some of my expenses money to the privateers,' claims Kawasaki team manager Harald Eckl. 'The works teams don't really need this money. It's better to give it to the privateers to help them cover their costs, as in the GPs. Without this, 500s would have died already.' He would present his ideas to Flammini in forthcoming negotiations between the organiser and the manufacturers.

Flammini has ideas of his own. These include allowing some degree of leeway concerning modifications to the frame and engine bottom end. The frame rule would work in the Japanese bikes' favour by allowing them to modify the handling characteristics of their machinery without having to homologate a new model.

However, these suggestions found little favour with the teams and will probably not be implemented. The manufacturers have been more receptive to proposals for lowering the homologation numbers. At present, the Japanese are required to build 500 units of a particular model in order to clear it for World Superbike duty. But with the 750 cc sportsbike market shrinking, the Japanese are reluctant to take such commercial risks. This is the main reason why Team Yamaha will have to soldier on with the ageing YZF 750 next year: Yamaha Japan feels that the market simply does not exist for 500 state-of-the-art race replicas. If next year's homologation requirements should be brought down to Ducati's level of 200 units, that would help the Japanese produce more accessible privateer machines.

Whatever the eventual solution, these suggestions and ideas show that the problem is being taken seriously by Flammini. And so it should be. After all, two-times World Champion Carl Fogarty won his first World Superbike race on a production Ducati paid for out of his own pocket. In today's championship, such a rags-to-riches story seems like an improbable fairy-tale.

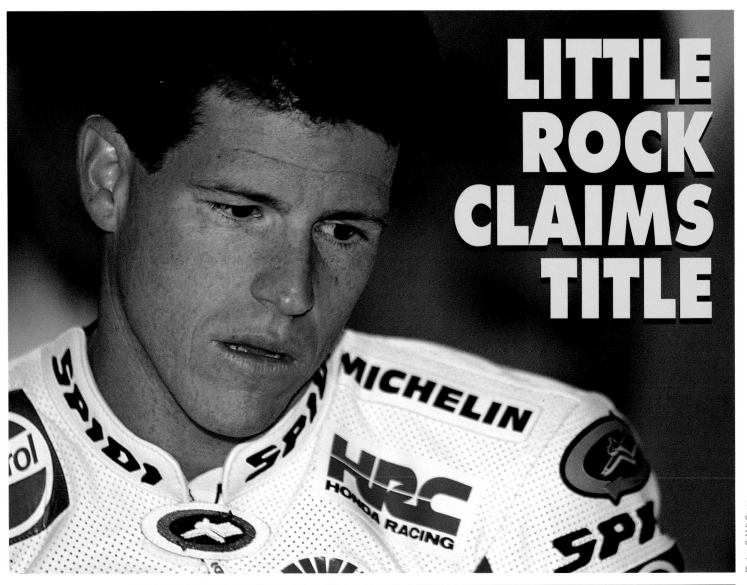

LITTLE ROCK CLAIMS TITLE

Photos: Gold & Goose

Profile of the 1997 Superbike World Champion

JOHN Kocinski had a lot to prove coming into World Superbike. He was the first major Grand Prix star since the early days of the series to make the switch to four-strokes, so his results would be bound to fuel the intense 'Superbike versus Grand Prix' arguments that have sprung up in recent years. But it was undoubtedly to himself that Kocinski had the most to prove. After a career of failed seasons, unrealised potential and often eccentric behaviour, the bad boy of motor cycle racing had a lot to atone for.

Unfortunately, his first foray into World Superbikes turned out to be the perfect example of a typical Kocinski season. He started 1996 by winning the first two races...and ended it by blaming Ducati for failing to get the expected results and falling out with his team manager, Virginio Ferrari.

There was no reason for this year to be any different. The Honda has traditionally been harder to ride than the Ducati and Kocinski would face some very determined men. Carl Fogarty was out to show that he could still be World Champion on the Ducati, after a troubled year at Honda. And Castrol Honda veteran Aaron Slight was desperate not to be upstaged by his new team-mate.

But John Kocinski's approach has always set him apart from other racers.

Even though Fogarty and Slight seemed obsessed by him, Kocinski was concentrating on other things. He was revelling in Honda's slick organisation and settling into his team extremely well. 'This is the first time in a long time that I can honestly say that I've had a team behind me,' he claimed. 'When I won the 250 cc GP championship in 1990, I felt at home with the team I had. Since then, I've just been thrown into these situations where I didn't know anybody and everyone was more concerned about making money than winning.'

Kocinski will readily admit that he's a very demanding rider to work with, and that only Honda could keep up with his expectations. 'My standards as a rider have always been very high and I think that's what caused a lot of the problems in the past. I expect so much and other people simply didn't want to work that hard. But Honda probably want to do it more than I do so I've spent all year trying to catch up to their level and that's been really fun. I've made a very nice home here (at Honda) and I intend to stay here until I retire.'

Even though he won the first race, Kocinski's 1997 season did not typically go downhill from there. Quite the opposite, in fact. He started out some way off the pace but was helped by an extraor-

dinary run of wet races which gave him time to adapt to the Honda. 'Part of being a World Champion is being able to ride in all the conditions,' Kocinski quickly reminds those who suggest that rain gave him the title. 'Whatever the weather, I was always close to the top of the tables. I just seemed to be more consistent than everyone else.'

Kocinski was also more focused than his rivals. Slight failed to maintain his early season momentum and the championship soon turned into a Fogarty/Kocinski duel. But while Fogarty crashed himself out of contention, Kocinski stayed on target. 'I never worried about or raced against Carl Fogarty,' he explained. 'I raced against myself. I tried so hard every week to give good information to Honda to improve my bike. It might have looked like it, but I never fought with Carl or anybody out there. I just fought with myself and tried to achieve my own goals. By doing that, I became World Champion.'

Many suspected it, but it has still taken Kocinski seven years to show that he is indeed one of the decade's great motor cycle champions. He is the first rider to be crowned in both Grands Prix and World Superbike. He has shown that, with the right backing, his talent will shine through and that he can stay consistent over a full season.

Kocinski is justifiably proud of his achievements and does not take kindly to suggestions that he won because the Honda was the best bike this year. 'Carl told everybody that he was a guy who could win on anything,' Kocinski snaps. 'But I guess he realised he couldn't win on the Honda!'

His sharp tongue combined with a tendency to be extremely aggressive on the track have not won Kocinski many friends. He remains one of the most controversial characters in the paddock, a trait highlighted by his behaviour on the last lap of the last race at Sentul. Even his own team was dismayed when he took Simon Crafar out. 'I think it's fair to say that everyone in the paddock regrets the way the season ended,' commented Castrol Honda team manager Neil Tuxworth.

Still, the 1997 World Superbike Champion showed himself to be strong both on and off the track. In taking this title, Kocinski must have silenced a few of his critics. More importantly, as far as his career is concerned, Kocinski has earned Honda's gratitude by finally making the RC45 a champion. Now all Kocinski needs to make his racing career truly exceptional is a 500 GP title. 'That would really be quite special,' he admits.

PHILLIP ISLAND

OALA HOM

BUILDER
RJ. & CA. KENT
REG. H.I.A. & H.G.F.L.

PHILLIP ISLAND

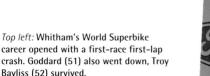

THE 1997 season started where the previous one left off, at Australia's picturesque Phillip Island circuit. There were surprises in store from the word go. Kawasaki new boy Akira Yanagawa stunned his rivals by setting a very fast provisional pole time. Aaron Slight managed to beat it in the last three minutes of the final session, but Yanagawa and team-mate Simon Crafar stayed second and third. 'We used our '97 spec bike for the first time a week ago,' revealed Crafar. 'But it looks like we have now closed the gap in power compared to the other four-cylinders.'

On Sunday, the heavens opened on southern Australia and the first race was a washout. John Kocinski led from the start while James Whitham, Pier Francesco Chili and Peter Goddard all crashed on the first lap. Chili injured his left shoulder, while Goddard broke his collarbone. By now Kocinski was being followed by Neil Hodgson, Scott Russell and Colin Edwards, but soon many of the field started biting the drenched Phillip Island dust. Hodgson went first, then Slight, Mike Hale, Russell and Edwards. This chaos left Kocinski with a comfortable lead. He won easily, ahead of Carl Fogarty, Crafar and Yanagawa. Russell managed to remount and take seventh.

The rain, which had stopped a few minutes before the start of the first race, held off for the second leg. Yanagawa led the first three laps ahead of Slight, Fogarty, Crafar, Hodgson and Edwards. Hodgson crashed on the fifth lap, leaving the others to swap places at almost every turn. Yanagawa had a spectacular crash on lap 15 when he ran off the track at high speed. Hale was forced to retire when his rear Michelin destroyed itself.

The action at the front was red hot. It soon became clear that this would go down to a last-lap fight between Edwards, Slight and Crafar – Fogarty had lost a little ground on this trio and had to make do with fourth. The closing moments of the race provided classic entertainment. Edwards had been leading, but Slight was right there and used his Honda's superior speed to devastating effect as he edged past the Yamaha in the last dash to the flag. 'Colin opened up a gap with two laps to go,' said Slight. 'But I managed to get him back under braking at Honda corner. Then I just had to stay with him around the final corner to beat him down the straight.'

The first winner of 1997 had a more difficult time in the dry. Kocinski finished seventh, behind Russell and Australian Troy Bayliss. 'We had some small problems in the dry during qualifying so I knew that I wouldn't be as fast in the second race,' confessed the American. Compared to Bayliss's two fifth places on his privateer Suzuki, the works Suzuki team's results looked decidedly poor. James Whitham scored Team Harris's only points of the week-end when he took 13th place in the second leg.

Top left: Whitham's World Superbike career opened with a first-race first-lap crash. Goddard (51) also went down, Troy Bayliss (52) survived.

Above centre: Two rostrums for Crafar showed that the revised Kawasaki team had strength for 1997.

Above and right: Colin Edwards made the second-race rostrum for Yamaha.

Left: The rewards of fame. Ex-GP recruit Neil Hodgson now had a factory ride, superstar shades, and travelled in a prestigious complimentary limousine.

Far left: Foggy was back on the Ducati after an unhappy Honda year. Would it once again be the combination?

Not if John Kocinski *(below)* had anything to do with it. He made the reverse switch, and won directly.

Round 1 PHILLIP ISLAND, Australia

23 March, 2.764-mile/4.448-km circuit

2 x 22 laps, 60.456 miles/97.856 km

Race 1

Pl. Name Nat. (Machine)	No.	Time & speed	Laps
1 John Kocinski, USA (Honda)	3	41m 16.551s	22
		88.428 mph/142.311 km/h	
2 Carl Fogarty, GB (Ducati)	4	41m 32.273s	22
3 Simon Crafar, NZ (Kawasaki)	6	41m 45.509s	22
4 Akira Yanagawa, J (Kawasaki)	8	41m 57.457s	22
5 Troy Bayliss, AUS (Suzuki)	52	42m 45.500s	22
6 Marty Craggill, AUS (Kawasaki)	32	41m 23.965s	21
7 Scott Russell, USA (Yamaha)	22	41m 28.785s	21
8 Andreas Meklau, A (Ducati)	13	41m 29.507s	21
9 Shawn Giles, AUS (Honda)*	21	41m 49.573s	21
10 Pere Riba Cabana, E (Honda)	17	41m 56.173s	21
11 Jason Love, AUS (Ducati)*	35	42m 10.747s	21
12 Igor Jerman, SLO (Kawasaki)	31	42m 18.052s	21
13 Benn Archibald, AUS (Kawasaki)	69	42m 29.513s	21
14 Greg Moss, AUS (Honda)*	38	43m 01.195s	21
15 Craig Stafford, AUS (Yamaha)*	48	42m 16.693s	20
16 Steve Martin, AUS (Suzuki)*	99	42m 25.336s	20
17 Stephen Tozer, AUS (Kawasaki)*	66	42m 12.408s	19
18 Simon Middleton, AUS (Kawasaki)*	34	42m 43.766s	19

DNF Graeme Wilshaw, AUS (Suzuki) 62, 16 laps; Piergiorgio Bontempi, I (Kawasaki) 15, 10 laps; Colin Edwards, USA (Yamaha) 45, 9 laps; Damon Buckmaster, AUS (Kawasaki) 44, 7 laps; Craig Connell, AUS (Ducati) 39, 7 laps; Mike Hale, USA (Suzuki) 11, 6 laps; Aaron Slight, NZ (Honda) 2, 5 laps; John Orchard, GB (TBA) 89, 4 laps; Neil Hodgson, GB (Ducati) 9, 3 laps; Peter Goddard, AUS (Suzuki) 51, 1 lap; James Whitham, GB (Suzuki) 12, 1 lap; Pier Francesco Chili, I (Ducati) 7, 1 lap; James Haydon, GB (Ducati) 14, 0 laps; David Emmerson, AUS (Suzuki) 42, 0 laps; Alistair Maxwell, AUS (Kawasaki) 41, 0 laps; Daniel Vanolini, AUS (Ducati) 79, 0 laps.

Fastest lap: Kocinski, 1m 49.306s, 91.069 mph/145.561 km/h.

Race 2

Pl. Name Nat. (Machine)	No.	Time & speed	Laps
1 Aaron Slight, NZ (Honda)	2	35m 33.917s	22
		102.626mph/165.162km/h	
2 Colin Edwards, USA (Yamaha)	45	35m 33.949s	22
3 Simon Crafar, NZ (Kawasaki)	6	35m 34.673s	22
4 Carl Fogarty, GB (Ducati)	4	35m 42.145s	22
5 Troy Bayliss, AUS (Suzuki)	52	35m 51.923s	22
6 Scott Russell, USA (Yamaha)	22	35m 56.570s	22
7 John Kocinski, USA (Honda)	3	35m 58.133s	22
8 Damon Buckmaster, AUS (Kawasaki)	44	36m 01.409s	22
9 Marty Craggill, AUS (Kawasaki)	32	36m 17.132s	22
10 Shawn Giles, AUS (Honda)*	49	36m 17.185s	22
11 Craig Connell, AUS (Ducati)*	39	36m 17.226s	22
12 Piergiorgio Bontempi, I (Kawasaki)	15	36m 23.763s	22
13 James Whitham, GB (Suzuki)	12	36m 39.483s	22
14 James Haydon, GB (Ducati)	14	36m 47.159s	22
15 Andreas Meklau, A (Ducati)	13	36m 51.669s	22
16 Jason Love, AUS (Ducati)*	35	36m 55.875s	22
17 Pere Riba Cabana, E (Honda)	17	37m 03.152s	22
18 David Emmerson, AUS (Suzuki)	42	35m 35.890s	21
19 Craig Stafford, AUS (Yamaha)*	48	36m 28.712s	21
20 Stephen Tozer, AUS (Kawasaki)*	66	36m 29.272s	21
21 John Orchard, GB (TBA)*	89	36m 32.231s	21

DNF Igor Jerman, SLO (Kawasaki) 31, 19 laps; Mike Hale, USA (Suzuki) 11, 15 laps; Akira Yanagawa, J (Kawasaki) 8, 14 laps; Graeme Wilshaw, AUS (Suzuki) 62, 14 laps; Steve Martin, AUS (Suzuki) 99, 13 laps; Greg Moss, AUS (Honda) 38, 8 laps; Benn Archibald, AUS (Kawasaki) 69, 5 laps; Neil Hodgson, GB (Ducati) 9, 4 laps; Simon Middleton, AUS (Kawasaki) 34, 4 laps; Alistair Maxwell, AUS (Kawasaki) 41, 1 lap; Daniel Vanolini, AUS (Ducati) 79, 0 laps; Peter Goddard, AUS (Suzuki) 51, 0 laps; Pier Francesco Chili, I (Ducati) 7, 0 laps.

Fastest lap: Edwards, 1m 36.078s, 103.607 mph/166.739 km/h.

Fastest qualifier: Slight, 1m 34.683s, 105.134 mph/169.196 km/h.
Lap record: Aaron Slight, NZ (Honda), 1m 35.442s (1996).
Championship points: 1 Kocinski, 34; **2** Fogarty, 33; **3** Crafar, 32; **4** Slight, 25; **5** Bayliss, 22; **6** Edwards, 20; **7** Russell, 19; **8** Craggill, 17; **9** Yanagawa, 13; **10** Meklau, 11; **11** Riba Cabana, 9; **12** Buckmaster, 8; **13** Bontempi and Jerman, 6; **15** Archibald and Whitham, 5.

* not eligible for championship points

MISANO

Far left: More rain, more crashes. James Haydon, another GP refugee, was one of many to fall victim to the conditions.

Left: Russell's shark's-fin helmet had a certain aptness. Here the returned former champion trails Pier Francesco Chili in the fight for the first-leg lead.

Main picture: Yanagawa and Bontempi lead the pack out of the spray.

Below (top to bottom): Whitham was strong again on the Suzuki, but fell again too; the paddock enjoys a respite from the rain; John Kocinski continued to start as he meant to go on, top points scorer of the weekend.

KAWASAKI'S fine performance at Phillip Island was no fluke. Akira Yanagawa proved that in the last minutes of the second qualifying session, when he set his first World Superbike pole ahead of Chili, Crafar and Fogarty.

Misano generally favours the Ducatis, but Fogarty was finding it hard to readjust to his bike. 'It's just a different bike to ride through the corners,' Foggy complained. 'It doesn't hold its line like it used to. That makes it hard for me, as my riding style is all about high corner speed.' Still, Carl had qualified in front of the two Castrol Hondas – Aaron Slight was fifth, John Kocinski sixth.

Once again, two dry practice days gave way to a wet and miserable race day. The difficult conditions caught out Yanagawa, who charged to the front straight away in race one but fell before the end of the first lap. Fogarty soon took over the lead, followed by Scott Russell, who had arrived at Misano a day late after being arrested for speeding in his Porsche Turbo back home.

Russell took over at the front when Fogarty slipped back and was overtaken by Chili. Rain or no rain, the Italian was obviously in no mood to let anyone take the glory on his home track. He was riding very hard indeed and soon eased into the lead.

With the first back-markers already in sight for the leaders, Mike Hale crashed his Suzuki. This was only the Texan's third race in the wet. His team-mate James Whitham, however, was doing much better. The Suzuki star was dicing for third with Fogarty, Kocinski and Slight.

Kocinski had managed to leave his rivals behind and now began to close on Russell. Meanwhile, just as Whitham looked set for a historic result, disaster struck when he lost the front of his GSX-R750 and went down.

Russell was on the move again and actually managed to get back ahead of Chili. Kocinski was also looking more dangerous by the minute as Russell and Chili swapped places yet again. With the race nearly over Colin Edwards, clearly not very comfortable in the rain, found himself being lapped! A moment later team-mate Russell crashed. 'With conditions as bad as that, it's easy to make a mistake,' Scott explained.

With the Yamaha rider's challenge over, Chili took victory ahead of Kocinski and Fogarty.

Race two was just as wet. Russell led from the start but was soon overhauled by Chili. Unfortunately, the Italian would soon be slowed by a mechanical problem. After holding on to the lead as long as he could, Chili slipped back and eventually retired. Russell, on his spare bike, showed none of his race one form and quickly lost places, eventually finishing in sixth. Kocinski was a runaway winner, looking every bit as impressive in the Misano rain as he had done in the wet first leg at Phillip Island.

Slight finished an uneventful race second, Fogarty was third. With Donington coming up, the double World Superbike champion still hadn't won a race.

Round 2   AUTODROMO SANTAMONICA, MISANO, Italy
20 April, 2.523-mile/4.060-km circuit
2 x 25 laps, 63.075 miles/101.500 km

Race 1

Pl. Name Nat. (Machine)	No.	Time & speed	Laps
1 Pier Francesco Chili, I (Ducati)	7	48m 44.232s	25
		77.644 mph/124.956 km/h	
2 John Kocinski, USA (Honda)	3	48m 58.426s	25
3 Carl Fogarty, GB (Ducati)	4	49m 48.354s	25
4 Aaron Slight, NZ (Honda)	2	50m 03.269s	25
5 Simon Crafar, NZ (Kawasaki)	6	50m 22.645s	25
6 Colin Edwards, USA (Yamaha)	45	48m 54.670s	24
7 Neil Hodgson, GB (Ducati)	9	49m 16.620s	24
8 Piergiorgio Bontempi, I (Kawasaki)	15	49m 21.637s	24
9 Pere Riba Cabana, E (Honda)	17	49m 28.497s	24
10 Christian Lavieille, F (Honda)	33	49m 33.840s	24
11 Giorgio Cantalupo, I (Ducati)*	57	50m 41.234s	24
12 Redamo Assirelli, I (Yamaha)*	72	50m 50.650s	24
13 Igor Jerman, SLO (Kawasaki)	31	49m 04.852s	23
14 Jiri Mrkyvka, CS (Honda)*	52	50m 16.191s	23
15 Bruno Scatola, I (Kawasaki)	59	50m 55.907s	22
16 Gerhard Esterer, A (Kawasaki)*	62	49m 10.421s	20
17 Luigi Aljinovic, CRO (Kawasaki)*	60	50m 23.941s	20

DNF Scott Russell, USA (Yamaha) 22, 24 laps; James Haydon, GB (Ducati) 14, 13 laps; James Whitham, GB (Suzuki) 12, 12 laps; Milos Madara, SK (Ducati) 64, 10 laps; Mike Hale, USA (Suzuki) 11, 9 laps; Vittorio Scatola, I (Honda) 70, 1 lap; Anton Gruschka, D (Yamaha) 73, 0 laps; Nikolaos Voukakis, GR (Kawasaki) 55, 0 laps; Akira Yanagawa, J (Kawasaki) 8, 0 laps; Lino Pittaluga, I (Yamaha) 58, 0 laps.

Fastest lap: Chili, 1m 53.651s, 79.911 mph/128.604 km/h.

Race 2

Pl. Name Nat. (Machine)	No.	Time & speed	Laps
1 John Kocinski, USA (Honda)	3	47m 44.390s	25
		79.266 mph/127.566 km/h	
2 Aaron Slight, NZ (Honda)	2	48m 16.253s	25
3 Carl Fogarty, GB (Ducati)	4	48m 24.933s	25
4 Neil Hodgson, GB (Ducati)	9	48m 31.885s	25
5 Akira Yanagawa, J (Kawasaki)	8	48m 37.338s	25
6 Scott Russell, USA (Yamaha)	22	48m 57.049s	25
7 Simon Crafar, NZ (Kawasaki)	6	49m 01.370s	25
8 Colin Edwards, USA (Yamaha)	45	49m 35.335s	25
9 Pere Riba Cabana, E (Honda)	17	47m 57.249s	24
10 Christian Lavieille, F (Honda)	33	48m 14.144s	24
11 James Haydon, GB (Ducati)	14	48m 22.773s	24
12 Mike Hale, USA (Suzuki)	11	48m 46.816s	24
13 Giorgio Cantalupo, I (Ducati)*	57	48m 18.729s	23
14 Bruno Scatola, I (Kawasaki)*	59	49m 20.008s	23
15 Jiri Mrkyvka, CS (Honda)*	52	49m 20.759s	23
16 Luigi Aljinovic, CRO (Kawasaki)*	60	48m 37.832s	22
17 Redamo Assirelli, I (Yamaha)*	72	49m 05.934s	22

DNF Piergiorgio Bontempi, I (Kawasaki) 15, 18 laps; Pier Francesco Chili, I (Ducati) 7, 13 laps; Anton Gruschka, D (Yamaha) 73, 12 laps; James Whitham, GB (Suzuki) 12, 9 laps; Igor Jerman, SLO (Kawasaki) 31, 5 laps; Milos Madara, SK (Ducati) 64, 3 laps; DNS Nikolaos Voukakis, GR (Kawasaki) 55; Vittorio Scatola, I (Honda) 70; Gerhard Esterer, A (Kawasaki) 62; Lino Pittaluga, I (Yamaha) 58.

Fastest lap: Kocinski, 1m 52.706s, 80.581 mph/129.682 km/h.

Fastest qualifier: Yanagawa, 1m 33.494s, 97.139 mph/156.330 km/h.
Lap record: John Kocinski, USA (Ducati), 1m 34.296s, 96.313 mph/155.001 km/h (1996).
Championship points: 1 Kocinski, 79; 2 Fogarty, 65; 3 Slight, 58; 4 Crafar, 52; 5 Edwards, 38; 6 Russell, 29; 7 Chili, 25; 8 Yanagawa, 24; 9 Riba Cabana, 23; 10 Bayliss and Hodgson, 22; 12 Craggill, 17; 13 Bontempi, 14; 14 Jerman and Meklau, 11.

* not eligible for championship points

DONINGTON

L AST year, Donington did more to fuel Superbike vs GP armchair arguments than any other single event. It was here that Troy Corser recorded an historic pole position time under Kevin Schwantz's long-standing GP lap record. But with Corser gone, the times stood still this year.

Neil Hodgson took his first World Superbike pole, but he was some three-tenths slower than Corser's 1996 time. Hodgson ended qualifying ahead of Aaron Slight. Carl Fogarty and Pier Francesco Chili made up the rest of the front row.

The first race looked set to be a Ducati benefit. For the first time this season, three red bikes dominated the beginning of the race in a way which brought back memories of previous years. Fogarty was in front, with Hodgson and Chili in close pursuit. Foggy looked set for his first win of the year, even though there was trouble brewing further back. Slight was recovering from a pretty useless start and clawing his way back up the field. At the same time, Crafar had managed to split the Yamaha pairing of Edwards and Russell. All three were soon overhauled by Slight, who slotted into fourth with Crafar following.

With the Kawasaki rider making his presence felt, Slight decided it was about time to mount a challenge for the rostrum. His charge was very impressive. First, he outbraked Chili at the esses. On the next lap, he lined up Hodgson at exactly the same place. One lap further on, still at the esses, it was Fogarty's turn to succumb to the Castrol Honda's convincing Racing CBS dual braking system.

Slight took his second win of the season, with Fogarty second. But there was still some thrilling action as third place was decided. Chili had already crashed himself out of contention. Crafar was fast catching Hodgson and managed to deprive him of a podium finish one lap from the end.

John Kocinski finished a disappointing tenth in the first leg, complaining of a lack of feel from the rear tyre. He took off in the lead for the second race, but could not stay in front for long, as Chili and Fogarty both came past him. Foggy went ahead, but Chili was not ready to give up without a fight. Kocinski had now been passed by Slight and was coming under pressure from Crafar.

Back at the front, Fogarty had managed to wear down Chili and the Italian dropped back within reach of Slight. King Carl was left to clinch his 40th World Superbike win. Second came down to a last-lap manoeuvre between Chili and Slight, with the New Zealander just missing out.

Home had been very good to Fogarty. Not only had he finally tasted victory again on the Ducati, but he left Donington as the new championship leader. A good omen coming into Hockenheim, where he had scored his first win on the Honda in 1996.

Top left: Honda versus Ducati, Slight versus Chili, under cloudless skies.

Bottom left: Fogarty, Hodgson and Chili give a display of Ducati power.

Top: Aaron Slight stays stony-faced under his own poster-sized gaze. That's the code of the Mohicans.

Above and left: Behind every good man, a good woman - and vice versa. Chili and family study the times, Michaela and Carl Fogarty await events.

Round 3 DONINGTON PARK, England

4 May, 2.500-mile/4.023-km circuit

2 x 25 laps, 62.500 miles/100.575 km

Race 1

Pl. Name Nat. (Machine)	No.	Time & speed	Laps
1 Aaron Slight, NZ (Honda)	2	39m 52.127s	25
		94.050 mph/151.359 km/h	
2 Carl Fogarty, GB (Ducati)	4	39m 53.810s	25
3 Simon Crafar, NZ (Kawasaki)	6	39m 56.578s	25
4 Neil Hodgson, GB (Ducati)	9	39m 56.781s	25
5 Colin Edwards, USA (Yamaha)	45	40m 01.475s	25
6 Scott Russell, USA (Yamaha)	22	40m 02.865s	25
7 Niall Mackenzie, GB (Yamaha)	41	40m 12.118s	25
8 James Whitham, GB (Suzuki)	12	40m 21.437s	25
9 John Reynolds, GB (Ducati)	33	40m 21.826s	25
10 John Kocinski, USA (Honda)	3	40m 22.227s	25
11 Piergiorgio Bontempi, I (Kawasaki)	15	40m 23.698s	25
12 Christer Lindholm, S (Yamaha)	16	40m 43.547s	25
13 Gregorio Lavilla, E (Ducati)	35	40m 56.269s	25
14 Sean Emmett, GB (Ducati)	44	41m 00.109s	25
15 Mike Hale, USA (Suzuki)	11	41m 00.846s	25
16 James Haydon, GB (Ducati)	14	41m 04.438s	25
17 Andreas Meklau, A (Ducati)	13	41m 04.622s	25
18 Pere Riba Cabana, E (Honda)	17	41m 24.766s	25
19 Christian Lavieille, F (Honda)	43	40m 06.930s	24
20 Igor Jerman, SLO (Kawasaki)	31	40m 17.037s	24
21 Anton Gruschka, D (Yamaha)*	54	41m 01.168s	24
22 Jiri Mrkyvka, CS (Honda)*	56	41m 20.323s	24
23 Paolo Malvini, I (Ducati)*	53	41m 20.897s	24

DNF Pier Francesco Chili, I (Ducati) 7, 21 laps; Giorgio Cantalupo, I (Ducati) 52, 7 laps; Brett Sampson, GB (Kawasaki) 77, 2 laps; **DNS** Eugene McManus, GB (Kawasaki) 25; Steve Hislop, GB (Ducati) 34.

Fastest lap: Chili, 1m 34.723s, 95.005 mph/152.896 km/h.

Race 2

Pl. Name Nat. (Machine)	No.	Time & speed	Laps
1 Carl Fogarty, GB (Ducati)	4	39m 48.996s	25
		94.173 mph/151.557 km/h	
2 Pier Francesco Chili, I (Ducati)	7	39m 52.888s	25
3 Aaron Slight, NZ (Honda)	2	39m 53.133s	25
4 Simon Crafar, NZ (Kawasaki)	6	39m 55.376s	25
5 John Kocinski, USA (Honda)	3	39m 57.211s	25
6 Colin Edwards, USA (Yamaha)	45	39m 59.159s	25
7 Scott Russell, USA (Yamaha)	22	39m 59.859s	25
8 Niall Mackenzie, GB (Yamaha)	41	40m 08.242s	25
9 Neil Hodgson, GB (Ducati)	9	40m 14.007s	25
10 James Whitham, GB (Suzuki)	12	40m 21.480s	25
11 John Reynolds, GB (Ducati)	33	40m 21.667s	25
12 Sean Emmett, GB (Ducati)	44	40m 37.014s	25
13 Gregorio Lavilla, E (Ducati)	35	40m 37.212s	25
14 James Haydon, GB (Ducati)†	14	40m 57.958s	25
15 Andreas Meklau, A (Ducati)	13	41m 12.849s	25
16 Pere Riba Cabana, E (Honda)	17	41m 31.172s	25
17 Christian Lavieille, F (Honda)	43	40m 00.591s	24
18 Igor Jerman, SLO (Kawasaki)	31	40m 04.801s	24
19 Anton Gruschka, D (Yamaha)*	54	40m 44.064s	24
20 Giorgio Cantalupo, I (Ducati)*	52	41m 01.630s	24
21 Paolo Malvini, I (Ducati)*	53	39m 59.705s	23
22 Jiri Mrkyvka, CS (Honda)*	56	41m 21.897s	23

DNF Piergiorgio Bontempi, I (Kawasaki) 15, 13 laps; Mike Hale, USA (Suzuki) 11, 11 laps; Brett Sampson, GB (Kawasaki) 77, 2 laps; Christer Lindholm, S (Yamaha) 16, 1 laps; **DNS** Steve Hislop, GB (Ducati) 34; Eugene McManus, GB (Kawasaki) 25.

Fastest lap: Fogarty, 1m 34.637s, 95.092 mph/153.035 km/h.
† *Later disqualified for weight irregularities.*

Fastest qualifier: Hodgson, 1m 33.748s, 95.993 mph/154.486 km/h.
Lap record: Troy Corser, AUS (Ducati), 1m 33.470s, 96.281 mph/154.950 km/h (1996).
Championship points: 1 Fogarty, 110; **2** Slight, 99; **3** Kocinski, 96; **4** Crafar, 81; **5** Edwards, 59; **6** Russell, 48; **7** Chili, 45; **8** Hodgson, 42; **9** Riba Cabana and Yanagawa, 24; **11** Bayliss, 22; **12** Bontempi and Whitham, 19; **14** Craggill and Mackenzie, 17.
* not eligible for championship points

Photos: Gold & Goose and Mark Wernham

HOCKENHEIM

Mark Wernham

Above: Hockenheim, as always, produced great slipstreaming battles. Here Russell's Yamaha hangs on to the back of a three-Duke train – Fogarty, Hodgson and Chili.

Right: Hodgson dives inside Fogarty, with Russell (22), Crafar (6) and Edwards (45) in close attendance.

Far right, top to bottom: Simon Crafar claimed pole at the German-based Kawasaki team's home GP; Whitham's third place was the Suzuki team's first-ever podium; Hodgson led race two until the last lap.

HOCKENHEIM always promises extremely close racing, with the Japanese fours getting the most out of their rev-happy engines on the long forest straights. Nevertheless, few expected to see Simon Crafar put his ZX-7R Kawasaki on pole. Even the amiable Kiwi was surprised. 'This is the last place I would have expected to get the first pole of my career,' he confessed.

But Crafar, along with team-mate Yanagawa, had received a new engine with better top-end performance. Sadly he would not benefit from his pole: his first race ended prematurely when his engine broke (he was second at the time, closing on early runaway leader Aaron Slight) and could only manage sixth in the second leg.

After Crafar disappeared Kocinski came out of nowhere, at impressive speed, to close the gap on Slight. With three laps to go, he sailed past Aaron and gave the 45,000-strong crowd something to get excited about. Despite the New Zealander's early domination, this would turn out to be a race with a thrilling finish.

Especially with the awesome battle for third going on a few metres behind. It was three Ducatis against a lone Yamaha as Fogarty, Hodgson and Chili ganged up on Scott Russell.

Slight looked certain to make his move on Kocinski on the last lap and that's exactly what he did, waiting for the critical right-hander leading into the Stadium so that the American would have no chance of coming back at him. Russell chose the same corner for his last-minute outbraking manoeuvre. There was nothing his three Ducati-mounted rivals could do to prevent him from taking his first podium as a Yamaha WSB factory rider. Fogarty finished ahead of Chili and Hodgson.

The second leg was even more intense. Hodgson led from the start, with Fogarty and Slight not far behind. For Kocinski, there was drama almost straight away. The second lap saw contact between him and Fogarty, Kocinski coming away with a broken fairing. He had to work hard to finish 14th and save a modest two points. But there was more disaster in store for the Castrol Honda team.

Unable to get past Hodgson and Fogarty, Slight grew impatient and went into the Sachskurve too hard. He crashed right in front of Fogarty, who had to go wide to avoid him. That gave Hodgson a bit of breathing space and allowed Yanagawa, Crafar and Whitham to come back.

Yanagawa went by Fogarty and started to close on Hodgson, taking Fogarty and Whitham with him. Neil led until the last lap, where he nearly crashed twice coming into the Stadium. Foggy needed no second invitation and pounced on his second win of the season.

Yanagawa was second as Whitham gave Lester Harris's Suzuki team their best-ever result and their first podium finish. Thanks to Slight's crash and Kocinski's poor result, Fogarty unexpectedly found himself with an almost comfortable championship lead. 'But the bike is far from perfect and we've still got a lot of work to do to win this championship,' he warned.

Round 4 HOCKENHEIM, Germany
8 June, 4.220-mile/6.792-km circuit

2 x 14 laps, 59.080 miles/95.088 km

Race 1			
Pl. Name Nat. (Machine)	No.	Time & speed	Laps
1 Aaron Slight, NZ (Honda)	3	28m 54.050s	14
		122.664 mph/197.409 km/h	
2 John Kocinski, USA (Honda)	2	28m 54.085s	14
3 Scott Russell, USA (Yamaha)	22	29m 00.451s	14
4 Carl Fogarty, GB (Ducati)	4	29m 00.451s	14
5 Pier Francesco Chili, I (Ducati)	7	29m 00.683s	14
6 Neil Hodgson, GB (Ducati)	9	29m 00.887s	14
7 Colin Edwards, USA (Yamaha)	45	29m 03.383s	14
8 Akira Yanagawa, J (Kawasaki)	8	29m 12.160s	14
9 Mike Hale, USA (Suzuki)	11	29m 12.318s	14
10 Andreas Meklau, A (Ducati)	13	29m 19.167s	14
11 Piergiorgio Bontempi, I (Kawasaki)	15	29m 19.423s	14
12 Christer Lindholm, S (Yamaha)	16	29m 32.397s	14
13 Jochen Schmid, D (Kawasaki)	21	29m 32.441s	14
14 James Whitham, GB (Suzuki)	12	29m 59.836s	14
15 Udo Mark, D (Suzuki)*	51	30m 02.809s	14
16 Igor Jerman, SLO (Kawasaki)	31	30m 07.952s	14
17 Christian Lavieille, F (Honda)	10	30m 32.798s	14
18 Anton Gruschka, D (Yamaha)*	59	30m 39.504s	14
19 Michal Bursa, CS (Kawasaki)*	69	30m 44.440s	14
20 Gerhard Esterer, A (Kawasaki)*	60	31m 00.637s	14
21 Giorgio Cantalupo, I (Ducati)*	63	31m 07.349s	14
22 Vittorio Scatola, I (Kawasaki)*	62	29m 45.827s	13
23 Harry Fath, D (Ducati)*	58	29m 47.826s	13
24 Ondrej Lelek, CS (Honda)*	71	30m 14.874s	13

DNF Andrea Mazzali, I (Ducati) 32, 11 laps; Pere Riba Cabana, E (Honda) 17, 10 laps; Simon Crafar, NZ (Kawasaki) 6, 6 laps; **DNS** James Haydon, GB (Ducati) 14; Michael Rudroff, D (Suzuki) 52; Gregorio Lavilla, E (Ducati) 35; Lothar Kraus, D (Kawasaki) 56.

Fastest lap: Kocinski, 2m 02.155s, 124.377 mph/200.165 km/h.

Race 2			
Pl. Name Nat. (Machine)	No.	Time & speed	Laps
1 Carl Fogarty, GB (Ducati)	4	28m 57.410s	14
		122.427 mph/197.027 km/h	
2 Akira Yanagawa, J (Kawasaki)	8	28m 58.107s	14
3 James Whitham, GB (Suzuki)	12	28m 58.809s	14
4 Scott Russell, USA (Yamaha)	22	29m 01.301s	14
5 Colin Edwards, USA (Yamaha)	45	29m 01.577s	14
6 Simon Crafar, NZ (Kawasaki)	6	29m 01.845s	14
7 Pier Francesco Chili, I (Ducati)	7	29m 05.295s	14
8 Neil Hodgson, GB (Ducati)	9	29m 08.295s	14
9 Jochen Schmid, D (Kawasaki)	21	29m 09.040s	14
10 Andreas Meklau, A (Ducati)	13	29m 14.850s	14
11 Piergiorgio Bontempi, I (Kawasaki)	15	29m 19.215s	14
12 Christer Lindholm, S (Yamaha)	16	29m 27.445s	14
13 Gregorio Lavilla, E (Ducati)	35	29m 30.922s	14
14 John Kocinski, USA (Honda)	3	29m 46.926s	14
15 Udo Mark, D (Suzuki)*	51	29m 47.130s	14
16 Igor Jerman, SLO (Kawasaki)	31	29m 54.795s	14
17 Anton Gruschka, D (Yamaha)*	59	30m 23.471s	14
18 Michal Bursa, CS (Kawasaki)*	69	30m 39.163s	14
19 Gerhard Esterer, A (Kawasaki)*	60	30m 44.488s	14
20 Giorgio Cantalupo, I (Ducati)*	63	30m 48.645s	14
21 Vittorio Scatola, I (Kawasaki)*	62	29m 16.388s	13
22 Pere Riba Cabana, E (Honda)	17	29m 41.677s	13
23 Ondrej Lelek, CS (Honda)*	71	29m 58.580s	13

DNF Mike Hale, USA (Suzuki) 11, 13 laps; Christian Lavieille, F (Honda) 10, 12 laps; Harry Fath, D (Ducati) 58, 11 laps; Aaron Slight, NZ (Honda) 2, 10 laps; Lothar Kraus, D (Kawasaki) 56, 6 laps; Andrea Mazzali, I (Ducati) 32, 2 laps; James Haydon, GB (Ducati) 14, 2 laps; **DNS** Michael Rudroff, D (Suzuki) 52.

Fastest lap: Fogarty, 2m 02.587s, 123.938 mph/199.459 km/h.

Fastest qualifier: Crafar, 2m 00.812s, 125.759 mph/202.390 km/h.
Lap record: Troy Corser, 2m 00.790s, 125.801 mph/202.457 km/h (1996).
Championship points: 1 Fogarty, 148; **2** Slight, 124; **3** Kocinski, 118; **4** Crafar, 91; **5** Edwards, 79; **6** Russell, 77; **7** Chili, 65; **8** Hodgson, 60; **9** Yanagawa, 52; **10** Whitham, 37; **11** Bontempi, 29; **12** Meklau, 25; **13** Riba Cabana, 24; **14** Bayliss, 22; **15** Craggill and Mackenzie, 17.

* not eligible for championship points

Photos: Gold & Goose and Mark Wernham

MONZA

A S far as Team Yamaha are concerned, Monza is their home race. The Belgarda workshops are located minutes away from the circuit. Edwards and Russell had tested at Monza a few days prior to the race, and a win looked a distinct possibility. So there was bitter disappointment in store when ex-GP racer Jean-Philippe Ruggia knocked Edwards off the track in Saturday's free practice. The American crashed, fracturing his wrist and, as he found out a few weeks later, breaking the plate that had been holding his collarbone together since his spill at Sugo last year. Even though Russell managed to score his first pole of the season at Monza, the team's morale was low.

Russell was first away when the lights turned green for race one. Fogarty had started from the second row but he outbraked about four riders at the first chicane to slip into second. By the end of that lap, Foggy was first ahead of Crafar, Russell and Chili. They were soon joined by Kocinski, Slight and Whitham, making it an incredible seven-rider battle for the lead.

There were constant, and sometimes dramatic, position changes. Kocinski went from fourth to first in one go and led the fourth lap. Crafar and Slight also led before handing back first place to Fogarty. But there was no respite for the Blackburn ace: Kocinski and Slight were becoming more and more menacing.

Four laps from the flag, the two Honda riders went into the lead and actually started pulling away. Back-markers split the leading group, with Russell, Whitham and Chili coming off worst and losing the tow. Fogarty, though, was pushing hard to claw his way back to Kocinski and Slight. It just had to be a close finish. Carl came out of the last turn first but was just beaten across the line by the two Hondas. 'It's great to win at Monza,' said Kocinski. 'This place is so historic and is known throughout the world.'

Soon after the first leg the thunderclouds burst, and although the rain stopped just before the second race, the track was soaked. The early laps were like a dream come true for English fans, with Fogarty leading and Whitham obviously enjoying the conditions. On lap three Whitham was running side by side with Fogarty on the start/finish straight before going into the lead. Foggy stayed right with him, but the improving conditions allowed Kocinski and Chili to close on the two Brits.

The four men were soon together and dominating the race. Whitham and Fogarty seemed unable to maintain their early pace, though, and were eventually passed by both Kocinski and Chili.

The popular Italian was in a class of his own. Since 1995, Chili has always won at least one race at the Monza round and this year would prove to be no exception. He increased his lead with every lap to claim his second win of the season. Kocinski held second, while Whitham managed to get the better of Fogarty for third.

Above: More rain in race two suited Whitham, who pipped old pal and new rival Fogarty for a second rostrum place in succession.

Left: As usual, local hero Pier Francesco Chili obliged the Monza fans with a fine home win.

Above left: Aaron Slight in high-speed action. Once again, the New Zealander was playing second fiddle to his Honda team-mate.

Below left: All the track, and more. Scott Russell goes kerb-hopping in pursuit of pole position.

Below: A pile of tattered bodywork marked the end of Colin Edwards's season. Knocked off in practice, his injuries meant he did not race again all year.

Round 5 MONZA, Italy

22 June, 3.585-mile/5.770-km circuit
2 x 18 laps, 64.530 miles/103.860 km

Race 1

Pl. Name Nat. (Machine)	No.	Time & speed	Laps
1 John Kocinski, USA (Honda)	3	32m 41.944s	18
		118.417 mph/190.574 km/h	
2 Aaron Slight, NZ (Honda)	2	32m 41.949s	18
3 Carl Fogarty, GB (Ducati)	4	32m 41.952s	18
4 Simon Crafar, NZ (Kawasaki)	6	32m 42.326s	18
5 Scott Russell, USA (Yamaha)	22	32m 42.573s	18
6 James Whitham, GB (Suzuki)	12	32m 48.717s	18
7 Pier Francesco Chili, I (Ducati)	7	32m 49.028s	18
8 Akira Yanagawa, J (Kawasaki)	8	32m 49.079s	18
9 Piergiorgio Bontempi, I (Kawasaki)	15	32m 54.324s	18
10 Mike Hale, USA (Suzuki)	11	32m 56.631s	18
11 Andreas Meklau, A (Ducati)	13	32m 58.428s	18
12 James Haydon, GB (Ducati)	14	33m 32.725s	18
13 Jochen Schmid, D (Kawasaki)	21	33m 38.655s	18
14 Jean-Philippe Ruggia, F (Yamaha)	20	33m 39.212s	18
15 Igor Jerman, SLO (Kawasaki)	31	33m 39.233s	18
16 Jean-Marc Deletang, F (Yamaha)	27	33m 42.495s	18
17 Udo Mark, D (Suzuki)*	51	33m 43.294s	18
18 Pere Riba Cabana, E (Honda)	17	34m 06.705s	18
19 Anton Gruschka, D (Yamaha)*	59	32m 42.254s	17
20 Giorgio Cantalupo, I (Ducati)*	63	32m 42.255s	17
21 Redamo Assirelli, I (Yamaha)*	68	32m 55.233s	17
22 Paolo Malvini, I (Ducati)*	72	33m 06.473s	17
23 Lino Pittaluga, I (Yamaha)	34	33m 09.250s	1
24 Gerhard Esterer, A (Kawasaki)*	60	33m 12.614	
25 Paolo Bosetti, I (Ducati)*	74	33m 38.0	

DNF Luigi Aljinovic, CRO (Ducati) 69, 16 laps;
chetti, I (Kawasaki) 35, 9 laps; Bruno Scato
61, 8 laps; Emmanouill Pallis, GRE (D
Michal Bursa, CS (Kawasaki) 75, 4 laps.

Fastest lap: Slight, 1m 47.476
km/h.

Fastest qualifier: Russe
Lap record: Pier Fran
Championship po
79; 8 Whitham
Bayliss, 22.

Race 2

Pl. Name Nat. (Machine)	No.	Time & speed	Laps
1 Pier Francesco Chili, I (Ducati)	7	36m 46.817s	18
		105.278 mph/169.428 km/h	
2 John Kocinski, USA (Honda)	3	36m 48.657s	18
3 James Whitham, GB (Suzuki)	12	36m 53.905s	18
4 Carl Fogarty, GB (Ducati)	4	36m 55.165s	1
5 Aaron Slight, NZ (Honda)	2	37m 27.241	
6 Piergiorgio Bontempi, I (Kawasaki)	15	37m 32.	
7 Simon Crafar, NZ (Kawasaki)	6	37m	
8 Scott Russell, USA (Yamaha)	22	3	
9 Mike Hale, USA (Suzuki)	11		
10 Jochen Schmid, D (Kawasaki)			
11 Pere Riba Cabana, E (Hond			
12 Udo Mark, D (Suzuki)*			
13 James Haydon, GB (D			
14 Jean-Marc Deleta			
15 Giorgio Cant			
16 Igor Jerma			
17 Michal			
18 Ant			
19 G			
2			

LAGUNA

Above: Miguel DuHamel had one chance to show the world what he could do – and he made the most of it, running with the leaders in fine style.

Top left: Hodgson legs it Supercross style at the notorious Corkscrew – 'like dropping off the edge of the world'.

Left: Fogarty overcame his lack of enthusiasm for the tortuous Laguna Seca swoops to keep Kocinski within reach.

Right: Kocinski was determined to be king at his home track. He succeeded, to become the season's first double winner.

SECA

KOCINSKI seemed almost over-confident at Laguna Seca. 'I'm sure I'll be on top of the podium,' he claimed before the race week-end even started.

The odds did look in John's favour. He'd been fastest in pre-season testing at Laguna and had set a blistering pole there last season. Surprisingly, the times were about a second slower this year. Even more of a surprise was Chili's practice performance: he took pole away from Kocinski in the last seconds of the second session.

The usual spate of local riders made a strong showing. Reigning American Superbike champion Doug Chandler set provisional pole on Friday and ended up third fastest on Saturday. Miguel DuHamel was fifth fastest and Suzuki's Aaron Yates was in ninth place, well ahead of James Whitham (16th) and Mike Hale (18th). The factory Suzuki pairing only scored points in the first race, Whitham crashing in the second while Hale retired with front brake problems.

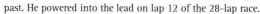

The lights never turned green for the first race, which caught several riders out. But not Kocinski. He led DuHamel, Hodgson, Chandler and Chili into the first turn.

Hodgson had missed Monza after badly breaking his knee while practising on his motocross bike – his presence at Laguna was down to sheer guts and determination. While DuHamel challenged Kocinski for the lead, Hodgson fought with Chili for third. Chandler was going backwards and would finish fifth. Chili's engine went on lap five, leaving Fogarty fourth and charging. Foggy went by Hodgson and DuHamel and was soon all over Kocinski's back wheel – at a track which he admitted he'd not liked in the past. He powered into the lead on lap 12 of the 28-lap race.

Four laps later, Hodgson crashed. That left DuHamel third, with Crafar and Russell behind him. With three laps to go Kocinski gave the 43,000-strong crowd something to cheer about as he got his Honda sideways in the first turn and outbraked Fogarty. Kocinski just managed to stay in front and win ahead of Fogarty, with DuHamel some eight seconds back in third. Slight could only finish seventh, behind Russell.

Race two was a lot less exciting, with Kocinski leading from start to finish and never really challenged. Fogarty took five laps to move up to second but then he stayed there. The real battle was for third. DuHamel had taken over the position on lap four, when Chandler retired with suspected transmission failure. The Honda rider was hassled by Chili, but after a while the Italian faded, finishing a distant sixth.

But there was no respite for DuHamel. Russell had come back and was now all over him. In the end, DuHamel just managed to hold third. Slight finished a dire tenth.

With half of the season gone, Slight was beginning to lag behind Kocinski and Fogarty for the title chase. 'I am bitterly disappointed,' admitted the Kiwi, 'but I am not giving up yet.' Still, with Brands Hatch coming up, Foggy looked set to extend his title lead. 'It's about time that I won again,' he said. 'Brands is the perfect place to start.'

Round 6 LAGUNA SECA, USA

13 July, 2.243-mile/3.610-km circuit

2 x 28 laps, 62.804 miles/101.080 km

Race 1

Pl. Name Nat. (Machine)	No.	Time & speed	Laps
1 John Kocinski, USA (Honda)	3	41m 00.380s	28
		91.900 mph/147.899 km/h	
2 Carl Fogarty, GB (Ducati)	4	41m 00.519s	28
3 Miguel DuHamel, CAN (Honda)	5	41m 09.087s	28
4 Simon Crafar, NZ (Kawasaki)	6	41m 14.618s	28
5 Doug Chandler, USA (Kawasaki)	10	41m 19.310s	28
6 Scott Russell, USA (Yamaha)	22	41m 19.951s	28
7 Aaron Slight, NZ (Honda)	2	41m 20.604s	28
8 James Whitham, GB (Suzuki)	12	41m 31.975s	28
9 Piergiorgio Bontempi, I (Kawasaki)	15	41m 31.994s	28
10 Akira Yanagawa, J (Kawasaki)	8	41m 32.186s	28
11 Steve Crevier, CAN (Honda)	41	41m 35.902s	28
12 Tom Kipp, USA (Yamaha)	16	41m 36.342s	28
13 Pascal Picotte, CAN (Suzuki)	34	41m 42.604s	28
14 Mike Hale, USA (Suzuki)	11	41m 47.587s	28
15 Igor Jerman, SLO (Kawasaki)	31	42m 27.418s	28
16 Michael Krynock, USA (Suzuki)	69	42m 29.295s	27

DNF James Haydon, GB (Ducati) 14, 20 laps; Mat Mladin, AUS (Ducati) 36, 17 laps; Neil Hodgson, GB (Ducati) 9, 16 laps; Dave Sadowski, USA (Ducati) 25, 14 laps; Aaron Yates, USA (Suzuki) 20, 11 laps; Pier Francesco Chili, I (Ducati) 7, 5 laps; **DNS** Andreas Meklau, A (Ducati) 13.

Fastest lap: Fogarty, 1m 27.148s, 92.662 mph/149.125 km/h.

Race 2

Pl. Name Nat. (Machine)	No.	Time & speed	Laps
1 John Kocinski, USA (Honda)	3	40m 57.308s	28
		92.015 mph/148.084 km/h	
2 Carl Fogarty, GB (Ducati)	4	41m 02.170s	28
3 Miguel DuHamel, CAN (Honda)	5	41m 05.862s	28
4 Scott Russell, USA (Yamaha)	22	41m 05.920s	28
5 Akira Yanagawa, J (Kawasaki)	8	41m 07.835s	28
6 Pier Francesco Chili, I (Ducati)	7	41m 16.895s	28
7 Piergiorgio Bontempi, I (Kawasaki)	15	41m 28.802s	28
8 Tom Kipp, USA (Yamaha)	16	41m 29.991s	28
9 Neil Hodgson, GB (Ducati)	9	41m 30.069s	28
10 Aaron Slight, NZ (Honda)	2	41m 31.175s	28
11 Aaron Yates, USA (Suzuki)	20	41m 38.256s	28
12 Steve Crevier, CAN (Honda)	41	41m 09.338s	27
13 Igor Jerman, SLO (Kawasaki)	31	41m 21.055s	27
14 Michael Krynock, USA (Suzuki)	69	42m 38.114s	27

DNF Mat Mladin, AUS (Ducati) 36, 21 laps; James Haydon, GB (Ducati) 14, 9 laps; James Whitham, GB (Suzuki) 12, 9 laps; Simon Crafar, NZ (Kawasaki) 6, 6 laps; Pascal Picotte, CAN (Suzuki) 34, 6 laps; Doug Chandler, USA (Kawasaki) 10, 3 laps; Mike Hale, USA (Suzuki) 11, 2 laps; **DNS** Dave Sadowski, USA (Ducati) 25; Andreas Meklau, A (Ducati) 13.

Fastest lap: Kocinski, 1m 27.092s, 92.722 mph/149.221 km/h.

Fastest qualifier: Chili, 1m 26.628s, 93.218 mph/150.020 km/h.
Lap record: Wataru Yoshikawa, J (Yamaha), 1m 26.926s (1996).
Championship points: 1 Fogarty, 217; **2** Kocinski, 213; **3** Slight, 170; **4** Crafar, 126; **5** Russell, 119; **6** Chili, 109; **7** Edwards, 79; **8** Yanagawa, 77; **9** Whitham, 71; **10** Hodgson, 67; **11** Bontempi, 62; **12** DuHamel, 32; **13** Meklau, 30; **14** Riba Cabana, 29; **15** Hale, 27.
* not eligible for championship points

BRANDS

Mark Wernham

THE Laguna Seca and Brands Hatch rounds were separated by the most important four-stroke event of the year: the Suzuka Eight Hour endurance race. Most of the top Superbike riders were there, with the notable exception of the Ducatis.

It was at Suzuka that Colin Edwards realised he probably wouldn't race again this season. His injuries were more troublesome than expected and would require surgery and several weeks' convalescence. Edwards was replaced by Briton Chris Walker for the remaining European rounds.

Suzuka had been wet, bringing yet more rain to riders who had already endured the wettest-ever first half of a season. Still, Brands looked set to be run in the dry. The track had recently been resurfaced and was much smoother than before. Using a new EPROM chip to smooth the Ducati's power curve and thus make the bike easier to ride, Pier Francesco Chili dominated practice. He was fastest in every session and became the first man to clinch two poles this season.

But on race day things just refused to go as planned. The first leg had to be stopped after two laps when privateer Graeme Ritchie slid off. He was airlifted to hospital with serious injuries, to which sadly he later succumbed.

Hodgson led the restart from Kocinski and Niall Mackenzie, both the latter benefiting from the stoppage. Kocinski had been lying tenth when the race was stopped; Mackenzie hadn't even started – a footpeg had broken on his 1996 factory Yamaha during warm-up, forcing him to go back to the pits.

Kocinski challenged Hodgson for the lead, but Mackenzie made a mistake and dropped to 11th. The leaders were now being caught by Fogarty, Crafar, Chili and Russell.

On the fifth lap disaster struck again as Fogarty nearly high-sided out of Druids. Crafar was just behind him and there was nothing he could do to avoid the flailing Ducati. Both riders fell. That left Chili and Kocinski to challenge Hodgson, with Russell not far behind.

Hodgson was unable to keep up the pace and soon found himself fourth. Mackenzie, meanwhile, was slicing his way back up to the front: he soon passed Hodgson to challenge Russell and Kocinski. Chili was already out of reach. He'd cleared off as soon as he'd hit the front and would never be seen again.

Russell slid into second, while Kocinski tried to contain Mackenzie. The Scot outbraked him on the last lap to secure a popular third, but he was later excluded when fuel irregularities were discovered with his 1996 factory Yamaha.

The second race looked set to go Chili's way as well, with the Italian leading a very determined Fogarty and an even more aggressive Crafar. On lap seven, however, Fogarty forced his way past and took Chili's front wheel away, causing the Italian to crash. Foggy was now at the front, with Crafar and Hodgson in hot pursuit. But, once again, proceedings had to be halted when the rain started pouring down. After a 15-minute wet practice session, the race was restarted for 15 laps.

One-race Honda Britain rider Michael Rutter was the undisputed star. He shot to the front and built up an impressive lead over Fogarty and Kocinski. Always a demon in the wet, Kocinski fought Fogarty all the way and managed to finish the race in front of him. But on aggregate time Fogarty won the second leg, with Kocinski second and Rutter a magnificent third.

Above, from left: **Kocinski exults in second place, after outpointing title rival Fogarty at home;** Foggy fans were in defiant mood, in between discussing teething problems; the man himself fell under Crafar's front wheel in the first race, as Hodgson and Kocinski led the early stages.

Left: Niall Mackenzie and son Taylor. A home–hero one-race third, he was later excluded for fuel irregularities.

Below: **Step forward Michael Rutter,** whose third in the rain was a magnificent performance.

Below, far left: **Different ways to fly a Duke,** demonstrated by Fogarty (4) and Chili.

Round 7   BRANDS HATCH, England

3 August, 2.6002-mile/4.185-km circuit

2 x 25 laps, 65.010 miles/104.620 km

Race 1

Pl. Name Nat. (Machine)	No.	Time & speed	Laps
1 Pier Francesco Chili, I (Ducati)	7	36m 23.452s	25
		107.188 mph/172.502 km/h	
2 Scott Russell, USA (Yamaha)	22	36m 25.524s	25
3 Niall Mackenzie, GB (Yamaha)†	41	36m 25.993s	25
4 John Kocinski, USA (Honda)	3	36m 26.460s	25
5 Neil Hodgson, GB (Ducati)	9	36m 29.284s	25
6 Akira Yanagawa, J (Kawasaki)	8	36m 29.308s	25
7 Aaron Slight, NZ (Honda)	2	36m 29.556s	25
8 James Whitham, GB (Suzuki)	12	36m 45.259s	25
9 Piergiorgio Bontempi, I (Kawasaki)	15	36m 45.525s	25
10 Mike Hale, USA (Suzuki)	11	36m 55.516s	25
11 Chris Walker, GB (Yamaha)	42	37m 04.418s	25
12 Michael Rutter, GB (Honda)	40	37m 10.379s	25
13 Ray Stringer, GB (Kawasaki)*	71	37m 36.338s	25
14 Pere Riba Cabana, E (Honda)	17	37m 36.684s	25
15 Brett Sampson, GB (Kawasaki)*	77	36m 47.232s	24
16 Phil Giles, GB (Kawasaki)	35	36m 49.864s	24
17 Steve Marks, GB (Kawasaki)*	69	37m 13.897s	24
18 Giorgio Cantalupo, I (Ducati)*	52	37m 29.803s	24
19 Nigel Nottingham, GB (Yamaha)*	67	37m 49.672s	24
20 Jiri Mrkyvka, CS (Honda)*	61	36m 45.249s	23
21 Richard Defago, GB (Kawasaki)*	57	36m 45.290s	23

DNF Sean Emmett, GB (Ducati) 44, 18 laps; Anton Gruschka, D (Yamaha) 54, 18 laps; Igor Jerman, SLO (Kawasaki) 31, 10 laps; Steve Hislop, GB (Kawasaki) 34, 7 laps; James Haydon, GB (Ducati) 14, 5 laps; Carl Fogarty, GB (Ducati) 4, 4 laps; Simon Crafar, NZ (Kawasaki) 6, 4 laps; **DNS** Graeme Ritchie, GB (Ducati) 59.

Fastest lap: Mackenzie, 1m 26.525s, 108.195 mph/174.123 km/h (record).
† *Later excluded for fuel irregularities.*

Race 2

Pl. Name Nat. (Machine)	No.	Time & speed	Laps
1 Carl Fogarty, GB (Ducati)	4	39m 31.922s	25
		98.671 mph/158.795 km/h	
2 John Kocinski, USA (Honda)	3	39m 36.676s	25
3 Michael Rutter, GB (Honda)	40	39m 47.791s	25
4 Akira Yanagawa, J (Kawasaki)	8	39m 49.410s	25
5 Scott Russell, USA (Yamaha)	22	39m 49.421s	25
6 Neil Hodgson, GB (Ducati)	9	39m 50.190s	25
7 Simon Crafar, NZ (Kawasaki)	6	39m 54.595s	25
8 Aaron Slight, NZ (Honda)	2	39m 56.008s	25
9 James Whitham, GB (Suzuki)	12	39m 57.537s	25
10 Chris Walker, GB (Yamaha)	42	40m 04.421s	25
11 Mike Hale, USA (Suzuki)	11	40m 30.641s	25
12 Piergiorgio Bontempi, I (Kawasaki)	15	41m 06.333s	25
13 Pere Riba Cabana, E (Honda)	17	41m 14.349s	25
14 Phil Giles, GB (Kawasaki)	35	41m 45.195s	25
15 Igor Jerman, SLO (Kawasaki)	31	40m 04.819s	24
16 Ray Stringer, GB (Kawasaki)*	71	40m 34.539s	24
17 Nigel Nottingham, GB (Yamaha)*	67	40m 58.368s	24
18 Steve Marks, GB (Kawasaki)*	69	41m 32.414s	24
19 Anton Gruschka, D (Yamaha)*	54	41m 50.003s	24
20 Richard Defago, GB (Kawasaki)*	57	42m 21.184s	24
21 Jiri Mrkyvka, CS (Honda)*	61	41m 33.897s	23
22 Giorgio Cantalupo, I (Ducati)*	52	40m 49.384s	22

DNF Sean Emmett, GB (Ducati) 44, 10 laps; Steve Hislop, GB (Kawasaki) 34, 7 laps; Pier Francesco Chili, I (Ducati) 7, 6 laps; Niall Mackenzie, GB (Yamaha) 41, 5 laps; James Haydon, GB (Ducati) 14, 0 laps; Brett Sampson, GB (Kawasaki) 77, 0 laps.

Fastest lap: Fogarty, 1m 26.366s, 108.394 mph/174.443 km/h (record).

Fastest qualifier: Chili, 1m 25.960s, 108.906 mph/175.267 km/h.
Previous lap record: John Kocinski, USA (Ducati), 1m 28.022s, 106.340 mph/171.140 km/h (1996).
Championship points: 1 Kocinski, 249; **2** Fogarty, 242; **3** Russell, 188; **4** Slight, 150; **5** Crafar, 135; **6** Chili, 134; **7** Yanagawa, 101; **8** Hodgson, 90; **9** Whitham, 87; **10** Edwards, 79; **11** Bontempi, 74; **12** Hale, 39; **13** Riba Cabana, 36; **14** DuHamel, 32; **15** Meklau, 30.   * *not eligible for championship points*

A1-RING

Mark Wernham

Mark Wernham

FOR the first time this season, the World Superbike regulars had to get acquainted with a new track. Zeltweg had been a World Championship venue from 1988 to 1994, but that was on the old circuit. Renamed the A1-Ring, the new track had undergone extensive changes. They didn't stop Pier Francesco Chili, though: he clinched his third consecutive pole position in the final moments of the second qualifying session.

Yanagawa had set the pace up to that point, and he stayed second. The first row was completed by the two main world title contenders, with Kocinski ending up just ahead of Fogarty.

Chili, Yanagawa and Fogarty charged up to the front as the first race started. Slight, Kocinski and Crafar followed a short distance behind. Hodgson had started well but lost ground after a few laps and was soon fighting for seventh with Scott Russell.

Yanagawa looked set to give Kawasaki their first win of the season, as he led going into the last lap. But Fogarty managed to get by him and just stay ahead of the green bike until the chequered flag.

Slight ended the lean streak he'd been enduring since Laguna Seca by taking third. 'Maybe people will stop asking what's wrong with me now,' he commented. Chili and Kocinski crossed the finish line just behind him.

Fogarty's title chances were now looking good. So far, Kocinski had never seemed quite able to match Fogarty's pace in the dry. But the skies looked threatening as the second leg started. Kocinski took the lead, but Fogarty and Yanagawa soon charged past him. At this point, Hodgson had already retired after outbraking himself in the first corner.

The two leaders pulled away as Chili, Kocinski, Crafar and Slight gave chase. While Fogarty did his best to distance himself from Yanagawa, Chili crashed out, taking the luckless Crafar with him. This was the second time in two meetings that the Kawasaki rider had found himself on the ground through no fault of his own. Chili was unscathed; Crafar suffered a badly bruised leg which needed treatment right up to the Assen round, two weeks later.

With light rain beginning to fall, the race suddenly took on a different face. Suddenly, Kocinski was on a charge. Within moments, he'd gone from a distant fourth to new race leader.

Seeing the number 3 Honda sail past him, Fogarty lost his cool. He tried a desperate pass while braking into a slow corner and rammed Kocinski. Carl crashed, but John managed to stay upright even though he was forced off the track. With the RC45's tailpiece in ruins, Kocinski rejoined the race.

Yanagawa could not have hoped for a better scenario. He shot back into the lead. Slight followed him closely and looked threatening on the last lap, but he was unable to prevent Yanagawa from taking his first World Superbike win.

Kocinski secured third and kept the championship lead. Russell was fourth, but a long way off, after a race-long battle with Piergiorgio Bontempi.

Above: The eyes of a winner. Yanagawa's first win was also Kawasaki's first of the year. *Above left:* The Japanese rider leads Chili, Fogarty and the pack en route to victory.

Left: First race winner Fogarty and runner-up Yanagawa are happy to show their hair; Slight (on the left) keeps his crop-top hidden.

Far left: John Kocinski – the mask didn't slip; his points lead stretched.

Round 8   A1-Ring, Zeltweg, Austria
17 August, 2.684-mile/4.319-km circuit
2 x 25 laps, 67.100 miles/107.970 km

Race 1

Pl. Name Nat. (Machine)	No.	Time & speed	Laps
1 Carl Fogarty, GB (Ducati)	4	38m 11.804s	25
		105.390 mph/169.609 km/h	
2 Akira Yanagawa, J (Kawasaki)	8	38m 12.101s	25
3 Aaron Slight, NZ (Honda)	2	38m 12.419s	25
4 Pier Francesco Chili, I (Ducati)	7	38m 12.894s	25
5 John Kocinski, USA (Honda)	3	38m 13.285s	25
6 Simon Crafar, NZ (Kawasaki)	6	38m 14.940s	25
7 Scott Russell, USA (Yamaha)	22	38m 27.750s	25
8 Neil Hodgson, GB (Ducati)	9	38m 39.302s	25
9 Piergiorgio Bontempi, I (Kawasaki)	15	38m 44.960s	25
10 James Whitham, GB (Suzuki)	12	38m 46.519s	25
11 Mike Hale, USA (Suzuki)	11	38m 55.484s	25
12 Chris Walker, GB (Yamaha)	42	38m 59.612s	25
13 Udo Mark, D (Suzuki)*	64	39m 03.966s	25
14 Jochen Schmid, D (Kawasaki)	21	39m 24.319s	25
15 Andreas Meklau, A (Ducati)	13	39m 28.092s	25
16 Pere Riba Cabana, E (Honda)	17	39m 46.574s	24
17 Igor Jerman, SLO (Kawasaki)	31	38m 27.021s	24
18 Anton Gruschka, D (Yamaha)*	54	38m 49.552s	24
19 Giorgio Cantalupo, I (Ducati)*	52	39m 10.097s	24
20 Gerhard Esterer, A (Kawasaki)*	55	39m 35.424s	24
21 Ondrej Lelek, CS (Honda)*	58	38m 46.768s	23
22 Ossi Niederkirche, A (Suzuki)	37	39m 01.817s	23
23 Toni Rechberger, A (Yamaha)*	62	39m 10.172s	23
24 Ali Guettouche, A (Kawasaki)*	57	39m 56.140s	23
25 Jiri Mrkyvka, CS (Honda)*	61	39m 04.018s	22

NC Johann Wolfsteiner, A (Kawasaki) 39, 14 laps; **DNF** Gregorio Lavilla, E (Ducati) 35, 16 laps; Redamo Assirelli, I (Yamaha) 72, 14 laps; James Haydon, GB (Ducati) 14, 10 laps; Christian Hausle, A (Ducati) 36, 0 laps; J. Bichler, A (Ducati) 43, 0 laps; **DNS** Hermann Schmid, A (Ducati) 38.

Fastest lap: Yanagawa, 1m 30.945s, 106.232 mph/170.964 km/h (record).

Race 2

Pl. Name Nat. (Machine)	No.	Time & speed	Laps
1 Akira Yanagawa, J (Kawasaki)	8	38m 18.104s	25
		105.101 mph/169.144 km/h	
2 Aaron Slight, NZ (Honda)	2	38m 18.225s	25
3 John Kocinski, USA (Honda)	3	38m 25.368s	25
4 Scott Russell, USA (Yamaha)	22	38m 37.563s	25
5 Piergiorgio Bontempi, I (Kawasaki)	15	38m 37.749s	25
6 James Whitham, GB (Suzuki)	12	38m 49.156s	25
7 Mike Hale, USA (Suzuki)	11	38m 49.549s	25
8 Andreas Meklau, A (Ducati)	13	38m 50.711s	25
9 Udo Mark, D (Suzuki)*	64	39m 02.238s	25
10 Chris Walker, GB (Yamaha)	42	39m 19.429s	25
11 Jochen Schmid, D (Kawasaki)	21	39m 23.751s	25
12 Pere Riba Cabana, E (Honda)	17	39m 33.713s	25
13 Igor Jerman, SLO (Kawasaki)	31	39m 34.595s	25
14 Anton Gruschka, D (Yamaha)*	54	39m 26.766s	24
15 Gerhard Esterer, A (Kawasaki)*	55	39m 44.483s	24
16 Christian Hausle, A (Ducati)*	36	39m 46.327s	24
17 Giorgio Cantalupo, I (Ducati)*	52	38m 20.247s	23
18 Jiri Mrkyvka, CS (Honda)*	61	38m 35.988s	23
19 Johann Wolfsteiner, A (Kawasaki)	39	38m 36.596s	23
20 Ali Guettouche, A (Kawasaki)*	57	38m 37.006s	23
21 Ondrej Lelek, CS (Honda)*	58	38m 37.743s	23
22 Ossi Niederkircher, A (Suzuki)	37	39m 00.183s	23
23 Toni Rechberger, A (Yamaha)*	62	39m 08.786s	23

DNF Carl Fogarty, GB (Ducati) 4, 18 laps; James Haydon, GB (Ducati) 14, 18 laps; Simon Crafar, NZ (Kawasaki) 6, 7 laps; Pier Francesco Chili, I (Ducati) 7, 7 laps; Redamo Assirelli, I (Yamaha) 72, 6 laps; J. Bichler, A (Ducati) 43, 6 laps; Gregorio Lavilla, E (Ducati) 35, 3 laps; Neil Hodgson, GB (Ducati) 9, 1 lap; **DNS** Hermann Schmid, A (Ducati) 38.

Fastest lap: Yanagawa, 1m 30.660s, 106.566 mph/171.502 km/h (record).

Fastest qualifier: Chili, 1m 30.806s, 106.395 mph/171.266 km/h.
Previous lap record: none.
Championship points: 1 Kocinski, 276; **2** Fogarty, 267; **3** Slight, 224; **4** Russell, 172; **5** Chili, 147; **6** Yanagawa, 146; **7** Crafar, 145; **8** Whitham, 103; **9** Hodgson, 98; **10** Bontempi, 92; **11** Edwards, 79; **12** Hale, 53; **13** Riba Cabana, 42; **14** Meklau, 40; **15** DuHamel, 32.   * *not eligible for championship points*

Photos: Gold & Goose and Mark Wernham

ASSEN

Left and bottom: Fogarty's fans won the propaganda war by plundering the cupboard marked 'Vulgar Abuse'. But it was Kocinski *(below)* who won the first race, breaking Fogarty's run.

Far left, above: Fogarty at work at his favourite circuit. *Far left, below:* Chili in full flow. On form, he joined the chief title rivals on the rostrum in both races.

CARL Fogarty hadn't lost a race at Assen since 1993 – eight straight wins had made the double Superbike World Champion the undisputed king of the Dutch circuit.

'Yes, this is my favourite track,' he admitted during practice. 'But if I can't win, I'll just have to settle for seconds and thirds.' A sensible attitude with a third title slowly slipping through his fingers. But nobody was fooled. Come race day he would be gunning for victory, as always.

If anything, the Ducati ace was even more determined after practice. Kocinski had grabbed pole on the very last lap of the last session and Fogarty was not impressed.

But Kocinski did not profit. As the first race began and Fogarty shot into the lead, the American was left floundering in midfield. 'Another start like that and I deserve to be fired!' John commented after the race. 'I worked hard all weekend to get that pole and just wasted it.'

Fogarty set about putting as much distance as possible between himself and his rival. He was followed by Russell, Yanagawa and Slight. Whitham had made a strong start but was soon passed by a hard-charging Chili. Unable to hold Foggy's pace, Yanagawa slipped back as Chili moved up.

Soon Fogarty, Chili, Russell and Slight had broken away from the rest of the pack. But Kocinski was riding superbly. He moved into fifth ahead of Whitham, Yanagawa and Hodgson, then started reeling in Russell.

On the eighth lap of this 16-lap first leg, Kocinski passed Russell. Two laps later, he lined up Slight with a very daring pass on the outside of the second Castrol Honda. It was now only a matter of time before Kocinski caught Fogarty.

On the penultimate lap, the Honda eased into the lead. Fogarty stayed in close proximity, but Kocinski just kept the pressure on and, for the first time in years, King Carl lost a round at Assen!

If his first race start was a sacking offence, then surely Kocinski should have been shot after the second. The American managed to fluff it yet again and left himself with a lot of catching up to do.

Whitham had been quickest off the line, so quick in fact that he was called into the pits for a ten second stop-and-go penalty. He eventually finished 11th.

Despite the Suzuki's lightning start, Fogarty was soon in the lead with Chili right behind him. Simon Crafar and Akira Yanagawa weren't far off, until Slight flew past them and into third.

Just as in the first race, Kocinski wasted no time in recovering from his awful start and took fourth on lap six. But little changed after that, except for John getting the better of his team-mate.

Fogarty was delighted with his race win but recognized that, with Kocinski still five points ahead, there was a long way to go. 'I have to leave Albacete ahead in the championship to keep my title hopes alive,' he warned. 'Sugo and Sentul should favour the Hondas.'

Round 9   ASSEN, Holland
31 August, 3.759-mile/6.049-km circuit
2 x 16 laps, 60.144 miles/96.784 km

Race 1

Pl. Name Nat. (Machine)	No.	Time & speed	Laps
1 John Kocinski, USA (Honda)	3	33m 34.731s	16
		107.458 mph/172.937 km/h	
2 Carl Fogarty, GB (Ducati)	4	33m 34.874s	16
3 Pier Francesco Chili, I (Ducati)	7	33m 35.432s	16
4 Aaron Slight, NZ (Honda)	2	33m 41.094s	16
5 Neil Hodgson, GB (Ducati)	9	33m 43.162s	16
6 Scott Russell, USA (Yamaha)	22	33m 45.501s	16
7 James Whitham, GB (Suzuki)	12	33m 48.271s	16
8 Akira Yanagawa, J (Kawasaki)	8	33m 48.297s	16
9 Simon Crafar, NZ (Kawasaki)	6	33m 51.333s	16
10 Chris Walker, GB (Yamaha)	42	34m 02.379s	16
11 Mike Hale, USA (Suzuki)	11	34m 06.008s	16
12 Pere Riba Cabana, E (Honda)	17	34m 37.063s	16
13 Jochen Schmid, D (Kawasaki)	21	34m 37.518s	16
14 Udo Mark, D (Suzuki)*	53	34m 37.764s	16
15 Erkka Korpiaho, SF (Kawasaki)	46	34m 40.381s	16
16 Igor Jerman, SLO (Kawasaki)	31	34m 40.690s	16
17 Michael Rudroff, D (Suzuki)*	57	35m 00.548s	16
18 Rainer Janisch, D (Suzuki)*	56	35m 07.812s	16
19 Juha Berner, SF (Kawasaki)	49	35m 40.829s	16
20 Anton Gruschka, D (Yamaha)*	52	33m 47.059s	16
21 Joop Bosch, NL (Kawasaki)*	60	33m 53.970s	15
22 Heinz Platacis, NL (Kawasaki)*	64	34m 00.394s	15
23 Giorgio Cantalupo, I (Ducati)*	51	34m 01.964s	15
24 Gijsbert Spilt, NL (Ducati)*	61	34m 21.631s	15
25 Ondrej Lelek, CS (Honda)*	79	34m 24.288s	15

DNF James Haydon, GB (Ducati) 14, 13 laps; Jiri Mrkyvka, CS (Honda) 68, 10 laps; Piergiorgio Bontempi, I (Kawasaki) 15, 0 laps; Eskil Suter, F (Honda) 47, 0 laps; **DNS** Steve Marks, GB (Kawasaki) 69.

Fastest lap: Chili, 2m 04.583s, 108.612 mph/174.794 km/h (record).

Race 2

Pl. Name Nat. (Machine)	No.	Time & speed	Laps
1 Carl Fogarty, GB (Ducati)	4	33m 31.289s	16
		107.642 mph/173.233 km/h	
2 Pier Francesco Chili, I (Ducati)	7	33m 32.220s	16
3 John Kocinski, USA (Honda)	3	33m 34.277s	16
4 Aaron Slight, NZ (Honda)	2	33m 35.909s	16
5 Neil Hodgson, GB (Ducati)	9	33m 44.715s	16
6 Simon Crafar, NZ (Kawasaki)	6	33m 47.179s	16
7 Akira Yanagawa, J (Kawasaki)	8	33m 52.229s	16
8 Scott Russell, USA (Yamaha)	22	34m 02.255s	16
9 Chris Walker, GB (Yamaha)	42	34m 06.254s	16
10 Piergiorgio Bontempi, I (Kawasaki)	15	34m 12.010s	16
11 James Whitham, GB (Suzuki)	12	34m 21.796s	16
12 Jochen Schmid, D (Kawasaki)	21	34m 33.285s	16
13 Udo Mark, D (Suzuki)	53	34m 33.589s	16
14 Igor Jerman, SLO (Kawasaki)	31	34m 33.747s	16
15 Pere Riba Cabana, E (Honda)	17	34m 34.204s	16
16 Rainer Janisch, D (Suzuki)*	56	35m 08.337s	16
17 Erkka Korpiaho, SF (Kawasaki)	46	35m 19.192s	16
18 Michael Rudroff, D (Suzuki)*	57	35m 38.168s	16
19 Juha Berner, SF (Kawasaki)	49	33m 36.850s	15
20 Jiri Mrkyvka, CS (Honda)*	68	34m 04.061s	15
21 Heinz Platacis, NL (Kawasaki)*	64	34m 04.326s	15
22 Steve Marks, GB (Kawasaki)	69	34m 04.768s	15
23 Ondrej Lelek, CS (Honda)*	79	34m 13.854s	15

DNF Joop Bosch, NL (Kawasaki) 60, 13 laps; Anton Gruschka, D (Yamaha) 52, 12 laps; Mike Hale, USA (Suzuki) 11, 11 laps; Giorgio Cantalupo, I (Ducati) 51, 11 laps; Eskil Suter, F (Honda) 47, 7 laps; Gijsbert Spilt, NL (Ducati) 61, 4 laps; James Haydon, GB (Ducati) 14, 0 laps.

Fastest lap: Chili, 2m 04.649s, 108.554 mph/174.701 km/h.

Fastest qualifier: Kocinski, 2m 04.061s, 109.069 mph/175.529 km/h.
Previous lap record: John Kocinski, USA (Ducati), 2m 04.629s, 108.572 mph/174.729 km/h (1996).
Championship points: 1 Kocinski, 317; **2** Fogarty, 312; **3** Slight, 250; **4** Russell, 190; **5** Chili, 183; **6** Yanagawa, 163; **7** Crafar, 162; **8** Hodgson, 120; **9** Whitham, 117; **10** Bontempi, 98; **11** Edwards, 79; **12** Hale, 58; **13** Riba Cabana, 48; **14** Meklau, 40; **15** Walker, 36. * not eligible for championship points

ALBACETE

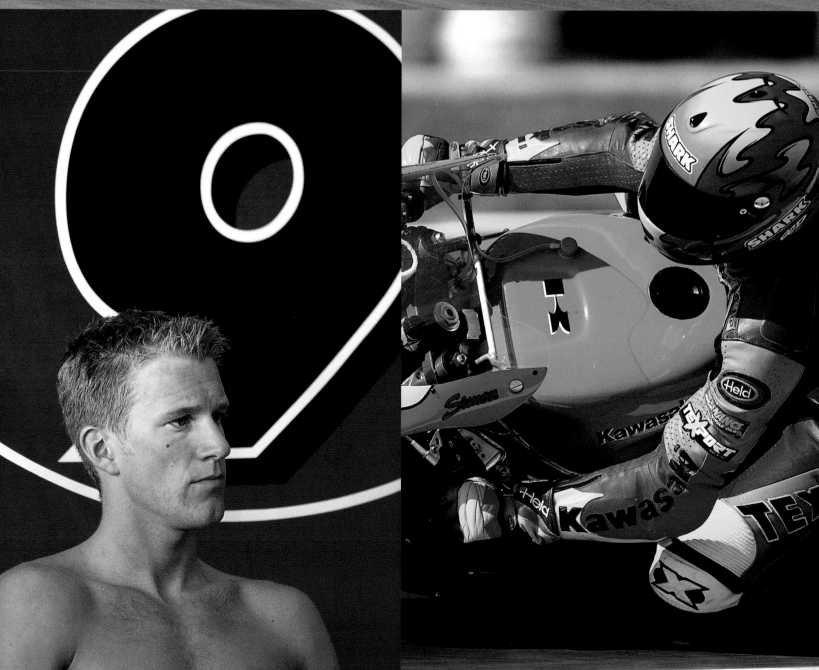

Left: Kocinski leads the field for another double victory. He left Spain with a 55-point lead. But Albacete was disastrous for Fogarty *(below)*.

Bottom, left to right: Elusive targets – Neil Hodgson was still waiting for a good finish; Simon Crafar for that elusive win; Scott Russell for more speed from the Yamaha.

IF Kocinski's Assen pole wasn't enough to show that he was now really at home on the Honda, then his practice performance at Albacete certainly proved the point. On a track that has traditionally favoured the Ducatis, Kocinski and his Honda once again headed the time sheet. 'I am more comfortable than ever on the bike,' confirmed the American. Still struggling with handling problems, Fogarty was just one-tenth of a second off his rival's time and qualified second ahead of Crafar and Slight.

Fogarty had to finish ahead of Kocinski to keep his titles hopes high, and his first race start fitted that strategy perfectly as he led from Crafar, Slight, Whitham and Kocinski. Foggy and Crafar soon broke away from the pack, with Kocinski and Slight in close pursuit. But John was on a charge, clawing his way back to take the lead from Carl by half-distance.

There was drama further back as Russell was hit by Whitham and both riders ended their race in the gravel trap, while up front it looked like Fogarty might be settling for second. Then, with a few laps to go, he began closing on Kocinski – and it all went terribly wrong. The Ducati hit one bump too many, and down it crashed. 'I was on the limit anyway,' claimed Fogarty. 'There was nothing I could do.'

With his main rival for the race and the championship out of the picture, Kocinski had little trouble taking the win ahead of Slight and Crafar. Yanagawa and Chili had been involved in a battle for fourth but the Japanese rider managed to pull out a substantial lead over Frankie by the flag.

Whitham was quick off the mark at the start of race two and tucked in behind Kocinski, who had taken the holeshot. But Crafar was on a mission. He wasted no time passing Whitham and then shadowed Kocinski for a couple of laps before snatching the lead.

Carl, meanwhile, was fighting back from an unfortunate first-lap incident in which he was forced off the track by another rider's crash. A tribute to the Fogarty skill and reflexes, he had managed to avoid crashing as he ploughed into the gravel trap. But by the time he rejoined the race he was last, and facing an uphill struggle to get back into contention.

He managed to fight his way through the ranks and back up to 11th. But then he crashed again. 'The front just went,' the dejected Englishman commented. 'But after my first race crash, I knew my title chances were probably over anyway.'

In true champion's style, Kocinski took maximum advantage of Fogarty's misfortune by robbing Crafar of the lead and going on to win his second race of the day. His team-mate Slight was third, with Yanagawa fourth once again.

Kocinski left Albacete with a huge 55-point lead over Fogarty – an extremely comfortable position, with only four races left.

Round 10   ALBACETE, Spain
21 September, 2.199-mile/3.539-km circuit
2 x 26 laps, 57.174 miles/92.014 km

Race 1

Pl.	Name Nat. (Machine)	No.	Time & speed	Laps
1	John Kocinski, USA (Honda)	3	40m 22.586s	26
			84.963 mph/136.734 km/h	
2	Aaron Slight, NZ (Honda)	2	40m 28.614s	26
3	Simon Crafar, NZ (Kawasaki)	6	40m 31.038s	26
4	Akira Yanagawa, J (Kawasaki)	8	40m 36.311s	26
5	Pier Francesco Chili, I (Ducati)	7	40m 42.772s	26
6	Piergiorgio Bontempi, I (Kawasaki)	15	40m 49.035s	26
7	Gregorio Lavilla, E (Ducati)	35	40m 50.076s	26
8	Mike Hale, USA (Suzuki)	11	40m 50.502s	26
9	Jochen Schmid, D (Kawasaki)	21	41m 07.320s	26
10	Chris Walker, GB (Yamaha)	42	41m 08.303s	26
11	Pere Riba Cabana, E (Honda)	17	41m 10.154s	26
12	Udo Mark, D (Suzuki)*	53	41m 37.081s	26
13	Igor Jerman, SLO (Kawasaki)	31	41m 41.794s	26
14	Giorgio Cantalupo, I (Ducati)*	51	40m 49.839s	25
15	Jiri Mrkyvka, CS (Honda)*	57	41m 04.272s	25
16	Anton Gruschka, D (Yamaha)*	52	41m 07.449s	25
17	Gilson Scudeler, BR (Ducati)*	63	41m 34.154s	25
18	Erkka Korpiaho, SF (Kawasaki)	46	41m 55.003s	25
19	Ondrej Lelek, CS (Honda)*	56	42m 53.856s	25
20	Vladimir Karban, S (Suzuki)*	71	42m 55.863s	25

DNF Carl Fogarty, GB (Ducati) 4, 21 laps; James Whitham, GB (Suzuki) 12, 8 laps; Scott Russell, USA (Yamaha) 22, 8 laps; James Haydon, GB (Ducati) 14, 3 laps; Neil Hodgson, GB (Ducati) 9, 1 lap.

Fastest lap: Kocinski, 1m 32.334s, 85.737 mph/137.981 km/h.

Race 2

Pl.	Name Nat. (Machine)	No.	Time & speed	Laps
1	John Kocinski, USA (Honda)	3	40m 21.958s	26
			84.985 mph/136.770 km/h	
2	Simon Crafar, NZ (Kawasaki)	6	40m 23.374s	26
3	Aaron Slight, NZ (Honda)	2	40m 24.060s	26
4	Akira Yanagawa, J (Kawasaki)	8	40m 24.266s	26
5	Scott Russell, USA (Yamaha)	22	40m 36.541s	26
6	Piergiorgio Bontempi, I (Kawasaki)	15	40m 36.914s	26
7	Pier Francesco Chili, I (Ducati)	7	40m 53.131s	26
8	Neil Hodgson, GB (Ducati)	9	41m 07.432s	26
9	Mike Hale, USA (Suzuki)	11	41m 07.503s	26
10	James Whitham, GB (Suzuki)	12	41m 09.459s	26
11	Chris Walker, GB (Yamaha)	42	41m 10.849s	26
12	Jochen Schmid, D (Kawasaki)	21	41m 10.990s	26
13	Pere Riba Cabana, E (Honda)	17	41m 11.399s	26
14	Udo Mark, D (Suzuki)*	53	41m 25.177s	26
15	James Haydon, GB (Ducati)	14	41m 33.548s	26
16	Erkka Korpiaho, SF (Kawasaki)	46	41m 51.679s	26
17	Giorgio Cantalupo, I (Ducati)*	51	40m 48.041s	25
18	Jiri Mrkyvka, CS (Honda)*	57	40m 50.433s	25
19	Anton Gruschka, D (Yamaha)*	52	40m 53.265s	25
20	Igor Jerman, SLO (Kawasaki)	31	41m 13.640s	25
21	Gilson Scudeler, BR (Ducati)*	63	41m 17.384s	25
22	Ondrej Lelek, CS (Honda)*	56	41m 56.732s	25
23	Vladimir Karban, S (Suzuki)*	71	40m 25.418s	24

DNF Carl Fogarty, GB (Ducati) 4, 14 laps; Gregorio Lavilla, E (Ducati) 35, 0 laps.

Fastest lap: Crafar, 1m 32.258s, 85.808 mph/138.095 km/h.

Fastest qualifier: Kocinski, 1m 31.350s, 86.661 mph/139.467 km/h.
Lap record: Troy Corser, AUS (Ducati), 1m 31.714s, 86.317 mph/138.914 km/h (1996).
Championship points: 1 Kocinski, 367; **2** Fogarty, 312; **3** Slight, 286; **4** Chili, 203; **5** Russell, 201; **6** Crafar, 198; **7** Yanagawa, 189; **8** Hodgson, 128; **9** Whitham, 123; **10** Bontempi, 118; **11** Edwards, 79; **12** Hale, 73; **13** Riba Cabana, 56; **14** Walker, 47; **15** Schmid, 46.
* not eligible for championship points

Photos: Gold & Goose

SUGO

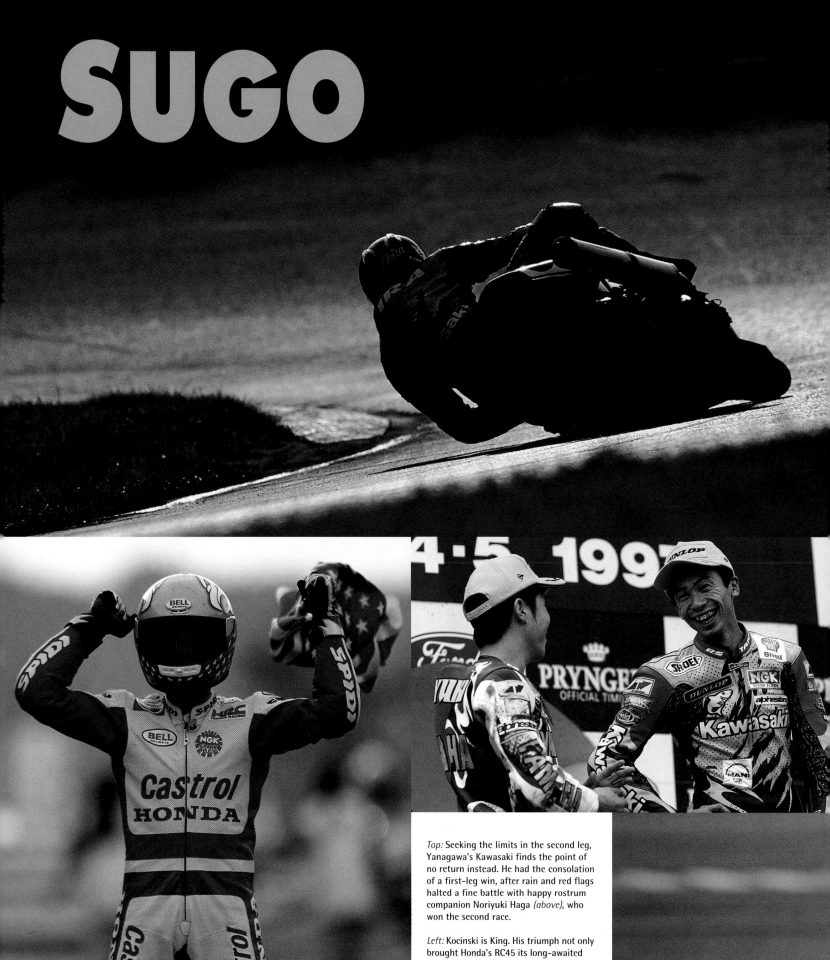

Top: Seeking the limits in the second leg, Yanagawa's Kawasaki finds the point of no return instead. He had the consolation of a first-leg win, after rain and red flags halted a fine battle with happy rostrum companion Noriyuki Haga *(above)*, who won the second race.

Left: Kocinski is King. His triumph not only brought Honda's RC45 its long-awaited first title victory, it also rekindled the former 250 World Champion's flagging career.

Above right and centre: Kocinski's pit board tells him the crucial news. Fogarty is out, and the title is his. On the rostrum with Crafar *(left)* and Haga, the rider from Little Rock finally succumbed to the emotion.

Right: One-race wonder Haga succeeded where Yamaha's regular riders Russell and Edwards had failed, giving the marque its only win of the year at his home circuit.

RACES in Japan are always special. As elsewhere, the local talent is on show, eager to compete against the world regulars. But in Japan the local talent rides on full factory equipment.

Thus Sugo was not the best place for Fogarty to try and save the title. It takes a lot of time to get to know this tight and technical course and with his Ducati's handling still problematic, the British star faced a difficult week-end.

As if to prove that point, he qualified a lowly 13th, Kocinski faring a little better and ending practice in eighth. The Japanese ruled, as expected, with Yanagawa taking pole ahead of 1996 World Superbike regular Wataru Yoshikawa. Third fastest was Noriyuki Haga, standing in for a still-injured Colin Edwards.

Haga was keen to take advantage of this opportunity and shot into the lead at the start of the first race. The newly crowned Japanese Superbike champion was followed by Kawasaki team-mates Yanagawa and Crafar. But Haga was determined to break away and upped the pace. Only Yanagawa followed, leaving Crafar a safe third.

The race behind was all action as Kitagawa, Yoshikawa, Fujiwara and Takeishi led Slight, Kocinski and Fogarty. Foggy was obviously struggling and never left the back of this chasing group.

Up front, Yanagawa was right with Haga and managed to pass him. The pair swapped places a few times and looked set for a serious bout of last-lap heroics but, with three laps to go, the red flags came out. It had started to rain and the race was being stopped – just at the right moment for Yanagawa, who had passed Haga a lap before and was therefore declared the winner.

But what of the championship? Kocinski finished 9th, four places ahead of Fogarty. It was still not enough to give him the title.

Race two was chaotic from the start. Bontempi crashed at Turn One, breaking his foot and taking several other riders out in the process, Chili and Yoshikawa among the fallen.

Haga once again took an early lead but, this time, he held on to it until the flag. A somewhat ironical situation, for it had taken a substitute to give the Yamaha factory team their first World Superbike victory.

Crafar leapt into second place, followed by Kitagawa, Kocinski, Fujiwara and Slight. Fogarty, meanwhile, was in deep trouble. Twelfth on lap one, he was moving through the field rather too slowly to have a realistic chance of threatening Kocinski's position. Especially as the American was gaining on Kitagawa and soon eased into third. (Kitagawa would not finish the race: the Japanese collided with a hard-charging Scott Russell who had come up from 14th on the starting grid.)

Then it was Fogarty's turn to crash, thus ending all hopes of beating Kocinski for the title. The American came home in third, behind Crafar, and stood tearfully on the podium as he celebrated his and Castrol Honda's first World Superbike crown.

Round 11   SUGO, Japan
5 October, 2.335-mile/3.737-km circuit

Race 1 (21 laps, 49.035 miles/78.477 km)

Pl. Name Nat. (Machine)	No.	Time & speed	Laps
1 Akira Yanagawa, J (Kawasaki)	8	31m 53.323s	21
		91.750 mph/147.658 km/h	
2 Noriyuki Haga, J (Yamaha)	41	31m 53.356s	21
3 Simon Crafar, NZ (Kawasaki)	6	31m 57.429s	21
4 Keiichi Kitagawa, J (Suzuki)	37	32m 05.225s	21
5 Wataru Yoshikawa, J (Yamaha)*	51	32m 11.668s	21
6 Aaron Slight, NZ (Honda)	2	32m 12.218s	21
7 Shinya Takeishi, J (Kawasaki)	39	32m 13.396s	21
8 Katsuaki Fujiwara, J (Suzuki)	38	32m 13.696s	21
9 John Kocinski, USA (Honda)	3	32m 13.986s	21
10 Tamaki Serizawa, J (Suzuki)	34	32m 14.589s	21
11 Shinichi Ito, J (Honda)*	52	32m 14.702s	21
12 Pier Francesco Chili, I (Ducati)	7	32m 14.886s	21
13 Carl Fogarty, GB (Ducati)	4	32m 15.465s	21
14 Scott Russell, USA (Yamaha)	22	32m 15.800s	21
15 Norihiko Fujiwara, J (Yamaha)	36	32m 19.947s	21
16 Yuichi Takeda, J (Honda)	40	32m 27.310s	21
17 Akira Ryo, J (Kawasaki)	35	32m 27.409s	21
18 Neil Hodgson, GB (Ducati)	9	32m 28.226s	21
19 John Reynolds, GB (Ducati)	33	32m 29.365s	21
20 Sean Emmett, GB (Ducati)	44	32m 39.378s	21
21 Mike Hale, USA (Suzuki)	11	32m 43.864s	21
22 Manabu Kamada, J (Honda)*	61	32m 50.246s	21
23 Pere Riba Cabana, E (Honda)	17	32m 52.697s	21
24 Ichirou Asai, J (Ducati)*	55	32m 59.471s	21
25 Makoto Suzuki, J (Ducati)	14	33m 00.112s	21
26 Syuya Arai, J (Honda)*	60	33m 03.901s	21
27 Shinya Nakatani, J (Kawasaki)	54	33m 06.963s	21
28 Igor Jerman, SLO (Kawasaki)	31	32m 35.597s	20

DNF Piergiorgio Bontempi, I (Kawasaki) 15, 8 laps; **DNS** Katsunori Hasegawa, J (Yamaha) 58; Kousuke Akiyoshi, J (Suzuki) 53; James Whitham, GB (Suzuki) 12.

Fastest lap: Yanagawa, 1m 30.338s, 92.535 mph/148.920 km/h (record).

Race 2 (25 laps, 58.375 miles/93.425 km)

Pl. Name Nat. (Machine)	No.	Time & speed	Laps
1 Noriyuki Haga, J (Yamaha)	41	38m 04.349s	25
		91.486 mph/147.232 km/h	
2 Simon Crafar, NZ (Kawasaki)	8	38m 07.025s	25
3 John Kocinski, USA (Honda)	3	38m 10.232s	25
4 Aaron Slight, NZ (Honda)	2	38m 14.714s	25
5 Katsuaki Fujiwara, J (Suzuki)	38	38m 17.203s	25
6 Tamaki Serizawa, J (Suzuki)	34	38m 20.231s	25
7 Yuichi Takeda, J (Honda)	40	38m 36.915s	25
8 Akira Ryo, J (Kawasaki)	35	38m 43.506s	25
9 Sean Emmett, GB (Ducati)	44	38m 51.808s	25
10 Mike Hale, USA (Suzuki)	11	38m 57.794s	25
11 Makoto Suzuki, J (Ducati)	14	39m 02.751s	25
12 Ichirou Asai, J (Ducati)*	55	39m 05.667s	25
13 Manabu Kamada, J (Honda)*	61	39m 06.843s	25
14 Igor Jerman, SLO (Kawasaki)	31	39m 07.703s	25
15 Pere Riba Cabana, E (Honda)	17	39m 12.037s	25
16 Syuya Arai, J (Honda)*	60	39m 17.506s	25
17 Shinya Nakatani, J (Kawasaki)	54	38m 30.064s	24

DNF Shinya Takeishi, J (Kawasaki) 39, 24 laps; Carl Fogarty, GB (Ducati) 4, 20 laps; Keiichi Kitagawa, J (Suzuki) 37, 17 laps; Scott Russell, USA (Yamaha) 22, 17 laps; Neil Hodgson, GB (Ducati) 9, 9 laps; Akira Yanagawa, J (Kawasaki) 8, 7 laps; John Reynolds, GB (Ducati) 33, 1 lap; Shinichi Ito, J (Honda) 52, 1 lap; Wataru Yoshikawa, J (Yamaha) 51, 0 laps; Pier Francesco Chili, I (lDucati) 7, 0 laps; Piergiorgio Bontempi, I (Kawasaki) 15, 0 laps; Norihiko Fujiwara, J (Yamaha) 36, 0 laps; **DNS** Katsunori Hasegawa, J (Yamaha) 58; Kousuke Akiyoshi, J (Suzuki) 53; James Whitham, GB (Suzuki) 11.

Fastest lap: Haga, 1m 30.786s, 92.078 mph/148.185 km/h.

Fastest qualifier: Yanagawa, 1m 30.170s, 92.707 mph/149.198 km/h.
Previous lap record: Takuma Aoki, J (Honda), 1m 31.044s, 91.830 mph/147.786 km/h (1996).
Championship points: 1 Kocinski, 391; **2** Fogarty, 317; **3** Slight, 310; **4** Crafar, 234; **5** Yanagawa, 214; **6** Chili, 209; **7** Russell, 205; **8** Hodgson, 128; **9** Whitham, 123; **10** Bontempi, 118; **11** Edwards and Hale, 79; **13** Riba Cabana, 59; **14** Walker, 47; **15** Schmid, 46. *not eligible for championship points*

Photos: Gold & Goose

SENTUL

Left: Already the champion, Kocinski meant to end the year in a blaze of glory. Riding with maximum aggression, he almost took out team-mate Slight in a tooth-and-nail first race, and succeeded in doing the same to Crafar in race two. With some justice, he also crashed himself.

Right: Team-mates Whitham and Hale remain cheerful despite their Suzukis' uncompetitiveness.

Below (top and centre): Crafar leads the Hondas. Robbed of two potential wins, he remained the unluckiest man in the class. In the background, Chili is in trouble, and Hodgson pays the price.

Bottom: Fogarty took a surprise win from Yanagawa *(right)* and Haga in race two which put him second overall.

WITH the title already decided, the last round might have been boring. It was anything but. John Kocinski suffered bad food poisoning on Friday night. 'I was up all night vomiting and I had a high fever,' he explained after practice. 'The doctors in the Clinica Mobile put me on a drip this morning and I have to thank them for being able to ride at all.' Despite his weakened condition, Kocinski set another pole ahead of Fogarty and Chili.

Sitting on the outside of the front row, Slight was first off the line when the lights turned green for the season's penultimate race. But Kocinski and Crafar came past him before the first lap was over. Crafar soon took the lead ahead of Kocinski, Slight and Fogarty.

Chili, Hodgson and Yanagawa led the second group but on lap five, Chili outbraked himself at the chicane, shooting across the gravel trap and back onto the track just ahead of Hodgson. The riders collided, with Hodgson going down. Chili managed to continue, only to retire a few moments later.

Crafar was still leading on lap ten when his front tyre chunked and tore off the Kawasaki's front mudguard on the start-finish straight. The unluckiest of the World Superbike contenders had once again been cruelly robbed of a potential win.

Earlier, Slight had moved ahead of Kocinski but the American seemed to find his second wind now that the Honda team-mates were fighting for the lead. With the heat and the Sentul dust making the track very slippery, Slight was spectacular as he slid his RC45 into every corner. Still, Kocinski found a way past.

An incredible fight ensued, with Slight not giving Kocinski an inch. The pair were locked together as they entered the final lap. Aaron fought his way past, but Kocinski was not giving up. He almost took the Kiwi out in a very aggressive pass two corners from the end, to secure his ninth win of the season.

Fogarty was third, two seconds behind the leaders.

Kocinski and Crafar once again took control at the start of the second leg. Fogarty followed, while Slight was stuck in between the Yamahas of Russell and Haga. Crafar took the lead on lap two and held on to it, but Kocinski was never far behind. Both riders pulled away from Fogarty.

Meanwhile, the race for fourth was spectacular. Stunning Haga was the star of the chasing group with his wild overtaking moves on Slight and Russell. Yanagawa was also moving up after a bad start. Soon, all four riders were mixing it up in an incredible battle which saw them continually swapping places.

The last lap had to be intense. Crafar and Kocinski were still at each other's throats, with the Kawasaki man leading, but two corners from the end Kocinski tried the same pass that had won him the first race. Unfortunately, this time he didn't get away with it and hit Crafar. Both men crashed, handing Fogarty an unexpected win and the number two plate for 1998.

Yanagawa just beat Haga for second, with Slight fourth ahead of Russell.

Round 12   SENTUL, Indonesia
12 October, 2.464-mile/3.965-km circuit
2 x 25 laps, 61.600 miles/99.125 km

Race 1

Pl. Name Nat. (Machine)	No.	Time & speed	Laps
1 John Kocinski, USA (Honda)	3	36m 51.314s	25
		100.274 mph/161.375 km/h	
2 Aaron Slight, NZ (Honda)	2	36m 51.369s	25
3 Carl Fogarty, GB (Ducati)	4	36m 53.437s	25
4 Akira Yanagawa, J (Kawasaki)	8	36m 58.363s	25
5 Noriyuki Haga, J (Yamaha)	41	37m 04.744s	25
6 Scott Russell, USA (Yamaha)	22	37m 19.621s	25
7 John Reynolds, GB (Ducati)	33	37m 20.716s	25
8 Mike Hale, USA (Suzuki)	11	37m 27.277s	25
9 James Whitham, GB (Suzuki)	12	37m 30.167s	25
10 Igor Jerman, SLO (Kawasaki)	31	37m 40.409s	25
11 Pere Riba Cabana, E (Honda)	17	37m 45.331s	25
12 Makoto Suzuki, J (Ducati)	14	37m 51.328s	25
13 Yudhe Kusuma, IND (Kawasaki)	77	37m 17.218s	23

DNF Simon Crafar, NZ (Kawasaki) 6, 11 laps; Joenaidy Gozali, IND (Kawasaki) 75, 7 laps; Pier Francesco Chili, I (Ducati) 7, 5 laps; Neil Hodgson, GB (Ducati) 9, 5 laps; Christian Lavieille, F (Honda) 10, 5 laps; Sean Emmett, GB (Ducati) 44, 3 laps.

Fastest lap: Kocinski, 1m 27.568s, 101.286 mph/163.004 km/h.

Race 2

Pl. Name Nat. (Machine)	No.	Time & speed	Laps
1 Carl Fogarty, GB (Ducati)	4	36m 37.726s	25
		100.893 mph/162.372 km/h	
2 Akira Yanagawa, J (Kawasaki)	8	36m 45.493s	25
3 Noriyuki Haga, J (Yamaha)	41	36m 45.523s	25
4 Aaron Slight, NZ (Honda)	2	36m 45.704s	25
5 Scott Russell, USA (Yamaha)	22	36m 46.566s	25
6 James Whitham, GB (Suzuki)	12	37m 04.355s	25
7 Neil Hodgson, GB (Ducati)	9	37m 06.555s	25
8 Sean Emmett, GB (Ducati)	44	37m 07.670s	25
9 Igor Jerman, SLO (Kawasaki)	31	37m 24.210s	25
10 Makoto Suzuki, J (Ducati)	14	37m 27.990s	25
11 Pere Riba Cabana, E (Honda)	17	37m 29.413s	25
12 Christian Lavieille, F (Honda)	10	37m 34.359s	24
13 Yudhe Kusuma, IND (Kawasaki)	77	37m 31.440s	23

DNF Simon Crafar, NZ (Kawasaki) 6, 24 laps; John Kocinski, USA (Honda) 3, 24 laps; Mike Hale, USA (Suzuki) 11, 10 laps; Joenaidy Gozali, IND (Kawasaki) 75, 7 laps; Pier Francesco Chili, I (Ducati) 7, 4 laps; John Reynolds, GB (Ducati) 33, 2 laps.

Fastest lap: Kocinski, 1m 27.151s, 101.771 mph/163.784 km/h (record).

Fastest qualifier: Kocinski, 1m 26.839s, 102.137 mph/164.373 km/h.
Previous lap record: Carl Fogarty, GB (Ducati), 1m 28.064s, 100.717 mph/162.088 km/h (1994).
Final World Championship points: see page 196.

* not eligible for championship points

Photos: Gold & Goose

CONSISTENCY COUNTS FOR SUZUKI

ENDURANCE WORLD CHAMPIONSHIP REVIEW

by Kel Edge

THE grime-splattered blue and white bike screamed into the pits, heralding a flurry of controlled activity that saw a change of rider, tyres, oil top-up and full tank of fuel in about the amount of time it takes to read this sentence. As Australian Peter Goddard sped down the pit lane and back into action, teammate Doug Polen slowly pulled off his gloves and helmet, took out his earplugs and went over to the monitor to check on the standings. With his helmet removed, the signs of tiredness and lack of sleep were plainly visible, but behind the bloodshot eyes, there was a look of determination and desire that had led him to a World Championship title at the age of 37. 'Not bad for an old guy, huh?' he said to Suzuki France team manager Dominic Meilland before walking off to grab an hour and a half's rest prior to his next stint aboard the GSX-R750. It was Suzuki's first world title with the new GSX-R750 and Doug Polen and Peter Goddard had given the Japanese factory reason to celebrate after two years of World Superbike racing without a win.

It was a season that Kawasaki, with their faster bike, had expected to win, but Suzuki (with Polen and Goddard) proved that Endurance racing is not all about being fastest – consistency

counts as well. Winning the first two 24-hour races (and the double points that went with them) set them up nicely – as did Kawasaki's two DNFs! The other challenges, from the French-based Yamaha and Honda teams, never amounted to much. They both missed a race – Yamaha at Spa and Honda France at Suzuka, which was packed with Japanese factory teams anyway.

The World Endurance Championship has always been the poor relation of the three road racing titles, but the fans (particularly in France) love it. How else do you explain crowds of 80,000 or more turning up for Le Mans and the Bol d'Or? In Japan, too, the Suzuka Eight Hour drew huge crowds despite appalling weather and a dearth of top GP stars. Even in Belgium, with some of the best French teams missing, the crowd is pretty reasonable. So what is the attraction?

Maybe the Endurance World Championship is well attended precisely because it is not like GPs or World Superbikes. Endurance races are far more than just a 20- or 30-lap sprint, they are an event, of which the track action forms only a part. And because of these extra attractions – funfairs, rock concerts and all the other sideshows – fans come to Le Mans, Spa, Suzuka and the Bol d'Or in droves to have two or three days of fun

Le Mans 24 Hours
Round 1, 12-13 April 1997

The fun started in France where a record 80,000 crowd witnessed a tense struggle between Suzuki and Kawasaki, with Yamaha and Honda in close attendance. Suzuki and Yamaha entered two bikes each. 'Big Guns' Doug Polen and Peter Goddard were on the number one Suzuki, partnered by Frenchman Eric Gomez, with Bruno Bonhuil, Florian Ferracci and Gilles Ferstler on the second GSX-R. Yamaha also went for a bit of 'foreign' glamour – Japanese rider Norihiko Fujiwara teamed with locals Eric Mahé and Jean-Louis Battistini in one team, with Swede Christer Lindholm joining Jean-Philippe Ruggia and Jean-Marc Deletang in the other. Honda's sole entry consisted of 1996 USA AMA Superbike champion Canadian Miguel DuHamel, together with Endurance regulars Christian Lavieille and Jean-Michel Mattioli, while Kawasaki kept 1996 Endurance champ Brian Morrison with Italian Piergiorgio Bontempi and home-grown Jehan D'Orgeix. Apart from Morrison, British interest was minimal – there was only one UK team entered, Phase One Kawasaki with Dave Goodley, David Jefferies and Kiwi Andrew Stroud. But it wasn't going to be a good race for any of the British riders.

Kawasaki was on pole, but DuHamel got the drop on the field and led them

all away, with Polen and D'Orgeix close behind. The lead changed hands several times in the hectic opening 15 minutes until a two-bike crash caused the first appearance of the pace car while oil and debris were cleared from the track. Thirty-five minutes later racing resumed, and at the end of the first hour it was the Yamaha of Deletang, Ruggia and Lindholm in the lead. But almost immediately the pace car was back in action again – this time for only 15 minutes – and the order closed up as five of the factory bikes scrapped for the lead. Suzuki and Kawasaki traded places at the top of the leaderboard, with Yamaha close by until Battistini crashed the YZF and was forced to pit – losing half an hour repairing the damage. Honda were also in trouble. Mattioli's crash, and subsequent time in the pits, dropped them way down the standings, but even worse off was Phase One. Their ZXR dropped a valve and normally that would have been the end of the race. But unbelievably the mechanics whipped the engine out of the chassis, changed the head and barrel and the team were back on track less than one-and-a-half hours later.

After Kawasaki and Honda both retired with mechanical failures Polen, Goddard and Gomez enjoyed a trouble-free ride (apart from a worrying

Doug Polen takes the factory Suzuki to victory at Le Mans – the first of two wins for the former Superbike champion and his veteran team-mate Peter Goddard, and crucial for their ultimate championship success.

Below: GP rider Tohru Ukawa won the prestigious Suzuka Eight Hour for Honda.

almost the entire race but looked to have it in the bag until half an hour from the end when the ZXR's motor blew up. Kawasaki's second DNF in a row gave Polen, Goddard and Gomez an unexpected, but welcome, victory – and one that effectively decided the outcome of the title. Second went to Lavieille, Costes and Mertens (Honda), with French privateers Ullmann, Gabriele and Bronec (Yamaha) third.

Suzuka Eight Hour
Round 3, 27 July 1997
Honda were taking this race seriously. They arrived at Suzuka mob-handed with no less than five factory bikes and plenty of top quality riders, including two of the Aoki brothers, Ito, Ukawa, Slight, Okada, Kocinski and Barros. Yamaha for once were well represented, with 1996 winners Edwards and Haga (though Edwards didn't race in the end, due to injury), Russell and Corser, Yoshikawa and Fujiwara, plus French duo Deletang and Ruggia. Suzuki's Polen and Goddard found their GSX-R in Lucky Strike colours, with full factory support, but were under no illusions about the enormity of the task ahead. There were two other factory Suzukis plus four factory Kawasakis (including Rymer and Bontempi on one and Crafar and Yanagawa on another) – all adding up to the strongest grid of the year.

But the dominating factor of the event turned out to be typhoon called 'Rosie' that swept in on Friday, caused the cancellation of Saturday practice and then hung around long enough to alter the complexion of the race. Race day dawned dark, wet and miserable and that's pretty much how it stayed during the eight-hour sprint. By the end of the first lap Kawasaki's curse had struck again: Rymer and Bontempi were out. Terry slid off in the difficult conditions and remounted, without realising that the radiator had been punctured and lost water. It was only a matter of time before the engine cried out 'No more!'

Kocinski and Barros mastered the wet conditions better than most and would've won the race were it not for two unscheduled pit stops early on. A misted visor and a problem with a rear tyre cost them dearly and they dropped all the way down to 55th before fighting their way grittily back into contention. Pre-race favourites Slight and Okada had gambled on a particular bike set-up – incorrectly as it turned out – and spent the whole race chasing a rostrum when they should've been chasing a win. But Honda honour was restored, because Ito and Ukawa had a problem-free ride and took victory at the end of eight soggy

hours. Their factory Honda never missed a beat and they finished a clear two minutes ahead of Kocinski and Barros. Ryo and Takeishi's Kawasaki splashed into third, depriving Russell and Corser's Yamaha of a rostrum place with less than 15 minutes remaining.

In the magnificent fireworks display that traditionally climaxes the event, it was almost forgotten that Polen and Goddard's fifth place was, with Gomez missing, theoretically enough to take the title – as long, that is, as Gomez was their team member at the Bol d'Or. If he raced in another team which won and Polen and Goddard failed to make the top ten, then he would take the title instead.

Bol d'Or 24 Hours
Round 4, 20-21 September 1997
No surprise, then, when Suzuki France team manager Dominic Meilland announced that Gomez would not be riding with Polen and Goddard. Instead, Gomez teamed up with Coutelle and Bonhuil while Ferstler took the ride with Polen and Goddard. Nobody could take the title away from Suzuki – but Meilland wanted his fellow-countryman Gomez to have a chance of taking top honours.

Suzuki were looking for a clean

sweep of the three 24-hour 'classics', but it was finally Kawasaki's turn to come good, with Rymer, Morrison and D'Orgeix winning a thriller of a race by just over a minute after a record-breaking 692 laps. They fought throughout with the Honda of DuHamel, Lavieille and Costes and although the RC45 led for most of the night, a holed radiator and a crash by Lavieille gave Kawasaki just the cushion they needed. Third went to Hislop, Lindholm and van den Bossche on one of the factory Yamahas, with Gomez, Coutelle and Bonhuil's Suzuki fourth.

It had been a difficult race for Polen and Goddard, who had been forced to put in extra sessions on the bike during the night when Ferstler was 11 seconds off the pace. The American also suffered a stomach problem and then, later on, the Suzuki's exhaust had to be replaced – all causing anxious moments in the pits. Despite these niggles Polen and Goddard managed to bring the bike home in fifth place, one lap down on their Suzuki team-mates, but enough to give the duo the 1997 World Endurance Championship title by a healthy seven points – just reward for a season of hard work and consistent riding.

Photos: Kel Edge

moment with a broken exhaust in the last three hours) for the rest of the race. The two Yamahas chased the Suzuki valiantly, but the gap was too great and Polen, Goddard and Gomez ran out comfortable winners, by ten laps, from Deletang, Ruggia and Lindholm, with the second Yamaha some eight laps further back. First blood to Suzuki, then, but more importantly it was the new GSX-R750's first international race victory and just cause for celebration.

Spa 24 Hours
Round 2, 12-13 July 1997
The picturesque Ardennes circuit was home to round two – a round that Kawasaki had to win if they were to have any chance of retaining the title. The race clashed with a World Superbike round in the USA, so Bontempi was missing from the Kawasaki line-up, but his place was more than adequately filled by Londoner Terry Rymer. With DuHamel also on Superbike duty, Honda were forced to make changes and Lavieille found himself partnered by two new riders – Frenchman William Costes and local hero Stéphane Mertens. With Yamaha absent, the race was between the three factory bikes – Suzuki, Kawasaki and Honda.

It was a gruelling contest and one that Kawasaki should have won. They ran neck and neck with Suzuki for

WEBSTER'S SPECIAL BREW

by John McKenzie

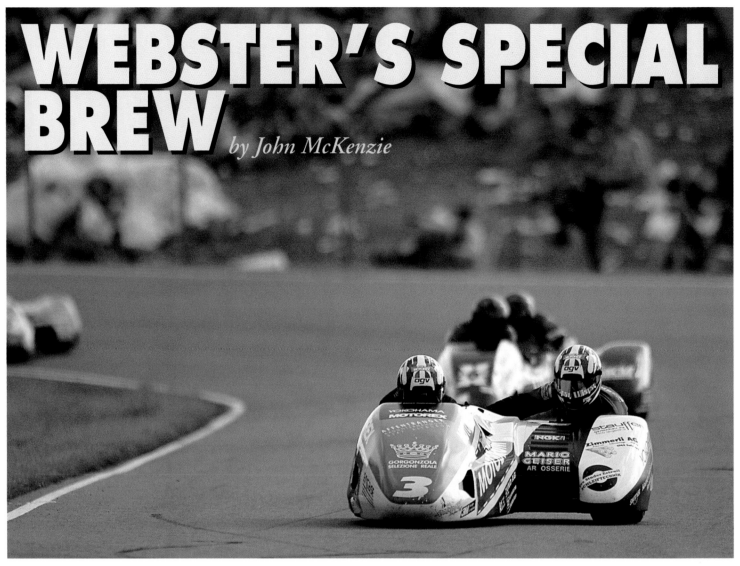

A reduction in status to the FIM-ISRA World Cup may prove to be another nail in the coffin for sidecars, but in the meantime, for the riders, it was largely business as usual. The line-up differed little, apart from the notable absence of 1995 and 1996 World Champion Darren Dixon, who decided to go Superbike racing in Britain. The big five – Steve Webster, Rolf Biland, Klaus Klaffenböck, Derek Brindley and Paul Güdel – offered up the usual sidecar feast of thrills, still criminally ignored by the British press.

After successful early ISRA testing at Paul Ricard, Webster and passenger David James started as favourites and, as the season progressed, Steve for once had luck running his way when he needed it to make a return to dominating form.

Round 1
Hungaroring, Hungary
25 May 1997
Pole-qualifier Steve Webster scorched to his first World Championship win since Sweden in 1993, and his first with David James. In a tough battle Webster fought to the front by lap 15, eventually coming home to beat arch rival Rolf Biland by four seconds over 24 hot and humid laps of the twisty Hungaroring.

Third-placed Klaffenböck was miffed enough about it to lodge a protest, claiming Webster's speed was down to methanol in the fuel. However, he left the track before paying the £800 fee,

leaving a shadow cast over the result. When the fuel of the top three was checked – unofficially – Webbo's ISRA-supplied lead-free pump juice not surprisingly proved legal. The only fuel to test non-standard was Klaffenböck's...

It set up a tension between the Austrian and British crews that was to last all season.

Round 2
A1-Ring, Zeltweg, Austria
31 May 1997
With Webster again on pole, and after another hurly-burly start, Swiss veteran Biland called upon his massive experience to establish a lead at half race distance and defend it like the old pro he truly is. A calculated victory margin of 5.5 seconds brought his 82nd World Championship win and a seven-point title lead.

The action was in the battle for the runner-up spot and in a blanket finish only three-tenths of a second separated eventual second-place man Klaffenböck from Güdel in third and Webster in fourth.

Round 3
Assen, Holland
28 June 1997
At the start, Klaffenböck got the jump but Webster settled into his slipstream until halfway into the second lap when he nosed his Pneu Bösiger LCR through on the inside of the 160 mph flat-in-top left-hand kink on the back straight.

By lap ten, third-placed Biland was out with water in his cylinders and Webster's lead over Klaffenböck was 6.5 seconds and rising.

At the end of 17 laps the unruffled Webster took the flag with a massive 25-second advantage over runner-up Klaffenböck, and was almost a minute clear of third-placed Güdel, having lapped everyone up to sixth place. The win was Webster's first at Assen since 1989.

Round 4
Most, Czech Republic
13 July 1997
After qualifying on pole again, getting his best start in living memory and pulling out ten seconds in eight laps, Webster seemed to be heading for certain victory – until his ADM engine expired with a broken piston.

With the points leader out Klaffenböck inherited the lead and was pressed all the way by Güdel. The Swiss brothers seemed to have it under control, tucked behind Klaffy, staying on his tail before slipstreaming past on the main straight. But Klaffenböck, in brilliant form, forced his way through at the chicane on the final lap to take his first ever and richly deserved World Championship win, and shoot to the top of the title table.

Derek Brindley grabbed third, his first podium in a strong year for the Briton, who was partnered throughout by Switzerland's Adolf Hänni.

Round 5
Nürburgring, Germany
20 July 1997
Rain stopped play soon after the beginning of the race, and the restart was deemed to be a 'wet race'. However, when the green light went on Biland set off at a cracking pace, with Klaffenböck and Webster following.

Webster passed the Austrians for second place on lap three, and although Biland had tried to make a break Steve harried him ceaselessly before scything through on the inside on lap 11. From then on it was vintage Webster as he reeled off consistently fast laps to pull way and win by six seconds – though Klaffenböck still led in the points.

Round 6
Anderstorp, Sweden
10 August 1997
Ten years and one day since he won his first World Championship Webbo was back on top at Anderstorp, continuing his dominating form with a sixth consecutive pole and his fourth victory of the season. But his 14-second winning margin belied an eventful afternoon.

Once again it was Biland, Klaffenböck and Webster vying for the lead. At half race distance it was almost crunch time – literally. Trying for an inside line, Steve had to panic-brake to avoid a collision as Klaffenböck closed the gap. His wheels locked, and he spun to a stalled standstill facing oncoming

Left: Still rolling along. Steve Webster claimed a fifth sidecar championship – now a 'World Cup' rather than a 'World Championship'. Here he leads Klaus Klaffenböck at Assen.

Right: Webster and partner David James (eyes closed) after the Dutch win, flanked by *(left)* Klaus Klaffenböck and Christian Parzer, and *(right)* the Güdel brothers.

Bottom: In Austria, home hero Klaffenböck leads eventual winner Biland (2), Webster (3) and the Güdels (4).

traffic before executing a hasty three-point turn and resuming the chase.

Meanwhile, at the front, after Biland's BRM engine had given up, Klaffenböck inherited a lead which he held for only two laps before he too was forced to retire with a broken crankshaft, handing the lead on to the Güdels. Striving to get back into contention Webster, with a clear track, absolutely flew. With nine laps to go he had Güdel in his sights, reeling him in at around 1.5 seconds a lap. With three laps left, and as Güdel started to suffer gearbox problems, Webster sped past to take the flag unchallenged.

Round 7
Brno, Czech Republic
31 August 1997
Another broken engine spoiled Biland's hopes of a win with only four laps of the race remaining, after Rolf employed his usual strategy of building and defending a lead of a handful of seconds.

That handed it over to Webster, who had been hard pressed by Klaffenböck

in the early stages. Webster went on to amass a comfortable winning margin of six seconds, and stretch his lead to a strong-looking 21 points over the Austrian with only two races to go. Third place went to the Güdels, with Derek Brindley in fourth – the same positions they occupied in the points table, Biland having slipped to fifth overall as a result of his engine problems.

Round 8
Autodromo Grobnik, Rijeka
21 September 1997
Steve Webster MBE and passenger David James clinched the 1997 FIM-ISRA Sidecar World Cup in the closest-ever finish in the history of World Championship sidecar racing. Webster led for only the very last six inches of the 100-km, 24-lap race: he won by the incredible margin of two-thousandths of a second, with third-placed Paul and Charly Güdel a mere tenth of a second further back. It was Steve's 29th career victory and clinched his fifth world title in 11 seasons.

With Klaffenböck slamming the door on Webster almost every lap from half-distance, the climax had built up steadily. As they crossed the finish line for the penultimate time Steve again pulled alongside and, as Klaffy tried to cover the move, the two outfits touched.

Going onto the last lap it seemed that the Austrian might have done enough to hold Webbo. But he wasn't prepared for a final frantic five seconds. As the two outfits streaked down to the final left-hander – with the Güdel brothers merely inches behind – Klaffenböck went wide, forcing Webster deep and almost allowing the Güdels in. As they exited the corner and accelerated into the final right kink approaching the pits Webster had already started to put his killer punch into action.

'I thought we could get him there on acceleration and so for the last three laps I practised the line out of the corner, edging right over to the edge of the track and almost onto the pit-lane entrance – and it worked out!' said a joyous Web-

ster. 'It feels just great to be World Champion again and I'm so pleased to win it like this and not have to take it to the last round. Just brilliant!'

On the rostrum Klaffenböck looked utterly bemused, no doubt wondering just what he had to do to beat Webster.

Round 9
Cartagena, Spain
26 October 1997
With the title already decided, interest centred on the final points table and, in particular, which team would be runners-up – Klaffenböck or the Güdels. A small grid of just ten outfits contested the 26-lap race, with the Swiss Güdel brothers taking the victory, and second place in the championship, by nearly 13 seconds from second-placed Derek Brindley, with Switzerland's Markus Bösiger in third. Klaffenböck could only finish fifth.

British and Swiss teams once again filled the lower championship placings, with Mark Reddington and Stuart Muldoon achieving some solid results.

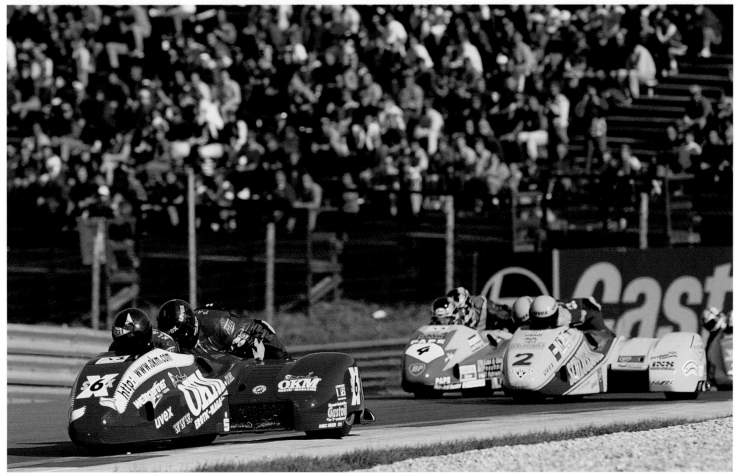

Mark Wernham

Consistency wins titles, as three-times AMA champion Doug Chandler *(left and below)* proved. He took just one race win on the Muzzy Kawasaki; Miguel DuHamel *(right)* won four times on the Honda, but lost out in the end.

CHANDLER
ROPES IN HIS RIVALS

by Paul Carruthers

WHEN it comes right down to it, Doug Chandler will one day be able to sit down and tell his grandchildren that he won his third AMA Superbike National Championship in 1997. Miguel DuHamel won't have such a yarn to spin. Neither will Mat Mladin. That Chandler won the title while only winning a single race when DuHamel and Mladin won four apiece won't change the story. Chandler took the title and that's really all that matters when history lessons are taught.

He did so by playing the rules to perfection. The current AMA points-paying system rewards consistency more than aggression – and no one is more consistent than Chandler. He did what he had to do. He won early on, watched as his championship rivals faltered through either crashes or mechanical failures, and then marched on to his second straight title. For him, to have taken unnecessary risks that could have led to failure would have been stupid. Diehard racing fans may believe that Chandler wasn't the fastest rider in this year's AMA series because he won less often, but Chandler's bank manager certainly won't complain. If Doug wasn't the fastest, he was definitely the best.

There's no denying that DuHamel and his Smokin' Joe's Honda and Mladin and his Fast By Ferracci Ducati did win more often than Chandler and his Muzzy Kawasaki. But ask them both if they'd trade their wins for Chandler's number 1 plate – and, odds are, they would.

In all, the 1997 AMA Superbike season was good. Live television in certain markets, ten factory riders on five different makes of motor cycle and close racing made it a season to remember. With factory-backed teams scheduled to field 16 or 17 riders on top-notch equipment for 1998, it is a series that arguably rivals the World Superbike Championship as the premier four-stroke series in the world. All of the top players – including Chandler, DuHamel and Mladin – will return.

While an AMA season generally begins with spectators hurriedly turn-ing the pages of their programmes in an effort to find out who these men on different motor cycles are, the 1997 season started without much in the way of change.

Doug Chandler was back to defend his title on his trusty Muzzy Kawasaki, though the team now featured young Tommy Hayden as its back-up rider. Hayden wasn't just new to the team, he was new to the series after hanging up his dirt-track steel shoe to give road racing his full-time attention. If he was willing to pay attention, he could get enough information from his insight-ful team-mate to speed up any road racing career.

The Smokin' Joe's Honda team also featured much of the same. It was led by Miguel DuHamel, the French Canadian who came so painfully close to winning the title last year after a season-long battle with Chandler. Fellow-Canadian Steve Crevier joined DuHamel on the factory Hondas, though Crevier's stay on the team was much more tenuous, his spot for 1998 having already been handed to upstart Ben Bostrom. Crevier's season would be an open audition to see if he could find another ride for 1998.

Yoshimura Suzuki was set to run a three-rider team in 1997, with former Fast By Ferracci man Larry Pegram joining returnees Aaron Yates and Pascal Picotte – both of whom had won AMA Superbike Nationals last year. All three would also spearhead the company's hopes of capturing the all-important 600 cc Supersport crown on its new GSX-R600. To do so, they'd have to match wits with DuHamel and his trusty Honda CBR600...more on that later.

Harley-Davidson was back for more, again with two riders returning from the previous season. Thomas Wilson and former AMA Grand National Champion Chris Carr were attempting to build on last year's sporadically promising efforts with the VR1000, but by season's end things were worse instead of better. Though the bike seems to be improving, the results didn't come with it. Wilson banged his head in a crash at Daytona and it took him a while to recover; Carr simply didn't get to speed until very late in the season. For 1998, the team will make a rider change, bringing Picotte in to lead the team while Carr departs. Wilson stays.

Next up was Yamaha, sans Vance & Hines. After making a decision to take the team in-house for 1997, Yamaha left team owner Terry Vance out in the cold. He wasn't cold for long. Vance quickly worked his way to the top of the Ducati food chain and by Laguna Seca had a very impressive-looking Vance & Hines Ducati effort to run. His only rider was Thomas Stevens, until the last race of the season when he imported Swede Christer Lindholm. Then came the announcement during the off-season that Vance would take the gamble of all gambles by bringing troubled Anthony Gobert to the AMA Championship for a run at the title on a Ducati. Stay tuned.

Back to Yamaha. Without Vance, Yamaha also decided to cut back to one rider – Tom Kipp, in a returning role from seasons past. Kipp would have an up-and-down season that would eventually sour both parties enough to make them part company. Kipp will ride a Ferracci Ducati in 1998, while Yamaha are putting their eggs in Rich Oliver's basket.

Ferracci's Ducati team looked on paper to be the favourite heading into the '97 season. After all, they had acquired the services of Australian Mat Mladin, hot from a successful AMA debut season on a Yoshimura Suzuki. Mladin was promised big things and was hoping an AMA title would bring him a Ducati World Superbike ride for 1998. Neither would materialise, though Mladin could never be faulted for not giving it his absolute best. He was joined by Gerald Rothman Jnr, the former Supersport winner having a disastrous year that would eventually knock him out of the AMA's premier class for 1998.

The season began not in Daytona, but at Phoenix International Raceway (after a two-year hiatus) and it began with a bang that belonged to the bright red Ducati V-twin ridden by Mladin.

In his first race for Eraldo Ferracci,

Mladin was impressive indeed. He qualified on pole and dominated every inch of the race. In the end he was nine seconds ahead of DuHamel, who had worked his way past Chandler on the last lap – drawing first blood in the two rivals' battle for the championship. But, alas, there were now three major players in the hunt.

Behind them came Picotte and the Harley of Wilson, off to a good start that would quickly turn sour with his Daytona crash.

With its 200 miles of wide-open racing, gas stops and tyre changes, Daytona is obviously a very different proposition from any of the other rounds in the AMA Championship. But what really makes it different is the man who owns the facility. Bill France? Forget it. The title to the land on which Daytona International Speedway was built should have one name at the very top: Scott Russell.

Heading into the 1997 200-miler, Russell had already earned the decoration 'Mr Daytona'. This year's race only added further to the Russell legend in south Florida.

Scott came to Daytona armed with a basically unfamiliar Yamaha YZ750, after having signed on the dotted line to campaign a factory Yamaha in the World Superbike Championship. As always, Daytona is the first step in the staircase of Russell's racing year. It mattered not that the Georgian native was riding a Yamaha. After all, he'd won the 200 on a Kawasaki (three times) and had come so very close on a Suzuki last year – so why not a Yamaha? Hey, when you own the place, what difference does it make?

Russell started his Daytona 200

defence in typical fashion, shattering the lap record en route to his third pole position and claiming the gold Rolex chronograph that accompanies the honour. He did it very late in his qualifying session and with the usual flair that Scott continually bestows on the classic tri-oval.

And it was just a prelude of things to come. On Sunday he simply ran away and hid, turning the race into a rather dull parade until late on when a pace car came out to liven things up a bit (while also allowing workers to clear up debris from a messy crash). But not even that could help arouse the race, for Chandler was more concerned with being caught from behind than he was at making a run at Russell. Always thinking, Chandler was already in championship-winning mode. Russell could have the 200, Chandler wanted to make certain of coming away from the race with the gobs of points that second place would bring.

In the end, Chandler was able to hold off Russell's team-mate, Colin Edwards II. And he was happy with that, knowing full well that his championship rivals had suffered through the tough times that only Daytona can bring.

Mladin fared worse than any. His Ducati had failed him early, developing an oil leak on only the third lap. The team fixed the bike while the others circulated, and the Australian rejoined the race some eight laps behind. To add insult to injury, he then crashed in turn one, finally bringing an end to his miserable Daytona experience. The points leader going in, he left Daytona only eighth on points. The result would haunt him all season long.

DuHamel, meanwhile, could only

muster seventh as tyre-related problems forced him to pit four times (Russell pitted twice). Still, at the end of the day, he was somewhat relieved to have done that well.

DuHamel's team-mate Crevier risked a late-race tyre change for softer rubber and the gamble paid off. He stormed his way around Picotte and Kipp to finish fourth, with those two finishing fifth and sixth, respectively.

The third round of the series brought racers to what is generally regarded as one of the true 'racing' venues on the schedule – Laguna Seca Raceway. In 1996, the championship took a serious turn at Laguna Seca when DuHamel crashed out of the lead and was forced to watch as Chandler rode away to victory and the points lead. Chandler had won, but DuHamel was faster.

Not so in 1997. This one was Chandler's. From the first time a wheel was turned in anger on the scenic track in the hills of the Monterey Peninsula, Chandler was quick. In fact, he was the only rider to crack into 1m 26s, lapping at 1m 26.851s – under the best lap turned in the 1996 World Superbike round at Laguna Seca. The race featured more of the same. He watched DuHamel's unsuccessful attempt at making a break at the front, and he watched as Mladin tried in vain to catch him from behind. Then he simply put his head down and motored away, winning by 13 seconds and sending a demoralising message to his competition.

'The hardest thing was watching Doug go away – he's got the lead in the championship and he's the one I've got to catch. I really needed to beat him,' said Mladin, who had finished second

ahead of DuHamel, Crevier...and, surprisingly, Bostrom in his first superbike ride of the year.

With just three rounds under his belt, Chandler had something of a comfortable cushion. He led DuHamel by 13 points and Mladin, still recovering from Daytona and fifth overall, by 30.

The fourth round of the series was a good news/bad news scenario for Mladin. The good news: Mladin won his second race of the season on the ultra-fast 'Four Miles of Fun' that is Road America. The bad news: Chandler finished second.

It was DuHamel, though, who put the Honda on pole for the first time all year. But it was Mladin who had the better of it come race day. In the way of fast tracks, close racing was what we got at Road America. A quartet of riders battled away at the front for the majority of the 16-lap final, with the race picking up speed to lap record pace in the end. By then, the battle had been whittled down to just two: Mladin and Chandler, the two former Cagiva 500 cc Grand Prix team-mates lapping at qualifying speeds that left the others behind.

It came down to the very end. Mladin got the better breaks in traffic and held on to become the season's first two-time winner. 'I think Mat just had his package a bit better than mine this weekend,' Chandler said. But Doug still had 26 points and two riders between himself and the Australian in the table. Third went to Yates, his early-season woes with the Suzuki apparently behind him. He'd got the better of DuHamel as the French Canadian battled a chunking rear Dunlop. At the end it featured a 2-in. wide tat-

Mat Mladin won four times on the Fast by Ferracci Ducati, but the Australian's title challenge was spoiled by niggling mechanical problems at the other races.

Below: Scott Russell returned to reclaim Daytona in his first ride on the Yamaha. It was the ex-Superbike champion's fourth win at the Florida tri-oval.

tered strip down its centre and he was fortunate to have finished. Fifth went to Crevier, who was continuing his consistent season.

Mladin maintained his serious charge at the championship by decisively winning the fifth round (and halfway mark) of the series at New Hampshire International Speedway. By winning his third race in five tries and his second in two weeks, Mladin left New England just 19 points behind Chandler, the defending champion finishing fourth after choosing a rear tyre that was too hard.

And everything that Mladin gained, DuHamel lost. The Honda rider crashed while running third on the 20th lap, his simple front-end low-side costing him dearly. It was his first race crash since Laguna Seca in April 1996 – and this one would prove equally as costly to his championship aspirations.

Yates was second, with Crevier a surprising third. Mladin's win moved him into second in the series standings, while DuHamel's non-finish dropped him to sixth – a whopping 44 points behind Chandler.

DuHamel wasn't giving up. At Brainerd International Raceway, he was scintillating. As hard as it was to imagine, it was his first win in just over a year. The drubbing he gave his rivals at the Minnesota track left many wondering if he'd ever lose again.

DuHamel didn't earn pole, though he could have used the championship point that goes with it; that went to Picotte. But on Sunday he more than made up for it, DuHamel pulling away early to win by 3.45 seconds in what was really only a delusion of closeness. He'd led by 10 seconds before slowing slightly near the end of the race to secure his 13th career win.

The battle was for second and – more importantly – the chase for the National Championship. Mladin and Chandler battled throughout for the runner-up spot, with Picotte sandwiched between them for the majority of the race. But then there were four, with Yamaha's Kipp joining in late to beat them all for second place. 'There are riders and there are racers – today I was a racer,' Kipp said.

Behind Kipp came Mladin, gaining a few valuable points on Chandler, who finished a disappointed fifth. The Californian was forced into using his back-up (and slower) bike on Sunday to make certain of finishing. Picotte had got the better of him to finish fourth. Now the gap from Chandler to Mladin was down to just 15 points.

In what was without doubt the most thrilling AMA Superbike National of the season, DuHamel and Chandler battled to the bitter end at the Mid-Ohio Sports Car Course, with DuHamel winning a mad dash to the finishing line by just 0.120 of a second.

Initially the race featured more than just these two. Early on, Mladin was also a protagonist; and later Yates joined in after fighting his way through from a botched start. In the end Mladin faded to fourth with a misfire, and Yates just couldn't keep pace. So it came down to two, and two was plenty. Neither could find an advantage, until on the last lap DuHamel, in nothing-to-lose mood, got the better of Chandler – who was again thinking championship all the way. Both were happy...and rightfully so.

Not so happy was Mladin, his fourth place putting him 20 points down on friendly rival Chandler with only three races to go. And now DuHamel was back on a roll; he trailed Mladin by just 12 points.

Three in a row? No problem for DuHamel as the AMA series visited Pikes Peak International Raceway in the mountains of Colorado for the first time. Despite wrecking the bike on which he'd won the previous two AMA Superbike Nationals during Friday's practice, DuHamel was still able to win his third straight race, a win that moved him into a tie with Wayne Rainey for second on the all-time AMA Superbike victory list with 16.

Chandler, however, was continuing his march to the title with a second-place finish on the rough-and-tumble 1.315-mile race track. Still more concerned with Mladin than with DuHamel, second to the Australian's fourth suited him just fine. He might have lost the battle, but the most consistent man in the series was still winning the war. Chandler left Colorado 25 points ahead of Mladin and there were just two races remaining. The fat lady was warming up...

And so was DuHamel. In fact, warming up was a tad understated. The man was red-hot. At Sears Point Raceway, in northern California's wine country, DuHamel won his fourth straight race – but he still had little chance of taking the title. That, no doubt, would go to Chandler in the season finale. Doug had finished a conservative fourth at Sears Point, beaten home by Canadians Crevier and Picotte in an All-Canada winners' celebration.

And Mladin? Well, early on he appeared to be in a good position, but it all went wrong as he struggled with boiling brake fluid that made braking precarious at best. He later ran straight instead of turning for the first corner, and limped home a disappointing sixth.

Now only one race remained – and Chandler led DuHamel by 20 points. This one was over.

After announcing that he was leaving Ferracci's Ducati team to rejoin Suzuki for 1998, Mladin went out and gave the Italians something to think about, winning the last race of the season for the Michelin-shod Ducati team. He fought off a cooked rear tyre and relentless pressure from DuHamel to win his fourth race of the season, though it was little consolation as Chandler tip-toed his way to eighth place and the National Championship.

The season ended, fittingly enough, with a classic race for the win. Mladin went out in front early, knowing that his Michelins wouldn't go the distance. His plan was to open a big lead and nurse it to the finish. It worked, but just barely as DuHamel and Yates closed to within half a second at the finish line.

'I felt we could have run up there if needed, but the guys were kinda hanging it out a bit and I didn't want to be in the middle of anything,' Chandler said. 'I just sat back.'

In other AMA Championship action, it was DuHamel winning his third consecutive 600 cc Supersport title, despite the best efforts of a horde of Suzukis. It was also DuHamel's fifth championship in the class. Jason Pridmore, the son of three-times AMA Superbike champ Reg Pridmore, won the 750 cc Supersport title, riding a Suzuki GSX-R750.

Naturally, the 250 cc Grand Prix series was won by Rich Oliver – still undefeated after two seasons and 20 races. Oliver's title will be his last on 250s as he has made the commitment to switch full time to Superbike racing in 1998 and 1999. Kiwi Andrew Stroud on an Erion Racing CBR900 won the much-ridiculed Formula Xtreme title.

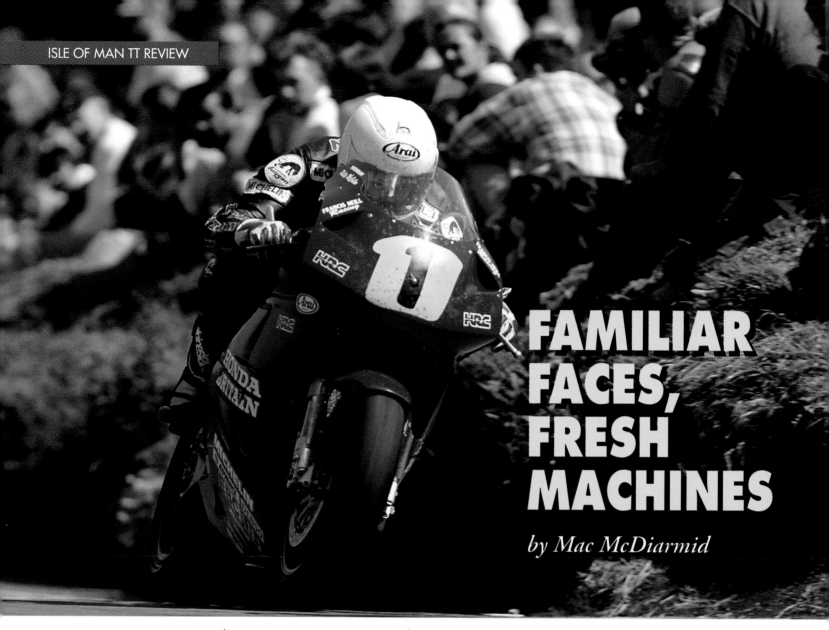

FAMILIAR FACES, FRESH MACHINES

by Mac McDiarmid

NEXT year marks the Honda Motor Company's 50th birthday, and already a huge TT party is planned at the circuit where the company first made its international mark. Yet if Honda were keeping their powder dry in anticipation of 1998's celebrations, it certainly didn't show. Excluding the sidecar and single cylinder classes, 60 top ten places are up for grabs at this year's Isle of Man festival. Of these, Big Aitch snatched no less than 44. What on earth can they achieve when they really try?

To some extent this startling statistic is a reflection of Honda Britain's continued support for the TT races, when the interest of other UK importers is desultory in comparison. But, confronted with up to 226 miles of the most punishing circuit in the world, they also make some rather suitable machines. When, for instance, did a well-prepared RC45 last break down? And is any Supersport 600 better suited to Island life than the enduring CBR? Certainly not on the evidence of this year's Junior TT, when nine of the top ten places went to such machines.

It was the same in almost every division: Lightweight, seven out of ten; Formula One 6/10; Senior 7/10; Ultra-Lightweight 10/10; Production, a relatively poor showing – just 5/10 for the dear old 'Blade. And who would you put money on to break up this near-monopoly? Not BMW, surely. Yet a BMW it was which romped home in the Singles division, giving Bavaria its first

manufacturer's award since Georg Meier in 1939. Next year, Ascot-Pullin.

Almost as surprising was the weather. Practice week began clear, warm and cloudless, and just got better and better. 'It'll rain come race week, always does,' suggested the Jonahs, but if there was a bigger threat than Phillip McCallen in the Formula One, it was heat-stroke. Not until the final two days did the Cloak of Mannan – Manx fog to you – intervene, causing the Production event to be shortened to two laps. But, by then, most of us were glad of a little respite from the strange yellow orb in the sky.

Some events were more expected. McCallen once again dominated affairs, but does a mere three wins, a year after he claimed a record four, betoken a man on the slide? We think not, although the slide he took through Quarry Bends in the Lightweight race will surely lose him some sleep. Joey Dunlop scored another for the oldies, taking his all-time tally to 22 wins in the race his compatriot baled out of so spectacularly. Ian Simpson finally won a TT, which was as novel as it was expected and deserved. And Ian Lougher finally won another one, of which pretty much the same can be said.

PRACTICE

An unexpected buzz surrounded the larger classes - the buzz of pukka two-stroke racing machines. Expectations of the NSR500-V V-twins ridden by Joey Dunlop and Jim Moodie were high. The concept of a 250-style lightness and agility allied to strong top-end performance caused many to suggest that the Grand Prix twins could be the perfect Isle of Man tool. Indeed, if any machine could rejuvenate Joey Dunlop's Senior and F1 career, surely it was the 135 bhp NSR twin.

In the event 'pole' position went, as is usual these days, to Phillip McCallen's Honda RC45. Behind him, Michael Rutter sneaked another RC45 into second place at an impressive 120.98 mph, confirming his position as one of the men most likely to join the next generation of TT masters.

Behind this duo matters were slightly more interesting. Jim Moodie, riding a Suzuki 750 in the F1 and an NSR500-V in the Senior, was comfortably quicker – by a full 18 seconds – on the latter. The unfamiliar machine 'felt really good, light and easy to ride. I should be able to go well on it.' Joey Dunlop, meanwhile, of whom great things had been hoped, proved marginally quicker on the relatively ponderous RC45. The only other big two-stroke in the field, Nigel Davies's ex-John Reynolds V4 Yamaha, fared even less well when the Welshman dumped it at Braddan Bridge, breaking his ankle and foot.

If Phillip McCallen had hopes of equalling his 1996 haul of four TT wins in a week, in the other classes he certainly wasn't getting things all his own way, for he topped the leaderboard in none of them. In the Junior (600 cc Supersport) class his CBR600 was pipped by four seconds by the similar machine of Ian Simpson, arguably the classiest rider in the field never to win a

TT. Only Simpson broke 117 mph, with McCallen, Rutter, Moodie, Bob Jackson and Adrian Archibald all slotting in laps at 116 mph in what promised to be a stirring race.

In the Production class, too, McCallen had to give best, this time to the quiet Kiwi, Loren Poole, riding a Yamaha Thunderace. Alan Bennallick placed third, with Simpson's Red Bull Ducati a promising fourth and improving session by session.

Practice in the smaller divisions proved a romp for Ian Lougher, whose Hondas topped their class in both the Lightweight (250 cc) and Ultra-Lightweight (125 cc) classes. Second in the 250 cc division, predictably, was McCallen, with Jim Moodie third on one of his rare two-stroke outings. Ulsterman Gary Dynes was fourth with Shaun Harris fifth and John McGuiness sixth. Lougher's rivals in the Ultra-Lightweight looked likely to be the usual suspects such as Denis McCullough, Glen English and Gavin Lee, although the man they all most feared – Joey Dunlop – languished half a minute in arrears in ninth place.

Thumper specialist Dave Morris put his BMW fractionally ahead of the Singles field. In the Sidecar class, Rob Fisher stood head and shoulders above the rest, lapping at 110.24 mph on his Baker Yamaha, almost 3 mph faster than Ian Bell.

Practice week's most poignant moment came when former winner Nick Jefferies damaged knee ligaments when he crashed at Greeba Castle dur-

Phillip McCallen's Senior win was his third of this year's TT – and also showed that in the right hands, the heavyweight RC45 Honda could beat the new 500 V-twin.

Below: Michael Rutter was second in the F1 race, confirming his potential as a future TT star.

ing Junior practice on Wednesday morning. The 45-year-old Yorkshireman had already announced that 1997 would be the last TT of his distinguished career, and it was less than fitting that his swan-song should be made on crutches. Jefferies had already paid tribute to the lives of racing friends claimed by the Island, and tragically another joined their ranks when Colin Gable died at Ballagarey during Monday evening's practice.

FORMULA ONE

The TT's opening event got under way under cloudless skies and in 80 degree heat, but it was Phillip McCallen who scorched the Manx earth fastest of all. The 33-year-old took the lead from fast-starting Joey Dunlop at Ramsey on lap one, extending his lead remorselessly to win by 93.7 seconds. It was the Portadown man's third Formula One success, and it looked every bit as easy as before.

Prior to the race, McCallen had asserted that a 125 mph lap was possible on his World Superbike-spec Honda Britain RC45. In the event, he was not pushed hard enough for such an effort to be necessary.

Michael Rutter, suffering from the heat and the after-effects of a car crash, placed second, his best TT result

After 30 years of trying, Roy Hanks claimed a first TT win.

Below: Joey Dunlop took his TT tally to 22 wins with victory in the Lightweight.

to date. Joey Dunlop's early challenge evaporated at his first pit stop when his Honda's rear wheel nut jammed, costing him 70 precious seconds and dropping him from the leaderboard. He recovered to take sixth place.

Forty-two-year-old Bob Jackson confirmed his growing reputation as the TT's Mr Dependable by bringing his McAdoo Kawasaki into third, preventing Honda making a clean sweep of the first six places. A fellow-Cumbrian, Marc Flynn, placed a superb fifth on the RC45 vacated by Nick Jefferies, with slow-starting Ian Simpson's Honda in between. All owed a little to fortune. Simon Beck held a comfortable third place but ran out of fuel a tantalising 400 metres from his second pit stop. The Preston man pushed his Kawasaki in, rejoining in a state of near-collapse to claim an eventual ninth place.

SIDECARS: RACE A

It seemed for all the world that the worst possible strategy for Sidecar Race A was actually to lead it. From the flag, pre-race favourite Rob Fisher roared into an early lead, setting the fastest lap of the race from a standing start. Then, on lap two, the engine of his Baker Yamaha self-destructed. Ian Bell rashly inherited the lead on another Yamaha, until he in turn was sidelined when his outfit punctured at Windy Corner, also on the second lap. This handed the luckless advantage to Greg Lambert, who had the satisfac-

tion of leading after two laps before his Honda blew up.

Enter Roy Hanks, who's been chasing a first TT win for 30 years, longer than many of his rivals have been alive. The 49-year-old Brummie shrugged off the omens to carry his lead to the flag by a slim 2.2 seconds from Vince Biggs. Only then did we realise that Hanks had enjoyed family help. Biggs also happens to be the uncle of Hanks's passenger Phil. For good measure, both the second- and third-placed passengers have previously chaired for Roy, whose nephew, Tom Hanks, steered the third outfit home. Perhaps the Monopolies Commission should investigate?

SIDECARS: RACE B

If Roy Hanks had to wait half a lifetime for his first TT success, nephew Tom's TT career has been an exercise in impatience. In adding second place in Race B to his third in Race A, the 28-year-old took the overall Sidecar award in only his second year as a driver. The race itself was Rob Fisher's opportunity to put matters right after the disappointment of Race A, which he did in imperious style to win by 64.4 seconds. Having defied doctor's orders to race after injuring his right leg in crashing at Cadwell Park the previous month, Fisher led from start to finish. His fastest lap, at 110.45 mph, was almost 2 mph faster than any of his rivals, while his average race speed was nearly 3 mph faster than Saturday's Race A.

LIGHTWEIGHT

Joey Dunlop may only be an occasional racer these days, but on occasions he's good. Victory in the Lightweight event pushed his all-time tally to 22 wins, and in the process proved that younger hot-shots like McCallen can take nothing for granted. 'Yer Maun' was pushed hard for the first half of the race by his compatriot, but it was the younger man who was found wanting. Only two seconds adrift at the half-distance pit stop, McCallen elected to change tyres, putting him 18 seconds in arrears. He was pushing to make up this deficit when he crashed out at over 120 mph at Quarry Bends. Dunlop, who did not change wheels, struggled with a sliding rear tyre in the latter stages but by then was over 40 seconds ahead of runner-up Ian Lougher and cruised home to a comfortable win more reminiscent of his heyday.

Behind Dunlop, Lougher, John McGuiness, Shaun Harris and Gary Dynes waged a titanic battle for the minor places. Lougher survived a partial seizure, Kiwi Harris struggled with a right footrest broken when he cranked his Trollope Yamaha hard over to pass a back-marker and Dynes battled with a faulty gearbox. Only McGuiness enjoyed a relatively trouble-free ride on the one Aprilia to finish, claiming third place and the fastest lap of the race at 116.83 mph.

ULTRA-LIGHTWEIGHT

And about time, too. Despite two previous wins, Ian Lougher's TT career has never quite taken off since he set the 250 cc lap record during that memorable dice with Steve Hislop in 1990. This year the likeable 31-year-old Welshman made amends in winning the delayed 125 cc event by 2.6 seconds after a sizzling race-long tussle with Ulster's Denis McCullough. McCullough led for most of the race, and even at Windy Corner on the final lap Lougher's signals indicated that he was two seconds in arrears. 'I just squeezed every piece of my body

Double Red Photography

behind the fairing...I couldn't have gone any faster,' he said afterwards. McCullough was handicapped by a faulty filler cap which splashed petrol in his face for much of the race.

An uncharacteristically assertive Lougher said afterwards that 'A lot of people said my wins were down to other riders having bad luck and I couldn't win purely on riding ability. Well, they can crawl back under their stones now. I think I've proved what I can do.' Lougher also posted a new lap record on his RS125R Honda, 109.25 mph, narrowly ahead of Mark Baldwin's time from 1995.

Lougher's feat was welcome, but the most sentimental result was Robert Dunlop's third place on his return to TT racing after the near-fatal crash when his RC45's rear wheel collapsed at Ballaugh in 1994. A rostrum place was particularly welcome for the Ulsterman following a long struggle to overcome medical objections to his racing. Fourth was Glen English. Pre-race favourite Joey Dunlop struggled with a bike which was down on top speed to finish a disappointing tenth.

SINGLE CYLINDER

Singles specialist Dave Morris gave BMW their first solo TT win since Georg Meier's victory on a supercharged twin in 1939. Yet, in truth, this was a lacklustre race, with only 16 finishers from a slim field of 23. Southampton-based Morris overhauled early leader Chris McGahan on lap two to finish a comfortable 40 seconds ahead of John Barton's Ducati Supermono, with Steve Linsdell's Yamaha third. The four-year-old singles class is assured of running in 1998, but its long-term future must surely depend on more rousing support.

Nigel Kinrade

JUNIOR (600 SUPERSPORT)

It doesn't seem that long ago since we speculated on the first 120 mph lap on a full-on racing machine (in fact it was Steve Hislop in 1989). Now they're almost doing it on souped-up roadster middleweights. In taking his maiden TT victory on the V & M CBR600 Honda, Ian Simpson posted a new lap record at 119.86 mph, eclipsing the 118.94 mph mark set by McCallen last year. From Ramsey to Ramsey on laps two to three he was unofficially timed at over 120 mph. The Dumfries man also established a new race record at 118.41 mph.

Ironically, Simpson was drafted into the V & M squad – for which his father now works as a mechanic – only after regular rider Iain Duffus pulled out due to injuries received at Snetterton the previous month. His victory came 21 years after his father, Bill, scored his only TT win on a 250 Yamaha, in 1976. 'Simmo' was a six-year-old spectator that day. Yet for all that the result was a novelty, the Scot's progress was imperious as he led from start to finish.

Phillip McCallen scored a brave second place despite a badly swollen left hand, a legacy of his Lightweight TT crash. Another legacy was an uncharacteristic note of caution: 'I must have lost about half a minute [through Quarry Bends]. Every time I came through I could see my tyre marks from Monday. I was too cautious.'

A superb late charge over the Mountain brought Michael Rutter third by just 0.2 seconds from Derek Young. Joey Dunlop secured fifth ahead of Bob Jackson, while Jim Moodie, one of the pre-race favourites, struggled with a misfiring Suzuki to finish 11th.

PRODUCTION

For the second year in succession the pairing of Phillip McCallen and the Motorcycle City Fireblade proved unbeatable in the newest TT division. In a race cut from three to two laps because of poor weather, in which riders had to contend with treacherous damp patches, the Ulsterman held off a determined challenge from Ian Simpson's Red Bull Ducati 916 to clock his second win of the week.

Simpson had led at Glen Helen on lap one, but McCallen clawed out a five-second margin by Ramsey Hairpin. It looked all over when he had extended this to 14 seconds one lap later, but Simpson charged hard over the Mountain, as McCallen eased the pace, narrowing the Honda man's advantage to just 7.6 seconds at the flag. Both riders were wary of damp stretches over the Mountain, but 'Simmo' observed that 'Phillip must have been going really quick despite the damp. I just couldn't catch him.'

Simon Beck brought his Fireblade home a contented third, some consolation for his Formula One disappointment. 'A lot of people have been saying the Fireblade was too twitchy for the Island, but mine was excellent.'

Despite the shortened race distance, Marc Flynn had probably the most eventful race of the week. The Cumbrian survived a second-lap spill at Ramsey Hairpin to finish fourth overall, and first 750 home. Marshals had to help him bump-start his GSX-R750 Suzuki, then he had to ride the 12

miles of the Mountain section without a visor. (Lucky he still had it on lap one when he struck a pigeon at 150 mph near Glen Helen.) Whether he could read his signals is unclear, but at the flag Jim Hodson's Thunderace was just 1.3 seconds adrift, with Derek Young a further 4.3 seconds behind in sixth on yet another 'Blade. Next year, Honda party or no, it could all be very different, with likely new production contenders from Kawasaki, Suzuki and Yamaha.

SENIOR

To no one's great surprise – with the possible exception of the Quarry Bends' marshals – Phillip McCallen duly claimed another TT hat-trick in taking victory in the blue riband Senior TT. But if spectators expected a cake-walk, Michael Rutter and Jim Moodie had other ideas.

Early leader Rutter's challenge ended abruptly at Signpost Corner on lap one when he crashed due to oil spewed onto his rear tyre. This left McCallen just five seconds ahead of Moodie, coming to terms with the power of his NSR500-V twin. When both men pitted at the end of lap two, Bob Jackson took the lead on a ZX-7R Kawasaki fitted with a massive 32-litre tank requiring him to make only a single refuelling stop. McCallen retook the lead when Jackson pitted one lap later, nine seconds up on Moodie.

But pit stops have never been McCallen's strength, and yet again the pit-lane gremlins struck during his second refuelling halt. A petrol delivery problem allowed Moodie to claw back to within 4.8 seconds of the Ulsterman. Meanwhile 'one-stop' Jackson retook third, overtaking Ian Simpson and Simon Beck as they pitted for the second time.

Although we didn't know it, Moodie was having problems of his own. The Glaswegian reported afterwards that the £90,000 NSR was misfiring and down on acceleration. Certainly McCallen claimed to have been well in control, with signals keeping him apprised of his rival's progress. On the final lap – his fastest at 122.22 mph – he pulled out a further eight seconds to win by 8.7s at the flag. Simpson brought his RC45 into third, with Jackson's big-tank strategy allowing him to edge Simon Beck into fifth.

Nigel Kinrade

Don Morley

Photos: Dave Collister

The perils of TT racing are vividly illustrated in this practice crash sequence at Braddan Bridge. Welsh rider Nigel Davies was one of a handful of riders on a GP-spec two-stroke – a V4 Yamaha. He was lucky to escape with ankle and foot fractures after losing the rear wheel, sliding over the kerb, and slamming into the bales protecting the stone wall.

Opposite page. Top left: Denis McCullough came so close in the Ultra-Lightweight class.
Ian Simpson *(middle)* won the Junior on the 600 Honda, and came within an ace of a 120 mph lap...on a production bike!
Bottom left: Dave Morris won the Singles race, giving BMW their first TT win since 1939.
Bottom right: Phillip McCallen sweeps to Production TT victory on the Honda Fireblade. Hondas won every solo TT except the Singles this year.

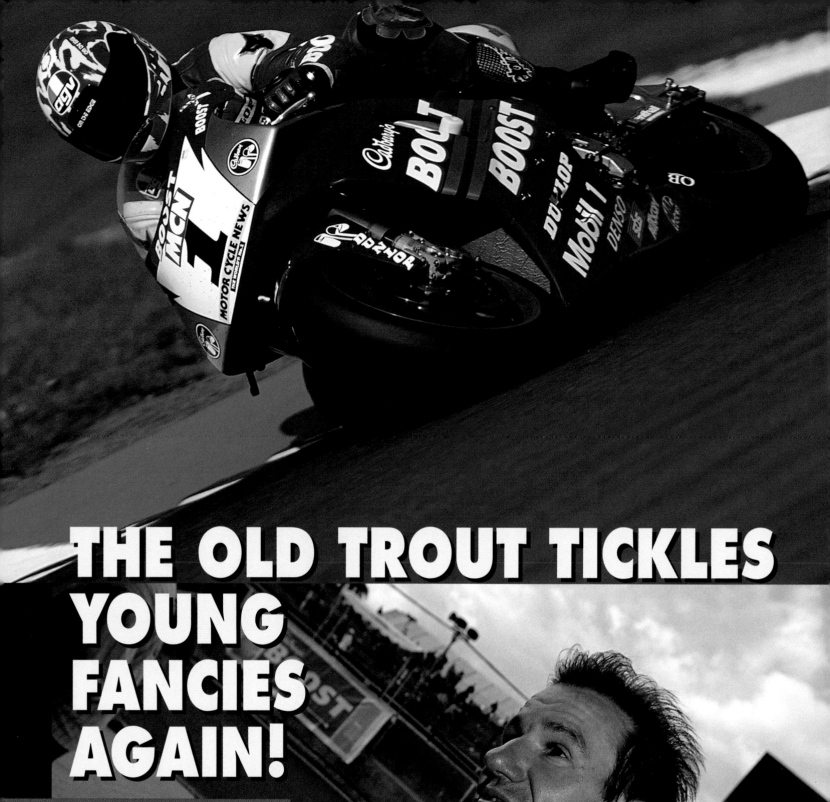

THE OLD TROUT TICKLES YOUNG FANCIES AGAIN!

BRITISH NATIONAL RACING REVIEW

by Gordon Ritchie

Niall Mackenzie *(left, on and off his Yamaha)* again proved you can't teach an old dog new tricks. Or (as some wag wrote on his T-shirt) an old trout.

THE 1996 season had represented a major success for the Motor Cycle Circuit Racing Control Board and marked possibly the biggest upturn of both enthusiast and general public interest in bike racing for a couple of decades. The quality BBC TV coverage of the Motor Cycle News British Superbike series was a major factor in the triumphant return of big-time domestic racing, and the crowd figures consistently beat all-time records. What a success! We'd never had it so good since Harold Macmillan was a lad.

The trick for '97 was to keep all that new-found interest growing. Hence, this year, there were eleven two-leg Superbike races, more extensive TV coverage on both terrestrial and satellite channels, and national support races at virtually all Superbike Championship meetings to heighten the spectacle and extend the meetings from two days to three. And the crowds responded in their droves.

Trouble was, reigning champion Niall Mackenzie was a virtual cert to retain his title. Last season only the similarly equipped and mercurially brilliant James Whitham had been able to mount a serious challenge to Mackenzie's immense skill and ten years of GP experience. With his 1996 playmate gone to World Superbikes, and the all-conquering Cadbury's Boost Yamaha YZF with even more factory parts, Niall was looking invincible before he'd even crossed Hadrian's Wall for his first Border raid at Donington.

So strong was his position at one pre-season stage it looked like the only serious threat would have to come from his team-mate – whoever that might be.

Fortunately for us, if sadly for them, there were enough quality riders beating a refugee trail back to the UK after unsuccessful GP or WSB sorties to constitute a mini-flood: John Reynolds, Sean Emmett, Chris Walker and, it looked for a while, James Haydon. In addition, there were enough good UK-based riders, like Michael Rutter, Matt Llewellyn, Jim Moodie, Terry Rymer and Steve Hislop, to make the second-rider choice a genuinely difficult decision for Boost team chief Rob McElnea and Yamaha UK race boss, Jeff Turner.

The final selection of Chris Walker was seen by some as a gamble. His talent was undoubted, his ability to attract controversy (after messily dumping his '96 Old Spice Ducati ride for an Elf 500 GP saddle) still fresh in some minds. Others expected a titanic crash-fest in between brilliant performances. We got a bit of everything from Chris in the event – but mostly consistency and maturity.

In fairness, not all the aforementioned riders were strictly up for grabs by the Boost Boys, partly because all that TV coverage in 1996 had attracted new teams of unheard-of affluence and presence, usually toting works and semi-works support from their respective importers.

John Reynolds, for instance, was going into partnership with 1995 British Superbike champion Steve Hislop on 1997 works Ducati 996 Corsas, under the banner of Reve Red Bull Ducati; a new/old team, run by former British champion Roger Marshall and bankrolled by main sponsor Red Bull and Reynolds's firm friend, Ben Atkins. And what a bankroll. One million pounds was the claim, and the set-up looked every penny of it.

Kawasaki Motors UK, the official importer, was right back in the big time after suffering through the non-works Nemesis debacle in '96, fielding an in-house team headed by Terry Rymer and ex-Thunderbike World 600 series top runner, Iain Macpherson. Now here was a gamble: works pressure, slick tyres and 150 bhp for a guy who'd never even sat on a Superbike before.

Honda fielded but a single V & M-tended RC45 for Michael Rutter, their sparse Superbike presence a world removed from their virtually omnipotent support of the other main championship classes.

Suzuki increased their level of commitment (albeit without much in the way of ex-WSB equipment) for the biggest dealer team in the business, Crescent Suzuki. The FORRM Team of the Year 1996, managed by Paul Denning, belied their outward status by fielding multiple British Superbike champion Jim Moodie and former national champion, Matt Llewellyn, on the fast-but-fickle GSX-R750s.

The works entries were rounded off by the very dark horses in the Groundwork South East Ducati team, headed by ex-500 GP and WSB rider Sean Emmett. In truth it was more a mega-private team than a works-supported effort, but team manager Colin Seeley opted for taking on the big boys with his brace of 996 Corsas and the talents of experienced tuner and crew chief, John Hackett.

The rest (and there were a lot of them) competed for the newly formed Privateer Championship, which offered not only points towards the overall series, but a separate championship table and minor, rather than invisible, amounts of TV coverage to entice smaller sponsors. Sabre Airways-backed Ray Stringer looked hot favourite for this class, with De Walt Ducati's Dean Ashton the one most likely to spoil the Kawasaki rider's party. The privateer field also boasted Darren Dixon, former British solo champion in the days of RG500s – and World Sidecar Champion to boot.

Come the first race at Donington Park in April some infrequent visitors to the racing world could be forgiven for thinking they'd passed through a glitch in the space-time continuum and had arrived a few weeks early for the World Superbike Championship round. The paddock area looked like any WSB paddock, with transporters, mobile hospitality units, corporate branding and a seething mass of humanity as far as the eye could see, if

not entirely believe. Not bad when you consider that British racing was showing all the signs of slow death a bare two years previously.

In fact, the only thing which looked like spoiling the spectacle of the MCRCB's multi-ring circus after Donington was that man Mackenzie. Thirty-five, married, a father of two, and with a tidy bank balance after his years of racing at the highest level, Mackenzie had laid the ghost of his disastrous final GP season with his British Superbike win in 1996; we could only wonder how he worked up the necessary enthusiasm and motivation to do it all over again. At Donington, though, Niall showed all the speed of a man racing the devil for his very soul – and it looked like his salvation was assured after overcoming his characteristically diabolical starts to notch up the first of the five double wins he would accrue over the season.

Eternal damnation seemed to beckon for the rest, but it only took until the next round, at the awesome high-speed armco tunnel of Oulton Park, for Mackenzie to be toppled – by his team-mate Walker in the first race and by John Reynolds in the second. Walker dealt himself out of the chance of his first double, to go with his first Superbike win, after experiencing the most spectacular high-speed crash anyone could remember seeing – anywhere. Somehow his Yamaha conspired to spit him off while he was coasting the brow of the hill at the Avenue at a piffling 150 mph. The ensuing high-side was positively orbital for both man and machine, and Chris was lucky to escape with just a cracked bone and torn ligaments in his feet – even if they did rule him out of the chance to shine at the WSB round at Donington the week after.

Reynolds's win in the second leg seemed to set him up nicely for a season-long challenge for the title.

Or not.

An eighth place (after a clash with double DNF man Rymer) and a mechanical retirement shuffled him down the pack again after a disastrous visit to Snetterton. With Macpherson out with a non-bike-related injury, Kawasaki's pride was only restored by the one-off inclusion of World Endurance champion Brian Morrison, who sorted them out a pair of very respectable sixth places. Matt Llewellyn put the good speed of his Crescent Suzuki to equally good effect in race two, taking what turned out to be the team's only podium of the year. Michael Rutter even overcame head and rib injuries sustained in a Saturday evening car smash to take a third on his ultra-fast RC45. A 1-2 for each of the Boost Boys, however, saw them leave Snetterton in an already commanding position in the championship, with Mackenzie fully 19 points ahead of his younger team-mate.

Walker cut that back to nine points after surviving the tropical monsoons which literally engulfed the Brands Hatch Indy Circuit in June, even if he

only managed second and fifth. The entire meeting looked under threat from the elements at one point, with extensive flooding causing races to be stopped, foreshortened or rendered farcical by the appalling rain.

Sean Emmett had the misfortune to puncture his intermediate rear on the warm-up lap of race one, forcing his GSE Ducati team to fit a slick in the wet conditions and pray. Emmett later claimed 'That was a tyre from God,' after defying floods of biblical proportions to win the first race with seeming ease from Walker.

Mackenzie, showing signs of the only real chink in his almost impregnable armour, had two uncomfortable rides on the wet and changeable surface to finish eighth and fourth. No such problems for Macpherson, who was now getting the hang of this Superbike lark: he scored his first podium of the year, behind Rutter and John Reynolds, as the Nottinghamshire rider took his and Reve Red Bull Ducati's second win of the year. As things transpired, it would be Reynolds's last.

The flat-out sweeps of Thruxton proved to be a stern challenge to all the main Superbike combatants, none more so than Steve Hislop. Despite joining his team-mate Reynolds on the podium at the inaugural round at Donington, Hislop had been having serious problems adapting to the Ducati, in the same way as he did during his championship-winning year of 1995. Or adapting the Ducati to suit him, maybe. Thus we saw the improbable sight of Hislop way down in 12th and then 18th (and last!) places at Thruxton, followed in short order by the sound of boot on backside as he was 'invited' to leave the team with immediate effect.

It was business as usual for the other top men, though, with Mackenzie winning both legs from Rymer and Walker, then Rymer and Reynolds.

The second Oulton-based round of the year saw further controversy. Terry Rymer's already slim chances of overall title success (plus having to miss the next round at Mallory, due to Kawasaki's desire to use his Endurance experience in the Suzuka Eight Hour) were finally crushed when he was excluded from the points, along with team-mate Macpherson, in the baking heat of race one. The team had removed the front mudguards in an attempt to stop the engines overheating; a protest was lodged, and Rymer's third and Macpherson's eighth places were stripped from them. This made little difference to Mackenzie (36 years young on race eve) and John Reynolds, who were 1-2 in both races, while two eventual third places for Chris Walker (the second of them after Rymer crashed out in spectacular fashion) at least kept him within spitting distance of Mackenzie. If he could spit 50 points and two race wins, that is.

With only a week between Oulton II and Mallory, the Kawasaki mechanics had their work cut out to fettle

Above: Second Yamaha rider Chris Walker leads Rymer, Mackenzie and Michael Rutter at Brands Hatch – the Superbike season had some fine racing.

More ex-GP riders came home to a booming season. John Reynolds (left) had mixed fortunes on the Red Bull Ducati; Sean Emmett (below) found the going far from easy on his Groundwork South East Ducati.

Right: Jim Moodie ponders his problems in the Suzuki pit garage.

Mark Wernham

Mark Wernham

Clive Challinor

Scott Smart *(left)* took the 250 cc championship after a titanic battle with Jason Vincent.

Below left: Ray Stringer was top Superbike privateer on his Kawasaki.

Rymer's crashed ZX-7RR in readiness for its one-off replacement rider...Steve Hislop. Another Colin Wright gamble, and one which paid off: the fired-up Hizzie scored vengeful third- and second-place finishes. Macpherson added to Kawasaki's deep joy with a career-best second place in race one, but the Mackenzie steamroller chugged on with two wins – again. Reynolds suffered a nasty shoulder injury in a practice crash at the ultra-fast Gerrards bend, ruling him out of the next six races, killing his title chances – and passing the flickering Red Bull Ducati torch to new team-mate, and former champion, Ian Simpson.

Come his home round at Knockhill it looked like Mackenzie's luck was finally about to peter out when he suffered a broken ankle in a first race collision with Moodie and Emmett. The measure of his determination this season can be seen from the fact that he strapped up his ankle for race two, borrowed an oversized boot, and promptly won. This to the increasing delight of the Scottish crowd, who had earlier seen Macpherson hold off Hislop's privately entered Sabre Kawasaki and score his first British Superbike win.

The still-injured Mackenzie was in further trouble, though, in the second race at Cadwell Park two weeks later, when he crashed in the Woodland (i.e. next to no run-off) section in damp conditions and broke his wrist. Rain-man Rutter won that one, to no one's surprise but V & M Honda's delight. Mackenzie had only managed a poor seventh in the first leg, won by Simpson, and the break was considered serious enough to threaten his fitness for the penultimate round at Brands Hatch.

Ray Stringer, on the other hand, could have had the rest of term off if he chose, having secured the Privateer Championship at Cadwell from Brett Sampson. Despite Stringer's domination, a fair few others had their moment on the top step of the podium and the victory lap with the works lads, namely, Dean Ashton, Andy Ward, Darren Dixon, Andy Hatton and David Jefferies.

But come the end of the day at Brands Hatch, three weeks after Cadwell, Mackenzie had won his championship as well, and in fine style for a man with a heavily braced wrist. He took a pair of close wins over the returned Reynolds and Emmett in the closest-fought races of the entire season.

So Mackenzie retained his title, as expected, but the increased competition forced him to win the series the hard way, by overcoming not just a myriad of well-equipped and competitive rivals, but the pain of fresh injury on two separate occasions. Even so, he felt aggrieved at missing the second half of a celebratory double at the last round at Donington, after clashing with Hislop, but couldn't begrudge the win to his team-mate Walker, who triumphed despite severe tonsillitis and a viral infection.

The bad news, for everyone else, is that Mac's back next year, competitive equipment permitting. The good news is that any young rider wishing to make it on a world stage still has a truly world class act to measure himself against in the UK.

Mind you, one of those young riders has already bypassed that route this year. James Toseland, a 16-year-old schoolboy, positively burst onto the UK racing scene, starting in the CB500 Cup competition – and ending the year as champion of that class and third in the frighteningly competitive Shell Advance Supersport 600 series. His youthful exuberance won him more 600 races (four) from his eight starts than any of the others could muster in eleven; premature ejection (i.e. crashes while leading) lost him two more. In fact he was so impressive he was snapped up mid-season by the works Castrol Honda team to head their World Supersport Championship challenge in 1998.

Understandably the mass of media attention was focused on Toseland most of the time, but that's not to belittle the achievements of eventual Supersport 600 champion, Paul 'Marra' Brown, on his RS Performance/Semi-com Sanyo Honda. Marra kept his head while all about him lost theirs, at some stage or other, and he took the title with one round to go.

If you wanted to see strength-in-depth racing, on evenly matched machinery, then the British 600 championship was your gig, with at least ten riders in with very realistic chances of winning the title. Honda spent big in this class, with all the top riders except Crescent Suzuki's Jim Moodie and John Crawford running in well-supported CBR600-equipped teams. Virtually season-long tyre problems and a very controversial win for Toseland over Crawford in the last round (the general consensus that he overtook under a yellow flag twice was not punished for some reason) prevented the Suzuki squad from breaking Honda's 11/11 scoreline, much to the disbelief of all who felt the brace of GSX-Rs were more than worthy challengers to the CBR horde.

If the two four-stroke British championship classes were decided before the last round, the Shell Advance 250 and 125 cc classes were nail-biters until the final corners. Scott Smart finally overcame his fellow Honda RS250 rival Jason Vincent by a two-point margin after a right ding-dong battle which saw them win nine of the 14 races between them. They even managed to beat the rest of a quality field despite both missing a Brands Hatch double-header due to Euro Championship commitments. GPs beckon for these two, surely. Highest placed Aprilia rider was double Brands winner Woolsey Coulter, in fourth, with Mark Coats, John McGuiness and Maurice Ruddock the other race victors.

Darren Barton may have made a victorious return to British 125 racing after

Clive Challinor

Double Red Photography

Darren Barton returned from a difficult year in GPs to claim the 125 title.

Below left: Famous dad, future famous son? Leon Haslam, here with dad Ron, was a racing prodigy at 14.

James Toseland made a huge impression in his debut season, scoring four victories in the Supersport 600 championship *(bottom)* in addition to winning the CB500 Cup.

a disastrous year in GPs, but the total domination he exercised in his last UK campaign was not to be repeated, as Fernando Mendes, teenager Chris Burns, Jason Davis, Paul Robinson and Rodney Fee all won races in the 14-round series.

With Burns especially impressive in his debut British Championship year (before he went off on an ill-starred GP adventure with UGT Honda), it could have come down to a three-way scrap for the title on Finals Day at Donington. However, Barton's 21-point lead over Mendes could not be overcome, despite Mendes finishing second to Burns and Barton only netting fifth.

'The People' National Championships, for 125 GP and 600 Supersport classes, were for the most part incorporated into the main Superbike rounds, increasing the chances of eventual winners Andi Notman (125) and Jonti Hobday (600) being noticed by the bigger teams.

Such was the reasoning behind the Honda CB500 National and Newcomers' Cup Championships. The idea, blatantly cribbed from the French, was to equip all-comers with identical CB500 Honda twins and see who came out on top. James Toseland decimated the hopefuls in the national series and Chris Sherring did similar damage to the other newcomers' aspirations, despite a nasty mid-season arm break.

Motorcycle City's Superteen Championship continued on its Aprilia-dominated way in 1997, and was another class only decided on the last day of school. Steve Brogan got the nod over

his only real title challenger, Paul Jones, despite yielding the last five straight race wins to his Liverpudlian neighbour. Karl Harris was the only other race winner, at Oulton Park in April.

Twelve wins from 16 starts gave 14-year-old Leon Haslam (yes that Haslam, son of Ron) the Carnell Gilera National Scooter Championship by a mile from Carl Ogdon. Winning the only round

of the CB500 Newcomers' Cup he competed in has helped bring Haslam to people's attention on merit, rather than by family association, and he will compete in the 125 British Championship next season on a Honda Britain kitted RS.

A change of machinery for competitors in the Triumph Speed Triple one-make Challenge, to the new T509, had the curious effect of making lap times slower for the most part, but didn't prevent Jason Emmett from winning by the narrow margin of 2.5 points from Alan Batson. The eight-round series still attracted some big names (Paul Brown, Matt Llewellyn, David Jefferies) with its equally big prize money, but it degenerated into a shambolic affair at both Thruxton and the Brands Hatch World Superbike round when delayed race programmes meant rescheduling to other meetings because of noise curfews.

Other than the British Championship classes themselves, the biggest interest in national racing, for manufacturers, spectators and riders alike, was in the Bike Trader Production Powerbike Championship. Despite taking place over only seven rounds the series attracted support from all the major manufacturers and importers and included such luminaries as eventual champion Ian Simpson (Red Bull Reve Ducati 916 SPS), Jim Moodie (Electronic Arts GSX-R750 Suzuki), Michael Rutter (V & M Honda Fireblade), John Crawford, Paul Brown, Dave Heal, Iain Duffus, Phillip McCallen, Mike Edwards, Matt Llewellyn – to name but a few of the more famous. Simpson was assured the win after Moodie retired from the final round, run during the Donington Park GP weekend.

All in all, a very successful year for British racing, which should advance

its cause still further next year when more TV, an additional British Superbike meeting at the remodelled Silverstone (making a round dozen) and an Aprilia 250 Challenge series are on the cards. The latter should fling new and more experienced riders together into a class using more race-friendly tackle than the present Triumphs or CB500s.

Not everything in the garden is rosy, however. Track safety is still not up to scratch at many venues. Most British riders now shun the TT and the Irish road circuits, only to race on many tracks which can barely be called safer in some parts. How can air-fence be necessary at the Brands Hatch WSB race, for instance, yet be deemed superfluous at British Superbike meetings? Facilities for the ever-increasing paddock community have not kept pace with the efforts made by all the teams to improve the sport's professionalism and presentation. Further, the adoption of control fuel seems an unnecessary expense – and robbed Mackenzie of a brilliant third-place finish at the Brands Hatch World Superbike round when it proved too octane-friendly for the WSB regs it is supposed to follow.

There are other complaints from those who actually provide the show and they are real and valid (and will be ignored at the MCRCB's long-term peril). Nothing, though, can overshadow the fact that British domestic racing is enjoying a renaissance on an unheard-of scale: the MCN British Superbike Championship can now lay claim to being the strongest four-stroke race series on the planet – this side of full-on World Superbike competition, of course. Seven different race winners, from five different teams, on four different makes of machine are proof of that. From zeros to heroes in two-and-a-half years. Not too shabby really, is it?

Mark Wernham

1997 SUPERBIKE WORLD CHAMPIONSHIP POINTS

Position	Rider	Nationality	Machine	Phillip Island/1	Phillip Island/2	Misano/1	Misano/2	Donington Park/1	Donington Park/2	Hockenheim/1	Hockenheim/2	Monza/1	Monza/2	Laguna Seca/1	Laguna Seca/2	Brands Hatch/1	Brands Hatch/2	A1-Ring/1	A1-Ring/2	Assen/1	Assen/2	Albacete/1	Albacete/2	Sugo/1	Sugo/2	Sentul/1	Sentul/2	Points total
1	John Kocinski	USA	Honda	25	9	20	25	6	11	20	2	25	20	25	25	16	20	11	16	25	16	25	25	8	16	25	–	416
2	Carl Fogarty	GB	Ducati	20	13	16	16	20	25	13	25	16	13	20	20	–	25	25	–	20	25	–	–	5	–	16	25	358
3	Aaron Slight	NZ	Honda	–	25	13	20	25	16	25	–	20	11	9	6	10	8	16	20	13	13	20	16	11	13	20	13	343
4	Akira Yanagawa	J	Kawasaki	13	–	–	11	–	–	8	20	8	–	6	11	11	13	20	25	8	9	13	25	13	13	20	–	247
5	Simon Crafar	NZ	Kawasaki	16	16	11	9	16	13	–	10	13	9	13	–	–	9	10	–	7	10	16	20	16	20	–	–	234
6	Scott Russell	USA	Yamaha	9	10	–	10	10	9	16	13	11	8	10	13	20	11	9	13	10	8	–	11	4	–	10	11	226
7	Pier Francesco Chili	I	Ducati	–	–	25	–	–	20	11	9	9	25	–	10	25	–	13	–	16	20	11	9	6	–	–	–	209
8	James Whitham	GB	Suzuki	–	5	–	–	8	6	2	16	10	16	8	–	9	7	6	10	9	5	–	6	–	–	7	10	140
9	Neil Hodgson	GB	Ducati	–	–	9	13	13	7	10	8	–	–	7	13	10	8	–	11	11	–	8	–	–	–	–	9	137
10	Piergiorgio Bontempi	I	Kawasaki	–	6	8	–	5	–	5	5	7	10	7	9	8	4	7	11	–	6	10	10	–	–	–	–	118
11	Mike Hale	USA	Suzuki	–	–	–	–	4	1	–	7	–	6	7	2	–	7	5	5	9	5	–	8	7	–	6	8	87
12	Colin Edwards	USA	Yamaha	–	20	10	8	11	10	9	11	–	–	–	–	–	–	–	–	–	–	–	–	–	–	–	–	79
13	Noriyuki Haga	J	Yamaha	–	–	–	–	–	–	–	–	–	–	–	–	–	–	–	–	–	–	–	–	20	25	11	16	72
14	Pere Riba Cabana	E	Honda	7	2	7	7	–	1	–	–	5	–	–	4	3	1	5	4	2	5	3	–	3	5	5	–	69
15	Igor Jerman	SLO	Kawasaki	6	–	5	–	–	–	1	1	1	2	1	3	–	1	–	4	1	3	4	–	–	4	6	7	50
16	Chris Walker	GB	Yamaha	–	–	–	–	–	–	–	–	–	–	–	–	6	6	4	7	6	7	6	5	–	–	–	–	47
17	Jochen Schmid	D	Kawasaki	–	–	–	–	–	–	3	7	3	6	–	–	–	–	3	6	3	4	7	4	–	–	–	–	46
18	Andreas Meklau	A	Ducati	8	3	–	–	–	2	6	6	5	–	–	–	–	–	2	8	–	–	–	–	–	–	–	–	40
19	Miguel DuHamel	CAN	Honda	–	–	–	–	–	–	–	–	–	–	16	16	–	–	–	–	–	–	–	–	–	–	–	–	32
20	Troy Bayliss	AUS	Suzuki	11	11	–	–	–	–	–	–	–	–	–	–	–	–	–	–	–	–	–	–	–	–	–	–	22
21 =	Sean Emmett	GB	Ducati	–	–	–	–	2	4	–	–	–	–	–	–	–	–	–	–	–	–	–	–	–	7	–	8	21
21 =	John Reynolds	GB	Ducati	–	–	–	–	7	5	–	–	–	–	–	–	–	–	–	–	–	–	–	–	–	–	9	–	21
21 =	Michael Rutter	GB	Honda	–	–	–	–	–	–	–	–	–	–	–	–	5	16	–	–	–	–	–	–	–	–	–	–	21
24	Katsuaki Fujiwara	J	Suzuki	–	–	–	–	–	–	–	–	–	–	–	–	–	–	–	–	–	–	–	–	9	11	–	–	20
25	James Haydon	GB	Ducati	–	4	–	5	–	–	4	4	–	–	–	–	–	–	–	–	–	–	2	–	–	–	–	–	19
26	Gregorio Lavilla	E	Ducati	–	–	–	–	3	3	–	3	–	–	–	–	–	–	–	–	9	–	–	–	–	–	–	–	18
27 =	Tamaki Serizawa	J	Suzuki	–	–	–	–	–	–	–	–	–	–	–	–	–	–	–	–	–	–	–	–	7	10	–	–	17
27 =	Niall Mackenzie	GB	Yamaha	–	–	–	–	9	8	–	–	–	–	–	–	–	–	–	–	–	–	–	–	–	–	–	–	17
27 =	Marty Craggill	AUS	Kawasaki	10	7	–	–	–	–	–	–	–	–	–	–	–	–	–	–	–	–	–	–	–	–	–	–	17
30	Christian Lavieille	F	Honda	–	–	6	6	–	–	–	–	–	–	–	–	–	–	–	–	–	–	–	–	–	–	–	4	16
31	Makoto Suzuki	J	Ducati	–	–	–	–	–	–	–	–	–	–	–	–	–	–	–	–	–	–	–	–	–	5	4	6	15
32	Keiichi Kitagawa	J	Suzuki	–	–	–	–	–	–	–	–	–	–	–	–	–	–	–	–	–	–	–	–	13	–	–	–	13
33 =	Tom Kipp	USA	Yamaha	–	–	–	–	–	–	–	–	–	–	4	8	–	–	–	–	–	–	–	–	–	–	–	–	12
33 =	Christer Lindholm	S	Yamaha	–	–	–	–	4	–	4	4	–	–	–	–	–	–	–	–	–	–	–	–	–	–	–	–	12
35 =	Yuichi Takeda	J	Honda	–	–	–	–	–	–	–	–	–	–	–	–	–	–	–	–	–	–	–	–	2	9	–	–	11
35 =	Doug Chandler	USA	Kawasaki	–	–	–	–	–	–	–	–	–	–	11	–	–	–	–	–	–	–	–	–	–	–	–	–	11
37	Shinya Takeishi	J	Kawasaki	–	–	–	–	–	–	–	–	–	–	–	–	–	–	–	–	–	–	–	–	–	10	–	–	10
38 =	Akira Ryo	J	Kawasaki	–	–	–	–	–	–	–	–	–	–	–	–	–	–	–	–	–	–	–	–	–	–	1	8	9
38 =	Steve Crevier	CAN	Honda	–	–	–	–	–	–	–	–	–	–	5	4	–	–	–	–	–	–	–	–	–	–	–	–	9
40	Damon Buckmaster	AUS	Kawasaki	–	8	–	–	–	–	–	–	–	–	–	–	–	–	–	–	–	–	–	–	–	–	–	–	8
41	Erkka Korpiaho	SF	Kawasaki	–	–	–	–	–	–	–	–	–	–	–	–	–	–	–	–	2	1	3	1	–	–	–	–	7
42	Yudhe Kusuma	IND	Kawasaki	–	–	–	–	–	–	–	–	–	–	–	–	–	–	–	–	–	–	–	–	–	–	3	3	6
43 =	Phil Giles	GB	Kawasaki	–	–	–	–	–	–	–	–	–	–	–	–	3	2	–	–	–	–	–	–	–	–	–	–	5
43 =	Aaron Yates	USA	Suzuki	–	–	–	–	–	–	–	–	–	–	–	5	–	–	–	–	–	–	–	–	–	–	–	–	5
43 =	Benn Archibald	AUS	Kawasaki	5	–	–	–	–	–	–	–	–	–	–	–	–	–	–	–	–	–	–	–	–	–	–	–	5
46 =	Norihiko Fujiwara	J	Yamaha	–	–	–	–	–	–	–	–	–	–	–	–	–	–	–	–	–	–	–	–	3	–	–	–	3
46 =	Christian Hausle	A	Ducati	–	–	–	–	–	–	–	–	–	–	–	–	–	–	–	3	–	–	–	–	–	–	–	–	3
46 =	Pascal Picotte	CAN	Suzuki	–	–	–	–	–	–	–	–	–	–	3	–	–	–	–	–	–	–	–	–	–	–	–	–	3
46 =	Jean-Marc Deletang	F	Yamaha	–	–	–	–	–	–	–	3	–	–	–	–	–	–	–	–	–	–	–	–	–	–	–	–	3
50 =	Johann Wolfsteiner	A	Kawasaki	–	–	–	–	–	–	–	–	–	–	–	–	–	–	–	2	–	–	–	–	–	–	–	–	2
50 =	Jean-Philippe Ruggia	F	Yamaha	–	–	–	–	2	–	–	–	–	–	–	–	–	–	–	–	–	–	–	–	–	–	–	–	2
52 =	Ossi Niederkircher	A	Suzuki	–	–	–	–	–	–	–	–	–	–	–	–	–	–	–	–	1	–	–	–	–	–	–	–	1
52 =	David Emmerson	AUS	Suzuki	–	1	–	–	–	–	–	–	–	–	–	–	–	–	–	–	–	–	–	–	–	–	–	–	1

OTHER MAJOR RESULTS

Compiled by Kay Edge

Endurance World Championship

24 HEURES DU MANS, Bugatti Circuit, Le Mans, France, 12-13 April.
Endurance World Championship, round 1. 758 laps of the 2.756-mile/4.435-km circuit, 2089.048 miles/3361.730 km
1 Eric Gomez/Doug Polen/Peter Goddard, F/USA/AUS (Suzuki GSX-R), 23h 59m 05.810s, 87.091 mph/141.160 km/h.
2 Jean-Marc Deletang/Jean-Philippe Ruggia/Christer Lindholm, F/F/S (Yamaha YZF), 748 laps; **3** Eric Mahé/Norihiko Fujiwara/Jean-Louis Battistini, F/J/F (Yamaha YZF), 740; **4** Christophe Guyot/André Lussiana/Michel Simeon, F/F/B (Kawasaki ZXR), 740; **5** Philippe Dobé/Christian Haquin/Jean-François Cortinovis, F/F/F (Kawasaki ZXR), 734; **6** Thierry Paillot/Olivier Ullmann/Vincent Vivoli, F/F/F (Suzuki GSX-R), 718; **7** Philippe Monneret/Emmanuel Maubon/Michel Amalric, F/F/F (Yamaha YZF), 717; **8** Gilles Ferstler/Bruno Bonhuil/Florian Ferracci, F/F/F (Suzuki GSX-R), 717; **9** Jean-Pierre Schneider/Stéphane Gabriele/Alain Bronec, F/F/F (Yamaha YZF), 714; **10** Eric L'Herbette/Wilfrid Veille/Philippe Denis, F/F/F (Kawasaki ZXR), 710; **11** M. Rieder/C. Kuenzi/Eric Monot, CH/CH/F (Kawasaki ZXR), 703; **12** Joel Petit/Patrick Dubois/Jean-Louis Tranois, F/F/F (Honda RC45), 702; **13** D. Beauvais/O. Pean/F. Mussard, F/F/F (Suzuki GSX-R), 702; **14** B. Destoop/F. Henninot/H. Teixeira, F/F/F (Honda), 701; **15** Bernard Cuzin/Jean Marchand/Jerome Couturier, F/F/F (Honda RC45), 699.
Fastest lap: Brian Morrison/Piergiorgio Bontempi/Jehan D'Orgeix, GB/I/F (Kawasaki ZXR), 1m 45.695s, 93.862 mph/151.057 km/h.
Championship points: 1 Goddard, Gomez and Polen, 50; **4** Deletang, Lindholm and Ruggia, 40.

24 HEURES DE LIÈGE, Spa-Francorchamps, Belgium, 12-13 July.
Endurance World Championship, round 2. 541 laps of the 4.340-mile/6.985-km circuit, 2347.940 miles/3778.885 km
1 Eric Gomez/Doug Polen/Peter Goddard, F/USA/AUS (Suzuki GSX-R), 24h 00m 31.694s, 97.563 mph/157.013 km/h.
2 Christian Lavieille/William Costes/Stéphane Mertens, F/F/B (Honda RC45), 533 laps; **3** Olivier Ullmann/Stéphane Gabriele/Alain Bronec, F/F/F (Yamaha YZR), 518; **4** A. Laranjeira/T. Pereira/Michel Graziano, P/P/F (Suzuki GSX-R), 517; **5** Bernard Cuzin/Jerome Couturier/Jean Marchand, F/F/F (Honda RC45), 510; **6** Joel Petit/Gérald Muteau/Jean-Louis Tranois, F/F/F (Honda RC45), 509; **7** F. Girardot/C. Laurent/Emmanuel Lentaigne, F/F/F (Honda), 498; **8** P. Carrara/T. Pochon/C. Desmaria, F/F/F (Suzuki GSX-R), 493; **9** D. Beauvais/O. Pean/F. Mussard, F/F/F (Suzuki GSX-R), 490; **10** J.-F. Le Glatin/Claude-Alain Jaggi/D. Crassous, F/CH/F (Ducati), 487; **11** F. Beltermann/Thomas Rothig/Kai Schlieper, D/D/D (Yamaha YZF); **12** T. Beaumont/E. Chevallier/Xavier Fabra, F/F/F (Kawasaki ZXR), 486; **13** Werner Graf/Peter Knutti/B. Muller, CH/CH/CH (Kawasaki ZXR), 484; **14** S. Strauch/K. Kaspers/R. Altzschner, D/D/D (Suzuki GSX-R), 484; **15** J. Mommen/Y. Tonquang/P. Adrien, B/B/B (Honda), 483.
Fastest lap: not available.
Championship points: 1 Goddard, Gomez and Polen, 100; **4** Ullmann, 52; **5** Bronec and Gabriele, 46.

SUZUKA EIGHT HOURS, Suzuka International Circuit, Japan, 27 July.
Endurance World Championship, round 3. 186 laps of the 3.644-mile/5.864-km circuit, 677.784 miles/1090.704 km
1 Shinichi Ito/ITohru Ukawa, J/J (Honda RC45), 8h 02m 03.722s, 84.351 mph/135.75 km/h.
2 John Kocinski/Alex Barros, USA/BR (Honda RC45), 186 laps; **3** Akira Ryo/Shinya Takeishi, J/J (Kawasaki ZX-7RR), 185; **4** Scott Russell/Troy Corser, USA/AUS (Yamaha YZF), 185; **5** Peter Goddard/Doug Polen, AUS/USA (Suzuki GSX-R), 184; **6** Tadayuki Okada/Aaron Slight, J/NZ (Honda RC45), 184; **7** Simon Crafar/Akira Yanagawa, NZ/J (Kawasaki ZX-7RR), 183; **8** Wataru Yoshikawa/Norihiko Fujiwara, J/J (Yamaha YZF), 180; **9** Youichi Takeda/Daijiro Kato, J/J (Honda RC45), 180; **10** Jean-Marc Deletang/Jean-Philippe Ruggia, F/F (Yamaha YZF), 179; **11** Tomohiko Kaneyasu/Yukio Nukumi, J/J (Honda RC45), 177; **12** Shinya Nakatani/Ryuji Tsuruta, J/J (Kawasaki ZX-7RR), 176; **13** Takatoshi Onishi/Takashi Minoda, J/J (Yamaha YZF), 176; **14** Takaharu Kishida/Masaki Tokunaga, J/J (Honda RC45), 176; **15** Haruchika Aoki/Manabu Kamada, J/J (Honda RC45), 176.
Fastest lap: Ito/Ukawa, 2m 28.838s, 88.129 mph/141.830 km/h.
Championship points: 1 Goddard and Polen, 111; **3** Gomez, 100; **4** Ullmann, 52; **5** Bronec, Deletang, Gabriele and Ruggia, 46.

61e BOL D'OR, Circuit Paul Ricard, France, 20-21 September.
Endurance World Championship, round 4. 692 laps of the 2.361-mile/3.800-km circuit, 1633.812 miles/2629.600 km
1 Brian Morrison/Terry Rymer/Jehan D'Orgeix, GB/GB/F (Kawasaki ZX-7RR), 24h 00m 42.285s.
2 Christian Lavieille/William Costes/Miguel DuHamel, F/F/CAN (Honda RC45), 692 laps; **3** Steve Hislop/Christer Lindholm/Arnaud van den Bossche, GB/S/F (Yamaha YZF), 688; **4** Eric Gomez/Stéphane Coutelle/Bruno Bonhuil, F/F/F (Suzuki GSX-R), 687; **5** Doug Polen/Peter Goddard/Gilles Ferstler, USA/AUS/F (Suzuki GSX-R), 686; **6** Sébastien Charpentier/Nicolas Dussauge/Bertrand Stey, F/F/F (Honda), 676; **7** Christophe Guyot/André Lussiana/S. Scarnato, F/F/F (Kawasaki ZXR), 673; **8** Jean-François Damide/F. Foret/Jean-François Braut, F/F/F (Honda), 667; **9** Yves Caille/Philippe Pinchedez/Thierry Paillot, F/F/F (Honda), 665; **10** A. Laranjeira/T. Pereira/Michel Graziano, P/P/F (Suzuki GSX-R), 663; **11** Joel Petit/Olivier Ullmann/Jean-François Cortinovis, F/F/F (Honda RC45), 660; **12** Jean-Jacques Lovichi/Daewen/Alain Kempener, F/B/B (Honda), 653; **13** Philippe Monneret/Emmanuel Maubon/Christophe Mouzin, F/F/F (Yamaha YZF), 651; **14** Stefan Ambord/Eric Monot/C. Kuenzi, CH/F/CH (Kawasaki ZXR), 646; **15** Bernd Scheiff/Kurt Gasser/Michel Nickmans, B/CH/B (Yamaha YZF), 639.
Fastest lap: Rymer, 1m 59.21s, 109.330 mph/175.950 km/h.

Final World Championship points

1=	Peter Goddard, AUS	133
1=	Doug Polen, USA	133
3	Eric Gomez, F	126
4=	William Costes, F	80
4=	Christian Lavieille, F	80
6	Christer Lindholm, S	72

7 Olivier Ullmann, F, 62; **8**=Jehan D'Orgeix, F, Brian Morrison, GB and Terry Rymer, GB, 50; **11**=Alain Bronec, F, Jean-Marc Deletang, F, Stéphane Gabriele, F and Jean-Philippe Ruggia, F, 46; **15**=Christophe Guyot, F and André Lussiana, F, 44.

FIM-ISRA Sidecar World Cup

HUNGARORING, Hungary, 25 May. 2.465-mile/3.968-km circuit.
FIM-ISRA Sidecar World Cup, round 1 (24 laps, 59.160 miles/95.232 km)
1 Steve Webster/David James, GB/GB (LCR-ADM R4), 42m 23.123s, 84.938 mph/136.694 km/h.
2 Rolf Biland/Kurt Waltisperg, CH/CH (LCR-BRM-Swissauto); **3** Klaus Klaffenböck/Christian Parzer, A/A (LCR-ADM R4); **4** Paul Güdel/Charly Güdel, CH/CH (LCR-BRM-Swissauto); **5** Derek Brindley/Adolf Hänni, GB/CH (LCR-ADM R4); **6** Mark Reddington/Andy Hetherington, GB/GB (LCR-ADM R4); **7** Markus Neumann/Peter Höss, D/D (LCR-ADM R4); **8** Dave Molyneux/Peter Hill, GB/GB (Windle-ADM R4); **9** Markus Schlosser/Daniel Hauser, CH/CH (LCR-BRM-Swissauto); **10** Ian Wilford/Steve English, GB/GB (LCR-ADM R4); **11** Stuart Muldoon/Jeff Haines, GB/GB (LCR-ADM R4); **12** Roger Body/Andy Peach, GB/GB (LCR-BRM-Swissauto).
Fastest lap: Biland, 1m 44.219s, 85.168 mph/137.065 km/h.
Championship points: 1 S. Webster, 25; **2** Biland, 20; **3** Klaffenböck, 16; **4** Güdel, 13; **5** D. Brindley, 11; **6** Reddington, 10.

A1-RING, Zeltweg, Austria, 31 May. 2.684-mile/4.319-km circuit.
FIM-ISRA Sidecar World Cup, round 2 (24 laps, 64.416 miles/103.656 km)
1 Rolf Biland/Kurt Waltisperg, CH/CH (LCR-BRM-Swissauto), 38m 53.380s, 99.372 mph/159.923 km/h.
2 Klaus Klaffenböck/Christian Parzer, A/A (LCR-ADM R4); **3** Paul Güdel/Charly Güdel, CH/CH (LCR-BRM-Swissauto); **4** Steve Webster/David James, GB/GB (LCR-ADM R4); **5** Steve Abbott/Jamie Biggs, GB/GB (Windle-ADM R4); **6** Derek Brindley/Adolf Hänni, GB/CH (LCR-ADM R4); **7** Markus Bösiger/Jurg Egli, CH/CH (LCR-ADM R4); **8** Dave Molyneux/Peter Hill, GB/GB (Windle-ADM R4); **9** Roger Body/Andy Peach, GB/GB (LCR-BRM-Swissauto); **10** Stuart Muldoon/Chris Gusman, GB/GB (LCR-ADM R4); **11** Billy Gällros/Peter Berglund, S/S (LCR-NGK 500).
Fastest lap: Biland, 1m 35.845s, 102.044 mph/162.224 km/h.
Championship points: 1 Biland, 45; **2** S. Webster, 38; **3** Klaffenböck, 36; **4** Güdel, 29; **5** D. Brindley, 21; **6** Molyneux, 16.

ASSEN RACING CIRCUIT, Holland, 28 June. 3.759-mile/6.049-km circuit.
FIM-ISRA Sidecar World Cup, round 3 (17 laps, 63.903 miles/102.833 km)
1 Steve Webster/David James, GB/GB (LCR-ADM R4), 36m 48.148s, 104.174 mph/167.651 km/h.
2 Klaus Klaffenböck/Christian Parzer, A/A (LCR-ADM R4); **3** Paul Güdel/Charly Güdel, CH/CH (LCR-BRM-Swissauto); **4** Derek Brindley/Adolf Hänni, GB/CH (LCR-ADM R4); **5** Barry Brindley/Phillip Biggs, GB/GB (Windle-ADM R4); **6** Stuart Muldoon/Chris Gusman, GB/GB (LCR-ADM R4); **7** Roger Lovelock/Gary Partridge, GB/GB (LCR-Yamaha); **8** Markus Bösiger/Jurg Egli, CH/CH (LCR-ADM R4); **9** Martin Whittington/Paul Woodhead, GB/GB (LCR-Yamaha); **10** Reiner Koster/Torsten Gries, CH/D (LCR-ADM R4); **11** Eise Hummel/Frits Goris, NL/NL (LCR-Krauser); **12** Roger Body/Andy Peach, GB/GB (LCR-BRM-Swissauto).
Fastest lap: S. Webster, 2m 07.799s, 105.879 mph/170.396 km/h.
Championship points: 1 S. Webster, 63; **2** Klaffenböck, 56; **3** Biland and Güdel, 45; **5** D. Brindley, 34; **6** Muldoon, 21.

AUTODROM MOST, Czech Republic, 13 July. 2.577-mile/4.148-km circuit.
FIM-ISRA Sidecar World Cup, round 4 (24 laps, 61.848 miles/99.552 km)
1 Klaus Klaffenböck/Christian Parzer, A/A (LCR-ADM R4), 37m 19.958s, 99.418 mph/159.998 km/h.
2 Paul Güdel/Charly Güdel, CH/CH (LCR-BRM-Swissauto); **3** Derek Brindley/Adolf Hänni, GB/CH (LCR-ADM R4); **4** Markus Bösiger/Jurg Egli, CH/CH (LCR-ADM R4); **5** Markus Schlosser/Daniel Hauser, CH/CH (LCR-BRM-Swissauto); **6** Rolf Biland/Kurt Waltisperg, CH/CH (LCR-BRM-Swissauto); **7** Mark Reddington/Andy Hetherington, GB/GB (LCR-ADM R4); **8** Stuart Muldoon/Chris Gusman, GB/GB (LCR-ADM R4); **9** Kevin Webster/Rob McIntosh, GB/GB (LCR-ADM R4); **10** Markus Neumann/Peter Höss, D/D (LCR-ADM R4); **11** Roger Lovelock/Gary Partridge, GB/GB (LCR-Yamaha); **12** Wolfram Centner/Mike Helbig, D/D (LCR-ADM R4); **13** Reiner Koster/Torsten Gries, CH/D (LCR-ADM R4); **14** Barry Fleury/Jane Fleury, NZ/NZ (LCR-FRT R4); **15** Peter Schröder/Patrick Kramer, CH/CH (LCR-Krauser).
Fastest lap: Steve Webster/David James, GB/GB (LCR-ADM R4), 1m 31.209s, 101.732 mph/163.721 km/h.
Championship points: 1 Klaffenböck, 81; **2** Güdel, 65; **3** S. Webster, 63; **4** Biland, 55; **5** D. Brindley, 50; **6** Bösiger, 30.

NÜRBURGRING, Germany, 20 July. 2.827-mile/4.550-km circuit.
FIM-ISRA Sidecar World Cup, round 5 (23 laps, 65.021 miles/104.650 km)
1 Steve Webster/David James, GB/GB (LCR-ADM R4), 40m 22.422s, 96.637 mph/155.522 km/h.
2 Rolf Biland/Kurt Waltisperg, CH/CH (LCR-BRM-Swissauto); **3** Klaus Klaffenböck/Christian Parzer, A/A (LCR-ADM R4); **4** Paul Güdel/Charly Güdel, CH/CH (LCR-BRM-Swissauto); **5** Derek Brindley/Adolf Hänni, GB/CH (LCR-ADM R4); **6** Markus Schlosser/Daniel Hauser, CH/CH (LCR-BRM-Swissauto); **7** Markus Neumann/Peter Höss, D/D (LCR-ADM R4); **8** Mark Reddington/Andy Hetherington, GB/GB (LCR-ADM R4); **9** Benny Janssen/Frans Geurts van Kessel, NL/NL (LCR-Stredor); **10** Ralph Bohnhorst/Eckhart Rösinger, D/D (LCR-Yamaha); **11** Kevin Webster/Rob McIntosh, GB/GB (LCR-ADM R4); **12** Jari Nikkanen/Juha Joutsen, SF/SF (Windle-ADM R4); **13** Jörg Steinhausen/Frank Schmidt, D/D (LCR-ADM R4); **14** Roger Lovelock/Gary Partridge, GB/GB (LCR-Yamaha); **15** Ian Wilford/Steve English, GB/GB (LCR-ADM R4).
Fastest lap: S. Webster, 1m 42.939s, 98.874 mph/159.123 km/h.
Championship points: 1 Klaffenböck, 97; **2** S. Webster, 88; **3** Güdel, 78; **4** Biland, 75; **5** D. Brindley, 61; **6** Bösiger, 30.

ANDERSTORP RACEWAY, Sweden, 10 August. 2.501-mile/4.025-km circuit.
FIM-ISRA Sidecar World Cup, round 6 (24 laps, 60.024 miles/96.600 km)
1 Steve Webster/David James, GB/GB (LCR-ADM R4), 38m 54.480s, 92.566 mph/148.970 km/h.
2 Paul Güdel/Charly Güdel, CH/CH (LCR-BRM-Swissauto); **3** Derek Brindley/Adolf Hänni, GB/CH (LCR-ADM R4); **4** Markus Bösiger/Jurg Egli, CH/CH (LCR-ADM R4); **5** Stuart Muldoon/Chris Gusman, GB/GB (LCR-ADM R4); **6** Jari Nikkanen/Juha Joutsen, SF/SF (LCR-ADM R4); **7** Kevin Webster/Rob McIntosh, GB/GB (LCR-ADM R4); **8** Markus Schlosser/Daniel Hauser, CH/CH (LCR-BRM-Swissauto); **9** Roger Body/Andy Peach, GB/GB (LCR-BRM-Swissauto); **10** Barry Fleury/Jane Fleury, NZ/NZ (LCR-FRT R4); **11** Mark Reddington/Andy Hetherington, GB/GB (LCR-ADM R4); **12** Billy Gällros/Peter Berglund, S/S (LCR-NGK 500); **13** Wolfram Centner/Mike Helbig, D/D (LCR-ADM R4).
Fastest lap: S. Webster, 1m 35.270s.
Championship points: 1 S. Webster, 113; **2** Güdel, 98; **3** Klaffenböck, 97; **4** D. Brindley, 77; **5** Biland, 75; **6** Bösiger, 43.

AUTODROMO BRNO, Czech Republic, 31 August. 3.357-mile/5.403-km circuit.
FIM-ISRA Sidecar World Cup, round 7 (19 laps, 63.783 miles/102.657 km)
1 Steve Webster/David James, GB/GB (LCR-ADM R4), 40m 38.890s, 94.156 mph/151.530 km/h.
2 Klaus Klaffenböck/Christian Parzer, A/A (LCR-ADM R4); **3** Paul Güdel/Charly Güdel, CH/CH (LCR-BRM-Swissauto); **4** Derek Brindley/Adolf Hänni, GB/CH (LCR-ADM R4); **5** Markus Bösiger/Jurg Egli, CH/CH (LCR-ADM R4); **6** Markus Schlosser/Daniel Hauser, CH/CH (LCR-BRM-Swissauto); **7** Mark Reddington/Andy Hetherington, GB/GB (LCR-ADM R4); **8** Jurg Schmid/Roger Maurer, CH/CH (LCR-BRM-Swissauto); **9** Jörg Steinhausen/Frank Schmidt, D/D (LCR-ADM R4); **10** Kevin Webster/Rob McIntosh, GB/GB (LVR-ADM R4); **11** Wolfram Centner/Mike Helbig, D/D (LCR-ADM R4); **12** Peter Schröder/Patrick Kramer, CH/CH (LCR-Krauser); **13** Kurt Liechti/Daniel Locher, CH/CH (LCR-Yamaha).
Fastest lap: Rolf Biland/Kurt Waltisperg, CH/CH (LCR-BRM-Swissauto), 2m 06.234s, 95.744 mph/154.085 km/h.
Championship points: 1 S. Webster, 138; **2** Klaffenböck, 117; **3** Güdel, 114; **4** D. Brindley, 90; **5** Biland, 75; **6** Bösiger, 54.

AUTODROMO GROBNIK, Rijeka, 21 September. 2.590-mile/4.168-km circuit.
FIM-ISRA Sidecar World Cup, round 8 (24 laps, 62.160 miles/100.032 km)
1 Steve Webster/David James, GB/GB (LCR-ADM R4), 37m 08.717s.
2 Klaus Klaffenböck/Christian Parzer, A/A (LCR-ADM R4); **3** Paul Güdel/Charly Güdel, CH/CH (LCR-BRM-Swissauto); **4** Rolf Biland/Kurt Waltisperg, CH/CH (LCR-BRM-Swissauto); **5** Markus Bösiger/Jurg Egli, CH/CH (LCR-ADM R4); **6** Markus Schlosser/Daniel Hauser, CH/CH (LCR-BRM-Swissauto); **7** Mark Reddington/Andy Hetherington, GB/GB (LCR-ADM R4); **8** Roger Lovelock/Peter Hill, GB/GB (LCR-Yamaha); **9** Stuart Muldoon/Chris Gusman, GB/GB (LCR-ADM R4); **10** Roger Body/Andy Peach, GB/GB (LCR-BRM-Swissauto); **11** Reiner Koster/Oscar Combi, CH/I (LCR-ADM R4).

Fastest lap: S. Webster, 1m 31.297s, 102.123 mph/164.351 km/h.
Championship points: **1** S. Webster, 163; **2** Klaffenböck, 137; **3** Güdel, 130; **4** D. Brindley, 90; **5** Biland, 88; **6** Bösiger, 65.

CIRCUITO DE CARTAGENA, Spain, 26 October. 2.162-mile/3.480-km circuit.
FIM-ISRA Sidecar World Cup, round 9 (26 laps, 56.212 miles/90.480 km)
1 Paul Güdel/Charly Güdel, CH/CH (LCR-BRM-Swissauto), 43m 09.162s, 78.171 mph/125.804 km/h.
2 Derek Brindley/Adolf Hänni, GB/CH (LCR-ADM R4); **3** Markus Bösiger/Jurg Egli, CH/CH (LCR-ADM R4); **4** Markus Schlosser/Daniel Hauser, CH/CH (LCR-BRM-Swissauto); **5** Klaus Klaffenböck/Christian Parzer, A/A (LCR-ADM R4); **6** Mark Reddington/Andy Hetherington, GB/GB (LCR-ADM R4); **7** Markus Neumann/Peter Höss, D/D (LCR-ADM R4).
Fastest lap: Steve Webster/David James, GB/GB (LCR-ADM R4), 1m 37.351s, 79.964 mph/128.689 km/h.

Final Sidecar World Cup Championship points

1	Steve Webster, GB	163
2	Paul Güdel, CH	155
3	Klaus Klaffenböck, A	148
4	Derek Brindley, GB	110
5	Rolf Biland, CH	88
6	Markus Bösiger, CH	81

7 Markus Schlosser, CH, 69; **8** Mark Reddington, GB, 60; **9** Stuart Muldoon, GB, 47; **10** Markus Neumann, D, 33; **11** Roger Body, GB, 28; **12** Kevin Webster, GB, 27; **13** Roger Lovelock, GB, 24; **14** Dave Molyneux, GB, 16; **15=**Reiner Koster, CH and Jari Nikkanen, SF, 14.

AMA National Championship Road Race Series (Superbike)

PHOENIX INTERNATIONAL RACEWAY, Goodyear, Arizona, 16 February 1997. 52.120 miles/83.879 km
1 Mat Mladin (Ducati); **2** Miguel DuHamel (Honda); **3** Doug Chandler (Kawasaki); **4** Pascal Picotte (Suzuki); **5** Thomas Wilson Jnr (Harley-Davidson); **6** Steve Crevier (Honda); **7** Larry Pegram (Suzuki); **8** Aaron Yates (Suzuki); **9** Tripp Nobles (Harley-Davidson); **10** Tommy Hayden (Kawasaki).

DAYTONA INTERNATIONAL SPEEDWAY, Daytona Beach, Florida, 9 March 1997. 200 miles/321.869 km
1 Scott Russell (Yamaha); **2** Doug Chandler (Kawasaki); **3** Colin Edwards (Yamaha); **4** Steve Crevier (Honda); **5** Pascal Picotte (Suzuki); **6** Tom Kipp (Yamaha); **7** Miguel DuHamel (Honda); **8** Larry Pegram (Suzuki); **9** Aaron Yates (Suzuki); **10** Paul Harrell (Yamaha).

LAGUNA SECA RACEWAY, Monterey, California, 20 April 1997. 66.640 miles/107.247 km
1 Doug Chandler (Kawasaki); **2** Mat Mladin (Ducati); **3** Miguel DuHamel (Honda); **4** Steve Crevier (Honda); **5** Ben Bostrom (Honda); **6** Pascal Picotte (Suzuki); **7** Chris Carr (Harley-Davidson); **8** Aaron Yates (Suzuki); **9** Thomas Stevens (Ducati); **10** Tommy Hayden (Kawasaki).

ROAD AMERICA, Elkhart Lake, Wisconsin, 8 June 1997. 64 miles/102.998 km
1 Mat Mladin (Ducati); **2** Doug Chandler (Kawasaki); **3** Aaron Yates (Suzuki); **4** Miguel DuHamel (Honda); **5** Steve Crevier (Honda); **6** Pascal Picotte (Suzuki); **7** Tom Kipp (Yamaha); **8** Ben Bostrom (Honda); **9** Larry Pegram (Suzuki); **10** Gerald Rothman Jnr (Ducati).

NEW HAMPSHIRE INTERNATIONAL SPEEDWAY, Loudon, New Hampshire, 15 June 1997. 62.400 miles/100.423 km
1 Mat Mladin (Ducati); **2** Aaron Yates (Suzuki); **3** Steve Crevier (Honda); **4** Doug Chandler (Kawasaki); **5** Tom Kipp (Yamaha); **6** Pascal Picotte (Suzuki); **7** Chris Carr (Harley-Davidson); **8** Gerald Rothman Jnr (Ducati); **9** Larry Pegram (Suzuki); **10** Tripp Nobles (Harley-Davidson).

BRAINERD INTERNATIONAL RACEWAY, Brainerd, Minnesota, 29 June 1997. 63 miles/101.389 km
1 Miguel DuHamel (Honda); **2** Tom Kipp (Yamaha); **3** Mat Mladin (Ducati); **4** Pascal Picotte (Suzuki); **5** Doug Chandler (Kawasaki); **6** Steve Crevier (Honda); **7** Thomas Stevens (Ducati); **8** Aaron Yates (Suzuki); **9** Larry Pegram (Suzuki); **10** Tommy Hayden (Kawasaki).

MID-OHIO SPORTS CAR COURSE, Lexington, Ohio, 20 July 1997. 62.400 miles/100.423 km
1 Miguel DuHamel (Honda); **2** Doug Chandler (Kawasaki); **3** Aaron Yates (Suzuki); **4** Mat Mladin (Ducati); **5** Pascal Picotte (Suzuki); **6** Tom Kipp (Yamaha); **7** Thomas Wilson Jnr (Harley-Davidson); **8** Steve Crevier (Honda); **9** Ben Bostrom (Honda); **10** Tommy Hayden (Kawasaki).

PIKES PEAK INTERNATIONAL RACEWAY, Fountain, Colorado, 17 August 1997. 62.400 miles/100.423 km
1 Miguel DuHamel (Honda); **2** Doug Chandler (Kawasaki); **3** Tom Kipp (Yamaha); **4** Mat Mladin (Ducati); **5** Steve Crevier (Honda); **6** Pascal Picotte (Suzuki); **7** Aaron Yates (Suzuki); **8** Thomas Wilson Jnr (Harley-Davidson); **9** Thomas Stevens (Ducati); **10** Chris Carr (Harley-Davidson).

SEARS POINT RACEWAY, Sonoma, California, 31 August 1997. 63 miles/101.389 km
1 Miguel DuHamel (Honda); **2** Steve Crevier (Honda); **3** Pascal Picotte (Suzuki); **4** Doug Chandler (Kawasaki); **5** Tom Kipp (Yamaha); **6** Mat Mladin (Ducati); **7** Jason Pridmore (Suzuki); **8** Thomas Stevens (Ducati); **9** Rich Oliver (Yamaha); **10** Larry Pegram (Suzuki).

LAS VEGAS MOTOR SPEEDWAY, Las Vegas, Nevada, 5 October 1997. 62 miles/99.779 km
1 Mat Mladin (Ducati); **2** Miguel DuHamel (Honda); **3** Aaron Yates (Suzuki); **4** Thomas Stevens (Ducati); **5** Steve Crevier (Honda); **6** Christer Lindholm (Ducati); **7** Tom Kipp (Yamaha); **8** Doug Chandler (Kawasaki); **9** Chris Carr (Harley-Davidson); **10** Larry Pegram (Suzuki).

Final Championship points

1	Doug Chandler	304
2	Miguel DuHamel	292
3	Mat Mladin	288
4	Steve Crevier	269
5	Aaron Yates	239

6 Pascal Picotte, 239; **7** Tom Kipp, 213; **8** Larry Pegram, 186; **9** Paul Harrell, 159; **10** Tripp Nobles, 151.

Isle of Man Tourist Trophy Races

ISLE OF MAN TOURIST TROPHY COURSE, 26 May-6 June. 37.73-mile/60.72-km course
Lancaster Insurance Services Formula One TT (6 laps, 226.38 miles/364.32 km)
1 Phillip McCallen (Honda RC45), 1h 53m 16.8s, 119.90 mph/192.96 km/h.
2 Michael Rutter (Honda RVF750), 1h 54m 52.5s; **3** Bob Jackson (Kawasaki 750), 1h 55m 03.2s; **4** Ian Simpson (Honda RC45), 1h 55m 05.6s; **5** Marc Flynn (Honda RC45), 1h 55m 59.7s; **6** Joey Dunlop (Honda RC45), 1h 56m 29.4s; **7** Alan Bennallick (Honda RC30), 1h 57m 50.4s; **8** David Goodley (Kawasaki 750), 1h 58m 24.1s; **9** Simon Beck (Kawasaki 750), 1h 59m 38.5s; **10** Paul Orritt (Yamaha 750), 2h 00m 16.7s; **11** Dave Leach (Kawasaki 750), 2h 01m 23.5s; **12** David Madsen-Mygdal (Kawasaki 750), 2h 01m 50.8s.
Fastest lap: McCallen, 18m 24.4s, 122.98 mph/197.92 km/h.

'The People' Lightweight TT (4 laps, 150.92 miles/242.88 km)
1 Joey Dunlop (Honda RS250R), 1h 18m 20.1s, 115.59 mph/186.02 km/h.
2 Ian Lougher (Honda RS250), 1h 19m 07.0s; **3** John McGuiness (Aprilia RSV 250), 1h 19m 08.4s; **4** Shaun Harris (Yamaha 250), 1h 19m 10.7s; **5** Gary Dynes (Honda RS250), 1h 19m 31.9s; **6** Derek Young (Honda RS250R), 1h 19m 49.3s; **7** Ian Simpson (Honda RS250), 1h 20m 05.3s; **8** Richard Coates (Yamaha TZ250), 1h 20m 26.7s; **9** Jason Griffiths (Honda RS250), 1h 21m 09.6s; **10** Neil Richardson (Honda RS250), 1h 21m 17.0s; **11** Ashley Law (Honda RS250), 1h 21m 30.7s; **12** Tony Duncan (Yamaha TZ250), 1h 21m 43.6s; **13** Owen McNally (Aprilia 250), 1h 21m 57.6s; **14** Stanley Rea (Honda RS250), 1h 22m 17.3s.
Fastest lap: McGuiness, 19m 22.6s, 116.83 mph/188.02 km/h.

Ultra-Lightweight TT (4 laps, 150.92 miles/242.88 km)
1 Ian Lougher (Honda 125), 1h 23m 55.4s, 107.89 mph/173.63 km/h.
2 Denis McCullough (Honda 125), 1h 23m 57.5s; **3** Robert Dunlop (Honda 125), 1h 24m 30.9s; **4** Glen English (Honda 125), 1h 24m 37.9s; **5** Owen McNally (Honda 125), 1h 25m 13.0s; **6** Gavin Lee (Honda 125), 1h 25m 15.2s; **7** Gary Dynes (Honda 125), 1h 25m 51.0s; **8** Noel Clegg (Honda 125), 1h 26m 13.9s; **9** Chris Richardson (Honda 125), 1h 26m 18.0s.
Fastest lap: Lougher, 20m 43.2s, 109.25 mph/175.82 km/h (record).

Single Cylinder TT (4 laps, 150.92 miles/242.88 km)
1 David Morris (BMW F650), 1h 21m 58.2s, 110.46 mph/177.77 km/h.
2 John Barton (Ducati 598), 1h 23m 37.6s; **3** Steve Linsdell (Yamaha 680), 1h 24m 01.5s; **4** Johannes Kehrer (MUZ Skorpion), 1h 24m 08.3s; **5** Danny Shimmin (Matchless 648), 1h 27m 33.0s.
Fastest lap: Morris, 20m 11.9s, 112.07 mph/180.36 km/h.

Junior TT (4 laps, 150.92 miles/242.88 km)
1 Ian Simpson (Honda CBR600), 1h 16m 28.3s, 118.41 mph/190.56 km/h.
2 Phillip McCallen (Honda 600), 1h 16m 57.8s; **3** Michael Rutter (Honda 600), 1h 17m 21.7s; **4** Derek Young (Honda 600), 1h 17m 21.9s; **5** Joey Dunlop (Honda 600), 1m 17m 42.6s; **6** Bob Jackson (Honda 600), 1h 17m 51.6s; **7** Adrian Archibald (Honda 600), 1h 18m 07.9s; **8** Paul Dedman (Kawasaki ZX-6R), 1h 18m 51.0s; **9** Simon Beck (Honda 600), 1h 18m 56.4s; **10** Thomas Montano (Honda CBR600), 1h 19m 10.4s; **11** Jim Moodie (Suzuki GSX-R600V), 1h 19m 16.6s; **12** Simon Smith (Honda CBR600), 1h 19m 22.0s; **13** Chris Heath (Honda 600), 1h 20m 01.2s.
Fastest lap: Simpson, 18m 53.2s, 119.86 mph/192.90 km/h (record).

Sega Production TT (2 laps, 75.46 miles/121.44 km)
1 Phillip McCallen (Honda CBR900), 38m 39.4s, 117.12 mph/188.49 km/h.
2 Ian Simpson (Ducati 916), 38m 47.0s; **3** Simon Beck (Honda 900 Fireblade), 39m 08.3s; **4** Marc Flynn (Suzuki GSX-R750), 39m 28.9s; **5** Jim Hodson (Yamaha YZF1000), 39m 30.2s; **6** Derek Young (Honda CBR900RR), 39m 34.5s; **7** Alan Bennallick (Honda 900 Fireblade), 39m 35.8s; **8** Paul Hunt (Yamaha YZF1000), 39m 41.4s; **9** Michael Rutter (Honda CBR900RR), 39m 43.5s; **10** Jim Moodie (Suzuki GSX-R750), 39m 59.8s; **11** Dennis Winterbottom (Bimota YB11 1000), 40m 00.3s; **12** Chris Heath (Honda CBR900), 40m 06.1s; **13** Adrian Archibald (Honda CBR900), 40m 13.4s.
Fastest lap: McCallen, 19m 15.6s, 117.53 mph/189.15 km/h.

A. McAlpine Construction (IOM) Senior TT (6 laps, 226.38 miles/364.32 km)
1 Phillip McCallen (Honda RC45), 1h 53m 36.6s, 119.55 mph/192.40 km/h.
2 Jim Moodie (Honda V-twin), 1h 53m 45.3s; **3** Ian Simpson (Honda RC45), 1h 54m 30.2s; **4** Bob Jackson (Kawasaki 750), 1h 54m 50.6s; **5** Simon Beck (Kawasaki 750), 1h 55m 04.4s; **6** Derek Young (Honda RC45), 1h 55m 28.5s; **7** Joey Dunlop (Honda RC45), 1h 56m 01.3s; **8** David Goodley (Kawasaki 750), 1h 56m 04.0s; **9** Alan Bennallick (Honda RC30), 1h 57m 12.7s; **10** Chris Heath (Honda 600), 1h 58m 00.3s; **11** Adrian Archibald (Honda 600), 1h 58m 13.6s; **12** Paul Dedman (Kawasaki ZX-6R), 1h 58m 29.6s; **13** Steve Linsdell (Yamaha), 1h 58m 51.1s.
Fastest lap: McCallen, 18m 31.3s, 122.22 mph/196.69 km/h.

Sidecar TT: Race A (3 laps, 113.19 miles/182.16 km)
1 Roy Hanks/Phillip Biggs (Ireson NRH), 1h 03m 29.7s, 106.95 mph/172.12 km/h.
2 Vince Biggs/Graham Biggs (Molyneux Yamaha 600), 1h 03m 31.9s; **3** Tom Hanks/Steve Wilson (Hanks Yamaha), 1h 03m 37.1s; **4** John Holden/Ian Watson (Jacobs 600), 1h 03m 52.8s; **5** Kenny Howles/Doug Jewell (Ireson Yamaha), 1h 04m 02.5s; **6** Allan Schofield/Andrew Thornton (Astra Yamaha 600), 1h 04m 17.8s; **7** Gary Horspole/Kevin Leigh (Shelbourne Honda), 1h 04m 24.8s; **8** Geoff Bell/Lee Farrington (Bell Yamaha), 1h 05m 09.0s; **9** Steve Norbury/Andrew Smith (Shelbourne Yamaha), 1h 06m 03.4s; **10** Joe Martin/Kate Harrington (Windle Yamaha), 1h 06m 11.4s; **11** Rob Cameron/Paul Randall (Hartgate Honda), 1h 06m 11.8s; **12** Mick Boddice Jnr/Chris Hollis (Windle Honda), 1h 06m 39.6s; **13** Lars Schwartz/Colin Hardman (Ireson Yamaha), 1h 06m 52.4s.
Fastest lap: Rob Fisher/Rick Long (Baker Yamaha), 20m 43.5s, 109.23 mph/175.79 km/h.

Sidecar TT: Race B (3 laps, 113.19 miles/182.16 km)
1 Rob Fisher/Rick Long (Baker Yamaha), 1h 01m 47.8s, 109.89 mph/176.85 km/h.
2 Tom Hanks/Steve Wilson (Hanks Yamaha), 1h 02m 52.2s; **3** Ian Bell/Neil Carpenter (Bell Yamaha), 1h 03m 05.6s; **4** Roy Hanks/Phillip Biggs (Ireson NRH), 1h 03m 25.0s; **5** Gary Horspole/Kevin Leigh (Shelbourne Honda), 1h 03m 56.8s; **6** John Holden/Ian Watson (Jacobs 600), 1h 04m 03.4s; **7** Rob Cameron/Paul Randall (Hartgate Honda), 1h 04m 12.7s; **8** Mick Boddice Snr/Dave Wells (Honda 600), 1h 04m 29.8s; **9** Geoff Bell/Lee Farrington (Bell Yamaha), 1h 05m 00.0s; **10** Steve Norbury/Andrew Smith (Shelbourne Yamaha), 1h 05m 41.9s; **11** Joe Martin/Kate Harrington (Windle Yamaha), 1h 05m 51.4s; **12** Tony Baker/Ian Simons (Baker Yamaha), 1h 06m 43.2s; **13** Eddy Wright/Rod Pearce (Windle), 1h 06m 50.9s.
Fastest lap: Fisher/Long, 20m 29.7s, 110.45 mph/177.75 km/h.

Motor Cycle News British Superbike Championship

DONINGTON PARK GRAND PRIX CIRCUIT, 13 April. 2.500-mile/4.023-km circuit.
MCN British Superbike Championship, round 1 (2 x 15 laps, 37.500 miles/60.345 km)
Race 1
1 Niall Mackenzie (Yamaha), 24m 05.290s, 93.40 mph/150.32 km/h.
2 John Reynolds (Ducati); **3** Steve Hislop (Ducati); **4** Chris Walker (Yamaha); **5** Jim Moodie (Suzuki); **6** Terry Rymer (Kawasaki); **7** Sean Emmett (Ducati); **8** Iain Macpherson (Kawasaki); **9** Michael Rutter (Honda); **10** Ray Stringer (Kawasaki); **11** Andy Hatton (Ducati); **12** Dean Ashton (Ducati); **13** Andrew Ward (Ducati); **14** Roger Bennett (Kawasaki); **15** Darren Dixon (Kawasaki).
Fastest lap: Reynolds, 1m 35.382s, 94.35 mph/151.85 km/h.

Race 2
1 Niall Mackenzie (Yamaha), 24m 12.727s, 92.92 mph/149.55 km/h.
2 Chris Walker (Yamaha); **3** Sean Emmett (Ducati); **4** Terry Rymer (Kawasaki); **5** Jim Moodie (Suzuki); **6** Michael Rutter (Honda); **7** Matt Llewellyn (Suzuki); **8** Dean Ashton (Ducati); **9** Ray Stringer (Kawasaki); **10** Andrew Ward (Ducati); **11** Brett Sampson (Kawasaki); **12** Graham Ward (Kawasaki); **13** Colin Hipwell (Kawasaki); **14** Nigel Nottingham (Yamaha); **15** Jon Ward (Ducati).
Fastest lap: Mackenzie, 1m 35.782s, 93.96 mph/151.21 km/h.
Championship points: **1** Mackenzie, 50; **2** Walker, 33; **3** Emmett, 25; **4** Rymer, 23; **5** Moodie, 22; **6** Reynolds, 20.

OULTON PARK CIRCUIT, 27 April. 2.769-mile/4.458-km circuit.
MCN British Superbike Championship, round 2 (2 x 15 laps, 41.535 miles/66.870 km)
Race 1
1 Chris Walker (Yamaha), 24m 05.915s, 103.41 mph/166.42 km/h.
2 John Reynolds (Ducati); **3** Terry Rymer (Kawasaki); **4** Sean Emmett (Ducati); **5** Niall Mackenzie (Yamaha); **6** Matt Llewellyn (Suzuki); **7** Jim Moodie (Suzuki); **8** Michael Rutter (Honda); **9** Iain Macpherson (Kawasaki); **10** Ray Stringer (Kawasaki); **11** Andy Hatton (Ducati); **12** Graham Ward (Kawasaki); **13** Brett Sampson (Kawasaki); **14** Andrew Ward (Ducati); **15** Roger Bennett (Kawasaki).
Fastest lap: Reynolds, 1m 35.301s, 104.59 mph/168.33 km/h.

Race 2
1 John Reynolds (Ducati), 24m 03.863s, 103.55 mph/166.66 km/h.
2 Terry Rymer (Kawasaki); **3** Niall Mackenzie (Yamaha); **4** Steve Hislop (Ducati); **5** Sean Emmett (Ducati); **6** Matt Llewellyn (Suzuki); **7** Jim Moodie (Suzuki); **8** Iain Macpherson (Kawasaki); **9** Ray Stringer (Kawasaki); **10** Brett Sampson (Kawasaki); **11** Andy Hatton (Ducati); **12** Dean Ashton (Ducati); **13** Graham Ward (Kawasaki); **14** Darren Dixon (Kawasaki); **15** Nigel Nottingham (Yamaha).
Fastest lap: Mackenzie, 1m 34.603, 105.37 mph/169.57 km/h (record).
Championship points: **1** Mackenzie, 77; **2** Reynolds, 65; **3** Rymer, 59; **4** Walker, 58; **5** Emmett, 49; **6** Moodie, 40.

SNETTERTON CIRCUIT, 11 May. 1.952-mile/3.141-km circuit.
MCN British Superbike Championship, round 3
Race 1 (18 laps, 35.136 miles/56.538 km)
1 Niall Mackenzie (Yamaha), 20m 45.073s, 101.59 mph/163.49 km/h.
2 Chris Walker (Yamaha); **3** Michael Rutter (Honda); **4** Matt Llewellyn (Suzuki); **5** Jim Moodie (Suzuki); **6** Brian Morrison (Kawasaki); **7** Sean Emmett (Ducati); **8** John Reynolds (Ducati); **9** Andy Hatton (Ducati); **10** Lee Dickinson (Kawasaki); **11** Ray Stringer (Kawasaki); **12** Andrew Ward (Ducati); **13** Steve Hislop (Ducati); **14** Dean Ashton (Ducati); **15** Neil Cray (Kawasaki).
Fastest lap: Mackenzie, 1m 07.948s, 103.42 mph/166.43 km/h (record).

Race 2 (15 laps, 29.280 miles/47.115 km)
1 Chris Walker (Yamaha), 17m 32.165s, 100.18 mph/161.22 km/h.
2 Niall Mackenzie (Yamaha); **3** Matt Llewellyn (Suzuki); **4** Jim Moodie (Suzuki); **5** Sean Emmett (Ducati); **6** Brian Morrison (Kawasaki); **7** Andy Hatton (Ducati); **8** Ray Stringer (Kawasaki); **9** Michael Rutter (Honda); **10** Tom Knight (Ducati); **11** Darren Dixon (Kawasaki); **12** Dean Ashton (Ducati); **13** Colin Hipwell (Kawasaki); **14** David Higgins (Suzuki).
Fastest lap: Mackenzie, 1m 08.926s, 101.95 mph/164.07 km/h.
Championship points: **1** Mackenzie, 122; **2** Walker, 103; **3** Reynolds, 73; **4** Emmett, 69; **5** Moodie, 64; **6** Rymer, 59.

BRANDS HATCH INDY CIRCUIT, 22 June. 1.2036-mile/1.937-km circuit.
MCN British Superbike Championship, round 4 (2 x 24 laps, 28.886 miles/46.488 km)
Race 1
1 Sean Emmett (Ducati), 21m 15.831s, 81.50 mph/131.17 km/h.
2 Chris Walker (Yamaha); **3** Terry Rymer (Kawasaki); **4** Michael Rutter (Honda); **5** Iain Macpherson (Kawasaki); **6** Dean Ashton (Ducati); **7** Andrew Ward (Ducati); **8** Niall Mackenzie (Yamaha); **9** Darren Dixon (Kawasaki); **10** Matt Llewellyn (Suzuki); **11** Steve Hislop (Ducati); **12** Brett Sampson (Kawasaki); **13** Andy Hatton (Ducati); **14** Steve Marks (Kawasaki); **15** David Higgins (Suzuki).
Fastest lap: Emmett, 50.732s, 85.40 mph/137.45 km/h.

Race 2
1 John Reynolds (Ducati), 21m 08.043s, 82.00 mph/131.98 km/h.
2 Michael Rutter (Honda); **3** Iain Macpherson (Kawasaki); **4** Niall Mackenzie (Yamaha); **5** Chris Walker (Yamaha); **6** Sean Emmett (Ducati); **7** Steve Hislop (Ducati); **8** Jim Moodie (Suzuki); **9** Darren Dixon (Kawasaki); **10** Brett Sampson (Kawasaki); **11** Andrew Ward (Ducati); **12** Dean Ashton (Ducati); **13** Matt Llewellyn (Suzuki); **14** Ray Stringer (Kawasaki); **15** Graham Ward (Kawasaki).
Fastest lap: Reynolds, 50.952s, 85.04 mph/136.85 km/h.
Championship points: **1** Mackenzie, 143; **2** Walker, 134; **3** Emmett, 104; **4** Reynolds, 98; **5** Rutter, 81; **6** Rymer, 75.

THRUXTON CIRCUIT, 6 July. 2.356-mile/3.792-km circuit.
MCN British Superbike Championship, round 5 (2 x 17 laps, 40.052 miles/64.464 km)
Race 1
1 Niall Mackenzie (Yamaha), 22m 26.700s, 107.06 mph/172.30 km/h.
2 Terry Rymer (Kawasaki); **3** Chris Walker (Yamaha); **4** Iain Macpherson (Kawasaki); **5** John Reynolds (Ducati); **6** Jim Moodie (Suzuki); **7** Michael Rutter (Honda); **8** Matt Llewellyn (Suzuki); **9** Ray Stringer (Kawasaki); **10** Brett Sampson (Kawasaki); **11** Graham Ward (Kawasaki); **12** Steve Hislop (Ducati); **13** Peter Graves (Ducati); **14** Andrew Ward (Ducati); **15** Tom Knight (Ducati).

Fastest lap: Mackenzie, 1m 18.291s, 108.33 mph/174.34 km/h (record).

Race 2
1 Niall Mackenzie (Yamaha), 22m 31.193s, 106.71 mph/171.73 km/h.
2 Terry Rymer (Kawasaki); 3 John Reynolds (Ducati); 4 Iain Macpherson (Kawasaki); 5 Chris Walker (Yamaha); 6 Jim Moodie (Suzuki); 7 Sean Emmett (Ducati); 8 Matt Llewellyn (Suzuki); 9 Ray Stringer (Kawasaki); 10 Michael Rutter (Honda); 11 Graham Ward (Kawasaki); 12 Brett Sampson (Kawasaki); 13 Jim Hodson (Kawasaki); 14 Andrew Ward (Ducati); 15 Dean Ashton (Ducati).
Fastest lap: Mackenzie, 1m 18.527s, 108.00 mph/173.82 km/h.
Championship points: 1 Mackenzie, 193; 2 Walker, 161; 3 Reynolds, 125; 4 Rymer, 115; 5 Emmett, 113; 6 Rutter, 96.

OULTON PARK CIRCUIT, 20 July. 2.769-mile/4.458-km circuit.
MCN British Superbike Championship, round 6 (2 x 15 laps, 41.535 miles/66.870 km)
Race 1
1 Niall Mackenzie (Yamaha), 23m 54.184s, 104.25 mph/167.78 km/h.
2 John Reynolds (Ducati); 3 Chris Walker (Yamaha); 4 Michael Rutter (Honda); 5 Matt Llewellyn (Suzuki); 6 Jim Moodie (Suzuki); 7 Ray Stringer (Kawasaki); 8 Ian Simpson (Ducati); 9 Brett Sampson (Kawasaki); 10 Graham Ward (Kawasaki); 11 Peter Graves (Ducati); 12 Darren Dixon (Kawasaki); 13 Andrew Ward (Ducati); 14 Jim Hodson (Kawasaki); 15 Colin Hipwell (Kawasaki).
Fastest lap: Mackenzie, 1m 34.767s, 105.18 mph/169.28 km/h.

Race 2
1 Niall Mackenzie (Yamaha), 23m 54.694s, 104.22 mph/167.72 km/h.
2 John Reynolds (Ducati); 3 Chris Walker (Yamaha); 4 Michael Rutter (Honda); 5 Iain Macpherson (Kawasaki); 6 Sean Emmett (Ducati); 7 Jim Moodie (Suzuki); 8 Matt Llewellyn (Suzuki); 9 Ray Stringer (Kawasaki); 10 Brett Sampson (Kawasaki); 11 Peter Graves (Ducati); 12 Andrew Ward (Ducati); 13 Darren Dixon (Kawasaki); 14 Lee Dickinson (Kawasaki); 15 James Bunton (Yamaha).
Fastest lap: Reynolds, 1m 34.653s, 105.31 mph/169.48 km/h.
Championship points: 1 Mackenzie, 243; 2 Walker, 193; 3 Reynolds, 165; 4 Emmett, 123; 5 Rutter, 122; 6 Rymer, 115.

MALLORY PARK CIRCUIT, 27 July. 1.370-mile/2.205-km circuit.
MCN British Superbike Championship, round 7
Race 1 (23 laps, 31.510 miles/46.575 km)
1 Niall Mackenzie (Yamaha), 18m 52.920s, 100.12 mph/161.13 km/h.
2 Iain Macpherson (Kawasaki); 3 Steve Hislop (Kawasaki); 4 Sean Emmett (Ducati); 5 Jim Moodie (Suzuki); 6 Chris Walker (Yamaha); 7 Ray Stringer (Kawasaki); 8 Michael Rutter (Honda); 9 Ian Simpson (Ducati); 10 Dean Ashton (Ducati); 11 Graham Ward (Kawasaki); 12 Lee Dickinson (Kawasaki); 13 Darren Dixon (Kawasaki); 14 Peter Graves (Ducati); 15 Steve Marks (Kawasaki).
Fastest lap: Mackenzie, 48.625s, 101.42 mph/163.23 km/h.

Race 2 (17 laps, 23.290 miles/37.485 km)
1 Niall Mackenzie (Yamaha), 13m 57.004s, 100.17 mph/161.21 km/h.
2 Steve Hislop (Kawasaki); 3 Chris Walker (Yamaha); 4 Michael Rutter (Honda); 5 Jim Moodie (Suzuki); 6 Ray Stringer (Kawasaki); 7 Ian Simpson (Ducati); 8 Brett Sampson (Kawasaki); 9 Dean Ashton (Ducati); 10 Lee Dickinson (Kawasaki); 11 Andrew Ward (Ducati); 12 Peter Graves (Ducati); 13 Steve Marks (Kawasaki); 14 Darren Dixon (Kawasaki); 15 Colin Hipwell (Kawasaki).
Fastest lap: Mackenzie, 48.754s, 101.16 mph/162.80 km/h.
Championship points: 1 Mackenzie, 293; 2 Walker, 219; 3 Reynolds, 165; 4 Rutter, 143; 5 Emmett, 136; 6 Moodie, 133.

KNOCKHILL CIRCUIT, 10 August. 1.300-mile/2.092-km circuit.
MCN British Superbike Championship, round 8 (2 x 24 laps, 31.200 miles/50.208 km)
Race 1
1 Iain Macpherson (Kawasaki), 20m 59.908s, 89.14 mph/143.47 km/h.
2 Steve Hislop (Kawasaki); 3 Michael Rutter (Honda); 4 Chris Walker (Yamaha); 5 Terry Rymer (Kawasaki); 6 Ian Simpson (Ducati); 7 David Jefferies (Ducati); 8 Ray Stringer (Kawasaki); 9 Andrew Ward (Ducati); 10 Brett Sampson (Kawasaki); 11 Nigel Nottingham (Yamaha); 12 Colin Hipwell (Kawasaki).
Fastest lap: Macpherson, 51.945s, 90.09 mph/144.99 km/h.

Race 2
1 Niall Mackenzie (Yamaha), 20m 57.778s, 89.30 mph/143.71 km/h.
2 Chris Walker (Yamaha); 3 Iain Macpherson (Kawasaki); 4 Steve Hislop (Kawasaki); 5 Matt Llewellyn (Suzuki); 6 Terry Rymer (Kawasaki); 7 Jim Moodie (Suzuki); 8 Ian Simpson (Ducati); 9 Ray Stringer (Kawasaki); 10 David Jefferies (Ducati); 11 Andrew Ward (Ducati); 12 Brett Sampson (Kawasaki); 13 Roger Bennett (Kawasaki); 14 Colin Hipwell (Kawasaki).
Fastest lap: Mackenzie, 51.574s, 90.74 mph/146.03 km/h (record).

Championship points: 1 Mackenzie, 318; 2 Walker, 252; 3 Reynolds, 165; 4 Rutter, 159; 5 Macpherson, 148; 6 Moodie, 142.

CADWELL PARK CIRCUIT, 25 August. 2.170-mile/3.472-km circuit.
MCN British Superbike Championship, round 9
Race 1 (18 laps, 39.060 miles/62.496 km)
1 Ian Simpson (Ducati), 28m 51.723s, 81.20 mph/130.67 km/h.
2 Michael Rutter (Honda); 3 Terry Rymer (Kawasaki); 4 Iain Macpherson (Kawasaki); 5 Chris Walker (Yamaha); 6 Sean Emmett (Ducati); 7 Niall Mackenzie (Yamaha); 8 Jim Moodie (Suzuki); 9 Andrew Ward (Ducati); 10 Ray Stringer (Kawasaki); 11 Matt Llewellyn (Suzuki); 12 Dean Ashton (Ducati); 13 Brett Sampson (Kawasaki); 14 Jim Hodson (Kawasaki); 15 Scott Hanney (Suzuki).
Fastest lap: Rutter, 1m 34.982s, 82.24 mph/132.36 km/h.

Race 2 (16 laps, 34.720 miles/55.552 km)
1 Michael Rutter (Honda), 25m 29.822s, 81.70 mph/131.48 km/h.
2 Chris Walker (Yamaha); 3 Sean Emmett (Ducati); 4 Iain Macpherson (Kawasaki); 5 Ian Simpson (Ducati); 6 David Jefferies (Ducati); 7 Andrew Ward (Ducati); 8 Brett Sampson (Kawasaki); 9 Matt Llewellyn (Suzuki); 10 Ray Stringer (Kawasaki); 11 Colin Hipwell (Kawasaki); 12 Steve Hislop (Kawasaki).
Fastest lap: Macpherson, 1m 32.715s, 84.25 mph/135.60 km/h.
Championship points: 1 Mackenzie, 327; 2 Walker, 283; 3 Rutter, 204; 4 Macpherson, 174; 5 Reynolds, 165; 6 Emmett, 162.

BRANDS HATCH GRAND PRIX CIRCUIT, 14 September. 2.6002-mile/4.185-km circuit.
MCN British Superbike Championship, round 10 (2 x 15 laps, 39.003 miles/62.775 km)
Race 1
1 Niall Mackenzie (Yamaha), 22m 03.222s, 106.11 mph/170.77 km/h.
2 John Reynolds (Ducati); 3 Sean Emmett (Ducati); 4 Michael Rutter (Honda); 5 Terry Rymer (Kawasaki); 6 Jim Moodie (Suzuki); 7 Iain Macpherson (Kawasaki); 8 Steve Hislop (Kawasaki); 9 Ray Stringer (Kawasaki); 10 Ian Simpson (Ducati); 11 Chris Walker (Yamaha); 12 Dave Heal (Honda); 13 David Jefferies (Ducati); 14 Brett Sampson (Kawasaki); 15 Pete Jennings (Kawasaki).
Fastest lap: Reynolds, 1m 27.078s, 107.49 mph/173.00 km/h.

Race 2
1 Niall Mackenzie (Yamaha), 22m 04.962s, 105.97 mph/170.54 km/h.
2 Sean Emmett (Ducati); 3 Chris Walker (Yamaha); 4 John Reynolds (Ducati); 5 Terry Rymer (Kawasaki); 6 Michael Rutter (Honda); 7 Steve Hislop (Kawasaki); 8 Ray Stringer (Kawasaki); 9 Ian Simpson (Ducati); 10 Dave Heal (Honda); 11 David Jefferies (Ducati); 12 Brett Sampson (Kawasaki); 13 Graham Ward (Kawasaki); 14 Andrew Ward (Ducati); 15 Steve Marks (Kawasaki).
Fastest lap: Emmett, 1m 26.874s, 107.75 mph/173.40 km/h.
Championship points: 1 Mackenzie, 377; 2 Walker, 304; 3 Rutter, 227; 4 Emmett and Reynolds, 198; 6 Macpherson, 183.

DONINGTON PARK SHORT CIRCUIT, 28 September. 1.957-mile/3.149-km circuit.
MCN British Superbike Championship, round 11
Race 1 (16 laps, 31.312 miles/50.384 km)
1 Niall Mackenzie (Yamaha), 18m 57.460s, 99.11 mph/159.51 km/h.
2 John Reynolds (Ducati); 3 Chris Walker (Yamaha); 4 Terry Rymer (Kawasaki); 5 Iain Macpherson (Kawasaki); 6 Matt Llewellyn (Suzuki); 7 Michael Rutter (Honda); 8 Steve Hislop (Kawasaki); 9 Dave Heal (Honda); 10 Dean Thomas (Honda); 11 Dean Ashton (Ducati); 12 Brett Sampson (Kawasaki); 13 Graham Ward (Kawasaki); 14 Andrew Ward (Ducati); 15 Roger Bennett (Kawasaki).
Fastest lap: Reynolds, 1m 10.165s, 100.42 mph/161.61 km/h.

Race 2 (15 laps, 29.355 miles/47.235 km)
1 Chris Walker (Yamaha), 17m 40.779s, 99.63 mph/160.35 km/h.
2 Sean Emmett (Ducati); 3 Terry Rymer (Kawasaki); 4 Iain Macpherson (Kawasaki); 5 Matt Llewellyn (Suzuki); 6 Michael Rutter (Honda); 7 John Reynolds (Ducati); 8 Dean Thomas (Honda); 9 Ray Stringer (Kawasaki); 10 Dave Heal (Honda); 11 Brett Sampson (Kawasaki); 12 Andrew Ward (Ducati); 13 Graham Ward (Kawasaki); 14 Juha Berner (Kawasaki); 15 Roger Bennett (Kawasaki).
Fastest lap: Walker, 1m 10.130s, 100.47 mph/161.69 km/h (record).

Final MCN British Superbike Championship points

1	Niall Mackenzie	402
2	Chris Walker	345
3	Michael Rutter	246
4	John Reynolds	227
5	Sean Emmett	218

6 Iain Macpherson, 207; 7 Terry Rymer, 203; 8 Jim Moodie, 190; 9 Steve Hislop, 148; 10 Matt Llewellyn, 146; 11 Ray Stringer, 139; 12=Brett Sampson and Ian Simpson, 91; 14 Andy Ward, 81; 15 Dean Ashton, 59.

Shell Advance British Championship

DONINGTON PARK CIRCUIT, 13 April. 2.500-mile/4.023-km circuit.
Shell Advance 125 cc British Championship, round 1 (18 laps, 45.000 miles/72.414 km)
1 Rodney Fee (Honda), 31m 01.276s, 87.03 mph/140.07 km/h.
2 Fernando Mendes (Honda); 3 Phelim Owens (Honda); 4 Darren Barton (Honda); 5 Robin Appleyard (Honda); 6 Ian Lougher (Honda); 7 Chris Palmer (Honda); 8 Jason Davis (Honda); 9 Damien Cahill (Honda); 10 Gavan Morris (Honda); 11 Steve Patrickson (Honda); 12 Daniel Tarratt (Honda); 13 Paul Robinson (Honda); 14 Nick Sergent (Honda); 15 Tom Tunstall (Honda).
Fastest lap: Fee, 1m 42.174s, 88.08 mph/141.75 km/h.
Championship points: 1 Fee, 25; 2 Mendes, 20; 3 Owens, 16; 4 Barton, 13; 5 Appleyard, 11; 6 Lougher, 10.

Shell Advance 250 cc British Championship, round 1 (2 x 12 laps, 30.000 miles/48.276 km)
Race 1
1 Scott Smart (Honda), 19m 49.057s, 90.82 mph/146.17 km/h.
2 Jason Vincent (Honda); 3 Woolsey Coulter (Aprilia); 4 Steve Sawford (Honda); 5 John McGuiness (Aprilia); 6 Callum Ramsay (Honda); 7 Shane Norval (Honda); 8 Gary May (Yamaha); 9 Adrian Clarke (Honda); 10 Robin Milton (Honda); 11 Mark Coates (Honda); 12 Dean Johnson (Honda); 13 John Creith (Honda); 14 G. Winterbottom (Honda); 15 Philip Stead (Yamaha).
Fastest lap: Vincent, 1m 38.117s, 91.72 mph/147.62 km/h.

Race 2
1 Scott Smart (Honda), 19m 39.366s, 91.57 mph/147.37 km/h.
2 Jason Vincent (Honda); 3 Steve Sawford (Honda); 4 John McGuiness (Aprilia); 5 Mark Coates (Honda); 6 Robin Milton (Honda); 7 Shane Norval (Honda); 8 Gary May (Yamaha); 9 Callum Ramsay (Honda); 10 Adrian Clarke (Honda); 11 Dean Johnson (Honda); 12 John Creith (Honda); 13 Mark Chapman (Yamaha); 14 John Pearson (Honda); 15 Philip Stead (Yamaha).
Fastest lap: Smart, 1m 37.260s, 92.53 mph/148.92 km/h.
Championship points: 1 Smart, 50; 2 Vincent, 40; 3 Sawford, 29; 4 McGuiness, 24; 5 Norval, 18; 6 Ramsay, 17.

Shell Advance Supersport 600 Championship, round 1 (18 laps, 45.000 miles/72.414 km)
1 Phillip McCallen (Honda), 30m 24.845s, 88.77 mph/142.86 km/h.
2 Dean Thomas (Honda); 3 Jim Moodie (Suzuki); 4 David Wood (Kawasaki); 5 Dave Heal (Honda); 6 Pete Jennings (Honda); 7 Iain Duffus (Honda); 8 Paul Brown (Honda); 9 Phil Borley (Honda); 10 Phil Giles (Yamaha); 11 Mark Wainwright (Honda); 12 Adam Lewis (Yamaha); 13 Steve Plater (Honda); 14 Andy Tinsley (Honda); 15 Simon Smith (Honda).
Fastest lap: McCallen, 1m 40.016s, 89.98 mph/144.81 km/h.
Championship points: 1 McCallen, 25; 2 Thomas, 20; 3 Moodie, 16; 4 Wood, 13; 5 Heal, 11; 6 Jennings, 10.

OULTON PARK CIRCUIT, 27 April. 2.769-mile/4.458-km circuit.
Shell Advance 125 cc British Championship, round 2 (18 laps, 49.842 miles/80.244 km)
1 Fernando Mendes (Honda), 31m 44.946s, 94.19 mph/151.58 km/h.
2 Jason Davis (Honda); 3 Phelim Owens (Honda); 4 Darren Barton (Honda); 5 Steve Patrickson (Honda); 6 Darran Gawley (Aprilia); 7 Chris Burns (Honda); 8 Gavan Morris (Honda); 9 Chris Palmer (Honda); 10 Alan Green (Honda); 11 Andi Notman (Honda); 12 Ian Lougher (Honda); 13 Tom Tunstall (Honda); 14 David Dawson (Honda); 15 Daniel Tarratt (Honda).
Fastest lap: Mendes, 1m 44.445s, 95.44 mph/153.59 km/h.
Championship points: 1 Mendes, 45; 2 Owens, 32; 3 Davis, 28; 4 Barton, 26; 5 Fee, 25; 6 Palmer and Patrickson, 16.

Shell Advance 250 cc British Championship, round 2 (18 laps, 49.842 miles/80.244 km)
1 Scott Smart (Honda), 30m 02.574s, 99.54 mph/160.19 km/h.
2 Mark Coates (Honda); 3 Steve Sawford (Honda); 4 Robin Milton (Honda); 5 Fernando Mendes (Honda); 6 Adrian Clarke (Honda); 7 Callum Ramsay (Honda); 8 G. Winterbottom (Honda); 9 Lee Masters (Honda); 10 Adrian Coates (Yamaha); 11 John Creith (Honda); 12 Stuart Edwards (Honda); 13 Dean Johnson (Honda); 14 Stephen Thompson (Honda); 15 Shane Norval (Honda).
Fastest lap: Smart, 1m 38.638s, 101.06 mph/162.64 km/h.
Championship points: 1 Smart, 75; 2 Sawford, 45; 3 Vincent, 40; 4 M. Coates, 36; 5 Milton, 29; 6 Ramsay, 26.

Shell Advance Supersport 600 Championship, round 2 (18 laps, 49.842 miles/80.244 km)
1 Ian Simpson (Honda), 30m 26.878s, 98.21 mph/158.06 km/h.
2 Dave Heal (Honda); 3 Steve Plater (Honda); 4 Pete Jennings (Honda); 5 Paul Brown (Honda); 6 John Crawford (Suzuki); 7 Iain Duffus (Honda); 8 Simon Smith (Honda); 9 Adam Lewis (Yamaha); 10 Kevin Mawdsley (Honda); 11 Howard Whitby (Honda); 12 Stuart Wickens (Honda); 13 Dean Thomas (Honda); 14 Colin Gable (Honda); 15 Paul Dedman (Kawasaki).
Fastest lap: Phillip McCallen (Honda), 1m 39.775s, 99.90 mph/160.78 km/h.
Championship points: 1 Heal, 31; 2 McCallen and Simpson, 25; 4 Thomas and Jennings, 22; 6 Brown and Plater, 19.

SNETTERTON CIRCUIT, 11 May. 1.952-mile/3.141-km circuit.
Shell Advance 125 cc British Championship, round 3
Race 1 (12 laps, 23.424 miles/37.692 km)
1 Paul Robinson (Honda), 17m 39.849s, 79.56 mph/128.04 km/h.
2 Alan Green (Honda); 3 Steve Patrickson (Honda); 4 Chris Palmer (Honda); 5 Stephen Lee (Honda); 6 George Bedford (Honda); 7 Fernando Mendes (Honda); 8 Marcus Johnston (Honda); 9 Chris Burns (Honda); 10 Pete Jennings (Honda); 11 David Dawson (Honda); 12 Robert Chilcott (Honda); 13 Paul Notman (Aprilia); 14 Jeremy Goodall (Honda); 15 Robin Appleyard (Honda).
Fastest lap: Robinson, 1m 25.897s, 81.80 mph/131.75 km/h.

Race 2 (10 laps, 19.520 miles/31.410 km)
1 Darren Barton (Honda), 12m 53.076s, 90.89 mph/146.28 km/h.
2 Phelim Owens (Honda); 3 Fernando Mendes (Honda); 4 Robin Appleyard (Honda); 5 Steve Patrickson (Honda); 6 Kenny Tibble (Honda); 7 Chris Burns (Honda); 8 Damien Cahill (Honda); 9 Gavan Morris (Honda); 10 Pete Jennings (Honda); 11 Daniel Tarratt (Honda); 12 Paul Robinson (Honda); 13 Tom Tunstall (Honda); 14 Chris Palmer (Honda); 15 Alan Green (Honda).
Fastest lap: Mendes, 1m 16.065s, 92.38 mph/148.67 km/h (record).
Championship points: 1 Mendes, 70; 2 Owens, 52; 3 Barton, 51; 4 Patrickson, 43; 5 Palmer, 31; 6 Davis, 28.

Shell Advance 250 cc British Championship, round 3 (20 laps, 39.040 miles/62.820 km)
1 Mark Coates (Honda), 25m 43.495s, 91.05 mph/146.53 km/h.
2 Jason Vincent (Honda); 3 Scott Smart (Honda); 4 Steve Sawford (Honda); 5 Rob Frear (Yamaha); 6 John McGuiness (Aprilia); 7 Shane Norval (Honda); 8 Adrian Clarke (Honda); 9 Robin Milton (Honda); 10 Stephen Thompson (Honda); 11 Lee Masters (Yamaha); 12 Callum Ramsay (Honda); 13 Woolsey Coulter (Aprilia); 14 Stuart Edwards (Honda); 15 Gary May (Yamaha).
Fastest lap: Clarke, 1m 14.203s, 94.70 mph/152.40 km/h.
Championship points: 1 Smart, 91; 2 M. Coates, 61; 3 Vincent, 60; 4 Sawford, 58; 5 Milton, 36; 6 McGuiness, 34.

Shell Advance Supersport 600 Championship, round 3 (18 laps, 35.136 miles/56.538 km)
1 Dean Thomas (Honda), 22m 03.803s, 95.55 mph/153.77 km/h.
2 Jim Moodie (Suzuki); 3 Paul Brown (Honda); 4 Phil Borley (Honda); 5 Ian Simpson (Honda); 6 Dave Heal (Honda); 7 Adam Lewis (Yamaha); 8 Phil Giles (Honda); 9 John Crawford (Suzuki); 10 Steve Plater (Honda); 11 Colin Gable (Honda); 12 Pete Jennings (Honda); 13 Paul Breslin (Yamaha); 14 Simon Smith (Honda); 15 Danny Beaumont (Yamaha).
Fastest lap: Moodie, 1m 12.625s, 96.76 mph/155.72 km/h.
Championship points: 1 Thomas, 48; 2 Heal, 41; 3 Moodie and Simpson, 36; 5 Brown, 35; 6 Jennings, 27.

BRANDS HATCH INDY CIRCUIT, 22 June. 1.2036-mile/1.937-km circuit.
Shell Advance 125 cc British Championship, round 4 (23 laps, 27.683 miles/44.551 km)
1 Jason Davis (Honda), 21m 36.471s, 76.86 mph/123.70 km/h.
2 Darran Gawley (Aprilia); 3 Pete Jennings (Honda); 4 Chris Burns (Honda); 5 Phelim Owens (Honda); 6 Steve Patrickson (Honda); 7 Gareth Jones (Honda); 8 Alan Green (Honda); 9 David Mateer (Honda); 10 Stephen Lee (Honda); 11 Daniel Tarratt (Honda); 12 David Dawson (Honda); 13 Darren Barton (Honda); 14 Fernando Mendes (Honda); 15 Sanjay Sharma (Honda).
Fastest lap: Davis, 57.857s, 80.45 mph/129.47 km/h.
Championship points: 1 Mendes, 72; 2 Owens, 63; 3 Barton, 54; 4 Davis and Patrickson, 53; 6 Burns, 38.

Shell Advance 250 cc British Championship, round 4
Race 1 (15 laps, 18.054 miles/29.055 km)
1 Woolsey Coulter (Aprilia), 13m 37.082s, 79.54 mph/128.01 km/h.
2 Simon Turner (Honda); 3 John McGuiness (Aprilia); 4 John Creith (Honda); 5 Rob Frear (Yamaha); 6 Gary May (Yamaha); 7 Callum Ramsay (Honda); 8 Steve Sawford (Honda); 9 Stuart Edwards (Honda); 10 Tim Levy (Honda); 11 Dean Johnson (Honda); 12 Lee Masters (Yamaha); 13 Brendan Marchesi (Aprilia); 14 Adrian Clarke (Honda); 15 Greg Fowler (Honda).
Fastest lap: Coulter, 52m 234s, 82.95 mph/133.49 km/h.

Race 2 (10 laps, 12.036 miles/19.370 km)
1 Woolsey Coulter (Aprilia), 8m 48.513s, 81.98 mph/131.94 km/h.
2 John McGuiness (Aprilia); 3 Simon Turner (Honda); 4 Rob Frear (Yamaha); 5 Adrian

Coates (Honda); **6** Callum Ramsay (Honda); **7** Mark Burr (Yamaha); **8** Stuart Edwards (Honda); **9** John Creith (Honda); **10** Dean Johnson (Honda); **11** Tim Levy (Honda); **12** Greg Fowler (Honda); **13** Adrian Clarke (Honda); **14** Steve Sawford (Honda); **15** Lee Masters (Yamaha).
Fastest lap: McGuiness, 51.680s, 83.84 mph/134.93 km/h.
Championship points: **1** Smart, 91; **2** McGuiness, 70; **3** Coulter, 69; **4** Sawford, 68; **5** M. Coates, 61; **6** Vincent, 60.

Shell Advance Supersport 600 Championship, round 4 (24 laps, 28.886 miles/46.488 km)
1 Paul Brown (Honda), 22m 00.924s, 78.72 mph/126.69 km/h.
2 Ian Simpson (Honda); **3** Howard Whitby (Honda); **4** Danny Beaumont (Yamaha); **5** James Toseland (Honda); **6** Steve Plater (Honda); **7** Phil Borley (Honda); **8** Dave Rathbone (Honda); **9** Dave Heal (Honda); **10** Dan Harris (Suzuki); **11** Adam Lewis (Yamaha); **12** Phil Giles (Honda); **13** Simon Smith (Honda); **14** Lee Morton (Honda); **15** Jago Chapman (Honda).
Fastest lap: Whitby, 53.144s, 81.53 mph/131.21 km/h.
Championship points: **1** Brown, 60; **2** Simpson, 52; **3** Heal and Thomas, 48; **5** Moodie, 36; **6** Plater, 35.

THRUXTON CIRCUIT, 6 July. 2.356-mile/3.792-km circuit.
Shell Advance 125 cc British Championship, round 5 (20 laps, 47.120 miles/75.840 km)
1 Darren Barton (Honda), 28m 19.898s, 99.78 mph/160.59 km/h.
2 Phelim Owens (Honda); **3** Fernando Mendes (Honda); **4** Robin Appleyard (Honda); **5** Chris Burns (Honda); **6** Jason Davis (Honda); **7** Rodney Fee (Honda); **8** Chris Palmer (Honda); **9** Pete Jennings (Honda); **10** Tom Tunstall (Honda); **11** Daniel Tarratt (Honda); **12** Alan Green (Honda); **13** Darran Gawley (Aprilia); **14** Gavin Lee (Honda); **15** Steve Patrickson (Honda).
Fastest lap: Appleyard, 1m 23.558s, 101.50 mph/163.35 km/h (record).
Championship points: **1** Mendes, 88; **2** Owens, 83; **3** Barton, 79; **4** Davis, 63; **5** Patrickson, 54; **6** Burns, 49.

Shell Advance 250 cc British Championship, round 5 (20 laps, 47.120 miles/75.840 km)
1 Jason Vincent (Honda), 27m 07.271s, 104.24 mph/167.76 km/h.
2 Scott Smart (Honda); **3** Phelim Owens (Aprilia); **4** Adrian Coates (Honda); **5** Callum Ramsay (Honda); **6** Adrian Clarke (Honda); **7** Steve Sawford (Honda); **8** Lee Masters (Yamaha); **9** Stuart Edwards (Honda); **10** John Pearson (Honda); **11** Mark Chapman (Yamaha); **12** Max Vincent (Honda); **13** Anna Wilkin (Yamaha).
Fastest lap: J. Vincent, 1m 20.165s, 105.80 mph/170.27 km/h.
Championship points: **1** Smart, 111; **2** J. Vincent, 85; **3** Sawford, 77; **4** McGuiness, 70; **5** Coulter, 69; **6** M. Coates, 61.

Shell Advance Supersport 600 Championship, round 5 (17 laps, 40.052 miles/64.464 km)
1 Paul Brown (Honda), 23m 28.653s, 102.35 mph/164.72 km/h.
2 Phillip McCallen (Honda); **3** Mike Edwards (Honda); **4** Jim Moodie (Suzuki); **5** Dean Thomas (Honda); **6** Ian Simpson (Honda); **7** Steve Plater (Honda); **8** Gary Weston (Yamaha); **9** Phil Borley (Honda); **10** Howard Whitby (Honda); **11** Dave Heal (Honda); **12** Ian Cobby (Honda); **13** Phil Giles (Honda); **14** Chris Heath (Honda); **15** John Crawford (Suzuki).
Fastest lap: Plater, 1m 21.695s, 103.82 mph/167.08 km/h (record).
Championship points: **1** Brown, 85; **2** Simpson, 66; **3** Thomas, 59; **4** Heal, 53; **5** Moodie, 49; **6** McCallen, 45.

OULTON PARK CIRCUIT, 20 July. 2.769-mile/4.458-km circuit.
Shell Advance 125 cc British Championship, round 6 (18 laps, 49.842 miles/80.244 km)
1 Darren Barton (Honda), 31m 06.372s, 96.13 mph/154.72 km/h.
2 Robin Appleyard (Honda); **3** Jason Davis (Honda); **4** Phelim Owens (Honda); **5** Darran Gawley (Aprilia); **6** Pete Jennings (Honda); **7** Fernando Mendes (Honda); **8** Alan Green (Honda); **9** Paul Notman (Aprilia); **10** Kenny Tibble (Honda); **11** Chris Palmer (Honda); **12** Daniel Tarratt (Honda); **13** Damien Cahill (Honda); **14** George Bedford (Honda); **15** Steve Patrickson (Honda).
Fastest lap: Chris Burns (Honda), 1m 42.201s, 97.53 mph/156.97 km/h (record).
Championship points: **1** Barton, 104; **2** Mendes, 97; **3** Owens, 96; **4** Davis, 79; **5** Appleyard, 58; **6** Patrickson, 55.

Shell Advance 250 cc British Championship, round 6 (18 laps, 49.842 miles/80.244 km)
1 Scott Smart (Honda), 29m 18.655s, 102.02 mph/164.19 km/h.
2 Jason Vincent (Honda); **3** Woolsey Coulter (Aprilia); **4** John McGuiness (Aprilia); **5** Steve Sawford (Honda); **6** John Pearson (Honda); **7** Adrian Clarke (Honda); **8** Gary Haslam (Aprilia); **9** G. Winterbottom (Honda); **10** Martin Johnson (Honda); **11** Derek Welch (Yamaha); **12** Carl Salvage (Honda); **13** Mark Burr (Yamaha); **14** Alan McGregor (Honda); **15** Paul Ellis (Yamaha).
Fastest lap: Smart, 1m 36.802s, 102.97 mph/165.72 km/h (record).
Championship points: **1** Smart, 136; **2** J. Vincent, 105; **3** Sawford, 88; **4** Coulter, 85; **5** McGuiness, 83; **6** M. Coates, 61.

Shell Advance Supersport 600 Championship, round 6 (17 laps, 47.073 miles/75.786 km)
1 Paul Brown (Honda), 28m 31.311s, 99.02 mph/159.36 km/h.
2 Mike Edwards (Honda); **3** Ian Simpson (Honda); **4** Steve Plater (Honda); **5** Dave Heal (Honda); **6** Howard Whitby (Honda); **7** Phillip McCallen (Honda); **8** James Toseland (Pallot); **9** Dave Rathbone (Honda); **10** Andy Pallot (Honda); **11** Pete Jennings (Honda); **12** Andy Tinsley (Honda); **13** Mark Wainwright (Honda); **14** Stuart Wickens (Honda); **15** Chris Heath (Honda).
Fastest lap: Edwards, 1m 39.599s, 100.08 mph/161.07 km/h (record).
Championship points: **1** Brown, 110; **2** Simpson, 82; **3** Heal, 64; **4** Thomas, 59; **5** Plater, 57; **6** McCallen, 54.

MALLORY PARK CIRCUIT, 27 July. 1.370-mile/2.205-km circuit.
Shell Advance 125 cc British Championship, round 7 (2 x 15 laps, 20.550 miles/33.075 km)
Race 1
1 Fernando Mendes (Honda), 12m 58.566s, 95.02 mph/152.92 km/h.
2 Chris Burns (Honda); **3** Robin Appleyard (Honda); **4** Steve Patrickson (Honda); **5** Jason Davis (Honda); **6** Damien Cahill (Honda); **7** Phelim Owens (Honda); **8** Darren Barton (Honda); **9** Pete Jennings (Honda); **10** Darran Gawley (Aprilia); **11** Alan Green (Honda); **12** Gavan Morris (Honda); **13** Daniel Tarratt (Honda); **14** Tom Tunstall (Honda); **15** David Mateer (Honda).
Fastest lap: Burns, 51.007s, 96.69 mph/155.61 km/h.

Race 2
1 Chris Burns (Honda), 12m 58.530s, 95.02 mph/152.92 km/h.
2 Darren Barton (Honda); **3** Damien Cahill (Honda); **4** Pete Jennings (Honda); **5** Phelim Owens (Honda); **6** Steve Patrickson (Honda); **7** Gavan Morris (Honda); **8** Fernando Mendes (Honda); **9** Daniel Tarratt (Honda); **10** Darran Gawley (Aprilia); **11** Jason Davis (Honda); **12** Kenny Tibble (Honda); **13** Chris Palmer (Honda); **14** Paul Robinson (Honda); **15** David Mateer (Honda).
Fastest lap: Burns, 50.984s, 96.73 mph/155.68 km/h.
Championship points: **1** Barton, 132; **2** Mendes, 130; **3** Owens, 116; **4** Davis, 95; **5** Burns, 94; **6** Patrickson, 78.

Shell Advance 250 cc British Championship, round 7 (30 laps, 41.100 miles/66.150 km)
1 Jason Vincent (Honda), 24m 43.698s, 99.72 mph/160.48 km/h.
2 Scott Smart (Honda); **3** John McGuiness (Aprilia); **4** Steve Sawford (Honda); **5** Alan Patterson (Honda); **6** Gary May (Yamaha); **7** Stuart Edwards (Honda); **8** Gary Haslam (Aprilia); **9** Max Vincent (Honda); **10** Adrian Coates (Honda); **11** Callum Ramsay (Honda); **12** Adrian Clarke (Honda); **13** John Pearson (Honda); **14** Ryan Farquhar (Honda); **15** Dean Johnson (Honda).
Fastest lap: J. Vincent, 48.832s, 100.99 mph/162.54 km/h (record).
Championship points: **1** Smart, 156; **2** J. Vincent, 130; **3** Sawford, 101; **4** McGuiness, 99; **5** Coulter, 85; **6** Ramsay, 65.

Shell Advance Supersport 600 Championship, round 7 (25 laps, 34.250 miles/55.125 km)
1 James Toseland (Honda), 21m 17.240s, 96.53 mph/155.36 km/h.
2 Paul Brown (Honda); **3** Steve Plater (Honda); **4** Howard Whitby (Honda); **5** Phil Borley (Honda); **6** Phillip McCallen (Honda); **7** Dean Thomas (Honda); **8** Ian Simpson (Honda); **9** Dave Heal (Honda); **10** Phil Giles (Honda); **11** Andy Pallot (Honda); **12** John Crawford (Suzuki); **13** Andy Tinsley (Honda); **14** Bill Hutcheson (Honda); **15** Simon Smith (Honda).
Fastest lap: Brown, 50.557s, 97.55 mph/156.99 km/h (record).
Championship points: **1** Brown, 130; **2** Simpson, 90; **3** Plater, 73; **4** Heal, 71; **5** Thomas, 68; **6** McCallen, 64.

KNOCKHILL CIRCUIT, 10 August. 1.300-mile/2.092-km circuit.
Shell Advance 125 cc British Championship, round 8 (2 x 15 laps, 19.500 miles/31.380 km)
Race 1
1 Chris Burns (Honda), 14m 11.114s, 82.48 mph/132.73 km/h.
2 Pete Jennings (Honda); **3** Darren Barton (Honda); **4** Robin Appleyard (Honda); **5** Gavan Morris (Honda); **6** Chris Palmer (Honda); **7** Kenny Tibble (Honda); **8** Paul Notman (Honda); **9** Darran Gawley (Aprilia); **10** Daniel Tarratt (Honda); **11** Damien Cahill (Honda); **12** George Bedford (Honda); **13** Steve Patrickson (Honda); **14** David Mateer (Honda); **15** Tom Tunstall (Honda).
Fastest lap: Burns, 56.002s, 83.56 mph/134.49 km/h.

Race 2
1 Chris Burns (Honda), 14m 12.839s, 82.31 mph/132.47 km/h.
2 Darren Barton (Honda); **3** Fernando Mendes (Honda); **4** Alan Green (Honda); **5** Robin Appleyard (Honda); **6** Pete Jennings (Honda); **7** Darran Gawley (Aprilia); **8** Gavan Morris (Honda); **9** Jason Davis (Honda); **10** Kenny Tibble (Honda); **11** Chris Palmer (Honda); **12** George Bedford (Honda); **13** Daniel Tarratt (Honda); **14** Steve Patrickson (Honda); **15** Marcus Johnston (Honda).
Fastest lap: Burns, 55.866s, 83.77 mph/134.81 km/h (record).
Championship points: **1** Barton, 168; **2** Mendes, 146; **3** Burns, 144; **4** Owens, 116; **5** Davis, 102; **6** Appleyard, 98.

Shell Advance 250 cc British Championship, round 8 (29 laps, 37.700 miles/60.668 km)
1 John McGuiness (Aprilia), 26m 13.609s, 86.24 mph/138.80 km/h.
2 Steve Sawford (Honda); **3** Callum Ramsay (Honda); **4** Woolsey Coulter (Aprilia); **5** Gary May (Yamaha); **6** John Creith (Honda); **7** Adrian Coates (Honda); **8** Adrian Clarke (Honda); **9** Stephen Thompson (Honda); **10** Alan McGregor (Honda); **11** Tim Levy (Honda); **12** Dean Johnson (Honda); **13** Gary Jackson (Honda); **14** Mike Walker (Yamaha).
Fastest lap: Coulter, 53.256s, 87.87 mph/141.42 km/h.
Championship points: **1** Smart, 156; **2** J. Vincent, 130; **3** McGuiness, 124; **4** Sawford, 121; **5** Coulter, 98; **6** Ramsay, 81.

Shell Advance Supersport 600 Championship, round 8 (30 laps, 39.000 miles/62.760 km)
1 James Toseland (Honda), 27m 29.097s, 85.13 mph/137.01 km/h.
2 Paul Brown (Honda); **3** Phillip McCallen (Honda); **4** Jim Moodie (Suzuki); **5** Ian Simpson (Honda); **6** Phil Borley (Honda); **7** Howard Whitby (Honda); **8** Steve Plater (Honda); **9** Dave Heal (Honda); **10** Dave Rathbone (Honda); **11** Simon Smith (Honda); **12** Paul Breslin (Yamaha); **13** Gordon Whitaker (Suzuki); **14** Andy Pallot (Honda); **15** Phil Giles (Honda).
Fastest lap: Mike Edwards (Honda), 54.284s, 86.21 mph/138.74 km/h.
Championship points: **1** Brown, 150; **2** Simpson, 101; **3** Plater, 81; **4** McCallen, 80; **5** Heal, 78; **6** Toseland, 69.

CADWELL PARK CIRCUIT, 25 August. 2.170-mile/3.472-km circuit.
Shell Advance 125 cc British Championship, round 9 (20 laps, 43.400 miles/69.440 km)
1 Jason Davis (Honda), 32m 58.568s, 78.96 mph/127.08 km/h.
2 George Bedford (Honda); **3** Fernando Mendes (Honda); **4** Gavan Morris (Honda); **5** Darran Gawley (Honda); **6** Steve Patrickson (Honda); **7** Chris Palmer (Honda); **8** Daniel Tarratt (Honda); **9** Damien Cahill (Honda); **10** Paul Notman (Honda); **11** Mark Davies (Honda); **12** Tom Tunstall (Honda); **13** Robert Chilcott (Honda); **14** Marcus Johnston (Honda); **15** George Wakefield (Honda).
Fastest lap: Morris, 1m 36.047s, 81.33 mph/130.89 km/h.
Championship points: **1** Barton, 168; **2** Mendes, 162; **3** Burns, 144; **4** Davis, 127; **5** Owens, 116; **6** Appleyard, 98.

Shell Advance 250 cc British Championship, round 9 (2 x 12 laps, 26.040 miles/41.664 miles)
Race 1
1 Maurice Ruddock (Aprilia), 20m 32.479s, 76.06 mph/122.40 km/h.
2 Max Vincent (Honda); **3** Steve Sawford (Honda); **4** Scott Smart (Honda); **5** Jason Vincent (Honda); **6** Simon Turner (Honda); **7** Adrian Coates (Honda); **8** Adrian Clarke (Honda); **9** Lea Gourlay (Honda); **10** Callum Ramsay (Honda); **11** Alex Hutchinson (Honda); **12** John Pearson (Honda); **13** Mark Chapman (Yamaha); **14** Dean Johnson (Honda); **15** Davy Morgan (Honda).
Fastest lap: Ruddock, 1m 39.856s, 78.23 mph/125.90 km/h.

Race 2
1 Jason Vincent (Honda), 18m 44.155s, 83.39 mph/134.20 km/h.
2 Scott Smart (Honda); **3** Woolsey Coulter (Aprilia); **4** Steve Sawford (Honda); **5** Maurice Ruddock (Aprilia); **6** Max Vincent (Honda); **7** Adrian Clarke (Honda); **8** Simon Turner (Honda); **9** Callum Ramsay (Honda); **10** G. Winterbottom (Honda); **11** Tim Levy (Honda); **12** Stephen Thompson (Honda); **13** John Pearson (Honda); **14** Davy Morgan (Honda); **15** Stuart Hall (Yamaha).
Fastest lap: J. Vincent, 1m 30.549s, 86.27 mph/138.84 km/h.
Championship points: **1** Smart, 189; **2** J. Vincent, 166; **3** Sawford, 150; **4** McGuiness, 124; **5** Coulter, 114; **6** Ramsay, 94.

Shell Advance Supersport 600 Championship, round 9 (20 laps, 43.400 miles/69.440 km)
1 Ian Simpson (Honda), 33m 50.928s, 76.93 mph/123.80 km/h.
2 Howard Whitby (Honda); **3** Paul Brown (Honda); **4** David Wood (Kawasaki); **5** Dean Thomas (Honda); **6** Dave Rathbone (Honda); **7** Gordon Whitaker (Suzuki); **8** Andy Tinsley (Honda); **9** Dave Heal (Honda); **10** Mark Wainwright (Honda); **11** Douglas Cowie (Honda); **12** Ian Campbell (Honda); **13** Paul Dedman (Kawasaki); **14** Chris Heath (Honda).
Fastest lap: Simpson, 1m 39.546s, 78.47 mph/126.29 km/h.
Championship points: **1** Brown, 166; **2** Simpson, 126; **3** Heal, 85; **4** Plater, 81; **5** McCallen, 80; **6** Thomas and Whitby, 79.

BRANDS HATCH GRAND PRIX CIRCUIT, 14 September. 2.6002-mile/4.185-km circuit.
Shell Advance 125 cc British Championship, round 10 (18 laps, 46.804 miles/75.330 km)
1 Darren Barton (Honda), 28m 35.683s, 98.20 mph/158.04 km/h.
2 Alan Green (Honda); **3** Pete Jennings (Honda); **4** Paul Jones (Aprilia); **5** Robin Appleyard (Honda); **6** Fernando Mendes (Honda); **7** Chris Palmer (Honda); **8** Damien Cahill (Honda); **9** Paul Robinson (Honda); **10** Paul Notman (Honda); **11** Andi Notman (Honda); **12** Steve Patrickson (Honda); **13** Tom Tunstall (Honda); **14** David Mateer (Honda); **15** Daniel Tarratt (Honda).
Fastest lap: Jones, 1m 33.151s, 100.48 mph/161.72 km/h (record).
Championship points: **1** Barton, 193; **2** Mendes, 172; **3** Burns, 144; **4** Davis, 127; **5** Owens, 116; **6** Jennings, 111.

Shell Advance 250 cc British Championship, round 10 (18 laps, 46.804 miles/75.330 km)
1 Jason Vincent (Honda), 27m 02.017s, 103.87 mph/167.17 km/h.
2 Woolsey Coulter (Aprilia); **3** John McGuiness (Aprilia); **4** Scott Smart (Honda); **5** Callum Ramsay (Honda); **6** Max Vincent (Honda); **7** Steve Sawford (Honda); **8** Adrian Coates (Honda); **9** Gavin Lee (Yamaha); **10** Stuart Edwards (Honda); **11** Adrian Clarke (Honda); **12** John Pearson (Honda); **13** Adam Marshall (Honda); **14** Tim Levy (Honda); **15** Philip Stead (Yamaha).
Fastest lap: J. Vincent, 1m 28.958s, 105.22 mph/169.34 km/h (record).
Championship points: **1** Smart, 202; **2** J. Vincent, 191; **3** Sawford, 159; **4** McGuiness, 140; **5** Coulter, 134; **6** Ramsay, 105.

Shell Advance Supersport 600 Championship, round 10 (18 laps, 46.804 miles/75.330 km)
1 James Toseland (Honda), 27m 42.606s, 101.34 mph/163.09 km/h.
2 John Crawford (Suzuki); **3** Howard Whitby (Honda); **4** Ian Simpson (Honda); **5** Phil Giles (Honda); **6** Dean Thomas (Honda); **7** Dave Heal (Honda); **8** Simon Smith (Honda); **9** Phil Borley (Honda); **10** Andy Tinsley (Honda); **11** Jago Chapman (Honda); **12** Mark Wainwright (Honda); **13** Stuart Wickens (Honda); **14** Lee Dickinson (Honda); **15** Mark Horner (Honda).
Fastest lap: Toseland, 1m 31.533s, 102.26 mph/164.58 km/h (record).
Championship points: **1** Brown, 166; **2** Simpson, 139; **3** Whitby, 95; **4** Toseland and Heal, 94; **6** Thomas, 89.

DONINGTON PARK SHORT CIRCUIT, 28 September. 1.957-mile/3.149-km circuit.
Shell Advance 125 cc British Championship, round 11 (20 laps, 39.140 miles/62.980 km)
1 Chris Burns (Honda), 25m 24.234s, 92.45 mph/148.79 km/h.
2 Fernando Mendes (Honda); **3** Jason Davis (Honda); **4** Robin Appleyard (Honda); **5** Darren Barton (Honda); **6** Damien Cahill (Honda); **7** Chris Palmer (Honda); **8** Paul Jones (Aprilia); **9** Paul Notman (Aprilia); **10** Alan Green (Honda); **11** George Bedford (Honda); **12** Andi Notman (Honda); **13** Steve Patrickson (Honda); **14** Tom Tunstall (Honda); **15** Daniel Tarratt (Honda).
Fastest lap: Burns, 1m 15.478s, 93.35 mph/150.24 km/h (record).

Shell Advance 250 cc British Championship, round 11 (20 laps, 39.140 miles/62.980 km)
1 Jason Vincent (Honda), 24m 11.989s, 97.05 mph/156.19 km/h.
2 Woolsey Coulter (Aprilia); **3** Scott Smart (Honda); **4** John McGuiness (Aprilia); **5** Callum Ramsay (Honda); **6** Max Vincent (Honda); **7** Steve Sawford (Honda); **8** John Creith (Honda); **9** Adrian Clarke (Honda); **10** John Pearson (Honda); **11** Alan McGregor (Honda); **12** Gary Haslam (Aprilia); **13** Dean Johnson (Honda); **14** Gavin Lee (Yamaha); **15** Philip Stead (Yamaha).
Fastest lap: J. Vincent, 1m 11.527s, 98.51 mph/158.54 km/h (record).

Shell Advance Supersport 600 Championship, round 11 (20 laps, 39.140 miles/62.980 km)
1 James Toseland (Honda), 24m 43.711s, 94.98 mph/152.85 km/h.
2 John Crawford (Suzuki); **3** Steve Plater (Honda); **4** Paul Brown (Honda); **5** Dean Thomas (Honda); **6** Phil Borley (Honda); **7** Dave Rathbone (Honda); **8** Phil Giles (Honda); **9** Simon Smith (Honda); **10** Dave Heal (Honda); **11** David Wood (Kawasaki); **12** Karl Harris (Honda); **13** Paul Breslin (Yamaha); **14** Iain Duffus (Honda); **15** Shane Byrne (Honda).
Fastest lap: Toseland, 1m 13.418s, 95.97 mph/154.45 km/h (record).

Final 125 cc British Championship points

1	Darren Barton	204
2	Fernando Mendes	192
3	Chris Burns	169
4	Jason Davis	143
5	Robin Appleyard	122

6 Phelim Owens, 116; **7** Pete Jennings, 111; **8** Steve Patrickson, 100; **9** Alan Green, 91; **10** Chris Palmer, 89; **11** Darran Gawley, 83; **12** Damien Cahill, 74; **13** Gavan Morris, 66; **14** Daniel Tarratt, 53; **15** George Bedford, 45.

Final 250 cc British Championship points

1	Scott Smart	218
2	Jason Vincent	216
3	Steve Sawford	168
4	Woolsey Coulter	154
5	John McGuiness	153

6 Callum Ramsay, 116; **7** Adrian Clarke, 96; **8** Adrian Coates, 62; **9=**Mark Coates and Max Vincent, 61; **11** Simon Turner, 54; **12** John Creith, 50; **13** Gary May, 48; **14** Stuart Edwards, 43; **15** John Pearson, 38.

Final Supersport 600 Championship points

1	Paul Brown	179
2	Ian Simpson	139
3	James Toseland	119
4=	Dave Heal	100
4=	Dean Thomas	100

6 Steve Plater, 97; **7** Howard Whitby, 95; **8** Phillip McCallen, 80; **9** Phil Borley, 74; **10=**John Crawford and Jim Moodie, 62; **12** Phil Giles, 47; **13** Dave Rathbone, 40; **14** Mike Edwards, 36; **15** Simon Smith, 35.